# Feminist Ethics

**The International Research Library of Philosophy**
***Series Editor: John Skorupski***

*Metaphysics and Epistemology*

**Identity** *Harold Noonan*
**Personal Identity** *Harold Noonan*
**Scepticism** *Michael Williams*
**Infinity** *A.W. Moore*
**Theories of Truth** *Paul Horwich*
**Knowledge and Justification, Vols I & II** *Ernest Sosa*
**Spacetime** *Jeremy Butterfield, Mark Hogarth, Gordon Belot*
**A Priori Knowledge** *Albert Casullo*

*Future Volumes*: Substance and Causation; Necessity; The Existence and Knowability of God; Faith, Reason and Religious Language.

*The Philosophy of Mathematics and Science*

**The Ontology of Science** *John Worrall*
**Mathematical Objects and Mathematical Knowledge** *Michael D. Resnik*
**Theory, Evidence and Explanation** *Peter Lipton*

*Future Volumes*: Proof and its Limits; Probability; The Philosophy of the Life Sciences; The Philosophy of History and the Social Sciences; Rational Choice.

*The Philosophy of Logic, Language and Mind*

**Understanding and Sense, Vols I and II** *Christopher Peacocke*
**Metaphysics of Mind** *Peter Smith*
**The Limits of Logic** *Stewart Shapiro*
**Events** *Roberto Casati, Achille C. Varzi*
**Consciousness** *Frank Jackson*
**Reason, Emotions and the Will** *R. Jay Wallace*

*Future Volumes*: Truth and Consequence; Modality, Quantification, High-order Logic; Reference and Logical Form; The Nature of Meaning; Functionalism; Interpretation; Intentionality and Representation.

*The Philosophy of Value*

**Consequentialism** *Philip Pettit*
**Punishment** *Antony Duff*
**Meta-ethics** *Michael Smith*
**Duty and Virtue** *Onora O'Neill*
**Human Sexuality** *Igor Primoratz*
**The Ethics of the Environment** *Andrew Brennan*
**Medical Ethics** *R.S. Downie*
**Feminist Ethics** *Moira J. Gatens*
**Public Reason** *Fred D'Agostino, Jerry Gaus*

*Future Volumes*: Aesthetics; The Foundations of the State; Justice; Liberty and Community.

# Feminist Ethics

*Edited by*

Moira Gatens

*Associate Professor of Philosophy*
*University of Sydney*



**Ashgate**

DARTMOUTH

Aldershot • Brookfield USA • Singapore • Sydney

Published by
Dartmouth Publishing Company Limited
Ashgate Publishing Limited
Gower House
Croft Road
Aldershot
Hants GU11 3HR
England

Ashgate Publishing Company
Old Post Road
Brookfield
Vermont 05036
USA

**British Library Cataloguing in Publication Data**
Feminist ethics. – (The international research library of philosophy)
1. Feminist ethics
I. Gatens, Moira
170.8′2

**Library of Congress Cataloging-in-Publication Data**
Feminist ethics / edited by Moira Gatens.
p. cm. — (International research library of philosophy)
ISBN 1–85521–979–4 (hb)
1. Feminist ethics. I. Gatens, Moira. II. Series.
BJ1395.F445 1998
170′.82—dc21 98–2545
CIP

ISBN 1 85521 979 4

Printed and bound by Athenaeum Press, Ltd.,
Gateshead, Tyne & Wear.

# Contents

# Acknowledgements

The editor and publishers wish to thank the following for permission to use copyright material.

Blackwell Publishers UK for the essays: Susan Mendus (1993), 'Different Voices, Still Lives: Problems in the Ethics of Care', *Journal of Applied Philosophy*, **10**, pp. 17–27. Copyright © Society for Applied Philosophy, 1993, Blackwell Publishers; Seyla Benhabib (1986), 'The Generalized and the Concrete Other: The Kohlberg–Gilligan Controversy and Feminist Theory', *Praxis International*, **5**, pp. 402–24; Nancy Fraser (1986), 'Toward a Discourse Ethic of Solidarity', *Praxis International*, **5**, pp. 425–29.

Blackwell Publishers USA for the essay: Annette C. Baier (1994), 'What Do Women Want in a Moral Theory?', in Annette Baier (ed.), *Moral Prejudices: Essays on Ethics*, Cambridge, MA: Harvard University Press, pp. 1–18. Originally published in *Nous*, **XIX**, pp. 53–63 by Blackwell Publishers, Inc. Copyright © 1985 Blackwell Publishers, Inc.

Cambridge University Press and The Royal Institute of Philosophy for the essay: Jonathan Dancy (1992), 'Caring about Justice', *Philosophy*, **67**, pp. 447–66.

Cornell University Press for the essay: Marilyn Friedman (1993), 'Liberating Care', in *What Are Friends For? Feminist Perspectives on Personal Relationships and Moral Theory*, Ithaca: Cornell University Press, pp. 142–83. Used by permission of the publisher, Cornell University Press.

Daedalus for the essay: Mary G. Dietz (1987), 'Context Is All: Feminism and Theories of Citizenship', *Daedalus*, **116**, pp. 1–24.

Carol Gilligan (1995), 'Hearing the Difference: Theorizing Connection', *Hypatia*, **10**, pp. 120–27. Copyright © 1995 by Carol Gilligan.

Harvard Educational Review for the essay: Carol Gilligan (1977), 'In a Different Voice: Women's Conceptions of Self and of Morality', *Harvard Education Review*, **47**, pp. 481–517. Copyright © 1977 by the President and Fellows of Harvard College. All rights reserved.

Virginia Held (1995), 'The Meshing of Care and Justice', *Hypatia*, **10**, pp. 128–32. Copyright © 1995 by Virginia Held.

Harvard Journal of Law and Public Policy for the essay: Jeremy Waldron (1988), 'When Justice Replaces Affection: The Need for Rights', *Harvard Journal of Law and Public Policy*, **11**, pp. 625–47.

The Journal of Philosophy for the essay: Cheshire Calhoun (1988), 'Justice, Care, Gender Bias', *Journal of Philosophy*, **LXXXV**, pp. 451–63. Copyright © 1988 The Journal of Philosophy, Inc.

Kluwer Academic Publishers for the essay: Susan Hekman (1993), 'Moral Voices, Moral Selves: About Getting it Right in Moral Theory', *Human Studies*, **16**, pp. 143–62. Copyright © 1993 Kluwer Academic Publishers. Printed in the Netherlands with kind permission from Kluwer Academic Publishers.

Littlefield, Adams & Co. for the essay: Mary Fainsod Katzenstein and David D. Laitin (1987), 'Politics, Feminism, and the Ethics of Caring', in Eva Feder Kittay and Diana T. Meyers (eds), *Women and Moral Theory*, Totowa, NJ: Rowman and Littlefield Publishers, Inc., pp. 261–81. Copyright © 1987 by Roman & Littlefield.

Uma Narayan (1995), 'Colonialism and Its Others: Considerations On Rights and Care Discourses', *Hypatia*, **10**, pp. 133–40. Copyright © 1995 Uma Narayan.

New York University Press for the essays: Jane Mansbridge (1993), 'Feminism and Democratic Community', in John W. Chapman and Ian Shapiro (eds), *Democratic Community, NOMOS*, **XXXV**, New York: New York University Press, pp. 339–95. Copyright © 1993 by New York University; Robert E. Goodin (1996), 'Structures of Political Order: The Relational Feminist Alternative', in Ian Shapiro and Russell Hardin (eds), *Political Order, NOMOS*, **XXXVIII**, pp. 498–521. Copyright © 1996 by New York University.

North American Society for Social Philosophy for the essays: Nel Noddings (1990), 'Feminist Fears in Ethics', *Journal of Social Philosophy*, **21**, pp. 25–33; Kathleen League (1993), 'Individualism, Class, and the Situation of Care: An Essay on Carol Gilligan', *Journal of Social Philosophy*, **24**, pp. 69–79. Copyright © 1993 Journal of Social Philosophy.

Philosophy and Phenomenological Research for the essay: Virginia Held (1990), 'Feminist Transformations of Moral Theory', *Philosophy and Phenomenological Research*, **L**, pp. 321–44.

Joan C. Tronto (1995), 'Care as a Basis for Radical Political Judgments', *Hypatia*, **10**, pp. 141–49. Copyright © 1995 Joan Tronto.

The University of Chicago Press for the essays: Susan Moller Okin (1989), 'Reason and Feeling in Thinking About Justice', *Ethics*, **99**, pp. 229–49. Copyright © 1989 by The University of Chicago. All rights reserved; Owen Flanagan and Kathryn Jackson (1987), 'Justice, Care, and Gender: The Kohlberg–Gilligan Debate Revisited', *Ethics*, **97**, pp. 622–37. Copyright © 1987 by The University of Chicago. All rights reserved.

University Press of Kansas for the essay: Elizabeth V. Spelman (1991), 'The Virtue of Feeling and the Feeling of Virtue', in Claudia Card (ed.), *Feminist Ethics*, Lawrence: University Press of Kansas, pp. 213–32. Copyright © 1991 by the University Press of Kansas.

# Series Preface

The International Research Library of Philosophy collects in book form a wide range of important and influential essays in philosophy, drawn predominantly from English-language journals. Each volume in the Library deals with a field of inquiry which has received significant attention in philosophy in the last 25 years, and is edited by a philosopher noted in that field.

No particular philosophical method or approach is favoured or excluded. The Library will constitute a representative sampling of the best work in contemporary English-language philosophy, providing researchers and scholars throughout the world with comprehensive coverage of currently important topics and approaches.

The Library is divided into four series of volumes which reflect the broad divisions of contemporary philosophical inquiry:

- Metaphysics and Epistemology
- The Philosophy of Mathematics and Science
- The Philosophy of Logic, Language and Mind
- The Philosophy of Value

I am most grateful to all the volume editors, who have unstintingly contributed scarce time and effort to this project. The authority and usefulness of the series rests firmly on their hard work and scholarly judgement. I must also express my thanks to John Irwin of the Dartmouth Publishing Company, from whom the idea of the Library originally came, and who brought it to fruition; and also to his colleagues in the Editorial Office, whose care and attention to detail are so vital in ensuring that the Library provides a handsome and reliable aid to philosophical inquirers.

John Skorupski
General Editor
University of St. Andrews
Scotland

# Series Preface

# Introduction

The last quarter-century has witnessed an extraordinary flourishing of feminist writing in all disciplines, including philosophy. Contemporary feminist philosophy is a highly diverse field of research and, even within feminist ethics, a single volume will inevitably fail to capture this diversity. There are many important approaches within feminist ethics which are not represented here and others which are mentioned only in passing. These omissions are necessary if the reader is to gain a sense of the complexity of at least one strand of contemporary feminist ethics and an inkling of the manner in which this strand is beginning to be woven into mainstream Anglo-American moral philosophy. I have not included, for example, essays whose primary focus is so-called 'Continental' philosophy,[1] as such a task would itself require an entire volume. Therefore I have opted to present 27 essays which have made significant contributions to what has become known as the 'care/justice debate' in contemporary moral philosophy. While contemporary feminist ethics cannot be confined to this debate, many of the issues raised by it overlap with feminists' concerns in political philosophy, in theories of human nature and in epistemology, as well as ethics.[2] Wherever possible, I have selected essays which reflect the breadth of these concerns and the common feminist view that moral philosophy cannot be treated in isolation from epistemology and political philosophy.

A major catalyst for the care/justice debate was the 'different voice' which Carol Gilligan claimed to hear when conducting empirical research on patterns of moral reasoning employed by women facing moral quandaries (for example, the decision to have an abortion). Gilligan, a psychologist, set forth her findings in 1982 in *In a Different Voice: Psychological Theory and Women's Development*. Gilligan was a student of Lawrence Kohlberg, an influential psychologist who claimed to have identified six stages of human moral development, ranging from simple obedience to those in authority (stage 1) through to the mature ability to autonomously self-legislate in moral matters (stage 6). A neo-Kantian, Kohlberg was committed to a Rawlsian view of justice. (See Gilligan, Chapter 4, and Dancy, Chapter 9, for a more detailed description of Kohlberg's stages). Given Kohlberg's reliance on Kantian and Rawlsian notions of justice, it is perhaps not surprising that a debate which began in psychology came to resonate with feminists who were challenging the gender bias in traditional moral philosophy.

Kohlberg's account of human moral development was one in which women were seen to have not only a *different* moral sense from men but moreover, one deemed immature or *inferior*.[3] Gilligan claimed that Kohlberg's research methods were flawed and, further, that although women do indeed employ a different style of moral reasoning from men, there are no legitimate grounds on which to judge it as inferior. Gilligan proposed that, whereas men tend to approach moral issues from a perspective which assumes a set of principles within whose terms moral judgements should be made, women are more likely to approach moral problems in a particularistic and contextual fashion.[4] Along with other feminist theorists, Gilligan explained women's more contextual approach to moral problems by reference to their feeling more connected to others and their tendency to be responsive to the needs and feelings of others.

Gilligan's findings were consistent with other strands of feminist theory which held that the mothering practices of Western societies have significant effects on the development of male and female children and result in the stereotypical qualities of masculinity and femininity associated with adult men and women, respectively. For example, in *The Reproduction of Mothering: Psychoanalysis and the Sociology of Gender*, Nancy Chodorow (1978) argued that each generation reproduces the conditions of women's subordination through its childrearing practices. Relying on psychoanalytic approaches to child development, Chodorow asserted that young children initially base their identities on the person, or persons, from whom they receive nurturance. In Western cultures that person is almost always the child's mother. For boys this identification is sex-inappropriate and they must switch identification to the sex-appropriate father. Identification with the father may prove difficult because his work is likely to make him absent from the home for long periods. Boys experience this forced separation from the mother as traumatic and the resulting sense of self is likely to be defensively separate. The young boy must learn, according to this view, that he is not like the mother nor destined for a similar social role. Chodorow argued that masculine hostility towards women, and towards things associated with femininity, may be understood as a reaction to the fact that men must repudiate the initial sex-inappropriate identification which they had made when they were boys. Girls, on the other hand, lack the motivation to separate themselves from their mothers and so develop a sense of self which is marked by a strong connectedness to, and empathy with, others. In contemporary feminist thought this is called the 'relational' view of the self.

The relational view of the self has been very influential in feminist theories of sexual difference and has been used to explain women's different standpoints in areas as diverse as epistemology (see Harding, 1986), political theory (see Nedelsky, Chapter 20 in this volume) and, of course, ethics. It underpins the arguments for sex-specific approaches to moral philosophy described in Nel Noddings (1984), Sara Ruddick (1990), Sarah Hoagland (1988), and Virginia Held (1993). The idea of a 'different voice' has also become influential in applied ethics where Gilligan's views have been applied to nursing (see, for example, Khuse, 1995), education (Brabeck, 1989) and law (Menkel-Meadow, 1985).

However, the primary focus of this volume will be the controversy concerning the merits of the care approach compared to those of the justice approach in normative ethics.[5] In contemporary philosophy, the justice stance is closely identified with the influential view put forward by John Rawls in *A Theory of Justice* (1971) and, more recently, in *Political Liberalism* (1993), both of which receive a good deal of criticism in this volume. Feminists have accused Rawls of failing to include relations between the sexes and familial relations within the purview of his theory of justice (see Okin (1989) and Chapter 3 in this volume). From Mary Wollstonecraft (1792) to the present, feminists have argued that philosophies of justice have focused on (men's) rights in the public sphere at the expense of (women's) responsibilities and duties in the domestic sphere. Feminist philosophers often define care ethics by directly contrasting the 'different voice' of women to the Rawlsian 'voice' of justice. They have claimed that, whereas the justice stance is concerned to identify universal principles of justice, the care stance will stress responsiveness to the specific context in which a moral question arises. For the justice ethicist, mature moral selves are capable of impartially applying universally valid principles to particular cases. The care stance, on the other hand, not only acknowledges the affective relations obtaining between persons but, further, will see these relations as relevant to the adequate resolution of concrete ethical questions or dilemmas. Finally, whereas the care stance tends to focus on responsibilities and duties of care which arise through one's relation to others, the justice stance tends to focus on the rights of the individual.

Many philosophers have claimed that the care/justice contrast is overdrawn and argue that the two stances are compatible since they are merely the two sides of any single moral situation. Others, however, follow Gilligan when she states that the two perspectives are more like the ambiguous figure of the 'duck-rabbit' – one may see the rabbit or the duck, but not both at the same (see Gilligan, 1987 and also Flanagan and Jackson, Chapter 6 in this volume, who criticize the use of this 'Gestalt' metaphor).

Of course, feminists are not the only group to have criticized Rawls's approach to ethics and politics. Communitarians such as Michael Sandel (1982) and Michael Walzer (1983) have rejected the individualistic, contractarian base of the justice approach, stressing that individuals are formed in communities from which they acquire their sense of self and their moral values. Likewise, virtue ethicists such as Alasdair MacIntyre (1981, 1988) are critical of Rawlsian approaches for failing to note that virtues assume social practices and historical contexts in which particular kinds of ethical behaviour may, or may not, flourish. The distinctiveness of the feminist approach derives from the critical stance it takes toward communitarian and virtue ethics as well as to liberalism. Community values are often conservative with regard to women's 'proper place' and virtues, historically, have been gendered in ways that are unappealing to feminists. So, while feminist ethics may agree on some points with communitarians, and on others, with virtue ethics, it nevertheless finds aspects of those views incompatible with the feminist commitment to the equal treatment of women (see Mansbridge, Chapter 19 in this volume).

According to many feminists, communitarianism and virtue ethics suffer from the same problem as liberalism: namely that they fail to take adequate account of women's life experiences and the specific moral perspective to which those experiences have given rise. On most feminist views, women's relational sense of self and their greater empathy with others are seen to be socially constructed rather than innate. For example, Virginia Held (1989, 1990, 1993) maintains that women's traditional association with the tasks of caring for the young, the aged and the infirm have made them more sensitive to the needs of others. Held, along with many others, eschews any essential or natural basis to the performance of such tasks and, echoing Chodorow, suggests that if men took up an equal share of caring tasks, then this may lead to the merging of the different moral perspectives of the sexes.

The essays in this volume are thematically organized into five Parts. Part I provides the reader with some background to feminist thought in ethics, and in particular to the ethics of care approach. In the opening essay, Held argues that the traditional organization of society has led to the gendering of reason and emotion, the public and the private spheres. This situation has produced quite different senses of self and morality for men and women. In Chapter 2 Annette Baier asks what women want in a moral theory, and answers that perhaps a 'theory' is precisely what women do *not* want. Baier stresses that fostering trust rather than following rules may be more conducive to the promotion of moral relations between the sexes and a just society. The essay by Susan Moller Okin (Chapter 3) serves to introduce the reader to feminist criticisms of Kantian and Rawlsian morality while, at the same time, offering a sketch of Okin's broader project of recasting Rawls's theory of justice in order that it may accommodate these criticisms. The last two essays in this Part are by Gilligan and Cheshire Calhoun, respectively. The former is an early essay that anticipates the main themes of Gilligan's book,

*In A Different Voice*. It also offers a clear and succinct account of Kohlberg's six stages of moral judgement. The latter offers a brief but cogent account of why Gilligan's research, and the gender bias which it uncovered, should matter to all moral philosophers.

Part II begins by focusing on the debate that has been generated by the care approach in contemporary ethics and ends with essays that open up that debate to broader issues. In Chapter 6 Owen Flanagan and Kathryn Jackson argue that care and justice are not incompatible perspectives but rather different aspects of a moral situation which may be considered together by a moral reasoner of either sex. They argue for a rich and pluralist conception of moral personalities that would resist both a single ideal 'type' and the reduction of this plurality to only two 'voices'. In the following chapter Susan Mendus takes the care/justice debate into the public arena where, she argues, the assumption of face-to-face caring relations are inappropriate to the large, anonymous, post-industrial modern societies in which we live. However, she argues that the care approach does highlight an important tension between the liberal theorists' valuing of choice and autonomy, on one hand, and the communitarians' insistence on unchosen community and connectedness, on the other. In Mendus's view, feminist care ethics has the potential to make a significant contribution to contemporary moral thought by plotting a path between these two extremes.[6] Nel Noddings (Chapter 8) confronts criticisms often put to feminist care ethics – namely, that it essentializes sexual difference, that it offers support to the arcane view that women are incapable of acting in accordance with principles, and that it rejects the values of autonomy and impartiality. Noddings provides a good summary of these common criticisms while defending feminist ethics against them. In Chapter 9 Jonathan Dancy takes the claim that the two genders entertain distinct moral perspectives to be confused and suggests that the core of feminist ethics is particularism, which combines both care and the claims of justice. Part II closes with Jeremy Waldron's essay which puts a strong case for the need for Kantian rights as a necessary fallback for those occasions when caring relations are absent or break down.

In the 1980s feminist theory came under attack for repeating the very gestures of exclusion for which feminists had criticized Western philosophy.[7] Part III examines these issues by bringing together essays which challenge the assumed homogeneity of Gilligan's 'different voice'. These essays converge on issues concerning differences among women – especially differences of race and class. In Chapter 11 Elizabeth Spelman draws attention to social contexts in which some women patently failed to show care, concern or feelings of connectedness towards others (for example, slavery, Nazi Germany). She argues that feminist ethics must resist the temptation to romanticize women's nature and acknowledge that women (as well as men) sometimes fail to care for others. Uma Narayan (Chapter 12) deepens this line of criticism by stressing the importance of identifying *who* defines human needs in the context of colonialism, in which colonizers often describe their relation to the colonized in terms of 'care' or 'protection'. Kathleen League, in the following chapter, accuses Gilligan of importing middle-class bias into her interpretations of the moral dilemmas of the young women whom she studies while, in Chapter 14, Seyla Benhabib questions Rawls's and Kohlberg's commitment to the 'generalized other' who is 'disembedded [from any particular community, or time] and disembodied'. Benhabib argues that such a standpoint is incapable of considering the differences of race, sex, class and culture that are central to the complex identities of concrete individuals and puts forward the view that an adequate moral theory would need to take account of both the generalized other (the justice stance) and the concrete other (the care stance). Drawing on the work of Jürgen

Habermas, she suggests the model of a 'communicative ethic of need interpretations' which does not assume, but rather produces through dialogue and interaction, a commitment to universal norms. Nancy Fraser's response to this relational concept of identity, in Chapter 15, is to suggest that Benhabib's model of a communicative ethic may be expanded to include collectivities, allowing the development of an 'ethic of solidarity'.

Carole Pateman has stated that '[t]he dichotomy between the private and the public is central to almost two centuries of feminist writing and political struggle; it is, ultimately, what the feminist movement is about (Pateman, 1989, p. 118). Too often moral theorists have confined their ethical and political enquiries to relations in the public sphere. Part IV considers some common feminist criticisms of the public–private distinction, and its corollary, the division of human life into personal (the family) and political (the state) compartments. Relations of care and dependency are generally taken to be relations relevant to the familial or domestic sphere. On the other hand, relations between strangers in the public sphere are understood to be regulated according to rights rather than affection or care. This Part is framed by the question: could care provide the basis for political life and interaction? What are the political implications of promoting an ethic of care in the public sphere? How can one acknowledge human dependency without undermining the traditional ethical value of the autonomy of the individual? Many of the essays in Part IV argue that the care and the autonomy stances are not necessarily opposed. In Chapter 16 Katzenstein and Laitin set out three conditions which would need to be met if care ethics is to have a non-reactionary place in political life. The following essay by Mary Dietz cautions against the political implications of those versions of care ethics which privilege the mother–child relation. Dietz insists that an adequate theory of citizenship cannot have its basis in the particular activities of some subset of citizens (that is, women). Joan Tronto's brief essay (Chapter 18) considers the practical import of utilizing a care approach in politics. The last three essays in this Part, by Jane Mansbridge, Robert Goodin and Eva Feder Kittay, respectively, each open out the care/justice debate to the broader political arena. Mansbridge (Chapter 19) uses feminist insights to analyse terms central to political and moral theory (for example, autonomy, community, obligation, power) and argues that feminism is capable of forging new forms of thought that avoid the pitfalls of both liberalism and communitarianism. Goodin (Chapter 20) considers feminist objections to the centrality of rights in the liberal political order along with the feminist preference for fostering communities based in relations of trust. He argues that if rights are conceived as the necessary background to the fostering of trust and fair-dealing between persons then liberalism and relational feminism may be reconciled. In Chapter 22 Kittay criticizes both Rawls and traditional political theory for failing to attend to human dependency. She offers detailed criteria of adequacy which any political theory must meet if it is to acknowledge the private sphere, in which caring relations take place, as one to which questions of moral worth and political equality can be addressed.

Part V is framed by the question: must we choose between the care and justice perspectives? Margaret Walker's opening essay presents a challenge to contemporary moral theory: does contemporary feminist moral philosophy constitute an alternative 'epistemology'? In a similar vein, Susan Hekman (Chapter 24) suggests that Gilligan's thesis, and feminist research built upon it, signals a new discourse of morality, capable of theorizing multiple moral voices in new ways.[8] Gilligan's recent essay, presented as Chapter 25, puts the claim that her earlier work may be understood as introducing a 'paradigm shift' in the way that morality is conceived, and Held (Chapter 26) reflects upon the progress of the care/justice debate and states that the reconciliation of the two approaches should involve fitting the justice stance within care, which she sees as the more fundamental moral value. The volume ends with an essay by Marilyn Friedman which offers a critical overview of the now vast literature on care ethics.

## Acknowledgements

I would like to thank Robert E. Goodin, Genevieve Lloyd and Paul Patton for their generous and valuable advice during the preparation of this volume. Many thanks to Justine McGill and Kim Castle for providing excellent research assistance.

## Notes

1 See, for example, Irigaray (1993). For an accessible introduction to this field of research see Diprose (1994). Note too that the essays in this volume by Seyla Benhabib (Chapter 14), Nancy Fraser (Chapter 15) and Susan Hekman (Chapter 24) productively bring together elements from both 'analytic' and 'continental' approaches in philosophy.
2 There are a number of anthologies which address these issues. See: Bell (1993); Card (1991); Browning Cole and Coultrap-McQuin (1992); Frazer *et al.* (1992); Held (1995); Kittay and Meyers (1987); Larrabee (1993); Okin and Mansbridge (1994); and Tong (1993).
3 For Kohlberg's later reflections on the alleged gender bias in his theory of moral development see Kohlberg *et al.* (1983).
4 Such statements are obviously generalizations and many of the authors in this volume challenge the claim.
5 For an account of my own views on this debate, see Gatens (1995).
6 See Young (1990) for a feminist account of justice which attempts to acknowledge both community and autonomy.
7 For a representative account of these criticisms see Lugones and Spelman (1983).
8 For a more detailed account of Hekman's views see Hekman (1995).

## References

Bell, Linda A. (ed.) (1993), *Rethinking Ethics in the Midst of Violence: A Feminist Approach to Freedom*, Totowa, NJ: Rowman & Littlefield.

Brabeck, Mary M. (ed.) (1989), *Who Cares? Theory, Research, and Educational Implications of the Ethic of Care*, New York: Praeger.

Browning Cole, Eva and Coultrap-McQuin, Susan (eds) (1992), *Explorations in Feminist Ethics: Theory and Practice*, Bloomington/Indianapolis: Indiana University Press.

Card, Claudia (ed.) (1991), *Feminist Ethics*, Lawrence: University of Kansas Press.

Chodorow, Nancy (1978), *The Reproduction of Mothering: Psychoanalysis and the Sociology of Gender*, Berkeley: University of California Press.

Diprose, Rosalyn (1994), *The Bodies of Women: Ethics, Embodiment and Sexual Difference*, London and New York: Routledge.

Frazer, Elizabeth, Hornsby, Jennifer and Lovibond, Sabina (eds) (1992), *Ethics: A Feminist Reader*, Oxford/Cambridge, MA: Blackwell.

Gatens, Moira (1995), 'Between the Sexes: Care or Justice?', in Brenda Almond (ed.), *Introducing Applied Ethics*, Oxford: Blackwell.

Gilligan, Carol (1982), *In a Different Voice: Psychological Theory and Women's Development*, Cambridge, MA: Harvard University Press.

Gilligan, Carol (1987), 'Moral Orientation and Moral Development', in Eva F. Kittay and Diana T. Meyers (eds), *Women and Moral Theory*, Totowa, NJ: Rowman & Littlefield.

Harding, Sandra (1986), *The Science Question in Feminism*, Ithaca, NY: Cornell University Press.

Hekman, Susan J. (1995), *Moral Voices, Moral Selves: Carol Gilligan and Feminist Moral Theory*, Cambridge: Polity Press.

Held, Virginia (1989), 'Birth and Death', *Ethics*, **99** (2), pp. 362–88.

Held, Virginia (1990), 'Mothering versus Contract', in Jane J. Mansbridge (ed.), *Beyond Self-Interest*, Chicago: University of Chicago Press.

Held, Virginia (1993), *Feminist Morality: Transforming Culture, Society, and Politics*, Chicago: University of Chicago Press.

Held, Virginia (ed.) (1995), *Justice and Care: Essential Readings in Feminist Ethics*, Boulder, CO: Westview Press.

Hoagland, Sarah Lucia (1988), *Lesbian Ethics: Towards a New Value*, Palo Alto, California: Institute of Lesbian Studies.

Irigary, Luce (1993), *An Ethics of Sexual Difference*, trans. Carolyn Burke and Gillian C. Gill, Ithaca, NY: Cornell University Press.

Khuse, Helga (1995), 'Clinical Ethics and Nursing: "Yes" to Caring, but "No" to a Female Ethics of Care', *Bioethics*, **9** (3–4), pp. 207–19.

Kittay, Eva Feder and Meyers, Diana T. (eds) (1987), *Woman and Moral Theory*, Totowa, NJ: Rowman & Littlefield.

Kohlberg, Lawrence, Levine, C. and Hewar, A. (1983), *Moral Stages: A Current Formulation and Response to Critics*, New York: Karger,

Larrabee, Mary Jeanne (ed.) (1993), *An Ethic of Care: Feminist and Interdisciplinary Perspectives*, New York/London: Routledge.

Lugones, Maria and Spelman, Elizabeth (1983), 'Have We Got a Theory for You! Feminist Theory, Cultural Imperialism and the Demand for the "Woman's Voice"', *Women's Studies International Forum*, **6** (6), pp. 573–81.

MacIntyre, Alasdair (1981), *After Virtue: A Study in Moral Theory*, Notre Dame: University of Notre Dame Press.

MacIntyre, Alasdair (1988), *Whose Justice? Which Rationality?*, Notre Dame: University of Notre Dame Press.

Menkel-Meadow, Carrie (1985), 'Portia in a Different Voice', *Berkeley Women's Law Journal*, **1** (1), pp. 39–63.

Noddings, Nel (1984), *Caring: A Feminine Approach to Ethics and Moral Education*, Berkeley: University of California Press.

Okin, Susan Moller (1989), *Justice, Gender and the Family*, New York: Basic Books.

Okin, Susan Moller and Mansbridge, Jane (eds) (1994), *Feminism, Volume II*, Aldershot/Brookfield: Edward Elgar.

Pateman, Carole (1989), *The Disorder of Women: Democracy, Feminism and Political Theory*, Cambridge, MA: Polity Press.

Rawls, John (1971), *A Theory of Justice*, Cambridge, MA: Harvard University Press.

Rawls, John (1993), *Political Liberalism*, New York: Columbia University Press.

Ruddick, Sarah (1990), *Maternal Thinking: Towards a Politics of Peace*, London: The Women's Press.

Sandel, Michael J. (1982), *Liberalism and the Limits of Justice*, Cambridge: Cambridge University Press.

Tong, Rosemary (1993), *Feminine and Feminist Ethics*, Belmont, CA: Wadsworth.

Walzer, Michael (1983), *Spheres of Justice*, New York: Basic Books.

Wollstonecraft, M. (1975), *Vindication of the Rights of Woman* [1792], Harmondsworth: Penguin.

Young, Iris M. (1990), *Justice and the Politics of Difference*, Princeton, NJ: Princeton University Press.

# Part I
# Feminism, Women and Moral Theory

[1]

*Philosophy and Phenomenological Research*
Vol. L, Supplement, Fall 1990

# Feminist Transformations of Moral Theory

VIRGINIA HELD
*City University of New York, Graduate School and Hunter College*

The history of philosophy, including the history of ethics, has been constructed from male points of view, and has been built on assumptions and concepts that are by no means gender-neutral.[1] Feminists characteristically begin with different concerns and give different emphases to the issues we consider than do non-feminist approaches. And, as Lorraine Code expresses it, "starting points and focal points shape the impact of theoretical discussion."[2] Within philosophy, feminists often start with, and focus on, quite different issues than those found in standard philosophy and ethics, however "standard" is understood. Far from providing mere additional insights which can be incorporated into traditional theory, feminist explorations often require radical transformations of existing fields of inquiry and theory.[3] From a feminist point of view, moral theory along with almost all theory will have to be transformed to take adequate account of the experience of women.

I shall in this paper begin with a brief examination of how various fundamental aspects of the history of ethics have not been gender-neutral. And I shall discuss three issues where feminist rethinking is transforming moral concepts and theories.

## The History of Ethics

Consider the ideals embodied in the phrase "the man of reason." As Genevieve Lloyd has told the story, what has been taken to characterize the man of reason may have changed from historical period to historical

[1] See e.g. Cheshire Calhoun, "Justice, Care, Gender Bias," *The Journal of Philosophy* 85 (September, 1988): 451-63.

[2] Lorraine Code, "Second Persons," in *Science, Morality and Feminist Theory*, ed. Marsha Hanen and Kai Nielsen (Calgary: University of Calgary Press, 1987), p. 360.

[3] See e.g. *Revolutions in Knowledge: Feminism in the Social Sciences*, ed. Sue Rosenberg Zalk and Janice Gordon-Kelter (Boulder: Westview Press, forthcoming).

period, but in each, the character ideal of the man of reason has been constructed in conjunction with a rejection of whatever has been taken to be characteristic of the feminine. "Rationality," Lloyd writes, "has been conceived as transcendence of the 'feminine,' and the 'feminine' itself has been partly constituted by its occurrence within this structure."[4]

This has of course fundamentally affected the history of philosophy and of ethics. The split between reason and emotion is one of the most familiar of philosophical conceptions. And the advocacy of reason "controlling" unruly emotion, of rationality guiding responsible human action against the blindness of passion, has a long and highly influential history, almost as familiar to non-philosophers as to philosophers. We should certainly now be alert to the ways in which reason has been associated with male endeavor, emotion with female weakness, and the ways in which this is of course not an accidental association. As Lloyd writes, "From the beginnings of philosophical thought, femaleness was symbolically associated with what Reason supposedly left behind — the dark powers of the earth goddesses, immersion in unknown forces associated with mysterious female powers. The early Greeks saw women's capacity to conceive as connecting them with the fertility of Nature. As Plato later expressed the thought, women 'imitate the earth.'"[5]

Reason, in asserting its claims and winning its status in human history, was thought to have to conquer the female forces of Unreason. Reason and clarity of thought were early associated with maleness, and as Lloyd notes, "what had to be shed in developing culturally prized rationality was, from the start, symbolically associated with femaleness."[6] In later Greek philosophical thought, the form/matter distinction was articulated, and with a similar hierarchical and gendered association. Maleness was aligned with active, determinate, and defining form; femaleness with mere passive, indeterminate, and inferior matter. Plato, in the *Timaeus*, compared the defining aspect of form with the father, and indefinite matter with the mother; Aristotle also compared the form/matter distinction with the male/female distinction. To quote Lloyd again, "This comparison . . . meant that the very nature of knowledge was implicitly associated with the extrusion of what was symbolically associated with the feminine."[7]

---

[4] Genevieve Lloyd, *The Man of Reason: 'Male' and 'Female' in Western Philosophy* (Minneapolis: University of Minnesota Press, 1984), p. 104.

[5] Ibid., p. 2.

[6] Ibid., p. 3.

[7] Ibid., p. 4. For a feminist view of how reason and emotion in the search for knowledge might be reevaluated, see Alison M. Jaggar, "Love and Knowledge: Emotion in Feminist Epistemology," *Inquiry* 32 (June, 1989): 151-76.

The associations, between Reason, form, knowledge, and maleness, have persisted in various guises, and have permeated what has been thought to be moral knowledge as well as what has been thought to be scientific knowledge, and what has been thought to be the practice of morality. The associations between the philosophical concepts and gender cannot be merely dropped, and the concepts retained regardless of gender, because gender has been built into them in such a way that without it, they will have to be different concepts. As feminists repeatedly show, if the concept of "human" were built on what we think about "woman" rather than what we think about "man," it would be a very different concept. Ethics, thus, has not been a search for universal, or truly human guidance, but a gender-biased enterprise.

Other distinctions and associations have supplemented and reinforced the identification of reason with maleness, and of the irrational with the female; on this and other grounds "man" has been associated with the human, "woman" with the natural. Prominent among distinctions reinforcing the latter view has been that between the public and the private, because of the way they have been interpreted. Again, these provide as familiar and entrenched a framework as do reason and emotion, and they have been as influential for non-philosophers as for philosophers. It has been supposed that in the public realm, man transcends his animal nature and creates human history. As citizen, he creates government and law; as warrior, he protects society by his willingness to risk death; and as artist or philosopher, he overcomes his human mortality. Here, in the public realm, morality should guide human decision. In the household, in contrast, it has been supposed that women merely "reproduce" life as natural, biological matter. Within the household, the "natural" needs of man for food and shelter are served, and new instances of the biological creature that man is are brought into being. But what is distinctively human, and what transcends any given level of development to create human progress, are thought to occur elsewhere.

This contrast was made highly explicit in Aristotle's conceptions of polis and household; it has continued to affect the basic assumptions of a remarkably broad swath of thought ever since. In ancient Athens, women were confined to the household; the public sphere was literally a male domain. In more recent history, though women have been permitted to venture into public space, the associations of the public, historically male sphere with the distinctively human, and of the household, historically a female sphere, with the merely natural and repetitious, have persisted. These associations have deeply affected moral theory, which has often supposed the transcendent, public domain to be relevant to the foundations of morality in ways that the natural behavior of women in the household could not be. To take some recent and representative examples, David Heyd, in his discussion of supererogation, dismisses a mother's sacrifice for her child as an example of the supererogatory because it belongs, in his view, to "the sphere of natural relationships and instinctive feelings (which lie outside morality)."[8] J. O. Urmson had earlier taken a similar position. In his discussion of supererogation, Urmson said, "Let us be clear that we are not now considering cases of natural affection, such as the sacrifice made by a mother for her child; such cases may be said with some justice not to fall under the concept of morality . . ."[9] And in a recent article called "Distrusting Economics," Alan Ryan argues persuasively about the questionableness of economics and other branches of the social sciences built on the assumption that human beings are rational, self-interested calculators; he discusses various examples of non self-interested behavior, such as of men in wartime, which show the assumption to be false, but nowhere in the article is there any mention of the activity of mothering, which would seem to be a fertile locus for doubts about the usual picture of rational man.[10] Although Ryan does not provide the kind of explicit reason offered by Heyd and Urmson for omitting the context of mothering from consideration as relevant to his discussion, it is difficult to understand the omission without a comparable assumption being implicit here, as it so often is elsewhere. Without feminist insistence on the relevance for morality of the experience in mothering, this context is largely ignored by moral theorists. And yet, from a gender-neutral point of view, how can this vast and fundamental domain of human experience possibly be imagined to lie "outside morality"?

The result of the public/private distinction, as usually formulated, has been to privilege the points of view of men in the public domains of state and law, and later in the marketplace, and to discount the experience of women. Mothering has been conceptualized as a primarily biological activity, even when performed by humans, and virtually no moral theory in the history of ethics has taken mothering, as experienced by women, seriously as a source of moral insight, until feminists in recent years have

---

8 David Heyd, *Supererogation: Its Status in Ethical Theory* (New York: Cambridge University Press, 1982), p. 134.

9 J. O. Urmson, "Saints and Heroes," in *Essays in Moral Philosophy*, ed. A. I. Melden (Seattle: University of Washington Press, 1958), p. 202. I am indebted to Marcia Baron for pointing out this and the previous example in her "Kantian Ethics and Supererogation," *The Journal of Philosophy* 84 (May, 1987): 237-62.

10 Alan Ryan, "Distrusting Economics," *New York Review of Books* (May 18, 1989): 25-27. For a different treatment, see *Beyond Self-Interest*, ed. Jane Mansbridge (Chicago: University of Chicago Press, 1990).

begun to.[11] Women have been seen as emotional rather than as rational beings, and thus as incapable of full moral personhood. Women's behavior has been interpreted as either "natural" and driven by instinct, and thus as irrelevant to morality and to the construction of moral principles, or it has been interpreted as, at best, in need of instruction and supervision by males better able to know what morality requires and better able to live up to its demands.

The Hobbesian conception of reason is very different from the Platonic or Aristotelian conceptions before it, and from the conceptions of Rousseau or Kant or Hegel later; all have in common that they ignore and disparage the experience and reality of women. Consider Hobbes' account of man in the state of nature contracting with other men to establish society. These men hypothetically come into existence fully formed and independent of one another, and decide on entering or staying outside of civil society. As Christine Di Stefano writes, "What we find in Hobbes's account of human nature and political order is a vital concern with the survival of a self conceived in masculine terms . . . This masculine dimension of Hobbes's atomistic egoism is powerfully underscored in his state of nature, which is effectively built on the foundation of denied maternity."[12] In *The Citizen*, where Hobbes gave his first systematic exposition of the state of nature, he asks us to "consider men as if but even now sprung out of the earth, and suddenly, like mushrooms, come to full maturity, without all kind of engagement with each other."[13] As Di Stefano says, it is a most incredible and problematic feature of Hobbes's state of nature that the men in it "are not born of, much less nurtured by, women, or anyone else."[14] To abstract from the complex web of human reality an abstract man for rational perusal, Hobbes has, Di Stefano continues, "expunged human reproduction and early nurturance, two of the most basic and typically female-identified features of distinctively human life, from his account of basic human nature. Such a strategy ensures that he can present a thoroughly atomistic subject . . ."[15] From the point of view of women's experience, such a subject or self is unbelievable and mis-

---

[11] See especially *Mothering: Essays in Feminist Theory*, ed. Joyce Trebilcot (Totowa, New Jersey: Rowman and Allanheld, 1984); and Sara Ruddick, *Maternal Thinking: Toward a Politics of Peace* (Boston: Beacon Press, 1989).

[12] Christine Di Stefano, "Masculinity as Ideology in Political Theory: Hobbesian Man Considered," *Women's Studies International Forum* (Special Issue: *Hypatia*), Vol. 6, No. 6 (1983): 633-44, p. 637.

[13] Thomas Hobbes, *The Citizen: Philosophical Rudiments Concerning Government and Society*, ed. B. Gert (Garden City, New York: Doubleday, 1972 (1651)), p. 205.

[14] Di Stefano, op. cit., p. 638.

[15] Ibid.

leading, even as a theoretical construct. The Leviathan, Di Stefano writes, "is effectively comprised of a body politic of orphans who have reared themselves, whose desires are situated within and reflect nothing but independently generated movement. . . . These essential elements are natural human beings conceived along masculine lines."[16]

Rousseau, and Kant, and Hegel, paid homage to the emotional power, the aesthetic sensibility, and the familial concerns, respectively, of women. But since in their views morality must be based on rational principle, and women were incapable of full rationality, or a degree or kind of rationality comparable to that of men, women were deemed, in the view of these moralists, to be inherently wanting in morality. For Rousseau, women must be trained from childhood to submit to the will of men lest their sexual power lead both men and women to disaster. For Kant, women were thought incapable of achieving full moral personhood, and women lose all charm if they try to behave like men by engaging in rational pursuits. For Hegel, women's moral concern for their families could be admirable in its proper place, but is a threat to the more universal aims to which men, as members of the state, should aspire.[17]

These images, of the feminine as what must be overcome if knowledge and morality are to be achieved, of female experience as naturally irrelevant to morality, and of women as inherently deficient moral creatures, are built into the history of ethics. Feminists examine these images, and see that they are not the incidental or merely idiosyncratic suppositions of a few philosophers whose views on many topics depart far from the ordinary anyway. Such views are the nearly uniform reflection in philosophical and ethical theory of patriarchal attitudes pervasive throughout human history. Or they are exaggerations even of ordinary male experience, which exaggerations then reinforce rather than temper other patriarchal conceptions and institutions. They distort the actual experience and aspirations of many men as well as of women. Annette Baier recently speculated about why it is that moral philosophy has so seriously overlooked the trust between human beings that in her view is an utterly central aspect of moral life. She noted that "the great moral theorists in our tradition not only are all men, they are mostly men who had minimal adult dealings with (and so were then minimally influenced by)

[16] Ibid., p. 639.

[17] For examples of relevant passages, see *Philosophy of Woman: Classical to Current Concepts*, ed. Mary Mahowald (Indianapolis: Hackett, 1978); and *Visions of Women*, ed. Linda Bell (Clifton, New Jersey: Humana, 1985). For discussion, see Susan Moller Okin, *Women in Western Political Thought* (Princeton, New Jersey: Princeton University Press, 1979); and Lorenne Clark and Lynda Lange, eds., *The Sexism of Social and Political Theory* (Toronto: University of Toronto Press, 1979).

women."[18] They were for the most part "clerics, misogynists, and puritan bachelors," and thus it is not surprising that they focus their philosophical attention "so single-mindedly on cool, distanced relations between more or less free and equal adult strangers . . ."[19]

As feminists, we deplore the patriarchal attitudes that so much of philosophy and moral theory reflect. But we recognize that the problem is more serious even than changing those attitudes. For moral theory as so far developed is incapable of correcting itself without an almost total transformation. It cannot simply absorb the gender that has been "left behind," even if both genders would want it to. To continue to build morality on rational principles opposed to the emotions and to include women among the rational will leave no one to reflect the promptings of the heart, which promptings can be moral rather than merely instinctive. To simply bring women into the public and male domain of the polis will leave no one to speak for the household. Its values have been hitherto unrecognized, but they are often moral values. Or to continue to seek contractual restraints on the pursuits of self-interest by atomistic individuals, and to have women join men in devotion to these pursuits, will leave no one involved in the nurturance of children and cultivation of social relations, which nurturance and cultivation can be of greatest moral import.

There are very good reasons for women not to want simply to be accorded entry as equals into the enterprise of morality as so far developed. In a recent survey of types of feminist moral theory, Kathryn Morgan notes that "many women who engage in philosophical reflection are acutely aware of the masculine nature of the profession and tradition, and feel their own moral concerns as women silenced or trivialized in virtually all the official settings that define the practice."[20] Women should clearly not agree, as the price of admission to the masculine realm of traditional morality, to abandon our own moral concerns as women.

And so we are groping to shape new moral theory. Understandably, we do not yet have fully worked out feminist moral theories to offer. But we can suggest some directions our project of developing such theories is taking. As Kathryn Morgan points out, there is not likely to be a "star" feminist moral theorist on the order of a Rawls or Nozick: "There will be no individual singled out for two reasons. One reason is that vital moral and theoretical conversations are taking place on a large dialectical scale as the

---

[18] Annette Baier, "Trust and Anti-Trust," *Ethics* 96 (1986): 231-60, pp. 247-48.

[19] Ibid.

[20] Kathryn Pauly Morgan, "Strangers in a Strange Land: Feminists Visit Relativists" in *Perspectives on Relativism*, ed. D. Odegaard and Carole Stewart (Toronto: Agathon Press, 1990).

feminist community struggles to develop a feminist ethic. The second reason is that this community of feminist theoreticians is calling into question the very model of the individualized autonomous self presupposed by a star-centered male-dominated tradition . . . We experience it as a common labour, a common task."[21]

The dialogues that are enabling feminist approaches to moral theory to develop are proceeding. As Alison Jaggar makes clear in her useful overview of them, there is no unitary view of ethics that can be identified as "feminist ethics." Feminist approaches to ethics share a commitment to "rethinking ethics with a view to correcting whatever forms of male bias it may contain."[22] While those who develop these approaches are "united by a shared project, they diverge widely in their views as to how this project is to be accomplished."[23]

Not all feminists, by any means, agree that there are distinctive feminist virtues or values. Some are especially skeptical of the attempt to give positive value to such traditional "feminine virtues" as a willingness to nurture, or an affinity with caring, or reluctance to seek independence. They see this approach as playing into the hands of those who would confine women to traditional roles.[24] Other feminists are skeptical of all claims about women as such, emphasizing that women are divided by class and race and sexual orientation in ways that make any conclusions drawn from "women's experience" dubious.[25]

Still, it is possible, I think, to discern various important focal points evident in current feminist attempts to transform ethics into a theoretical and practical activity that could be acceptable from a feminist point of view. In the glimpse I have presented of bias in the history of ethics, I focused on what, from a feminist point of view, are three of its most questionable aspects: 1) the split between reason and emotion and the devaluation of emotion; 2) the public/private distinction and the relegation of the private to the natural; and 3) the concept of the self as constructed from a male

[21] Kathryn Morgan, "Women and Moral Madness," in *Science, Morality and Feminist Theory*, ed. Hanen and Nielsen, p. 223.

[22] Alison M. Jaggar, "Feminist Ethics: Some Issues For The Nineties," *Journal of Social Philosophy* 20 (Spring/Fall 1989), p. 91.

[23] Ibid.

[24] One well-argued statement of this position is Barbara Houston, "Rescuing Womanly Virtues: Some Dangers of Moral Reclamation," in *Science, Morality and Feminist Theory*, ed. Hanen and Nielsen.

[25] See e.g. Elizabeth V. Spelman, *Inessential Woman: Problems of Exclusion in Feminist Thought* (Boston: Beacon Press, 1988). See also Sarah Lucia Hoagland, *Lesbian Ethics: Toward New Value* (Palo Alto, California: Institute of Lesbian Studies, 1989); and Katie Geneva Cannon, *Black Womanist Ethics* (Atlanta, Georgia: Scholars Press, 1988).

point of view. In the remainder of this article, I shall consider further how some feminists are exploring these topics. We are showing how their previous treatment has been distorted, and we are trying to reenvision the realities and recommendations with which these aspects of moral theorizing do and should try to deal.

## I. Reason and Emotion

In the area of moral theory in the modern era, the priority accorded to reason has taken two major forms. A) On the one hand has been the Kantian, or Kantian-inspired search for very general, abstract, deontological, universal moral principles by which rational beings should be guided. Kant's Categorical Imperative is a foremost example: it suggests that all moral problems can be handled by applying an impartial, pure, rational principle to particular cases. It requires that we try to see what the general features of the problem before us are, and that we apply an abstract principle, or rules derivable from it, to this problem. On this view, this procedure should be adequate for all moral decisions. We should thus be able to act as reason recommends, and resist yielding to emotional inclinations and desires in conflict with our rational wills.

B) On the other hand, the priority accorded to reason in the modern era has taken a Utilitarian form. The Utilitarian approach, reflected in rational choice theory, recognizes that persons have desires and interests, and suggests rules of rational choice for maximizing the satisfaction of these. While some philosophers in this tradition espouse egoism, especially of an intelligent and long-term kind, many do not. They begin, however, with assumptions that what are morally relevant are gains and losses of utility to theoretically isolatable individuals, and that the outcome at which morality should aim is the maximization of the utility of individuals. Rational calculation about such an outcome will, in this view, provide moral recommendations to guide all our choices. As with the Kantian approach, the Utilitarian approach relies on abstract general principles or rules to be applied to particular cases. And it holds that although emotion is, in fact, the source of our desires for certain objectives, the task of morality should be to instruct us on how to pursue those objectives most rationally. Emotional attitudes toward moral issues themselves interfere with rationality and should be disregarded. Among the questions Utilitarians can ask can be questions about which emotions to cultivate, and which desires to try to change, but these questions are to be handled in the terms of rational calculation, not of what our feelings suggest.

Although the conceptions of what the judgments of morality should be based on, and of how reason should guide moral decision, are different in Kantian and in Utilitarian approaches, both share a reliance on a highly abstract, universal principle as the appropriate source of moral guidance, and both share the view that moral problems are to be solved by the application of such an abstract principle to particular cases. Both share an admiration for the rules of reason to be appealed to in moral contexts, and both denigrate emotional responses to moral issues.

Many feminist philosophers have questioned whether the reliance on abstract rules, rather than the adoption of more context-respectful approaches, can possibly be adequate for dealing with moral problems, especially as women experience them.[26] Though Kantians may hold that complex rules can be elaborated for specific contexts, there is nevertheless an assumption in this approach that the more abstract the reasoning applied to a moral problem, the more satisfactory. And Utilitarians suppose that one highly abstract principle, The Principle of Utility, can be applied to every moral problem no matter what the context.

A genuinely universal or gender-neutral moral theory would be one which would take account of the experience and concerns of women as fully as it would take account of the experience and concerns of men. When we focus on the experience of women, however, we seem to be able to see a set of moral concerns becoming salient that differs from those of traditional or standard moral theory. Women's experience of moral problems seems to lead us to be especially concerned with actual relationships between embodied persons, and with what these relationships seem to require. Women are often inclined to attend to rather than to dismiss the particularities of the context in which a moral problem arises. And we often pay attention to feelings of empathy and caring to suggest what we ought to do rather than relying as fully as possible on abstract rules of reason.

Margaret Walker, for instance, contrasts feminist moral "understanding" with traditional moral "knowledge." She sees the components of the former as involving "attention, contextual and narrative appreciation, and communication in the event of moral deliberation."[27] This alternative moral epistemology holds that "the adequacy of moral understanding decreases as its form approaches generality through abstraction."[28]

---

[26] For an approach to social and political as well as moral issues that attempts to be context-respectful, see Virginia Held, *Rights and Goods. Justifying Social Action* (Chicago: University of Chicago Press, 1989).

[27] Margaret Urban Walker, "Moral Understandings: Alternative 'Epistemology' for a Feminist Ethics," *Hypatia* 4 (Summer, 1989): 15-28, p. 19.

[28] Ibid., p. 20. See also Iris Marion Young, "Impartiality and the Civic Public. Some Implications of Feminist Critiques of Moral and Political Theory," in Seyla Benhabib and Drucilla Cornell, *Feminism as Critique* (Minneapolis: University of Minnesota Press, 1987).

The work of psychologists such as Carol Gilligan and others has led to a clarification of what may be thought of as tendencies among women to approach moral issues differently. Rather than interpreting moral problems in terms of what could be handled by applying abstract rules of justice to particular cases, many of the women studied by Gilligan tended to be more concerned with preserving actual human relationships, and with expressing care for those for whom they felt responsible. Their moral reasoning was typically more embedded in a context of particular others than was the reasoning of a comparable group of men.[29] One should not equate tendencies women in fact display with feminist views, since the former may well be the result of the sexist, oppressive conditions in which women's lives have been lived. But many feminists see our own consciously considered experience as lending confirmation to the view that what has come to be called "an ethic of care" needs to be developed. Some think it should supercede "the ethic of justice" of traditional or standard moral theory. Others think it should be integrated with the ethic of justice and rules.

In any case, feminist philosophers are in the process of reevaluating the place of emotion in morality in at least two respects. First, many think morality requires the development of the moral emotions, in contrast to moral theories emphasizing the primacy of reason. As Annette Baier notes, the rationalism typical of traditional moral theory will be challenged when we pay attention to the role of parent. "It might be important," she writes, "for father figures to have rational control over their violent urges to beat to death the children whose screams enrage them, but more than control of such nasty passions seems needed in the mother or primary parent, or parent-substitute, by most psychological theories. They need to love their children, not just to control their irritation,"[30] So the emphasis in many traditional theories on rational control over the emotions, "rather than on cultivating desirable forms of emotion,"[31] is challenged by feminist approaches to ethics.

Secondly, emotion will be respected rather than dismissed by many feminist moral philosophers in the process of gaining moral understanding. The experience and practice out of which feminist moral theory can be expected to be developed will include embodied feeling as well as

---

[29] See especially Carol Gilligan, *In a Different Voice. Psychological Theory and Women's Development* (Cambridge, Massachusetts: Harvard University Press, 1988); and Eva Feder Kittay and Diana T. Meyers eds., *Women and Moral Theory* (Totowa, New Jersey: Rowman and Allanheld, 1987).

[30] Annette Baier, "The Need for More Than Justice," in *Science, Morality and Feminist Theory*, ed. Hanen and Nielsen, p. 55.

[31] Ibid.

thought. In a recent overview of a vast amount of writing, Kathryn Morgan states that "feminist theorists begin ethical theorizing with embodied, gendered subjects who have particular histories, particular communities, particular allegiances, and particular visions of human flourishing. The starting point involves valorizing what has frequently been most mistrusted and despised in the western philosophical tradition . . ."[32] Among the elements being reevaluated are feminine emotions. The "care" of the alternative feminist approach to morality appreciates rather than rejects emotion. The caring relationships important to feminist morality cannot be understood in terms of abstract rules or moral reasoning. And the "weighing" so often needed between the conflicting claims of some relationships and others cannot be settled by deduction or rational calculation. A feminist ethic will not just acknowledge emotion, as do Utilitarians, as giving us the objectives toward which moral rationality can direct us. It will embrace emotion as providing at least a partial basis for morality itself, and for moral understanding.

Annette Baier stresses the centrality of trust for an adequate morality.[33] Achieving and maintaining trusting, caring relationships is quite different from acting in accord with rational principles, or satisfying the individual desires of either self or other. Caring, empathy, feeling with others, being sensitive to each other's feelings, all may be better guides to what morality requires in actual contexts than may abstract rules of reason, or rational calculation, or at least they may be necessary components of an adequate morality.

The fear that a feminist ethic will be a relativistic "situation ethic" is misplaced. Some feelings can be as widely shared as are rational beliefs, and feminists do not see their views as reducible to "just another attitude."[34] In her discussion of the differences between feminist medical ethics and non-feminist medical ethics, Susan Sherwin gives an example of how feminists reject the mere case by case approach that has come to predominate in nonfeminist medical ethics. The latter also rejects the excessive reliance on abstract rules characteristic of standard ethics, and in this way resembles feminist ethics. But the very focus on cases in isolation from one another deprives this approach from attending to general features in the institutions and practices of medicine that, among other faults, systematically contribute to the oppression of women.[35] The dif-

[32] Kathryn Pauly Morgan, "Strangers in a Strange Land . . . ," p. 2.

[33] Annette Baier, "Trust and Anti-Trust."

[34] See especially Kathryn Pauly Morgan, "Strangers in a Strange Land . . ."

[35] Susan Sherwin, "Feminist and Medical Ethics: Two Different Approaches to Contextual Ethics," *Hypatia* 4 (Summer, 1989): 57-72.

ference of approach can be seen in the treatment of issues in the new reproductive technologies, where feminists consider how the new technologies may further decrease the control of women over reproduction.

This difference might be thought to be one of substance rather than of method, but Sherwin shows the implications for method also. With respect to reproductive technologies one can see especially clearly the deficiencies of the case by case approach: what needs to be considered is not only choice in the purely individualistic interpretation of the case by case approach, but control at a more general level and how it affects the structure of gender in society. Thus, a feminist perspective does not always counsel attention to specific case vs. appeal to general considerations, as some sort of methodological rule. But the general considerations are often not the purely abstract ones of traditional and standard moral theory, they are the general features and judgments to be made about cases in actual (which means, so far, patriarchal) societies. A feminist evaluation of a moral problem should never omit the political elements involved; and it is likely to recognize that political issues cannot be dealt with adequately in purely abstract terms any more than can moral issues.

The liberal tradition in social and moral philosophy argues that in pluralistic society and even more clearly in a pluralistic world, we cannot agree on our visions of the good life, on what is the best kind of life for humans, but we can hope to agree on the minimal conditions for justice, for coexistence within a framework allowing us to pursue our visions of the good life.[36] Many feminists contend that the commitment to justice needed for agreement *in actual conditions* on even minimal requirements of justice is as likely to demand relational feelings as a rational recognition of abstract principles. Human beings can and do care, and are capable of caring far more than at present, about the sufferings of children quite distant from them, about the prospects for future generations, and about the well-being of the globe. The liberal tradition's mutually disinterested rational individualists would seem unlikely to care enough to take the actions needed to achieve moral decency at a global level, or environmental sanity for decades hence, as they would seem unable to represent caring relationships within the family and among friends. As Annette Baier puts it, "A moral theory, it can plausibly be claimed, cannot regard concern for new and future persons as an optional charity left for those with a taste for it. If the morality the theory endorses is to sustain itself, it must provide for its own continuers, not just take out a loan on a carefully

[36] See especially the work of John Rawls and Ronald Dworkin; see also Charles Larmore, *Patterns of Moral Complexity* (Cambridge: Cambridge University Press, 1987).

encouraged maternal instinct or on the enthusiasm of a self-selected group of environmentalists, who make it their business or hobby to be concerned with what we are doing to mother earth."[37]

The possibilities as well as the problems (and we are well aware of some of them) in a feminist reenvisioning of emotion and reason need to be further developed, but we can already see that the views of nonfeminist moral theory are unsatisfactory.

### II. The Public and the Private

The second questionable aspect of the history of ethics on which I focused was its conception of the distinction between the public and the private. As with the split between reason and emotion, feminists are showing how gender-bias has distorted previous conceptions of these spheres, and we are trying to offer more appropriate understandings of "private" morality and "public" life.

Part of what feminists have criticized has been the way the distinction has been accompanied by a supposition that what occurs in the household occurs as if on an island beyond politics, whereas the personal is highly affected by the political power beyond, from legislation about abortion to the greater earning power of men, to the interconnected division of labor by gender both within and beyond the household, to the lack of adequate social protection for women against domestic violence.[38] Of course we recognize that the family is not identical to the state, and we need concepts for thinking about the private or personal, and the public or political. But they will have to be very different from the traditional concepts.

Feminists have also criticized deeper assumptions about what is distinctively human and what is "natural" in the public and private aspects of human life, and what is meant by "natural" in connection with women.[39] Consider the associations that have traditionally been built up: the public realm is seen as the distinctively human realm in which man transcends his animal nature, while the private realm of the household is seen as the natural region in which women merely reproduce the spe-

[37] Annette Baier, "The Need for More Than Justice," pp. 53-54.

[38] See e.g. Linda Nicholson, *Gender and History. The Limits of Social Theory in the Age of the Family* (New York: Columbia University Press, 1986); and Jean Bethke Elshtain, *Public Man, Private Woman* (Princeton, New Jersey: Princeton University Press, 1981). See also Carole Pateman, *The Sexual Contract* (Stanford, California: Stanford University Press, 1988).

[39] See e.g. Susan Moller Okin, *Women in Western Political Thought*. See also Alison M. Jaggar, *Feminist Politics and Human Nature* (Totowa, New Jersey: Rowman and Allanheld, 1983).

cies.[40] These associations are extraordinarily pervasive in standard concepts and theories, in art and thought and cultural ideals, and especially in politics.

Dominant patterns of thought have seen women as primarily mothers, and mothering as the performance of a primarily biological function. Then it has been supposed that while engaging in political life is a specifically human activity, women are engaged in an activity which is not specifically human. Women accordingly have been thought to be closer to nature than men,[41] to be enmeshed in a biological function involving processes more like those in which other animals are involved than like the rational discussion of the citizen in the polis, or the glorious battles of noble soldiers, or the trading and rational contracting of "economic man." The total or relative exclusion of women from the domain of public life has then been seen as either inevitable or appropriate.

The view that women are more determined by biology than are men is still extraordinarily prevalent. It is as questionable from a feminist perspective as many other traditional misinterpretations of women's experience. Human mothering is an extremely different activity from the mothering engaged in by other animals. The work and speech of men is recognized as very different from what might be thought of as the "work" and "speech" of other animals. Human mothering is fully as different from animal mothering. Of course all human beings are animal as well as human. But to whatever extent it is appropriate to recognize a difference between "man" and other animals, so would it be appropriate to recognize a comparable difference between "woman" and other animals, and between the activities — including mothering — engaged in by women and the behavior of other animals.

Human mothering shapes language and culture, it forms human social personhood, it develops morality. Animal behavior can be highly impressive and complex, but it does not have built into it any of the consciously chosen aims of morality. In creating human social persons, human mothering is different in kind from merely propagating a species. And human mothering can be fully as creative an activity as those activities traditionally thought of as distinctively human, because to create *new* persons, and new types of *persons*, can surely be as creative as to make new objects, products, or institutions. *Human* mothering is no more "natural" or "primarily biological" than is any other human activity.

[40] So entrenched is this way of thinking that it was even reflected in Simone de Beauvoir's pathbreaking feminist text *The Second Sex*, published in 1949. Here, as elsewhere, feminists have had to transcend our own early searches for our own perspectives.

[41] See e.g. Sherry B. Ortner, "Is Female to Male as Nature is to Culture?" in *Woman, Culture, and Society*, ed. Michelle Z. Rosaldo and Louise Lamphere (Stanford: Stanford University Press, 1974).

Consider nursing an infant, often thought of as the epitome of a biological process with which mothering is associated and women are identified. There is no reason to think of human nursing as any more simply biological than there is to think of, say, a businessmen's lunch this way. Eating is a biological process, but what and how and with whom we eat are thoroughly cultural. Whether and how long and with whom a woman nurses an infant, are also human, cultural matters. If men transcend the natural by conquering new territory and trading with their neighbors and making deals over lunch to do so, women can transcend the natural by choosing not to nurse their children when they could, or choosing to nurse them when their culture tells them not to, or singing songs to their infants as they nurse, or nursing in restaurants to overcome the prejudices against doing so, or thinking human thoughts as they nurse, and so forth. Human culture surrounds and characterizes the activity of nursing as it does the activities of eating, or governing, or writing, or thinking.

We are continually being presented with images of the humanly new and creative as occuring in the public realm of the polis, or the realms of marketplace or of art and science outside the household. The very term 'reproduction' suggests mere repetition, the "natural" bringing into existence of repeated instances of the same human animal. But human reproduction is not repetition.[42] This is not to suggest that bringing up children in the interstices of patriarchal society, in society structured by institutions supporting male dominance, can achieve the potential of transformation latent in the activity of human mothering. But the activity of creating new social persons and new kinds of persons is potentially the most transformative human activity of all. And it suggests that morality should concern itself first of all with this activity, with what its norms and practices ought to be, and with how the institutions and arrangements throughout society and the world ought to be structured to facilitate the right kinds of development of the best kinds of new persons. The flourishing of children ought to be at the very center of moral and social and political and economic and legal thought, rather than, as at present, at the periphery, if attended to at all.

Revised conceptions of public and private have significant implications for our conceptions of human beings and relationships between them. Some feminists suggest that instead of seeing human relationships in terms of the impersonal ones of the "public" sphere, as standard political and moral theory has so often done, we might consider seeing human relationships in terms of those experienced in the sphere of the "private," or

[42] For further discussion and an examination of surrounding associations, see Virginia Held, "Birth and Death," in *Ethics* 99 (January 1989): 362-88.

of what these relationships could be imagined to be like in post-patriarchal society.[43] The traditional approach is illustrated by those who generalize, to other regions of human life than the economic, assumptions about "economic man" in contractual relations with other men. It sees such impersonal, contractual relations as paradigmatic, even, on some views, for moral theory. Many feminists, in contrast, consider the realm of what has been misconstrued as the "private" as offering guidance to what human beings and their relationships should be like even in regions beyond those of family and friendship. Sara Ruddick looks at the implications of the practice of mothering for the conduct of peace politics.[44] Marilyn Friedman and Lorraine Code consider friendship, especially as women understand it, as a possible model for human relationships.[45] Others see society as non-contractual rather than as contractual.

Clearly, a reconceptualization is needed of the ways in which every human life is entwined with personal and with social components. Feminist theorists are contributing imaginative work to this project.

### III. The Concept of Self

Let me turn now to the third aspect of the history of ethics which I discussed and which feminists are re-envisioning: the concept of self. One of the most important emphases in a feminist approach to morality is the recognition that more attention must be paid to the domain between, on the one hand, the self as ego, as self-interested individual, and, on the other hand, the universal, everyone, others in general.[46] Traditionally, ethics has dealt with these poles of individual self and universal all. Usually, it has called for impartiality against the partiality of the egoistic self; sometimes it has defended egoism against claims for a universal perspective. But most standard moral theory has hardly noticed as morally significant the intermediate realm of family relations and relations of friendship, of group ties and neighborhood concerns, especially from the point of view of women. When it has noticed this intermediate realm it has often seen its attachments as threatening to the aspirations of the Man of Reason, or as subversive of "true" morality. In seeing the problems of ethics as problems of reconciling the interests of the self with what would be right or

---

[43] See e.g., Virginia Held, "Non-contractual Society: A Feminist View," in *Science, Morality and Feminist Theory*, ed. Hanen and Nielsen.

[44] Sara Ruddick, *Maternal Thinking*.

[45] See Marilyn Friedman, "Feminism and Modern Friendship: Dislocating the Community," *Ethics* 99 (January 1989): 275-90; and Lorraine Code, "Second Persons."

[46] See Virginia Held, "Feminism and Moral Theory," in *Women and Moral Theory*, ed. Kittay and Meyers.

best for "everyone," standard ethics has neglected the moral aspects of the concern and sympathy which people actually feel for particular others, and what moral experience in this intermediate realm suggests for an adequate morality.

The region of "particular others" is a distinct domain, where what can be seen to be artificial and problematic are the very egoistic "self" and the universal "all others" of standard moral theory. In the domain of particular others, the self is already constituted to an important degree by relations with others, and these relations may be much more salient and significant than the interests of any individual self in isolation.[47] The "others" in the picture, however, are not the "all others," or "everyone," of traditional moral theory; they are not what a universal point of view or a view from nowhere could provide.[48] They are, characteristically, actual flesh and blood other human beings for whom we have actual feelings and with whom we have real ties.

From the point of view of much feminist theory, the individualistic assumptions of liberal theory and of most standard moral theory are suspect. Even if we would be freed from the debilitating aspects of dominating male power to "be ourselves" and to pursue our own interests, we would, as persons, still have ties to other persons, and we would at least in part be constituted by such ties. Such ties would be part of what we inherently are. We are, for instance, the daughter or son of given parents, or the mother or father of given children, and we carry with us at least some ties to the racial or ethnic or national group within which we developed into the persons we are.

If we look, for instance, at the realities of the relation between mothering person (who can be female or male) and child, we can see that what we value in the relation cannot be broken down into individual gains and losses for the individual members in the relation. Nor can it be understood in universalistic terms. Self-development apart from the relation may be much less important than the satisfactory development of the relation. What matters may often be the health and growth of and the development of the relation-and-its-members in ways that cannot be understood in the

---

47 See Seyla Benhabib, "The Generalized and the Concrete Other. The Kohlberg-Gilligan Controversy and Moral Theory," in *Women and Moral Theory*, ed. Kittay and Meyers. See also Caroline Whitbeck, "Feminist Ontology: A Different Reality," in *Beyond Domination*, ed. Carol Gould (Totowa, New Jersey: Rowman and Allanheld, 1983).

48 See Thomas Nagel, *The View from Nowhere* (New York: Oxford University Press, 1986). For a feminist critique, see Susan Bordo, "Feminism, Postmodernism, and Gender-Skepticism," in *Feminism/Postmodernism*, ed. Linda Nicholson (New York: Routledge, 1989).

individualistic terms of standard moral theories designed to maximize the satisfaction of self-interest. The universalistic terms of moral theories grounded in what would be right for "all rational beings" or "everyone" cannot handle, either, what has moral value in the relation between mothering person and child.

Feminism is of course not the only locus of criticism of the individualistic and abstractly universalistic features of liberalism and of standard moral theory. Marxists and communitarians also see the self as constituted by its social relations. But in their usual form, Marxist and communitarian criticisms pay no more attention than liberalism and standard moral theory to the experience of women, to the context of mothering, or to friendship as women experience it.[49] Some recent nonfeminist criticisms, such as offered by Bernard Williams, of the impartiality required by standard moral theory, stress how a person's identity may be formed by personal projects in ways that do not satisfy universal norms, yet ought to be admired. Such views still interpret morality from the point of view of an individual and his project, not a social relationship such as that between mothering person and child. And recent nonfeminist criticisms in terms of traditional communities and their moral practices, as seen for instance in the work of Stuart Hampshire and Alasdair MacIntyre, often take traditional gender roles as given, or provide no basis for a radical critique of them.[50] There is no substitute, then, for feminist exploration of the area between ego and universal, as women experience this area, or for the development of a refocused concept of relational self that could be acceptable from a feminist point of view.

Relationships can be evaluated as trusting or mistrustful, mutually considerate or selfish, harmonious or stressful, and so forth. Where trust and consideration are appropriate, which is not always, we can find ways to foster them. But understanding and evaluating relationships, and encouraging them to be what they can be at their best, require us to look at relationships between actual persons, and to see what both standard moral

---

[49] On Marxist theory, see e.g. *Women and Revolution*, ed. Lydia Sargent (Boston: South End Press, 1981); Alison Jaggar, *Feminist Politics and Human Nature;* and Ann Ferguson, *Blood at the Root. Motherhood, Sexuality and Male Dominance* (London: Pandora, 1989). On communitarian theory, see Marilyn Friedman, "Feminism and Modern Friendship . . . ," and also her paper "The Social Self and the Partiality Debates," presented at the Society for Women in Philosophy meeting in New Orleans, April 1990.

[50] Bernard Williams, *Moral Luck* (Cambridge: Cambridge University Press, 1981); *Public and Private Morality*, ed. Stuart Hampshire (Cambridge: Cambridge University Press, 1978); Alasdair MacIntyre, *After Virtue. A Study in Moral Theory* (Notre Dame, Indiana: University of Notre Dame Press, 1981). For discussion see Susan Moller Okin, *Justice, Gender, and the Family* (New York: Basic Books, 1989).

theories and their nonfeminist critics often miss. To be adequate, moral theories must pay attention to the neglected realm of particular others in the actual relationships and actual contexts of women's experience. In doing so, problems of individual self-interest vs. universal rules may recede to a region more like background, out-of- focus insolubility or relative unimportance. The salient problems may then be seen to be how we ought best to guide or to maintain or to reshape the relationships, both close and more distant, that we have, or might have, with actual other human beings. Particular others can be actual children in need in distant continents, or the anticipated children of generations not yet even close to being born. But they are not "all rational beings" or "the greatest number," and the self that is in relationships with particular others and is composed to a significant degree by such relations is not a self whose ego must be pitted against abstract, universal claims. Developing the needed guidance for maintaining and reshaping relationships presents enormous problems, but a first step is to recognize how traditional and nonfeminist moral theory of both an individualistic and communitarian kind falls short in providing it.

The concept of the relational self which is evolving within feminist thought is leading to interesting inquiry in many fields. An example is the work being done at the Stone Center at Wellesley College.[51] Psychologists there have posited a self-in-relation theory and are conducting empirical inquiries to try to establish how the female self develops. They are working with a theory that a female relational self develops through a mutually empathetic mother-daughter bond.

The work has been influenced by Jean Baker Miller's re-evaluation of women's psychological qualities as strengths rather than weaknesses. In her book *Toward a New Psychology of Women*, published in 1976, Miller identified women's "great desire for affiliation" as one such strength.[52] Nancy Chodorow's *The Reproduction of Mothering*, published in 1978, has also had a significant influence on the work done at the

[51] On the Stone Center concept of the self see especially Jean Baker Miller, "The Development of Women's Sense of Self," Wellesley, Massachusetts: Stone Center Working Paper No. 12; Janet Surrey, "The 'Self-in-Relation': A Theory of Women's Development" (Wellesley, Massachusetts: Stone Center Working Paper No. 13); and Judith Jordan, "The Meaning of Mutuality" (Wellesley, Massachusetts: Stone Center Working Paper No. 23). For a feminist but critical view of this work, see Marcia Westkott, "Female Relationality and the Idealized Self," *American Journal of Psychoanalysis* 49 (September, 1989): 239-50.

[52] Jean Baker Miller, *Toward a New Psychology of Women* (Boston: Beacon Press, 1976).

Stone Center, as it has on much feminist inquiry.[53] Chodorow argued that a female affiliative self is reproduced by a structure of parenting in which mothers are the primary caretakers, and sons and daughters develop differently in relation to a parent of the same sex, or a parent of different sex, as primary caretaker. Daughters develop a sense of self by identifying themselves with the mother; they come to define themselves as connected to or in relation with others. Sons, in contrast, develop a sense of self by differentiating themselves from the mother; they come to define themselves as separate from or unconnected to others. An implication often drawn from Chodorow's work is that parenting should be shared equally by fathers and mothers so that children of either sex can develop with caretakers of both same and different sex.

In 1982, Carol Gilligan, building on both Miller and Chodorow, offered her view of the "different voice" with which girls and women express their understanding of moral problems.[54] Like Miller and Chodorow, Gilligan valued tendencies found especially in women to affiliate with others and to interpret their moral responsibilities in terms of their relationships with others. In all, the valuing of autonomy and individual independence over care and concern for relationships, was seen as an expression of male bias. The Stone Center has tried to elaborate and to study a feminist conception of the relational self. In a series of Working Papers, researchers and clinicians have explored the implications of this conception for various issues in women's psychology (e.g. power, anger, work inhibitions, violence, eating patterns) and for therapy.

The self as conceptualized in these studies is seen as having both a need for recognition and a need to understand the other, and these needs are seen as compatible. They are created in the context of mother-child interaction, and are satisfied in a mutually empathetic relationship. This does not require a loss of self, but a relationship of mutuality in which self and other both express intersubjectivity. Both give and take in a way that not only contributes to the satisfaction of their needs as individuals, but also affirms the "larger relational unit" they compose.[55] Maintaining this larger relational unit then becomes a goal, and maturity is seen not in terms of individual autonomy but in terms of competence in creating and sustaining relations of empathy and mutual intersubjectivity.

The Stone Center psychologists contend that the goal of mutuality is rarely achieved in adult male-female relationships because of the traditional gender system. The gender system leads men to seek autonomy and power over others, and to undervalue the caring and relational connected-

[53] Nancy Chodorow, *The Reproduction of Mothering: Psychoanalysis and the Sociology of Gender* (Berkeley: University of California Press, 1978).

[54] Carol Gilligan, *In a Different Voice*.

[55] J. V. Jordan, "The Meaning of Mutuality," p. 2.

ness that is expected of women. Women rarely receive the nurturing and empathetic support they provide. Accordingly, these psychologists look to the interaction that occurs in mother-daughter relationships as the best source of insight into the promotion of the healthy, relational self. This research provides an example of exploration into a refocused, feminist conception of the self, and into empirical questions about its development and implications.

In a quite different field, that of legal theory, a refocused concept of self is leading to reexaminations of such concepts as property and autonomy and the role these have played in political theory and in constitutional law. For instance, the legal theorist Jennifer Nedelsky questions the imagery that is dominant in constitutional law and in our conceptions of property: the imagery of a bounded self, a self contained within boundaries and having rights to property within a wall allowing it to exclude others and to exclude government. The boundary metaphor, she argues, obscures and distorts our thinking about human relationships and what is valuable in them. "The boundedness of selves," Nedelsky writes, "may seem to be a self-evident truth, but I think it is a wrong-headed and destructive way of conceiving of the human creatures law and government are created for."[56] In the domain of the self's relation to the state, the central problem, she argues, is not "maintaining a sphere into which the state cannot penetrate, but fostering autonomy when people are already within the sphere of state control or responsibility."[57] What we can from a feminist perspective think of as the male "separative self" seems on an endless quest for security behind such walls of protection as those of property. Property focuses the quest for security "in ways that are paradigmatic of the efforts of separative selves to protect themselves through boundaries . . ."[58] But of course property is a social construction, not a thing; it requires the involvement of the state to define what it is and to defend it. What will provide what it seeks to offer will not be boundaries and exclusions, but constructive relationships.

In an article on autonomy, Nedelsky examines the deficiencies in the concept of self with which so much of our political and legal thinking about autonomy has been developed. She well recognizes that of course feminists are centrally concerned with freedom and autonomy, with enabling women to live our own lives. But we need a language with which to express these concerns which will also reflect "the equally important

[56] Jennifer Nedelsky, "Law, Boundaries, and the Bounded Self," *Representations* 30 (Spring, 1990): 162-89, at 167.

[57] Ibid., p. 169.

[58] Ibid., p. 181.

feminist precept that any good theorizing will start with people in their social contexts. And the notion of social context must take seriously its constitutive quality; social context cannot simply mean that individuals will, of course, encounter one another."[59] The problem, then, is how to combine the claim of the constitutiveness of social relations with the value of self-determination. Liberalism has been the source of our language of freedom and self-determination, but it lacks the ability to express comprehension of "the reality we know: the centrality of relationships in constituting the self."[60]

In developing a new conception of autonomy that avoids positing self-sufficient and thus highly artificial individuals, Nedelsky point out first that "the capacity to find one's own law can develop only in the context of relations with others (both intimate and more broadly social) that nurture this capacity, and second, that the 'content' of one's own law is comprehensible only with reference to shared social norms, values, and concepts."[61] She sees the traditional liberal view of the self as implying that the most perfectly autonomous man is the most perfectly isolated, and finds this pathological.

Instead of developing autonomy through images of walls around one's property, as does the Western liberal tradition and as does U. S. constitutional law, Nedelsky suggests that "the most promising model, symbol, or metaphor for autonomy is not property, but childrearing. There we have encapsulated the emergence of autonomy through relationship with others . . . Interdependence [is] a constant component of autonomy."[62] And she goes on to examine how law and bureaucracies can foster autonomy within relationships between citizen and government. This does not entail extrapolating from intimate relations to largescale ones; rather, the insights gained from experience with the context of childrearing allow us to recognize the relational aspects of autonomy. In work such as Nedelsky's we can see how feminist reconceptualizations of the self can lead to the rethinking of fundamental concepts even in terrains such as law, thought by many to be quite distant from such disturbances.

To argue for a view of the self as relational does not mean that women need to remain enmeshed in the ties by which they are constituted. In recent decades, especially, women have been breaking free of relation-

---

59 Jennifer Nedelsky, "Reconceiving Autonomy: Sources, Thoughts and Possibilities," *Yale Journal of Law and Feminism* 1 (Spring, 1989): 7-36, p. 9. See also Diana T. Meyers, *Self, Society, and Personal Choice* (New York: Columbia University Press, 1989).

60 Ibid.

61 Ibid., p. 11.

62 Ibid., p. 12. See also Mari J. Matsuda, "Liberal Jurisprudence and Abstracted Visions of Human Nature," *New Mexico Law Review* 16 (Fall, 1986): 613-30.

ships with parents, with the communities in which they grew up, and with men, relationships in which they defined themselves through the traditional and often stifling expectations of others.[63] These quests for self have often involved wrenching instability and painful insecurity. But the quest has been for a new and more satisfactory relational self, not for the self-sufficient individual of liberal theory. Many might share the concerns expressed by Alison Jaggar that disconnecting ourselves from particular others, as ideals of individual autonomy seem to presuppose we should, might make us *in*capable of morality, rather than capable of it, if, as so many feminists think, "an ineliminable part of morality consists in responding emotionally to particular others."[64]

I have examined three topics on which feminist philosophers and feminists in other fields are thinking anew about where we should start and how we should focus our attention in ethics. Feminist reconceptualizations and recommendations concerning the relation between reason and emotion, the distinction between public and private, and the concept of the self, are providing insights deeply challenging to standard moral theory. The implications of this work are that we need an almost total reconstruction of social and political and economic and legal theory in all their traditional forms as well as a reconstruction of moral theory and practice at more comprehensive, or fundamental, levels.*

[63] See e.g. *Women's Ways of Knowing. The Development of Self, Voice, and Mind*, by Mary Field Belenky, Blyth McVicker Clinchy, Nancy Rule Goldberger, and Jill Mattuck Tarule (New York: Basic Books, 1986).

[64] Alison Jaggar, "Feminist Ethics: Some Issues for the Nineties," p. 11.

* This paper is based in part on my Truax Lectures on "The Prospect of Feminist Morality" at Hamilton College on November 2 and 9, 1989. Early versions were also presented at Colgate University; at Queens University in Kingston, Ontario; at the University of Kentucky; and at the New School for Social Research. I am grateful to all who made possible these occasions and commented on the paper at these times, and to Alison Jaggar, Laura Purdy, and Sara Ruddick for additional discussion.

# [2]

# WHAT DO WOMEN WANT IN A MORAL THEORY?

When I finished reading Carol Gilligan's *In a Different Voice,*[1] I asked myself the obvious question for a philosopher reader: what differences should one expect in the moral philosophy done by women, supposing Gilligan's sample of women to be representative and supposing her analysis of their moral attitudes and moral development to be correct? Should one expect women to want to produce moral theories, and if so, what sort of moral theories? How will any moral theories they produce differ from those produced by men?

Obviously one does not have to make this an entirely a priori and hypothetical question. One can look and see what sort of contributions women have made to moral philosophy. Such a look confirms, I think, Gilligan's findings. What one finds *is* a bit different in tone and approach from the standard sort of moral philosophy as done by men following in the footsteps of the great moral philosophers (all men). Generalizations are extremely rash, but when I think of Philippa Foot's work on the moral virtues, Elizabeth Anscombe's work on intention and on modern moral philosophy, Iris Murdoch's philosophical writings, Ruth Barcan Marcus's work on moral dilemmas, the work of the radical feminist moral philosophers who are not content with orthodox Marxist lines of thought, Jenny Teichman's book on illegitimacy, Susan Wolf's articles, Claudia Card's essay on mercy, Sabina Lovibond's writings, Gabriele Taylor's work on pride, love, and on integrity, Cora Diamond's and

Mary Midgeley's work on our attitude toward animals, Sissela Bok's work on lying and on secrecy, Virginia Held's work, the work of Alison Jaggar, Marilyn Frye, and many others, I seem to hear a different voice from the standard moral philosophers' voice. I hear the voice Gilligan heard, made reflective and philosophical. What women want in moral philosophy is what they are providing. And what they are providing seems to me to confirm Gilligan's theses about women. One has to be careful here, of course, for not all important contributions to moral philosophy by women fall easily into the Gilligan stereotype or its philosophical extension. Nor has it been only women who have been proclaiming discontent with the standard approach in moral philosophy and trying new approaches. Michael Stocker, Alasdair MacIntyre, and Ian Hacking when he assesses the game-theoretic approach to morality,[2] all should be given the status of honorary women, if we accept the hypothesis that there are some moral insights for whatever reason women seem to attain more easily or more reliably than men do. Still, exceptions confirm the rule, so I shall proceed undaunted by these important exceptions to my generalizations.

If Hacking is right, preoccupation with prisoner's and prisoners' dilemmas is a big boys' game, and a pretty silly one too. It is, I think, significant that women have not rushed into the field of game-theoretic moral philosophy, and that those who have dared enter that male locker room have said distinctive things there. Edna Ullmann Margalit's book *The Emergence of Norms* put prisoner's dilemma in its limited moral place. Supposing that at least part of the explanation for the relatively few women in this field is disinclination rather than disability, one might ask if this disinclination also extends to the construction of moral theories. For although we find out what sort of moral philosophy women want by looking to see what they have provided, if we do that for moral theory, the answer we get seems to be "none." None of the contributions to moral philosophy by women really counts as a moral theory, nor is seen as such by its author.

Is it that reflective women, when they become philosophers, want to do without moral theory, want no part in the construction of such theories? To conclude this at this early stage, when we have only a few generations of women moral philosophers to judge from, would be rash indeed. The term "theory" can be used in wider and narrower ways, and in its widest sense a moral theory is simply an internally consistent fairly comprehensive account of what morality is and when and why it merits our acceptance and support. In that wide sense, a moral theory is something it would take a skeptic, or one who believes that our intellectual vision is necessarily blurred or distorted when we let it try to take in too much, to be an antitheorist. Even if there were some truth in the latter claim, one might compatibly with it still hope to build up a coherent total account by a mosaic method, assembling a lot of smaller-scale works until one had built up a complete account—say, taking the virtues or purported virtues one by one until one had a more or less complete account. But would that sort of comprehensiveness in one's moral philosophy entitle one to call the finished work a moral theory? If it would, then many women moral philosophers today can be seen as engaged in moral theory construction. In the weakest sense of "theory," as a coherent near-comprehensive account, there are plenty of incomplete theories to be found in the works of women moral philosophers. And in *that* sense of theory, most of what are recognized as the current moral theories are also incomplete, because they do not yet purport to be really comprehensive. Wrongs to animals and wrongful destruction of our physical environment are put to one side by John Rawls, and in most "liberal" theories there are only hand waves concerning our proper attitude toward our children, toward the ill, toward our relatives, friends, and lovers.

Is comprehensiveness too much to ask of a moral theory? The paradigm examples of moral theories—those that are called by their authors "moral theories"—are distinguished not by the comprehensiveness of their internally coherent account but by the *sort* of coherence which is aimed at over a fairly broad area. Their method is not the mosaic method but the broad brushstroke method. Moral theories, as we know them, are, to change the art form, vaults rather than walls—they are not built by assembling painstakingly made brick after brick. In *this* sense of theory—a fairly tightly systematic account of a large area of morality, with a keystone supporting all the rest—women moral philosophers have not yet, to my knowledge, produced moral theories or claimed that they have.

Leaving to one side the question of what purpose (other than good clean intellectual fun) is served by such moral theories, and supposing for the sake of argument that women can, if they wish, systematize as well as the next man and, if need be, systematize in a mathematical fashion as well as the next mathematically minded moral philosopher, then what key concept or guiding motif might hold together the structure of a moral theory hypothetically produced by a reflective woman, Gilligan-style, who has taken up moral theorizing as a calling? What would be a suitable central question, principle, or concept to structure a moral theory which might accommodate those moral insights which women tend to have more readily than men, and to answer those moral questions which, it seems, worry women more than men? I hypothesized that the women's theory, expressive mainly of women's insights and concerns, would be an ethics of love, and this hypothesis seems to be Gilligan's too, since she has gone on from *In a Different Voice* to write about the limitations of Freud's understanding of love as women know it.[3] But presumably women theorists will be like enough to men to want their moral theory to be acceptable to all, so acceptable both to reflective women and to reflective men. Like any good theory, it will need not to ignore the partial truth of previous theories. It must therefore accommodate both the insights men have more easily than women and those women have more easily than men. It should swallow up its predecessor theories. Women moral theorists, if any, will have this very great advantage over the men whose theories theirs supplant, that they can stand on the shoulders of male moral theorists, as no man has yet been able to stand on the shoulders of any female moral theorist. There can be advantages as well as handicaps in being latecomers. So women theorists will need to connect their ethics of love with what has been the men theorists' preoccupation, namely, obligation.

The great and influential moral theorists have in the modern era taken *obligation* as the key and the problematic concept, and have asked what justifies treating a person as morally bound or obliged to do a particular thing. Since to be bound is to be unfree, by making obligation central one at the same time makes central the question of the justification of coercion, of forcing or trying to force someone to act in a particular way. The concept of obligation as justified limitation of freedom does just what one wants a good theoretical concept to do—to divide up the field (as one looks at different ways one's freedom may be limited, freedom in different spheres, different sorts and versions and levels of justification) and at the same time to hold the subfields together. There must in a theory be some generalization and some speciation or diversification, and a good rich key concept guides one both in recognizing the diversity and in recognizing the unity in it. The concept of obligation has served this function very well for the area of morality it covers, and so we have some fine theories about that area. But as Aristotelians and Christians, as well as women, know, there is a lot of morality *not* covered by that concept, a lot of very great importance even for the area where there are obligations.

This is fairly easy to see if we look at what lies behind the perceived obligation to keep promises. Unless there is some good moral reason why someone should assume the responsibility of rearing a child to be *capable* of taking promises seriously, once she understands what a promise is, the obligation to obey promises will not effectively tie her, and any force applied to punish her when she breaks promises or makes fraudulent ones will be of questionable justice. Is there an *obligation* on someone to make the child into a morally competent promisor? If so, on whom? Who has failed in his or her obligations when, say, war orphans who grew up without parental love or any other love arrive at legal adulthood very willing to be untrue to their word? Who failed in what obligation in all those less extreme cases of attempted but unsuccessful moral education? The parents who didn't produce promise-keeping offspring? Those who failed to educate the parents in how to educate their children (whoever it might be who could plausibly be thought to have the responsibility for training parents to fulfill their obligations)? The liberal version of our basic moral obligations tends to be fairly silent on who has what obligations to new members of the moral community, and it would throw most theories of the justification of obligations into some confusion if the obligation to rear one's children lovingly were added to the list of obligations. Such evidence as we have about the conditions in which children do successfully "learn" the morality of the community of which they are members suggests that we cannot substitute "conscientiously" for "lovingly" in this hypothetical extra needed obligation. But an obligation to love, in the strong sense needed, would be an embarrassment to the theorist, given most accepted versions of "ought implies can."

It is hard to make fair generalizations here, so I shall content myself with indicating how this charge I am making against the current men's moral theories, that their version of the justified list of obligations does not ensure the proper care of the young and so does nothing to ensure the stability of the morality in question over several generations, can be made against what I regard as the best of the men's recent theories, Rawls's theory of justice. One of the great strengths of Rawls's theory is the careful attention given to the question of how just institutions produce the conditions for their continued support, across generations, and in particular of how the sense of justice will arise in children, once there are minimally just institutions structuring the social world into which they are born. Rawls, more than most moral theorists, has attended to the question of the stability of his just society, given what we know about child development. But Rawls's sensitive account of the conditions for the development of that sense of justice needed for the maintenance of his version of a just society takes it for granted that there will be loving parents rearing the children in whom the sense of justice is to develop. "The parents, we may suppose, love the child, and in time the child comes to love and trust the parents." Why may we suppose this? Not because compliance with Rawls's version of our obligations and duties will ensure it. Rawls's theory, like so many other theories of obligation, in the end must take out a loan not only on the natural duty of parents to care for children (which he will have no trouble including) but on the natural *virtue* of parental love (or even a loan on the maternal instinct?). The virtue of being a *loving* parent must supplement the natural duties and the obligations of justice, if the just society is to last beyond the first generation. And as Nancy Chodorow's work indicates, the loving parents must also accept a certain division of child-care responsibility if their version of the obligations and virtues of men and of women is, along with their version of the division of labor accompanying that allocation of virtues, to be passed on.

Reliance on a recognized obligation to turn oneself into a good parent or else to avoid becoming a parent would be a problematic solution. Good parents tend to be the children of good parents, so this obligation would collapse into the obligation to avoid parenthood unless one expected to be a good parent. That, given available methods of contraception, may itself convert into the obligation, should one expect not to be a good parent, to sexual abstinence, or sterilization, or resolute resort to abortion when contraception fails.

The conditional obligation to abort, and in effect also the conditional obligation to sterilization, falls on the women. There may be conditions in which the rational moral choice is between obligatory sexual abstinence and obligatory sterilization, but obligatory abortion, such as women in China now face, seems to me a moral monster. I do not believe that liberal moral theorists will be able to persuade reflective women that a morality that in any conditions makes abortion obligatory, as distinct from permitted or advisable or, on occasion, best, is in their own as well as their male fellows' long-term self-interest. It would be tragic if such moral questions in the end came to the question of whose best interests to sacrifice, men's or women's. I do not believe they *do* come to this, but should they, then justice would require that, given the long history of the subordination of women's to men's interests, men's interests be sacrificed. Justice, of course, never decides these issues unless power reinforces justice, so I am not predicting any victory for women, should it ever come to a fight over obligatory abortion or over who is to face obligatory sterilization.

No liberal moral theorist, as far as I know, is advocating obligatory abortion or obligatory sterilization when necessary to prevent the conception of children whose parents do not expect to love them. My point rather is that they escape this conclusion only by avoiding the issue of what is to ensure that new members of the moral community do get the loving care they need to become morally competent persons. Liberal moral theories assume that women either will provide loving maternal care, or will persuade their mates to provide loving paternal care, or when pregnant will decide for abortion, encouraged by their freedom-loving men. These theories, in other words, exploit the culturally encouraged maternal instinct and/or the culturally encouraged docility of women. The liberal system would receive a nasty spanner in its works should women use their freedom of choice as regards abortion to choose *not* to abort, and then leave their newborn children on their fathers' doorsteps. That would test liberal morality's ability to provide for its own survival.

At this point it may be objected that every moral theory must make some assumptions about the natural psychology of those on whom obligations are imposed. Why shouldn't the liberal theory count on a continuing sufficient supply of good loving mothers, as it counts on continuing self-interest and, perhaps, on a continuing supply of pugnacious men who are able and willing to become good soldiers, without turning any of these into moral *obligations?* Why waste moral resources recognizing as obligatory or as virtuous what one can count on getting without moral pressure? If, in the moral economy, one can get enough good mothers and good warriors "for free," why not gladly exploit what nature and cultural history offer? I cannot answer this question fully here, but my argument does depend upon the assumption that a decent morality will *not* depend for its stability on forces to which it gives no moral recognition. Its account books should be open to scrutiny, and there should be no unpaid debts, no loans with no prospect of repayment. I also assume that once we are clear about these matters and about the interdependencies involved, our principles of justice will not allow us to recognize either a special obligation on every woman to initiate the killing of the fetus she has conceived, should she and her mate be, or think they will be, deficient in parental love, or a special obligation on every young man to kill those his elders have labeled enemies of his country. Both such "obligations" are prima facie suspect, and difficult to make consistent with any of the principles supposedly generating obligations in modern moral theories. I also assume that, on reflection, we will not want to recognize as *virtues* the character traits of women and men which lead them to supply such life and death services "for free." Neither maternal servitude, nor the resoluteness needed to kill off one's children to prevent their growing up unloved, nor the easy willingness to go out and kill when ordered to do so by authorities seems to me to be a character trait a decent morality will encourage by labeling it a virtue. But the liberals' morality must somehow encourage such traits if its stability depends on enough people showing them. There is, then, understandable motive for liberals' avoidance of the question of whether such qualities are or are not morally approved of, and of whether or not there is any obligation to act as one with such character traits would act.

It is symptomatic of the bad faith of liberal morality as understood by many of those who defend it that issues such as whether to fight or not to fight, to have or not to have an abortion, or to be or not to be an unpaid maternal drudge are left to individual conscience. Since there is no coherent guidance liberal morality can give on these issues, which clearly are *not* matters of moral indifference, liberal morality tells each of us, "the choice is yours," hoping that enough will choose to be self-sacrificial life providers and self-sacrificial death dealers to suit the purposes of the rest.

Rawls's theory does explicitly face the question of the moral justification of refusal to bear arms, and of how a just society justly provides for its own defense. The hardships imposed on conscripted soldiers are, he says, a necessary evil, and the most that just institutions can do is to "make sure that the risks of suffering from those misfortunes are more or less evenly shared by all members of society over the course of their life, and that there is no avoidable class bias in selecting those who are called for duty." What of sex/gender bias? Or is that assumed to be unavoidable? Rawls's principles seem to me to imply that women should be conscripted, if anyone is (and I think that is right), but since he avoids the questions of justice between men and women one does not know whether he intended this implication. His suggestion that one argument in favor of a conscripted army is that it is less likely to be an instrument of unjustified foreign adventures will become even stronger, I believe, if half the conscripts are women. Like most male moral theorists, Rawls does not discuss the morality of having children, refusing to have them, refusing to care for them, nor does he discuss how just institutions might equalize the responsibilities involved in ensuring that there be new members of society and that they become morally competent members of it, so one does not know whether he accepts a gender-based division of social service here, leaving it to the men to do the dangerous defensive destruction of life and cities, while the support of new life, and any costs going or contrived to go with that, are left to the women. I hope that is not what he meant.

I do not wish, by having myself spoken of these two traditionally gender-based allocations of responsibility (producing and caring for new human life and the destruction of the lives of those officially labeled enemies) together, to leave the impression that I see any parallel between them except that they have both been treated as gender based and that both present embarrassments for liberal moral theory. Not all allocations of responsibility are allocations of burdens, and parenthood, unlike unchosen military life, need not be seen as essentially burden bearing. Good mothers and good soldiers make contributions of very different sorts and sort of importance to the ongoing life of a moral community, and they should not be seen, as they sometimes are, as fair mutual substitutes, as forms of social service. Good mothers will always be needed by a moral community, in the best conditions as well as the worst; the need for good military men, though foreseeably permanent, is a sign of some failure of our morality, a failure of our effectively acted upon moral laws to be valid theorems for the conservation of men in multitudes. Nor do the burdens of soldiering have any real analogue in the case of motherhood, which today *need* not impose real costs on the mother. If there are significant costs—loss of career opportunity, improperly recompensed drudgery in the home, or health risks—this is due to bad but largely remediable social arrangements, as the failure of parents to experience any especially parental satisfactions may be also due to bad but remediable socially produced attitudes toward parental responsibility. We do not, I think, want our military men to enjoy killing the enemy and destroying their cities, and any changes we made in social customs and institutions to make such pleasures more likely would be deplorable ones. Military life in wartime should always be seen as a sacrifice, while motherhood should never need to be seen as self-sacrificial service. If it is an honor and a privilege to bear arms for one's country, as we understandably tell our military conscripts and volunteers, part of the honor is being trusted with activities that are a necessary evil, being trusted not to enjoy their evil aspects, and being trusted to see the evil as well as the necessity. Only if we contrive to make the bringing into the world of new persons as nasty a business as killing already present persons will there be any just reason to exclude young women from conscripted armies or to exclude men from equal parental responsibility.

Granted that the men's theories of obligation need supplementation, to have much chance of integrity and coherence, and that the women's hypothetical theories will want to cover obligation as well as love, then what concept brings them together? My tentative answer is—the concept of appropriate trust, oddly neglected in moral theory. This concept also nicely mediates between reason and feeling, those tired old candidates for moral authority, since to trust is neither quite to believe something about the trusted nor necessarily to feel any emotion toward them—but to have a belief-informed and action-influencing attitude. To make it plausible that the neglected concept of appropriate trust is a good one for the enlightened moral theorist to make central, I need to show, or begin to show, how it could include obligation, indeed shed light on obligations and their justification, as well as include love, the other moral concerns of Gilligan's women, and many of the topics women moral philosophers have chosen to address, mosaic fashion. I would also need to show that it could connect all of these in a way which holds out promise both of synthesis and of comprehensive moral coverage. A moral theory which looked at the conditions for proper trust of all the various sorts we show, and at what sorts of reasons justify inviting such trust, giving it, and meeting it, would, I believe, not have to avoid turning its gaze on the conditions for the survival of the practices it endorses, so it could avoid that unpleasant choice many current liberal theories seem to have—between incoherence and bad faith. I do not pretend that we will easily agree once we raise the questions I think we should raise, but at least we may have a language adequate to the expression of both men's and women's moral viewpoints.

My trust in the concept of trust is based in part on my own attempts to restate and consider what is right and what wrong with men's theories, especially Hume's, which I consider the best of the lot. I have found myself reconstructing his account of the artifices of justice as an account of the progressive enlargement of a climate of trust, and have found that a helpful way to see it. It has some textual basis, but is nevertheless a reconstruction, and one I have found, immodestly, an improvement. So it is because I have tried the concept and explored its dimensions a bit—the variety of goods we may trust others not to take from us, the sort of security or insurance we have when we do, the sorts of defenses or potential defenses we lay down when we trust, the various conditions for reasonable trust of various types—that I am hopeful about its power as a theoretical, and not just an exegetical, tool. I also found myself needing to use it when I made a brief rash attempt at that women's topic, caring (invited in by a male philosopher,[4] I should say). I am reasonably sure that trust does generalize some central moral features of the recognition of binding obligations and moral virtues and of loving, as well as of other important relations between persons, such as teacher-pupil, confider-confidante, worker to co-worker in the same cause, and professional to client. Indeed it is fairly obvious that love, the main moral phenomenon women want attended to, involves trust, so I anticipate little quarrel when I claim that, if we had a moral theory spelling out the conditions for appropriate trust and distrust, that would include a morality of love in all its variants—parental love, love of children for their parents, love of family members, love of friends, of lovers in the strict sense, of co-workers, of one's country and its figureheads, of exemplary heroines and heroes, of goddesses and gods.

Love and loyalty demand maximal trust of one sort, and maximal trustworthiness, and in investigating the conditions for maximal trust and maximal risk we must think about the ethics of love. More controversial may be my claim that the ethics of obligation will also be covered. I see it as covered because to recognize a set of obligations is to trust some group of persons to instill them, to demand that they be met, possibly to levy sanctions if they are not, and this is to trust persons with very significant coercive power over others. Less coercive but still significant power is possessed by those shaping our conception of the virtues and expecting us to display them, approving when we do, disapproving and perhaps shunning us when we do not. Such coercive and manipulative power over others requires justification, and is justified only if we have reason to trust those who have it to use it properly and to use the discretion which is always given when trust is given in a way which serves the purpose of the whole system of moral control, and not merely self-serving or morally improper purposes. Since the question of the justification of coercion becomes, at least in part, the question of the wisdom of trusting the coercers to do their job properly, the morality of obligation, in as far as it reduces to the morality of coercion, is covered by the morality of proper trust. Other forms of trust may also be involved, but trusting enforcers with the use of force is the most problematic form of trust involved.

The coercers and manipulators are, to some extent, all of us, so to ask what our obligations are and what virtues we should exhibit is to ask what it is reasonable to trust us to demand, expect, and contrive to get from one another. It becomes, in part, a question of what powers we can in reason trust ourselves to exercise properly. But self-trust is a dubious or limit case of trust, so I prefer to postpone the examination of the concept of proper self-trust at least until proper trust of others is more clearly understood. Nor do we distort matters too much if we concentrate on those cases where moral sanctions and moral pressure and moral manipulation is not self-applied but applied to others, particularly by older persons to younger persons. Most moral pressuring that has any effect goes on in childhood and early youth. Moral sanctions may continue to be applied, formally and informally, to adults, but unless the criminal courts apply them it is easy enough for adults to ignore them, to brush them aside. It is not difficult to become a sensible knave, and to harden one's heart so that one is insensible to the moral condemnation of one's victims and those who sympathize with them. Only if the pressures applied in the morally formative stage have given one a heart that rebels against the thought of such ruthless independence of what others think will one see any reason *not* to ignore moral condemnation, not to treat it as mere powerless words and breath. Condemning sensible knaves is as much a waste of breath as arguing with them—all we can sensibly do is to try to protect children against their influence, and ourselves against their knavery. Adding to the criminal law will not be the way to do the latter, since such moves will merely challenge sensible knaves to find new knavish exceptions and loopholes, not protect us from sensible knavery. Sensible knaves are precisely those who exploit us without breaking the law. So the whole question of when moral pressure of various sorts, formative, reformative, and punitive, ought to be brought to bear by whom is subsumed under the question of whom to trust when and with what, and for what good reasons.

In concentrating on obligations, rather than virtues, modern moral theorists have chosen to look at the cases where more trust is placed in enforcers of obligations than is placed in ordinary moral agents, the bearers of the obligations. In taking, as contractarians do, contractual obligations as the model of obligations, they concentrate on a case where the very minimal trust is put in the obligated person, and considerable punitive power entrusted to the one to whom the obligation is owed (I assume here that Hume is right in saying that when we promise or contract, we formally subject ourselves to the penalty, in case of failure, of never being trusted as a promisor again). This is an interesting case of the allocation of trust of various sorts, but it surely distorts our moral vision to suppose that *all* obligations, let alone all morally pressured expectations we impose on others, conform to that abnormally coercive model. It takes very special conditions for it to be safe to trust persons to inflict penalties on other persons, conditions in which either we can trust the penalizers to have the virtues necessary to penalize wisely and fairly, or else we can rely on effective threats to keep unvirtuous penalizers from abusing their power—that is to say, rely on others to coerce the first coercers into proper behavior. But that reliance too will either be trust or will have to rely on threats from coercers of the coercers of coercers, and so on. Morality on this model becomes a nasty, if intellectually intriguing, game of mutual mutually corrective threats. The central question of who should deprive whom of what freedom soon becomes the question of whose anger should be dreaded by whom (the theory of obligation), supplemented perhaps by an afterthought on whose favor should be courted by whom (the theory of the virtues).

Undoubtedly some important part of morality does depend in part on a system of threats and bribes, at least for its survival in difficult conditions when normal goodwill and normally virtuous dispositions may be insufficient to motivate the conduct required for the preservation and justice of the moral network of relationships. But equally undoubtedly life will be nasty, emotionally poor, and worse than brutish (even if longer), if that is all morality is, or even if that coercive structure of morality is regarded as the backbone, rather than as an available crutch, should the main support fail. For the main support has to come from those we entrust with the job of rearing and training persons so that they can be trusted in various ways, some trusted with extraordinary coercive powers, some with public decision-making powers, all trusted as parties to promise, most trusted by some who love them and by one or more willing to become co-parents with them, most trusted by dependent children, dependent elderly relatives, sick friends, and so on. A very complex network of a great variety of sorts of trust structures our moral relationships with our fellows, and if there is a *main* support to this network it is the trust we place in those who respond to the trust of new members of the moral community, namely, children, and prepare them for new forms of trust.

A theory which took as its central question "Who should trust whom with what, and why?" would not have to forgo the intellectual fun and games previous theorists have had with the various paradoxes of morality—curbing freedom to increase freedom, curbing self-interest the better to satisfy self-interest, not aiming at happiness in order to become happier. For it is easy enough to get a paradox of trust to accompany or, if I am right, to generalize the paradoxes of freedom, self-interest, and hedonism. To trust is to make oneself or to let oneself be more vulnerable than one might have been to harm from others—to give them an opportunity to harm one, in the confidence that they will not take it, because they have no good reason to.[5] Why would one take such a risk? For risk it always is, given the partial opaqueness to us of the reasoning and motivation of those we trust and with whom we cooperate. Our confidence may be, and quite often is, misplaced. That is what we risk when we trust. If the best reason to take such a risk is the expected gain in security which comes from a climate of trust, then in trusting we are always giving up security to get greater security, exposing our throats so that others become accustomed to not biting. A moral theory which made proper trust its central concern could have its own categorical imperative, could replace obedience to self-made laws and freely chosen restraint on freedom with security-increasing sacrifice of security, distrust in the promoters of a climate of distrust, and so on.

Such reflexive use of one's central concept, negative or affirmative, is an intellectually satisfying activity which is bound to have appeal to those system lovers who want to construct moral theories, and it may help them design their theory in an intellectually pleasing manner. But we should beware of becoming hypnotized by our slogans or of sacrificing truth to intellectual elegance. Any theory of proper trust should not *prejudge* the question of when distrust is proper. We might find more objects of proper distrust than just the contributors to a climate of reasonable distrust, just as freedom should be restricted not just to increase human freedom but to protect human life from poisoners and other killers. I suspect, however, that all the objects of reasonable distrust are more reasonably seen as falling into the category of ones who contribute to a decrease in the scope of proper trust than can all who are reasonably coerced be seen as themselves guilty of wrongful coercion. Still, even if all proper trust turns out to be for such persons and on such matters as will increase the scope or stability of a climate of reasonable trust, and all proper distrust for such persons and on such matters as increase the scope of reasonable distrust, overreliance on such nice reflexive formulae can distract us from asking all the questions about trust which need to be asked if an adequate moral theory is to be constructed around that concept. These questions should include when to *respond* to trust with *un*trustworthiness, when and when not to invite trust, as well as when to give and refuse trust. We should not assume that promiscuous trustworthiness is any more a virtue than is undiscriminating distrust. It is appropriate trustworthiness, appropriate trustingness, appropriate encouragement to trust which will be virtues, as will be judicious untrustworthiness, selective refusal to trust, discriminating discouragement of trust.

Women are particularly well placed to appreciate these last virtues, since they have sometimes needed them to get into a position even to consider becoming moral theorizers. The long exploitation and domination of women by men depended on men's trust in women and women's trustworthiness to play their allotted role and so to perpetuate their own and their daughters' servitude. However keen women now are to end the lovelessness of modern moral philosophy, they are unlikely to lose sight of the cautious virtue of appropriate distrust or of the tough virtue of principled betrayal of the exploiters' trust.

Gilligan's girls and women saw morality as a matter of preserving valued ties to others, of preserving the conditions for that care and mutual care without which human life becomes bleak, lonely, and after a while, as the mature men in her study found, not self-affirming, however successful in achieving the egoistic goals which had been set. The boys and men saw morality as a matter of finding workable traffic rules for self-assertors, so that they not needlessly frustrate one another and so that they could, should they so choose, cooperate in more positive ways to mutual advantage. Both for the women's sometimes unchosen and valued ties with others and for the men's mutual respect as sovereigns and subjects of the same minimal moral traffic rules (and for their more voluntary and more selective associations of profiteers), trust is important. Both men and women are concerned with cooperation, and the dimensions of trust-distrust structure the different cooperative relations each emphasize. The various considerations which arise when we try to defend an answer to any question about the appropriateness of a particular form of cooperation with its distinctive form of trust or distrust, that is, when we look into the terms of all sorts of cooperation, at the terms of trust in different cases of trust, at what are fair terms and what are trust-enhancing and trust-preserving terms, are suitably many and richly interconnected. A moral theory (or family of theories) that made trust its central problem could do better justice to men's and women's moral intuitions than do the going men's theories. Even if we don't easily agree on the answer to the question of who should trust whom with what, who should accept and who should meet various sorts of trust, and why, these questions might enable us better to reason morally together than we can when the central moral questions are reduced to those of whose favor one must court and whose anger one must dread. But such programmatic claims as I am making will be tested only when women standing on the shoulders of men, or men on the shoulders of women, or some theorizing Tiresias actually works out such a theory. I am no Tiresias, and have not foresuffered all the labor pains of such a theory. I aim here only to fertilize.

## POSTSCRIPT

This essay was written before Carol Gilligan had withdrawn the suggestion in *A Different Voice* that there is some intrinsic connection between being female and taking up the care perspective. This essay refers to the early, and not to the revised, Gilligan views, as does Essay 4.

Some clarification may be in order to explain why I conferred on Alasdair MacIntyre the title of honorary woman, when to feminists such as Susan Moller Okin[6] he represents a particularly extreme version of patriarchal thinking. It was MacIntyre's anti-Kantian writings that made me regard him as an ally, and also his nostalgia for a virtues-centered variant of ethics. But I agree with Okin that his increasingly explicit defense of a patriarchal religious tradition does make the honor that I did him look undeserved.

# NOTES

## 1. WHAT DO WOMEN WANT IN A MORAL THEORY?

1. Carol Gilligan, *In a Different Voice: Psychological Theory and Women's Development* (Cambridge, Mass.: Harvard University Press, 1982).
2. Ian Hacking, "Winner Take Less," a review of *The Evolution of Cooperation* by Robert Axelrod, *New York Review of Books*, vol. 31, June 28, 1984.
3. Carol Gilligan, "The Conquistador and the Dark Continent: Reflections on the Psychology of Love," *Daedalus*, 113 (Summer 1984): 75–95.
4. "Caring about Caring," a response to Harry Frankfurt's "What We Care About," both in "Matters of the Mind," *Synthese*, 53 (November 1982): 257–290. My paper is also included in my *Postures of the Mind: Essays on Mind and Morals* (Minneapolis, Minn.: University of Minnesota Press, 1985).
5. I defend this claim about trust in Essay 6.
6. Susan Moller Okin, *Justice, Gender, and the Family* (New York: Basic Books, 1989), esp. chap. 3.

# [3]

# Reason and Feeling in Thinking about Justice*

*Susan Moller Okin*

Recent feminist scholarship has challenged the corpus of Western political thought in two new ways. Some works focus first on either the absence or the assumed subordination of women in a political theory, and then go on to ask how the theory would have to change in order to include women on an equal basis with men. Some focus more immediately on how the gendered structure of the societies in which theorists have lived has shaped their central ideas and arguments and consider how these ideas and arguments are affected by the adoption of a feminist perspective.[1] In this paper, I hope to contribute something to the second project. I raise, though do not by any means fully answer, some questions about the effects that assumptions about the gendered structure of society have had on thinking about social justice. In so doing, I suggest that some recent distinctions that have been made between an ethic of justice and an ethic of care may be at least overdrawn, if not false. They may obfuscate rather than aid our attempts to achieve a moral and political theory that we can find acceptable in a world in which gender is becoming an increasingly indefensible mode of social organization.[2]

* This paper has benefited from the comments and criticisms of Sissela Bok, Joshua Cohen, George Pearson Cross, Amy Gutmann, Robert O. Keohane, Will Kymlicka, Robert L. Okin, John Rawls, Nancy Rosenblum, Cass R. Sunstein, Joan Tronto, and Iris Young. Nevertheless, I regret that I have not been able to respond adequately to all of their objections and suggestions.

1. Works falling primarily within the first category include Lorenne Clark and Lynda Lange, *The Sexism of Social and Political Thought* (Toronto: University of Toronto Press, 1979); Jean Bethke Elshtain, *Public Man, Private Woman: Women in Social and Political Thought* (Princeton, N.J.: Princeton University Press, 1981); and Susan Moller Okin, *Women in Western Political Thought* (Princeton, N.J.: Princeton University Press, 1979). Works within the second include Mary O'Brien, *The Politics of Reproduction* (London: Routledge & Kegan Paul, 1981); and Judith H. Stiehm, ed., *Women's Views of the Political World of Men* (Dobbs Ferry, N.Y.: Transnational Publishers, 1984). The essays in Carole Pateman and Elizabeth Gross, eds., *Feminist Challenges: Social and Political Theory* (Boston: Northeastern University Press, 1987) span both categories.

2. For example, see Carol Gilligan, *In a Different Voice* (Cambridge, Mass.: Harvard University Press, 1982); and Nel Noddings, *Caring: A Feminine Approach to Ethics and Moral Education* (Berkeley and Los Angeles: University of California Press, 1984). See Owen Flanagan and Kathryn Jackson, "Justice, Care and Gender: The Kohlberg-Gilligan Debate

*Ethics* 99 (January 1989): 229–249

I shall focus on two major philosophers—primarily Rawls, and Kant as a major influence on him—and consider how their assumptions about the division of labor between the sexes, with women taking care of the realm of human nurturance, have a fundamental effect upon their accounts of moral subjects and the development of moral thinking. This is exemplified in their tendencies to separate reason from feelings and to require that moral subjects be abstracted, in their deliberations, from the contextuality and contingencies of actual human life.

John Rawls's *A Theory of Justice* has been the inspiration, in one way or another, for much of contemporary moral and political theory.[3] I am not going to focus primarily here on what it says—or, as it happens, mostly does not say—about women and gender. I am going to focus on the effects of assumptions about gender on central aspects of the theory. I shall first outline Kant's and Rawls's contrasting accounts of how one learns to be a moral person. I shall then argue that, despite this important area of contrast, the strong influence of Kant leads to Rawls's expressing his major ideas primarily in the language of rational choice. This leaves them unnecessarily open to two criticisms: that they involve unacceptably egoistic assumptions about human nature and that they are of little relevance to actual people thinking about justice.[4] Whereas Rawls's theory is sometimes viewed as excessively rationalistic, individualistic, and abstracted from real human beings, I will argue that, at its center (though frequently obscured by Rawls himself) is a voice of responsibility, care, and concern for others. This paper is, in part, an attempt to develop a feminist approach to social justice, which centers on a reinterpretation of Rawls's central concept, the original position.

In another sense, however, the paper is a feminist *critique* of Rawls. For he, unlike Kant but in line with a long tradition of political and moral philosophers including Rousseau, Hegel, and Tocqueville, regards the

---

Revisited," *Ethics* 97 (1987): 622–37, for a valuable alternative approach to this issue, which focuses on recent moral development theory, especially the Kohlberg-Gilligan debate, and provides an excellent selective list of references to what has rapidly become a vast literature. See also Gertrud Nunner-Winkler, "Two Moralities? A Critical Discussion of an Ethic of Care and Responsibility versus an Ethic of Rights and Justice," in *Morality, Moral Behavior, and Moral Development*, ed. W. Kurtines and J. Gewirtz (New York: Wiley, 1984), pp. 348–61; Joan Tronto, "'Women's Morality': Beyond Gender Difference to a Theory of Care," *Signs: Journal of Women in Culture and Society* 12 (1987): 644–63; and Lawrence Blum, "Gilligan and Kohlberg: Implications for Moral Theory," *Ethics* 98 (1988): 472–91.

3. John Rawls, *A Theory of Justice* (Cambridge, Mass.: Harvard University Press, 1971). Subsequent references to this book (*TOJ*) will be given parenthetically in the text.

4. Thomas Nagel, "Rawls on Justice," in *Reading Rawls*, ed. Norman Daniels (New York: Basic, 1974), pp. 1–16 (reprinted from *Philosophical Review*, vol. 72 [1973]), makes the former argument; Michael J. Sandel, *Liberalism and the Limits of Justice* (Cambridge: Cambridge University Press, 1982) makes both arguments; the latter argument is made by both Alasdair MacIntyre, *After Virtue* (Notre Dame, Ind.: Notre Dame University Press, 1981); and Michael Walzer, *Spheres of Justice* (New York: Basic, 1983), and *Interpretation and Social Criticism* (Cambridge, Mass.: Harvard University Press, 1987).

family as a school of morality, a primary socializer of just citizens. At the same time, along with others in the tradition, he neglects the issue of the justice or injustice of the gendered family itself. The result is a central tension within the theory, which can be resolved only by opening up the question of justice within the family.

## THE KANTIAN HERITAGE

Why did Rawls cast his theory, or much of it, in the language of rational choice? Why did he present it this way rather than as a theory that requires empathy even on the part of those artificial moral agents who inhabit the original position, and that requires not only empathy but far-reaching benevolence on the part of ordinary human beings who are prepared to abide by the principles of justice? Only the Kantian heritage can explain these things. The way Rawls presents his theory of justice reflects both Kant's stress on autonomy and rationality as the defining characteristics of moral subjects and his rigid separation of reason from feeling and refusal to allow feeling any place in the formulation of moral principles. Rawls says of Kant, "He begins with the idea that moral principles are the object of rational choice. . . . Moral philosophy becomes the study of the conception and outcome of a suitably defined rational decision" (*TOJ*, p. 251).[5] He frequently and explicitly acknowledges the connections between his theory and Kant's. The concept of the veil of ignorance, he says, is implicit in Kant's works, and the concept of the original position is an attempt to interpret Kant's conception of moral principles as formulated under "conditions that characterize men as free and equal rational beings" (*TOJ*, p. 252).

The Kantian connection, I suggest, made it extremely difficult for Rawls to acknowledge any role for empathy or benevolence in the formulation of his principles of justice and, instead, impelled him in the direction of rational choice. Kant is abundantly clear that feelings are to have no place in the foundations of morality. "No moral principle is based," he says, "as people sometimes suppose, on any *feeling* whatsoever. . . . For feeling, no matter by what it is aroused, always belongs to the order of *nature*."[6] He does not say so here, but he clearly means "nature, as contrasted with freedom." Kant so rejects the idea that feelings have anything to do with moral motivation that he considers that an act that is in accordance with duty, but is performed out of love or sympathetic inclination, has "no genuinely moral worth." It is only when such actions are performed from duty—because the moral law requires them—that they have moral content.[7]

5. See also John Rawls, "Kantian Constructivism in Moral Theory," *Journal of Philosophy* 77 (1980): 515–72.

6. Immanuel Kant, *The Doctrine of Virtue, pt. 2: Metaphysic of Morals*, trans. Mary J. Gregor (New York: Harper & Row, 1964), p. 33.

7. Immanuel Kant, *Groundwork of the Metaphysic of Morals*, trans. H. Paton (1948; reprint, New York: Harper & Row, 1964), pp. 66–67.

Kant is able to conclude that feeling and love have no part in the foundations of morality only because he neglects a very important type of human love. In *The Doctrine of Virtue,* he classifies love into two types. One he calls "practical love" or benevolence; this, he says, sometimes *results* from the performance of the duty to help others. Kant discusses the saying "you *ought* to *love* your neighbour as yourself." He says it "does not mean: you should immediately (first) love him and (afterwards) through the medium of this love do good to him. It means, rather: *do good* to your fellow-man, and this will give rise to love of man in you."[8] Such moral feelings, far from leading to principles of morality, can only follow from principles established independently of them. Kant does not, however, regard them as morally insignificant, since the moral feeling that follows from the thought of the law can be a significant factor in making us conscious of our obligations.[9] The other type of feeling Kant recognizes is called "pathological feeling" or attraction. "Pathological," as used here, does not mean that there is anything *wrong* with it, as it would signify in modern usage, but simply that it is "affective." As contrasted with moral feeling, which "can only follow from the thought of the law," pathological feeling "precedes the thought of the law." Being contingent and subject to change, belonging to the order of nature rather than to the order of autonomy or reason, however, this type of feeling can play no part in the formulation of the moral law.

Kant's brief account of moral education, as presented near the end of *The Doctrine of Virtue,* reflects this account of the relation (or, rather, comparative lack of it) between feelings and moral thinking. The moral catechism Kant presents in the form of a dialogue between teacher and pupil is, as he says, "developed from ordinary human reason." The teacher questions the pupil, and then "the answer which he methodically draws from the pupil's reason must be written down and preserved in precise terms which cannot easily be altered, and so be committed to the pupil's *memory.*" These memorized pieces of reasoning are then supplemented by "*good example*" on the teacher's part, as well as his pointing out the "*cautionary* example" of others.[10] Subsequent to formulating principles on the basis of reason, the pupil becomes conditioned, by imitation, into virtuous inclination and action.

This arid presentation of moral education is closely related to Kant's incomplete account of the varieties of human love, which in turn is made possible by the fact that women play only a peripheral role in his philosophy. His reduction of love to two types, the moral feeling of benevolence that follows from the recognition of duty, and the affective love that he calls "mere inclination," leaves out at least one very important kind of love. This is the love that is typified by parent/child relations, under favorable

8. Kant, *The Doctrine of Virtue,* pp. 62–63.
9. Ibid., p. 59.
10. Ibid., pp. 151–52; emphasis in the original.

circumstances at any rate. It is usually made up of elements of affective love and of benevolence, but it also involves far more. The benevolence in it does not spring from the recognition of duty, and the affection in it is usually far from being "mere inclination," with the fickleness suggested by those terms. It is a kind of love that develops over time and that has its origins in attachment so close that, for the young infant, it constitutes complete psychological identification. It is fed by attachment, continued intimacy, and interdependence. On the other hand, it is a kind of love that has disastrous consequences if there is no willingness on the part of the parent to recognize and to appreciate differences between the child and her- or himself. This kind of love is fundamental to human life and relationship since it is the first kind of love we experience (if our circumstances are fortunate) regardless of our sex, and it has, of course, constituted throughout history a much larger part of women's than of men's experience.

Kant seems to have been unable to perceive either the moral relevance or the moral potential of this kind of love. This is probably due to the fact that, accepting without question the gendered division of labor that prevailed around him, he defined a moral world that excluded women. That may seem too extreme a statement. Let me point out, however, that while in most of his central works of moral philosophy Kant defines the moral subjects of whom he speaks as not only human beings but also "all rational beings as such," in less noticed works from the earliest to the last, he makes it clear that women are not sufficiently rational and autonomous to be moral subjects. In an early essay, entitled *Observations on the Feeling of the Beautiful and Sublime*, he says of women that their "philosophy is not to reason, but to sense."[11] Their virtue, unlike men's, is to be inspired by the desire to please; for them, he asserts, there is to be "nothing of duty, nothing of compulsion, nothing of obligation!"[12] In one of his very last works, the *Anthropology from a Pragmatic Point of View*, although, most uncharacteristically, he says that male and female are both rational beings, he takes back any thought of moral autonomy in the case of a married woman, by pointing out that she is necessarily subject to her husband and a legal minor. "To make oneself behave like a minor," he says, "degrading as it may be, is, nevertheless, very comfortable."[13] It is not difficult to tell, from such remarks, where women stand (perhaps it is more appropriate to say "where women *sit*") on Kant's moral scale.

11. Immanuel Kant, *Observations on the Feeling of the Beautiful and Sublime*, trans. John T. Goldthwait (Berkeley: University of California Press, 1960), p. 79. Kant's word is *empfinden*. It is sometimes, with equal appropriateness, translated as "to feel." I am grateful to Suzanne Altenberger for advice on this matter.

12. Ibid., sec. 3, p. 81.

13. Immanuel Kant, *Anthropology from a Pragmatic Point of View*, trans. Victor Lyle Dowdell (Carbondale: Southern Illinois University Press, 1978), pp. 216, 105.

Thus the moral division of labor between the sexes is very clear in Kant's writings. The virtues he assigns to women, as appropriate for their role in the gendered social structure, and particularly within the family, are virtues ranked far lower than the virtues assigned to men. As Lawrence Blum says about the moral rationalist, in a discussion of Kant and Hegel: "It is the male qualities whose highest expression he naturally takes as his model. In the same way it is natural for him to ignore or underplay the female qualities as they are found in his society—sympathy, compassion, emotional responsiveness. He fails to give these qualities adequate expression within his moral philosophy. The moral rationalist philosopher thus both reflects the sexual value hierarchy of his society and indirectly gives it a philosophic grounding and legitimation."[14]

Thus, Kant neglected the moral significance of an extremely important kind of human love, and of the moral qualities that can arise from it, because of his devaluing of women and exclusion of them from the realm of moral subjects. While endorsing what Blum says above, Jean Grimshaw has recently argued, in her excellent book *Philosophy and Feminist Thinking*, that, although Kant implicitly excludes women from his philosophical ideals, he "could, without inconsistency, have retained his view about 'moral worth', but changed his view of women."[15] I do not think he could, for though women are so peripheral as to be virtually absent from his moral world, the role they are assumed to play behind the scenes would appear to be necessary for its continuance. Women as Kant perceived them, inspired by feeling and by the desire to please, provide both the essential nurturance required for human development, and a realm of existence without which the moral order he prescribes for the world outside the family seems intolerable in its demands.[16] Kant's exclusion of women is of significance not only for women; it has a distorting effect on his moral philosophy as a whole.

To the extent that it derives from Kant in some of its basic assumptions about what it means to be a moral subject, Rawls's theory of justice suffers to some extent from this same distortion. As I will argue, Rawls is unwilling to call explicitly on the human qualities of empathy and benevolence in the working out of his principles of justice and in his lengthy description of the process of deliberation that leads to them. However, his original

14. Lawrence Blum, "Kant's and Hegel's Moral Rationalism: A Feminist Perspective," *Canadian Journal of Philosophy* 12 (1982): 296–97.

15. Jean Grimshaw, *Philosophy and Feminist Thinking* (Minneapolis: University of Minnesota Press, 1986), p. 49.

16. A possible response to this might be to suggest that a twentieth-century Kantian, not regarding the remaining social subordination of women as natural, would view both men and women as equally moral subjects with the same moral worth. But unless the conceptions of a moral subject and moral worth were to be relevantly adapted, this would result in family life's being governed by principles as strictly rationalist as the moral world outside rather than as providing a haven from this world, as Kant seems to have envisaged.

position consists of a combination of assumptions—mutual disinterest and the veil of ignorance—that, as he says, "achieves the same purpose as benevolence" (*TOJ*, p. 148). Before going on to discuss this, however, let us look at Rawls's account of how people develop a sense of justice. For despite his Kantian assumptions about rationality and autonomy, and the related rational choice language of much of his theory, Rawls's account of moral development is very different from Kant's and indicates clearly that rationality is not a sufficient basis on which to found or sustain his theory of justice.

## RAWLS AND THE SENSE OF JUSTICE: THE SIGNIFICANCE OF GENDER

There is little indication, throughout most of *A Theory of Justice*, that the modern liberal society to which the principles of justice are to be applied is deeply and pervasively gender structured. As I shall argue, this neglect of gender has major implications for the practical feasibility of Rawls's principles of justice. In particular, there is very little mention of the family, the linchpin of the gender structure. Although Rawls, for good reason, mentions the "monogamous family" in his initial list of major institutions that constitute the "basic structure" to which the principles of justice are to apply, he never applies the two principles of justice to it. In fact, his assumption that those in the original position are "heads of families" prevents him from doing this (*TOJ*, p. 128). A central tenet of the theory, after all, is that justice characterizes institutions whose members could hypothetically have agreed to their structure and rules from a position in which they did not know which place in the structure they were to occupy. But since those in the original position are all heads of families, they are not in a position to settle questions of justice *within* families. In fact, if we discard the "heads of families" assumption, take seriously the notion that those in the original position are ignorant of their sex as well as their other individual characteristics, and apply the principles of justice to the gender structure and the family arrangements of our society, considerable changes are clearly called for.[17]

Instead, apart from being briefly mentioned as the link between generations necessary for Rawls's "savings principle," and as an obstacle to fair equality of opportunity, the family appears in Rawls's theory in only one context (albeit one of considerable importance): as the earliest school of moral development. Rawls argues, in a much neglected section of part 3 of *A Theory of Justice*, that a just, well-ordered society will be stable only if its members continue to develop a sense of justice—"a strong and normally effective desire to act as the principles of justice require" (*TOJ*, p. 454). He specifically turns his attention to the question

17. Susan Moller Okin, "Justice and Gender," *Philosophy and Public Affairs* 16 (1987): 42–72.

of childhood moral development, aiming to indicate the major steps by which a sense of justice is acquired.

In this context, Rawls *assumes* that families are just, though he has provided no reasons for us to accept this assumption (*TOJ*, p. 490). Moreover, these supposedly just families play a fundamental role in moral development. The love of parents for their children, coming to be reciprocated in turn by the child, is important in his account of the development of a sense of self-worth. By loving the child and being "worthy objects of his admiration, . . . they arouse in him a sense of his own value and the desire to become the sort of person that they are" (*TOJ*, p. 465). Healthy moral development in early life, Rawls argues, depends upon love, trust, affection, example, and guidance (*TOJ*, p. 466).

Later in moral development, at the stage he calls "the morality of association," Rawls perceives the family, which he describes in gendered terms, as a "small association, normally characterized by a definite hierarchy, in which each member has certain rights and duties" (*TOJ*, p. 467). It is the first of many associations in which, by moving through a sequence of roles and positions, our moral understanding increases. The crucial aspect of the sense of fairness that is learned during this stage is the capacity to take up the different points of view of others and to see things from their perspectives. We learn to perceive, from what they say and do, what other people's ends, plans, and motives are. Without this experience, Rawls says, "we cannot put ourselves into another's place and find out what we would do in his position," which we need to be able to do in order "to regulate our own conduct in the appropriate way by reference to it" (*TOJ*, p. 469). Participation in different roles in the various associations of society leads to the development of a person's "capacity for fellow feeling" and to "ties of friendship and mutual trust" (*TOJ*, p. 470). Rawls says that, just as in the first stage certain natural attitudes develop toward the parents, "so here ties of friendship and confidence grow up among associates. In each case certain natural attitudes underlie the corresponding moral feelings: a lack of these feelings would manifest the absence of these attitudes" (*TOJ*, p. 471).

This whole account of moral development is strikingly unlike that of Kant, for whom any feelings that did not follow from independently established moral principles were morally suspect. Unlike Kant, with his arid, intellectualized account of moral learning, Rawls clearly acknowledges the importance of feelings in the development of the capacity for moral thinking. In accounting for his third and final stage of moral development, where persons are supposed to become attached to the principles of justice themselves, Rawls says that "the sense of justice is continuous with the love of mankind" (*TOJ*, p. 476). At the same time, he allows for the fact that we have particularly strong feelings about those to whom we are closely attached and says that this is rightly reflected in our moral judgments: even though "our moral sentiments display an independence from the accidental circumstances of our world, . . . our natural attachments to particular persons and groups still have an appropriate place" (*TOJ*, p. 475). His differences from Kant's views are clear from his indications that empathy, or imagining oneself into the place of others, plays a major role in moral development. It is not surprising that he turns away from Kant, to moral philosophers such as Adam Smith, Elizabeth Anscombe, Philippa Foot, and Bernard Williams, in developing his ideas about the moral emotions or sentiments (*TOJ*, pp. 479 ff.).

In Rawls's summary of his three psychological laws of moral development (*TOJ*, pp. 490–91), the fundamental importance of loving parenting for the development of a sense of justice is manifest. The three laws, Rawls says, are "not merely principles of association or of reinforcement . . . [but] assert that the active sentiments of love and friendship, and even the sense of justice, arise from the manifest intention of other persons to act for our good. Because we recognize that they wish us well, we care for their well-being in return" (*TOJ*, p. 494). Each of the laws of moral development, as set out by Rawls, depends upon the one before it, and the first assumption of the first law is: "given that family institutions are just. . . ." Unlike Kant, with his nameless, but no doubt male, tutor, Rawls frankly admits that the whole of moral development rests upon the loving ministrations of those who raise small children from the earliest stages, and on the moral character of the environment in which this takes place. At the foundation of the development of the sense of justice, then, are an activity and a sphere of life that—though by no means necessarily so—have throughout history been predominantly the activity and the sphere of women.

Rawls does not explain the basis of his assumption that family institutions are just. If gendered family institutions are *not* just but are, rather, a relic of caste or feudal societies in which roles, responsibilities, and resources are distributed, not in accordance with the two principles of justice but in accordance with innate differences that are imbued with enormous social significance, then Rawls's whole structure of moral development seems to be built on uncertain ground. Unless the households in which children are first nurtured, and see their first examples of human interaction, are based on equality and reciprocity rather than on dependence and domination, as is too often in fact the case, how can whatever love they receive from their parents make up for the injustice they see before their eyes in the relationship between these same parents? Unless they are parented equally by adults of both sexes, how will children of both sexes come to develop a sufficiently similar and well-rounded moral psychology as to enable them to engage in the kind of deliberation about justice that is exemplified in the original position? And finally, unless the household is connected by a continuum of associations to the larger communities within which people are supposed to develop fellow feelings for each other, how will they grow up with the capacity for enlarged sympathies such as are clearly required for the practice of justice?

On the one hand, Rawls's neglect of justice within the family is clearly in tension with his own theory of moral development, which *requires* that families be just. On the other hand, his conviction that the development of a sense of justice depends on attachments to and feelings for other persons, originating in the family, is in tension with the "rational choice" language that he frequently employs in laying out his theory of justice. I shall now look at this prevailing mode of interpreting Rawls and then go on to suggest an alternative account of the original position, which is both consistent with much that he says about it and much more compatible with his own account of moral development. It is this alternative account of what goes on in the original position that leads me to suggest that one is not forced to choose between an ethic of justice and an ethic of sympathy or care, nor between an ethic that emphasizes universality and one that takes account of differences.

## THE ORIGINAL POSITION

The original position is at the heart of Rawls's theory of justice. It is both his most important contribution to moral and political theory and the focus of most of the controversy and disputes that the theory still attracts more than fifteen years after its publication. How the original position is understood and interpreted is extremely important for both the internal coherence and the persuasiveness of the theory. First I shall lay out briefly the set of conditions that Rawls calls the original position. Then I shall look at the way that Rawls presents it, at least some of the time, a presentation that I think has led to some of the criticisms that have been made of it. Then I will explain my alternative reading, which I think is faithful to Rawls's essential meaning. This alternative reading suggests that Rawls is far from being a moral rationalist and that feelings such as empathy and benevolence are at the very foundation of his principles of justice. The alternative reading, I suggest, leaves the original position, and indeed the whole theory, less susceptible to criticism.

In sum, Rawls's specifications for the original position are as follows: the parties are rational and mutually disinterested, and while no limits are placed on the *general* information available to them, they deliberate behind a "veil of ignorance" that conceals from them all knowledge of their individual characteristics: "No one knows his place in society, his class position or social status, nor does anyone know his fortune in the distribution of natural assets and abilities, his intelligence, strength, and the like. [Nor do the parties know] their conceptions of the good or their special psychological propensities" (*TOJ*, p. 12). The critical force of the original position can be appreciated from the fact that some interesting critiques of Rawls's theory have resulted from others' interpreting the original position more radically or broadly than its creator did. Beitz has argued, for example, that there is no justification for not extending its application to the population of the entire planet, which would lead to challenging virtually everything that is currently assumed in the dominant "statist" conception of international relations.[18] Some of us, feminist critics, have suggested that if we do away with the "heads of families" assumption, and take seriously the fact that those behind the veil of ignorance cannot know their *sex*, we must engage in a radical questioning of the gender structure, which Rawls himself leaves virtually unmentioned.[19]

In *A Theory of Justice* itself, Rawls foresees that problems will arise if readers focus separately on each of the assumptions made about parties in the original position, rather than taking the device as a whole. He warns that the theory may be interpreted as based on egoism if the mutual disinterest assumption is taken in isolation from the other specifications: "the feeling that this conception of justice is egoistic is an illusion fostered by looking at but one of the elements of the original position" (*TOJ*, p. 148).[20] He also addresses in advance those who are likely to ask, having taken note of what would be decided in the original position, what relevance it may have for actual human beings who know who they are and what their social position is. He responds like this:

> The conditions embodied in the description of this situation are ones that we do in fact accept. Or if we do not, then we can be persuaded to do so by philosophical considerations of the sort occasionally introduced. Each aspect of the original position can be given a supporting explanation. Thus what we are doing is to combine into one conception the totality of conditions that we are ready upon due reflection to recognize as reasonable in our conduct with respect to one another. Once we grasp this conception, we can at any time look at the social world from the required point of view. [*TOJ*, p. 587][21]

On the other hand, in a recent response to critics, Rawls says something that does not seem easy to reconcile with this conception of the original position as an explicitly moral point of view that we can adopt in real life by thinking in the appropriate way. He first reiterates the ideas expressed in the passage I just quoted, by saying that we can enter the original position at any time, simply by reasoning for principles of justice as we would if constrained by its restrictions (on our knowledge, motivations, and so on). But then he adds to this the following: "When, in this way, we simulate being in this position, our reasoning no more commits us to a metaphysical doctrine about the nature of the self than our playing a game like Monopoly commits us to thinking that we are landlords

18. Charles Beitz, *Political Theory and International Relations* (Princeton, N.J.: Princeton University Press, 1979).

19. See Jane English, "Justice between Generations," *Philosophical Studies* 31 (1977): 91–104; Deborah Kearns, "A Theory of Justice—and Love: Rawls on the Family," *Politics* 18 (1983): 36–42; and Okin, "Justice and Gender."

20. See also Rawls, "Kantian Constructivism," p. 527.

21. See also ibid., p. 518.

engaged in a desperate rivalry, winner take all."[22] This juxtaposition of the original position as a moral point of view, a way of reasoning about principles of justice, with the original position as analogous to a game, without moral significance, identifies a tension in the way the original position is presented throughout Rawls's works. In order to see what leads to such criticisms as I have mentioned above, and to consider how they can be fully answered, it is important to look at each side of this tension, in turn.

First, I shall look at how central aspects of the Kantian heritage—especially the presentation of moral subjects as, above all, rational, autonomous, and freed from contingency—influence Rawls in the direction of perceiving what he is doing as a branch of rational choice theory. Given this interpretation, the Monopoly analogy is perfectly appropriate. Then I shall sketch out an alternative reading of the theory, and of the original position in particular, which explains better what it is that makes it into an appropriate "moral point of view" that we can be persuaded to accept. I shall pay particular attention to the question, What do we have to be like, in order to be prepared to take up this point of view and to formulate our principles of justice in accordance with its demands? This is the crucial issue on which I think some parts of Rawls's theory are misleading, due to his identification with Kantian ways of thinking about the foundations of principles of justice and right.

## THE "RATIONAL CHOICE" INTERPRETATION AND ITS IMPLICATIONS

Rawls states early on and repeats a number of times throughout his construction of the theory of justice that it is "a part, perhaps the most important part, of the theory of rational choice" (*TOJ*, p. 16). Recently, he has said that this was a "very misleading" error and that "there is no thought of trying to derive the content of justice within a framework that uses an idea of the rational as the sole normative idea."[23] Once we look at the implications of the rational choice reading of the theory, I

22. John Rawls, "Justice as Fairness: Political, not Metaphysical," *Philosophy and Public Affairs* 14 (1985): 239.

23. Rawls, "Justice as Fairness," p. 237, n. 20. Rawls's movement in this direction is already clearly apparent in the first of the Dewey lectures (Rawls, "Kantian Constructivism"), where he pays much attention to the distinction between the rational and the reasonable. Here, the rational still denotes the advantage of the individual, as in rational choice theory, but the reasonable is defined by moral conceptions such as reciprocity and mutuality. Principles are reasonable only if they are publicly acceptable by moral persons as fair terms of cooperation among them. Rawls seems to draw a clear distinction between thinking about justice and thinking about rational choice when he says: "Familiar principles of justice are examples of reasonable principles, and familiar principles of rational choice are examples of rational principles. The way the Reasonable is presented in the original position leads to the two principles of justice" (p. 530). He also states clearly that, in his theory, "the Reasonable presupposes and subordinates the Rational" (p. 530). See especially pp. 517–22 and pp. 528–30.

suggest that we will be able to see why Rawls has reconsidered it. Purging the theory of the rational choice connection and its implications strengthens it and renders it far less vulnerable to some of its critics.[24]

Let us first look at how Rawls conceives of his theory as a branch of rational choice theory. First, he associates the rationality and mutual disinterest of the parties with rational choice theory (*TOJ*, pp. 13–14). The actors in such a theory are assumed to be egoists, and while Rawls specifies that his parties are not to be understood as egoists in the colloquial sense of being interested only in such things as wealth, prestige, and domination, they *are* to be conceived of as "not taking an interest in one another's interests" (*TOJ*, p. 13). The rationality of the parties is also specified as that standard in economic or other rational choice theory—as instrumental rationality, or "taking the most effective means to given ends" (*TOJ*, p. 14). Rawls explains a number of times that these assumptions are made about the parties in the original position in order that the theory not depend on strong assumptions. He says, for example, that "the original position is meant to incorporate widely shared and yet weak conditions. A conception of justice should not presuppose . . . extensive ties of natural sentiment. At the basis of the theory, one tries to assume as little as possible" (*TOJ*, p. 129; see also pp. 18 and 583). At this point, however, one needs to take heed of Rawls's own warning not to focus on the individual assumptions made about the parties in the original position but to look at the concept as a whole. Rawls claims that each of the assumptions "should by itself be natural and plausible; some of them may seem innocuous or even trivial" (*TOJ*, p. 18). The question is, however, how weak do the assumptions look when considered *together?* And is it possible, considering them together, still to conceive of the theory as an example of rational choice theory?

In rational choice theory, choice under certainty requires the individual to have both vast quantities of relevant knowledge about the environment and a well-organized and stable system of preferences.[25] It is on the basis of these, but especially the knowledge of his or her "independent utility

24. See n. 4 above. In addition, a number of rational choice theorists have criticized Rawls's conclusions as much too egalitarian to have emerged from a situation of rational choice (see, e.g., David Gauthier, *Morals by Agreement* [Oxford: Clarendon Press, 1986], pp. 245–67).

25. Conventional rational choice theory distinguishes three modes of deliberation and choice, correlated with three different sets of assumptions about what is known by the actors. Choice under certainty depends on the actors knowing with certainty the outcome of each choice and the utility of that outcome. Choice under risk occurs when all the possible outcomes and their utility are known, as well as the probabilities of their occurrence. Choice under uncertainty occurs when knowledge of the probabilities is absent or incomplete. These nomenclatures are not always strictly adhered to. Rather confusingly, the actor's preparedness to take risks is a more important factor in the case of the third set of assumptions (see John C. Harsanyi, *Rational Behavior and Bargaining Equilibrium in Games and Social Situations* [Cambridge: Cambridge University Press, 1977], chap. 3). I am grateful to Richard Arneson for helping me to correct some confusions in this part of the paper.

function" that individuals are presumed able to choose, from the alternatives open, the option that will permit each to reach the highest attainable point on his or her preference scale. In conditions where this knowledge about individual preferences is presumed not available, reasoning in accordance with abstract probabilities comes into play. We must compare the specifications of Rawls's original position with these assumptions.

In Rawls's account of the original position, mutual disinterest and instrumental rationality feature only in conjunction with the veil of ignorance. On the one hand, the parties try to maximize what rational choice theory calls their "utility functions." They realize that, as individuals *having* distinct ends and interests (even though these are not revealed to them) they all have an equal stake in promoting and protecting what Rawls calls the "primary goods"—those basic liberties and goods that are prerequisite for the pursuit of distinct ends and interests. In this respect, then, as Rawls acknowledges, there might as well be just one person behind the veil of ignorance since the deliberations of all are identical. On the other hand, the parties do not have any knowledge of their separate, distinct, individual interests. Rawls says of them that "in choosing between principles each tries as best he can to advance *his interests*," and that he will rank the options "according to how well they further *his purposes*," and so on (*TOJ*, pp. 142, 143; emphasis added). But what sense does it make to talk of mutually disinterested individuals pursuing their interests when, to the extent that their interests are distinct and differentiated, they have no knowledge of them? Clearly, choice under certainty, which requires both the knowledge of outcomes and of the utility of these outcomes, is ruled out. The branches of rational choice theory that remain potentially applicable are choice under risk and choice under uncertainty.

Choice under risk, however, involves taking into account the probability of the occurrence of different outcomes. Rawls does not allow this to happen, by specifying that the veil of ignorance "excludes all but the vaguest knowledge of likelihoods. The parties have no basis for determining the probable nature of their society, or their place in it" (*TOJ*, p. 155). As he points out, this stipulation means that the parties "have strong reasons for being wary of probability calculations if any other course is open to them" (*TOJ*, p. 155). Thus choice under risk is ruled out. Rawls says, indeed, that "the veil of ignorance leads directly to the problem of choice under uncertainty" (*TOJ*, p. 172). There is, however, no generally accepted theory of rational choice under uncertainty, and we must still ask: How *do* the parties deliberate, in coming to their conclusions?

Rawls further reduces the applicability of rational choice theory by specifying that the parties are to have no knowledge of their aversion from or propensity for taking risks. By prohibiting the parties from having any knowledge of *either* the probabilities themselves *or* their own attitudes toward taking chances, Rawls decisively rules out the modes of deliberation that rational choice theory typically turns to under such conditions as otherwise defined. When he specifies the situation as one of choice under uncertainty, he suggests another possible mode of reasoning: "Of course, it is possible to regard the parties as perfect altruists and to assume that they reason as if they are certain to be in the position of each person. This interpretation of the initial situation removes the element of risk and uncertainty" (*TOJ*, p. 172). Rawls does not consider himself to be taking this route, believing as he does that it leads to classic utilitarianism rather than to the two principles of justice.[26] But, as I shall argue, because he reduces the knowledge of those in the original position to the point where they cannot employ probabilistic reasoning and cannot be assumed to take risks, Rawls *does* have to rely on empathy, benevolence, and equal concern for others as for the self, in order to have the parties come up with the principles they choose, especially the difference principle. This takes him far from anything in rational choice theory.

Rawls compares the assumptions he makes about those in the original position with other assumptions that include benevolence. He considers whether his own theory requires that the parties be moved by benevolence or by an interest in one another's interests. And he states clearly that "the combination of mutual disinterest and the veil of ignorance *achieves the same purpose as benevolence*. For this combination of conditions *forces each person in the original position to take the good of others into account*" (*TOJ*, p. 148; emphasis added). It is important to pause and think about this statement. For what it means is that it is only because those in the original

26. In sec. 30 of *A Theory of Justice* Rawls discusses the ethical position that would be adopted by a perfect altruist (a person "whose desires conform to the approvals of . . . a rational and impartial sympathetic spectator"). Imagining himself in the place of each person in turn, the perfect altruist is supposed to arrive at classical utilitarian conclusions since "sympathetically imagined pains cancel out sympathetically imagined pleasures, and the final intensity of approval corresponds to the net sum of positive feeling" (p. 187). It is not clear to me why the imagining of the altruist should involve the conflation of all persons into one that results in adoption of the classical principle of utility. I agree with Nagel (Thomas Nagel, *The Possibility of Altruism* [Princeton, N.J.: Princeton University Press, 1978], p. 138), who concludes that "this situation is unimaginable, and in so far as it is not, it completely distorts the nature of the competing claims." Rawls then imagines the benevolent person in another way—as one who "is to imagine that he is to divide into a plurality of persons whose life and experience will be distinct in the usual way . . . [with] no conflation of desires and memories into those of one person." Under *these* conditions, Rawls thinks that "the two principles of justice . . . seem a relatively more plausible choice than the classical principle of utility" (p. 191). It seems completely reasonable that a benevolent spectator who imagined experiencing the distinct lives of all those concerned separately (the only way that makes any sense to me) would be more likely to adopt the two principles than the classical principle of utility. It is implausible to expect that the pains experienced in one life would be balanced off by the pleasures experienced in another—even if lived by the same person (see Nagel, *The Possibility of Altruism*, pp. 140–42). Rawls argues that a party in the original position, who knows that he will live *one* of the lives, but does not know *which* one, will be even less likely to favor aggregative solutions, or to trade off the pains of some against the pleasures of others. But he resists the idea that such a party needs benevolence since he considers that the veil of ignorance and mutual disinterestedness serve as its functional equivalents.

position are assumed to be behind the veil of ignorance that they can be presented as the "rational, mutually disinterested" agents characteristic of rational choice theory. They can be perceived as thinking only for themselves, *only* because they do not know *which self* they will turn out to be and, therefore, must consider the interests of all possible selves equally.

Having stated that his assumptions achieve the same purpose as that of benevolence, Rawls goes on to argue that his assumption of mutual disinterest and the veil of ignorance has enormous advantages over the assumption of benevolence plus knowledge since the "latter is so complex that no definite theory at all can be worked out." Too much information is required, and unanswered questions remain about the "relative strength of benevolent desires." His assumptions, by contrast, he says, have the "merits of simplicity and clarity," as well as the advantage of being "weak stipulations" (*TOJ*, pp. 148–49). The illusion that the stipulations are weak is not hard to dispel; it is only if they are considered in isolation from each other (just what Rawls warns us against) that they can be seen as weak. In fact, the veil of ignorance is *such* a demanding stipulation that it converts what would, without it, be self-interest into benevolence or the equal concern for others. As for the advantage of simplicity and clarity, when we look at the original position in the only way in which it is intelligible (which is far distant from any rational choice theory), we find that it cannot escape most of the complexities of benevolence plus knowledge. To be sure, the issue of "the relative strength of benevolent desires" is not a problem for those behind the veil of ignorance: since one does not know which person one will turn out to be, one's rational self-interest presumably directs one to being equally concerned for each. But in order to think reasonably in the original position, one must presumably have knowledge of the essential aspects of the lives of persons of all different imaginable types and in all different imaginable social positions. In the absence of knowledge about their own particular characteristics, those in the original position cannot think from the position of *nobody* (as Rawls's desire for simplicity might suggest); they must think from the position of *everybody*, in the sense of *each in turn*. This is far from a simple demand.[27]

In fact, when we consider the reasoning engaged in by the parties in the original position, we can see that this *is* what they do. For example,

27. In a later discussion, Rawls again suggests significant differences between the reasoning of the parties and the self-interest characteristic of conventional rational choice theory. He says: "In the original position we may describe the parties either as the representatives (or trustees) of persons with certain interests or as themselves moved by these interests. It makes no difference either way, although the latter is simpler and I shall usually speak in this vein" (Rawls, "Kantian Constructivism," pp. 524–25). As I have suggested, the latter description is not simpler. For in a situation in which the identity and particular characteristics of the self are unknown there is no difference between self-interest and the representation of the interests of others. Whichever description Rawls chooses, the complexities are the same, and neither can be equated with the situation in rational choice theory.

in formulating the principle that protects equal liberty of conscience, Rawls makes it clear that the parties, who of course do not know what their moral or religious convictions are, "must choose principles that secure the integrity of their religious and moral freedom" (*TOJ*, p. 206). But in the absence of knowledge about the self, including the absence of probabilities, the only way to do this is to imagine oneself in the position of those whose religious practices and beliefs or lack thereof will require most tolerance on the part of others—the religiously "least advantaged," one might call them. It is not easy for an essentially nonreligious person, trying to imagine her- or himself into the original position, to adopt the standpoint of a fundamentalist believer; nor is it easy for a devoutly religious person to imagine the situation of a nonbeliever in a highly religious society. To do either requires, at the very least, both strong empathy and a preparedness to listen carefully to the very different points of view of others.

This method of thinking in the original position is most obviously required in the formulation of the difference principle. There, the maximin rule "directs our attention to the worst that can happen under any proposed course of action, and to decide in the light of that" (*TOJ*, p. 154). In considering permissible inequalities, "one looks at the system from the standpoint of the least advantaged representative man" (*TOJ*, p. 151). And, of course, once we challenge Rawls's traditional belief that questions about justice can be resolved by "heads of families," the "least advantaged representative woman," who is likely to be considerably *worse* off, has to be considered equally. Especially for those accustomed by class position, race, and sex to privilege, wealth, and power, a real appreciation of the point of view of the worst-off is likely to require considerable empathy and capacity to listen to others.[28]

On this interpretation, the original position is *not* an abstraction from all contingencies of human life, as some of Rawls's critics, and even Rawls himself at his most Kantian, present it. It is, rather, as Rawls's own theory of moral development strongly indicates, much closer to an appreciation and concern for social and other human *differences*. Neither does it seem that the theory requires us to regard ourselves as "independent in the sense that our identity is never tied to our aims and attachments," as Sandel says that it does.[29] For there is nothing implausible or inconsistent about requiring us to distance ourselves from our particular aims and

28. For a very interesting discussion of the problems of considering "the other" in moral and social theory, see Joan Tronto, "Rationalizing Racism, Sexism, and Other Forms of Prejudice: Otherness in Moral and Feminist Theory" (Hunter College of the City University of New York, Department of Political Science, New York, 1987, typescript). Compare Kenneth Arrow, *Collected Papers: Social Choice and Justice* (Cambridge, Mass.: Harvard University Press, Belknap Press, 1983), pp. 98, 113–14, for doubts about whether different people with different life experiences can ever have the same information, and can therefore achieve the criterion of universalizability that is required by a theory of justice.

29. Sandel, p. 179.

attachments for the purpose of arriving at principles of justice, while acknowledging that we may to some extent identify with them as we go about living our lives. The original position requires that, as moral subjects, we consider the identities, aims, and attachments of every other person, however different they may be from ourselves, as of equal concern with our own. If we, who *do* know who we are, are to think *as if* we were in the original position, we must develop considerable capacities for empathy and powers of communicating with others about what different human lives are like. But these alone are not enough to maintain in us a sense of justice. Since we know who we are, and what are our particular interests and conceptions of the good, we need as well a great commitment to benevolence; to *caring* about each and every other as much as about ourselves.

Rawls states clearly in several passages that abiding by the principles of justice that would be chosen in the original position requires motivations on the part of real human beings—especially the powerful and privileged—that are far from being self-interested: "To be sure, any principle chosen in the original position may require a large sacrifice for some. The beneficiaries of clearly unjust institutions (those founded on principles that have no claim to acceptance) may find it hard to reconcile themselves to the changes that will have to be made" (*TOJ*, p. 176). But he also speaks of a sense in which abiding by the principles of justice is in the self-interest of all—in the sense of *moral* self-interest. In the well-ordered, just society, "everyone's acting to uphold just institutions is for the good of each. . . . When all strive to comply with these principles and each succeeds, then individually and collectively their nature as moral persons is most fully realized, and with it their individual and collective good" (*TOJ*, p. 528).

All this takes us very far from the language of rational choice, which may explain Rawls's subsequent rejection of his own initial characterization of his theory. In such language, there is no room for a distinction between self-interest and moral self-interest. As I have suggested, Rawls's theory is much better interpreted as a theory founded upon the notion of equal concern for others than as a theory in which "mutual disinterest" has any significance, except as but *one* of several assumptions in a construction that serves not simply as a "device of representation" (as he has called the original position) but also as a device of empathy and benevolence. Indeed, such an interpretation is supported by much of Rawls's own text, and especially by his theory of moral development. On the other hand, it requires that the theory be purged of all suggestions that it is a part of rational choice theory.

It will perhaps be useful to place my reinterpretation of Rawls in the context of the contrasting arguments of several other feminist theorists. For it challenges the views of some who have found such theories of justice to be either incomplete or unacceptable from a feminist point of view. Gilligan, for example, in her critique of the moral development theory of the Kohlberg school (which owes much to Rawls's work on justice), contrasts the morality of care, contextuality, and concern for others with the morality of justice, rights, and rules. She associates the former voice primarily with women and the latter with men.[30] As I have argued elsewhere, many of the respondents whom Gilligan identifies as speaking in the "different voice" use it to express as fully universalizable a morality of social concern as respondents who express themselves in the language of justice and rights.[31] Thus the implication frequently drawn from her work, that women's morality tends to be more particularistic and contextual, appears to be unfounded. Here, by arguing that Rawls's theory of justice is itself centrally dependent upon the capacity of moral persons to be concerned about and to demonstrate care for others, especially others who are most different from themselves, I have presented another piece of argument that questions the wisdom of distinguishing between an ethic of care and an ethic of justice.

In Noddings's view, justice has been much overrated as the fundamental virtue, and principles have been overvalued as a tool for thinking about ethical problems.[32] These mistaken emphases are attributed to an overly individualistic and abstract male bias in moral philosophy. Justice itself, according to this view, should be at least supplemented, if not supplanted, by an ethic of caring, in which one's responsibility to care for those close to one takes priority over or entirely replaces what have generally been regarded as obligations to a broader range of people, or even humanity at large. While the feminist interpretation of Rawls that I have presented above argues that feelings such as caring and concern for others are essential to the formulation of principles of justice, it does not suggest that such principles can be replaced by contextual caring thinking. The problem, I suggest, is not principles or rules per se but the ways in which they have often been arrived at. If the principles of justice are founded, as I have suggested that Rawls's are, not on mutual disinterest and detachment from others but on empathy and concern for others—including concern for the ways in which others are different from ourselves—they will not be likely to lead to destructive rules that have tragic consequences when applied to those we love.[33]

The argument presented above also contrasts with recent work on theories of justice by Young and Benhabib. Young argues that the ideal of impartiality and universality in moral reasoning is misguided and works in opposition to feminist and other emancipatory politics because it attempts to eliminate otherness and difference and creates a false dichotomy between reason and feeling.[34] She thus finds Rawls's theory

30. Gilligan.

31. Susan Moller Okin, "Thinking Like a Woman," in *Theoretical Perspectives on Sexual Difference*, ed. Deborah Rhode (New Haven, Conn.: Yale University Press, in press).

32. Noddings.

33. Compare ibid., p. 44.

34. Iris Marion Young, "Toward a Critical Theory of Justice," *Social Theory and Practice* 7 (1981): 279–301, and "Impartiality and the Civic Public," in *Feminism as Critique*, ed. Seyla Benhabib and Drucilla Cornell (Minneapolis: University of Minnesota Press, 1987).

to be as rationalist, monological, and abstracted from particularity as Kant's. Benhabib makes the closely related claim that, in universalistic moral theories, such as Kohlberg's and Rawls's, "ignoring the standpoint of the concrete other leads to epistemic incoherence." In Rawls's original position, she claims, "The *other as different from the self*, disappears. . . . Differences are not denied; they become irrelevant." With only a "generalized other," Benhabib remarks, "what we are left with is an empty mask that is everyone and no one."[35]

I have attempted here to respond to such feminist critiques of Rawlsian thinking about justice by disputing the dichotomies they draw between justice and care, in the works of Gilligan and Noddings, and, in the works of Benhabib and Young, between impartiality and universalizability on the one hand, and the recognition of otherness and difference on the other. I have argued that Rawls's theory of justice is most coherently interpreted as a moral structure founded on the equal concern of persons for each other as for themselves, a theory in which empathy with and care for others, as well as awareness of their differences, are crucial components. It is, certainly, the case that Rawls's construction of the original position is designed so as to eliminate from the formulation of the principles of justice biases that might result from particular attachments to others, as well as from particular facts about the self. Surely impartiality in this sense is a reasonable requirement to make of a theory of justice.[36] But nevertheless, as I have argued here, the only coherent way in which a party in the original position can think about justice is through empathy with persons of all kinds in all the different positions in society, but especially with the least well-off in various respects. To think as a person in the original position is not to be a disembodied nobody. This, as critics have rightly pointed out, would be impossible. Rather, it is to think from the point of view of everybody, of every "concrete other" whom one might turn out to be.

For real people, who of course *know* who they are, to think *as if* in the original position requires that they have well-developed capacities for empathy, care, and concern for others—certainly not self-interest and instrumental rationality. In order to develop the sense of justice that is required of people if a well-ordered society is to have any hope of

35. Seyla Benhabib, "The Generalized and the Concrete Other," in Benhabib and Cornell, eds., p. 89 and passim.

36. The pitfalls of rejecting the goals of impartiality and/or universalizability, and of associating women or feminist theory with such a position, seem to me to be underestimated in the arguments made by Benhabib, Noddings, and Young, as well as in the implications drawn by Gilligan from her data. As I have argued elsewhere, to the extent that findings about women's moral development are interpreted to mean that women are more attached than men to particular others and less able to be impartial or to universalize in their moral thinking, they seem not only to misread the data but to reinforce the negative stereotyping of women that has been employed to exclude them from political rights and positions of public authority (Susan Moller Okin, "Thinking Like a Woman").

being achieved or, once achieved, preserved, human beings must be nurtured and socialized in an environment that best develops these capacities in them. By acknowledging the importance of such feelings for the development of a sense of justice, Rawls breaks away from the rationalist Kantian mode of thinking that casts a strong influence over much of his theory. To the extent that these aspects of the theory are emphasized, and it is thereby freed from some of its most Kantian language and assumptions, it is less open to some of the criticisms that have been made of it—and especially of its central concept, the original position. But such an emphasis at the same time draws attention to the fact that the theory as it stands contains an internal paradox. Because of Rawls's assumptions about the gendered family, he has not applied the principles of justice to the realm of human nurturance, which is so crucial for the achievement and the maintenance of justice.

# [4]

# *In a Different Voice: Women's Conceptions of Self and of Morality*

CAROL GILLIGAN
*Harvard University*

*As theories of developmental psychology continue to define educational goals and practice, it has become imperative for educators and researchers to scrutinize not only the underlying assumptions of such theories but also the model of adulthood toward which they point. Carol Gilligan examines the limitations of several theories, most notably Kohlberg's stage theory of moral development, and concludes that developmental theory has not given adequate expression to the concerns and experience of women. Through a review of psychological and literary sources, she illustrates the feminine construction of reality. From her own research data, interviews with women contemplating abortion, she then derives an alternative sequence for the development of women's moral judgments. Finally, she argues for an expanded conception of adulthood that would result from the integration of the "feminine voice" into developmental theory.*

The arc of developmental theory leads from infantile dependence to adult autonomy, tracing a path characterized by an increasing differentiation of self from other and a progressive freeing of thought from contextual constraints. The vision of Luther, journeying from the rejection of a self defined by others to the assertive boldness of "Here I stand" and the image of Plato's allegorical man in the cave, separating at last the shadows from the sun, have taken powerful hold on the psychological understanding of what constitutes development. Thus, the individual, meeting fully the developmental challenges of adolescence as set for him by Piaget, Erikson, and Kohlberg, thinks formally, proceeding from theory to fact, and defines both the self and the moral autonomously, that is, apart from the identification and conventions that had comprised the particulars of his childhood world. So

The research reported here was partially supported by a grant from the Spencer Foundation. I wish to thank Mary Belenky for her collaboration and colleagueship in the abortion decision study and Michael Murphy for his comments and help in preparing this manuscript.

*Harvard Educational Review* Vol. 47 No. 4 November 1977

equipped, he is presumed ready to live as an adult, to love and work in a way that is both intimate and generative, to develop an ethical sense of caring and a genital mode of relating in which giving and taking fuse in the ultimate reconciliation of the tension between self and other.

Yet the men whose theories have largely informed this understanding of development have all been plagued by the same problem, the problem of women, whose sexuality remains more diffuse, whose perception of self is so much more tenaciously embedded in relationships with others and whose moral dilemmas hold them in a mode of judgment that is insistently contextual. The solution has been to consider women as either deviant or deficient in their development.

That there is a discrepancy between concepts of womanhood and adulthood is nowhere more clearly evident than in the series of studies on sex-role stereotypes reported by Broverman, Vogel, Broverman, Clarkson, and Rosenkrantz (1972). The repeated finding of these studies is that the qualities deemed necessary for adulthood—the capacity for autonomous thinking, clear decision making, and responsible action—are those associated with masculinity but considered undesirable as attributes of the feminine self. The stereotypes suggest a splitting of love and work that relegates the expressive capacities requisite for the former to women while the instrumental abilities necessary for the latter reside in the masculine domain. Yet, looked at from a different perspective, these stereotypes reflect a conception of adulthood that is itself out of balance, favoring the separateness of the individual self over its connection to others and leaning more toward an autonomous life of work than toward the interdependence of love and care.

This difference in point of view is the subject of this essay, which seeks to identify in the feminine experience and construction of social reality a distinctive voice, recognizable in the different perspective it brings to bear on the construction and resolution of moral problems. The first section begins with the repeated observation of difference in women's concepts of self and of morality. This difference is identified in previous psychological descriptions of women's moral judgments and described as it again appears in current research data. Examples drawn from interviews with women in and around a university community are used to illustrate the characteristics of the feminine voice. The relational bias in women's thinking that has, in the past, been seen to compromise their moral judgment and impede their development now begins to emerge in a new developmental light. Instead of being seen as a developmental deficiency, this bias appears to reflect a different social and moral understanding.

This alternative conception is enlarged in the second section through consideration of research interviews with women facing the moral dilemma of whether to continue or abort a pregnancy. Since the research design allowed women to define as well as resolve the moral problem, developmental distinctions could be derived directly from the categories of women's thought. The responses of women to structured interview questions regarding the pregnancy decision formed the basis for describing a developmental sequence that traces progressive differentiations in their understanding and judgment of conflicts between self and other. While the sequence of women's moral development follows the three-level progression of all

*In a Different Voice*
CAROL GILLIGAN

social developmental theory, from an egocentric through a societal to a universal perspective, this progression takes place within a distinct moral conception. This conception differs from that derived by Kohlberg from his all-male longitudinal research data.

This difference then becomes the basis in the third section for challenging the current assessement of women's moral judgment at the same time that it brings to bear a new perspective on developmental assessment in general. The inclusion in the overall conception of development of those categories derived from the study of women's moral judgment enlarges developmental understanding, enabling it to encompass better the thinking of both sexes. This is particularly true with respect to the construction and resolution of the dilemmas of adult life. Since the conception of adulthood retrospectively shapes the theoretical understanding of the development that precedes it, the changes in that conception that follow from the more central inclusion of women's judgments recast developmental understanding and lead to a reconsideration of the substance of social and moral development.

## Characteristics of the Feminine Voice

The revolutionary contribution of Piaget's work is the experimental confirmation and refinement of Kant's assertion that knowledge is actively constructed rather than passively received. Time, space, self, and other, as well as the categories of developmental theory, all arise out of the active interchange between the individual and the physical and social world in which he lives and of which he strives to make sense. The development of cognition is the process of reappropriating reality at progressively more complex levels of apprehension, as the structures of thinking expand to encompass the increasing richness and intricacy of experience.

Moral development, in the work of Piaget and Kohlberg, refers specifically to the expanding conception of the social world as it is reflected in the understanding and resolution of the inevitable conflicts that arise in the relations between self and others. The moral judgment is a statement of priority, an attempt at rational resolution in a situation where, from a different point of view, the choice itself seems to do violence to justice.

Kohlberg (1969), in his extension of the early work of Piaget, discovered six stages of moral judgment, which he claimed formed an invariant sequence, each successive stage representing a more adequate construction of the moral problem, which in turn provides the basis for its more just resolution. The stages divide into three levels, each of which denotes a significant expansion of the moral point of view from an egocentric through a societal to a universal ethical conception. With this expansion in perspective comes the capacity to free moral judgment from the individual needs and social conventions with which it had earlier been confused and anchor it instead in principles of justice that are universal in application. These principles provide criteria upon which both individual and societal claims can be impartially assessed. In Kohlberg's view, at the highest stages of development morality is freed from both psychological and historical constraints, and the individual can judge independently of his own particular needs and of the values of those around him.

That the moral sensibility of women differs from that of men was noted by Freud (1925/1961) in the following by now well-quoted statement:

> I cannot evade the notion (though I hesitate to give it expression) that for women the level of what is ethically normal is different from what it is in man. Their superego is never so inexorable, so impersonal, so independent of its emotional origins as we require it to be in men. Character-traits which critics of every epoch have brought up against women—that they show less sense of justice than men, that they are less ready to submit to the great exigencies of life, that they are more often influenced in their judgments by feelings of affection or hostility—all these would be amply accounted for by the modification in the formation of their super-ego which we have inferred above. (pp. 257–258)

While Freud's explanation lies in the deviation of female from male development around the construction and resolution of the Oedipal problem, the same observations about the nature of morality in women emerge from the work of Piaget and Kohlberg. Piaget (1932/1965), in his study of the rules of children's games, observed that, in the games they played, girls were "less explicit about agreement [than boys] and less concerned with legal elaboration" (p. 93). In contrast to the boys' interest in the codification of rules, the girls adopted a more pragmatic attitude, regarding "a rule as good so long as the game repays it" (p. 83). As a result, in comparison to boys, girls were found to be "more tolerant and more easily reconciled to innovations" (p. 52).

Kohlberg (1971) also identifies a strong interpersonal bias in the moral judgments of women, which leads them to be considered as typically at the third of his six-stage developmental sequence. At that stage, the good is identified with "what pleases or helps others and is approved of by them" (p. 164). This mode of judgment is conventional in its conformity to generally held notions of the good but also psychological in its concern with intention and consequence as the basis for judging the morality of action.

That women fall largely into this level of moral judgment is hardly surprising when we read from the Broverman et al. (1972) list that prominent among the twelve attributes considered to be desirable for women are tact, gentleness, awareness of the feelings of others, strong need for security, and easy expression of tender feelings. And yet, herein lies the paradox, for the very traits that have traditionally defined the "goodness" of women, their care for and sensitivity to the needs of others, are those that mark them as deficient in moral development. The infusion of feeling into their judgments keeps them from developing a more independent and abstract ethical conception in which concern for others derives from principles of justice rather than from compassion and care. Kohlberg, however, is less pessimistic than Freud in his assessment, for he sees the development of women as extending beyond the interpersonal level, following the same path toward independent, principled judgment that he discovered in the research on men from which his stages were derived. In Kohlberg's view, women's development will proceed beyond Stage Three when they are challenged to solve moral problems that

*In a Different Voice*
CAROL GILLIGAN

require them to see beyond the relationships that have in the past generally bound their moral experience.

What then do women say when asked to construct the moral domain; how do we identify the characteristically "feminine" voice? A Radcliffe undergraduate, responding to the question, "If you had to say what morality meant to you, how would you sum it up?," replies:

> When I think of the word morality, I think of obligations. I usually think of it as conflicts between personal desires and social things, social considerations, or personal desires of yourself versus personal desires of another person or people or whatever. Morality is that whole realm of how you decide these conflicts. A moral person is one who would decide, like by placing themselves more often than not as equals, a truly moral person would always consider another person as their equal . . . in a situation of social interaction, something is morally wrong where the individual ends up screwing a lot of people. And it is morally right when everyone comes out better of.[1]

Yet when asked if she can think of someone whom she would consider a genuinely moral person, she replies, "Well, immediately I think of Albert Schweitzer because he has obviously given his life to help others." Obligation and sacrifice override the ideal of equality, setting up a basic contradiction in her thinking.

Another undergraduate responds to the question, "What does it mean to say something is morally right or wrong?," by also speaking first of responsibilities and obligations:

> Just that it has to do with responsibilties and obligations and values, mainly values. . . . In my life situation I relate morality with interpersonal relationships that have to do with respect for the other person and myself. [Why respect other people?] Because they have a consciousness or feelings that can be hurt, an awareness that can be hurt.

The concern about hurting others persists as a major theme in the responses of two other Radcliffe students:

> [Why be moral?] Millions of people have to live together peacefully. I personally don't want to hurt other people. That's a real criterion, a main criterion for me. It underlies my sense of justice. It isn't nice to inflict pain. I empathize with anyone in pain. Not hurting others is important in my own private morals. Years ago, I would have jumped out of a window not to hurt my boyfriend. That was pathological. Even today though, I want approval and love and I don't want enemies. Maybe that's why there is morality—so people can win approval, love and friendship.

> My main moral principle is not hurting other people as long as you aren't going against your own conscience and as long as you remain true to yourself. . . . There are many moral issues such as abortion, the draft, killing, stealing, monogamy, etc. If something is a controversial issue like these, then I always say it is up to the individual. The individual has to decide and then follow his own con-

[1] The Radcliffe women whose responses are cited were interviewed as part of a pilot study on undergraduate moral development conducted by the author in 1970.

> science. There are no moral absolutes. . . . Laws are pragmatic instruments, but they are not absolutes. A viable society can't make exceptions all the time, but I would personally. . . . I'm afraid I'm heading for some big crisis with my boyfriend someday, and someone will get hurt, and he'll get more hurt than I will. I feel an obligation to not hurt him, but also an obligation to not lie. I don't know if it is possible to not lie and not hurt.

The common thread that runs through these statements, the wish not to hurt others and the hope that in morality lies a way of solving conflicts so that no one will get hurt, is striking in that it is independently introduced by each of the four women as the most specific item in their response to a most general question. The moral person is one who helps others; goodness is service, meeting one's obligations and responsibilities to others, if possible, without sacrificing oneself. While the first of the four women ends by denying the conflict she initially introduced, the last woman anticipates a conflict between remaining true to herself and adhering to her principle of not hurting others. The dilemma that would test the limits of this judgment would be one where helping others is seen to be at the price of hurting the self.

The reticence about taking stands on "controversial issues," the willingness to "make exceptions all the time" expressed in the final example above, is echoed repeatedly by other Radcliffe students, as in the following two examples:

> I never feel that I can condemn anyone else. I have a very relativistic position. The basic idea that I cling to is the sanctity of human life. I am inhibited about impressing my beliefs on others.
>
> I could never argue that my belief on a moral question is anything that another person should accept. I don't believe in absolutes. . . . If there is an absolute for moral decisions, it is human life.

Or as a thirty-one-year-old Wellesley graduate says, in explaining why she would find it difficult to steal a drug to save her own life despite her belief that it would be right to steal for another: "It's just very hard to defend yourself against the rules. I mean, we live by consensus, and you take an action simply for yourself, by yourself, there's no consensus there, and that is relatively indefensible in this society now."

What begins to emerge is a sense of vulnerability that impedes these women from taking a stand, what George Eliot (1860/1965) regards as the girl's "susceptibility" to adverse judgments of others, which stems from her lack of power and consequent inability to do something in the world. While relativism in men, the unwillingness to make moral judgments that Kohlberg and Kramer (1969) and Kohlberg and Gilligan (1971) have associated with the adolescent crisis of identity and belief, takes the form of calling into question the concept of morality itself, the women's reluctance to judge stems rather from their uncertainty about their right to make moral statements or, perhaps, the price for them that such judgment seems to entail. This contrast echoes that made by Matina Horner (1972), who differentiated the ideological fear of success expressed by men from the personal conflicts about succeeding that riddled the women's responses to stories of competitive achievement.

## *In a Different Voice*

CAROL GILLIGAN

> Most of the men who responded with the expectation of negative consequences because of success were not concerned about their masculinity but were instead likely to have expressed existential concerns about finding a "non-materialistic happiness and satisfaction in life." These concerns, which reflect changing attitudes toward traditional kinds of success or achievement in our society, played little, if any, part in the female stories. Most of the women who were high in fear of success imagery continued to be concerned about the discrepancy between success in the situation described and feminine identity. (pp. 163–164)

When women feel excluded from direct participation in society, they see themselves as subject to a consensus or judgment made and enforced by the men on whose protection and support they depend and by whose names they are known. A divorced middle-aged woman, mother of adolescent daughters, resident of a sophisticated university community, tells the story as follows:

> As a woman, I feel I never understood that I was a person, that I can make decisions and I have a right to make decisions. I always felt that that belonged to my father or my husband in some way or church which was always represented by a male clergyman. They were the three men in my life: father, husband, and clergyman, and they had much more to say about what I should or shouldn't do. They were really authority figures which I accepted. I didn't rebel against that. It only has lately occurred to me that I never even rebelled against it, and my girls are much more conscious of this, not in the militant sense, but just in the recognizing sense. . . . I still let things happen to me rather than make them happen, than to make choices, although I know all about choices. I know the procedures and the steps and all. [Do you have any clues about why this might be true?] Well, I think in one sense, there is less responsibility involved. Because if you make a dumb decision, you have to take the rap. If it happens to you, well, you can complain about it. I think that if you don't grow up feeling that you ever had any choices, you don't either have the sense that you have emotional responsibility. With this sense of choice comes this sense of responsibility.

The essence of the moral decision is the exercise of choice and the willingness to accept responsibility for that choice. To the extent that women perceive themselves as having no choice, they correspondingly excuse themselves from the responsibility that decision entails. Childlike in the vulnerability of their dependence and consequent fear of abandonment, they claim to wish only to please but in return for their goodness they expect to be loved and cared for. This, then, is an "altruism" always at risk, for it presupposes an innocence constantly in danger of being compromised by an awareness of the trade-off that has been made. Asked to describe herself, a Radcliffe senior responds:

> I have heard of the onion skin theory. I see myself as an onion, as a block of different layers, the external layers for people that I don't know that well, the agreeable, the social, and as you go inward there are more sides for people I know that I show. I am not sure about the innermost, whether there is a core, or whether I have just picked up everything as I was growing up, these different influences. I think I have a neutral attitude towards myself, but I do think in terms of good and bad. . . . Good—I try to be considerate and thoughtful of other people and I try to be fair in situations and be tolerant. I use the words but I try and work

> them out practically. . . . Bad things—I am not sure if they are bad, if they are altruistic or I am doing them basically for approval of other people. [Which things are these?] The values I have when I try to act them out. They deal mostly with interpersonal type relations. . . . If I were doing it for approval, it would be a very tenuous thing. If I didn't get the right feedback, there might go all my values.

Ibsen's play, *A Doll House* (1879/1965), depicts the explosion of just such a world through the eruption of a moral dilemma that calls into question the notion of goodness that lies at its center. Nora, the "squirrel wife," living with her husband as she had lived with her father, puts into action this conception of goodness as sacrifice and, with the best of intentions, takes the law into her own hands. The crisis that ensues, most painfully for her in the repudiation of that goodness by the very person who was its recipient and beneficiary, causes her to reject the suicide that she had initially seen as its ultimate expression and chose instead to seek new and firmer answers to the adolescent questions of identity and belief.

The availability of choice and with it the onus of responsibility has now invaded the most private sector of the woman's domain and threatens a similar explosion. For centuries, women's sexuality anchored them in passivity, in a receptive rather than active stance, where the events of conception and childbirth could be controlled only by a withholding in which their own sexual needs were either denied or sacrificed. That such a sacrifice entailed a cost to their intelligence as well was seen by Freud (1908/1959) when he tied the "undoubted intellectual inferiority of so many women" to "the inhibition of thought necessitated by sexual suppression" (p. 199). The strategies of withholding and denial that women have employed in the politics of sexual relations appear similar to their evasion or withholding of judgment in the moral realm. The hesitance expressed in the previous examples to impose even a belief in the value of human life on others, like the reluctance to claim one's sexuality, bespeaks a self uncertain of its strength, unwilling to deal with consequence, and thus avoiding confrontation.

Thus women have traditionally deferred to the judgment of men, although often while intimating a sensibility of their own which is at variance with that judgment. Maggie Tulliver, in *The Mill on the Floss* (Eliot, 1860/1965) responds to the accusations that ensue from the discovery of her secretly continued relationship with Phillip Wakeham by acceding to her brother's moral judgment while at the same time asserting a different set of standards by which she attests her own superiority:

> I don't want to defend myself. . . . I know I've been wrong—often continually. But yet, sometimes when I have done wrong, it has been because I have feelings that you would be the better for if you had them. If *you* were in fault ever, if you had done anything very wrong, I should be sorry for the pain it brought you; I should not want punishment to be heaped on you. (p. 188)

An eloquent defense, Kohlberg would argue, of a Stage Three moral position, an assertion of the age-old split between thinking and feeling, justice and mercy, that underlies many of the clichés and stereotypes concerning the difference between the sexes. But considered from another point of view, it is a moment of con-

*In a Different Voice*
CAROL GILLIGAN

frontation, replacing a former evasion, between two modes of judging, two differing constructions of the moral domain—one traditionally associated with masculinity and the public world of social power, the other with femininity and the privacy of domestic interchange. While the developmental ordering of these two points of view has been to consider the masculine as the more adequate and thus as replacing the feminine as the individual moves toward higher stages, their reconciliation remains unclear.

## The Development of Women's Moral Judgment

Recent evidence for a divergence in moral development between men and women comes from the research of Haan (Note 1) and Holstein (1976) whose findings lead them to question the possibility of a "sex-related bias" in Kolhberg's scoring system. This system is based on Kohlberg's six-stage description of moral development. Kohlberg's stages divide into three levels, which he designates as preconventional, conventional, and postconventional, thus denoting the major shifts in moral perspective around a center of moral understanding that equates justice with the maintenance of existing social systems. While the preconventional conception of justice is based on the needs of the self, the conventional judgment derives from an understanding of society. This understanding is in turn superseded by a postconventional or principled conception of justice where the good is formulated in universal terms. The quarrel with Kohlberg's stage scoring does not pertain to the structural differentiation of his levels but rather to questions of stage and sequence. Kohlberg's stages begin with an obedience and punishment orientation (Stage One), and go from there in invariant order to instrumental hedonism (Stage Two), interpersonal concordance (Stage Three), law and order (Stage Four), social contract (Stage Five), and universal ethical principles (Stage Six).

The bias that Haan and Holstein question in this scoring system has to do with the subordination of the interpersonal to the societal definition of the good in the transition from Stage Three to Stage Four. This is the transition that has repeatedly been found to be problematic for women. In 1969, Kohlberg and Kramer identified Stage Three as the characteristic mode of women's moral judgments, claiming that, since women's lives were interpersonally based, this stage was not only "functional" for them but also adequate for resolving the moral conflicts that they faced. Turiel (1973) reported that while girls reached Stage Three sooner than did boys, their judgments tended to remain at that stage while the boys' development continued further along Kohlberg's scale. Gilligan, Kohlberg, Lerner, and Belenky (1971) found a similar association between sex and moral-judgment stage in a study of high-school students, with the girls' responses being scored predominantly at Stage Three while the boys' responses were more often scored at Stage Four.

This repeated finding of developmental inferiority in women may, however, have more to do with the standard by which development has been measured than with the quality of women's thinking per se. Haan's data (Note 1) on the Berkeley Free Speech Movement and Holstein's (1976) three-year longitudinal study of adolescents and their parents indicate that the moral judgments of women differ from those of men in the greater extent to which women's judgments are tied to feelings of empathy and compassion and are concerned more with the resolution of "real-life" as opposed to hypothetical dilemmas (Note 1, p. 34). However, as long as the categories by which development is assessed are derived within a male perspective from male research data, divergence from the masculine standard can be seen only as a failure of development. As a result, the thinking of women is often classified with that of children. The systematic exclusion from consideration of alternative criteria that might better encompass the development of women indicates not only the limitations of a theory framed by men and validated by research samples disproportionately male and adolescent but also the effects of the diffidence prevalent among women, their reluctance to speak publicly in their own voice, given the constraints imposed on them by the politics of differential power between the sexes.

In order to go beyond the question, "How much like men do women think, how capable are they of engaging in the abstract and hypothetical construction of reality?" it is necessary to identify and define in formal terms developmental criteria that encompass the categories of women's thinking. Such criteria would include the progressive differentiations, comprehensiveness, and adequacy that characterize higher-stage resolution of the "more frequently occurring, real-life moral dilemmas of interpersonal, empathic, fellow-feeling concerns" (Haan, Note 1, p. 34), which have long been the center of women's moral judgments and experience. To ascertain whether the feminine construction of the moral domain relies on a language different from that of men, but one which deserves equal credence in the definition of what constitutes development, it is necessary first to find the places where women have the power to choose and thus are willing to speak in their own voice.

When birth control and abortion provide women with effective means for controlling their fertility, the dilemma of choice enters the center of women's lives. Then the relationships that have traditionally defined women's identities and framed their moral judgments no longer flow inevitably from their reproductive capacity but become matters of decision over which they have control. Released from the passivity and reticence of a sexuality that binds them in dependence, it becomes possible for women to question with Freud what it is that they want and to assert their own answers to that question. However, while society may affirm publicly the woman's right to choose for herself, the exercise of such choice brings her privately into conflict with the conventions of femininity, particularly the moral equation of goodness with self-sacrifice. While independent assertion in judgment and action is considered the hallmark of adulthood and constitutes as well the standard of masculine development, it is rather in their care and concern for others that women have both judged themselves and been judged.

The conflict between self and other thus constitutes the central moral problem for women, posing a dilemma whose resolution requires a reconciliation between femininity and adulthood. In the absence of such a reconciliation, the moral prob-

*In a Different Voice*
CAROL GILLIGAN

lem cannot be resolved. The "good woman" masks assertion in evasion, denying responsibility by claiming only to meet the needs of others, while the "bad woman" forgoes or renounces the commitments that bind her in self-deception and betrayal. It is precisely this dilemma—the conflict between compassion and autonomy, between virtue and power—which the feminine voice struggles to resolve in its effort to reclaim the self and to solve the moral problem in such a way that no one is hurt.

When a woman considers whether to continue or abort a pregnancy, she contemplates a decision that affects both self and others and engages directly the critical moral issue of hurting. Since the choice is ultimately hers and therefore one for which she is responsible, it raises precisely those questions of judgment that have been most problematic for women. Now she is asked whether she wishes to interrupt that stream of life which has for centuries immersed her in the passivity of dependence while at the same time imposing on her the responsibility for care. Thus the abortion decision brings to the core of feminine apprehension, to what Joan Didion (1972) calls "the irreconcilable difference of it—that sense of living one's deepest life underwater, that dark involvement with blood and birth and death" (p. 14), the adult questions of responsibility and choice.

How women deal with such choices has been the subject of my research, designed to clarify, through considering the ways in which women construct and resolve the abortion decision, the nature and development of women's moral judgment. Twenty-nine women, diverse in age, race, and social class, were referred by abortion and pregnancy counseling services and participated in the study for a variety of reasons. Some came to gain further clarification with respect to a decision about which they were in conflict, some in response to a counselor's concern about repeated abortions, and others out of an interest in and/or willingness to contribute to ongoing research. Although the pregnancies occurred under a variety of circumstances in the lives of these women, certain commonalities could be discerned. The adolescents often failed to use birth control because they denied or discredited their capacity to bear children. Some of the older women attributed the pregnancy to the omission of contraceptive measures in circumstances where intercourse had not been anticipated. Since the pregnancies often coincided with efforts on the part of the women to end a relationship, they may be seen as a manifestation of ambivalence or as a way of putting the relationship to the ultimate test of commitment. For these women, the pregnancy appeared to be a way of testing truth, making the baby an ally in the search for male support and protection or, that failing, a companion victim of his rejection. There were, finally, some women who became pregnant either as a result of a failure of birth control or intentionally as part of a joint decision that later was reconsidered. Of the twenty-nine women, four decided to have the baby, one miscarried, twenty-one chose abortion, and three remained in doubt about the decision.

In the initial part of the interview, the women were asked to discuss the decision that confronted them, how they were dealing with it, the alternatives they were considering, their reasons for and against each option, the people involved, the conflicts entailed, and the ways in which making this decision affected their self-concepts and their relationships with others. Then, in the second part of the interview, moral judgment was assessed in the hypothetical mode by presenting for resolution three of Kohlberg's standard research dilemmas.

While the structural progression from a preconventional through a conventional to a postconventional moral perspective can readily be discerned in the women's responses to both actual and hypothetical dilemmas, the conventions that shape women's moral judgments differ from those that apply to men. The construction of the abortion dilemma, in particular, reveals the existence of a distinct moral language whose evolution informs the sequence of women's development. This is the language of selfishness and responsibility, which defines the moral problem as one of obligation to exercise care and avoid hurt. The infliction of hurt is considered selfish and immoral in its reflection of unconcern, while the expression of care is seen as the fulfillment of moral responsibility. The reiterative use of the language of selfishness and responsibility and the underlying moral orientation it reflects sets the women apart from the men whom Kohlberg studied and may be seen as the critical reason for their failure to develop within the constraints of his system.

In the developmental sequence that follows, women's moral judgments proceed from an initial focus on the self at the *first level* to the discovery, in the transition to the *second level,* of the concept of responsibility as the basis for a new equilibrium between self and others. The elaboration of this concept of responsibility and its fusion with a maternal concept of morality, which seeks to ensure protection for the dependent and unequal, characterizes the *second level* of judgment. At this level the good is equated with caring for others. However, when the conventions of feminine goodness legitimize only others as the recipients of moral care, the logical inequality between self and other and the psychological violence that it engenders create the disequilibrium that initiates the *second* transition. The relationship between self and others is then reconsidered in an effort to sort out the confusion between conformity and care inherent in the conventional definition of feminine goodness and to establish a new equilibrium, which dissipates the tension between selfishness and responsibility. At the *third level,* the self becomes the arbiter of an independent judgment that now subsumes both conventions and individual needs under the moral principle of nonviolence. Judgment remains psychological in its concern with the intention and consequences of action, but it now becomes universal in its condemnation of exploitation and hurt.

*Level I: Orientation to Individual Survival*

In its initial and simplest construction, the abortion decision centers on the self. The concern is pragmatic, and the issue is individual survival. At this level, "should" is undifferentiated from "would," and others influence the decision only through their power to affect its consequences. An eighteen-year-old, asked what she thought when she found herself pregnant, replies: "I really didn't think anything except that I didn't want it. [Why was that?] I didn't want it, I wasn't ready for it, and next year will be my last year and I want to go to school."

Asked if there was a right decision, she says, "There is no right decision. [Why?]

*In a Different Voice*
CAROL GILLIGAN

I didn't want it." For her the question of right decision would emerge only if her own needs were in conflict; then she would have to decide which needs should take precedence. This was the dilemma of another eighteen-year-old, who saw having a baby as a way of increasing her freedom by providing "the perfect chance to get married and move away from home," but also as restricting her freedom "to do a lot of things."

At this first level, the self, which is the sole object of concern, is constrained by lack of power; the wish "to do a lot of things" is constantly belied by the limitations of what, in fact, is being done. Relationships are, for the most part, disappointing: "The only thing you are ever going to get out of going with a guy is to get hurt." As a result, women may in some instances deliberately choose isolation to protect themselves against hurt. When asked how she would describe herself to herself, a nineteen-year-old, who held herself responsible for the accidental death of a younger brother, answers as follows:

> I really don't know. I never thought about it. I don't know. I know basically the outline of a character. I am very independent. I don't really want to have to ask anybody for anything and I am a loner in life. I prefer to be by myself than around anybody else. I manage to keep my friends at a limited number with the point that I have very few friends. I don't know what else there is. I am a loner and I enjoy it. Here today and gone tomorrow.

The primacy of the concern with survival is explicitly acknowledged by a sixteen-year-old delinquent in response to Kohlberg's Heinz dilemma, which asks if it is right for a desperate husband to steal an outrageously overpriced drug to save the life of his dying wife:

> I think survival is one of the first things in life and that people fight for. I think it is the most important thing, more important than stealing. Stealing might be wrong, but if you have to steal to survive yourself or even kill, that is what you should do. . . . Preservation of oneself, I think, is the most important thing; it comes before anything in life.

### *The First Transition: From Selfishness to Responsibility*

In the transition which follows and criticizes this level of judgment, the words selfishness and responsibility first appear. Their reference initially is to the self in a redefinition of the self-interest which has thus far served as the basis for judgment. The transitional issue is one of attachment or connection to others. The pregnancy catches up the issue not only by representing an immediate, literal connection, but also by affirming, in the most concrete and physical way, the capacity to assume adult feminine roles. However, while having a baby seems at first to offer respite from the loneliness of adolescence and to solve conflicts over dependence and independence, in reality the continuation of an adolescent pregnancy generally compounds these problems, increasing social isolation and precluding further steps toward independence.

To be a mother in the societal as well as the physical sense requires the assumption of parental responsibility for the care and protection of a child. However, in order to be able to care for another, one must first be able to care responsibly for oneself. The growth from childhood to adulthood, conceived as a move from selfishness to responsibility, is articulated explicitly in these terms by a seventeen-year-old who describes her response to her pregnancy as follows:

> I started feeling really good about being pregnant instead of feeling really bad, because I wasn't looking at the situation realistically. I was looking at it from my own sort of selfish needs because I was lonely and felt lonely and stuff. . . . Things weren't really going good for me, so I was looking at it that I could have a baby that I could take care of or something that was part of me, and that made me feel good . . . but I wasn't looking at the realistic side . . . about the responsibility I would have to take on . . . I came to this decision that I was going to have an abortion [because] I realized how much responsibility goes with having a child. Like you have to be there, you can't be out of the house all the time which is one thing I like to do . . . and I decided that I have to take on responsibility for myself and I have to work out a lot of things.

Stating her former mode of judgment, the wish to have a baby as a way of combating loneliness and feeling connected, she now criticizes that judgment as both "selfish" and "unrealistic." The contradiction between wishes for a baby and for the freedom to be "out of the house all the time"—that is, for connection and also for independence—is resolved in terms of a new priority, as the criterion for judgment changes. The dilemma now assumes moral definition as the emergent conflict between wish and necessity is seen as a disparity between "would" and "should." In this construction the "selfishness" of willful decision is counterposed to the "responsibility" of moral choice:

> What I want to do is to have the baby, but what I feel I should do which is what I need to do, is have an abortion right now, because sometimes what you want isn't right. Sometimes what is necessary comes before what you want, because it might not always lead to the right thing.

While the pregnancy itself confirms femininity—"I started feeling really good; it sort of made me feel, like being pregnant, I started feeling like a woman"—the abortion decision becomes an opportunity for the adult exercise of responsible choice.

> [How would you describe yourself to yourself?] I am looking at myself differently in the way that I have had a really heavy decision put upon me, and I have never really had too many hard decisions in my life, and I have made it. It has taken some responsibility to do this. I have changed in that way, that I have made a hard decision. And that has been good. Because before, I would not have looked at it realistically, in my opinion. I would have gone by what I wanted to do, and I wanted it, and even if it wasn't right. So I see myself as I'm becoming more mature in ways of making decisions and taking care of myself, doing something for myself. I think it is going to help me in other ways, if I have other decisions to make put upon me, which would take some responsibility. And I would know that I could make them.

In the epiphany of this cognitive reconstruction, the old becomes transformed in

*In a Different Voice*
**CAROL GILLIGAN**

terms of the new. The wish to "do something for myself" remains, but the terms of its fulfillment change as the decision affirms both femininity and adulthood in its integration of responsibility and care. Morality, says another adolescent, "is the way you think about yourself . . . sooner or later you have to make up your mind to start taking care of yourself. Abortion, if you do it for the right reasons, is helping yourself to start over and do different things."

Since this transition signals an enhancement in self-worth, it requires a conception of self which includes the possibility for doing "the right thing," the ability to see in oneself the potential for social acceptance. When such confidence is seriously in doubt, the transitional questions may be raised but development is impeded. The failure to make this first transition, despite an understanding of the issues involved, is illustrated by a woman in her late twenties Her struggle with the conflict between selfishness and responsibility pervades but fails to resolve her dilemma of whether or not to have a third abortion.

> I think you have to think about the people who are involved, including yourself. You have responsibilities to yourself . . . and to make a right, whatever that is, decision in this depends on your knowledge and awareness of the responsibilities that you have and whether you can survive with a child and what it will do to your relationship with the father or how it will affect him emotionally.

Rejecting the idea of selling the baby and making "a lot of money in a black market kind of thing . . . because mostly I operate on principles and it would just rub me the wrong way to think I would be selling my own child," she struggles with a concept of responsibility which repeatedly turns back on the question of her own survival. Transition seems blocked by a self-image which is insistently contradictory:

> [How would you describe yourself to yourself?] I see myself as impulsive, practical—that is a contradiction—and moral and amoral, a contradiction. Actually the only thing that is consistent and not contradictory is the fact that I am very lazy which everyone has always told me is really a symptom of something else which I have never been able to put my finger on exactly. It has taken me a long time to like myself. In fact there are times when I don't, which I think is healthy to a point and sometimes I think I like myself too much and I probably evade myself too much, which avoids responsibility to myself and to other people who like me. I am pretty unfaithful to myself. . . I have a hard time even thinking that I am a human being, simply because so much rotten stuff goes on and people are so crummy and insensitive.

Seeing herself as avoiding responsibility, she can find no basis upon which to resolve the pregnancy dilemma. Instead, her inability to arrive at any clear sense of decision only contributes further to her overall sense of failure. Criticizing her parents for having betrayed her during adolescence by coercing her to have an abortion she did not want, she now betrays herself and criticizes that as well. In this light, it is less surprising that she considered selling her child, since she felt herself to have, in effect, been sold by her parents for the sake of maintaining their social status.

*The Second Level: Goodness as Self-Sacrifice*

The transition from selfishness to responsibility is a move toward social participation. Whereas at the first level, morality is seen as a matter of sanctions imposed by a society of which one is more subject than citizen, at the second level, moral judgment comes to rely on shared norms and expectations. The woman at this level validates her claim to social membership through the adoption of societal values. Consensual judgment becomes paramount and goodness the overriding concern as survival is now seen to depend on acceptance by others.

Here the conventional feminine voice emerges with great clarity, defining the self and proclaiming its worth on the basis of the ability to care for and protect others. The woman now constructs the world perfused with the assumptions about feminine goodness reflected in the stereotypes of the Broverman et al. (1972) studies. There the attributes considered desirable for women all presume an other, a recipient of the "tact, gentleness and easy expression of feeling" which allow the woman to respond sensitively while evoking in return the care which meets her own "very strong need for security" (p. 63). The strength of this position lies in its capacity for caring; its limitation is the restriction it imposes on direct expression. Both qualities are elucidated by a nineteen-year-old who contrasts her reluctance to criticize with her boyfriend's straightforwardness:

> I never want to hurt anyone, and I tell them in a very nice way, and I have respect for their own opinions, and they can do the things the way that they want, and he usually tells people right off the bat. . . . He does a lot of things out in public which I do in private. . . . it is better, the other [his way], but I just could never do it.

While her judgment clearly exists, it is not expressed, at least not in public. Concern for the feelings of others imposes a deference which she nevertheless criticizes in an awareness that, under the name of consideration, a vulnerability and a duplicity are concealed.

At the second level of judgment, it is specifically over the issue of hurting that conflict arises with respect to the abortion decision. When no option exists that can be construed as being in the best interest of everyone, when responsibilities conflict and decision entails the sacrifice of somebody's needs, then the woman confronts the seemingly impossible task of choosing the victim. A nineteen-year-old, fearing the consequences for herself of a second abortion but facing the opposition of both her family and her lover to the continuation of the pregnancy, describes the dilemma as follows:

> I don't know what choices are open to me; it is either to have it or the abortion; these are the choices open to me. It is just that either way I don't . . . I think what confuses me is it is a choice of either hurting myself or hurting other people around me. What is more important? If there could be a happy medium, it would be fine, but there isn't. It is either hurting someone on this side or hurting myself.

While the feminine identification of goodness with self-sacrifice seems clearly to dictate the "right" resolution of this dilemma, the stakes may be high for the woman herself, and the sacrifice of the fetus, in any event, compromises the altruism of an abortion motivated by a concern for others. Since femininity itself is in conflict in an abortion intended as an expression of love and care, this is a resolution which readily explodes in its own contradiction.

"I don't think anyone should have to choose between two things that they love," says a twenty-five-year-old woman who assumed responsibility not only for her lover but also for his wife and children in having an abortion she did not want:

> I just wanted the child and I really don't believe in abortions. Who can say when life begins. I think that life begins at conception and . . . I felt like there were changes happening in my body and I felt very protective . . . [but] I felt a responsibility, my responsibility if anything ever happened to her [his wife]. He made me feel that I had to make a choice and there was only one choice to make and that was to have an abortion and I could always have children another time and he made me feel if I didn't have it that it would drive us apart.

The abortion decision was, in her mind, a choice not to choose with respect to the pregnancy—"That was my choice, I had to do it." Instead, it was a decision to subordinate the pregnancy to the continuation of a relationship that she saw as encompassing her life—"Since I met him, he has been my life. I do everything for him; my life sort of revolves around him." Since she wanted to have the baby and also to continue the relationship, either choice could be construed as selfish. Furthermore, since both alternatives entailed hurting someone, neither could be considered moral. Faced with a decision which, in her own terms, was untenable, she sought to avoid responsibility for the choice she made, construing the decision as a sacrifice of her own needs to those of her lover. However, this public sacrifice in the name of responsibility engendered a private resentment that erupted in anger, compromising the very relationship that it had been intended to sustain.

> Afterwards we went through a bad time because I hate to say it and I was wrong, but I blamed him. I gave in to him. But when it came down to it, I made the decision. I could have said, 'I am going to have this child whether you want me to or not,' and I just didn't do it.

Pregnant again by the same man, she recognizes in retrospect that the choice in fact had been hers, as she returns once again to what now appears to have been missed opportunity for growth. Seeking, this time, to make rather than abdicate the decision, she sees the issue as one of "strength" as she struggles to free herself from the powerlessness of her own dependence:

> I think that right now I think of myself as someone who can become a lot stronger. Because of the circumstances, I just go along like with the tide. I never really had anything of my own before . . . [this time] I hope to come on strong and make a big decision, whether it is right or wrong.

Because the morality of self-sacrifice had justified the previous abortion, she now must suspend that judgment if she is to claim her own voice and accept responsibility for choice.

She thereby calls into question the underlying assumption of Level Two, which leads the woman to consider herself responsible for the actions of others, while holding others responsible for the choices she makes. This notion of reciprocity, backwards in its assumptions about control, disguises assertion as response. By reversing responsibility, it generates a series of indirect actions, which leave everyone feeling manipulated and betrayed. The logic of this position is confused in that the morality of mutual care is embedded in the psychology of dependence. Assertion becomes personally dangerous in its risk of criticism and abandonment, as well as potentially immoral in its power to hurt. This confusion is captured by Kohlberg's (1969) definition of Stage Three moral judgment, which joins the need for approval with the wish to care for and help others.

When thus caught between the passivity of dependence and the activity of care, the woman becomes suspended in an immobility of both judgment and action. "If I were drowning, I couldn't reach out a hand to save myself, so unwilling am I to set myself up against fate" (p. 7), begins the central character of Margaret Drabble's novel, *The Waterfall* (1971), in an effort to absolve herself of responsibility as she at the same time relinquishes control. Facing the same moral conflict which George Eliot depicted in *The Mill on the Floss,* Drabble's heroine proceeds to relive Maggie Tulliver's dilemma but turns inward in her search for the way in which to retell that story. What is initially suspended and then called into question is the judgment which "had in the past made it seem better to renounce myself than them" (Drabble, p. 50).

*The Second Transition: From Goodness to Truth*

The second transition begins with the reconsideration of the relationship between self and other, as the woman starts to scrutinize the logic of self-sacrifice in the service of a morality of care. In the interview data, this transition is announced by the reappearance of the word selfish. Retrieving the judgmental initiative, the woman begins to ask whether it is selfish or responsible, moral or immoral, to include her own needs within the compass of her care and concern. This question leads her to reexamine the concept of responsibility, juxtaposing the outward concern with what other people think with a new inner judgment.

In separating the voice of the self from those of others, the woman asks if it is possible to be responsible to herself as well as to others and thus to reconcile the disparity between hurt and care. The exercise of such responsibility, however, requires a new kind of judgment whose first demand is for honesty. To be responsible, it is necessary first to acknowledge what it is that one is doing. The criterion for judgment thus shifts from "goodness" to "truth" as the morality of action comes to be assessed not on the basis of its appearance in the eyes of others, but in terms of the realities of its intention and consequence.

A twenty-four-year-old married Catholic woman, pregnant again two months following the birth of her first child, identifies her dilemma as one of choice: "You have to now decide; because it is now available, you have to make a decision. And if it wasn't available, there was no choice open; you just do what you have to do." In the absence of legal abortion, a morality of self-sacrifice was necessary in order to insure protection and care for the dependent child. However, when such sacrifice becomes optional, the entire problem is recast.

The abortion decision is framed by this woman first in terms of her responsibilities to others: having a second child at this time would be contrary to medical advice and would strain both the emotional and financial resources of the family. However, there is, she says, a third reason for having an abortion, "sort of an emotional reason. I don't know if it is selfish or not, but it would really be tying myself down and right now I am not ready to be tied down with two."

Against this combination of selfish and responsible reasons for abortion is her Catholic belief that

> . . . it is taking a life, and it is. Even though it is not formed, it is the potential, and to me it is still taking a life. But I have to think of mine, my son's and my husband's, to think about, and at first I think that I thought it was for selfish reasons, but it is not. I believe that too, some of it is selfish. I don't want another one right now; I am not ready for it.

The dilemma arises over the issue of justification for taking a life: "I can't cover it over, because I believe this and if I do try to cover it over, I know that I am going to be in a mess. It will be denying what I am really doing." Asking "Am I doing the right thing; is it moral?," she counterposes to her belief against abortion her concern with the consequences of continuing the pregnancy. While concluding that "I can't be so morally strict as to hurt three other people with a decision just because of my moral beliefs," the issue of goodness still remains critical to her resolution of the dilemma:

> The moral factor is there. To me it is taking a life, and I am going to take that upon myself, that decision upon myself and I have feelings about it, and talked to a priest . . . but he said it is there and it will be from now on, and it is up to the person if they can live with the idea and still believe they are good.

The criteria for goodness, however, move inward as the ability to have an abortion and still consider herself good comes to hinge on the issue of selfishness with which she struggles to come to terms. Asked if acting morally is acting according to what is best for the self or whether it is a matter of self-sacrifice, she replies:

> I don't know if I really understand the question. . . . Like in my situation where I want to have the abortion and if I didn't it would be self-sacrificing, I am really in the middle of both those ways . . . but I think that my morality is strong and if these reasons—financial, physical reality and also for the whole family involved—were not here, that I wouldn't have to do it, and then it would be a self-sacrifice.

The importance of clarifying her own participation in the decision is evident in her attempt to ascertain her feelings in order to determine whether or not she was "putting them under" in deciding to end the pregnancy. Whereas in the first transition, from selfishness to responsibility, women made lists in order to bring to their consideration needs other than their own, now, in the second transition, it is the needs of the self which have to be deliberately uncovered. Confronting the reality of her own wish for an abortion, she now must deal with the problem of selfishness and the qualification that she feels it imposes on the "goodness" of her decision. The primacy of this concern is apparent in her description of herself:

> I think in a way I am selfish for one thing, and very emotional, very . . . and I think that I am a very real person and an understanding person and I can handle life situations fairly well, so I am basing a lot of it on my ability to do the things that I feel are right and best for me and whoever I am involved with. I think I was very fair to myself about the decision, and I really think that I have been truthful, not hiding anything, bringing out all the feelings involved. I feel it is a good decision and an honest one, a real decision.

Thus she strives to encompass the needs of both self and others, to be responsible to others and thus to be "good" but also to be responsible to herself and thus to be "honest" and "real."

While from one point of view, attention to one's own needs is considered selfish, when looked at from a different perspective, it is a matter of honesty and fairness. This is the essence of the transitional shift toward a new conception of goodness which turns inward in an acknowledgement of the self and an acceptance of responsibility for decision. While outward justification, the concern with "good reasons," remains critical for this particular woman: "I still think abortion is wrong, and it will be unless the situation can justify what you are doing." But the search for justification has produced a change in her thinking, "not drastically, but a little bit." She realizes that in continuing the pregnancy she would punish not only herself but also her husband, toward whom she had begun to feel "turned off and irritated." This leads her to consider the consequences self-sacrifice can have both for the self and for others. "God," she says, "can punish, but He can also forgive." What remains in question is whether her claim to forgiveness is compromised by a decision that not only meets the needs of others but that also is "right and best for me."

The concern with selfishness and its equation with immorality recur in an interview with another Catholic woman whose arrival for an abortion was punctuated by the statement, "I have always thought abortion was a fancy word for murder." Initially explaining this murder as one of lesser degree—"I am doing it because I have to do it. I am not doing it the least bit because I want to," she judges it "not quite as bad. You can rationalize that it is not quite the same." Since "keeping the child for lots and lots of reasons was just sort of impractical and out," she considers her options to be either abortion or adoption. However, having previously given up one child for adoption, she says: "I knew that psychologically there was no way that I could hack another adoption. It took me about four-and-a-half years to get my head on straight; there was just no way I was going to go through it again." The decision thus reduces in her eyes to a choice between murdering the fetus or damaging herself. The choice is further complicated by the fact that by continuing the pregnancy she would hurt not only herself but also her parents, with whom she lived. In the face of these manifold moral contradictions, the psychological demand for honesty that arises in counseling finally allows decision:

*In a Different Voice*
CAROL GILLIGAN

> On my own, I was doing it not so much for myself; I was doing it for my parents. I was doing it because the doctor told me to do it, but I had never resolved in my mind that I was doing it for me. Because it goes right back to the fact that I never believed in abortions. . . . Actually, I had to sit down and admit, no, I really don't want to go the mother route now. I honestly don't feel that I want to be a mother, and that is not really such a bad thing to say after all. But that is not how I felt up until talking to Maureen [her counselor]. It was just a horrible way to feel, so I just wasn't going to feel it, and I just blocked it right out.

As long as her consideration remains "moral," abortion can be justified only as an act of sacrifice, a submission to necessity where the absence of choice precludes responsibility. In this way, she can avoid self-condemnation, since, "When you get into moral stuff then you are getting into self-respect and that stuff, and at least if I do something that I feel is morally wrong, then I tend to lose some of my self-respect as a person." Her evasion of responsibility, critical to maintaining the innocence necessary for self-respect, contradicts the reality of her own participation in the abortion decision. The dishonesty in her plea of victimization creates the conflict that generates the need for a more inclusive understanding. She must now resolve the emerging contradiction in her thinking between two uses of the term right: "I am saying that abortion is morally wrong, but the situation is right, and I am going to do it. But the thing is that eventually they are going to have to go together, and I am going to have to put them together somehow." Asked how this could be done, she replies:

> I would have to change morally wrong to morally right. [How?] I have no idea. I don't think you can take something that you feel is morally wrong because the situation makes it right and put the two together. They are not together, they are opposite. They don't go together. Something is wrong, but all of a sudden because you are doing it, it is right.

This discrepancy recalls a similar conflict she faced over the question of euthanasia, also considered by her to be morally wrong until she "took care of a couple of patients who had flat EEGs and saw the job that it was doing on their families." Recalling that experience, she says:

> You really don't know your black and whites until you really get into them and are being confronted with it. If you stop and think about my feelings on euthanasia until I got into it, and then my feelings about abortion until I got into it, I thought both of them were murder. Right and wrong and no middle but there is a gray.

In discovering the gray and questioning the moral judgments which formerly she considered to be absolute, she confronts the moral crisis of the second transition. Now the conventions which in the past had guided her moral judgment become subject to a new criticism, as she questions not only the justification for hurting others in the name of morality but also the "rightness" of hurting herself. However, to sustain such criticism in the face of conventions that equate goodness with self-sacrifice, the woman must verify her capacity for independent judgment and the legitimacy of her own point of view.

Once again transition hinges on self-concept. When uncertainty about her own worth prevents a woman from claiming equality, self-assertion falls prey to the old criticism of selfishness. Then the morality that condones self-destruction in the name of responsible care is not repudiated as inadequate but rather is abandoned in the face of its threat to survival. Moral obligation, rather than expanding to include the self, is rejected completely as the failure of conventional reciprocity leaves the woman unwilling any longer to protect others at what is now seen to be her own expense. In the absence of morality, survival, however "selfish" or "immoral," returns as the paramount concern.

A musician in her late twenties illustrates this transitional impasse. Having led an independent life which centered on her work, she considered herself "fairly strong-willed, fairly in control, fairly rational and objective" until she became involved in an intense love affair and discovered in her capacity to love "an entirely new dimension" in herself. Admitting in retrospect to "tremendous naiveté and idealism," she had entertained "some vague ideas that some day I would like a child to concretize our relationship . . . having always associated having a child with all the creative aspects of my life." Abjuring, with her lover, the use of contraceptives because, "as the relationship was sort of an ideal relationship in our minds, we liked the idea of not using foreign objects or anything artificial," she saw herself as having relinquished control, becoming instead "just simply vague and allowing events to just carry me along." Just as she began in her own thinking to confront "the realities of that situation"—the possibility of pregnancy and the fact that her lover was married—she found herself pregnant. "Caught" between her wish to end a relationship that "seemed more and more defeating" and her wish for a baby, which "would be a connection that would last a long time," she is paralyzed by her inability to resolve the dilemma which her ambivalence creates.

The pregnancy poses a conflict between her "moral" belief that "once a certain life has begun, it shouldn't be stopped artificially" and her "amazing" discovery that to have the baby she would "need much more [support] than I thought." Despite her moral conviction that she "should" have the child, she doubts that she could psychologically deal with "having the child alone and taking the responsibility for it." Thus a conflict erupts between what she considers to be her moral obligation to protect life and her inability to do so under the circumstances of this pregnancy. Seeing it as "my decision and my responsibility for making the decision whether to have or have not the child," she struggles to find a viable basis on which to resolve the dilemma.

Capable of arguing either for or against abortion "with a philosophical logic," she says, on the one hand, that in an overpopulated world one should have children only under ideal conditions for care but, on the other, that one should end a life only when it is impossible to sustain it. She describes her impasse in response to the question of whether there is a difference between what she wants to do and what she thinks she should do:

*In a Different Voice*
CAROL GILLIGAN

> Yes, and there always has. I have always been confronted with that precise situation in a lot of my choices, and I have been trying to figure out what are the things that make me believe that these are things I should do as opposed to what I feel I want to do. [In this situation?] It is not that clear cut. I both want the child and feel I should have it, and I also think I should have the abortion and want it, but I would say it is my stronger feeling, and that I don't have enough confidence in my work yet and that is really where it is all hinged, I think . . . [the abortion] would solve the problem and I know I can't handle the pregnancy.

Characterizing this solution as "emotional and pragmatic" and attributing it to her lack of confidence in her work, she contrasts it with the "better thought out and more logical and more correct" resolution of her lover who thinks that she should have the child and raise it without either his presence or financial support. Confronted with this reflected image of herself as ultimately giving and good, as self-sustaining in her own creativity and thus able to meet the needs of others while imposing no demands of her own in return, she questions not the image itself but her own adequacy in filling it. Concluding that she is not yet capable of doing so, she is reduced in her own eyes to what she sees as a selfish and highly compromised fight

> for my survival. But in one way or another, I am going to suffer. Maybe I am going to suffer mentally and emotionally having the abortion, or I would suffer what I think is possibly something worse. So I suppose it is the lesser of two evils. I think it is a matter of choosing which one I know that I can survive through. It is really. I think it is selfish, I suppose, because it does have to do with that. I just realized that. I guess it does have to do with whether I would survive or not. [Why is this selfish?] Well, you know, it is. Because I am concerned with my survival first, as opposed to the survival of the relationship or the survival of the child, another human being . . . I guess I am setting priorities, and I guess I am setting my needs to survive first. . . . I guess I see it in negative terms a lot . . . but I do think of other positive things; that I am still going to have some life left, maybe. I don't know.

In the face of this failure of reciprocity of care, in the disappointment of abandonment where connection was sought, survival is seen to hinge on her work which is "where I derive the meaning of what I am. That's the known factor." While uncertainty about her work makes this survival precarious, the choice for abortion is also distressing in that she considers it to be "highly introverted—that in this one respect, having an abortion would be going a step backward; going outside to love someone else and having a child would be a step forward." The sense of retrenchment that the severing of connection signifies is apparent in her anticipation of the cost which abortion would entail:

> Probably what I will do is I will cut off my feelings, and when they will return or what would happen to them after that, I don't know. So that I don't feel anything at all, and I would probably just be very cold and go through it very coldly. . . . The more you do that to yourself, the more difficult it becomes to love again or to trust again or to feel again. . . . Each time I move away from that, it

> becomes easier, not more difficult, but easier to avoid committing myself to a relationship. And I am really concerned about cutting off that whole feeling aspect.

Caught between selfishness and responsibility, unable to find in the circumstances of this choice a way of caring which does not at the same time destroy, she confronts a dilemma which reduces to a conflict between morality and survival. Adulthood and femininity fly apart in the failure of this attempt at integration as the choice to work becomes a decision not only to renounce this particular relationship and child but also to obliterate the vulnerability that love and care engender.

*The Third Level: The Morality of Nonviolence*

In contrast, a twenty-five-year-old woman, facing a similar disappointment, finds a way to reconcile the initially disparate concepts of selfishness and responsibility through a transformed understanding of self and a corresponding redefinition of morality. Examining the assumptions underlying the conventions of feminine self-abnegation and moral self-sacrifice, she comes to reject these conventions as immoral in their power to hurt. By elevating nonviolence—the injunction against hurting—to a principle governing all moral judgment and action, she is able to assert a moral equality between self and other. Care then becomes a universal obligation, the self-chosen ethic of a postconventional judgment that reconstructs the dilemma in a way that allows the assumption of responsibility for choice.

In this woman's life, the current pregnancy brings to the surface the unfinished business of an earlier pregnancy and of the relationship in which both pregnancies occurred. The first pregnancy was discovered after her lover had left and was terminated by an abortion experienced as a purging expression of her anger at having been rejected. Remembering the abortion only as a relief, she nevertheless describes that time in her life as one in which she "hit rock bottom." Having hoped then to "take control of my life," she instead resumed the relationship when the man reappeared. Now, two years later, having once again "left my diaphragm in the drawer," she again becomes pregnant. Although initially "ecstatic" at the news, her elation dissipates when her lover tells her that he will leave if she chooses to have the child. Under these circumstances, she considers a second abortion but is unable to keep the repeated appointments she makes because of her reluctance to accept the responsibility for that choice. While the first abortion seemed an "honest mistake," she says that a second would make her feel "like a walking slaughter-house." Since she would need financial support to raise the child, her initial strategy was to take the matter to "the welfare people" in the hope that they would refuse to provide the necessary funds and thus resolve her dilemma:

> In that way, you know, the responsibility would be off my shoulders, and I could say, it's not my fault, you know, the state denied me the money that I would need to do it. But it turned out that it was possible to do it, and so I was, you know, right back where I started. And I had an appointment for an abortion, and I kept calling and cancelling it and then remaking the appointment and cancelling it, and I just couldn't make up my mind.

*In a Different Voice*
CAROL GILLIGAN

Confronting the need to choose between the two evils of hurting herself or ending the incipient life of the child, she finds, in a reconstruction of the dilemma itself, a basis for a new priority that allows decision. In doing so, she comes to see the conflict as arising from a faulty construction of reality. Her thinking recapitulates the developmental sequence, as she considers but rejects as inadequate the components of earlier-stage resolutions. An expanded conception of responsibility now reshapes moral judgment and guides resolution of the dilemma, whose pros and cons she considers as follows:

> Well, the pros for having the baby are all the admiration that you would get from, you know, being a single woman, alone, martyr, struggling having the adoring love of this beautiful Gerber baby . . . just more of a home life than I have had in a long time, and that basically was it, which is pretty fantasyland; it is not very realistic. . . . Cons against having the baby: it was going to hasten what is looking to be the inevitable end of the relationship with the man I am presently with. . . . I was going to have to go on welfare, my parents were going to hate me for the rest of my life, I was going to lose a really good job that I have, I would lose a lot of independence . . . solitude . . . and I would have to be put in a position of asking help from a lot of people a lot of the time. Cons against having the abortion is having to face up to the guilt . . . and pros for having the abortion are I would be able to handle my deteriorating relation with S. with a lot more capability and a lot more responsibility for him and for myself . . . and I would not have to go through the realization that for the next twenty-five years of my life I would be punishing myself for being foolish enough to get pregnant again and forcing myself to bring up a kid just because I did this. Having to face the guilt of a second abortion seemed like, not exactly, well, exactly the lesser of the two evils but also the one that would pay off for me personally in the long run because by looking at why I am pregnant again and subsequently have decided to have a second abortion, I have to face up to some things about myself.

Although she doesn't "feel good about having a second abortion," she nevertheless concludes,

> I would not be doing myself or the child or the world any kind of favor having this child. . . . I don't need to pay off my imaginary debts to the world through this child, and I don't think that it is right to bring a child into the world and use it for that purpose.

Asked to describe herself, she indicates how closely her transformed moral understanding is tied to a changing self-concept:

> I have been thinking about that a lot lately, and it comes up different than what my usual subconscious perception of myself is. Usually paying off some sort of debt, going around serving people who are not really worthy of my attentions because somewhere in my life I think I got the impression that my needs are really secondary to other people's, and that if I feel, if I make any demands on other people to fulfill my needs, I'd feel guilty for it and submerge my own in favor of other people's, which later backfires on me, and I feel a great deal of resentment for other people that I am doing things for, which causes friction and the eventual

> deterioration of the relationship. And then I start all over again. How would I describe myself to myself? Pretty frustrated and a lot angrier than I admit, a lot more aggressive than I admit.

Reflecting on the virtues which comprise the conventional definition of the feminine self, a definition which she hears articulated in her mother's voice, she says, "I am beginning to think that all these virtues are really not getting me anywhere. I have begun to notice." Tied to this recognition is an acknowledgement of her power and worth, both previously excluded from the image she projected:

> I am suddenly beginning to realize that the things that I like to do, the things I am interested in, and the things that I believe and the kind of person I am is not so bad that I have to constantly be sitting on the shelf and letting it gather dust. I am a lot more worthwhile than what my past actions have led other people to believe.

Her notion of a "good person," which previously was limited to her mother's example of hard work, patience and self-sacrifice, now changes to include the value that she herself places on directness and honesty. Although she believes that this new self-assertion will lead her "to feel a lot better about myself" she recognizes that it will also expose her to criticism:

> Other people may say, 'Boy, she's aggressive, and I don't like that,' but at least, you know, they will know that they don't like that. They are not going to say, 'I like the way she manipulates herself to fit right around me.' . . . What I want to do is just be a more self-determined person and a more singular person.

While within her old framework abortion had seemed a way of "copping out" instead of being a "responsible person [who] pays for his mistakes and pays and pays and is always there when she says she will be there and even when she doesn't say she will be there is there," now, her "conception of what I think is right for myself and my conception of self-worth is changing." She can consider this emergent self "also a good person," as her concept of goodness expands to encompass "the feeling of self-worth; you are not going to sell yourself short and you are not going to make yourself do things that, you know, are really stupid and that you don't want to do." This reorientation centers on the awareness that:

> I have a responsibility to myself, and you know, for once I am beginning to realize that that really matters to me . . . instead of doing what I want for myself and feeling guilty over how selfish I am, you realize that that is a very usual way for people to live . . . doing what you want to do because you feel that your wants and your needs are important, if to no one else, then to you, and that's reason enough to do something that you want to do.

Once obligation extends to include the self as well as others, the disparity between selfishness and responsibility is reconciled. Although the conflict between self and other remains, the moral problem is restructured in an awareness that the occurrence of the dilemma itself precludes non-violent resolution. The abortion decision is now seen to be a "serious" choice affecting both self and others: "This is a life that I have taken, a conscious decision to terminate, and that is just very heavy, a very heavy thing." While accepting the necessity of abortion as a highly compromised resolution, she turns her attention to the pregnancy itself, which she now considers to denote a failure of responsibility, a failure to care for and protect both self and other.

As in the first transition, although now in different terms, the conflict precipitated by the pregnancy catches up the issues critical to development. These issues now concern the worth of the self in relation to others, the claiming of the power to choose, and the acceptance of responsibility for choice. By provoking a confrontation with these issues, the crisis can become "a very auspicious time; you can use the pregnancy as sort of a learning, teeing-off point, which makes it useful in a way." This possibility for growth inherent in a crisis which allows confrontation with a construction of reality whose acceptance previously had impeded development was first identified by Coles (1964) in his study of the children of Little Rock. This same sense of possibility is expressed by the women who see, in their resolution of the abortion dilemma, a reconstructed understanding which creates the opportunity for "a new beginning," a chance "to take control of my life."

For this woman, the first step in taking control was to end the relationship in which she had considered herself "reduced to a nonentity," but to do so in a responsible way. Recognizing hurt as the inevitable concomitant of rejection, she strives to minimize that hurt "by dealing with [his] needs as best I can without compromising my own . . . that's a big point for me, because the thing in my life to this point has been always compromising, and I am not willing to do that any more." Instead, she seeks to act in a "decent, human kind of way . . . one that leaves maybe a slightly shook but not totally destroyed person." Thus the "nonentity" confronts her power to destroy which formerly had impeded any assertion, as she consider the possibility for a new kind of action that leaves both self and other intact.

The moral concern remains a concern with hurting as she considers Kohlberg's Heinz dilemma in terms of the question, "who is going to be hurt more, the druggist who loses some money or the person who loses their life?" The right to property and right to life are weighed not in the abstract, in terms of their logical priority, but rather in the particular, in terms of the actual consequences that the violation of these rights would have in the lives of the people involved. Thinking remains contextual and admixed with feelings of care, as the moral imperative to avoid hurt begins to be informed by a psychological understanding of the meaning of nonviolence.

Thus, release from the intimidation of inequality finally allows the expression of a judgment that previously had been withheld. What women then enunciate is not a new morality, but a moral conception disentangled from the constraints that formerly had confused its perception and impeded its articulation. The willingness to express and take responsibility for judgment stems from the recognition of the psychological and moral necessity for an equation of worth between self and other. Responsibility for care then includes both self and other, and the obligation not to hurt, freed from conventional constraints, is reconstructed as a universal guide to moral choice.

The reality of hurt centers the judgment of a twenty-nine-year-old woman, married and the mother of a preschool child, as she struggles with the dilemma posed by a second pregnancy whose timing conflicts with her completion of an advanced degree. Saying that "I cannot deliberately do something that is bad or would hurt another person because I can't live with having done that," she nevertheless confronts a situation in which hurt has become inevitable. Seeking that solution which would best protect both herself and others, she indicates, in her definition of morality, the ineluctable sense of connection which infuses and colors all of her thinking:

> [Morality is] doing what is appropriate and what is just within your circumstances, but ideally it is not going to affect—I was going to say, ideally it wouldn't negatively affect another person, but that is ridiculous, because decisions are always going to affect another person. But you see, what I am trying to say is that it is the person that is the center of the decision making, of that decision making about what's right and what's wrong.

The person who is the center of this decision making begins by denying, but then goes on to acknowledge, the conflicting nature both of her own needs and of her various responsibilities. Seeing the pregnancy as a manifestation of the inner conflict between her wish, on the one hand, "to be a college president" and, on the other, "to be making pottery and flowers and having kids and staying at home," she struggles with contradiction between femininity and adulthood. Considering abortion as the "better" choice—because "in the end, meaning this time next year or this time two weeks from now, it will be less of a personal strain on us individually and on us as a family for me not to be pregnant at this time," she concludes that the decision has

> got to be, first of all, something that the woman can live with—a decision that the woman can live with, one way or another, or at least try to live with, and that it be based on where she is at and other people, significant people in her life, are at.

At the beginning of the interview she had presented the dilemma in its conventional feminine construction, as a conflict between her own wish to have a baby and the wish of others for her to complete her education. On the basis of this construction she deemed it "selfish" to continue the pregnancy because it was something "I want to do." However, as she begins to examine her thinking, she comes to abandon as false this conceptualization of the problem, acknowledging the truth of her own internal conflict and elaborating the tension which she feels between her femininity and the adulthood of her work life. She describes herself as "going in two directions" and values that part of herself which is "incredibly passionate and sensitive"—her capacity to recognize and meet, often with anticipation, the needs of others. Seeing her "compassion" as "something I don't want to lose" she regards it as endangered by her pursuit of professional advancement. Thus the self-deception of her initial presentation, its attempt to sustain the fiction of her own innocence, stems from her fear that to say that *she* does not want to have another baby at this time would be

> an acknowledgement to me that I am an ambitious person and that I want to

*In a Different Voice*
CAROL GILLIGAN

> have power and responsibility for others and that I want to live a life that extends from 9 to 5 every day and into the evenings and on weekends, because that is what the power and responsibility means. It means that my family would necessarily come second . . . there would be such an incredible conflict about which is tops, and I don't want that for myself.

Asked about her concept of "an ambitious person" she says that to be ambitious means to be

> power hungry [and] insensitive. [Why insensitive?] Because people are stomped on in the process. A person on the way up stomps on people, whether it is family or other colleagues or clientele, on the way up. [Inevitably?] Not always, but I have seen it so often in my limited years of working that it is scary to me. It is scary because I don't want to change like that.

Because the acquisition of adult power is seen to entail the loss of feminine sensitivity and compassion, the conflict between femininity and adulthood becomes construed as a moral problem. The discovery of the principle of nonviolence begins to direct attention to the moral dilemma itself and initiates the search for a resolution that can encompass both femininity and adulthood.

## Developmental Theory Reconsidered

The developmental conception delineated at the outset, which has so consistently found the development of women to be either aberrant or incomplete, has been limited insofar as it has been predominantly a male conception, giving lip-service, a place on the chart, to the interdependence of intimacy and care but constantly stressing, at their expense, the importance and value of autonomous judgment and action. To admit to this conception the truth of the feminine perspective is to recognize for both sexes the central importance in adult life of the connection between self and other, the universality of the need for compassion and care. The concept of the separate self and of the moral principle uncompromised by the constraints of reality is an adolescent ideal, the elaborately wrought philosophy of a Stephen Daedalus, whose flight we know to be in jeopardy. Erikson (1964), in contrasting the ideological morality of the adolescent with the ethics of adult care, attempts to grapple with this problem of integration, but is impeded by the limitations of his own previous developmental conception. When his developmental stages chart a path where the sole precursor to the intimacy of adult relationships is the trust established in infancy and all intervening experience is marked only as steps toward greater independence, then separation itself becomes the model and the measure of growth. The observation that for women, identity has as much to do with connection as with separation led Erikson into trouble largely because of his failure to integrate this insight into the mainstream of his developmental theory (Erikson, 1968).

The morality of responsibility which women describe stands apart from the morality of rights which underlies Kohlberg's conception of the highest stages of moral judgment. Kohlberg (Note 3) sees the progression toward these stages as resulting from the generalization of the self-centered adolescent rejection of societal morality into a principled conception of individual natural rights. To illustrate this progression, he cites as an example of integrated Stage Five judgment, "possibly moving to Stage Six," the following response of a twenty-five-year-old subject from his male longitudinal sample:

> [What does the word morality mean to you?] Nobody in the world knows the answer. I think it is recognizing the right of the individual, the rights of other individuals, not interfering with those rights. Act as fairly as you would have them treat you. I think it is basically to preserve the human being's right to existence. I think that is the most important. Secondly, the human being's right to do as he pleases, again without interfering with somebody else's rights. (p. 29)

Another version of the same conception is evident in the following interview response of a male college senior whose moral judgment also was scored by Kohlberg (Note 4) as at Stage Five or Six:

> [Morality] is a prescription, it is a thing to follow, and the idea of having a concept of morality is to try to figure out what it is that people can do in order to make life with each other livable, make for a kind of balance, a kind of equilibrium, a harmony in which everybody feels he has a place and an equal share in things, and it's doing that—doing that is kind of contributing to a state of affairs that go beyond the individual in the absence of which, the individual has no chance for self-fulfillment of any kind. Fairness; morality is kind of essential, it seems to me, for creating the kind of environment, interaction between people, that is prerequisite to this fulfillment of most individual goals and so on. If you want other people to not interfere with your pursuit of whatever you are into, you have to play the game.

In contrast, a woman in her late twenties responds to a similar question by defining a morality not of rights but of responsibility:

> [What makes something a moral issue?] Some sense of trying to uncover a right path in which to live, and always in my mind is that the world is full of real and recognizable trouble, and is it heading for some sort of doom and is it right to bring children into this world when we currently have an overpopulation problem, and is it right to spend money on a pair of shoes when I have a pair of shoes and other people are shoeless. . . . It is part of a self-critical view, part of saying, how am I spending my time and in what sense am I working? I think I have a real drive to, I have a real maternal drive to take care of someone. To take care of my mother, to take care of children, to take care of other people's children, to take care of my own children, to take care of the world. I think that goes back to your other question, and when I am dealing with moral issues, I am sort of saying to myself constantly, are you taking care of all the things that you think are important and in what ways are you wasting yourself and wasting those issues?

While the postconventional nature of this woman's perspective seems clear, her judgments of Kohlberg's hypothetical moral dilemmas do not meet his criteria for scoring at the principled level. Kohlberg regards this as a disparity between normative and metaethical judgments which he sees as indicative of the transition

*In a Different Voice*
CAROL GILLIGAN

between conventional and principled thinking. From another perspective, however, this judgment represents a different moral conception, disentangled from societal conventions and raised to the principled level. In this conception, moral judgment is oriented toward issues of responsibility. The way in which the responsibility orientation guides moral decision at the postconventional level is described by the following woman in her thirties:

> [Is there a right way to make moral decisions?] The only way I know is to try to be as awake as possible, to try to know the range of what you feel, to try to consider all that's involved, to be as aware as you can be to what's going on, as conscious as you can of where you're walking. [Are there principles that guide you?] The principle would have something to do with responsibility, responsibility and caring about yourself and others. . . . But it's not that on the one hand you choose to be responsible and on the other hand you choose to be irresponsible—both ways you can be responsible. That's why there's not just a principle that once you take hold of you settle—the principle put into practice here is still going to leave you with conflict.

The moral imperative that emerges repeatedly in the women's interviews is an injunction to care, a responsibility to discern and alleviate the "real and recognizable trouble" of this world. For the men Kohlberg studied, the moral imperative appeared rather as an injunction to respect the rights of others and thus to protect from interference the right to life and self-fulfillment. Women's insistence on care is at first self-critical rather than self-protective, while men initially conceive obligation to others negatively in terms of noninterference. Development for both sexes then would seem to entail an integration of rights and responsibilities through the discovery of the complementarity of these disparate views. For the women I have studied, this integration between rights and responsibilities appears to take place through a principled understanding of equity and reciprocity. This understanding tempers the self-destructive potential of a self-critical morality by asserting the equal right of all persons to care. For the men in Kohlberg's sample as well as for those in a longitudinal study of Harvard undergraduates (Gilligan & Murphy, Note 5) it appears to be the recognition through experience of the need for a more active responsibility in taking care that corrects the potential indifference of a morality of noninterference and turns attention from the logic to the consequences of choice. In the development of a postconventional ethic understanding, women come to see the violence generated by inequitable relationships, while men come to realize the limitations of a conception of justice blinded to the real inequities of human life.

Kohlberg's dilemmas, in the hypothetical abstraction of their presentation, divest the moral actors from the history and psychology of their individual lives and separate the moral problem from the social contingencies of its possible occurrence. In doing so, the dilemmas are useful for the distillation and refinement of the "objective principles of justice" toward which Kohlberg's stages strive. However, the reconstruction of the dilemma in its contextual particularity allows the understanding of cause and consequence which engages the compassion and tolerance considered by previous theorists to qualify the feminine sense of justice. Only when substance is given to the skeletal lives of hypothetical people is it possible to consider the social injustices which their moral problems may reflect and to imagine the individual suffering their occurrence may signify or their resolution engender.

The proclivity of women to reconstruct hypothetical dilemmas in terms of the real, to request or supply the information missing about the nature of the people and the places where they live, shifts their judgment away from the hierarchical ordering of principles and the formal procedures of decision making that are critical for scoring at Kohlberg's highest stages. This insistence on the particular signifies an orientation to the dilemma and to moral problems in general that differs from any of Kohlberg's stage descriptions. Given the constraints of Kohlberg's system and the biases in his research sample, this different orientation can only be construed as a failure in development. While several of the women in the research sample clearly articulated what Kohlberg regarded as a postconventional metaethical position, none of them were considered by Kohlberg to be principled in their normative moral judgments of his hypothetical moral dilemmas (Note 4). Instead, the women's judgments pointed toward an identification of the violence inherent in the dilemma itself which was seen to compromise the justice of any of its possible resolutions. This construction of the dilemma led the women to recast the moral judgment from a consideration of the good to a choice between evils.

The woman whose judgment of the abortion dilemma concluded the developmental sequence presented in the preceding section saw Kohlberg's Heinz dilemma in these terms and judged Heinz's action in terms of a choice between selfishness and sacrifice. For Heinz to steal the drug, given the circumstances of his life (which she inferred from his inability to pay two thousand dollars), he would have "to do something which is not in his best interest, in that he is going to get sent away, and that is a supreme sacrifice, a sacrifice which I would say a person truly in love might be willing to make." However, not to steal the drug "would be selfish on his part . . . he would just have to feel guilty about not allowing her a chance to live longer." Heinz's decision to steal is considered not in terms of the logical priority of life over property which justifies its rightness, but rather in terms of the actual consequences that stealing would have for a man of limited means and little social power.

Considered in the light of its probable outcomes—his wife dead, or Heinz in jail, brutalized by the violence of that experience and his life compromised by a record of felony—the dilemma itself changes. Its resolution has less to do with the relative weights of life and property in an abstract moral conception than with the collision it has produced between two lives, formerly conjoined but now in opposition, where the continuation of one life can now occur only at the expense of the other. Given this construction, it becomes clear why consideration revolves around the issue of sacrifice and why guilt becomes the inevitable concomitant of either resolution.

Demonstrating the reticence noted in the first section about making moral judgments, this woman explains her reluctance to judge in terms of her belief

> that everybody's existence is so different that I kind of say to myself, that might be something that I wouldn't do, but I can't say that it is right or wrong for that person. I can only deal with what is appropriate for me to do when I am faced with specific problems.

Asked if she would apply to others her own injunction against hurting, she says:

> See, I can't say that it is wrong. I can't say that it is right or that it's wrong because I don't know what the person did that the other person did something to hurt him . . . so it is not right that the person got hurt but it is right that the person who just lost the job has got to get that anger up and out. It doesn't put any bread on his table, but it is released. I don't mean to be copping out. I really am trying to see how to answer these questions for you.

Her difficulty in answering Kohlberg's questions, her sense of strain with the construction which they impose on the dilemma, stems from their divergence from her own frame of reference:

> I don't even think I use the words right and wrong anymore, and I know I don't use the word moral, because I am not sure I know what it means. . . . We are talking about an unjust society, we are talking about a whole lot of things that are not right, that are truly wrong, to use the word that I don't use very often, and I have no control to change that. If I could change it, I certainly would, but I can only make my small contribution from day to day, and if I don't intentionally hurt somebody, that is my contribution to a better society. And so a chunk of that contribution is also not to pass judgment on other people, particularly when I don't know the circumstances of why they are doing certain things.

The reluctance to judge remains a reluctance to hurt, but one that stems now not from a sense of personal vulnerability but rather from a recognition of the limitations of judgment itself. The deference of the conventional feminine perspective can thus be seen to continue at the postconventional level, not as moral relativism but rather as part of a reconstructed moral understanding. Moral judgment is renounced in an awareness of the psychological and social determinism of all human behavior at the same time as moral concern is reaffirmed in recognition of the reality of human pain and suffering.

> I have a real thing about hurting people and always have, and that gets a little complicated at times, because, for example, you don't want to hurt your child. I don't want to hurt my child but if I don't hurt her sometimes, then that's hurting her more, you see, and so that was a terrible dilemma for me.

Moral dilemmas are terrible in that they entail hurt; she sees Heinz's decision as "the result of anguish, who am I hurting, why do I have to hurt them." While the morality of Heinz's theft is not in question, given the circumstances which necessitated it, what is at issue is his willingness to substitute himself for his wife and become, in her stead, the victim of exploitation by a society which breeds and legitimizes the druggist's irresponsibility and whose injustice is thus manifest in the very occurrence of the dilemma.

The same sense that the wrong questions are being asked is evident in the response of another woman who justified Heinz's action on a similar basis, saying "I don't think that exploitation should really be a right." When women begin to make direct moral statements, the issues they repeatedly address are those of exploitation and hurt. In doing so, they raise the issue of nonviolence in precisely the same psychological context that brought Erikson (1969) to pause in his consideration of the truth of Gandhi's life.

In the pivotal letter, around which the judgment of his book turns, Erikson confronts the contradiction between the philosophy of nonviolence that informed Gandhi's dealing with the British and the psychology of violence that marred his relationships with his family and with the children of the ashram. It was this contradiction, Erikson confesses,

> which almost brought *me* to the point where I felt unable to continue writing *this* book because I seemed to sense the presence of a kind of untruth in the very protestation of truth; of something unclean when all the words spelled out an unreal purity; and, above all, of displaced violence where nonviolence was the professed issue. (p. 231)

In an effort to untangle the relationship between the spiritual truth of Satyagraha and the truth of his own psychoanalytic understanding, Erikson reminds Gandhi that "Truth, you once said, 'excludes the use of violence because man is not capable of knowing the absolute truth and therefore is not competent to punish' " (p. 241). The affinity between Satyagraha and psychoanalysis lies in their shared commitment to seeing life as an "experiment in truth," in their being

> somehow joined in a universal "therapeutics," committed to the Hippocratic principle that one can test truth (or the healing power inherent in a sick situation) only by action which avoids harm—or better, by action which maximizes mutuality and minimizes the violence caused by unilateral coercion or threat. (p. 247)

Erikson takes Gandhi to task for his failure to acknowledge the relativity of truth. This failure is manifest in the coercion of Gandhi's claim to exclusive possession of the truth, his "unwillingness to learn from *anybody anything* except what was approved by the 'inner voice' " (p. 236). This claim led Gandhi, in the guise of love, to impose his truth on others without awareness or regard for the extent to which he thereby did violence to their integrity.

The moral dilemma, arising inevitably out of a conflict of truths, is by definition a "sick situation" in that its either/or formulation leaves no room for an outcome that does not do violence. The resolution of such dilemmas, however, lies not in the self-deception of rationalized violence—"I was" said Gandhi, "a cruelly kind husband. I regarded myself as her teacher and so harassed her out of my blind love for her" (p. 233)—but rather in the replacement of the underlying antagonism with a mutuality of respect and care.

Gandhi, whom Kohlberg has mentioned as exemplifying Stage Six moral judgment and whom Erikson sought as a model of an adult ethical sensibility, instead is criticized by a judgment that refuses to look away from or condone the infliction of harm. In denying the validity of his wife's reluctance to open her home to strangers and in his blindness to the different reality of adolescent sexuality and temptation, Gandhi compromised in his everyday life the ethic of nonviolence to which in principle and in public he was so steadfastly committed.

The blind willingness to sacrifice people to truth, however, has always been the danger of an ethics abstracted from life. This willingness links Gandhi to the biblical Abraham, who prepared to sacrifice the life of his son in order to demonstrate the integrity and supremacy of his faith. Both men, in the limitations of their fatherhood, stand in implicit contrast to the woman who comes before Solomon and verifies her motherhood by relinquishing truth in order to save the life of her child. It is the ethics of an adulthood that has become principled at the expense of care that Erikson comes to criticize in his assessment of Gandhi's life.

This same criticism is dramatized explicitly as a contrast between the sexes in *The Merchant of Venice* (1598/1912), where Shakespeare goes through an extraordinary complication of sexual identity (dressing a male actor as a female character who in turn poses as a male judge) in order to bring into the masculine citadel of justice the feminine plea for mercy. The limitation of the contractual conception of justice is illustrated through the absurdity of its literal execution, while the "need to make exceptions all the time" is demonstrated contrapuntally in the matter of the rings. Portia, in calling for mercy, argues for that resolution in which no one is hurt, and as the men are forgiven for their failure to keep both their rings and their word, Antonio in turn foregoes his "right" to ruin Shylock.

The research findings that have been reported in this essay suggest that women impose a distinctive construction on moral problems, seeing moral dilemmas in terms of conflicting responsibilities. This construction was found to develop through a sequence of three levels and two transitions, each level representing a more complex understanding of the relationship between self and other and each transition involving a critical reinterpretation of the moral conflict between selfishness and responsibility. The development of women's moral judgment appears to proceed from an initial concern with survival, to a focus on goodness, and finally to a principled understanding of nonviolence as the most adequate guide to the just resolution of moral conflicts.

In counterposing to Kohlberg's longitudinal research on the development of hypothetical moral judgment in men a cross-sectional study of women's responses to actual dilemmas of moral conflict and choice, this essay precludes the possibility of generalization in either direction and leaves to further research the task of sorting out the different variables of occasion and sex. Longitudinal studies of women's moral judgments are necessary in order to validate the claims of stage and sequence presented here. Similarly, the contrast drawn between the moral judgments of men and women awaits for its confirmation a more systematic comparison of the responses of both sexes. Kohlberg's research on moral development has confounded the variables of age, sex, type of decision, and type of dilemma by presenting a single configuration (the responses of adolescent males to hypothetical dilemmas of conflicting rights) as the basis for a universal stage sequence. This paper underscores the need for systematic treatment of these variables and points toward their study as a critical task for future moral development research.

For the present, my aim has been to demonstrate the centrality of the concepts of responsibility and care in women's constructions of the moral domain, to indicate the close tie in women's thinking between conceptions of the self and conceptions of morality, and, finally, to argue the need for an expanded developmental theory that would include, rather than rule out from developmental consideration, the difference in the feminine voice. Such an inclusion seems essential, not only for explaining the development of women but also for understanding in both sexes the characteristics and precursors of an adult moral conception.

## Reference Notes


1. Haan, N. *Activism as moral protest: Moral judgments of hypothetical dilemmas and an actual situation of civil disobedience.* Unpublished manuscript, University of California at Berkeley, 1971.
2. Turiel, E. *A comparative analysis of moral knowledge and moral judgment in males and females.* Unpublished manuscript, Harvard University, 1973.
3. Kohlberg, L. *Continuities and discontinuities in childhood and adult moral development revisited.* Unpublished paper, Harvard University, 1973.
4. Kohlberg, L. Personal communication, August, 1976.
5. Gilligan, C., & Murphy, M. *The philosopher and the "dilemma of the fact": Moral development in late adolescence and adulthood.* Unpublished manuscript, Harvard University, 1977.


## References


Broverman, I., Vogel, S., Broverman, D., Clarkson, F., & Rosenkrantz, P. Sex-role stereotypes: A current appraisal. *Journal of Social Issues,* 1972, **28,** 59–78.

Coles, R. *Children of crisis.* Boston: Little, Brown, 1964.

Didion, J. The women's movement. *New York Times Book Review,* July 30, 1972, pp. 1–2; 14.

Drabble, M. *The waterfall.* Hammondsworth, Eng.: Penguin Books, 1969.

Eliot, G. *The mill on the floss.* New York: New American Library, 1965. (Originally published, 1860.)

Erikson, E. H. *Insight and responsibility.* New York: W. W. Norton, 1964.

Erikson, E. H. *Identity: Youth and crisis.* New York: W. W. Norton, 1968.

Erikson, E. H. *Gandhi's truth.* New York: W. W. Norton, 1969.

Freud, S. "Civilized" sexual morality and modern nervous illness. In J. Strachey (Ed.), *The standard edition of the complete psychological works of Sigmund Freud* (Vol. 9). London: Hogarth Press, 1959. (Originally published, 1908.)

Freud, S. Some psychical consequences of the anatomical distinction between the sexes. In J. Strachey (Ed.), *The standard edition of the complete psychological works of Sigmund Freud* (Vol. 19). London: Hogarth Press, 1961. (Originally published, 1925.)

Gilligan, C., Kohlberg, L., Lerner, J., & Belenky, M. Moral reasoning about sexual dilemmas: The development of an interview and scoring system. *Technical Report of the President's Commission on Obscenity and Pornography* (Vol. 1) [415 060–137]. Washington, D.C.: U.S. Government Printing Office, 1971.

Haan, N. Hypothetical and actual moral reasoning in a situation of civil disobedience. *Journal of Personality and Social Psychology,* 1975, **32,** 255–270.

Holstein, C. Development of moral judgment: A longitudinal study of males and females. *Child Development,* 1976, **47,** 51–61.

In a Different Voice
CAROL GILLIGAN

Horner, M. Toward an understanding of achievement-related conflicts in women. *Journal of Social Issues,* 1972, **29,** 157–174.

Ibsen, H. *A doll's house.* In *Ibsen plays.* Hammondsworth, Eng.: Penguin Books, 1965. (Originally published, 1879.)

Kohlberg, L. From is to ought: How to commit the naturalistic fallacy and get away with it in the study of moral development. In T. Mischel (Ed.), *Cognitive development and epistemology.* New York: Academic Press, 1971.

Kohlberg, L., & Gilligan, C. The adolescent as a philosopher: The discovery of the self in a postconventional world. *Daedalus,* 1971, **100,** 1051–1056.

Kohlberg, L., & Kramer, R Continuities and discontinuities in childhood and adult moral development. *Human Development,* 1969, **12,** 93–120.

Piaget, J. *The moral judgment of the child.* New York: The Free Press, 1965. (Originally published, 1932.)

Shakespeare, W. *The merchant of Venice.* In *The comedies of Shakespeare.* London: Oxford University Press, 1912. (Originally published, 1598.)

[5]

THE JOURNAL OF PHILOSOPHY

VOLUME LXXXV, NO. 9, SEPTEMBER 1988

# JUSTICE, CARE, GENDER BIAS

CAROL GILLIGAN poses two separable, though in her work not separate, challenges to moral theory. The first is a challenge to the adequacy of current moral theory that is dominated by the ethics of justice.[1] The ethics of justice, on her view, excludes some dimensions of moral experience, such as contextual decision making, special obligations, the moral motives of compassion and sympathy, and the relevance of considering one's own integrity in making moral decisions. The second is a challenge to moral theory's presumed gender neutrality. The ethics of justice is not gender neutral, she argues, because it advocates ideals of agency, moral motivation, and correct moral reasoning which women are less likely than men to achieve; and because the moral dimensions excluded from the ethics of justice are just the ones figuring more prominently in women's than men's moral experience.

The adequacy and gender bias charges are, for Gilligan, linked. She claims that the ethics of justice and the ethics of care are two different moral orientations.[2] Whereas individuals may use both orientations, the shift from one to the other requires a Gestalt shift, since "the terms of one perspective do not contain the terms of the other" (*ibid.*, p. 30). The exclusion of the care perspective from the ethics of justice simultaneously undermines the adequacy of the

[1] In referring to the 'ethics of justice' and the 'ethics of care', I do not assume that either one is some monolithic, unified theory; rather, I use these terms, as Gilligan suggests, to designate different orientations—loosely defined sets of concepts, themes, and theoretical priorities—which we understand sufficiently well to pick out who is speaking from which orientation, but which are not so rigid as to preclude a great deal of disagreement within each orientation.

[2] Carol Gilligan, "Moral Orientation and Moral Development," in *Women and Moral Theory*, Eva Feder Kittay and Diana T. Meyers, eds. (Totowa, NJ: Rowman & Littlefield, 1987).

0022-362X/88/8509/0451$01.30 

ethics of justice (it cannot give a complete account of moral life) and renders it gender-biased.

Some critics have responded by arguing that there is no logical incompatibility between the two moral orientations.[3] Because the ethics of justice does not in principle exclude the ethics of care (even if theorists within the justice tradition have had little to say about care issues), it is neither inadequate nor gender-biased. Correctly applying moral rules and principles, for instance, requires, rather than excludes, knowledge of contextual details. Both orientations are crucial to correct moral reasoning and an adequate understanding of moral life. Thus, the ethics of justice and the ethics of care are not in fact rivaling, alternative moral theories. The so-called ethics of care merely makes focal issues that are already implicitly contained in the ethics of justice.

Suppose the two are logically compatible. Would the charge of gender bias evaporate? Yes, so long as gender neutrality only requires that the ethics of justice could, consistently, make room for the central moral concerns of the ethics of care. But perhaps gender neutrality requires more than this. Since the spectre of gender bias in theoretical knowledge is itself a moral issue, we would be well advised to consider the question of gender bias more carefully before concluding that our moral theory speaks in an androgynous voice. Although we can and should test the ethics of justice by asking whether it could consistently include the central moral issues in the ethics of care, we might also ask what ideologies of the moral life are likely to result from the repeated inclusion or exclusion of particular topics in moral theorizing.

Theorizing that crystallizes into a tradition has nonlogical as well as logical implications. In order to explain why a tradition has the contours it does, one may need to suppose general acceptance of particular beliefs that are not logically entailed by any particular theory and might be denied by individual theorists were those beliefs articulated. When behavioral researchers, for example, focus almost exclusively on aggression and its role in human life, neglecting other behavioral motives, their doing so has the nonlogical implication that aggression is, indeed, the most important behavioral motive. This is

[3] The logical compatibility thesis is, for example, advanced by Jean Grimshaw, *Philosophy and Feminist Thinking* (Minneapolis: Minnesota UP, 1986); Owen Flanagan and Kathryn Jackson, "Justice, Care, and Gender: The Kohlberg-Gilligan Debate Revisited," *Ethics*, XCVII (1987): 622–637; Thomas E. Hill, Jr., "The Importance of Autonomy," in *Women and Moral Theory;* George Sher, "Other Voice, Other Rooms? Women's Psychology and Moral Theory," in *Women and Moral Theory*.

because only a belief like this would explain the rationality of this pattern of research. Such nonlogical implications become ideologies when politically loaded (as the importance of aggression is when coupled with observations about women's lower level of aggression).

When understood as directed at moral theory's nonlogical implications, the gender-bias charge takes a different form. Even if the ethics of justice could consistently accommodate the ethics of care, the critical point is that theorists in the justice tradition have not said much, except in passing, about the ethics of care, and are unlikely to say much in the future without a radical shift in theoretical priorities; and concentrating almost exclusively on rights of noninterference, impartiality, rationality, autonomy, and principles creates an ideology of the moral domain which has undesirable political implications for women. This formulation shifts the justice-care debate from one about logical compatibility to a debate about which theoretical priorities would improve the lot of women.

I see no way around this politicization of philosophical critique. If we hope to shape culture, and not merely to add bricks to a philosophical tower, we will need to be mindful of the cultural/political use to which our thoughts may be put after leaving our wordprocessors. This mindfulness should include asking whether our theoretical work enacts or discredits a moral commitment to improving the lot of women.

Starting from the observation that the ethics of justice has had centuries of workout, I want to ask what ideological implications a concentration on only some moral issues might have and which shifts in priorities might safeguard against those ideologies. This particular tack in trying to bring the ethics of care to center stage has the double advantage of, first, avoiding the necessity of making charges of conceptual inadequacy stick, since it does not matter what the ethics of justice *could* consistently talk about, only what it *does* talk about; and, second, of avoiding the question of what, from an absolute, ahistorical point of view moral theory ought to be most preoccupied with.

The following reflections on moral theorizing about the self, knowledge, motivation, and obligations are not meant to be exhaustive but only to suggest some reasons for taking the charge of gender bias in ethics seriously. I shall sometimes stray rather far afield from the ethics of care, since my aim is not to defend the ethics of care but to advocate some shifts in theoretical priorities.

## I. THE MORAL SELF

One concern of moral theory has been with broadening our sensitivities about who has morally considerable rights and interests. The ordinary individual confronts at least two obstacles to taking others' rights and interests seriously. One is his own self-interest, which inclines him to weigh his own rights and interests more heavily; the other is his identification with particular social groups, which inclines him to weigh the rights and interests of co-members more heavily than those of outsiders. Immanuel Kant had a lot to say about the former obstacle, David Hume about the latter. Sensitivity to our failure to weigh the rights and interests of all members of the moral community equally led moral theorists to focus, in defining the moral self, on constructing various pictures of the moral self's similarity to other moral selves in an effort to underscore our common humanity and thus our entitlement to equal moral consideration. Kant's identification of the moral self with the noumenal self, thus minus all empirical individuating characteristics, is one such picture. Emphases on shared human interests in life, health, etc., serve a similar purpose. And so does John Rawls's invocation of a "veil of ignorance."

Providing us with some way of envisioning our shared humanity, and thus our equal membership in the moral community, is certainly an important thing for moral theory to do. But too much talk about our similarities as moral selves, and too little talk about our differences has its moral dangers. For one, unless we are also quite knowledgeable about the substantial differences between persons, particularly central differences due to gender, race, and class, we may be tempted to slide into supposing that our common humanity includes more substantive similarities than it does in fact. For instance, moral theorists have assumed that moral selves have a prominent interest in property and thus in property rights. But property rights may have loomed large on the moral horizons of past moral theorists partly, or largely, because they were themselves propertied and their activities took place primarily in the public, economic sphere. Historically, women could not share the same interest in property and concern about protecting it, since they were neither legally entitled to hold it nor primary participants in the public, economic world.[4] And arguably, women do not now place the same priority on property. (I have in mind the fact that equal opportunity has had surprisingly little impact on either sex segregation in the workforce or on women's, but not men's, accommodating their work and work schedules to

[4] Annette Baier makes a similar point in "Trust and Antitrust," *Ethics*, XCVI (1986): 231–260. There she argues that understanding moral relations in terms of contracts and voluntary promises reflects the social lives of male moral theorists: "Contract is a device for traders, entrepreneurs, and capitalists, not for children, servants, indentured wives, and slaves" (p. 247).

childrearing needs. One explanation is that income matters less to women than other sorts of considerations. The measure of a woman, unlike the measure of a man, is not the size of her paycheck.) Seyla Benhabib[5] summarizes this point by suggesting that a singleminded emphasis on common humanity encourages a "substitutionalist universalism" where universal humanity "is defined surreptitiously by identifying the experiences of a specific group of subjects as the paradigmatic case of all humans" (*ibid.*, p. 158).

In addition to encouraging us to overlook how our basic interests may differ depending on our social location, the emphasis on common humanity, because it is insensitive to connections between interests, social location, and power, deters questions about the possible malformation of our interests as a result of their development within an inegalitarian social structure. Both dangers plague the role-reversal test, some version of which has been a staple of moral theorizing. Although the point of that test is to eliminate egoistic bias in moral judgments, without a sensitivity to how our (uncommon) humanity is shaped by our social structure, role-reversal tests may simply preserve, rather than eliminate, inequities. This is because role-reversal tests either take individuals' desires as givens, thus ignoring the possibility that socially subordinate individuals have been socialized to want the very things that keep them socially subordinate (e.g., Susan Brownmiller[6] argues that women have been socialized to want masochistic sexual relations); or, if they take into account what individuals ought to want, role-reversal tests typically ignore the way that social power structures may have produced an alignment between the concept of a normal, reasonable desire and the desires of the dominant group (so, for example, much of the affirmative action literature takes it for granted that women ought to want traditionally defined male jobs with no consideration of the possibility that women might prefer retailoring those jobs so that they are less competitive, less hierarchical, and more compatible with family responsibilities).

In short, without adequate knowledge of how very different human interests, temperaments, lifestyles, and commitments may be, as well as a knowledge of how those interests may be malformed as a result of power inequities, the very egoism and group bias that the focus on common humanity was designed to eliminate may slip in as a result of that focus.

[5] "The Generalized and Concrete Other: The Kohlberg-Gilligan Controversy and Moral Theory," in *Women and Moral Theory*, p. 158.

[6] *Against Our Will: Men, Women, and Rape* (New York: Simon & Schuster, 1975).

The objection here is not that a formal, abstract notion of the moral self's common humanity is wrong and ought to be jettisoned. Nor is the objection that a formal notion of the moral self logically entails a substitutionalist universalism. The objection is that repetitive stress on shared humanity creates an ideology of the moral self: the belief that our basic moral interests are not significantly, dissimilarly, and sometimes detrimentally shaped by our social location. Unless moral theory shifts its priority to knowledgeable discussions of human differences—particularly differences tied to gender, race, class, and power—lists and rank orderings of basic human interests and rights as well as the political deployment of those lists are likely to be sexist, racist, and classist.

## II. MORAL KNOWLEDGE

Central to moral theory has been the issue of how moral principles, and hence moral decisions in particular cases, are to be justified. We owe that interest in justification in large measure to the modern period's concern to find foundations for knowledge that are, in principle, accessible to any rational individual. The concern with justifying moral knowledge meant that some questions, but not others, were particularly important for moral theory to address. First, how should an adult who has acquired a wide variety of moral views as a result of his socialization into a particular cultural tradition go about evaluating those views? That is, how do we distinguish mere inherited prejudices from legitimate moral beliefs? Second, given that the correctness of particular moral judgments depends, in part, on the correctness of the general moral principles that we bring to bear on particular cases, how do we justify those general moral principles? In either case, the answer involves showing that our moral views and principles can survive various tests of rationality, e.g., that they are consistent and universalizable.

The danger of asking these questions lies not in their being the wrong questions, but in their being only some of the right questions for a moral epistemology. As adults, moral theorists may naturally find questions about distinguishing learned prejudices from justified moral beliefs more pertinent to their own lives. And certainly one of the capacities that we hope moral agents will acquire is the capacity to draw just those kinds of distinctions. But we may pay a price by too strongly emphasizing the acquisition of moral knowledge through individual, adult reflection. For one, this emphasis contributes to the idea that the self who is capable of moral knowledge is, in Benhabib's caustic words, "a mushroom behind a veil of ignorance"; that is, that the moral knower, like a mushroom, has neither mother nor father, nor childhood education (*op. cit,* p. 166). Thus, we may lose sight of the fact that our adult capacity for rational reflection, the size of our adult reflective task, and quite possibly our motivation to act on reflective judgments depend heavily on our earlier moral education. Whereas moral theory has not been altogether blind to the importance of moral education, few have given moral education a role comparable to that of adult reflection in the acquisition of moral knowledge. (Francis Hutcheson comes to mind as a notable exception.) The result is an ideology of moral knowledge: the belief that moral knowledge is not only justified but also acquired exclusively or most importantly through rational reflection. Women have special reason to be concerned about this ideology. Women's traditional role has included the moral education of children. The significance of women's work in transmitting moral knowledge and instilling a moral motivational structure (either well or poorly) is likely to remain invisible so long as the theoretical focus remains on adult acquisition of moral knowledge.

More importantly, stressing the corrective efficacy of individual, rational reflection creates a second ideology of moral knowledge: the belief that individual reflection, if it conforms to cannons of rationality, guarantees the truth of one's moral judgments. It is untrue that any rational individual who applies sufficient reflective elbow grease can adequately assess the justifiability of his moral views or go behind a veil of ignorance and come out with the correct moral principles. Our being motivated to raise questions of justification in the first place and our ability to address those questions once raised depends at least partially on the social availability of moral criticisms and of morally relevant information. The nineteenth century's moral injunction against women's pursuing advanced education was not simply the product of failed rational reflection. It was tied, on the one hand, to a societal assumption that women's unequal status was morally unproblematic; and, on the other hand, to medical misinformation about the connection between women's intellectual activity and the healthy functioning of their reproductive organs. Thus, moral questions about the policy of barring women from higher education were unlikely to be raised, since rationality does not require indiscriminately questioning any and all policies but only those reasonably open to question. Even if raised, they were unlikely to be answered in women's favor, since, at the time, there appeared to be morally relevant differences between men and women. Only women could harm themselves and produce mentally and physically defective children as a result of education.

Without an equal theoretical stress on the social determinants of moral knowledge—particularly the potential alignment of moral and factual beliefs with social power structures—the very reflective processes that were designed to criticize cultural prejudices may simply repeat those prejudices. In emphasizing moral interdependency over moral autonomy, the ethics of care provides the kind of theoretical focus that could make moral education and the social determinants of moral knowledge salient.

### III. MORAL MOTIVATION

Moral theorizing, particularly though not exclusively in the Kantian tradition, has focused on the motivating role of thoughts of duty, of what is right or what contributes to general happiness. Moral action should stem from a regard for morality itself rather than from nonmoral thoughts, self-interest, or happily altruistic emotions, since only a regard for morality itself provides a reliable spur to moral action, and only a regard for morality focuses our attention on the kinds of considerations that ensure right action.

One bone of contention in the justice-care debate has been over whether the requirement to have duty as one's motive necessarily excludes being motivated by care, sympathy, compassion, or the personally involved motives of love, loyalty, and friendship. Marcia Baron[7] has argued forcefully for the compatibility of duty with more personally involved motives. Central to her argument is the distinction between primary and secondary motives.

> A primary motive supplies the agent with the motivation to do the act in question, whereas a secondary motive provides limiting conditions on what may be done from other motives. Although qua secondary motive it cannot by itself move one to act, a secondary motive is nonetheless a motive, for the agent would not proceed to perform the action without the "approval" of the secondary motive (*ibid.*, p. 207).

Being motivated by duty as a secondary motive amounts to no more than the realization that one would not act on one's love or one's compassion if doing so conflicted with what morally ought to be done. Thus, being morally motivated by duty does not require taking an emotionally uninvolved, alienated stance toward others. It merely requires cautious willingness to refrain from action that conflicts with what one ought to do. Moreover, Baron argues that doing what one ought to do may well include cultivating one's capacity for sympathy and compassion, since merely "going through the motions" is often less than what duty requires.

I find Baron's argument convincing, and truer to Kant. But, even if a duty-centered ethics can consistently accommodate caring atti-

[7] "The Alleged Moral Repugnance of Acting from Duty," this JOURNAL, LXXXI, 4 (April 1984): 197–220.

tudes, one can still object that the repeated opposition of duty to self-interest creates an ideology of moral motivation: the belief that we are psychologically so constructed that duty must usually supply a *primary* motive.

Almost invariably in moral theory, it is the lack of other-directed attitudes which is cited as the largest motivational obstacle to doing what morality requires. Agents find it difficult to behave morally because (1) they are egoistic and are inclined initially to be motivated by self-interest and to weigh their own interests more heavily than others'; and (2) even where they stand to gain nothing by acting immorally, they are initially indifferent to others' welfare. Moral thoughts, particularly the thought of duty, combat egoism and indifference by supplying a primary motive to do what morality requires which we otherwise would lack. Thus, moral theory constructs an image of the moral agent as psychologically so constituted as to require that duty be his primary motive. Conceding, in the way Baron does, that duty may operate as a secondary motive in some people or on some occasions does nothing to counter this image of the agent's psychology.

The narratives of the women in Gilligan's study, however, suggest a very different motivational picture for women.[8] At the earliest stage of moral development, women may share this egoistic psychology. But, at later stages, it is an unreflective and often self-excluding sympathy for others which poses the main motivational obstacle. Far from the lure of self-interest, the motivational problem for adult women is how to place proper limits on the inclination to respond to others' needs. The problem is not one of getting duty to operate as a primary motive, but of how to get it to function properly as a *secondary* motive. Moral theories that emphasize conquering self-interest by cultivating a sense of duty (or by cultivating sympathy) only reinforce women's inclination to act on caring attitudes unchecked by considerations of duties to self or overriding duties to others. If women's elective underparticipation in the workforce, overassumption of familial duties, and nonreportage of date rape and marital abuse concern us morally and politically, we might do well to shift theoretical priority from the conflict between duty and self-interest to that between duty and care.

## IV. MORAL OBLIGATIONS

The concern of traditional moral theory with impartiality emerges variously out of a concern with countering self-interest, enlarging our sentiments, and introducing greater consistency into moral

[8] *In a Different Voice* (Cambridge: Harvard, 1982).

judgments. This, too, has been a bone of contention in the justice-care debate: Does a fully impartial ethics necessarily exclude special moral obligations to friends and family and thus exclude considerations that are more likely to figure centrally in women's actual moral thinking given their traditional and ongoing familial role? In defending the adequacy of the ethics of justice, George Sher[9] argues from a Rawlsian contractarian point of view that the selection of impartial rules may well include selecting rules that dictate special obligations.

> The contractors' ignorance does rule out the choice of principles that name either specific agents who are allowed or required to be partial or the specific recipients of their partiality. However, this is irrelevant; for the question is not whether any *given* person may or should display partiality to any other, but rather whether *all* persons may or should be partial to their wives, husbands, or friends. The relevant principles, even if licensing or dictating partiality, must do so impartially. Hence, there is no obvious reason why such principles could not be chosen even by contractors ignorant of the particulars of their lives.

Similarly, Kantians might argue from the idea of implicit promises made to family or friends, and utilitarians might argue from considerations of maximizing welfare, that it is possible to give preference to friends and families without giving up the idea that no one counts for more than one. I want to concede this point that the ethics of justice leaves logical room for special obligations.

But, when moral theory is largely silent about special obligations or brings them in as addenda, two ideologies of moral life get created: the first is the belief that it is self-evident that general obligations are morally more important than special obligations. This ideology is troubling, because the division of the moral world into general obligations governing public relations with relative strangers and special obligations governing personal relations with family and friends so closely parallels the genderized division of spheres into public and private. The value of women's private domestic work has been too quickly dismissed in the past by those who assumed that public productive labor is self-evidently more important than private reproductive labor. One might, then, reasonably worry about the way moral theory, perhaps inadvertently, confirms this quick dismissal of the private realm as "of course" less important.

The second ideology created by the repeated focus on general obligations is the belief that general obligations are experientially more frequently encountered; they deserve more attention because

[9] "Other Voices, Other Rooms?" *op. cit.*, p. 186.

questions about them come up more often. Women, however, in addition to typically being more involved in familial caretaking, overwhelmingly dominate service and caring jobs; and the interpersonal relationships in those jobs bear many of the same characteristics as do private, familial relationships. They are often ongoing, dependency relations and/or involve heightened expectations that the worker will have a special concern for and advocacy relation to the client/employer (e.g., teaching, daycare, nursing, social work, secretarial work, and airline stewardessing). Even in traditionally male jobs, both employers and clients may expect, in virtue of women's caring social role, more from women workers (for example, to be warmer and more supportive) than general moral obligations require. Given these kinds of considerations, theoretical emphasis on general obligations (which would incline one to think that special obligations are experientially less frequently encountered) quite naturally evokes the question "Whose moral experience is being described?" Moreover, so long as moral theory continues to depict public moral relations as though they were governed almost exclusively by general obligations, which leave a good deal of latitude for the pursuit of self-interest, we are unlikely to see that women's public moral lives, not just their private ones, leave less scope for the pursuit of self-interest than men's.

## THE CHARGE OF GENDER BIAS

I have argued that repeated focusing in moral theorizing on a restricted range of moral problems or concepts produces ideologies of the moral life which may infect our philosophical as well as our popular, cultural beliefs. I want to emphasize that this results from the cumulative effect of moral theorizing rather than from errors or omissions in particular ethical works considered individually. I also want to re-emphasize that those ideologies need have been neither explicitly articulated nor believed by any serious moral philosopher (though some surely have). They are, rather, "explanatory beliefs" whose general acceptance would have to be supposed in order to explain the rationality of the particular patterns of philosophical conversation and silence which characterize moral theory. The charge of gender bias is thus not addressed to individual thinkers so much as to the community of moral theorists or, alternatively, to a tradition of moral theorizing.

The call for a shift in theoretical priorities is simultaneously a call for a shift in our methods of evaluating moral theories. Evaluation is not exhausted by carefully scrutinizing individual theories, since in the process of theorizing in a philosophical community we unavoidably contribute to the establishment of a tradition of moral thinking which may implicitly, in virtue of common patterns of talk and silence, endorse views of the moral life which go beyond those of individual contributors. The nonlogical implications of theorizing patterns require evaluation as well.

But, if moral theory suffers from a lopsidedness that produces ideologies of the moral life, why be particularly concerned with eliminating *gender* bias? Would not the more basic, and broader, philosophical task be to eliminate bias in general? Would not a bias sensitive (but gender insensitive) critique do all the work? There is indeed an interesting coincidence between the critiques stemming out of Gilligan's work with critiques having no clear connection to it or feminist theory.[10] The call, coming out of the ethics of care, for a de-emphasis on the role of reflective, principled reasoning curiously coincides with an independent resuscitation of virtue ethics. Similarly, Gilligan's attention to personal integrity coincides with comparable but independent worries about the threats posed by an overly demanding moral theory to personal integrity. The same is true of philosophical demands for moral attention to the good life, compassion, and special obligations. Thus, sensitivity to gender issues would seem unnecessary for philosophical critiques whose consequence, though not intent, would be a gender neutral moral theory.

Perhaps, but I suspect not. Some moral issues are arguably more critical for women, and thus achieving gender neutrality is partly a matter of prioritizing those issues. But eliminating gender bias cannot be equated (though possibly reducing gender bias can) with simply prioritizing those "women's issues" irrespective of the content of the analysis of those issues. These same issues also have a place in men's moral experience. For that reason, male moral philosophers too may have cause to regret moral theory's neglect of special relations, virtue ethics, compassion and the problem of limiting compassionate impulses; and it is thus no surprise that some of the same critiques of moral theories are coming from both feminist and nonfeminist quarters. But, given that our lives are thoroughly genderized, there is no reason to suppose that gender bias cannot recur in the discussion of these "women's moral issues." Which virtues, after all, will we make focal—intellectual virtues or inter-

[10] I have in mind Bernard Williams, "Persons, Character, and Morality" and "Moral Luck," in *Moral Luck* (New York: Cambridge, 1981); and "Integrity," in *Utilitarianism: For and Against*, J. J. C. Smart and Bernard Williams, eds. (New York: Cambridge, 1973); Susan Wolf, "Moral Saints," this JOURNAL, LXXIX, 8 (August 1982): 419–429; Andrew Oldenquist, "Loyalties," this JOURNAL, LXXIX, 4 (April 1982): 173–193; Lawrence Blum, *Friendship, Altruism, and Morality* (London: Routledge & Kegan Paul, 1980).

personal virtues? And what will we say about individual virtues? Will we, as Annette Baier does (*op. cit.*), examine how virtues may undergo deformation in different ways depending on our place in power structures? Which kind of compassion will become paradigmatic: the impersonal, public compassion for strangers and unfortunate populations, or the personal, private compassion felt for friends, children, and neighbors? Will we repeat the same militaristic metaphors of conquest and mastery in describing conflicts between compassion and duty which have dominated descriptions of the moral agent's relation to his self-interest? And, in weighing the value of personal integrity against the moral claims of others, will we take into account the way that gender roles may affect both the value we attach to personal integrity and the weight we attach to others' claims?

The possibility of gender bias recurring in the process of redressing bias in moral theory derives from the fact that philosophical reasoning is shaped by extra-philosophic factors, including the social location of the philosophic reasoner and his audience as well as the contours of the larger social world in which philosophic thought takes place. It is naive to suppose that a reflective, rational, but gender-insensitive critique of moral theory will have the happy outcome of eliminating gender bias. So long as we avoid incorporating gender categories among the tools for philosophical analysis, we will continue running the risks, whether we work within or counter to the tradition, of importing gender bias into our philosophical reflection and of creating an ideology of the moral life.

CHESHIRE CALHOUN

College of Charleston

# Part II
# The Terms of the Debate: Care, Justice and Rights

[6]

# Justice, Care, and Gender: The Kohlberg-Gilligan Debate Revisited

*Owen Flanagan and Kathryn Jackson*

## I

In 1958, G. E. M. Anscombe wrote, "It is not profitable for us at present to do moral philosophy; that should be laid aside at any rate until we have an adequate philosophy of psychology, in which we are conspicuously lacking" (p. 186). Anscombe hinted (and she and many others pursued the hint) that the Aristotelian tradition was the best place to look for a richer and less shadowy conception of moral agency than either utilitarianism or Kantianism had provided.

In the same year Anscombe published "Modern Moral Philosophy," Lawrence Kohlberg completed his dissertation at the University of Chicago, a dissertation that laid the foundations for what has been the dominant program in moral psychology for the last twenty-odd years. The contrast between the sort of Aristotelian philosophical psychology Anscombe envisaged and Kohlberg's program could not have been starker. Anscombe recommended that the concepts of "*moral* obligation and *moral* duty . . . and of what is *morally* right and wrong, and of the *moral* sense of 'ought,' ought to be jettisoned . . . because they are survivors . . . from an earlier conception of ethics which no longer survives, and are only harmful without it" (p. 186). Kohlberg meanwhile claimed that people at the highest stage of moral development "answer [moral dilemmas] in moral words such as *duty* or *morally right* and use them in a way implying universality, ideals and impersonality" (1981, p. 22). And while Anscombe pointed to Aristotle as the possibility proof that ethics could be done with a more robust and realistic conception of moral agency than the will-o'-the-wisp Enlightenment conception which Iris Murdoch describes as "thin as a needle" (1970, p. 53) and Alasdair MacIntyre depicts as "ghostlike" (1982), Kohlberg derided Aristotelianism, calling it the "bag of virtues" model; and he explicitly rejected the view that personality is divided up "into cognitive abilities, passions or motives, and traits of

*Ethics* 97 (April 1987): 622–637

character." Instead, he proposed that virtue is one and "the name of this ideal form is justice" (1981, pp. 30–31). For Kohlberg the morally good person is simply one who reasons with, and acts on the basis of, principles of justice as fairness.

Despite the fact that Kohlberg's theory has come to dominate the thinking of moral psychologists (but hardly the thinking of moral philosophers who think about moral psychology), critics abound. One of the more widely known challenges to Kohlberg's theory comes from his colleague and former collaborator, Carol Gilligan. Over the past fifteen years, Gilligan has been listening to women and men talk about morality. Her book, *In a Different Voice* (1982), is both a challenge to the comprehensiveness of Kohlberg's theory and a revealing look at the way liberal society distributes various psychological competencies between the sexes. Gilligan describes a moral universe in which men, more often than women, conceive of morality as substantively constituted by obligations and rights and as procedurally constituted by the demands of fairness and impartiality, while women, more often than men, see moral requirements as emerging from the particular needs of others in the context of particular relationships. Gilligan has dubbed this latter orientation the "ethic of care," and she insists that the exclusive focus on justice reasoning has obscured both its psychological reality and its normative significance.

Whereas justice as fairness involves seeing others thinly, as worthy of respect purely by virtue of common humanity, morally good caring requires seeing others thickly, as constituted by their particular human face, their particular psychological and social self. It also involves taking seriously, or at least being moved by, one's particular connection to the other (see Flanagan and Adler 1983). Gilligan's claim is that once the dispositions that underlie such caring are acknowledged, the dominant conception of moral maturity among moral psychologists and moral philosophers will need to be reconceived (Gilligan 1983; also see Blum 1980).

The purpose of this essay is to gain some perspective on the philosophical stakes in the moral psychology debate by surveying and critically evaluating Gilligan's writings subsequent to her book—writings in which she attempts to extend, clarify, and defend her views—as well as recent work of Kohlberg's in which he responds to Gilligan's challenge. Some recent philosophical literature is also discussed.

## II

One issue in need of clarification is the precise nature of the ethic of care and its relation within moral personality to the ethic of justice. In her most recent writings, Gilligan characterizes the two ethics as "different ways of viewing the world" that "organize both thinking and feeling" (1986, in press *a*, in press *c*), and she returns continually to the imagery of a gestalt shift (e.g., the vase-face illusion) to make it clear that she thinks that the two ethics involve seeing things in different and competing ways. The justice orientation organizes moral perception by highlighting issues of fairness, right, and obligation. Indeed, a person entirely in the grip of the justice orientation may be able to see a problem as a moral problem only if such issues can be construed in it. The care orientation meanwhile focuses on other saliencies: on the interconnections among the parties involved, on their particular personalities, and on their weal and woe.

The claim is that typically one orientation dominates moral thinking and that the direction of dominance is gender linked. Recent research shows that while most people introduce both care and justice considerations when discussing moral problems, over two-thirds present three-quarters or more considerations in one mode or the other. Furthermore, men and women distribute themselves bimodally on the justice and care ends of the scale (Lyons 1983; Gilligan and Wiggans 1986).

It is significant that there are such differences in the way men and women conceive of the moral domain and in the way they choose to talk about the moral issues they confront in real life. But two things must be kept in mind. First, although one way of conceiving of moral problems dominates, most individuals use both orientations some of the time. Therefore the differences between two individuals with contrasting dominant orientations will be more like the differences between two people—one of whom tends to see physical objects in functional terms and only secondarily in aesthetic terms, and another person with reversed dominance—than like the difference between occupants of totally alien universes. Second, the data on how people in fact conceive of morality have no simple and direct implications on the issues of how the domain of morality is best conceived, what virtues and reasoning skills are required by morality, and how best a particular moral issue is construed.

One need not be committed to any implausible version of moral realism to maintain that the most defensible specification of the moral domain will include issues of both right and good, that moral life requires a multiplicity of virtues, and that the description under which a particular problem is best understood is at least partly constrained by the kind of problem it is. The first two points seem fairly obvious, so let's focus on the third.

In several places, Gilligan suggests that every problem that can be construed morally can be construed from either the justice or care orientation (Gilligan 1986; Gilligan and Wiggans 1986). Suppose this is right. Imagine someone who sees the problem of repaying or forgiving foreign loans as an issue of *love* between nations; or a mother who construes all positive interactions with her children as something they are *owed.* There may still be good reasons for preferring one construal over another. Generally speaking, there are two sorts of grounds that might recommend one construal over another and thus that might recommend educating moral agents to be disposed to make one interpretation rather than another. First, there might be normative reasons. Although a particular type of issue, say, parent-child relations, can be construed theoretically from the perspective of either of Gilligan's two orientations, the different construals lead to different kinds of worlds, one of which is more desirable than the other, all things considered. Second, there might be reasons having to do with our basic psychological makeup for making use of different dispositions and reasoning strategies for dealing with different kinds of problems. For example, if one accepts Hume's insight about the difficulty of widening fellow feeling indefinitely, then it makes sense to inculcate beliefs and principles which produce moral sensitivities in situations where no positive feelings exist among the parties.

The data Gilligan and her co-workers have gathered point to the existence of something like such a psychological division of labor with different kinds of moral problems drawing out different kinds of moral response. Recall that most people use both orientations some of the time and that the choice of orientation depends at least in part on the type of problem posed. Indeed, standard Kohlbergian dilemmas, such as the Heinz dilemma (should Heinz steal the drug which could help his dying wife from the avaricious pharmacist who will not sell it at a fair price?), generate the highest number of justice responses in both sexes; and hypothetical stories that highlight inequality or attachment result in higher rates of justice and care responses, respectively, for both men and women (Gilligan and Wiggans 1986). This is true despite continuous findings of gender differences in responses to open-ended questions about the nature of morality and one's own real-life dilemmas, as well as in the ratio of justice versus care responses to hypothetical moral dilemmas.

Such findings regarding the domain specificity of moral response, especially in light of the point about better and worse construals, indicate that although Gilligan's gestalt-shift metaphor is illuminating in three ways, it is unhelpful and misleading in two others. First, it is helpful in drawing attention to the fact that just as some people have trouble ever seeing one or the other available images in a gestalt illusion, so too there are some people who have trouble understanding talk of rights or alternatively talk of love; they just can't see what you are talking about. Second, the metaphor highlights the findings that for most individuals one way of seeing moral problems dominates the other way of seeing to some degree, and that the direction of dominance is correlated with gender. Finally, the metaphor draws attention to the fact that there are some moral problems—abortion, for example—the proper construal of which is deemed by all parties to be a matter of the greatest importance, but for which the proper construal is an issue of deeply incompatible perception.

There are undoubtedly also problems of less monumental importance for which there are no clear grounds for preferring one construal over the other. In one study by a member of Gilligan's group, teenagers of both sexes were good at switching from their preferred orientation when asked if there was another way to think about a certain problem, but all subjects believed that their preferred mode gave rise to the most defensible solution. Barring radical discrepancies from a normative point of view as to what action is prescribed or how things turn out, there may well be nothing definitive to say about the preferability of one construal over the other in many specific cases (although there might well be objections to general dominance of one orientation), since personal style, even if socially constructed and gender linked, has certain saving graces on the side of cognitive economy once it is in place. Or to put the point more contentiously: in some cases the preferred mode of moral construal may be the most defensible simply because it is preferred.

Nevertheless, what is misleading about the gestalt metaphor is that, just as not all visual stimuli are ambiguous in the way gestalt illusions are, so too not all moral issues are so open to alternative construals. To be sure, the psychological apparatus involved in moral appraisal involves learning and underdetermination in a way visual perception does not, and thus moral construal is more tradition sensitive than visual perception. But again there may be both normative reasons and reasons of cognitive economy for teaching moral agents to be sensitive to certain saliencies (e.g., anonymity among parties, prior explicit contracts) in such a way that these saliencies are more or less sufficient to generate one construal (e.g., a justice construal) rather than some other. As we have seen, some of Gilligan's own data indicate that something like this happens for at least some problems for both men and women.

The second and more important way the gestalt metaphor is misleading has to do with the fact that there is a deep and important difference between visual perception and moral construal which the metaphor obscures. Whereas it is impossible to see both the duck and the rabbit at the same time in the duck-rabbit illusion, it is not impossible to see both the justice and care saliencies in a moral problem and to integrate them in moral deliberation. This is because moral consideration, unlike visual perception, takes place over time and can involve the assimilation and accommodation of as much, and as messy, information as we like. It is wrong, therefore, to suggest, as Gilligan does in one place, that the two perspectives are "fundamentally incompatible" (Gilligan, in press *b;* also see Lyons 1983).

The point is that there is no logical reason why both care and justice considerations cannot be introduced, where relevant, into one and the same reasoning episode. *Heinz,* after all, should steal the drug because it is *his* wife; and his wife should get the drug because *any* human life is more important than any avaricious pharmacist's desire to make some extra money.

This is not to deny that in some cases construing a particular problem from both perspectives will block moral clarity about what should be done (see Flanagan and Adler 1983), nor is it to deny that for the sake of normative elegance and psychological stability it will be important to have some, even imperfect, decision procedure to resolve such conflicts. But, as we have suggested, one possibility is that the saliencies construable in a particular situation will make different sorts of considerations differentially relevant to that situation and, in that way, will keep intractability (but, possibly, not a sense of moral costs) to a minimum. The important point is that there is no impossibility in imagining persons who are both very fair and very caring and who, in addition, have finely honed sensitivities for perceiving moral saliencies and seeing particular problems as problems of certain multifarious kinds.

Thinking of moral psychology as variegated, as composed of a wide array of attitudes, dispositions, rules of thumb, and principles that are designed for multifarious sorts of situations, suggests a move in a more virtue-theoretical direction and, thus, a return to the sort of conceptual model that has been out of favor in the cognitive-developmental tradition since Piaget's *The Moral Judgment of the Child* (1932).[1] Indeed, the more plausibility one assigns to an Aristotelian conception of moral psychology, the more credible will be the suspicion that Gilligan's expansion of Kohlberg's model to include two general orientations is still insufficently fine grained to be adequate from either a psychological or normative point of view. There are three reasons for this. First, we still lack a clear (and remotely complete) taxonomy of the various dispositions—the cognitive and affective attitudes—that constitute the care orientation, and the same goes for the justice orientation. This failure to provide a more fine-grained analysis is more understandable for Kohlberg than for Gilligan. After all, Kohlberg believes that morality is decidedly not a matter of special-purpose virtues, dispositions, and reasoning strategies but, rather, consists of the application of a unified general-purpose style of thinking. But there is every reason to think that Gilligan's program would benefit from moving in a more virtue-theoretical direction insofar as the conception of moral agency she describes is potentially so much thicker than Kohlberg's, embedded as it is in self-conception and social context.

In the second place, we lack a careful analysis of the differences between good and morally problematic or even corrupt kinds of care. Care can be corrupt either because of qualitative features of the caring relationship (e.g., it is based on insincerity or coercion) or because of the relationship's content (e.g., the parties have bad aspirations for each other or give sensitive attention to meeting each other's corrupt needs and desires). (See Baier [1986]; Gilligan does some of this in her own attempt to emulate stage theory [1982, p. 105].)

Third, even if we accept the plausible view that moral psychology is neither totally modular (as in vulgar Aristotelianism) nor totally unified and general purpose (as in vulgar Kantianism) but, rather, is tiered, containing both virtuous and vicious dispositions to think and react in certain ways as well as a general higher-level moral orientation (which may or may not have power over the lower levels), there is good reason

1. The rest of cognitive psychology, of course, has gone increasingly homuncular.

to think that there are more than two such general orientations.[2] For example, Charles Taylor (1982) has described moral outlooks guided by the commitments to personal integrity, to perfection, and to liberation which cannot be assimilated under either of Gilligan's two rubrics, let alone under Kohlberg's one (see Miller [1985] for descriptions of some even more alien moral orientations); and it is hard to see how virtues like courage or moderation fall under either orientation.

The issues of the scope of morality and the range of realizable moral conceptions are of the utmost importance. What moral psychologists conceive of as possible determines how they understand and classify moral personalities. But if the possibility range is too narrowly conceived or too culture bound or too gripped by a contentious normative conception, actual psychological realities may be missed.

In addition to these issues, there is still the important question of precisely what sort of adjustment Gilligan thinks work such as hers warrants in our conception of moral maturity. She was not clear on this matter in her book, and her recent work still shifts between the ideas that the two ethics are incompatible alternatives to each other but are both adequate from a normative point of view; that they are complements of one another involved in some sort of tense interplay; and that each is deficient without the other and thus ought to be integrated.

One might think that our claim that there is no logical incompatibility between the two ethics and thus no logical problem with bringing both kinds of considerations to any problem (which is not to imply that the two sets of concepts can be applied without conflict in every place) means that there is nothing to block the tactic of pursuing the integrationist strategy less hesitantly. But here Gilligan has some interesting things to say about the psychological origins of the two orientations. Although there may be no logical incompatibility between the concepts of justice and care (and their suites), Gilligan suggests in many places that there is a deep-seated psychological tension between the two perspectives, a tension rooted in the fact that the two ethics are built out of etiologically distinct underlying competencies which make different and competing psychological demands on moral agents. It is the differences in origin and underlying cognitive and motivational structure which make integration of the two orientations in particular moral agents hard to realize and which, at the same time, explain the data on gender differences.

2. Both Gilligan and Kohlberg take narrative data to be a fairly accurate index of the more general orientation. This is problematic. The relationship between first-person speech acts and underlying psychology is a widely discussed issue in contemporary philosophy of mind and cognitive psychology, and there is reason to think that our deficiencies in giving accurate self-assessments run very deep. Confabulation is an especially salient worry when the speech acts are being offered in response to issues which connect so obviously as do moral problems with issues of self-worth and with how one is perceived by others. Gilligan and Kohlberg are strangely silent on such matters.

Gilligan accepts a roughly neo-Freudian account of early childhood. This account turns on two main variables: (1) the psychological situation of the child as both dependent and attached and (2) the typical differences between maternal and paternal relations with the child. The basic story goes like this: The child has continuous experiences of both her relative powerlessness vis-à-vis her parents and her powerful attachment to them. The experiences of powerlessness and inequality give rise to the search for independence and equality and thereby provide fertile ground for the notions of fairness and autonomy (and their opposites) to take root. Meanwhile, the experiences of deep attachment and connection, of moving and being moved by others, provide the ground for the dispositions that will guide later attachments—for compassion, love, and altruism. Together, "the different dynamics of early childhood inequality and attachment lay the groundwork for two moral visions—of justice and of care" (Gilligan and Wiggans 1986).

Even if one accepts that it is the alleged tension between the two kinds of early experiences that grounds the tension between the two ethics (one might be skeptical on grounds that there is a high degree of overlap between the two kinds of experiences), this tension does not explain the data on gender differences. Here Gilligan follows Nancy Chodorow's (1978) influential analysis of gender differentiation. Initially for children of both sexes, the relationship with the primary caretaker, typically the mother, is one of powerful attachment and identification. However, as the child gets older and begins the project of carving out a self-concept, she starts to identify strongly with her same-sex parent, and parents reinforce this identification. In the typical family where the mother has a greater nurturing role than the father, boys will have to shift their initial identification with the mother to the father. Girls, meanwhile, do not need to reorient their initial identification but only to intensify the one that already exists. This means that the project of separation is more salient and more pressing for boys than for girls. Furthermore, because of the mutual feelings of identification between mother and daughter, girls will have richer experience than boys with attachment and connectedness. According to Chodorow, "Boys . . . have to curtail their primary love and sense of empathic tie with their mother. A boy has been required to engage in more emphatic individuation and a more defensive firming of experienced ego boundaries . . . . Girls emerge from this period with a basis for 'empathy' built into their primary definition of self in a way that boys do not" (1978, pp. 166–67).

Assuming this story is true, it should be obvious, first, that there is nothing necessary (although there may be biological and social pressures in certain directions) about the way we arrange nurturance nor about the particular ways parents treat their male and female children, and thus the story is not required to turn out exactly the way it now does. If there were greater sharing in nurturance by both parents, the process of acquiring a self-concept would not make such different demands and rest on such different experiences for boys and girls. Resultant attitudes about autonomy, attachment, and so on might not be as different as they now are. But, second, the latter analysis does indicate why, given current practices (with their long cultural histories), we cannot be sanguine about the possibilities for inculcating moral sensibilities which support both a rich sense of justice and care and a well developed sense of autonomy and connection in one and the same agent.

Full-fledged integration aside, it is important to consider what role, if any, the experiences and dispositions which underlie each ethic have in contributing to morally good forms of the other. Again, it is important not to lose sight of the fact that the early experiences of powerlessness and attachment overlap.

Annette Baier has made some interesting suggestions in this regard. Her basic insight is similar to Hume's about the problem with Hobbes's state-of-nature hypothesis, namely, it ignores the fact that for any human interaction to take place, including even "a war of each against each," there must first be family and nurturance. Otherwise the helpless infant will not survive its first nights.

Baier argues first that theories of justice, including Rawls's, need to assume that there will be loving parents in order to ensure the stability of a just society and the development of a sense of justice in new members. "Rawls's theory like so many other theories of obligation, in the end must take out a loan not only on the natural duty of parents to care for children . . . but on the natural virtue of parental love . . . . The virtue of being a *loving* parent must supplement the natural duties and obligations, if the just society is to last beyond the first generation" (Baier 1985, unpublished section).

Second, Baier argues that the dispositions to be fair and to keep contracts presuppose (psychologically and normally, but not logically) that the agent has been cared for and has had experiences of trust. "Promises presuppose both experience of longer on-going trust relationships *not* necessarily initiated by any voluntary act (with parents or with friends) so that the advantages of such future-involving mutual trust be already clear, and also an already established climate of trust enabling one to choose to get close enough to a stranger to exchange words or goods or handshakes with him" (Baier 1986).

Baier's argument suggests the further insight that the moral disposition to be just normally presupposes not only that the agent is attached to certain abstract concepts and ideals, but also, more fundamentally, that he is attached to and cares for his community, and that he has a sense that his own good and that of those he cares for most is associated with general adherence to these ideals. Without such cares and attachments, first to those one loves and secondarily to some wider community to which one's projects and prospects are intimately joined, the moral disposition to justice—as opposed to the purely prudential disposition to justice—has no place to take root.

There is no objection in principle to using one set of virtues and dispositions to support or strengthen another set. The point is simply, as Baier puts it, that "a decent morality will *not* depend for its stability on forces to which it gives no moral recognition" (1985, unpublished section).

III

The question arises as to what Kohlberg makes of the ethic of care and the various dispositions and experiences that constitute it. What sort of recognition does he think this ethical perspective deserves? What is its relation to the conception of morality as justice that he more than anyone else has championed?

At first, Kohlberg (1982) flirted with the strategy of simply denying that there is such an ethic and thereby denying that there is anything of *moral* psychological importance to recognize. Kohlberg admits that initially he found Gilligan's work unwelcome and preferred to read it as concerned with ego psychology but not with moral psychology (1982, p. 514). This suggestion in itself displays a very unrealistic view about the isolation of moral psychology from overall personality.

Lately Kohlberg seems to have come around to seeing that Gilligan's challenge was more apt than he first admitted. In two long coauthored essays (both with Charles Levine and Alexandra Hewer) in the second volume of his collected papers (1984), Kohlberg attempts to set forth a more complete and satisfactory response to Gilligan's work. On an initial reading, Kohlberg appears to concede many of the main points of contention. Reflecting on his original theory, he writes, "I assumed that the core of morality and moral development was deontological; that is it was a matter of rights and duties or prescriptions" (p. 225). These "starting assumptions led to the design of a research instrument measuring reasoning about dilemmas of conflicting rights or the distribution of scarce resources, that is, justice concerns. We did not use dilemmas about prosocial concerns for others that were not frameable as rights conflicts" (p. 304). "We admit, however, that the emphasis on the virtue of justice in my work does not fully reflect all that is recognized as being part of the moral domain" (p. 227).

In speaking specifically of his standard measurement tool, Kohlberg says, "We do agree that our justice dilemmas do not pull for the care and response orientation, and we do agree that our scoring manual does not lead to a full assessment of this aspect of moral thinking" (1984, p. 343; see also pp. 305–7 and 622–23). Kohlberg now recommends, therefore, understanding his theory as a "rational reconstruction of justice reasoning: emphasizing the nomenclature 'justice reasoning,' since the . . . stages have more typically been called stages of moral development [by him]" (1984, p. 224).

Despite such concessions, it is really quite difficult to put one's finger on how Kohlberg now intends his theory to be interpreted, and sometimes what is conceded with one hand seems to be withdrawn with the other. Indeed, on a closer reading, it is hard to read Kohlberg as completely sincere in the latter concessions, for he also puts forward a variety of claims that are at odds with them.

For example, although Kohlberg now acknowledges that his theory is not comprehensive, he continues to promote a restricted conception of morality which belies this concession. In particular, he continues to make two common but questionable claims about the nature of morality. First, there is the claim that all moral judgments have certain formal features such as prescriptivity (i.e., they entail obligations) and universalizability (1984, pp. 293–96). Second, there is the claim that "*moral* judgments or principles have the central function of resolving interpersonal or social conflicts, that is, conflicts of claims or rights" (p. 216).

Both points are problematic. With regard to the first point, imagine a complex judgment about how one can best help a friend who is depressed. The judgment here will involve assessment of particular features of both parties. What one can do for a friend is, after all, determined in large part by the kinds of persons both are, the characteristic patterns of interaction between the two, and so on. It is implausible to think that there is anything interestingly universalizable about such a judgment or that there is necessarily any judgment of obligation involved. Indeed, where friendship or love truly exists, thinking about what one is obligated to do can, as Bernard Williams has put it in a related context, involve "one thought too many" (1981, p. 18).

With regard to the second point, the same example serves to show that it is simply not obvious that morality has the central function of resolving "conflicts of claims or rights." To be sure, this is an important function of moral theory, and the function most visible in public debates, but to conceive of this function as central and other functions of morality as peripheral is to beg the interesting question of how best to conceive of the domain of morality. There is too much moral energy expended on self-improvement and the refinement of character, on respectful interactions with loved ones, friends, and strangers, and on supererogation for such a claim to be acceptable without considerable defense. None is given.

At one point Kohlberg stresses that his conception of "morality as justice best renders our view of morality as universal. It restricts morality to a central minimal core, striving for universal agreement in the face of more relativist conceptions of the good" (1984, p. 306). And in many places he emphasizes that there are two senses of the word "moral"—one sense is that of "the moral point of view" with the alleged formal features, the other sense refers to "personal" issues—to things like friendship, family relations, supererogation, and so on (p. 232). Kohlberg points out that how one treats the latter issues is widely acknowledged to be a relative matter (but, one must stress, not completely relative).

Still two issues must be kept distinct. It is one thing to want to study a certain kind of moral thinking because it is more stable (the function of a theory of justice is, after all, to produce such stability in interpersonal relations among individuals who may have no personal connections) or because it is easier to talk about in terms of the theoretical framework of cognitive-developmental stage theory. Kohlberg (1984, pp. 236–49) makes it clear that one reason he prefers to study justice reasoning is that he thinks that there are "hard" stages, that is, stages which satisfy standard Piagetian criteria of universality, irreversibility, and so on, of justice reasoning (see Flanagan [1984] for doubts about this) but not of reasoning about personal issues. But such theoretical attractions are irrelevant to the issues of psychological realism, normative adequacy, and the domain of the moral.

Once Kohlberg's proprietary attempt to restrict our conception of the domain of the moral is seen for what it is, his "total disagreement" (1984, p. 342) with Gilligan regarding gender differences is of little moment. Kohlberg clings to the fact that such differences are minimal or nonexistent in studies using his standard justice dilemmas as the test instrument (see Walker [1984] for a review; but see Baumrind [in press] for a criticism of Walker). The fact remains that there are, as Kohlberg acknowledges (p. 350), gender differences in preferred orientation, in response ratios, and so on, even if there are none for one restricted type of moral problem. Such findings point to differences in moral psychology unless one implausibly restricts the domain of inquiry.

In several places Kohlberg tries a more interesting tactic than the one of restricting the conception of morality to what he studies. This tactic starts by accepting that "personal morality" is part of the domain of the moral (1984, pp. 234–35) but then moves to claim that justice lies in some subsuming relation to this morality. In speaking specifically of Gilligan's work, he says, "The two senses of the word *moral* do not represent two different moral orientations existing at the same level of generality and validity" (p. 232).

The overall strategy is to make an argument for the "primacy of justice," either by arguing that considerations of justice trump considerations of care when the two conflict or by arguing that justice is in some sense necessary for care but not the other way around (see Kohlberg 1981, p. xiii; Kohlberg 1984, p. 305).

The first idea, that the demands of justice must be met before all others, is a familiar one within the context of liberal political theory. However, it is important to emphasize that, even within the liberal tradition, the claim that justice is trump applies in the first instance to the arrangement of basic social institutions. Many liberal philosophers are hesitant about any simple and straightforward extension of the deontological constraints governing political practices to individual behavior.

Furthermore, even if one holds that considerations of justice are overriding at the individual level, nothing follows about how often considerations of justice are germane. If, as seems the case for most of us, the larger part of moral life takes place in situations and contexts in which considerations of justice are not especially relevant, then the "primacy of justice" might be an important principle to have, and sensitivities to issues of justice will need to be well honed; but the virtue of justice will not be doing most of the work in the actual moral lives of most persons.

The second idea—that justice is necessary for care—comes in two forms. First, there is the claim that conditions of social justice must obtain for the personal virtues associated with both justice and care to thrive. "It seems to us . . . that morally valid forms of caring and community presuppose prior conditions and judgments of justice" (Kohlberg 1984, p. 305). Second, there is the claim that the personal virtue of justice is necessary for the personal virtue of care. "In our view special obligations of care presuppose, but go beyond, the general duties of justice, which are necessary, but not sufficient for them" (p. 229). "More than justice is required for resolving many complex moral dilemmas, but justice is a necessary element of any morally adequate resolution of these conflicts" (p. 370).

The first point is important. There is something obviously right about the view that morality is not a purely individual project and that personal virtue takes root best in a just society. But once we push things back to the basic social conditions necessary for morality, we come again upon the point that all societies, just or unjust, stable or unstable, egalitarian or nonegalitarian, presuppose prior relations of care between new members and those members involved in child rearing. There is in the end something misleading in the widely held view that justice is the first virtue of society. Indeed, although it is wise to resist lexically ordering the basic virtues required for an ongoing morally good society or for a morally good personality, there is no incoherence in putting care first when it comes to creating the possibility conditions for family, wider community, and individual character in the first place.

The second claim that personal justice has some essential connection to the other virtues comes in several versions. The strongest and most implausible claim is that personal justice is sufficient for moral goodness overall. With the possible exception of Plato, no one has held this view. The reason is that it is easy to imagine someone who espouses and abides by some defensible conception of justice but who is morally deficient in other ways.

Kohlberg intends something weaker than the implausible sufficiency claim. His proposal, however, is ambiguous between two different claims: (1) that experiences of fairness and the development of the disposition to be just are necessary for the causal formation of whatever psychological competencies turn out to be associated with Gilligan's ethic of care, but not vice versa; and (2) that the display of any other virtue necessarily presupposes possession of the virtue of justice, but not vice versa. Showing either claim 1 or 2 would help support the claim that the two ethics do not "exist at the same level of generality and validity."

With regard to claim 1, we have already expressed the opinion that experiences of care and caring have an important role in laying the foundations for any ethical sense whatsoever (see Noddings [1984] for someone who makes too much of this point). Hence we already have grounds for doubting the claim that justice has some unique foundational status with regard to the formation of other virtues or to overall moral psychology.

When one focuses less on the basic experiences necessary for developing a moral sense and looks more closely at the sort of explicit moral instruction that takes place between parents and children (something neither Gilligan nor Kohlberg does), the claim that the acquisition of the personal virtue of justice has unique foundational status also seems implausible. To be sure, parents often say things like "Kate, look how sad David is; he deserves a turn too." But it is most plausible to read such statements as presupposing that some of the competencies, dispositions, and beliefs required by justice and care are required by morally good forms of either. It is hard to see how we could teach children about kindness without teaching them certain things about fairness, but it is equally hard to see how we could teach them about fairness without teaching them certain things about kindness and sensitivity to the aims and interests of others. The situation is one of mutual support rather than a necessary condition in only one direction.

The fact that normally both justice and care are built out of some of the same underlying competencies does not imply, however, that a mature sense of justice is necessary for the display of the other virtues or for responding to every particular moral problem (claim 2 above). First, there are some persons who we think of as virtuous in certain ways and in certain domains, but who we do not think are very fair or just; and the same holds true in the other direction. Second, it is possible to imagine individuals in whom beneficence is so sensitively and globally developed that the virtue of justice, as normally conceived, is not only unnecessary for the display of the other virtues, but is even unnecessary in situations in which ordinary persons with less saintly personalities would need to call upon it. Third, and setting such moral exotica aside, there are many moral problems which have nothing to do with justice. It is implausible, therefore, to think the personal virtue of justice is necessarily implicated in our dealings with such problems.

To question the truth of the necessary condition claim as a psychological thesis is not to deny what is normatively important about it. A morally good life overall requires fairness because the possession of the virtues associated with care might well, if not tempered by justice, result in immorality, for example, chauvinism, in certain circumstances. But the same holds true in the other direction.

In several places, Kohlberg tries to make the normative point but links it with the implausible psychological one. He says, "In our philosophic end point of moral reasoning, the hypothetical sixth stage, there occurs, we believe, an integration of justice and care that forms a single moral principle" (1984, p. 344). And elsewhere he claims that the two orientations converge at the highest stage because the "principle of persons as ends is common to both" (p. 356).

This way of talking is misleading in two respects. First, Kohlberg now acknowledges (1982, p. 523; 1984, p. 215) that his highest stage of moral development is purely hypothetical; that in over twenty-five years of research, he and his colleagues have been unable to confirm the existence of stage 6. This means that the claim that justice and care converge at the highest stage to "form a single moral principle" is a claim for which there is no empirical evidence. Second, it is extremely doubtful for reasons Gilligan and others (Blum 1980) have expressed, that a normatively adequate moral psychology is best thought of in terms of the possession of a single unified faculty and, even less plausibly, in terms of the possession of a "single moral principle."

Still, Gilligan's own view that morality consists of "two voices" needs further refinement, development, and defense before its full psychological and normative importance is clear. We need to know more about many things, including the precise nature and extent of the gender differences, the social causes of these differences, content effects, the fine-grained features of the ethic of care, the role of the competencies it makes use of in justice reasoning, and the plausibility of carving morality into only two voices.

## IV

The view that there is one ideal type of moral personality—a unique way moral psychology is best ordered and moral reasoning conducted—is the psychological side of the coin whose other face contains the image of morality as a unitary domain with a determinate and timeless nature. Much recent work in moral philosophy has questioned this view of morality as a clearly carved domain for which a unified theory can be produced. Such work suggests that our attitudes and expectations about underlying moral psychology may also need to be revised. Rejection of the doctrine of the "unity of the moral" (Taylor 1982) may also require rejection of its close relative—the doctrine that there is one ideal type of moral personality.

A reasonable hypothesis is that moral personality occurs at a level too open to both social and self-determination for us to expect there to be any unique and determinate set of dispositions, capacities, attitudes, and types of reasoning which ideally underwrite all moral responsiveness. This means that we will have to learn to tolerate, and perhaps applaud, a rich diversity of good moral personalities. The fact that this will be hard for those still in the grip of the doctrine of the "unity of the moral" in no way belies the possibility that this is the right road to go.

## REFERENCES

Anscombe, G. E. M. 1958. Modern Moral Philosophy. *Philosophy* 33:1–19. Reprinted in *Ethics,* ed. Judith J. Thomson and Gerald Dworkin, pp. 186–210. New York: Harper & Row, 1968.

Baier, Annette C. 1985. What Do Women Want in a Moral Theory? *Nous* 19:53–65, including a section omitted from published article that was provided by courtesy of the author.

Baier, Annette C. 1986. Trust and Antitrust. *Ethics* 96:231–60.

Baumrind, Diana. In press. Sex Differences in Moral Reasoning: Response to Walker's Conclusion That There Are None. *Child Development*.

Blum, Lawrence. 1980. *Friendship, Altruism, and Morality*. London: Routledge & Kegan Paul.

Chodorow, Nancy. 1978. *The Reproduction of Mothering*. Berkeley: University of California Press.

Flanagan, Owen. 1984. *The Science of the Mind*. Bradford Books Series. Cambridge, Mass.: MIT Press.

Flanagan, Owen, and Adler, Jonathan. 1983. Impartiality and Particularity. *Social Research* 50:576–96.

Gilligan, Carol. 1982. *In a Different Voice*. Cambridge, Mass.: Harvard University Press.

Gilligan, Carol. 1983. Do the Social Sciences Have an Adequate Theory of Moral Development? In *Social Sciences as Moral Inquiry*, ed. N. Hann, R. Bellah, P. Rabinow, and W. Sullivan, pp. 33–51. New York: Columbia University Press.

Gilligan, Carol. 1986. Reply to "On *In a Different Voice:* An Interdisciplinary Forum." *Signs* 11:324–33.

Gilligan, Carol. In press *a*. Remapping Development: The Power of Divergent Data. In *Value Presuppositions in Theories of Human Development*, ed. L. Cirillo and S. Wapner. Hillsdale, N.J.: Lawrence Erlbaum Associates.

Gilligan, Carol. In press *b*. Remapping the Moral Domain: New Images of the Self in Relationship. In *Reconstructing Individualism: Autonomy, Individuality and the Self in Western Thought*, ed. T. C. Heller, M. Sosna, and D. Wellbery. Stanford, Calif.: Stanford University Press.

Gilligan, Carol. In press *c*. Moral Orientation and Moral Development. In *Women and Moral Theory*, ed. Eva Feder Kittay and Diana T. Meyers. Totowa, N.J.: Rowman & Littlefield.

Gilligan, Carol, and Wiggans, Grant. 1986. The Origins of Morality in Early Childhood Relationships. Harvard University, typescript.

Kohlberg, Lawrence. 1981. *Essays on Moral Development*. Vol. 1, *The Philosophy of Moral Development*. New York: Harper & Row.

Kohlberg, Lawrence. 1982. A Reply to Owen Flanagan and Some Comments on the Puka-Goodpaster Exchange. *Ethics* 92:513–28.

Kohlberg, Lawrence, with Levine, Charles, and Hewer, Alexandra. 1984. Moral Stages: A Current Statement. Response to Critics. Appendix A. In *Essays on Moral Development*. Vol. 2, *The Psychology of Moral Development*, by Lawrence Kohlberg, pp. 207–386, 621–39. New York: Harper & Row.

Lyons, Nona Plessner. 1983. Two Perspectives: On Self, Relationships, and Morality. *Harvard Educational Review* 53:125–45.

MacIntyre, Alasdair. 1982. How Moral Agents Become Ghosts. *Synthese* 53:292–312.

Miller, Richard. 1985. Ways of Moral Learning. *Philosophical Review* 94:507–56.

Murdoch, Iris. 1970. *The Sovereignty of the Good*. Boston: Routledge & Kegan Paul.

Noddings, Nel. 1984. *Caring: A Feminine Approach to Ethics*. Berkeley and Los Angeles: University of California Press.

Piaget, Jean. 1932. *The Moral Judgment of the Child*. New York: Free Press.

Taylor, Charles. 1982. The Diversity of Goods. In *Utilitarianism and Beyond*, ed. Amartya Sen and Bernard Williams. Cambridge, Mass.: Harvard University Press.

Walker, Lawrence J. 1984. Sex Differences in the Development of Moral Reasoning: A Critical Review. *Child Development* 55:677–91.

Williams, Bernard. 1981. Persons, Character, and Morality. In *Moral Luck*, by Bernard Williams. Cambridge: Cambridge University Press.

# [7]

*Journal of Applied Philosophy, Vol.10, No. 1, 1993*

# Different Voices, Still Lives: Problems in the Ethics of Care

**SUSAN MENDUS**

ABSTRACT *Recent writings in feminist ethics have urged that the activity of caring is more central to women's lives than are considerations of justice and equality. This paper argues that an ethics of care, so understood, is difficult to extend beyond the local and familiar, and is therefore of limited use in addressing the political problems of the modern world. However, the ethics of care does contain an important insight: if references to care are understood not as claims about women's nature, but as reflections on the extent to which moral obligations are both unchosen and conflicting, then an ethics of care can supplement an ethics of justice, and can also provide a more realistic account of both men's and women's moral life.*

> The moral imperative . . . [for] women is an injunction to care, a responsibility to discern and alleviate the 'real and recognizable trouble' of this world. For men, the moral imperative appears rather as an injunction to respect the rights of others and thus to protect from interference the rights to life and self-fulfilment . . . The standard of moral judgement that informs [women's] assessment of the self is a standard of relationship, an ethic of nurturance, responsibility, and care. [1]

Since the publication of Carol Gilligan's *In A Different Voice* feminist theorists have embraced a distinction between an ethic of justice and an ethic of care. Moral theories couched in terms of rights, justice and abstract rationality have given way to moral theories which emphasise care, compassion and contextualisation. And it is widely argued that these latter values reflect women's lives and women's concerns far more accurately than do the abstract and atomistic values inherent in, for example, John Rawls' theory of justice, or Kantian conceptions of morality generally. As the quotation demonstrates, Gilligan's account, which is based on the findings of empirical psychological research, contends that the justice perspective is predominantly male, the care perspective predominantly female. But moral and political philosophy have ignored the findings of psychology and in consequence have emphasised the (male) perspective of justice to the near exclusion of (female) conceptions of care. In this respect they have shown a distinct gender bias, and feminists now urge the need for rectification and an acknowledgement of the moral (as well as the psychological) importance of the language of care.

However, in urging a move from abstraction to contextualisation, and from considerations of justice to considerations of care, feminist theorists tread on sensitive ground. From Aristotle to Hegel, woman's 'special' nature or 'different' voice has been used as the primary justification for her confinement to the domestic realm and her exclusion from political life. Thus, notoriously, Hegel tells us that 'When women hold the helm of government, the state is at once in jeopardy, because women regulate their actions not by the demands of universality but by arbitrary inclinations and opinions'. [2] Similarly, Rousseau declared that 'a perfect man and a perfect woman should no more be alike in mind than in face', [3] and western political philosophy is replete with similar examples of arguments which move from the assertion of woman's different, caring nature to the conclusion that she is unfitted for public life. Against this background, the aspiration to employ an ethic of care in pursuit of feminist ends must be treated with considerable caution.

The converse also applies: difference theorists not only appear to ally themselves with arguments which have been used to women's disadvantage, they also, and in the process, distance themselves from a long tradition of feminist theory and practice — a tradition which has embraced abstract rights as the most important single means of escaping from oppression. Anne Phillips says;

> The liberal language of individual rights and freedoms has a tremendous resonance for women . . . much of the personal impetus towards a feminist politics is to do with claiming the space to choose who and what you are — not to be defined, contained and dictated by notions of 'woman'. [4]

Thus, difference theory in general, and the ethics of care in particular, raise serious problems for feminists. My aim in this paper is to draw attention to those problems, and to suggest ways in which they might be avoided or overcome. Specifically, I shall argue that on the individual level the ethics of care runs the risk of adopting too unitary and static a conception of woman's identity, and of ignoring the conflicts inherent in women's lives. Connectedly, I shall suggest that on the political level the concept of care is too narrow to do the work required of it: considerations of care are largely limited to those whom we know, and are problematic if extended to the wider world of unknown others which is the central sphere of politics. Finally, however, I shall suggest that the ethics of care does identify important defects in justice theory: if interpreted not as a theory about the activity of caring, but as a theory of the passivity of life, it may provide the foundations for a political philosophy which recognises our need for just treatment in virtue of our inherent vulnerability. This conclusion serves, moreover, to suggest that we should not interpret 'the ethics of justice' and 'the ethics of care' as distinct and alternative ethical systems, but rather as complementary facets of any realistic account of morality.

**Care, Difference and Politics**

There are two features of an ethic of care to which I wish to draw attention: the first is its emphasis on the differences which divide people rather than the similarities which unite; the second is the centrality it accords to small-scale, face-to-face relationships. Each of these features promises to mitigate the impersonality associated with an ethic of justice but, I shall argue, the price is high. As we have seen, emphasis on difference threatens political exclusion: it has uncomfortable associations with the arguments of the great dead philosophers, who claimed that women's different nature justified their confinement to a separate domestic sphere, distinct from the sphere of politics. Moreover, emphasis on small, face-to-face relationships compounds the difficulty when once we recognise that political problems are characteristically large scale. Typically, they do not arise at the level of individual relationships, and therefore an ethic which concentrates on the small scale may have little to contribute to their solution. At the very least, argument will be needed to show whether and how the features characteristic of small-scale relationships may be extended in such a way as to inform political practice.

Firstly, then, an ethic of care as an ethic which emphasises difference rather than similarity. References to this feature can be found throughout feminist philosophy, and I shall mention just two places where the argument is prominent.

In her article, *Liberty and Equality from a Feminist Perspective*, Virginia Held asserts; '*We* give birth, and you do not. This is a radical difference, and the fact that you lack this capacity may distort your whole view of the social realm'. [5] And similarly Cheshire Calhoun argues that;

> Too much talk about our similarities as moral selves, and too little talk about our differences has its moral dangers . . . Unless moral theory shifts its priority to knowledgeable discussion of human differences — particularly differences tied to gender, race, class and power — lists and rank orderings of basic human interests and rights as well as the political deployment of those lists are likely to be sexist, racist and classist. [6]

An ethic of care, unlike an ethic of justice, takes the differences between people as central and as the appropriate starting point for both moral and political philosophy.

Secondly, and connectedly, the ethic of care concentrates on the particularities of actual relationships rather than the dictates of universal reason. Kittay and Meyers draw the contrast as follows;

> A morality of rights and abstract reason begins with a moral agent who is separate from others, and who independently elects moral principles to obey. In contrast, a morality of responsibility and care begins with a self who is enmeshed in a network of relations to others, and whose moral deliberation aims to maintain these relations. [7]

Unlike an ethic of justice, an ethic of care emphasises the extent to which people are at least partly constituted by their relationships with those around them. It is these relationships which define their moral responsibilities and which should therefore inform our discussions of moral and political life. Emphasis on the differences which divide people (particularly the differences which divide men and women), and on the importance of actual relationships as constitutive of individual identity and moral responsibility, are therefore central to the distinction between an ethic of justice and an ethic of care. There are, however, two ways in which these features are problematic. On the individual level, they imply a conception of female identity which is altogether too simplistic and unitary; and on a political level, they assume a kind of society wholly different from that which exists in the post-industrial world of the late twentieth century.

Insistence on female difference, specifically on the 'radical' differences which divide men and women, is often ambivalent between an assertion of biological difference, rooted in women's status as child *bearers*, and an assertion of social difference, rooted in women's traditional role as child *carers*. Proponents of the ethic of care tend to vacillate uneasily between the claim that women's biological nature as child bearers renders them especially sensitive to considerations of care and compassion, and the claim that women's status as child carers makes them more conscious of those considerations. But either way feminist politics is jeopardised, for the former account renders women prisoners of their own biology, and the latter advocates for all women a single, defining role which in fact only some women occupy.

Of course, in so far as an ethic of care points to the importance of virtues other than the virtue of justice, it is powerful and important. Held is surely right to note that equality and justice are only two virtues amongst many and that, in ordinary life, the claims of care and compassion may be more central and more compelling. But she and others go further, implying a deep and defining connection between an ethic of care and women's identity. For her, the specification of women's identity contains essential reference to birth, care, and the raising of children. The same is not true of men, and this difference, it is claimed, generates a dramatically different perspective on moral problems and moral responsibilities. Thus Held concludes;

> When we dare to give voice to how we think the world ought to be, we can imagine that whether one adopts the point of view of those who give birth or whether one does not may radically change one's perspective on most of what is most important. [8]

Well, we can imagine that, but it is a risky activity and not, on the whole, one which has delivered much by way of improvement in women's political condition. On the contrary, it is emphasis on common humanity *despite* difference which has served women far better, since it has provided standards of impartiality which are necessary in the pursuit of equality. [9]

There is, however, a further implication of the ethic of care which I wish to note here. This is that, in addition to emphasising differences *between* the moral perspectives of men and women, it also threatens to ignore the acute conflicts of identity which occur *within* the lives of many women. Thus, while Held correctly notes the extent to which considerations of care inform women's moral judgements, she is silent on the extent to which care, compassion and the raising of children also generate conflicts within women's lives as they strive, for example, to combine domestic duties with professional duties. In the modern world, being a mother is only one role which is occupied by many women, and this role must be reconciled with other, often incompatible, roles. Again, this is not to deny that, for example, considerations of compassion ought to enter into the workplace, or into wider society. It is simply to note that care is a problematic concept: at the individual level, it may become 'chronic self-denial', whilst at the political level it may serve as an inadequate (and financially expedient) substitute for justice.

Put bluntly, the identification of women with care has nostalgic overtones, and threatens to result in a dangerously romantic conception of domesticity: romantic, because it idealises the maternal role, while remaining almost wholly silent as to its frustrations. Dangerous, because it implies a conceptual link between maternal virtues and political virtues. In fact, however, the disanalogies between the two are quite striking, and it is far from clear how maternal virtues are related to political ones. Specifically, mother-child relationships are characterised by an intimacy wholly lacking in relationships between citizens. As Mary Dietz has pointed out;

> the bond among citizens is not like the love between a mother and child, for citizens are not intimately, but politically involved with each other . . . citizens do not, because they cannot, relate to one another as brother does to brother, or mother does to child. We look in the wrong place for a model of democratic citizenship if we look to the family (even when we have carefully defined the family). [10]

Moreover, the relationship between mother and child, unlike the relationship between citizens, is not one of equality, but one of hierarchy, and in this respect too the mother-child relationship is simply not analogous to the relationship between citizens. Maternal virtues are therefore different from citizen virtues both in respect of intimacy and in respect of hierarchy. Feminist emphasis on care and compassion thus generates three distinct but related worries: the first is that its emphasis on difference implies a view of women which, historically, has been associated with policies of political exclusion. The second is that it implies an over-simple, and static, view of female identity, which misdescribes women's role in modern life, and the third is that it appeals to an inappropriate analogy between familial and political relationships.

However, Dietz's argument that there is a difference of kind between familial and political relationships ignores the persuasive power of the analogy both for feminists and for communitarians. Feminists are not alone in urging that politics should be informed by the actual relationships which invest individuals' lives with meaning and significance, and it is here that the nostalgic nature of both feminism and (some forms of) communitarianism becomes most apparent.

By urging the centrality of face-to-face relationships, proponents of the ethics of care hope to render political life an extension of family life. This may be an appropriate aim in societies which are small-scale, and where face-to-face relationships are the norm. But in large, anonymous, post-industrial societies the analogy becomes diminishingly useful or plausible. In brief, an ethic of care seems best suited to small-scale societies where face-to-face relationships are the norm. But these societies are not the ones which we now have. Modern society is large, sprawling, and anonymous. And whilst we might wish that it were not so, the insistence on an ethic which emphasises actual relationships may nevertheless appear nostalgic and untrue to the realities of modern life.

In this respect, the problems inherent in an ethic of care are akin to the problems encountered by those forms of socialism which emphasise the importance of small communities and the face-to-face relationships which they foster. Speaking about these forms of socialism David Miller notes;

> Socialism became a popular ideology precisely in response to the breakup of traditional communities under the impact of the industrial revolution. It became popular because it promised to restore the coherent moral life found in disappearing communities, whilst at the same time providing all the material (and other) benefits of industrialization. But these two promises could never be fulfilled together. In industrial societies the appeal to community is always nostalgic and backward looking, whatever its proponents may think. [11]

And we may have a similar worry about the ethic of care, for in so far as this too promises to restore the coherence of moral life, it too is vulnerable to the charge of nostalgia and lack of realism about the facts of the modern world. The theoretical worry which is generated by these thoughts is simply that, in the modern world, the concept of care is too weak to do the work required of it: unsupported by considerations of justice and equality, care may simply not extend reliably beyond the immediacy of one's own family, or group, or clan, to the wider world of unknown others. If identity and morality are constituted by actual relationships of care between particular people, they will not easily translate to the wider political problems of world hunger, poverty and war, which involve vast numbers of unknown people. Writing on this subject, Michael Ignatieff says;

> We recognize our humanity in our differences, in our individuality, our history, in the faithful discharge of our particular culture of obligations. There is no identity we can recognize in our universality. There is no such thing as love of the human race, only the love of this person for that, in this time and not in any other. [12]

Ignatieff's concern (that we are psychologically unable to extend care beyond those whom we know) may be supplemented by a further concern, which is whether care remains a good when applied undiluted to large-scale, political problems. Perhaps our problem is not simply that it is psychologically difficult to care for those who are distant from and unknown to us, but rather that care may be morally transformed when it is extended to such contexts.

This point may be clarified if we concentrate less on the perspective of the carer, and more on the perspective of the recipient of care. The ethics of care draws our attention to qualities which are prominent in dealing with those whom we know and love, and it urges that, via an extension of sympathy, those same qualities may be extended to unknown others. Thus, we should construe our relationship to (unknown) fellow citizens on the model of our relationship to members of our own family. So expressed, the ethic of care merely urges an enlargement of the scope of individual sympathy. However, from the recipient's perspective, the situation may be rather different: to be the recipient of sympathy from a stranger can often be offensive and unwelcome. Often, what is desired is not the compassion of someone better off than ourselves, but rather a recognition of our claims in terms of justice and equality. The substitution of compassion for justice at the political level was, after all, responsible for some of the most morally disreputable aspects of Victorian Poor Law, and this should serve as a warning against unbridled enthusiasm for the extension of care in addressing the problems of politics in the modern world.

In making this last point, I am not suggesting that compassion from a stranger can never be welcome or appropriate. Nor am I suggesting that compassion from friends and family is always welcome. Rather, the point is simply that, on the political level, too much emphasis on care may serve to disguise the requirements of justice and equality. Anne Phillips makes a similar point in noting that

> the contrast between (male) abstraction and (female) specificity is running like wildfire through much contemporary feminist debate, and if the implication is that the latter is superior to the former then I simply do not agree. Compassion cannot substitute for the impartiality of justice and equality, for compassion is potentially limited to those we can understand — and hence those who are most like ourselves. For feminists in particular, this would be a risky road to pursue, and it was precisely the demand for equality across seemingly impassable barriers of incomprehension and difference that gave birth to the feminist tradition. [13]

In the political context, therefore, the language of care presents two threats: the first is that it will simply result (indeed, has resulted) in those who present themselves as caring being required to carry the entire burden of welfare provision: the history of care in the community has been the history of dependence on women, whose role as carers has substituted for state provision. Thus, in Britain, the 1981 White Paper (*Growing Older*) asserted that

> the primary sources of support and care for elderly people are informal and voluntary. These spring from the personal ties of kinship, friendship and neighbourhood . . . It is the role of public authorities to sustain and, where

necessary, develop — but never to displace — such support and care. Care *in* the community must increasingly mean care *by* the community. [14]

Where the family unit, or the neighbourhood, has been seen as the primary locus of care, women have taken a disproportionate responsibility for the provision of that care. And the situation is unlikely to be improved by feminist adherence to an ethic of care which emphasises women's 'natural' propensities in this area.

More worrying even than this, however, is the consideration that care is necessarily particularised. It is not mere lack of imagination, but logic (the logical problem inherent in legislating care or compassion) which precludes its extension beyond friends and family. Of course, we may well feel compassion for the inhabitants of 'Cardboard City', for the unemployed, or for the hungry, but it does not follow that this emotion, on its own, provides the best foundation for political policies of welfare. On the contrary, the development of the modern welfare state was self-consciously a development away from the model of rich caring for poor and towards a model of entitlement for all, whether rich or poor. Such a development need not be motivated by scepticism about people's willingness (or ability) to extend care to a wider public. It may also be motivated by the recognition that when care is so extended, it can imply a loss of dignity for the recipient, and a convenient way of disguising the fact that he or she has claims in justice.

Put bluntly, the dilemma which faces care theorists is this: if caring is contained within the family, it will tend to lead in the direction of increased insistence that women are the most appropriate carers. But if extended beyond the family to public policy, it will threaten a return to a conception of the welfare state which is based not on entitlement but on charity.

My concern about the ethic of care therefore has two facets: on an individual level, it gives a simplistic and static account of modern identity, one which ignores the conflict and fragmentation inherent in it; and on a wider, political level it renders problematic our response to the needs of strangers. Nevertheless, I believe that an ethic of care does contain important insights which can avoid these difficulties, and I therefore turn now to a proposed reconstruction which, I hope, will indicate the importance of care in moral and political philosophy.

## Care and the Case of Antigone

In criticising the language of care as a language appropriate for the political problems of modern society, I urged a distinction between the perspective of those who provide care, and the perspective of those who are the recipients of care. Displaying compassion for unknown others may seem (for the donor) merely a matter of enlarging and extending the virtue of sympathy. But receiving compassion from unknown others is often perceived (by the recipient) as morally different from receiving compassion from friends and family. Specifically, when care is institutionalised, it may undermine the claims of justice, and present entitlements as mere favours. By concentrating on the perspective of the donor rather than the recipient, therefore, an ethic of care runs the risk of mis-understanding its own central virtue.

Similarly, but more generally, we may wonder whether the ethics of care would acquire a different status if we were to shift attention from the 'active' to the 'passive', and think about care not as something chosen by the carer, but rather as an obligation upon the carer, which is often unchosen, yet remains an obligation. It is this issue which I shall now address.

Earlier in the paper I made reference to the contrast drawn by Kittay and Meyers between an ethic of care and an ethic of universal reason. They say;

> A morality of rights and abstract reason begins with a moral agent who is separate from others, and who independently elects moral principles to obey. In contrast, a morality of responsibility and care begins with a self who is enmeshed in a network of relations to others and whose moral deliberation aims to maintain these relations. [15]

As we have seen, proponents of an ethic of care then concentrate on the particularities of actual relationships and on the emotions and commitments which sustain them. In other words, they concentrate on the *activity* of the moral agent as one who exhibits qualities of care. But there is a second insight in the contrast, which often goes unremarked. This is that moral life may be a matter of what is given, just as much as it is a matter of what is chosen. What is characteristic of women's lives is not simply that they give priority to the activity of caring, but also that their traditional role as carers constrains their ability to determine their own lives: as carers, women are frequently victims of their circumstances, rather than creators of their lives. Thus, where a morality of rights emphasises the individual as *agent* (as one who *elects* moral principles to live by), feminist morality should emphasise the individual as *recipient* (as one who *recognises* and *accepts* obligations which must be discharged).

The classic example here is Antigone, who is the tragic victim of the conflicting obligations dictated by her roles as sister, daughter, and citizen. Sophocles' play is replete with references to these obligations and the effects of their claims upon Antigone. Thus, it begins with the cry 'O sister!', and Antigone goes on immediately to describe 'the death of our two brothers' and how she and Ismene are doomed to suffer 'for our father'. Modern feminists have sometimes interpreted Antigone's situation as one in which familial, or domestic considerations take priority over political ones. They understand her tragic choice as a choice of private over public virtue; of care over justice. Thus, Jean Elshtain argues that the play is to be seen as the drama of a woman pitted against 'the arrogant insistencies of statecraft', a defender of 'the domain of women' and 'primordial family morality'. [16] Faced with conflict, Antigone defies the abstract obligations of the state and rejects public life in favour of familial bonds: she rejects the 'male' language of justice in favour of the 'female' language of care. But read in this way, both the tragic nature of the play, and its political dimension, remain unexplained.

Responding to the demand for a political interpretation of Antigone's dilemma, Mary Dietz argues that Elshtain's account is both anachronistic (since the public-private distinction is essentially a liberal construct) and blind to the transformation of private into public which characterises Antigone's action. Dietz says;

> The reason why Antigone is a heroine and Ismene is not has nothing to do with 'private' or 'familial' virtues, for both sisters loved their brother. The difference between them has to do with political consciousness. Antigone understands that Creon's refusal to allow Polyneices's burial is not just a singular personal insult, but a collective political threat. The former may be countered with a 'modest silence' or supplication; the latter demands decisive political action. Antigone takes such action; Ismene does not. [17]

But neither Dietz nor Elshtain provides a full explanation of the essentially *tragic* nature of

Antigone's dilemma: it is not the battle between private and public, nor the transformation of private into public which makes Antigone a tragic heroine. For tragedy, what is required is reference to the inevitability and inescapability of her situation. The references to conflicting roles (sister, daughter, citizen) none of which may voluntarily be renounced, provide the clue to Antigone's tragedy and also, I suggest, to the way in which feminist theory may have application to political practice.

What is of crucial importance to the tragedy of Antigone is the extent to which the roles she occupies are multiple, unchosen, and in conflict. She is not simply the champion of domesticity who must suffer for her cause; nor is she merely the translator of private actions into political language. Her role is essentially one which is given rather than chosen — she is the bearer of inconsistent obligations which she neither controls nor chooses, yet which she must honour. Since her obligations conflict, she cannot discharge them all. But since they are all, and equally, obligations, she cannot renounce them without dishonour. Thus, the key moral distinction is not between the family and the polity, nor between the private and the public, but between the chosen and the given.

Antigone is characterised by her recognition of the 'givenness' of moral life and of the extent to which it renders us vulnerable to the inconsistent demands of different duties. If we understand feminist ethics as an ethic which emphasises this, then we will, I believe, be in a position to alleviate the two problems mentioned earlier: we will be able to construct an account of female identity which answers to the complex realities of women's lives, and we will have a more fruitful perspective on the relationship between feminist morality and the claims of politics.

This way of interpreting Antigone's situation enables us to distinguish between two distinct objections to an ethic of justice. We may note that justice is only one value amongst many, and that different kinds of people will give priority to different values. This objection, which has been emphasised by feminists, is powerful but also problematic, for it threatens to create an unbridgeable gulf both between men and women, and between those who are the natural recipients of our care (those who are close to us) and those who are not (those who are distant from us). Unless we can extend care indefinitely, an ethic of care, so understood, will remain unhelpful in dealing with political problems which concern a wider world of unknown others. But as we have seen, the indefinite extension of care is both psychologically and conceptually problematic.

By contrast, if our objection to an ethic of justice is to its assumption of voluntariness, then we may overcome both these problems. On this account, what is important about the experience of women is not simply that as mothers they care for their children, but also that, as mothers, they are the occupiers of a role. The duties associated with that role constrain women's ability to lead the life of an independent free chooser (they exhibit the incompleteness of an ethic of justice understood as an ethic of choice), and they also conflict with the duties associated with other roles. [18] Moreover, these features of moral life are neither a function of biological determinism nor of social conditioning. They are facts about human life quite generally, but facts which may be more apparent to women, particularly to women who straddle the public-private divide as they attempt to combine the role and status of mother with other roles and aspirations. Emphasis on mothers as the occupiers of roles thus suggests and reflects the unchosen nature of much of moral life: it suggests, with Antigone, that there are responsibilities which are ours 'whether we like it or not', and it suggests that those responsibilities may not always fit very easily together. Connectedly, if we understand an ethic of care as an ethic which emphasises the 'givenness' of moral life, we may also be better placed to avoid regressive or conservative political conclusions. Earlier I suggested that the asssertion of difference, coupled with the implication of moral superiority, may generate an ethic with distinctly elitist political implications. To avoid this, feminist ethics must eschew the language of difference and concentrate instead on the similarities which unite us all. But isn't this to revert to an ethic of justice, with all its associated problems of alienation and impersonality? Not necessarily.

An ethic of justice is characterised not simply by the centrality it accords to universality, but also by the emphasis it places on individual autonomy and the role of choice in the selection of moral ends. Feminist theorists have concentrated on the former and, in so doing, have drawn attention to psychological differences between the moral development of men and women. But the latter claim also stands in need of scrutiny. Communitarians, objecting to the prominence of choice in liberal theory, insist that we are 'partly defined by the communities we inhabit', that we are constituted by our attachments to others and by the social context in which those attachments occur. And these societal values and constitutive attachments are almost invariably interpreted as both valuable and benign. Thus Sandel notes that I may owe to others more than justice requires or even permits, 'not by reason of agreements I have made but instead in virtue of those more or less enduring attachments and commitments which taken together partly define the person I am'. [19] By drawing attention to the unchosen roles which we occupy, communitarians hope to exhibit the deficiences in the liberal conception of the self as autonomous chooser. But, so understood, communitarianism lacks a political dimension. The neighbourhoods, homes, and communities in which identity is formed are private not public arenas. And, as Kukathas and Pettit have recently pointed out, 'when political questions arise, they often do because of conflicts among these antecedently individuated communities and persons — among these already existing identities'. [20]

Thus, communitarianism recognises that our social and moral situation is often given rather than chosen, but is silent as to the conflicts which may occur between it and a wider public world. A feminist ethic of care can make good this defect if it responds *both* to liberalism's insistence on choice, *and* to communitarianism's neglect of conflict. Again, the experience of mothers may be useful in one of two ways: we may employ it to draw attention to the fact that obligations are not invariably chosen, and we may also employ it to draw attention to the fact that obligations are not always consistent. If feminist ethics simply extols maternal virtues, then it will conspire with communitarianism to exclude women from the political realm.

There are therefore three conditions which feminist ethics must satisfy if it is to have any hope of generating feminist politics. Firstly, it must avoid appeal to women's 'special' or 'different' voice, since the different voice is a domestic voice, and domestic virtues are deformed when they are translated to a public world. Secondly, and connectedly, it must reject liberal emphasis on the activity of moral life and concentrate instead on the extent to which moral obligations are associated with roles and are unchosen (in this sense, it must ally itself with the communitarian critics of liberalism). Finally, and most importantly, it must distance itself from communitarianism by insisting that the social contexts in which obligations arise are diverse and conflicting. They are the source of pain and, at the limit, of tragedy. Since historically women have often been defined by their social roles, this is a point which they are well-placed to make. It is not, however, a point unique to women, but a quite general point about human beings. Indeed, it is an unavoidable consequence of any attempt to move between different communities, and therefore a necessary condition of feminist theory's ability to deliver a practical politics which will do justice to the facts of women's lives. [21]

*Susan Mendus, Department of Politics, University of York, York YO1 5DD, UK*

## NOTES

[1] CAROL GILLIGAN, *In A Different Voice* (Cambridge, Mass.: Harvard University Press, 1982), 159–160.

[2] G. W. F. HEGEL, *The Philosophy of Right*, trans. T. M. Knox (Oxford: University Press, 1952), 264.

[3] J. J. ROUSSEAU *Emile*: *Oeuvres Completes de Jean-Jacques Rousseau*, IV, 693.

[4] ANNE PHILLIPS, 'So What's Wrong with the Individual?', *Socialism and the Limits of Liberalism*, Peter Osborne (ed.) (London: Verso, 1991), 147.

[5] VIRGINIA HELD 'Liberty and Equality from a Feminist Perspective', *Enlightenment, Rights and Revolution*, N. MacCormick and Z. Bankowski (eds.) (Aberdeen: University Press, 1989), 225.

[6] CHESHIRE CALHOUN 'Justice, Care, Gender Bias' *Journal of Philosophy*, LXXXV (1988), 456.

[7] EVA FEDER KITTAY and DIANA T. MEYERS (eds.) *Women and Moral Theory*, (U.S.A. Rowman and Littlefield, 1987), 10.

[8] op.cit. note 5, 225–226.

[9] For a full discussion of this point see ANNE PHILLIPS, op.cit., note 4.

[10] MARY DIETZ, 'Citizenship With a Feminist Face: The Problem With Maternal Thinking', *Political Theory*, 13 (1985), 31.

[11] DAVID MILLER, 'In What Sense Must Socialism Be Communitarian?' *Social Philosophy and Policy*, 5 (1989), 66–67.

[12] MICHAEL IGNATIEFF, *The Needs of Strangers* (London: Hogarth, 1984), 42.

[13] op.cit. note 4, 156.

[14] As quoted in GILLIAN PARKER *With Due Care and Attention: A Review of research on Informal Care* (London: Family Policy Studies Centre, 1985), 5.

[15] op.cit. note 7, 10.

[16] JEAN ELSHTAIN, 'Antigone's Daughters' *Democracy*, 2, (1982), 46–59. As quoted in Dietz, 'Citizenship With a Feminist Face'.

[17] op.cit. note 10, 29.

[18] David Miller has suggested to me that, in fact, Gilligan objects only to the conception of justice as a system of formal rules; not to the assumption of voluntariness in many theories of justice. His point draws attention to Gilligan's unwillingness to consider the possibility that there might be different conceptions of justice. I do not consider this here, but the point is admirably discussed by ANDREW MASON in *Journal of the Theory of Social Behaviour*, 1990.

[19] MICHAEL SANDEL, *Liberalism and the Limits of Justice* (Cambridge: University Press, 1982), 179.

[20] CHANDRAN KUKATHAS and PHILIP PETTIT, *Rawls: A Theory of Justice and Its Critics*, (Oxford and Cambridge: Polity, 1990), 109.

[21] I am grateful to David Miller for his incisive written comments on an earlier draft of this paper, and also to Sally Baldwin, Gillian Parker, Julia Twigg, and other members of the Social Policy Research Unit at the University of York for helpful discussions on the social policy of care. My thanks also go to the anonymous reader for the *Journal*, who provided very constructive suggestions for revision, which I have tried to incorporate.

# [8]

## FEMINIST FEARS IN ETHICS

Nel Noddings

An ethic of care has received considerable attention in the past few years. Some see the ethic as an important "female ethic." But others argue that the emphasis on gender in the ethics of care may impede progress toward an adequate moral theory [Flanagan and Jackson 1987; Okin 1989; Tronto 1987]. This objection is more a political concern than a theoretical one, although one could, of course, argue that a genderized ethic is necessarily inadequate theoretically. However feminists have long argued that political and theoretical concerns cannot be easily separated. Therefore, the fears that some feminists have expressed about the relation of an ethic of caring to women's betterment are important to feminism as a political movement and also, from a feminist perspective, to the development of an adequate ethical theory. In this paper I will discuss several fears that feminists have raised about the ethics of care and attempt to respond to them.

### 1. The Difference Debate

The main fear of feminists is that any theoretical position that claims a difference between women and men will inevitably work to women's disadvantage. Several of the fears to be discussed in later sections—fears particular to features of the ethic of care—can be subsumed under this major concern. In a society characterized by large differences in power between men and women, it is unlikely that anything claimed as distinctively or chiefly feminine (or female, or belonging to women) will be highly valued. Therefore, the claim that an ethic of care is properly identified with women is self-defeating. Tronto makes this point explicit: "It is a strategically dangerous position for feminists because the simple assertion of gender difference in a social context that identifies the male as normal contains an implication of the inferiority of the distinctly female" [1987: 646].

On careful thought, it turns out that arguments for sameness do not work very well either. To argue that there is no difference—that women are the same as men—is to subject women to standards developed entirely from the needs and experience of men. As Catherine MacKinnon has so forcefully pointed out, this approach (arguing for either sameness or difference) conceals "the substantive way in which man has become the measure of all things" [1987: 34]. MacKinnon advises concentration on the domination inherent in the cultural construction of gender and a vigorous campaign to redistribute power.

Although I agree with MacKinnon that we must find a way to eliminate domination, I think she is mistaken in supposing that this campaign can go on without a thorough examination of women's culture. By "women's culture" I mean the set of experiences more likely to be women's than men's and the meanings that women have attached to these experiences. Some political decisions can be made without such an examination. For example, any reasonable person ought to expect and demand equal pay for equal work. But other decisions require an analysis and re-evaluation of women's traditional experience. For example, what value should be put on the following: teaching and caring for young children, caring directly for the elderly, nursing and teaching as professions, volunteer vs. paid work, raising one's own children, and revising the school curriculum to reflect values traditionally associated with women? To discuss these matters reasonably, a recognition of difference is at least implied.

But what is the locus of this difference? I would not want to give an essentialist argument; that is, I reject the hypothesis that women and men are essentially, innately, different in emotional, intellectual, or moral makeup. However, it is obvious that women and men have had different kinds of experience and, further, our society's expectations and demands for their experience have differed. Thus, far more women than men have had actual experience in the areas listed above, and even when women have avoided such experience, they—and not men—have suffered consequences for that avoidance. For example, female academics early in this century were expected to resign their professional positions when they married, and they were considered "unnatural" if they were less than enthusiastic about resigning [Rossiter 1982]. It was believed that married women (especially mothers) could not be adequate professionals, but if a woman tried to demonstrate or actually succeeded in demonstrating her professional adequacy, she was demeaned and found to be inadequate as a woman.

The experience just described is clearly an example of the power differences MacKinnon emphasizes. But raising children, caring for the elderly, maintaining a supportive home environment, nursing, and teaching are not only activities identified with oppression. They are activities in which women have exercised agency, from which a distinctive morality may indeed emerge, and in which, we might argue, all human beings should be prepared to engage [Martin 1984, 1985, 1987]. They are activities in which all persons should be prepared to engage because they are the fundamental activities of human life.

I would not hesitate, then, to claim a substantial difference between men and women on the basis of experience and socialization, but here at least two problems arise—one seemingly easy to solve, the other enormously difficult. The first is one of language. In my own work, I have always intended to rely on women's experience, *not* women's nature, to build my arguments for an ethic of care. But I wasn't as careful earlier as I am now, and there are places where I've used the words "nature" and, more often, "naturally." I tried to explain this usage by referring to centuries of fairly stable experience that might indeed induce something like a "feminine nature." But now I think it may be best simply to avoid such language entirely.

A similar problem arises in the work of Carol Gilligan (1982) and Sara Ruddick (1980, 1989). Gilligan is often misunderstood as claiming that the "different voice" she identified in moral theory is women's voice—a voice different from men's. In fact, the voice is different from the one that speaks exclusively or emphatically in terms of rights and justice. But the different voice was discovered in conversations with women, and it probably is more often heard from women than from men. This predictable result can be traced to experience and socialization. Similarly, Ruddick has drawn fire for putting moral emphasis on maternal thinking, thereby—say her critics—excluding men. But Ruddick has said that men, too, are capable of maternal thinking. It is just that people not engaged in activities requiring attentive love to dependent beings are not likely to develop it; that is, maternal thought is unlikely to develop through mere intellectual processes. I said that this language problem is seemingly easy to solve, but in reality it is difficult, not only because avoiding misunderstanding requires constant vigilance but also because the favored, privileged language is largely a product of masculine experience.

The second problem is one of analyzing experience and socialization. I make a distinction between the two as noted earlier. Even a woman who rejects traditional female experience has been subjected to a process of socialization that can make her uncomfortable with nontraditional choices. As traditional patterns of socialization change, young women may feel pressed to reject traditional experience. (This is already happening to a small but important group of educated women.) Without a thorough analysis of women's traditional experience, a sorting of cherished values from those to be abandoned, and a conscious celebration of the best in women's culture, that culture may be lost. And with it goes the foundation of fully human life.

It may be relatively easy to socialize young women to upgrade their education in, say, mathematics and science. They, as traditional underdogs, have much to gain by doing so. But it will be extremely difficult to socialize young men to upgrade their education so that they are prepared to care for young children, give direct care to the elderly, nurse the ill, be the full psychological parents of their own children. In addition to putting a social stamp of approval on these activities—real men do these things!—we must also provide preparation through concrete experience in doing them.

Finally, traditional female experience has to be incorporated into the school curriculum. Socialization will operate in only one direction unless this happens, and the end result could be a world filled with females and males all thinking and behaving in traditional male ways. If anyone doubts that there is an enormous difference between male and female experience, let him or her take a close look at the school curriculum. The traditional interests of women, the undergirding of a whole human culture, are either absent entirely or relegated to classes for teenage mothers where they are often distorted by the alien structures of schooling.

We have to work with difference—not essential difference, but experiential difference. However, accepting and working with difference does not preclude pushing for changes in power relations as MacKinnon has advised. In particular, analysis of experiential difference guides us to the situations where power differences are most frightening. We are directed to look at the educational deprivation of our young men and the one-sided nature of schooling. Stressing difference is risky, but denying it may cost more than we can afford to pay—the possibility of achieving a full human identity.

To conclude this section: What do we mean when we refer to caring as a female ethic? Certainly we do not mean that it is one applicable only in women's traditional domains, nor do we mean that only women embrace it. We mean that it arises more reliably out of the logic of women's traditional experience than it does out of traditional male experience. If the ethic of care is valuable, that makes an argument for changing the experience of men, not for rejecting the experience of women.

## 2. Principles

Among the greatest fears of feminists is that the de-emphasis of principles in an ethic of care will re-activate men's charge that women can't use principles. Feminist philosophers are aware of that charge made continually since the days of Aristotle. Even Kant said; "I hardly believe that the fair sex is capable of principles,...." Recognizing this assessment and confessing herself fearful of maintaining or re-awakening it, Jean Grimshaw writes:

> I think there are real dangers that a representation of women's moral reasoning based on such a sharp opposition will merely become a shadow of the belief that women perceive and act intuitively, situationally, pragmatically, "from the heart," and that their processes of *reasoning*, if they exist at all, are nebulous and unfathomable. [1986: 211]

But we should not let fear drive ethical theory. To begin with, rationality and reasoning involve more than the identification of principles and their deductive application. To evaluate the use of principles as minimally useful in ethics is very different from confessing oneself unable to use them. Such evaluation itself requires careful reasoning. Further, there is some empirical evidence to back up the claim that caring may motivate people to appropriate moral action more reliably than reflection on principles. In their impressive study of rescuers (non-Jews who, at considerable personal risk, saved Jews during the Holocaust), the Oliners [1988] found that only about 11 percent acted from principle. All the others responded either directly out of compassion or from a sense of themselves as decent, caring people.

Is it possible, some theorists ask, that these people who report acting directly from compassion or sense of ethical self are really using implicit principles? I contend that there is a greater danger in arguing this way than in denying the use of principles. Grimshaw, in an otherwise rigorous and commendable analysis, suggests that women may in fact use principles implicitly. In support of her claim, she tells the story of her parents who both thought it was wrong for a man and woman to live together without being married. Her father backed up his rule against such behavior by deciding that he would not visit his daughter, for doing so would violate his principle against condoning morally wrong behavior. However, her mother continued to visit her daughter. Whereas I would say that her mother put persons over principles and employed caring as a mode of moral life, Grimshaw says that her mother held the same principle as her father but, in addition, used an implicit principle, "Consider whether your behavior will stand in the way of maintaining care and relationships" [209]. This additional principle, Grimshaw suggests, overrode the first and allowed her mother to continue visiting her daughter while at the same time expressing her disapproval of the living arrangement.

Now it seems to me that, considering what a Kantian might say, this account is clearly more dangerous than mine. I argue that a moral agent can act—thoughtfully, reflectively—in direct response to human need and feeling. One need not always refer to principles, and it may be that actual moral agents in real world activity rarely use them. But Grimshaw allows the implicit use of principles. Surely Kant would say that such use proves his point about women. For Kant, use of principles must be explicit. One only gets moral credit for acts done out of *commitment* to principle. This means that one must have formulated a principle, reflected on it, and willed oneself to live by it. "Implicit" use, for Kant, is no use at all!

The problem here seems to be a conflation of scientific and ethical principles. We might indeed describe the behavior of Grimshaw's mother and many other moral agents as "principled" in the sense that we can observe certain commendable regularities in it. We can predict with some reliability how those people will behave. But this does not imply that their behavior is chosen in commitment to a principle. An ethical principle does not merely describe behavior.

But, others might argue, there *does* seem to be an ethical principle operating in the ethic of care. It looks like this: Always act so as to create, maintain, or enhance caring relations. Why isn't this a principle? I concede that one might cast things in this way, but why do it? If this is a principle, it certainly does not provide the sort of procedural guidance given by Kant's categorical imperative. I cannot, using it, lock myself in my study and decide logically what must be done. It is not a principle that depends strictly on logical inference, and I cannot deduce from it a subset of absolutes on stealing, killing, lying, and the like. It can only remind me that I must stay in contact with those concerned about the problem at hand. I must remain receptive and responsive to needs and desires. What I might logically decide at the outset may be overturned as I listen to those I must care for. There is no recipe for caring and no algorithm for deciding.

Finally, there may be more danger than help in considering a "principle of care," for we are accustomed to think of principles as productive of decision-making procedures. This is exactly what an ethic of care rejects. There is no objection to the unproblematic, day-to-day use of principles as general guides to dependable behavior. Our objection is to the underlying premise that one can deduce from them particular behaviors or patterns of behavior that can rule over all of moral life. The truth seems to be almost the reverse. Because certain regularities of moral life have been established and observed, we are able to state certain "principles," but these principles are minimally useful in new and genuinely puzzling situations. Here we do better to rely on a way of being, a basic condition of receptivity or empathy, that connects us to living others.

### 3. Autonomy and Relatedness

Philosophers have discussed at least four meanings of autonomy [Christman 1988; Hill 1987]. The first, closely associated with impartiality in the Kantian tradition, will be discussed in the next section. A second is the notion of autonomy as a human right. An emphasis on relatedness arouses fears that women may sacrifice their right to autonomy by emphasizing connection, response, and relation in ethics. A third is the idea of autonomy as a moral ideal and, a fourth—similar to the third—is the notion of autonomy as an ego ideal. Acceptance or rejection of any of these interpretations raises special problems for feminists.

Consider autonomy as a human right. Here we suppose that every normal human adult has a right to make choices without coercion or undue interference. Certainly, this notion of autonomy enjoys widespread acceptance. But when we press the concept, difficulties arise. Exactly what is undue interference? When I make a choice that I suppose is truly my own, can I be sure that it *is* my own? Surely all of us are deeply influenced by individuals with whom we interact, and we are all—at least to some degree—unavoidably affected by socialization [Meyers 1987]. Thus a question arises whether there is such a thing as true autonomy to which we have a right.

Still, because we all like to think of ourselves as people who can make independent choices, we want to protect ourselves from invasions of our "autonomy." For women, claiming autonomy in this sense is especially important, because it has so long been explicitly denied to us. Rousseau, for example, insisted that a woman's goodness depended on her reputation, not on her autonomy. "It follows," he wrote, "that the principle of her education must be in this respect contrary to that of ours [males]: opinion is the tomb of man's virtue and the throne of woman's" [quoted in Okin 1979, 162]. The denial of a right to autonomy was grounded in a denial of women's capacity for it, and so when we reject the impartiality interpretation of autonomy (next section), we risk pulling the foundational carpet from under our feet as moral agents.

Here it is vital to understand that the Kantian description of autonomous capacity is not the only possible grounding for autonomy as a right. Indeed, many philosophers would grant all human beings the right to autonomy without demanding that they pass a strict Kantian test of rationality [see Hill 1987]. An ethic of caring suggests that we consider the capacity of entities to respond rather than a narrow capacity of autonomy based on reason. Each capacity considered would have to be one of which we approve or with which we sympathize; we would not, for example, respect the capacity to inflict suffering and vow not to interfere with it. However, if an entity has the capacity to solve problems, we are obliged not to strip its environment of the possibility for problem solving. If it can suffer, we must not inflict suffering, and we must alleviate it if we are in a position to do so. If it shows affection for its young, we must not separate it from its young or block the expression of affection. If it can express preferences, we must attend to the expression and be cautious in denying a preference.

This last raises a question that is thorny in all ethical theories. When is it permissible to violate another's autonomy for his or her own good? The abandonment of a holistic notion of autonomy in favor of a wide range of respected capacities for response may give some guidance on this problem. Thomas Hill [1987] suggests that there may be occasional conflicts between autonomy and compassion; that is, we may sometimes have to violate another's autonomy out of a clear sense of what is best for the other. In our alternative framework, caring directs us to consider the full range of an entity's capacities. Thus we may occasionally have to interfere with the capacity of persons to make choices in order to preserve their lives, restore their capacities to reflect, or maintain their capacities to relate. But such acts are not wholesale affronts to "autonomy." On the contrary, they are properly done in order to preserve valued capacities, and they must be justified on such grounds.

Let's consider now the notion of autonomy as a moral ideal. Hill [1987] suggests that we concentrate here on the idea of autonomy as self-governance. Again, there is widespread intuitive understanding of what "self-governance " means. It is what every elementary school teacher hopes to instill in her pupils. When they can behave well while teacher is out of the room, they have achieved what their teacher thinks of as self-governance. But, of course, questions immediately arise whether such behavior is truly autonomous or just the product of thorough socialization.

In traditional ethics, the ideal of self-governance requires a carefully constructed and meticulously analyzed set of rules and principles to which an agent will turn for moral guidance. This set is built by (or discovered by) and built into the moral agent through strictly logical processes. An ideal agent can set aside the effects of socialization by examining each effect reflectively—accepting those that pass the hard tests of logical reason and rejecting those that fail. The result, ideally, is a universal or 'true' ethical self that does not reflect the idiosyncrasies of particular individuals.

Feminists who prefer an ethic of care or a "communicative ethic" (Benhabib 1987) accuse traditional ethics of building on an epistemological blindness to the needs of particular others. Benhabib says that such blindness is "an internal inconsistency in universalistic moral theories" [91]: The methods required by universalizability ensure that a moral agent will *not* be able to take the standpoint of a particular other. All such an agent can take into account is the "generalized" other.

But, although advocates of caring or Benhabib's communicative ethics reject the notion of a generalized true self, they do not reject the idea that moral agents must have a way of monitoring and governing their own behavior. They reject, first, the notion of a universalistic true self and, second, the assumption that such governance must proceed by well defined rules. Diana Meyers [1987] suggests an alternative to impartial and universalistic reason in "responsibility reasoning." This form of reasoning is part of what Kari Waerness [1984] has called the "rationality of caring." It places the moral agent in a position of responsibility to assess needs, evaluate their legitimacy (from the explicit perspectives of all those involved), and respond in a way that creates, maintains, or enhances caring relations.

Meyers [1987] agrees that a person using responsibility reasoning needs a procedure to govern her or his moral decisions and behavior. She suggests "the person's sense of her own identity" [151] as a filter. I [Noddings 1984] have suggested the ethical ideal defined as a reflectively constructed set of memories of caring and being cared for. It contains our best and worst moments, each carefully evaluated for its effects on others and on us as carers. When we are faced with responsibility for the needs of others, we either respond spontaneously with care and compassion (and this *is* a moral response) or, in times of conflict or indecision, we consult our ethical ideal. How would I behave now if I were guided by my best moments as a carer?

It can be argued, then, that an ethic of care incorporates a procedure for self-governance. Further, the ethical ideal as described in *Caring* is a product of each individual's quest to enter and remain in caring relations. The ideal itself is not universalistic. It varies properly from individual to individual. But it escapes radical relativism because it is constructed on a universal desire for connection.

Although the ethic of care (or communication or responsibility) can satisfy the traditional demand for a governance procedure, I would caution against describing this as an entirely self-governing or autonomous procedure. The ethical ideal is highly sensitive to the needs, values and suggestions of others. Indeed, an ethic of care is built on a relational ontology that stresses address and response. This ethic requires an ethical ideal that remains open and sensitive to possible instruction. In dialogue with others, we may put a new construal on old memories. The ideal provides guidance and stability, but it never closes off the self in a proud and lonely autonomy. Thus it is not clear that self-governance *should* be the moral ideal. Rather, we seek something more like a well considered, shared, relational ideal of moral governance.

Finally, we must consider the sense of autonomy as ego ideal. An ethic of care induces fear in some feminists (e.g., Card 1990, Hoagland 1990, Houston 1990), because its relational emphasis seems to accept or even aggravate a lack of individuation. Women's ego boundaries have been described as permeable and fluid [Chodorow 1978] in contrast to those of males that are solid and clearly delineated. But, again, it is not clear that this is necessarily a weakness. A relational ego can be a disadvantage in an oppressive society and the fear of exploitation is justified, but, even in such a setting, consideration of relational strengths suggests optimal rather than absolute forms of individuation and an alternative to the form of ego development associated with individualism.

## 4. Impartiality

The association of impartiality with the moral point of view and, in particular, with the first meaning of autonomy noted in the prior section makes it difficult for feminists to reject it. By doing so, we risk denying the base on which autonomy as right and self-governance is built. But I have already suggested that it is a mistake to construe autonomy as one encompassing right and that some optimal form of relational or shared governance is not only closer to the reality of human interaction but, perhaps, more desirable morally than an absolute notion of self-governance.

Feminists are not alone in criticizing impartiality as the central tenet of ethics. For different reasons, both Bernard Williams [1981] and Alasdair MacIntyre [1981] criticize the impartiality criterion. Feminists who fear repercussions from the rejection of impartiality are rightly concerned about its association with biological women. Alison Jaggar [1989], for example, notes that I used the word "feminine" rather than "feminist" in writing about an ethic that rejects impartiality. She is right to object (and I wish I had never used the word), but the idea was to point to a difference in experience, not to a biological difference. If there is something vitally important in that experience, then it is as important to consider as Williams' projects or MacIntyre's communities.

This brings us back to the discussion with which we started. The forms of experience that give rise to caring as a moral orientation are today more available to women than to men. Hence the problematic association of women with ethics of care. But this is not, as we have already seen, a *necessary* association.

Does the rejection of impartiality contribute something positive to political philosophy and social thinking? This is too large a question to tackle here, but I can suggest a positive line of response. When we recognize that dealing with generalized others under a criterion of impartiality often leads to arrogant dismissal of their particular desires and values, to imposition of our own sense of the good on them, and to inadvertent maintenance of the structures of oppression, we have to ask how we can deal with *concrete* others at a distance. From the perspective of caring, we need to establish chains of concrete connection, to adopt a stance of receptivity, and to commit ourselves to "staying with" so that our attempts at caring can be completed. Here again it is necessary to recognize and celebrate difference—not to fear or ignore it. It is also necessary to recognize the limitations on individual attempts to care. We cannot, in any meaningful sense, care for every one. We can only be prepared to care, to recognize our interdependence in caring (sometimes all we can do is support others' efforts to care), and to behave politically in ways likely to establish structures that will support concrete caring relations.

### 5. Conclusion

I have described several feminist fears about ethics of caring and response, and I have argued that we should not let fear drive our attempts to construct an adequate moral theory. In particular, I have explored fears concerning gender difference, the use of principles, ambivalence about autonomy, and the rejection of impartiality. In every case, it seems to me that feminists have more to gain than to lose by pressing forward.

### References


Benhabib, Seyla. 1987. "The generalized and the concrete other." In *Feminism As Critique*, Seyla Benhabib and Drucilla Cornell, eds., 77-95. Minneapolis: University of Minnesota Press.

Card, Claudia. 1990. Caring and evil. *Hypatia* 5(1):101-108.

Chodorow, Nancy. 1978. *The Reproduction of Mothering*. Berkeley: University of California Press.

Christman, John. 1988. Constructing the inner citadel: Recent work on the concept of autonomy. *Ethics* 99(1):109-124.

Flanagan, Owen and Kathryn Jackson. 1987. Justice, care, and gender: The Kohlberg-Gilligan debate revisited. *Ethics* 97(3):622-637.

Gilligan, Carol J. 1982. *In A Different Voice*. Cambridge: Harvard University Press.

Grimshaw, Jean. 1986. *Philosophy and Feminist Thinking*. Minneapolis: University of Minnesota Press.

Hill, Thomas E., Jr. 1987. "The importance of autonomy." In *Women and Moral Theory*, Eva Feder Kittay and Diana T. Meyers, eds., 129-138. Totowa, NJ: Rowman & Littlefield.

Hoagland, Sarah Lucia. 1990. Some concerns about Nel Noddings' *Caring*. *Hypatia* 5(1):109-114.

Houston, Barbara. 1990. Caring and exploitation. *Hypatia* 5(1):115-119.

Jaggar, Alison M. 1989. Feminist ethics: Some issues for the nineties. *Journal of Social Philosophy* 20(1-2):91-107.

MacIntyre, Alasdair. 1981. *After Virtue*. Notre Dame: University of Notre Dame Press.

MacKinnon, Catherine A. 1987. *Feminism Unmodified*. Cambridge: Harvard University Press.

Martin, Jane Roland. 1984. Bringing women into educational thought. *Educational Theory* 34(4):341-354.

Martin, Jane Roland. 1985. *Reclaiming a Conversation*. New Haven, CT: Yale University Press.

Martin, Jane Roland. 1987. Transforming moral education. *Journal of Moral Education* 16(3):204-213.

Meyers, Diana T. 1987. "The socialized individual and individual autonomy: An intersection between philosophy and psychology." In *Women and Moral Theory*, Eva Feder Kittay and Meyers, eds., 139-153. Totowa, NJ: Rowman & Littlefield.

Noddings, Nel. 1984. *Caring: A Feminine Approach to Ethics and Moral Education*. Berkeley: University of California Press.

Okin, Susan Moller. 1979. *Women in Western Political Thought*. Princeton, NJ: Princeton University Press.

Okin, Susan Moller. 1989. Reason and feeling in thinking about justice. *Ethics* 99(2):229-249.

Oliner, Samuel P. & Pearl M. 1988. *The Altruistic Personality: Rescuers of Jews in Nazi Europe*. New York: The Free Press.

Rossiter, Margaret W. 1982. *Women Scientists in America: Struggles and Strategies to 1940*. Baltimore and London: Johns Hopkins University Press.

Ruddick, Sara. 1980. Maternal thinking. *Feminist Studies* 6(2):342-367.

Ruddick, Sara. 1989. *Maternal Thinking: Towards a Politics of Peace*. Boston: Beacon Press.

Tronto, Joan. 1987. Beyond gender difference to a theory of care. *Signs* 12(4):644-663.

Waerness, Kari. 1984. The rationality of caring. *Economic and Industrial Democracy* 5(2):185-212.

Williams, Bernard. 1981. *Moral Luck*. Cambridge: Cambridge University Press.

# [9]

# Caring about Justice

JONATHAN DANCY

## 1

In the post-Gilligan debate about the differences, if any, between the ways in which people of different genders see the moral world in which they live, I detect two assumptions. These can be found in Gilligan's early work, and have infected the thought of others. The first, perhaps surprisingly, is Kohlberg's Kantian account of one moral perspective, the one more easily or more naturally operated by men and which has come to be called the justice perspective. (What I mean by calling this Kantian will emerge shortly.) This is the perspective whose claims Gilligan initially found suspect, not because she thought it a distorted account of the way in which male subjects operated, but because she disputed its claims to be the only account or the best or dominant one. Throughout the ensuing debate Kohlberg's account has been left in place, and challenged not for correctness but only for uniqueness. The second assumption is that since there are two genders, and since the men operate successfully within one moral perspective, there may be a second perspective within which women feel themselves more at home. But there is not likely to be a third, because there are not three genders. But one might ask 'What if there were?'. Would the sort of genetic argument that Gilligan takes from Chodorow be one we could appeal to in order to show that there must be a distinctive perspective for each gender however many genders there are, so long as patterns of nurture and care differ recognizably for each?

Both these assumptions can and will be disputed. For the moment I point out how they combine in Gilligan to suggest that as well as the justice perspective there is another moral perspective, the care perspective. My main concern is to get clearer about the relation between the two perspectives, which involves getting clearer about the nature of each and about which elements of each are central to the contrast between the two. I am not alone in feeling that we have a very unclear understanding of what these two perspectives are supposed to be and how they go or do not go together.

The justice perspective is conceived of in a way that derives largely from Kohlberg's work. But in the literature one can find a very wide variety of different characterizations of it. Here is a list, culled from several sources:

## Jonathan Dancy

1. The key word in the justice perspective is 'obligation'. [The key word for the care perspective is 'need'.]

2. It is driven by a single moral principle—the principle of justice or fairness. It may have other subordinate principles, but this is the dominant one.

3. Its agents are thin Kantian agents, conceived as purely rational beings. If they have emotions, these are not necessary to them for the discovery of moral truth or the making of moral decisions.

4. Its agents are *equal* and *autonomous*. Each makes choices for all, thinking of others as choosers equal with itself in a kingdom of ends.

5. Its agents deal only with relationships of their own choosing (e.g. contracts *freely* entered into). [These last two points are in opposition to an ethic which is intended to concern itself with unequal relationships in which we do not find ourselves entirely by choice, such as the mother-child relationship.]

6. Moral agents are conceived as those who operate by a set of *principles*—the approach here is a principled approach. [This is different from 2, because one could accept 6 without accepting 2.]

7. Moral choice is conceived as the *subsumption* of the situation under one or several moral principles. To decide what to do, we decide which principle applies in our situation, and we then read off what to do from the principle. [This is distinct from 6, for one could hold that though we must have a set of principles, this is not how we are to use them, i.e. one could deny the subsumptive account of rational moral thought and decision offered here. However it is admittedly characteristic of principled accounts to accept a subsumptive account of rationality in general and of practical rationality in particular, assuming that it is only with such an account that we can see our practice as *consistent*. To be consistent is to follow rules consistently, and there must therefore be moral rules (principles) for us to follow if moral practice is to have the sort of consistency required for rationality.]

8. The approach requires a certain *detachment* for its proper operation. The rules are intended to operate impartially (in a way to be captured by the primacy of the rule of justice), and hence the best operator will be one who is not involved or engaged. Detachment is to be preferred to attachment in a moral judge, reliable *observation* of the feelings of others is to be preferred to *sympathy*.

9. The justice perspective, if operating properly, constitutes a *restraint* on us by holding us back from actions we would otherwise choose for their benefits to ourselves and despite the harm they would do to others. By accepting these restraints, we combine to create a society in which the minimum conditions for civilized life are maintained. This is the purpose of morality.

## Caring about Justice

10. The justice perspective is further justified by the fact that it can be expected, when operated properly, to provide *firm answers* even in tricky situations.

11. It therefore maximizes the chance of *agreement* on what is to be done in tricky situations. All can understand and operate the principles, and so where an answer is provided there is a good chance that all will agree on it.

All these eleven features have been commonly attributed to the justice perspective, but one should be wary of the list I have given, for two reasons. The first is that it is built around a conception of Kohlberg's, which has no obvious status. The second is that Kohlberg's fascination with Kant does not necessarily mean that his account of Kant is accurate. From the point of view of Kantian scholarship, several of the elements on my list could be disputed. For present purposes I leave them all in place and go on to look at the opposing perspective, the care perspective. Gilligan says a great many things about the care perspective, not always consistently, but it is clear at least that in her eyes the care perspective lacks all eleven of the features listed above. Instead of showing this one by one, I shall do it so far as possible in blocks. There is a general antipathy to moral principles in the care perspective. At one point Gilligan describes a moral judgment as 'a contextual judgment, bound to the particulars of time and place . . . and thus resisting a categorical formulation'[1]. All moral judgments are thought of in this way, it seems, and so there is no room for the appeal to moral principles that is embodied in items 2, 6 and 7. This does not in itself mean that justice does not appear in another role, as we shall see. Second, the sorts of agents that the care perspective concerns itself with are thick agents, with their emotions prominent in their moral make-up, engaged in relationships of inequality and often not by their own choice. So the care perspective lacks features 3–5. Next, the care perspective champions the virtues of engagement in contrast to detachment, supposing that without engagement, without a real sympathy for each of the persons concerned in the problem facing you, you are in no position to make a moral choice at all. The detached observer is therefore disqualified, not thereby validated as a competent judge of the situation. So the care perspective lacks feature 8. It also prides itself on aiming at more than a minimum level of social subsistence, holding that this sort of aim is compatible with a great deal of manufactured social misery and may even be one of its main causes. It is important to the care perspective that in a way its demands are unlimited. The amount of care that can be called for from us has no happy tendency to fall short of making a

[1] *In a Different Voice* (Cambridge, Mass.: Harvard University Press, 1982), 58–59.

**Jonathan Dancy**

real difference to our lives; so the ethic of care and that of self-sacrifice go together. So the care perspective lacks feature 9. As for the possibility of firm answers and general agreement on them, the care perspective views these as moral aims rather than as achievements without which the approach would be deemed inadequate as a procedure. Here we hear it suggested that if a situation does not admit of a resolution that would command the agreement of all interested parties, we should look to change the situation until we do get agreement. Whereas the justice perspective will give you a 'right' answer no matter how horrible the circumstances, the care perspective is likely to say that since there is no generally acceptable solution as things stand, we must work to change the problem until we get better chances of finding something on which we can all agree.

Before I ask some harder questions about the relation between these two perspectives, I want to say a little about how the difference between them is related to the differences between the genders. Gilligan and others no longer hold that one perspective is distinctive of female thinking and the other of male thinking[2]. Their view is now that each of us can operate with either perspective when called on to do so, and that any problem can be approached from either perspective if we wish. They also admit that some problems lend themselves to resolution from one perspective much more easily than they do from the other. This is because some problems are framed in such a way as to lie naturally within the justice perspective, and hence look as if they could hardly be successfully approached from the care perspective. To borrow the examples of others: the question how much of a foreign loan to cancel and how much to postpone lies naturally within the justice perspective; the question whether to postpone a family holiday so that one member can have needed surgery lies naturally within the care perspective. However there are residual asymmetries between the ways men and women approach moral problems, and this leads us to ask how such differences as there are might support asymmetrical relations of dominance, exploitation and oppression. The first suggestion here is that men are better than women are at framing rules, and so that the prominence of the justice perspective has the effect of imposing on women a series of moral perceptions which make their own perceptions seem wrong-headed and so undermine their moral confidence. However the evidence that men are better at framing rules seems to be a bit

[2] See C. Gilligan and G. Wiggins, 'The Origins of Morality in Early Childhood Relationships', in Kagan, J. and Launch, S. eds *The Emergence of Morality in Young Children* (Cambridge: Harvard, 1987), and O. Flanagan and K. Jackson, 'Justice, Care and Gender: The Post-Gilligan Debate Revisited', *Ethics* 97 (1987), 622–37.

thin; there is more evidence that men are more *inclined* to frame rules than women are. This leads me to suggest that the supposed link between the justice perspective and dominance is one which derives largely from the fact that the justice perspective is one which comes naturally to an already dominant group. If things had been different historically, I think we would be less inclined to think there is a conceptual link between the operation of the justice perspective and oppression. Is there any reason (other than historical ones) to think that the justice perspective is *intrinsically* likely to support oppression? The only reason I can come up with is that one can operate the justice perspective successfully without sympathy, whereas operators of the care perspective require a sympathy with the needs of all concerned which would interfere with whole-hearted oppression. But this is a distortion. Although the agents in the justice perspective are thin rational agents, their victims are not, and it would be impossible to operate the justice perspective successfully without a sympathetic knowledge of their feelings, aims, hopes and fears. It may be that the role of sympathy in the care perspective differs from that in the justice perspective, but that does not mean that the justice perspective can be operated without sympathy, nor that the operators are excused by their approach from taking the needs of those concerned as morally relevant to their choices. To think otherwise is to exaggerate the contrast between the justice perspective and the care perspective. So I am not convinced by this attempt to discover an intrinsic link between the justice perspective and sexual oppression.

There is however a different way in which one might argue for the existence of such a link. The justice perspective is concerned with the creation and maintenance of the basic conditions necessary for civilized life, and to that end sets up minimal constraints on autonomous and equal choosers. Its demands are limited in this way, and, crucially, it contains no resources for approving distinctively of actions that go beyond this in the direction of self-sacrifice. It provides no rationale for the thought that to sacrifice one's own interests and prospects (beyond set limits) is an act of superlative moral worth. Self-restraint is required, self-sacrifice is not recommended. So there is no conceptual room in the justice perspective for the supererogatory action, one which is not required but which is very highly valued. There is a limit to what is required, but actions beyond that are not, it seems, to be valued.

The care perspective is not so limited. Here the demands of care are not restrictions on our freedom of choice, but calls for a caring response from us which can perhaps never be perfectly satisfied. There will always be other people with a claim on our care, and new ways one could find of caring for them. Here there is no natural limit set to the requirements of care, and so the demand for self-sacrifice is there in the

**Jonathan Dancy**

nature of the system, not one for which we have to work hard to find a place.

Given this, the split between the care perspective and the justice perspective, when each is thought of as operated especially by one sex, works to perpetuate the domination of men over women. For women sense a demand to do more than some minimum necessary for civilized co-existence, while men are happy to stop at that. So the men can use this female characteristic to bind women to a self-sacrifice which the men themselves feel completely uncalled on to make. Viewed in this way, the care perspective is its own worst enemy (nearly). And it is hard to complain too vigorously about this if one admits the viability of the justice perspective, as most are inclined to do at the moment.

Despite the familiarity of this picture it involves several confusions. First, if the justice perspective makes sense, something like supererogation makes sense within it. Suppose that the central principle of justice is that one should treat all equally. Surely this can be enormously demanding. One way of treating all equally would be to require of each that they give away their goods to those less well off than themselves up to the point where the cost to them is as great as the benefit to the recipients. If this were an expression of the basic principle of justice (and, in the way of justice, it concerns the distribution of goods), we could no longer say that the justice perspective restricted itself to creating the minimum conditions necessary for social life. Element 9 of my original list would have fallen out. But that may simply show that this element was an extraneous addition, not one central to the initial conception of a justice perspective.

There are several other philosophies of ethics which may fairly claim to be versions of the justice perspective, some of which are as demanding in their own way as the care perspective is in its way. Utilitarianism, when suitably dressed up, is such a theory. But one of the classic complaints against utilitarianism has been exactly that it sets no limits to its claims on moral agents. It would certainly have a hard time setting limits to its demands in the way that element 9 of my list suggested.

Thoughts of basic co-operation and of setting constraints on action with that in mind are more closely associated with Kohlberg's middle stage of moral development, where moral rules are thought of as those sanctioned by convention. There is a strong tradition which restricts such conventions to basic minima (as in Rawls's theory of justice). There is no such element in the Kantian tradition (Kohlberg's highest stage); one of the very examples Kant deals with is the requirement to give such aid to others as in worse times I might need from them, and surely asks of me more than some minimum.

So I am not convinced that the justice perspective, when conceived in the sort of opposition to the care perspective that we have so far brought out, is intrinsically suited for the purposes of exploitation or domination. To make out the claim that there is a moral perspective operated by men which serves the purposes of sexual dominance, one has to look for a more radical account of the dominant perspective than any offered in Gilligan or in the post-Gilligan debate, which will see both the justice and the care perspective as expressions of a dominant and oppressive view. But this would be the beginnings of a more radical feminist ethic than any I shall be considering in this paper. (In a way my view is that the less radical views are internally unsatisfactory and that only a more radical position has the seeds of truth in it.)

## 2

I have tried to lay out the contrast between the justice perspective and the care perspective, as it has standardly been set out in the literature. I now turn to ask whether the picture presented is in fact a fair one. I started by trying to sound a warning note to the effect that Kohlberg's preoccupation with Kant should not be allowed to set the scene. There is no antecedent presumption that men are Kantians, though Kohlberg has now admitted that 'I assumed that the core of morality and of moral development was deontological'.[3] Given this assumption, he wrote his six stages in its terms. Alternative accounts of moral thinking, prominent in the philosophical literature but which find no place in Kohlberg's structures, include utilitarianism. We can move forward, and perhaps come to a better understanding of the relation between the justice perspective and the care perspective, by looking in greater detail at alternative versions of the justice perspective such as utilitarianism, culled directly from the philosophical literature. What we will find is firstly that not all versions are committed to all eleven elements that I originally attributed to the justice perspective (as we have already seen that utilitarianism is not committed to element 9), and so that the contrast Gilligan and others in this field have drawn between the justice perspective and the care perspective is in many respects a contrast between one version of the justice perspective—a Kantian one and not the best one at that—and some generic alternative. If we pursue this thought we have some better chance of narrowing down the differences between the justice perspective *as such* and the care perspective *as such*, rather than between some arbitrarily chosen versions of them. And in this way we should be able to see if there is anything distinctive about feminist ethics, or whether what we have been offered is just a new way of writing a theory with which we are already familiar.

[3] See L. Kohlberg, *The Psychology of Moral Development* (San Francisco: Harper and Row, 1984), 225.

## Jonathan Dancy

The obvious place to start is with utilitarianism. In fact one ought to start with consequentialism in general. Consequentialists assert that the moral worth of an action is entirely determined by its consequences. Utilitarianism is a restricted version of consequentialism, which tells us that there is only one thing about the consequences that matters, namely their effect on the general happiness. Consequentialism in general can be much more liberal in its account of what matters, in two directions. First, it can say that there are many distinct goods, of which happiness or well-being is only one. Second, it can stretch our conception of a consequence so as to say that the worth of an action is determined by the difference made to the world by that action's being done. This more liberal account allows us to say that a futile gesture, for instance, makes the world better just by being made; the occurrence of the gesture is a respect in which the world goes better. In both these ways consequentialism is intuitively more plausible than utilitarianism.

Which of the eleven elements will consequentialism accept? It does not accept element 1, at least not in the sense given to the notion of obligation by the tradition. Talk of obligation and duty is designed to be set against talk of value and consequences, just as deontology is opposed to consequentialism. It rejects elements 3–5; these are aspects of Kantianism. There is no suggestion that agents need to be restricted, thin persons, nor that morality is set up in the first place for equal, autonomous agents in situations of their own choosing. It also rejects element 9, as we have seen. On the other hand it accepts elements 6–7; there are principles here, and what is right and wrong is discovered by applying the principles to the case before us in a subsumptive way. It also accepts elements 10–11. One of the supposed advantages of consequentialism is just that it offers a decision procedure which is fair and universally operable. This leaves 8 and 2, both of which are tricky. There is some reason to accuse consequentialism of preferring detachment to engagement. The first reason is that as judge one's impartiality, required for a fair balance of the claims of the various parties, is threatened by involvement. A second reason is that the asymmetric relation of care, in which we prefer a good for those with whom we have relationships of friendship to a possibly greater good for those with whom we are not so bound up, is one for which it is hard to find a consequentialist justification. The sort of friendship and love on which one supposes the care perspective to be founded is not something of whose operations consequentialism can easily approve, even though it easily conceives of friendship as a good since lives without friendship are impoverished.

This leaves the crucial element, 2. Is it true that consequentialism is driven by a single moral principle, that of justice? One answer is that the sort of consequentialism we have been considering has a complex structure. It offers two high level principles, one of the good and one of the right. The former says simply 'Make the consequences of your actions as good as possible', and the other says 'Fair distributions of goods are themselves among the goods'. Beneath these two lie all the specifications of particular goods, including happiness and friendship, but probably also knowledge, fun, aesthetic experience and whatever else we want to add. Now the existence of the lower level principles does not disqualify consequentialism from being a version of the justice perspective, for if it did Kantianism would be disqualified too. There is plenty of room in Kant's theory for second-level, thick moral principles as well as the thin principle 'Treat other rational beings never merely as a means, but also as an end'. And I cannot see that the fact that there are two higher-level principles disqualifies consequentialism as a version of the justice perspective either, given the central place it ascribes to considerations of justice or fairness of distribution. So I reckon that consequentialism is near enough to element 2 to count squarely as a version of the justice perspective.

## 3

However consequentialism is not the only going alternative to Kant. There is a different theory, the theory of *prima facie* duties, which differs from both Kantianism and from consequentialism. The elaboration of this theory we owe to W. D. Ross.[4] The general idea is that moral principles such as 'Keep your promises', 'Pay your debts', and 'Do not let down those who are relying on you' do not tell us that whenever an action involves breaking a promise it is wrong. Rather, they say, the fact that it involves breaking one's promise counts against it, but only in a way that may be overridden if enough other features count in favour of it. Sometimes it is right to break your promise even though there is a moral principle 'Keep your promises'. All moral principles express what Ross calls *prima facie* duties; the principle 'Keep your promises' tells us that if you choose to keep a promise, your action is right to that extent—as far as that goes it is right—its being a promise-keeping counts in favour of it. Ross's principles differ from Kant's because they are not exceptionless; we can honour Ross's principles in the breach, as it were, which we could not do for Kant's. And Ross's theory differs from consequentialism in another way; it holds that many of the features that determine whether an action is right or wrong are not concerned with consequences at all. For instance, I may take an action

[4] W. D. Ross, *The Right and The Good* (Oxford: Clarendon Press. 1930), esp. ch. 2, and *The Foundations of Ethics* (Oxford: Clarendon Press, 1939).

## Jonathan Dancy

to be called for because I promised you to do it, and this consideration relates to the past, not to the future nor to the difference I will make to the world by my action, in the way that consequentialists would like to have us believe.

Crucial to Ross's theory is the fact that there is no short list of moral principles, and no way of ordering the many that there are. His view is just that there are all sorts of different things that can matter morally, and the only way to find out about them is to pay careful attention to your moral experience. How exactly do we come to know the truth of any moral principle? Some philosophers hold that we know the truth of such principles directly (it was sometimes said that we know them by a sort of moral intuition). For instance, it has been held that the principle 'One should treat all people equally' is self-evident, in the sense that you only have to consider it with an open mind and its truth will simply strike you. Ross does not believe any such thing. For him, as I said, the only way to come to know a principle is to discover its truth in moral experience. It happens like this: first one is faced with a case in which one has to make a decision what to do. Take a case of a traditional marriage. James and Sally are going out to dinner with some people that he knows but she doesn't know. He is keen not to offend these people and generally to make a good impression. Sally knows this. However time is getting on and they are already a bit late. She emerges, all ready for the fray, and asks him whether she is suitably dressed for the occasion. It is immediately clear to James that she is not. What is he to say? He has three choices. The first is to lie, and hope that the truth will not be apparent to her as soon as they walk into their hosts' house. The second is to tell the truth, so that she goes and puts on something else (making them even later). The third is to say that what she is wearing is not right but that it is too late to change it now because they are already late. This has the advantage of minimizing their lateness but only at the cost of completely poisoning the evening for her and generally causing her distress. Now what Ross wants to say about this is that James can see already three sorts of consideration that are mattering or making a difference here. The first is that it is better if they are not late. The second is that it is better not to lie about the dress. The third is that it is better not to distress his wife. These things are all in the story here; they all matter and he has just got to sort out which is more important than the others. So far everything James has noticed is restricted in its relevance to the case before him. But he can immediately move beyond that, for one can see that what matters here must matter wherever it occurs. It is important not to be late here, and this tells him that it is generally important not to be late. What has happened is that he has learnt the truth of a moral principle (which expresses a *prima facie duty*) in what he noticed in a particular case.

I hope that this gives enough of the flavour of the theory of *prima facie* duties for those who are not familiar with it. I now want to ask, as I asked of consequentialism, which elements originally attributed to *the* justice perspective it shares and which it rejects. First, it is a theory of *prima facie* duty, and so concerns itself primarily with obligation, though of course it uses a weaker sense of obligation than that traditionally associated with Kant. So element 1 is in. Element 2 is out, I think. It is true that there is a *prima facie* principle of justice in the theory, but the role it plays here is not significant or central enough for one to say that it is primarily a theory of justice. The *prima facie* principle 'Distribute goods fairly' is only one among a welter of others, and enjoys no special or higher-level role.

Elements 3–5 are also out. Ross's theory concerns itself with real people rather than with Kantian abstractions, so far as one can tell, and those real people occur in all the various relations of unequal power and in situations that are not of their own choosing. Element 6 is firmly in place, but element 7 is out, and this is important. Ross admits an unwieldy number of moral principles, but does not suppose that the way in which we come to decide what we ought to do is by subsuming the present case under one or other of them. To do this would be to suppose that in a case of conflict only one principle really applied, which he holds to be ludicrous. The problem as he sees it is not to find out which principle applies, but, knowing that all the principles into which this action is keyed apply equally, to decide where the balance of duty lies. In doing this we are not guided by the principles themselves. A principle of *prima facie* duty tells us that a feature matters or makes a difference, but it does not tell us how much it matters and it certainly does not tell us how much it puts into the balance in the present case, which may be affected by the question which other principles are also operating at the same time. So according to Ross our decision in a particular case is not reached by subsuming what we find here under a moral principle, but by looking as carefully as we can at the ways in which the features that matter here go together, in the hope of being able to decide which way the balance lies. A decision of this sort is unlikely to be easy, and there is no suggestion that the only approach possible is one likely to generate firm answers, and even less suggestion that there is likely to be convergence among dfferent judges on one among all the possible answers. So elements 10 and 11 are out. So is element 9. The sort of moral principles that Ross is dealing with may be less trenchant than those of Kant, but they combine to create very strong demands on responsible moral agents. There is no reason to think that the rationale for Rossian morality is the need for minimum conditions for social interaction. The many things that matter make such severe demands on us that if we were to meet them entirely our life

## Jonathan Dancy

would probably resemble that of the traditional present-day saints such as Mother Theresa.

This leaves element 8 to be determined. It seems to me here that Ross's view that in difficult cases there is no substitute for looking as carefully as we can at the details of the situation and allowing the demands it creates to impress themselves upon us is reason for supposing that for him detachment would not necessarily be the virtue it is elsewhere held to be. I do not think it could easily be rendered compatible with his general approach to hold that the sort of engagement necessary to feel in their full force the differing needs, hopes and fears of those involved is in itself likely to distort one's judgment, which is the standard reason for preferring detachment to engagement. Whatever impartiality is, it cannot be incompatible with the sort of interest in the situation which is necessary to discover what the choice is that is facing us.

So of all our elements the only ones claimed by Ross's theory are 1 and 6. Does this mean that it is not a version of the justice perspective? It certainly shares some features normally considered central to the justice perspective. It deals in moral principles, and its central concept is that of obligation; the moral life for it is one in which obligations are fulfilled rather than relationships maintained and care for others expressed naturally in our actions. To this extent it seems to be an expression of the justice perspective, though clearly not on the Kantian model. It is in its own way a *rule*-bound model, though not a *justice*-bound model. However it also has many features of the care perspective, namely the denial of elements 2–5 and 7–11. So pressing the question whether Ross's view is *really* a version of the justice perspective or of the care perspective leads one to suspect that we have not here a straightforward division between two conceptions but a spectrum of positions which extends so far from Kant at one end to Ross at the other. Given however that a full feminist ethic should deny all my eleven elements, there should be at least one position further from Kant than Ross is. And this is in fact what emerges. If Ross's view is not an early formulation of a feminist ethic, but a view which lies at the limit of the justice perspective, it will emerge that the distinctive aspect of feminist ethical stances will be their denial of element 6, of the need for or possibility of moral principles that play any role whatever in our moral thinking. For this claim was the only one which was common to all versions of the justice perspective.[5]

[5] There is of course an interesting question of method here: is it a reputable method of approach to suppose the central element of the justice approach to be that one which is common to all versions (supposing there to be only one)? One might claim that this approach constitutes a crude attitude towards theory, supposing theories to be *ad hoc* collections of mutually indifferent parts.

## Caring about Justice

[The more radical position of which I spoke earlier would not accept that element 6 is the only one common to all versions of the justice perspective. It would also claim that there is an adherence to a certain conception of the individual, which could and should be disputed. I agree with this; but the point here is that the care perspective, in the tradition with which I am principally concerned here, seems equally wedded to that conception. If this is right, it remains the case that the only element common to all contrasts between justice and care perspectives is element 6.]

**4**

Before moving to flesh out this suggestion, I want to pause to consider how what I have said so far relates to Gilligan's early investigations into the moral perceptions of 11-year old children—the research which she describes in the second chapter of her influential book and which is in conscious opposition to Kohlberg. What she suggests there is that of the two children she describes, the boy Jake and the girl Amy, Jake is bidding fair to turn into a fully-fledged Kantian while Amy is already operating, when allowed by her interlocutor's Kantian prejudices, within the care perspective. However the evidence she offers for this analysis does not seem to me anything like strong enough, as I think that an awareness of different versions of the justice perspective can help us to see.

The question posed to these two young people concerned Heinz, a man whose wife will die if she is not given a certain drug. Heinz cannot afford the drug because the druggist who has it is charging too high a price for it, and the question is whether he should steal the drug. Gilligan tells us extraordinarily little about the responses of Jake, but from the little she does tell us it seems clear to me that she is trying to force Jake into Kohlberg's Kantian mould. She says:

> Constructing the dilemma, as Kohlberg did, as a conflict between the values of property and life, [Jake] discerns the logical priority of life and uses that logic to justify his choice:
>
> > For one thing, a human life is worth more than money, and if the druggist only makes money, he is still going to live, but if Heinz doesn't steal the drug, his wife is going to die. (*Why is life worth more than money?*) Because the druggist can get a thousand more dollars from rich people with cancer, but Heinz can't get his wife again. (*Why not?*) Because people are all different and so you couldn't get Heinz's wife again.[6]

[6] *In a Different Voice*, 26.

**Jonathan Dancy**

Gilligan is keen to see Jake as operating *logically* so that she can run a certain contrast:

> Both children thus recognize the need for agreement but see it as mediated in different ways—he impersonally through systems of logic and law, she personally through communication in relationship.[7]

And the sort of logic she sees Jake as operating is deductive logic. The idea here is that Jake will commit himself to some universal ethical principle, and derive by deduction a prescription for action by applying it to the case before him, rather along the lines of the syllogism:

> All cows are brown
> This is a cow
> So this is brown

So Jake is to say:

> Life always comes before property
> I have to choose between her life and his property
> So her life must come first.

There is no doubt that Jake's first sentence *could* be read in this Kantian way, and confirming evidence for this reading might be found in what Gilligan calls Jake's fascination with the power of logic. She tells us that Jake

> locates truth in maths, which, he says is 'the only thing that is totally logical'. Considering the moral dilemma to be 'sort of like a math problem with humans,' he sets it up as an equation and proceeds to work out the solution. . . . Yet he is also aware of the limits of logic. Asked whether there is a right answer to moral problems, Jake replies that 'there can only be right or wrong in judgment,' since the parameters of action are variable and complex.[8]

Later Gilligan talks of Jake's 'ability to bring deductive logic to bear on the solution of moral dilemmas'.[9] But there is another way to read Jake, and that is not as an incipient Kantian, but as someone operating an ethic of *prima facie* duties. The first chinks in Gilligan's Kantian reading appear when we read that Jake thinks that 'the laws make mistakes, and you can't go writing up a law for everything that you can imagine'.[10] If Jake thinks this about the law of the land, we might be

[7] Ibid.,29.
[8] Ibid.,26–27.
[9] Ibid.,27.
[10] Ibid., 26.

pardoned the suspicion that he thinks it about the moral law also. And this sort of suspicion of universal principles which pretend all on their own to tell us what to do in a particular case is just the position that Ross adopts and which informs his whole attitude to ethics. It seems to me therefore more plausible to see Jake as trying to sort out for himself whch matters more here—Heinz's wife's life or the druggist's property. That he knows perfectly well which side the balance comes down on here does not mean that he is committed to holding that a single human life is worth more than any amount of money, especially when we consider the benefits which that money might be expected to bring.

Why then does Jake consider the moral dilemma to be a sort of math problem with humans? There are two distinctive features of maths, the first being that mathematical reasoning is deductive, the second being something we can see in ordinary problems of addition and subtraction, namely that one can put together the pluses and the minuses and get out an answer. I suggest that it is not the first but the second of these that characterizes Jake's approach to the moral dilemma, in a way entirely in conformity with Ross's account of moral thinking. For Ross, the pluses and minuses are put together in that sort of way to find out where the balance of duty lies, even though the eventual decision is not the product of deductive reasoning but of judgment. And, notably for one who is supposed to be impressed by the powers of deduction, Jake says exactly what Ross would say here, namely that 'there can only be right or wrong in judgment' because of the complexity of moral problems and their consequent ability to outrun any precisely formulated principles.

So I do not agree with Gilligan's diagnosis of Jake as an incipient Kantian, and I see all the talk about deductive logic which she uses to back it up as seriously mistaken. What then of Amy? Her first answer to the question whether Heinz should steal the drug is as follows:

> Well, I don't think so. I think there might be other ways besides stealing it, like if he could borrow the money or make a loan or something, but he really shouldn't steal the drug—but his wife shouldn't die either.[11]

Asked why he shouldn't steal the drug, she says:

> If he stole the drug, he might save his wife then, but if he did, he might have to go to jail, and then his wife might get sicker again, and he couldn't get more of the drug, and it might not be good. So, they should really just talk it out and find some other way to make the money.[12]

Gilligan comments on this that Amy 'considers neither property nor law but rather the effect that theft could have on the relationship

[11] Ibid., 28.
[12] Ibid., 28.

between Heinz and his wife . . . Amy envisions the wife's continuing need for her husband and the husband's continuing concern for his wife and seeks to respond to the druggist's need in a way that would sustain rather than sever connection . . . she ties the wife's survival to the preservation of relationships'. I think, however, that her keenness to establish the notion of connection as central to an ethic contrasted with the justice perspective has caused her to outrun the evidence here. First, Amy has made no mention of the druggist's *need*, nor so far as I can see has she focused on the wife's continuing need for her husband, except as a provider of money or drugs, nor on the effect of the theft on their relationship, nor on the husband's continuing concern for his wife in any special way. Instead she takes the view that stealing would just be wrong. Gilligan says:

> Asked again why Heinz should not steal the drug, she simply repeats, 'Because it's not right.'[13]

This firm adherence to an absolute moral principle is, if anything, Kantian. Of course Amy finds it hard to stick to her Kantian principle in the difficult situation offered her. So she tries to support it, lamely, with consequentialist considerations. She hasn't got any firm ones to offer, and so she resorts to thoughts about what might happen; stealing the drug might not work in the long run, since the wife might need the drug again and her husband might have got caught and put in jail. (Note that Jake's view was that if caught Heinz should not and would not be sent to jail.) These thoughts are not very impressive, but, knowing that stealing is wrong, Amy is convinced that Heinz shouldn't have to steal. There must therefore be another way out, and the only possibilities are to borrow the necessary money or somehow to appeal to the druggist. These manoeuvres have got to work, since otherwise Heinz would have to steal, and stealing is wrong. Amy gives me here the strong impression of being a Kantian who takes it that the world cannot contain situations in which a wrong action is called for—this is Kant in his most optimistic moments.

## 5

I now return to the question of the nature of a distinctively feminist ethic, an ethic of care rather than one of justice. The only feature we found common to all versions of the justice perspective was that they awarded some role to moral principles. I call any position that denies any role to principles moral particularism. Particularists assert that

[13] Ibid., 29.

## Caring about Justice

there is no room for moral principles, and that it is bad faith to try to make moral decisions by appeal to them. Such an appeal will normally involve failing to look hard enough at the case before one, but asking oneself instead how closely it resembles some previous case about which one has already made up one's mind, in the hope that one will not have to think further but can simply read off the answer here from what one thought there. This particularism is already fairly well worked out in moral theory.[14] Is there any difference between this approach to ethics and a care perspective?

One feature which the two positions have in common is a distrust of hypothetical cases. It was noticeable that Jake was happy to answer the questions put to him in the terms in which they were conceived; he saw nothing peculiar about the game he was being asked to play, and we must admit that the game of deciding what to do here by first looking at foreshortened hypothetical cases is a common one. However it is not one which Amy is keen on. She wants to know more and to probe to see whether there might not be some other way out. I have already given my account of why this is so. But we can forget the vicissitudes of Amy and concentrate instead on the ethic of care in its own right. Particularists and carers (to coin a name) agree that nothing substantial can be learnt from cases of these sorts, for nothing about a foreshortened case could possible tie our hands when we come to decide what to do in a real, rich case. What is more, the pretence that there is something to be said about thin hypothetical cases only makes sense for those who have a pack of moral principles which they can apply to any case, however thin, to generate an answer *pro tem*. So there is this common element between the two positions.

What difference might there be? The difference I see is that in its assertion that we should open ourselves to all the details of the case before us, without the bad faith of comparing that case to a preconceived set of principles, particularism does not lay any special stress on care, connections or relationships. But these three terms are among those one hears most often in Gilligan and in post-Gilligan work on the care perspective. Now it is clearly consistent with the general thrust of particularism to hold that these notions are very important indeed, for those who fail to see their centrality are people who will be blind to the real nature of the moral choices they have to face. But it would be consistent also with particularism to hold that care itself can be abused,

[14] For recent attempts in this direction, see John McDowell 'Virtue And Reason', *The Monist*, 62 (1979), 331–50, and 'Non-cognitivism and Rule-following', in *Wittgenstein: To Follow a Rule*, S. Holtzman and C. Leich (eds) (London: Routledge and Kegan Paul, 1981). See also my *Moral Reasons* (Blackwell, forthcoming).

and that acting out of care, or making the caring choice, need not always be the right choice. An instance that occurs to me here is that of the husband whose care for his wife is so great that it effectively suffocates her, preventing her from making something of herself for herself. We might think in such a case that it would have been better if he had acted more out of respect and less out of care. My own view, then, as an unregenerate particularist, is that if the ethic of care is narrower than would be required by particularism, it is too narrow. If the ethic of care is the feminist ethic, I think it would be better expanded to merge with a wider particularism—one which still retains a central place for considerations of care but which has something to put against them on occasions.

So the main contrast I find between the justice perspective and the care perspective is the contrast between what I have called principled approaches and particularist ones. Given that contrast, there are different versions of either side, and one has to take one's pick.

## 6

Finally, I turn to the question of the relationship between the justice perspective and the care perspective. It is common for feminist writers such as Gilligan and Baier to be conciliatory here, and admit that each perspective has something to offer, so that a rounded view would be one aware of the advantages of each. If asked how there can be room for two adequate approaches to ethics, they tend to admit that neither is completely adequate. Rather, each has defects for which the other can compensate. But we cannot simply go for an amalgam of the two, since there is an ineradicable tension between them. This tension is established by appeal to the elements on my original list, or simply by asking how one could hope to amalgamate two approaches, one of which thinks that moral principles are important and the other of which thinks they are not.

The problem that I have with this sort of British compromise is that I cannot see how to make it other than insincere. In my view these various versions of the justice perspective and the care perspective are competing for something, and if none of them wins we do not mend matters by adding a second one with its own defects to it. The story goes like this. First I am impressed by Ross's arguments against any subsumptive theory. We know that if there are many moral principles, several will apply in any interesting case, some urging us in one direction and some in the other. How one could hope to derive a prescription for action by subsumption alone in such a situation is a mystery to me. Nor do we improve matters by supposing that there is really only one moral principle, such as the great Kantian principle 'Treat other rational beings never merely as a means but always also as an end'. For principles of this type are merely formal; they do not have sufficient content to serve as a guide to action. A far better approach is that of Ross, where the relation between relevant principles and action is not one of subsumption. In saying this, however, we are not saying that Kantian ethics is adequate in many ways but needs supplementation from Rossian ethics. Rather we are holding that Ross's view, for all we have seen so far, is right and Kant's wrong. But now we notice that the way Ross retains room for moral principles in his theory is peculiar. The principles do no work in the theory at all other than to give us a sense that in moving from one case to the next we are intending to judge consistently. The notion of consistency as a requirement on moral judgment (a notion which I have not seen discussed at all in feminist writings) is captured in Ross's account by the assertion that if a feature makes a difference here it must make a difference everywhere. This is clearly an important matter. Note however that without this role the principles would be idle cogs, for Ross explicitly holds that our actual moral judgments are not made by applying principles to cases. And principles are not required for consistency either. There is an alternative account of consistency, which we owe to Wittgenstein, which gives no substantial place to rules or principles in its story of what it is to go on in the same way as before. What is more, it is possible to dispute the truth of Ross's central claim that what matters here must matter everywhere. To give just one example, there may be one action which is made right by the fact that it causes pleasure to most onlookers, even though it causes pain to some of those involved. But public hangings are thought the worse for this feature, not better. So it is not true that what matters here *must* matter in the same way everywhere. And this result is the main argument in favour of a particularist ethic. Again, we do not say that Ross's view is adequate but incomplete; we say that it is mistaken and should be replaced by a particularist ethic which is not mistaken.

Why should we accept that particularism is inadequate as a moral theory? One suggestion of Gilligan's is that one defect of the ethic of care is that it is liable to constant vacillation, because of its tendency to try to accommodate the points of view of everyone involved.[15] But this is a complaint that Ross, at least, could not make; his theory is vulnerable to the same charge, if it is a charge at all. And I do not view it as any sort of defect. Moral stances or perspectives are not created nor to be valued primarily for their ability to generate decisons quickly or automatically, and if moral problems are difficult we should be wary of any

[15] Gilligan and Wiggins, 'The Origins of Morality', op. cit.

theory that offers sharp procedures for cutting through the undergrowth. The undergrowth is not an impediment to a solution; it is the problem.

So the passage is from Kant, through Ross, to particularism. I suggest that particularism is the core element in a genuine feminist ethic, which can be an ethic of care since it gives caring a central place (but not *the* central place), but can also capture the claims of justice. Someone trying to sort out how to care here—someone trying to work out which present to give to which child, say—is trying to decide what would be fair; though that would perhaps not be the way she posed the problem to herself, for good reasons. This person is caring about justice in what she does, but of course justice here has lost the role it attempted to play in the justice perspective. A particularist perspective captures the claims both of care and of justice without essential tension. It is a feminist ethic, and it is the only ethic. In this sense, there is no room for a non-feminist ethic at all.

## Postscript

If particularism turns out eventually not to be a feminist ethic, this will not be for reasons that emerge in Gilligan, but because its Wittgensteinian sense of consistency is too strong still for feminist stomachs, since it gives the picture of someone travelling from situation to situation with a moral perspective from which all their judgments are to be made, on pain of inconsistency. (Of course such a person judges in full knowledge of the points of view of all concerned, a comparatively unimportant point of which Gilligan makes much.) The more radical view will hold that we all have different inconsistent perspectives between which we oscillate, so that there can be no single-track conception of consistency as a constraint on a *person's* moral outlook. Each person is in a way broken up into various perspectives, in choosing between which she chooses who she is (here) to be.

This is an interesting view which I do not here have space to discuss. But it is very different from the sort of liberal feminism that I have been talking about in this paper.[16]

*University of Keele*

[16] I am particularly grateful to Candace Vogler for helping me to understand the nature of a more radical feminist attitude in this area, and want also to thank David Bakhurst, Elisa Carse, Sarah Dancy and Christine Sypnowich for helpful discussion of earlier drafts.

# [10]

# WHEN JUSTICE REPLACES AFFECTION: THE NEED FOR RIGHTS

JEREMY WALDRON*

## I.

Why do individuals need rights? In a world crying out for a greater emphasis on fraternity and communal responsibility in social life, what is the point of an institution that legitimates the making of querulous and adversarial claims by individuals against their fellows? If human relations can be founded on affection, why is so much made in modern jurisprudence of formal and impersonal rights as a starting point for the evaluation of laws and institutions? In answering these questions, I take as my starting point a disagreement between the philosophers Kant and Hegel regarding the role of rights in marriage.

In his work on the philosophy of law, Immanuel Kant likened marriage to a contract between two people for "life-long reciprocal possession of their sexual faculties."[1] He was quick to add that, though it is a contract, it is "not on that account a matter of arbitrary will"; rather, it is a matter of necessity for anyone who wants to enjoy another person sexually. In sexual relations, Kant says, one party is used as an object by the other, and that *prima facie* is incompatible with the basic "Law of Humanity" prohibiting the use of any human agent as a mere means to the satisfaction of one's desires. That situation can be rectified "only . . . under the one condition that as the one Person is acquired by the other as a *res*, that same Person equally acquires the other reciprocally, and thus regains and re-establishes the rational Personality."[2] Kant went on to say that the reciprocity of rights that this solution presupposes leads to a requirement of monogamy, because in a polygamous regime, one of the partners may be giving more to the other than the

---

* Acting Professor of Law, University of California, Berkeley. B.A. Otago 1974, LL.B. Otago, 1978, D.Phil. Oxford 1986. An earlier version of this article was delivered as a public lecture at the University of Michigan in December 1986. I would like to thank Daniela Gabetti, Alan Gibbard, Don Herzog, John Kingdon, Larry Mohr, Peter Railton, Donald Regan, Jonathan Simon, and Kim Scheppele for their suggestions. I am also grateful to Kristin Luker, Philip Selznick, Judith Squires, and Susan Sterett, for conversations and comments on these issues.

1. I. KANT, THE PHILOSOPHY OF LAW: AN EXPOSITION OF THE FUNDAMENTAL PRINCIPLES OF JURISPRUDENCE AS THE SCIENCE OF RIGHT 110 (W. Hastie trans. 1887).
2. *Id.* at 110-11.

other is to her.[3] The contract has got to be a matter of *equal* right in order to satisfy the fundamental test of respect for persons.

Sometimes it seems that Kant was not content with this contractualist characterization of marriage. In one place, he went further and argued that the rights involved are like rights of property:

> The Personal Right thus acquired is at the same time, real in kind. This characteristic of it is established by the fact that if one of the married Persons run away or enter into the possession of another, the other is entitled, at any time, and incontestably, to bring such a one back to the former relation, as if that Person were a Thing.[4]

Many have thought that such ideas are perhaps better ignored in the overall assessment of Kant's philosophy of morals.

The Kantian view of marriage as a purely contractual arrangement was adamantly repudiated by Hegel—"shameful," he said, "is the only word for it."[5] Hegel conceded that marriage originates in a contract between two people and that therefore, in its dependence on their say-so to get it underway, it has some of the contingency and "arbitrariness" that are normally associated with contractual relations.[6] But, according to Hegel, rights and contract are far from telling us the complete story about the institution. For one thing, the public character of the marriage celebration (whether the ceremony is religious or civil)—the procedures of notification, licensing, witnessing, solemnization, registration, and so on—attest to a significance that goes far beyond a mere meeting of the wills or "the mutual caprice" of the prospective partners.[7] For another thing, the parties celebrate their marriage not merely as a *quid pro quo* but in order to attain a union of desire, affection, interest, and identity that goes far beyond anything that could possibly be specified in even the fine print of a contract. There is a world of difference, on this view, between the Kantian "contract for reciprocal use" and the "love, trust, and common sharing of their existence as individuals" which is what married partners com-

3. *Id.* at 111-12.
4. *Id.* at 111.
5. G.W.F. Hegel, Philosophy of Right 58, at ¶ 75 (T. Knox trans. 1967).
6. *Id.* at 111-12, at ¶ 162.
7. *Id.* at 113-14, at ¶ 164; *id.* at 262, at ¶ 161[A].

mit themselves to.[8] As Hegel puts it, if marriage begins in an agreement, "it is precisely a contract to transcend the standpoint of contract," that is, to transcend the standpoint of "individual self-subsistent units" making claims against one another, which is how contracting parties are normally understood.[9]

There are two distinct aspects to this critique. On the one hand, Hegel is attacking Kant's specific use of *contract* to characterize the marriage bond; the suggestion is that *this* legal concept is inappropriate in the particular context (though I imagine he would take even greater exception to Kant's use of the terminology of property!). On the other hand, he is also attacking the much broader target of Kant's pervasive legalism: the temptation, to which Kantians so often succumb, to reduce social institutions of all kinds to some formal array of legalistic rights and duties. Here it is not so much the idea of *contract*, but the more general idea of *a right*, that is out of place. This is the aspect of Hegel's critique that I will focus on, because I think it raises interesting and far-reaching issues about liberal rights-based approaches to social and communal relations.

Few of us would disagree with Hegel's basic point: Claims of right should have little part to play in the context of a normal loving marriage. If we hear one partner complaining to the other about a denial or withdrawal of conjugal *rights*, we know that something has already gone wrong with the interplay of desire and affection between the partners. The same would be true if people started talking about their *right* to a partner's fidelity, their *right* to be freed from child-care or domestic chores once in a while, their equal *right* to pursue a career, their *right* to draw equally on the family income, and so on. In each case, the substance of the claim may be indispensable for a happy and loving marriage in the modern world. But it is its presentation *as a claim*—that is, as an entitlement that one party presses peremptorily, querulously, and adversarially against the other—that would lead to our misgivings. We would certainly look for all these things in a marriage, but we would hope to see them upheld and conceded, not as matters of right, but as the natural outcome of the most intimate mutual concern and respect brought to bear by the partners on the common problems that they face. Even if rights like these were acknowledged as the

8. *Id.* at 112, at ¶ 163.
9. *Id.*

ground-rules of the relationship in some sort of formal agreement drawn up by the partners, there would still be something unpleasant about their *asserting* them as rights or, as the phrase goes, "*standing on their rights*" in the normal functioning of the relationship. Such behavior would be seen as a way of blocking and preventing warmth and intimacy, replacing relatively unbounded and immediate care and sensitivity with rigid and abstract formulas of justice.

The point can be generalized: To stand on one's rights is to distance oneself from those to whom the claim is made; it is to announce, so to speak, an opening of hostilities; and it is to acknowledge that other warmer bonds of kinship, affection, and intimacy can no longer hold. To do this in a context where adversarial hostility is inappropriate is a serious moral failing.[10] As Hegel put it in an Addition to the *Philosophy of Right*: "To have no interest except in one's formal right may be pure obstinacy, often a fitting accompaniment of a cold heart and restricted sympathies. It is uncultured people who insist most on their rights, while noble minds look on other aspects of the thing."[11]

## II.

Is there not anything, then, to be said for the Kantian position? I think there is this. Though marriage is certainly more than a matter of rights and correlative duties, and though one will not expect to hear claims of right in a happily functioning marriage, nevertheless the strength and security of the marriage commitment in the modern world depends in part on there being an array of legalistic rights and duties that the partners know they can fall back on, if ever their mutual affection fades. That is the idea I will consider in this paper.

I want to explore this idea against the background of some criticisms that have been made of rights-based liberalism. In

10. *See, e.g.*, Young, *Dispensing with Moral Rights*, 6 POLITICAL THEORY 63, 68 (1978):

> [O]ften not only is such an appeal to rights otiose, but it is morally jarring (rather than dignified) to insist on one's due . . . . This means of protecting what are conceived to be legitimate interests is, even if understandable, not morally desirable since it does nothing to mend the ruptured relations.

*See also* Louden, *Rights Infatuation and the Impoverishment of Theory*, 17 J. VALUE INQUIRY 87, 99 (1983) ("In extreme cases [of rights infatuation], a severe form of moral inertia takes over, at which point it becomes difficult to get the rights infatuationist to do anything but claim his rights.").

11. Hegel, *supra* note 5, at 235, at ¶ 37[A].

recent years, liberal theories have come under attack from socialists and communitarians for their implausible suggestion that the bonds of social life should be thought of as constituted primarily by the rights and rights-based relations of initially atomistic individuals.[12] I will consider how much of that attack would be mitigated or refuted if liberals were to concede that the structure of rights is not constitutive of social life, but instead to be understood as a position of fall-back and security in case other constituent elements of social relations ever come apart. To go back to the marriage example, I will suggest that there is a need for an array of formal and legalistic rights and duties, not to constitute the affective bond, but to provide each person with secure knowledge of what she can count on in the unhappy event that there turns out to be no other basis for her dealings with her erstwhile partner in the relationship. The importance of rights ought to be much easier to defend from this somewhat less inflated position.

But the argument is not merely a strategic retreat for liberals. Liberals are entitled to ask their communitarian critics how this important function of security is to be performed in a community that repudiates rights and legalism, and under the auspices of a theory that gives individual rights no part to play at all. Is it to be supposed that the intimate and affective relations that characterize various forms of community will never come apart, that affections will never change, and that people will never feel the urge to exit from some relationships and initiate others? If so, communitarianism in the modern world presents itself as naive or desperately dangerous, and probably both. Or is it supposed that a society will be pervaded by such a strong background sense of affection and responsibility, that we will be able to afford to allow people to change their intimate relations as they please without any attempt to articulate formally the terms on which they are to do so? That, for example, in the marriage case, we can somehow count on goodwill to provide for the continued care of person's partner or children if they need it? Again, if this is the view that communitarians rely on, they are dangerously underestimating both the possibility for

12. *See, e.g.*, LIBERALISM AND ITS CRITICS (M. Sandel ed. 1984) (hereinafter LIBERALISM); M. SANDEL, LIBERALISM AND THE LIMITS OF JUSTICE (1982); A. MACINTYRE, AFTER VIRTUE: A STUDY IN MORAL THEORY (1981); Taylor, *Atomism*, in POWERS, POSSESSIONS AND FREEDOM: ESSAYS IN HONOUR OF C.B. MACPHERSON (A. Kontos ed. 1979); R. UNGER, KNOWLEDGE AND POLITICS (1976).

things to go wrong between human beings, and the human need for some sort of background guarantee, on which, in the last resort, one can rely in the face of that possibility.

Before continuing it may be worth saying a word or two about *communitarianism*. The new communitarianism is by no means a rigidly defined body of thought; the term refers rather to a trend in modern critiques of liberal political philosophy. In the work of writers like Roberto Unger, Michael Sandel, Alasdair Macintyre, and Charles Taylor, liberal theories of rights have been attacked for their individualism, for the way they parade the desires and interests of the human individual as the be-all and end-all of politics, at the expense of notions like community, fraternity and a shared social good.[13] It is not that liberals ignore those values altogether; but it is alleged that they give them only an instrumental significance or treat them merely as particular moral causes which individuals may or may not espouse. Partly it is a matter of perspective on society. For liberal theories of rights, the point of reference is the "unencumbered" individual, who is free to shrug off his communal and other allegiances whenever he chooses. The relatively unaffectionate and formalistic language of rights and contract theory is said to be an expression of his essential detachability from affective commitments; its formalism expresses the facts deemed most important about his moral status, without reference to any content or community. Communitarians, on the other hand, take as their point of reference the shared lives of people who regard themselves as, in Sandel's words, "defined to some extent by the community of which they are a part"[14]—people who cannot imagine a standpoint of political judgment over and above their particular communal identity.

It is important to stress that community here is not an *abstract* idea; one's communal identity depends on the particularity of one's past. As Macintyre puts it, "I am someone's son or daughter, someone else's cousin or uncle; I am a citizen of this or that city, a member of this or that guild or profession."[15] Apart from the particularity of these attachments, there is said to be no standpoint for abstract political thought, communal or

13. There is a good general discussion of the communitarian critique in Gutman, *Communitarian Critics of Liberalism*, 14 PHIL. & PUB. AFF. 308 (1985).

14. *See* Sandel, *Introduction*, LIBERALISM, *supra* note 12, at 5.

15. A. MACINTYRE, *supra* note 12, 204-05. *See also* M. SANDEL, *supra* note 12, at 179.

individual. The discourse of this communitarian politics, then, will be informal and engaged rather than impersonal and abstract. Political thought will be a matter of the discovery and recognition of the particular social selves we are, rather than the deliberate choice and articulation of abstract principles of right. There are also other strands in the communitarian literature—notably a strand of civic republicanism that is by no means so clearly incompatible with the traditional liberal point of view—but these are the ones I deal with in this article.[16]

## III.

I chose marriage as my starting point because I wanted to illustrate two things. The first is the claim I have already outlined. The function of matrimonial law, with its contractual rules and formulas and rigid rights and duties, is not necessarily to constitute the marriage bond; its function is to provide a basis on which affective ties can be converted into legal responsibilities in the unhappy situation where affection can no longer be guaranteed.

But I also want to develop a second point. The structure of impersonal rules and rights not only provides a background guarantee; it also furnishes a basis on which people can act to initiate *new* relations with other people even from a position of alienation from the affective bonds of existing attachments and community. Impersonal rules and rights provide a basis for new beginnings and for moral initiatives which challenge existing affections, driving them in new directions or along lines that might seem uncomfortable or challenging to well-worn traditional folkways. Such initiatives may be valued on social as well as individual grounds: Not only do they make life bearable for alienated individuals by allowing them to start out in new directions, but they also provide a dynamic for social progress by challenging the existing types of relationships with new ones.[17] If we value these initiatives for either or both of these reasons, we have to ask: Under what conditions are they possible in human affairs? The traditional liberal reply is that people

16. For a discussion of civic republicanism, see H. ARENDT, ON REVOLUTION (1973), B. SMITH, POLITICS AND REMEMBRANCE: REPUBLICAN THEMES IN MACHIAVELLI, BURKE, AND TOCQUEVILLE (1985), and *Civic Republicanism and its Critics*, 14 POLITICAL THEORY 423 (1986) (symposium).

17. For the importance of new beginnings in human affairs, see H. ARENDT, THE HUMAN CONDITION 177-78 (1958).

must be free from legal coercion and social pressure so they can try out new experiments in living.[18] But other conditions may be necessary besides negative freedom. Can people take new initiatives in a social vacuum? Once men and women repudiate the existing affections of their community, are they in a position to develop new types of relationship without any help from social structures at all? If the answer is no, then there is a reason to ensure that *some* social structures at least should be established on a basis which distances them somewhat from existing communal affections. That may be the job of legal rules and legal rights: to constitute a non-affective framework for actions which are novel from a communal point of view. Without some such impersonal framework, the creative human desire for new initiatives faces a terrifying vacuum: If it is not to be stifled by existing community, it must take its chances in a world beyond community. But that would be a world unstructured by *any* basis for security and expectation.

I want to illustrate this with an example. At a superficial level, Shakespeare's *Romeo and Juliet* is a noble and lamentable tragedy of star-crossed "death-marked" love:[19] The fates bring the lovers together and, at the end, it is the fates who cruelly divide them. But *Romeo and Juliet* can also be read as a deeper text about the dangers that beset a new and unforeseen social initiative—in this case a romantic initiative—in circumstances where the only available structures for social action are those embedded in the affections and disaffections of the existing community. The bonds which tie together the members of the respective clans of Capulet and Montague, and which divide the clans from one another, are such as to rule out of the question the union that the young lovers seek. Driven by their need for each other, Juliet and Romeo seek to create a marriage for themselves outside those inhibiting bonds.

The tragedy is that this cannot reliably be done in that social world, for there is no framework of public or impersonal law, standing apart from communal attachments, of which people can avail themselves in circumstances like these. Even the apparent voice of order in the play—Prince Escalus—is presented as head of a third clan and himself deeply implicated in the dis-

18. J.S. Mill, On Liberty (Indianapolis ed. 1955).

19. W. Shakespeare, *Prologue, Romeo and Juliet*, in The Complete Works 379 (S. Wells & G. Taylor eds. 1986).

affection between Capulet and Montague.[20] So the lovers have to take their chances in a world outside the public realm. The arrangements they make are of necessity covert and clandestine. There is no public and hence no visible and reliable way of co-ordinating actions and expectations. There is no way of counting on any but their own resources in a world where formally and publicly their relationship does not exist. Secret letters go astray. Another marriage is contracted for Juliet because it is thought this one did not exist.[21] Communications break down, actions are misread, and timing fails as the lovers try to act in concert in a world that provides no structure or landmarks for co-ordination. Their only hope of success is for Juliet to assume "the form of death" to the social world in which she was brought up, and to resurrect herself in the giddy space of a world beyond the city walls.[22]

On the superficial reading, the lovers are cursed by wretched bad luck in the final Act. If only Friar Lawrence's letter had got through, if only Balthazar had seen Friar Lawrence before riding to talk with Romeo, if only Juliet had awoken a minute or two before Romeo took the poison—the tragedy might have been averted, and everyone might have lived happily ever after. But on the deeper reading, misunderstanding, lack of co-ordination, failure in planning and communication, mistiming, and eventual catastrophe are more or less inevitable. For action, there is, as Romeo discovers, "no world without Verona walls."[23] There is nothing outside the structures of their warring clans that these two can rely on—no points of salience, no common framework of expectations, and no public knowledge—just their own meagre resources and those of their understandably pusillanimous allies. Man is a social animal; only a

20. *Id.* at 412 (Act V, Scene 3—Prince Escalus: "And I, for winking at your discords too / Have lost a brace of kinsmen. All are punished.").

21. *Id.*, 402-03 (Act III, Scene 5):

Nurse: . . . Romeo
Is banished, and all the world to nothing
That he dares ne'er come back to challenge you.
Or, if he do, it needs must be by stealth.
. . . .
Beshrew my very heart,
I think you are happy in this second match,
For it excels your first; or if it did not,
Your first is dead, or 'twere as good he were
As living hence and you no use of him.

22. *Id.* at 412 (Act V, Scene 3).

23. *Id.* at 398 (Act III, Scene 3).

god can live outside a state. We do not have the resources in ourselves to co-ordinate our activity without some social structures.[24]

There are two morals one can draw from this story. The first is cautionary: Don't fall in love with someone from a hostile clan, or in other words, "Don't ever try to act outside the structures of your community." But the second moral, and the one I want to draw upon, is addressed not to young lovers, but to those of our colleagues who call for a return to a particularist communitarian form of politics: "Don't urge us to identify the structures for social action too closely with the affections of existing communities. For in a human world, the limits of those affections may sometimes leave people with nowhere to go, and no reliable basis on which they can take new initiatives or constitute bearable lives for themselves."

What this implies is that it is important for there to be a structure of rights that people can count on for organizing their lives, a structure which stands somewhat apart from communal or affective attachments and which can be relied on to survive as a basis for action no matter what happens to those attachments. In this regard, we are not just talking about a structure of claim-rights, but also a structure of what Hohfeld called "powers," or what Hart called secondary rules of change: some basis on which individuals or groups can reconstitute their relations to take new initiatives in social life without having to count on the affective support of the communities to which they have hitherto belonged.[25] Of course, we need not parade this as the most desirable basis for social action. The Veronan equivalent of marriage by a judge in a civil ceremony, which ought to have been available to Romeo and Juliet when their families failed to provide the necessary support, would seem a cold and arid setting for a wedding, compared to the lavish ceremony which a loving community might have made available to them. That the liberal can concede. The point is that the civil ceremony would have been better than nothing—better, that is, than the lovers being driven by the disaffection of their families

24. *Cf.* Aristotle, *Politics*, in 2 THE COMPLETE WORKS OF ARISTOTLE (J. Barnes ed. 1984) (Book I, Chapter 2) ("[M]an is by nature a political animal. And he who by nature and not by mere accident is without a state, is either a bad man or above humanity . . . .").

25. *See* W. HOHFELD, FUNDAMENTAL LEGAL CONCEPTIONS AS APPLIED IN JUDICIAL REASONING (1923); H.L.A. HART, THE CONCEPT OF LAW 27 n. (1961).

to take their chances in an outside world devoid of public structures upon which they could finally and in the last resort rely.[26]

## IV.

I have used the marriage example to illustrate these points, but I do not want to give the impression that marriage is my sole concern. There are other areas of law and politics that can be used to make related points about the indispensibility of individual rights.

One is the area of welfare rights. It is common to hear laments about the loss of face-to-face charity and caring, whether by individuals or in family groups, and its replacement in modern society by more impersonal systems of welfare agencies and formalized welfare entitlements. Certainly, there is a very important debate to be had about the nature and extent of our provision for need in society— one that I cannot go into here. But it may be worth pointing out why the replacement of face-to-face caring by more impersonal structures is not altogether the disaster that some people make it out to be.

Consider care for the elderly. Age brings with it a certain amount of dependence: As one gets older, one's capacity to secure an income diminishes while one's needs increase. There have been societies, perhaps ours in an earlier age, or China, both now and in the past, where the old have been able to count on the support of their adult children as their needs increase and their capacities diminish. That mode of caring strikes us as an attractive one, for it is based on ties of kinship, affection, and love, and it reciprocates in an almost symmetrical way the care that the parent once lavished on her children.

Moreover, it has the advantage of being personal: The care is between this particular old person and her children (who can be sensitive to the detail of her needs), rather than between old people and young people in general. Still, there are good reasons in the modern world why many old people feel less than confident about relying on their children's support. One problem is demographic: Even in kin-oriented societies such as China, there are proportionately fewer working adults to support an increasing population of the aged. But other problems

26. These reflections on *Romeo and Juliet* were first stimulated by Germaine Greer. *See* Greer, *Romeo and Juliet*, in 1 SHAKESPEARE IN PERSPECTIVE 22-23 (R. Sales ed. 1982).

go deeper into modern life. People's lives and careers are complex, shifting, and often risky and demanding. They cannot always guarantee a secure base for themselves, let alone provide an assurance of security for their parents. And people are torn by other motives in modern life which, though not intrinsically hostile to the provision of this care, make it somewhat less certain that this will be something they necessarily want to do.

To insist, then, in a communitarian spirit, that care for the aged should remain the responsibility of the family, we would have to accept either or maybe both of two costs. We would have to place limits on the *other* demands that adult children would be permitted to respond to, the risks they could run, and the mobility they could seek. (I suspect, by the way, that in the present state of things, this would involve limiting once again the capacity of *women* to move and flourish outside the home. A great many of the concerns about communitarianism articulated in this paper are above all *feminist* concerns.) Or, if we were not prepared to do that (and maybe even if we were), we would have to accept the cost of exposing the elderly to a certain amount of insecurity and uncertainty in addition to the other burdens of their age. Neither in this country nor in Europe have people been willing to accept those costs. Instead, we have opted for less personal, less affective modes of care. People are encouraged to purchase an income for their old age in the marketplace, so they can rely on a pension check from a finance house even if they cannot rely on the warm support of their children. And, as a fall-back position, the impersonal agencies of the state guarantee an income, either to all the elderly, or to those who have not made or have not been able to make impersonal provision for themselves. Thus, although we may not care for them on a face-to-face basis, we both provide impersonal structures to enable them to care for themselves, and respond collectively and impersonally as a society to the rights that they have to our support. Our choice of this impersonality is well described in an English context by Michael Ignatieff in his book, *The Needs of Strangers*:

> As we stand together in line at the post office, while they cash their pension cheques, some tiny portion of my income is transferred into their pockets through the numberless capillaries of the state. The mediated quality of our relationship seems necessary to both of us. They are dependent on the state, not upon me, and we are both glad of it. . . . My

> responsibilities towards them are mediated through a vast division of labour. In my name a social worker climbs the stairs to their rooms and makes sure they are as warm and as clean as they can be persuaded to be. When they get too old to go out, a volunteer will bring them a hot meal, make up their beds, and if the volunteer is a compassionate person, listen to their whispering streams of memory. When they can't go on, an ambulance will take them to the hospital, and when they die, a nurse will be there to listen to the ebbing of their breath. It is this solidarity among strangers, this transformation through the division of labour of needs into rights and rights into care that gives us whatever fragile basis we have for saying that we live in a moral community.[27]

It is not that a system of rights is the only imaginable way in which needs could be dealt with in a caring society. We could set things up in a way that encouraged old people to rely on the warm and loving support of their families. But even if we did that, I think we would still want to set up a system of rights as a fall-back—as a basis on which some *assurance* of support could be given, without risking the insecurity, resentment and indignity of leaving the elderly completely at "the uncertain mercy of their sons and daughters."[28]

## V.

These points suggest some more general reflections about the distribution of resources and well-being. There is a passage in the work of Karl Marx, and a tradition of Marxist thought, which criticizes philosophers who emphasize justice and individual rights in their accounts of social distribution. In his *Critique of the Gotha Programm*, Marx heaped derision on even egalitarian theories as proposals for the distribution of social wealth. He regarded all such proposals as "obsolete verbal rubbish"[29] so far as the reform of capitalism was concerned, and as too utopian and naive for the early stages of socialist construction. He was, however, prepared to predict that a time would come when people would lose their concern for justice and rights altogether:

> In a higher phase of communist society . . . after labour has become not only a means of life but life's prime want; after

27. M. Ignatieff, The Needs of Strangers 9-10 (1984).
28. *Id.* at 17.
29. Marx, *Critique of the Gotha Programme*, in Karl Marx: Selected Writings 569 (D. McLellan ed. 1977) (hereinafter Marx).

> the productive forces have also increased with the all-round development of the individual, and all the springs of co-operative wealth flow more abundantly—only then can the narrow horizon of bourgeois right be crossed in its entirety and society inscribe on its banners: From each according to his ability, to each according to his needs![30]

The suggestion here is precisely *not* that in a communist society people would have a *right* to the satisfaction of their needs. On the contrary, in a communist society we would be able to do away with rights as such altogether, and goods and services would be supplied naturally to needs and wants as they arose without the mediation of rigid individual entitlements. On the basis of this sort of talk, rights and rigid formulas of law have been regarded by many Marxists as essentially bourgeois forms destined to disappear with the rest of bourgeois society, including the restricted conditions of production which make that society possible. Bourgeois philosophers are therefore engaged, they say, in asking the wrong questions when they worry about what rights people would have in an ideal society.[31]

Some communitarians have echoed this theme. Sandel takes John Rawls to task for insisting on the primacy of distributive justice when Rawls himself acknowledges that justice makes sense only relative to circumstances in which resources are scarce and human sympathies limited. Sandel says it is easy to imagine small-scale communities in which neither of those conditions obtained: communities in which claims of justice and right would be replaced by spontaneous affection. In such a community, he says,

> Individual rights and fair decision procedures are seldom invoked, not because injustice is rampant but because their appeal is preempted by a spirit of generosity in which I am rarely inclined to *claim* my fair share. Nor does this generosity necessarily imply that I receive out of kindness a share that is equal to or greater than the share I would be entitled to under fair principles of justice. I may get less. The point is not that I get what I would otherwise get, only more spontaneously, but simply that questions of what I get and what I am due do not loom large in the context of this overall way

30. *Id.* at 568-69.

31. For a general discussion of the place of rights and justice in Marx's thought, see A. BUCHANAN, MARX AND JUSTICE: THE RADICAL CRITIQUE OF LIBERALISM (1982); MARX, JUSTICE, AND HISTORY (M. Cohen ed. 1980).

of life.[32]

I do not want to embark on a discussion of how far-fetched the Marxian idea of the "abolition of scarcity" is. We should note, however, that for the purposes of this argument, scarcity refers simply to the existence of opportunity costs in the use of resources, and that many economists would regard the idea of the "abolition" of opportunity costs as incoherent rather than merely improbable.[33] Nor do I want to make any comment on the changes in human sympathies that Sandel and Marx are relying on, except to say that as long as goods are scarce in the sense just outlined, anything other than a situation in which each person's altruistic affections and strategies overlap perfectly with those of everyone else is going to be a situation in which competition for resources and hence the circumstances of justice continue to prevail.

If anything, the competition may be more intense if we all become altruists. History indicates that passionate altruists tend to struggle much more ferociously for their ideals than those who are merely self-interested. And surely perfect uncompetitive altruism is unlikely (to say the least!) in a world in which, we are told, concern for others will be situated concretely in the particularity of each person's life rather than given abstractly as a general formula like the principle of utility.[34]

But even if we grant Sandel and Marx their assumptions, an unrepentant bourgeois philosopher might want to insist that there is *still* a place for rights in Marx's prosperous higher phase of communism and in Sandel's affectionate *gemeinschaft*. For it matters to people that they and their loved ones have enough to eat, it matters to them that they have access to at least some of the resources necessary for the pursuit of their own projects and aspirations, and it is likely to go on mattering sufficiently for them to want some greater *assurance* of that

32. M. SANDEL, *supra* note 12, at 33. *Cf.* J. RAWLS, A THEORY OF JUSTICE 126 n. (1971), and D. HUME, A TREATISE ON HUMAN NATURE 485 n. (L. Selby-Bigge ed. 1888).

33. *Cf.* A. NOVE, THE ECONOMICS OF FEASIBLE SOCIALISM 15-20 (1983). Marx's view was that the abolition of scarcity was a crucial prerequisite for socialism because without it and without what he called "a great increase in productive power . . . want is merely made general, and with destitution the struggle for necessities and all the old filthy business would necessarily be reproduced." Marx, *The German Ideology*, in MARX, *supra* note 29, at 171.

34. *See* citations *supra* note 15. For an explanation of how collective action problems may arise even among altruists, see D. PARFIT, REASONS AND PERSONS (1984).

other than merely the affections of their fellow citizens. Even if we concede that distribution can take place on the basis of spontaneous co-operation in circumstances of plenty, and even if we concede that it is desirable that it should take place on that basis, people will want some assurance that the circumstances that make this possible are going to continue. I cannot imagine that in any conceivable society on earth this is something they will be able to take for granted; everything we know warns us of the dangers of such trust and complacency, touching no doubt though it is. (Again the background question is: Are the socialists and communitarians asking us to think concretely or in terms of abstract possibilities?) So rights once again have at least a fall-back function to perform. People might want to have some sense of what they *could* claim as their due in the unhappy though no doubt unlikely case that goods become scarce, or affections turn out to be limited after all.[35]

## VI.

Interestingly, it is not only welfare rights that perform this fall-back function. A similar analysis is possible in the area of market relations—the area that liberals and their critics see as the domain *par excellence* of individual rights—as Marx described it, "a very Eden of the innate rights of man . . . the exclusive realm of Freedom, Equality, Property and Bentham."[36] At first sight, it is tempting to say about markets, not what we have said so far about rights—that they involve fall-back positions for social relations constituted by affection or community—but rather that markets involve an area of social relations that *is* actually constituted by structures of contract and individual right, an area in which there is no prominent component of affection or community at all. We know, of course, that this is

35. This raises an interesting question. When a theorist of justice evaluates the distribution of wealth in society, should she be concerned with what people are entitled to, or with what they actually get? The idea of rights as fall-back guarantees suggests the former rather than the latter, because what people actually get may depend on an interplay of factors, including affective factors, which are independent of their rights. But still there are reasons to be cautious about concentrating too exclusively on formal entitlements. Such concentration can too easily lead us to look only at *legal* entitlements, ignoring the fact that certain non-legal structures in society may determine not only what people actually get but also what they can rely on *in extremis*. There may also be a lot of interplay between people's sense of their formal entitlements and their sense of what they actually receive. Expectations are not fixed, and what may originally have been given out of affection may come in time to be regarded as a guarantee.

36. 1 K. Marx, Capital 280 (E. Mandel ed. 1976).

sociologically naive: A market cannot exist without an ethic of fidelity and without some underpinning for its property entitlements.[37] But still, the ethics, the ideology, and the force that make markets possible are not much more than what is presupposed by the idea of rights anyway, and the point is that they do not necessarily include any of the more robust and substantial ideas and affections associated in the modern mind with the idea of community.

Certainly the higher levels of the capitalist market—secondary capital markets, commodity markets, international trade and so on—have this character of being mainly rights-constituted (though even there the network of individual rights is supplemented by more or less rigid codes of professional honor among those who trade in them). Similarly, in more mundane markets, we buy and sell in department stores with little more to bond us to our market partners than reciprocal self-interest and the laws of contract. In these contexts, then, it is true that rights do not *underwrite* affective arrangements; rather, they *make possible* an enormous variety of arms-length dealings between people who are in almost all other respects strangers to one another.

The point can be put in terms of an analogy with the *Romeo and Juliet* argument. If we were limited to the structures of *gemeinschaft*, if there were a sense that economic transactions and economic co-operation had always to be predicated upon substantial and affectionate solidarity, then the result would indeed be a warm and caring society, but also a desperately primitive and impoverished one. Human life would not be solitary, but many of the devices by which we have succeeded in mitigating its poverty, its nastiness, its brutishness, and its brevity would be limited or unavailable.[38] The division of labour, national and international trade, commercial research and development, and above all the co-ordination of the activity of millions of different centers of production, distribution, and exchange would be impossible. Those who wanted to take an initiative and deal with strangers, or strike bargains with those they neither cared for nor expected to care for them, would, like Shakespeare's lovers, have to step outside the world of social structures and rule-governed expectations altogether, and

37. *See* E. Durkheim, The Division of Labour in Society (1933).
38. *See* A. Nove, *supra* note 33, at 4-26.

take their chances in an environment where there was nothing to count on but the unstructured self-interest of others. They would be stuck, as it were, in a perpetual black market.[39] Ground rules of rights and contract, on the other hand, conceived independently of communal bonds, make it possible for us to initiate dealings every day, directly or indirectly, with thousands of people we barely know, and to take advantage of their situation and abilities as they take advantage of ours, with the confidence that there are rules available to facilitate, structure, and secure these dealings even when there is no affection to base them on.[40]

Having said all that, it should be noted that there are many transactions, which we would call market transactions, that are not solely or explicitly constituted by rights and contracts. Transactions in the local store, for example, may be governed by implicit friendship and goodwill as much as by self-interest and legal obligation. Someone may ask, "Why can't all economic transactions be like that?" I think I have already given an answer, but it is important to stress that, even if they were, there would *still* be a role for rights to play. My grocer can deal with me in an informal, friendly way, sometimes giving me credit when I need it, or ordering some trivial item that I want, and so on, only if he has confidence that in the last resort he would be able to recover the money I owe if I abused his friendship, and that no-one else can take unfair advantage of the "goodwill" he has accumulated. He may hope (just like the partners to a normal marriage) that he never has to invoke these formal guarantees, but that is quite compatible with the proposition that his assurance of their existence is one of the reasons he is able to act as informally as he does. Once again, we find that, far from destroying or replacing affective ties, fall-back rights may be their pre-condition, at least in an imperfect world.

39. In environments like this—black markets—there are no structures of rules, and hence no basis for security, expectations and co-ordination in contractual dealings. That would be the fate of *all* dealings between strangers, if we were to insist on legitimating only those economic transactions that were clothed in the substantial affections of the community.

40. For a similar perspective on markets and affection, see A. SMITH, AN INQUIRY INTO THE NATURE AND CAUSES OF THE WEALTH OF NATIONS 18 (E. Cannan ed. 1976) ("In civilized society, [man] stands in need of the cooperation and assistance of great multitudes, while his whole life is scarce sufficient to gain the friendship of a few persons.").

## VII.

I want to conclude my analysis with a couple of more theoretical points about this particular approach to rights. The first is a modest disclaimer. This theory of rights as fallbacks is intended to explain some of the rights we rely on in social life, but it is not intended as a *comprehensive* theory of rights. There probably is something wrong with the idea that there has to be just *one* theory that generates and explains everything so far as rights are concerned. There may be several theories, and as a consequence, not all rights will necessarily have to have the same normative shape or moral importance.

In particular, the idea of rights as fall-backs should be distinguished from that of rights as setting minimum acceptable standards of behavior. The rights that one would have to fall back on when a marriage breaks up in bitterness may, for example, impose much higher standards of behavior than one might necessarily want to impose as *minima* for a happily functioning marriage. But I make this point mainly because I am not clear exactly how so-called "human" rights or constitutional guarantees would fit into my analysis. Consider, for example, Article Three of the European Convention on Human Rights: "No one shall be subjected to torture or to inhuman or degrading treatment or punishment."[41] Perhaps this could be squeezed into the framework of my analysis by saying that in ordinary political arrangements between state and citizen, the issue of torture simply does not arise; but that people need this as something to fall back on when normal politics collapse. Someone who wants to stress the affective side of political commitment—love for one's country, the patriotic cherishing of its constitution—would still have to leave room for that.

However, I think the "minimum standards" conception captures more accurately the sense of this provision. The claim is that the government in *all* its dealings with citizens, normal or abnormal, must never let its conduct descend to this level. Certainly citizens need to be able to rely on a *guarantee* that this will never happen; and there is that common element of guarantee in both conceptions. But the constitutional right is intended to operate as a *constant* constraint, not as something that can be

41. Art. 3, Convention for the Protection of Human Rights and Fundamental Freedoms, *reprinted in* A. ROBERTSON, HUMAN RIGHTS IN EUROPE 294-95 (1977).

relied on to come into the picture but only when other bases for political restraint have failed.

Either way, communitarians and other opponents of the rights tradition would do well to reflect on this need for articulated guarantees as part of the security that people require of their society. They are entitled to insist, of course, that liberals should think more seriously than many of them have about the communal structures that make rights possible as effective guarantees for all.[42] But that has not been the main point of this paper—the importance of community and communal bonds is conceded. The main point is that some rights, at least, would be necessary as fall-backs in many areas, even if on the whole we wanted to constitute normal social relations in those areas on a basis other than rights.

## VIII.

My final point is about the individualism of this analysis. Someone might accept the need for formal legalistic structures as fall-backs to underpin social relations that are constituted on other terms. But they may still question why it is necessary for those *in extremis* arrangements to be presented as rights *of an individual.* Surely groups and communities as such need to have something they can fall back on as well.

The point is a good one as far as it goes. *Romeo and Juliet* is not so much about the need for *individual* rights (though it can be expressed in those terms) as about the needs of *a couple*, needs that would of course be unintelligible apart from their involvement with one another. Similarly a village or local community, an ethnic group, or a family, may need to know what they can count on, and how they can organize their relations with other groups, once their affectionate bonds to their neighbors or to the larger society have been broken. In these contexts, we may want to talk about the rights of groups, or we may think that other less individual-oriented legal terms are appropriate.[43] Moreover, in other contexts, one affectionate or communal bond may be backed up by another: When a marriage

42. *See generally* Taylor, *supra* note 12.

43. On group rights, see N. Glazer, *Individual Rights, Against Group Rights*, in HUMAN RIGHTS (E. Kamenka & A. Tay eds. 1978). *See also* Waldron, *Can Communal Goods Be Human Rights?*, 28 ARCH. EUR. SOC. 296 (1987). For an excellent discussion of individualism in this context, see J. RAZ, THE MORALITY OF FREEDOM 104-32 (1986).

fails and a woman is violently assaulted by her husband, she may find greater security in the communal atmosphere of a Woman's Refuge than in the austere individualism of the law courts.

Still there is some point to stressing that a set of legal rules conceived as fall-backs will have to include rights for individual men and women whatever else it includes. For any given social relation, there is always the possibility that it may disintegrate completely, leaving a naked individual bereft of any substantial bond to others, wanting to know where she stands. To recognize this possibility is not necessarily to embrace ontological individualism.[44] It may still be true that the individual is the creation of the social, not the other way round, and that man, as Marx put it, is "an animal which can develop into an individual only in society."[45] All one needs to accept is that, as it were, individual *fall-out* from social relations is possible. And, indeed, if it is the case that the precipitated individual is going to be an incomplete and alienated being, confused, frightened, and truncated as a result of the social rupture, then surely the case for her protection and security in these unhappy circumstances is if anything even more substantial.

Of course, modernists among us accept something much more positive than this: that though an individual standing apart from all social relations is unimaginable, nevertheless it is a good thing that modern men and women feel able to distance themselves from, reflect upon, and consciously embrace or repudiate any or all of the relations that constitute their history.[46] Though we live in and for communities of one sort or another most of the time, our communal attachments are never so remote from our capacities as conscious, articulate, thinking, choosing, creating beings that we cannot subject them to scrutiny and consideration. Rights as fall-backs give us the vantage point from which that can be done. The point is not simply the liberal one about the importance of individuals' autonomously shaping their lives. It is also that these processes of individual thought, reflection, and change are source of many of the new beginnings in the world, including new communal beginnings.

44. For a discussion of the different meanings of the word "individualism," see S. LUKES, INDIVIDUALISM (1973).

45. Marx, *Grundrisse*, in MARX, *supra* note 29, at 346.

46. *See* M. BERMAN, ALL THAT IS SOLID MELTS INTO THE AIR: THE EXPERIMENT OF MODERNITY (1982); M. IGNATIEFF, *supra* note 27, at ch. 5.

We should be careful not to undermine the possibility of that.[47]

In recent communitarian literature, Sandel and others have condemned this image of the individual: They say it seems to "rule out in advance any end whose adoption or pursuit could engage or transform the identity of the self."[48] The modern liberal self is said to stand apart from its attachments, particularly those attachments which might involve "more or less expansive self-understandings" to take in one's connections with others as well.

> One consequence of this distance is to put the self beyond the reach of experience, to make it vulnerable, to fix its identity once and for all. No commitment could grip me so deeply that I could not understand myself without it. No transformation of life purposes and plans could be so unsettling as to disrupt the contours of my identity. No project could be so essential that turning away from it would call into question the person I am.[49]

Communal bonds, says Sandel, can never be *constitutive* of a liberal self, so long as it retains this facility for questioning them. He calls instead for a conception of the self that is at least capable of being identified completely and essentially with some communal history or commitment (taking for granted that we know what "completely" and "essentially" mean in this context).

The critique appears to be an attractive one, for it associates flexibility of attachments with shallowness. "To imagine a person incapable of constitutive attachments is . . . to imagine a person wholly without character, without depth."[50] The sense we get is that one who knows she can alter her attachments—the liberal individual—cannot possibly feel as intensely or wholehearted about them than one who knows she cannot. But that is a mistake, based at best on a simplistic view about the relation between the metaphysics of the self and the phenomenology of commitment, and at worst on the mere rhetorical power of ill-understood terms like "essence," "identity," and "constitutive." To retain the capacity to review our commitments, we do not always have to be *holding something back* from them. Having the capacity to reflect means *being able to make an*

47. *See* H. Arendt, *supra* note 17.
48. M. Sandel, *supra* note 12, at 64-65.
49. *Id.* at 62.
50. *Id.* at 179.

*effort* when one needs to, to wrench away and construct the necessary psychological distance. It does not require a continuous reserve of commitment and energy which *could* have been associated with one's attachment but is not, and it certainly does not mean sitting back all the time in the isolated citadel of self treating the attachment as a curious and contingent event in which one has no interest. In modern experience, intensity, whole-heartedness, and the sense of having identified comprehensively with a project or commitment, are as much features of the commitments that people *choose* and the ones they could give up *if* they wanted to, as of the commitments which people *discover* they have and find they cannot question—many moderns would say more so. To repeat a point I have made a number of times: Having something to fall back on if an attachment fails may be a *condition* of being able to identify intensely with one's attachments, rather than something which derogates from that intensity.

At any rate, these reflections at least make the nub of the controversy clear, between communitarians and their modernist opponents. The debate is not between those who see social life as constitutively communal and those who do not. Nor is it between community and the values of bare individualism. It is between those who, on the one hand, yearn for communal bonds so rigid that the question of what happens when they come apart will not arise or need to be faced, and, on the other hand, those who are, firstly, realistic enough to notice the tragedy of the broken bond and ask "What happens next?"; and, secondly, optimistic enough to embrace the possibility of the creative construction of new bonds and new connections, and ask "How is that possible?". Those are the battle-lines; in this article, I have tried to indicate the role that rights may play in that controversy.

# Part III
# How Many Different Voices?

# [11]

# *The Virtue of Feeling and the Feeling of Virtue*

ELIZABETH V. SPELMAN

> The mother who taught me what I know of tenderness and love and compassion taught me also the bleak rituals of keeping Negroes in their place.
>
> —*Lillian Smith*[1]

We cannot be said to have taken women seriously until we explore how women have treated each other. But that means, too, how we have mistreated each other. The history of women, including the history of feminism and feminists, is hardly free of some women doing violence to others, of some women miserably failing other women in need.

Most feminists would insist that the history of women cannot be well told unless its tellers are not embarrassed to investigate and describe women's emotional lives: our joys, our griefs, our hopes, our fears, our loves, our hates. But such insistence on the importance of feeling amounts simply to a ringing, one-sided celebration of women's virtues—in having emotions and recounting them—unless we are willing, as Lillian Smith was, to look at the expression of emotions among women that reveal the less glorious side of our lives together.

As is well documented, nineteenth-century white, middle-class suffragists were ready and willing to use racist arguments in the name of advancing what they called "women's interests."[2] Some white women routinely beat black women who were their slaves.[3] Nazi women gave their all in the effort to eliminate the Jewish population of Europe—which included, of course, Jewish women.[4] At an international conference on women's history not long ago in Amsterdam, the organizers were asked why what in the conference brochure was referred to as "women's history" still really amounted to "white women's history." One of the white women responded: "We have enough of a burden trying to get a feminist viewpoint across, why do we have to take on this extra burden?"[5] At a recent feminist gathering in Minnesota, an able-bodied woman expressed her deep disappointment at the complaints by women in wheelchairs that all the papers presumed that women are able-bodied: in effect she said, "Here we finally have some time and space to talk about just 'us,' and you insist that we talk about something else." Can we be confident that women who demand the strictest scrutiny of the conditions under which they work and of the fairness of their salaries show the same concern for the working conditions of the women who take care of their children or clean their condos?

I do not wish to suggest here that white, middle-class, able-bodied, heterosexual Christian women have a monopoly on the mistreatment of other women. And by using these examples rather than others, I run the risk of making the sins of some women more important than those of others and thereby simply reasserting the privileged position of certain women in Western feminism. But it is startling that something as basic as some women's inhumanity to other women has not been a central concern for the variety of inquiries included under the rubric "feminist ethics." We give lots of attention to men's oppression of women but far too few sustained examinations of women's oppression or exploitation of other women.[6] As Berenice Fisher put it, when commenting on the growing use of "guilt" at feminist conferences: "Although we frequently employed the language of "guilt," virtually no one paid attention to guilt as a moral issue, that is, to the realities of wrongdoing and the responsibilities and consequences entailed by it."[7] I want to offer a few reasons in brief for this virtual silence and then suggest a way we might explore the moral dimensions of women's treatment and mistreatment of one another as at least a necessary part of whatever we include under the rubric "feminist ethics."

Why has the question of women's treatment of each other not been a burning issue for much of feminism? First of all, one of the bad raps about themselves that many women have had to battle is the image that they are catty and callous toward each other, really interested only in men and their money or their prestige or their bodies or in some cases all of those. So perhaps it has seemed hard to make a publicly understandable feminist case about the oppression of women without simultaneously remaining mute on the topic of some women's oppression of or plain meanness toward other women. According to this way of thinking, it is, to begin with, too difficult psychologically to talk about oneself or other women as both victim and victimizer. For example, perhaps it is not easy to feel sympathy for the abused wives of white slave-owners and at the same time be critical of some of their actions toward their female (and male) slaves. Moreover, under such circumstances it is awfully inviting to lay the blame for our own or others' shortcomings at the feet of those who have victimized us or them. But however we might explain the reluctance or caution about discussing women's bad treatment of other women, taking those groups of women seriously requires that we do so.

There aren't only psychological motives for shying away from examining women's mistreatment of one another. Many of the tools of feminist thinking work against the possibility of our taking to be of much theoretical or practical concern the absence of care or the presence of hostility, hatred, and contempt among women.

First of all, many of us feminists have done little to shake a habit we share with many of our fellow citizens: talking loosely about "men and women" as if these men and women had no racial, class, or cultural identity; talking about "women and blacks" or "women and minorities" as if there were no black women or no women in the groups called "minorities"; comparing relations between "men and women" to those between "whites and blacks" or "rich and poor" or "colonizer and colonized," which precludes us from talking about differences among women—between white and black, or Anglo and Latina, or rich and poor, or colonizer and colonized. In addition, much feminist theory and history is filled with incessant comparisons between "women" on the one hand and "blacks," the "poor," "Jews," and so on, on the other. Think for example of talk about "women" being treated like "slaves." Whenever we talk that way we are not only making clear that the "women" we're referring to aren't themselves slaves; we're making it impossible to talk about how the women who weren't slaves treated those who were.

If we aren't encouraged to talk about differences among women, indeed prohibited from doing so by the very terms we use or the allegedly crucial comparisons we make, then it becomes very hard, or apparently only peripheral to our central concerns, to talk about how women treat each other. But *that*, it seems to me, is what feminist ethics ought to be about, whatever else it might be about: how women treat each other. For again we must ask whether we can be said to have taken women seriously if we have not explored how women have treated each other.

Moreover, the effort by some feminists to delineate an "ethics of care,"[8] as well as the struggle to get the role of emotions in human life taken seriously, paradoxically (but perhaps not so accidentally) has diverted our attention from the history of the lack of care of women for women and has almost precluded the possibility of our looking at anything but love and friendship in women's emotional responses to one another. Some passages from Jane Austen's *Emma* illustrate what I have in mind.

Emma, our lively young protagonist, is deep in a debate with Mr. George Knightley about the behavior of Frank Churchill. Young Churchill did not grow up with his father and stepmother, who are part of Emma and Knightley's social circle. A visit by Churchill to his father and stepmother has been long awaited. Emma and Knightley disagree in their assessment of Churchill's delay in making the trip:

> KNIGHTLEY: "I cannot believe that he has not the power of coming, if he made a point of it. It is too unlikely for me to believe it without proof. . . . If Frank Churchill had wanted to see his father, he would have contrived it between September and January. A man at his age—what is he? three or four-and-twenty—cannot be without the means of doing as much as that. It is impossible."
>
> EMMA: "You are the worst judge in the world, Mr. Knightley, of the difficulties of dependence. You do not know what it is to have tempers to manage. . . . It is very unfair to judge of anybody's conduct without an intimate knowledge of their situation. Nobody, who has not been in the interior of a family, can say what the difficulties of any individual of that family may be."
>
> KNIGHTLEY: "There is one thing, Emma, which a man can always do, if he chooses, and that is, his duty. . . . It is Frank Churchill's duty to pay this attention to his father."

EMMA: ". . . you have not an idea of what is requisite in situations directly opposite to your own. . . . I can imagine that if you, as you are . . . were to be transported and placed all at once in Mr. Frank Churchill's situation, you would be able to say and do just what you have been recommending for him; and it might have a very good effect . . . but then you would have no habits of early obedience and long observance to break through. To him who has, it might not be so easy to burst forth at once into perfect independence. . . . Oh, the difference of situation and habit! I wish you would try to understand what an amiable young man may be likely to feel in directly opposing [the other adults who had brought him up]."

KNIGHTLEY: "Your amiable young man is a very weak young man, if this be the first occasion of his carrying through a resolution to do right against the will of others. It ought to have been a habit with him, by this time, of following his duty, instead of consulting expediency."

EMMA: "We are both prejudiced! you against, I for him; and we have no chance of agreeing till he is really here."

KNIGHTLEY: "Prejudiced! I am not prejudiced."

EMMA: "But I am very much, and without being at all ashamed of it. My love for [his father and stepmother] gives me a decided prejudice in his favour."[9]

I think anyone interested in the work of Carol Gilligan and those influenced by her work would find the constrasts between Knightley's and Emma's judgments about Frank Churchill to be at least on the face of it illustrative of two conceptions of morality that seem to be quite distinct.[10]

Knightley's concern for principled behavior, impartial judgment, and everyone's getting their due seems to exemplify an "ethics of justice" (said to be more likely held by men than women). For Knightley, there are at least two principles that ought to be brought to bear: the duty Churchill has to his father and the importance of Knightley himself remaining unbiased in his judgment of Churchill. Whatever relationship Churchill has to his more immediate family, that can't be as important as his duty to his own father; whatever the particular facts of the circumstances Churchill finds himself in, such facts cannot be used by Churchill, or by anyone else, to mitigate the full weight of his duty.

Emma's insistence on the contextual details of the situation and her concern for the importance of the many relationships involved (Churchill and his immediate family, Churchill and his father and stepmother, Emma and Churchill, Emma and Knightley) seem characteristic of an "ethics of care" (said to be more likely held by women than men). For Emma, Churchill's formal "duty" here is irrelevant. And Emma's relationship to both Churchill and his father cannot be erased by some formal obligation she might be said to have to remain "unprejudiced." Knightley's principled judgment of Churchill is not well grounded: He doesn't know enough about what Churchill is capable of or about the crucial details of Churchill's relationship to his immediate family.

I do not here wish to enter into the ongoing and very rich conversation about such apparently contrasting ethical orientations.[11] Instead, I feel obliged to point out what readers may miss about Emma if they are interested in her only to the degree that her words and actions illustrate an "ethics of care" in contrast to an "ethics of justice."

In the chapter immediately following the one in which we overhear the animated discussion between Emma and Knightley, Emma and her friend Harriet are out for a walk. Jane Austen invites us to eavesdrop again, this time on Emma's private thoughts:

> They were just approaching the house where lived Mrs. and Miss Bates. . . . There was always sufficient reason for [calling upon them]; Mrs. and Miss Bates loved to be called on; and [Emma] knew she was considered by the very few who presumed ever to see imperfection in her, as rather negligent in that respect, and as not contributing what she ought to the stock of their scanty comforts.
>
> She had had many a hint from Mr. Knightley, and some from her own heart, as to her deficiency, but none were equal to counteract the persuasion of its being very disagreeable—a waste of time—tiresome women—and all the horror of being in danger of falling in with the second and third rate of Highbury, who were calling on them for ever, and therefore she seldom went near them.[12]

If we get thoroughly caught up in comparing Emma's unapologetically biased, very particularized caring for Frank Churchill with Knightley's rather stern, impersonal principled response, we may fail to ask a very important question: But for whom does Emma care? What kind of treatment does she give those she regards as her social and economic inferiors? The fact, if it is one, that some women in reflecting on their moral problems show care and a fine sense of complexity appreciative of context tells us nothing about *who* they think worthy of their care nor whose situation demands attention to details and whose does not.

Moreover, there are forms of care that are not only compatible with but in some contexts crucial to the maintenance of systematic inequalities among women. Judith Rollins describes in some detail the "maternalism" expressed by white female employers towards their black female domestic employees:

> The maternalism dynamic is based on the assumption of a superordinate-subordinate relationship. While maternalism may protect and nurture, it also degrades and insults. The "caring" that is expressed in maternalism might range from an adult-to-child to a human-to-pet kind of caring but, by definition (and by the evidence presented by my data), it is not human-to-equal-human caring. The female employer, with her motherliness and protectiveness and generosity, is expressing in a distinctly feminine way her lack of respect for the domestic as an autonomous, adult employee. While the female employer typically creates a more intimate relationship with a domestic than her male counterpart does, this should not be interpreted as meaning she values the human worth of the domestic any more highly than does the more impersonal male employer.[13]

I have said in effect that by my lights one of the most fruitful understandings of "feminist ethics" is the investigation of how women treat each other—how well or badly we do in relation to one another. I have also said that feminist interest in exploring an "ethics of care" and in emphasizing the importance of emotions in our lives paradoxically has encouraged us to *ignore* the absence of care by women for other women, to *disregard* the presence of "negative" emotional reactions by women to other women. I now want to make my remarks much more specific by focusing on the ways in which our emotions reveal the moral dimensions of our relationships—in particular, how our emotions reveal how seriously we take the concerns of others, what we take to be our responsibility for others' plight, and the extent to which we regard others as even having points of view we need to take seriously.

Our emotions, or at least some of them, can be highly revelatory of whom and what we care or don't care about. They provide powerful clues to the ways in which we take ourselves to be implicated in the lives of others and they in ours. As this example from Aristotle reveals, many of our emotions locate us in moral relation to one another: One who doesn't get angry when the occasion calls for it "is thought not to feel things nor to be pained by them, and since he does not get angry, he is thought unlikely to defend himself; and to endure being insulted, and put up with insult to one's friends, is slavish."[14] Aristotle is insisting that if under certain conditions we don't feel anger, we may have failed to show proper respect for ourselves or proper concern for our friends.

Here is another example of what I have in mind when speaking of our emotions as revelatory of ways in which we take ourselves to be implicated in the lives of others and they in ours. At my own educational institution and many others, there have been blatant displays of racism—for example, messages left by cowards in protective anonymity—telling black, Latina, and Chinese-American students in no uncertain terms that they don't belong at Smith College and that if they don't like the way they're treated, they should "go home." (These represent only the obvious tip of an iceberg that is melting with what the Supreme Court in a related context called "all deliberate speed.") I do not wish to go into details of how my institution or yours actually has responded to what, in a revealing phrase, typically are called "incidents" (a term that suggests, perhaps insists, that such events are infrequent and anomalous). But by way of beginning to show what our emotions tell us about our moral relations to each other and the contours and quality of our care for one another, I'd like to run through some possible responses.

1. Ivylawn College regrets the occurrence of racist incidents on its campus.
2. Ivylawn College is embarrassed by the occurrence of racist incidents on its campus.
3. Ivylawn College feels guilty about the occurrence of racist incidents on its campus.
4. Ivylawn College feels shame for the occurrence of racist incidents on its campus.[15]

Surely you already notice some significant difference—yet to be explored in detail—between regret, embarrassment, guilt, and shame. Think also of the difference between

5. Ivylawn College regrets the occurrence of racist incidents on its campus.
6. Ivylawn College regrets the harm done to those hurt by the recent events on its campus.

If the first set of contrasts reminds us that different emotions imply different notions of responsibility and depth of concern, the second reminds us that the same emotion can have different objects—what the emotions are about. In going into all these differences in more detail, I turn to Gabriele Taylor's *Pride, Shame, and Guilt: Emotions of Self-Assessment.*[16]

Gabriele Taylor is one of a number of contemporary philosophers who hold or operate on the basis of what has been dubbed the "cognitive theory" of the emotions. Though cognitivists differ among each other on certain details, they share the conviction that emotions cannot simply be feelings, like churnings in our stomachs, flutterings of our hearts, chokings in our throats. Though such feelings may accompany my regretting having hurt you or my sense of shame in having hurt you, the difference between my regret and my shame cannot be accounted for by reference to such feelings; nor can the difference between my regret in having hurt *you* and my regret in having hurt *my father.* There is a kind of logic to our emotions that has nothing to do with whatever dumb feelings may accompany them (in many cases there don't even seem to be such feelings anyway).

It is the central tenet of what is currently known as the "cognitive theory" of emotions that our emotions are not a clue to or sign of poppings and firings and other gyrations—mental or physical—within us but rather indicate how we see the world. For emotions typically have identificatory cognitive states. For example, what identifies my emotion as *anger* is among other things a belief that some unjust harm has been done; what makes my emotion a matter of *fear* is among other things my belief that danger is imminent. I shall not go into more detail about the cognitive theory here—you shall see more of it in reflective practice below—but it is perhaps worth making explicit that we could not regard our emotions as very interesting facts about us—in particular, as deeply connected to ourselves as moral agents—if emotions were simply events, things happening in us like headaches or bleeding gums.[17]

That said, let us return to our earlier examples of regret, embarrassment, guilt, and shame. As Gabriele Taylor reminds us, if I regret that something happened, then I must regard what happened as in some sense undesirable. But I need not regard what happened as anything morally troubling—for example, I may now regret not taking a few more days of vacation. Or I can feel regret for something for which I was in no way responsible—Gabriele Taylor's example is the passing of summer.[18] Moreover, even though regretting that something happened means I must take it to be in some sense undesirable, it is still possible for me to think that nevertheless all things considered it is not something I think should not have happened. And it is perfectly possible for me to regret it without being at all inclined to take any actions in consequence. This is why we can perfectly sincerely send our regrets—indeed, even our "deepest regrets"—that a party occurs on a night we're out of town. It might have been fun to go to the party, and I might be a bit apprehensive about hurting the feelings of or disappointing a good friend, but it is more important to do what takes me out of town and I don't want my friend to change the date of the party. In all these ways, Gabriele Taylor points out, regret is quite different from remorse. You can't feel remorse about something for which you do not believe yourself responsible, or about something that doesn't appear to you to be morally wrong, or about something you don't wish to undo or attend to in some way.

So if Ivylawn College or any other institution expresses *regret* that a "racist incident" happened on its campus, all it is doing so far is acknowledging that such an event took place and allowing that it was in some unspecified sense undesirable. But it is not in any way assuming responsibility for the "incident" or indicating that there is anything morally troubling about it (as opposed to its just being undesirable for its nuisance value in terms of college publicity); nor is it indicating that any action is in consequence required. Note, by the way, that precisely because regret has these features, there are certain built-in limitations on the description of *what* is regretted: Though it is perfectly possible to "regret" something described as a "racist *incident*," I'm sure no institution would publicly say that it "regretted" the murder of one student by another.

Having sketched out what the presence of regret means, we can keep on the back burner what the absence of it means—that is, not acknowledging that anything of note happened at all, let alone that it was in some way undesirable.

I shall then, without regret, move on to *embarrassment*. My guess is that most institutions are embarrassed by the occurrence of racism on their campuses, but they would not describe themselves in just that way. The reasons for this will become clear as we look at the logic of embarrassment (here again with Gabriele Taylor's help). Unlike regret, embarrassment necessarily involves a sense that one has been exposed and in consequence is subject to an adverse judgment of oneself in some respect. Suppose a man is embarrassed about beating his wife. His being embarrassed is fully compatible with his finding nothing wrong in the fact that he beats his wife. He judges himself adversely not because he thinks he has done something wrong but because he does not yet know how to respond to the audience to whom he is or imagines himself exposed. If all he feels is embarrassed, he doesn't need to do any basic repair work on himself, only figure out a way to deal with the audience—perhaps tell them it is none of their business, or insist that women need to be pushed around, or laugh it off. Perhaps he'll express regret that it is necessary to beat his wife in order to keep her in her place (so the expression of regret might cancel embarrassment). His concern is not about what he is doing to his wife but about the kind of impression he is making on others.

What then does it mean if Ivylawn College is *embarrassed* by the racist incidents on its campus—and why might it or any other institution be unlikely to publicly describe itself in this way? If an institution is embarrassed by the occurrence of racist remarks and other behavior, then what it finds troubling is not the behavior itself but the exposure of the behavior. If there is anything wrong with the institution, it is that it does not know how to prevent adverse publicity or deal well with it once public notice is taken. When an institution is embarrassed, and only embarrassed, it puts its public relations department to work; it works not on changing the institution but on changing the perception of the institution. Admitting to embarrassment is usually not a good way of dealing with embarrassment, for it simply brings attention to the situation that the embarrassed party does not want others to see.

You can feel *embarrassed* without thinking that you have done anything wrong or anything you shouldn't do, but in general[19] you can't feel *guilty* without believing that you have failed to live up to some kind of standard or that you have done something that is forbidden according to an accepted authority (including your conscience). (Of course you can be guilty without feeling guilty, but here we are talking only about feeling guilty). There is something I have done or failed to do. According to Gabriele Taylor, in feeling guilt I certainly am judging myself adversely, but my situation is not hopeless—I am not less of a person than I thought I was. I simply did something I think I shouldn't have done or failed to do something I think I ought to have done. There is a blot on my record—but then blots only are blots against the background of an otherwise still morally intact person. That is connected to the fact that there are things I can do to repair the damage I've done. Indeed, the action I take is geared to restoring the blot-free picture of myself—so, Gabriele Taylor insists, if I feel guilty about harming someone else, the thought is not so much that "I have harmed *her*" but rather "*I* have harmed her"[20] and hence disfigured myself to some extent. In response, I may want to do something about the harm I did to her but—to the extent that my concern is more about myself than about her—as a means of restoring my status in my own eyes.

Gabriele Taylor's analysis, then, implies that the man who beats his wife and feels guilty about it, unlike the man who merely feels embarrassed, does believe that he has done something he ought not to do, and feeling this way he is inclined to take action to alleviate the feeling of guilt. But his concern is not directly for his wife but for himself. If her pain is the occasion for his thinking he has violated something he stands for, his ceasing to beat her or his otherwise atoning for what he has done is the means to his self-rehabilitation.

Could Ivylawn College feel *guilty* about the racism on its campus? Of course this sounds odd—in a way that ascribing regret to the institution does not. This seems related to the fact that feeling guilty involves a sense of direct responsibility for the deed, so that to ascribe feelings of guilt to an institution really amounts to ascribing it to particular individuals within the institution. Institutions can have regret precisely because regrets don't entail responsibility and where there is responsibility we look for particular agents. The president of Ivylawn, for example, could talk about the college's having regrets without implying that she herself has them, but it would take a lot of work for her to say that the college feels guilty about something without giving the impression that she was talking about herself or other highly placed officials. It certainly is possible that there might be reports of various officials feeling "very bad" about what went on—not simply embarrassed, much more than regretful. Insofar as this means something like "feeling guilty," then if Gabriele Taylor is right such officials believe that while nothing is basically wrong with the institution or with them, they or the institution bear responsibility for the racist events. The emphasis in any action will be on redeeming the good name of the institution and attending to the hurt done the injured parties as the means to redeeming the good name of the institution.

Let us go on to *shame*. Suppose the man who beats his wife feels shame for doing so. How is that different from his feeling embarrassed or guilty? According to Gabriele Taylor,[21] the identificatory belief in shame is that I am not the person I thought I was or hoped I might be. It is not simply, as in embarrassment, that I wish I hadn't been seen doing something (even though I don't think I've done anything wrong) or, as in guilt, simply that I have failed to live up to a standard I adhere to. If I thought the latter, I could still entertain the possibility that I can set the record straight, for in such a case what troubles me about what I've done is quite local: I've *done* something I don't approve of, but I'm not *someone* I don't approve of. As Gabriele Taylor puts it: "When feeling guilty . . . the view I take of myself is entirely different from the view I take of myself when feeling shame: in the latter case I see myself as being all of a piece, what I have just done, I now see, fits only too well what I really am. But when feeling guilty I think of myself as having brought about a forbidden state of affairs and thereby in this respect disfigured a self which otherwise remains the same."[22] So if Mr. Husband feels shame about beating his wife, he must think that his action is revelatory of the person he in fact is even though he had thought or hoped that he was someone else, someone better than he turns out to be.

And thus if Ivylawn College should feel shame about the racism existing on its campus,[23] it would indicate that the college or the people identified as its representatives thought it wasn't the institution it hoped it was. The racism on the campus is revelatory of what the institution really is and not simply a sign that the college can't always live up to what it says it stands for.

Perhaps that is why an institution is unlikely to feel or admit to shame: It may be unable to countenance the possibility that at root it is not what it purports, even to itself, to be.

So, then, our emotions, or at least some of them, can be highly revelatory of who and what we care or don't care about. They provide powerful clues to the ways in which we take ourselves to be implicated in the lives of others and they in ours. And their *absence* provides such clues as much as their presence does. For example, the conference organizers referred to at the beginning of this chapter who were asked why no women of color were included in a gathering on "women's history" seemed to have no regrets about their decision, let alone embarrassment, guilt, or shame. From their vantage point, there was nothing undesirable about the focus of the conference, and though not in any way disclaiming responsibility for that focus, they made no room for the implication that they had done anything wrong or that the conference or they weren't what they understood it or themselves to be. Indeed, from the remarks quoted earlier, it appears that they began to argue that the complaints and demands of the women of color were groundless: The conference was about "women," not about race. And if anything, there is a strong note of annoyance in the remarks of the woman who insisted that talking about race was an "extra burden" for feminism and that the women of color were both missing the point and adding to the load already carried by the conveners.

Let us suppose that as a convener I come to feel regret as a result of listening to the comments of the women of color. What would that show about what I care about and how I take myself to be implicated in the lives of others and others in mine? Well, that depends of course on *what* I regret. Do I regret having hurt the women of color? Having been made uncomfortable myself? That my theory turns out not to be adequate? In this connection María Lugones recently noted that in her experience many feminists, when asked to explain how their accounts of "women's experiences" apply to women of color, express considerable concern about the inadequacy of their theories—but the focus of concern, María Lugones reluctantly concludes, is not how they have hurt women of color but rather that they need to tidy up their theories.[24]

It is not news that white feminist conferences and conversations have been peppered, sometimes even smothered, with expressions of guilt—sometimes in reaction to the very lack of regret (or perhaps some other emotion) for the exclusionary practices and policies I have described.[25] Indeed, a great deal has been made of white women's feelings of *guilt* in the face of charges by black women, Latinas, Japanese-American women, and others that our theories have been heavily tilted in the direction and to the exclusive benefit of white, middle-class women. Reflection on Gabriele Taylor's work leads me to make three comments about the discussions about this guilt. First, if Gabriele Taylor is right about the point of action taken to get rid of the feeling of guilt, then guilt is not an emotion that makes us attend well to the situation of those whose treatment at our hands we feel guilty about. We're too anxious trying to keep our moral slate clean. Second, I think it worth asking whether in any given case people are feeling guilt or simply embarrassment. If the latter, then there is no sense that one has failed in any way to act in accordance with what one stands for. There are no amends to make, only appearances to create.

Third, I think that there is a very neat fit between feeling guilty and a particular way of conceiving the relation between one's gender and one's racial identity. This friendly cohabitation throws some very interesting light on the concept of "white guilt." According to Gabriele Taylor, in feeling guilt rather than shame, it is possible for me to think of a part of myself as not living up to what the rest of me stands for. Insofar as I see myself as a "doer of a wicked deed," I see the hint of an alien self; in order to make sure such a self does not emerge, I need to do whatever it takes to "purge" myself of this alien self.[26] If I have a metaphysical position according to which my gender identity is thoroughly distinct from my racial identity (what I elsewhere call a form of "Tootsie Roll metaphysics")[27] I very handily can rely on a neat distinction between myself as woman and myself as white person. The woman part of me is perfectly okay; it's being white that is the source of my wrongdoing. I assert my privilege over women of color not insofar as I am a woman but insofar as I am white. Note then that unless I am prepared to think of my womanness and my whiteness as folded inextricably into the person I am, I can think of myself and my responsibility for my acts in the following way: What really counts about me is that I am a woman, and my deeds do not show that I am not any less of a woman than I thought I was; it's only insofar as I am white, which isn't nearly as important a part of me, that I have failed other women. It's not the woman in me that failed the woman in you; it's the white in me that failed (for example) the black in you. I, woman, feel nothing in particular; but I, white person, do feel guilt. If feminism focuses on the "woman" part of me and the "woman" part of you, conceived of as thoroughly distinct from my white part and your black part, feminism doesn't have to pay attention to our relations as white and black. We never have to confront each other woman to woman, then, only white to black or Anglo to Latina.

Feminist ethics, I have been insisting, must at least address the history of woman's inhumanity to woman. This part of the history of women is shameful. However, I am not proposing a daily regimen of shame-inducing exercises. Nor do I think that the deep self-doubt that is part of shame can serve as the immediate ground of a vibrant feminist politics, a politics that expresses and promotes real care and concern for all women's lives. But I do not see how women who enjoy privileged status over other women (whether it be based on race, class, religion, age, sexual orientation, or physical mobility) can come to think it desirable to lose that privilege (by force or consent) unless they see it not only as producing harm to other women but also as being deeply disfiguring to themselves. It is not simply, as it would be in the case of guilt, that the point of ceasing to harm others is to remove a disquieting blot from one's picture of oneself. The deeper privilege goes, the less self-conscious people are of the extent to which their being who they are, in their own eyes as well as in the eyes of others, is dependent upon the exploitation or degradation or disadvantage of others. Seeing myself as deeply disfigured by privilege and desiring to do something about it may be impossible without my feeling shame. The degree to which I am moved to undermine systems of privilege is closely tied to the degree to which I feel shame at the sort of person such privilege makes me or allows me to be.

In sum, then, I have been urging these considerations to keep those of us who are feminists from hastening to quickly to feel virtuous about attending to the virtues of feeling, the marvel of care. Whatever we mean by "feminist ethics," it ought not to make it difficult for us to examine and evaluate how women treat or mistreat each other. However, there are elements in feminism that make such examination difficult. For example, there is a tendency to focus on the contrast between an "ethics of care" and ethical systems that seem not to take care seriously. So far the contrast tells us nothing about who cares or does not care for whom. Moreover, since it has been claimed that an ethics of care is associated strongly though not exclusively with the way "women" think and act in the moral domain, it makes it very hard even to suggest that some women have failed to care for others, let alone that they have done violence to others. There is also a reliance on an understanding of care that obscures the fact that some forms of care are not only compatible with but crucial to the maintenance of systematic inequalities among women. In this connection, Judith Rollins's book about relations between white female employers and their black domestic employees is very insightful.[28] Among other things, Judith Rollins describes ways in which the employers insist on the privilege of "caring" for their employees in ways that reflect and sustain their power over them. Finally, there is a rampant terminology of contrasts between "women" on the one hand and "slaves" or "minorities" or "the poor" or "Jews" or whatever on the other. Such contrasts (and for that matter similarities) obscure differences between free women and slave women, gentile women and Jewish women, and so on, making it hard to talk about how one group of women treated others. This is reinforced by theories within feminism according to which women are the same *as women* and are oppressed the same *as women* and so if white women mistreat, say, black women, it is seen as how whites treat blacks, not how some women treat other women.

I have proposed one way of looking at some of the moral dimensions of women's treatment of one another. Some emotions are called "moral emotions" because having them involves or can involve moral assessment of oneself and others. In Gabriele Taylor's words, a moral emotion "requires a sense of value on the part of the agent, an awareness, more or less developed, of moral distinctions, of what is right or wrong, honorable or disgraceful."[29] Our having such emotions toward others can reveal whether, how, and to what extent we have treated them or think we have treated them well or poorly—so does our not having them. Moreover, our political and metaphysical theories give shape and structure to our emotional lives. For example, our assumptions about what *feminism* is about will influence our beliefs about what is appropriate and inappropriate to bring up at feminist conferences, which will in turn influence the possibility of our feeling anger, regret, remorse, embarrassment, guilt, or shame. (As Arnold Isenberg says: "When you lack what you do not want, there is no shame."[30]) And as I stated earlier, assumptions about the relation between our gender identity and other aspects of our identity such as our race, class, and religion can influence how we describe our responsibility for the way we treat other women.

NOTES

1. Lillian Smith, *Killers of the Dream* (New York: Norton, 1949, 1961), 27.

2. See, for example, Eleanor Flexner, *Century of Struggle* (New York: Atheneum, 1972), especially chap. 13; Ellen Carol DuBois, *Feminism and Suffrage* (Ithaca, N.Y.: Cornell University Press, 1978); Angela Davis, *Women, Race, and Class* (New York: Random, 1981); Paula Giddings, *When and Where I Enter: The Impact of Black Women on Race and Sex in America* (New York: Morrow, 1984).

3. See, for example, Linda Brent, *Incidents in the Life of a Slave Girl*, ed. L. Maria Child (New York: Harcourt Brace Jovanovich, 1973); Solomon Northrup, *Narrative of Solomon Northrup, Twelve Years a Slave* (Auburn, N.Y.: Derby and Miller, 1853), quoted in Gerda Lerner, ed., *Black Women in White America* (New York: Vintage, 1972), 51.

4. See, for example, Claudia Koonz, *Mothers in the Fatherland: Women, the Family, and Nazi Politics* (New York: St. Martin's Press, 1987).

5. *off our backs* (feminist newspaper), July 1986, 3.

6. See notes 1–5 above; also, for example, bell hooks, *Feminist Theory: From Margin to Center* (Boston: South End Press, 1984); Audre Lorde, *Sister/Outsider: Essays and Speeches* (Trumansburg, N.Y.: Crossing Press, 1984); Helen Longino and Valerie Miner, eds., *Competition: A Feminist*

*Taboo?* (New York: Feminist Press, 1987); Elly Bulkin, Minnie Bruce Pratt, and Barbara Smith, *Yours in Struggle: Three Feminist Perspectives on Anti-Semitism and Racism,* (Ithaca, N.Y.: Firebrand Books, 1984). Simone de Beauvoir, by the way, had quite a lot to say about women with race and class privilege undermining or failing to support other women in order to maintain their race and class privilege, but that part of her work is rarely highlighted—even by herself (see Spelman, *Inessential Woman: Problems of Exclusion in Feminist Thought* [Boston: Beacon Press, 1988], chap. 3).

7. Berenice Fisher, "Guilt and Shame in the Women's Movement: The Radical Ideal of Action and Its Meaning for Feminist Intellectuals," *Feminist Studies* 10, no. 2 (Summer 1984): 186.

8. See Carol Gilligan, *In a Different Voice: Psychological Theory and Women's Development* (Cambridge, Mass.: Harvard University Press, 1982); Eva Feder Kittay and Diana T. Meyers, eds., *Women and Moral Theory* (Totowa, N.J.: Rowman and Littlefield, 1987).

9. Jane Austen, *Emma* (New York: Bantam, 1981; first edition, 1816), 133–139.

10. These are not incompatible conceptions, according to Gilligan and others. See Eva Kittay and Diana Meyers, eds., *Women and Moral Theory.*

11. See, for example, ibid.; Lawrence A. Blum, "Gilligan and Kohlberg: Implications for Moral Theory," *Ethics* 98 (April 1988): 472–491.

12. Jane Austen, *Emma,* 139–140.

13. Judith Rollins, *Between Women: Domestics and Their Employers* (Philadelphia: Temple University Press, 1985), 186.

14. Aristotle, *The Nicomachean Ethics of Aristotle,* tr. Sir David Ross (London: Oxford University Press, 1925), 97.

15. Two problems emerge here, even in the presentation of 1–4: One is what it means for institutions, as opposed to individuals, to have such reactions; and the other is that as long as we focus on institutions, we don't have to think about what our own reactions are. But we'll get to these below.

16. Gabriele Taylor, *Pride, Shame, and Guilt: Emotions of Self-Assessment* (Oxford: Clarendon Press, 1985).

17. See Elizabeth V. Spelman, "Anger and Insubordination," in *Women, Knowledge, and Reality,* ed. Ann Garry and Marilyn Pearsall (Winchester, Mass.: Unwin Hyman, 1989), 263–273.

18. Although regretting that something happened differs in some important ways from regretting having done something—since the latter, not the former, entails responsibility for having done the thing in question—I can fully regret that something happened without in any way implicating myself in having brought it about.

19. In "Cognitive Emotions?" Chesire Calhoun discusses the repair work necessary for certain versions of the cognitive theory in light of the fact that sometimes "one's doxic life and one's emotional life part company" (in *What is an Emotion? Classic Readings in Philosophical Psychology,* ed. Chesire Calhoun and Robert C. Solomon [New York: Oxford University Press, 1984], 333).

20. Gabriele Taylor, *Pride, Shame, and Guilt,* 92.
21. Ibid., 68.
22. Ibid., 92.
23. Note how odd it would be to refer to that about which one feels shame as merely an "incident."
24. See chapter 2 of this volume.
25. It may seem as if this is at odds with my claim at the beginning of the chapter that the history of hostile or uncaring relationships among women has not gotten the sustained attention it deserves. But passing, even frequent, expressions of regret, embarrassment, guilt, or shame are hardly the same as a thorough examination of the meanings of those emotions in the history of the social and political relationships among women.
26. Gabriele Taylor, *Pride, Shame, and Guilt,* 134, 135.
27. See Elizabeth Spelman, *Inessential Woman,* passim.
28. Judith Rollins, *Between Women,* passim.
29. Gabriele Taylor, *Pride, Shame, and Guilt,* 107.
30. Arnold Isenberg, "Natural Shame and Natural Pride," in *Explaining Emotions,* ed. Amélie Oksenberg Rorty (Berkeley: University of California Press, 1981), 370.

# [12]

SYMPOSIUM ON CARE AND JUSTICE

# Colonialism and Its Others: Considerations On Rights and Care Discourses

UMA NARAYAN

*I point to a colonial care discourse that enabled colonizers to define themselves in relationship to "inferior" colonized subjects. The colonized, however, had very different accounts of this relationship. While contemporary care discourse correctly insists on acknowledging human needs and relationships, it needs to worry about who defines these often contested terms. I conclude that improvements along dimensions of care and of justice often provide "enabling conditions" for each other.*

I wish to think about certain aspects of the roles played by rights and care discourses in colonial times. I shall start with the following question: How did the vast majority of people in the colonizing countries motivate themselves to participate in the large-scale phenomena of slavery and colonialism, not only embracing the idea that distant lands and peoples should be subjugated, but managing to conceive of imperialism as an *obligation*, an obligation taken so seriously that by 1914 Europe "held a grand total of roughly 85 percent of the earth as colonies, protectorates, dependencies, dominions, and commonwealths"? (Said 1993, 8).

The answer to this question forces us to attend to the self-serving collaboration between elements of colonial rights discourse and care discourse. Pervasive racist stereotypes about the negative and inferior status of enslaved or colonized Others were used both to justify denial of the rights enjoyed by the colonizers, and to construct the colonized as childish and inferior subjects, in need of the paternalistic guidance and rule of their superiors (see Said 1993). In general terms, the colonizing project was seen as being *in the interests of*, *for the good of*, and as *promoting the welfare of* the colonized—notions that draw our

*Hypatia* vol. 10, no. 2 (Spring 1995) © by Uma Narayan

attention to the existence of a *colonialist* care discourse whose terms have some resonance with those of some contemporary strands of the ethic of care. Particular colonial practices were seen as concrete attempts to achieve these paternalistic ends. Coercive religious conversion was seen as promoting the *spiritual* welfare of the "heathen." Inducting the colonized into the economic infrastructures of colonialism was seen as conferring the *material* benefits of western science, technology and economic progress, the *cultural* benefits of western education, and the *moral* benefits of the work ethic. There were often marked gender dimensions to these projects—colonial attempts to get "native women" to conform to Victorian/Christian norms of respectable dress, sexuality, and family life were regarded as in the moral interests of the women (see Chauduri and Strobel 1992).

I am not denying there were powerful economic motivations underlying colonialism and slavery. However, justifications for colonialism and slavery in terms of crude self-interest alone seem to have been rare. These enterprises were made morally palatable by the rhetoric of responsibility and care for enslaved and colonized Others. Though such justifications have often been seen as attempts to convince the dominated of the appropriateness of their domination, I would argue that the central purpose of such arguments often is to make domination morally palatable to those engaged in the infliction of domination. While much of the contemporary discourse on an ethics of care focuses on the import of one's relationships to *particular others*, thinking about care-discourse in the colonial context highlights, in contrast, the roles it has historically played in justifying relationships of power and domination between *groups of people*, such as colonizers and colonized. The paternalistic moral vision of colonialism was sustained by the discourses of religion, philosophy, science, and art—cultural practices that collaborated to make a sense of western superiority part of the collective world view of people in the colonizing countries. (A large segment of western women's movements and working class movements of the time, such as those in England, were pro-empire.)

Colonial stereotypes about the hierarchy of races had similarities to existing theories of the hierarchy of gender—where attributes such as physical "weakness," smaller craniums, deficient rationality, and moral frailty were ascribed to western women, constructing them as the "weaker sex" in need of the care, support, and guidance of western men, not unlike the colonized. However, while western women's care-taking labor, namely domestic work and childcare responsibilities, were often rendered invisible qua work by being depicted as expressions of love and care for their families, the toil and labor of exploited slaves and colonized workers were often effaced instead by depicting their products as results of the efforts of colonial capitalists. John Stuart Mill provides a vivid example in *Principles of Political Economy*:

> These [outlying possessions of ours] are hardly to be looked upon as countries, but more properly as outlying agricultural or manufacturing estates. . . . Our West Indian colonies, for example, cannot be regarded as countries with a productive capital of their own, . . . [but are rather] the place where England finds it convenient to carry on the production of sugar, coffee and a few other tropical commodities. All the capital employed is English capital. (Mill 1965, 693)

What does attending to the colonial context teach us about discourses of rights and care? Among the more obvious lessons is that rights discourse was only seemingly universal, not extending to the colonized, among others. Another lesson is that care discourse can sometimes function ideologically, to justify or conceal relationships of power and domination. While it has been pointed out that much of the responsibility for informal as well as institutionalized caring falls on subordinate and relatively powerless members of society—often working class and minority women (Held 1995)—I want to add that "paternalistic caring" of the sort found in colonial discourse can also be wielded as a form of control and domination by the powerful and privileged. The colonial notion of "the white man's burden" included both a sense of obligation to confer the benefits of western civilization on the colonized, and a sense of being burdened with the responsibility for doing so—an obligation and responsibility rooted in a sense of being agents who had a world-historic mission to bring the light of civilization and progress to others inhabiting "areas of darkness"!

The seemingly universal, free, equal, independent, separate, and mutually disinterested individual of contract theory and of rights discourse has been criticized as being contrary to the experiences of most women. I wish to add that the contractual focus on relationships between equals, and on agents as independent, separate and mutually disinterested was only *part* of the liberal story. Another part of the story was that these same subjects had paternalistic obligations and responsibilities to "inferior Others," whether women in their own families or distant colonial peoples. Rights-discourse was constructed during the historical time when western countries were becoming increasingly interdependent with, unseparate from, and anything but disinterested in their unfree and unequal colonies, and most liberal political theorists had no difficulty endorsing colonialism. We would be mistaken if we read liberal rights-theorists as concerned only with contractual relationships between equals, or if we focus only on notions of agency pertinent to that side of their thought, since we would be ignoring their support for colonialism, and the more "missionary" notions of agency embedded in that facet of their worldview. If we recognize that the agent of liberal rights theory was also the agent of the colonial project, its independence, separateness and disinterestedness appear to be more qualified properties than the picture of the same agent that emerges if we ignore the colonial dimensions of liberal theory.

In the colonial worldview, white women too had their own version of the "white man's burden," in which caretaking roles played a large part. Many white women went to the colonies as wives, whose presence was meant to shield their husbands from the lurking dangers of miscegenation and of "going native" (see Zlotnick 1994). White women had their own brand of paternalistic roles towards the colonized, and often shared in roles that constructed the "natives" as children.

Many aspects of the self-perceptions of the colonizers seem to have depended heavily on their relationship to the colonized. The world-view of colonialism, as well as the moral and socio-political world-views of many colonized cultures, subscribed to a picture where several large groups of people were normatively defined in terms of their relationships as inferiors and subordinates vis-a-vis members of dominant groups. To be a slave, a colonized Other, an untouchable, a woman, has often been meant as having one's entire existence defined in terms of one's "proper place" with respect to those with power, which entailed obligations to acquiesce to relationships of domination.

This suggests that strands in contemporary care discourse that stress that we are all essentially interdependent and in relationship, while important, do not go far enough if they fail to worry about the *accounts* that are given of these interdependencies and relationships. The colonizers and the colonized, for example, while both acutely conscious of their relationship to each other, had very different accounts of what the relationship and its interdependencies amounted to, and whether they were morally justified. Many social movements and struggles on the part of subordinate groups, though often couched in terms of individual rights, were also attempts to renegotiate and change the prevailing relationships between social groups.

While I do not endorse reducing the value of any moral theory to its ideological uses, I would argue that we must attend to the ideological functions served by various moral theories. Pervasive structural relationships of power and powerlessness between groups, such as those between colonizers and the colonized, tend to foster ideological justifications for the maintenance of such relationships. While aspects of care discourse have the potential virtue of calling attention to vulnerabilities that mark relationships between differently situated persons, care discourse also runs the risk of being used to ideological ends where these "differences" are defined in self-serving ways by the dominant and powerful. Notions of differences in vulnerabilities and capabilities should be recognized as *contested terrain*, requiring critical attention to who defines these differences as well as their practical implications.

Ideological pictures of the nature of Self and Others, and of one's relationship to Others are problematic pictures shared by large historically constituted groups of individuals. It is not clear to me that any moral theory is immune to such ideological deployment, nor am I convinced that there is any moral faculty or set of moral practices, neither Humean "reflexion" nor Kantian "reason," whose careful and sustained cultivation *necessarily* liberates particular individuals from the historical effects of such ideologies. It seems to me that what such ideological pictures often yield to are not primarily theoretical moral self-corrections, based either on reason or on enlarged sympathies with Others, but to political contestations and moral challenges by groups who are victimized by the status quo. To challenge the paternalistic construction of femininity and of colonial subjectivity, western women and the colonized had to resort to insurgencies, rebellions, and protests, and had to *prove* themselves to be moral and political agents in order to make plausible their claims to such agency.

Two broad strategies were used both by western women and by the colonized in these contestations: (a) there were frequent assertions that western women or the colonized possessed the capacities and capabilities that entitled them to the same rights as white male colonizers, and (b) there were frequent redescriptions of the "paternalistic protective project" as one based instead on force and exploitation, inflicting misery on the powerless, and brutalizing those with power. The powerful role played by rights discourse in these emancipatory movements should not lead us to ignore their concurrent critique of the paternalistic colonial care-discourses that operated as justifications for their domination.

The alternative moral visions of the agency of women or of the colonized that developed in such political contestations, though they challenge the moral picture of the world held by the powerful, are not themselves immune to creating or reinforcing other relationships of power. A great deal has been written on how, for instance, the contemporary feminist movement has tended to be focused on the interests of middle-class white women, and about how drawing attention to the problems of women of color remains an ongoing problem. Anticolonial nationalist movements often displayed similar problems—in that nationalist discourses often constructed issues in a manner that marginalized colonized women. Several strands of Indian nationalism, for instance, associated Indian women with the preservation of Indian traditions, culture, and spirituality—a function that simultaneously gave them an *imagined function* in the nationalist agenda, but excluded them from *real participation* in many areas of work, politics, and public culture (Chatterjee 1990, 243). Thus, though I believe large-scale political movements have been historically crucial in bringing about certain forms of moral change and progress, these movements too generate problematic moral narratives. I would conclude that moral theories need to be evaluated not only in terms of their theoretical adequacy in accounting for the range of phenomena in our moral lives but also with regard to the instrumental political uses to which they lend themselves at concrete historical junctures.

I shall end with a few reflections on the relationship between rights and care discourses. The perspectives of colonialism, as well as those of many colonized cultures, and of many contemporary societies, provide several examples of what John Ladd refers to as the "Doctrine of Moral Disqualification," whereby groups with social power define members of other groups in ways that disqualify them for full membership in the moral community (Ladd 1991, 40). These definitions have been repeatedly used to justify the denial of rights to members of "disqualified" groups. These definitions have also been used to justify the failure to be genuinely attentive and responsive to the needs, interests, and welfare of the members of these groups. Dominant social definitions of what an untouchable or a slave was, did not encourage the powerful to care for the less powerful; and the same definitions were in fact inimical to the well-being of the less powerful, who were not, by these definitions, entitled to the means and opportunities for flourishing.

Justice concerns have been central to many social and political movements because asserting and gaining rights have been instrumental in transforming certain groups of people, however imperfectly, into fellow citizens whose concerns mattered, into people whose human worth mattered. However, as many slave-narratives well illustrate, much of the moral and political work that was necessary to change the "moral disqualification" inflicted on powerless groups consisted not only of claims to rights, but of attempts to call attention to the *suffering* inflicted on the powerless by the status quo. These political depictions of suffering can be seen as attempts to elicit the attentiveness and moral responsiveness of those with power, by redescribing the life situations of the powerless in ways that challenged the rationalizations of the powerful. The discourses of slave narratives, for example, make it difficult for members of dominant groups to continue to believe in the myth of happy slaves, content with their lot.

Joan Tronto may well be right in arguing that "one of the practical effects of the widespread adoption of a theory of care may be to make our concerns for justice less central" (Tronto 1995). I would like to add the converse claim, that a more serious commitment to and enforcement of the claims of justice might, at least in some cases, be a precondition for the possibility of adequately caring for and about some people. Tronto herself acknowledges that "*until* we care about something, the care process cannot begin" (Tronto 1995). Social relationships of domination often operate so as to make many who have power unable to *genuinely* care about the marginalized and powerless.

Although I am very sympathetic to the idea of a politics and of public policies that are more sensitive to *needs*, I am not sure we can arrive at what Tronto calls "a full account of human needs" without serious attention to considerations of justice that would enable the powerless to seriously participate in the social and political discourse where such needs are contested and defined. Once again, adequate attention to justice may, in some instances, be a precondition for adequately caring policies.

Virginia Held argues that though justice is an important moral value, much moderately good life has gone on without it, for instance, in families where there has been little justice but much care. She points out that we can have care without justice, but that, without care, there would be no persons to respect (Held 1995). I suggest that attending to what happens in some families also reveals situations in which without justice, care may fail to be provided. India, for instance, has an alarming and growing "deficit of women" in the population. Some of this is due to active acts of infanticide and female feticide. But the most significant cause seems to be what is called "the fatal neglect of female children" by their own families. In a nutshell, girl children are systematically and seemingly non-deliberately provided substantially less care—nutritional, medical, and so forth—than are boys (Sen 1990). My point is, in some families, without more justice, of a sort that changes the cultural meanings and material implications of having daughters, care will fail to be provided, and many female infants will not grow up to become adult bearers of rights.

Carol Gilligan's work suggests that rights and care perspectives provide alternative accounts of moral problems and decisions, and that shifting to a care perspective foregrounds moral issues of preserving and maintaining relationships that are often not well illuminated by a rights perspective. I understand both Tronto and Held as arguing that the care perspective is a wider or possibly more foundational framework, within which considerations of rights and justice constitute a subset—though admittedly an important one.

I would like to suggest yet another possibility. Improvements along dimensions of justice and rights might, in some cases such as the issue of fatal neglect of female children, provide what I shall call "enabling conditions" for the provision of adequate care. In other cases, improvements along care dimensions, such as attentiveness to and concern for human needs and human suffering, might provide the "enabling conditions" for more adequate forms of justice. For instance, attention to the needs, predicaments and suffering of the impoverished and destitute in affluent western societies might result in social policies that institutionalize welfare rights, rights to adequate medical care, and so forth.

I suggest that this is one possible dimension of the relationships between care and justice considerations, and not an over-arching account of their relationship. I am suggesting that, in particular contexts, struggles for greater justice may foster more adequate or richer forms of care and that in others, the cultivation of a care perspective might foster enhanced forms of justice. In some situations at least, justice and care perspectives might be seen less as contenders for theoretical primacy or moral and political adequacy and more as collaborators and allies in our practical and political efforts to make our world more conducive to human flourishing.

## REFERENCES

Chatterjee, Partha. 1990. The nationalist resolution of the women's question. In *Recasting women: Essays in Indian colonial history*, ed. Kumkum Sangari and Suresh Vaid. New Brunswick: Rutgers University Press.

Chaudhuri, Nupur, and Margaret Strobel, eds. 1992. *Western women and imperialism: Complicity and resistance*. Bloomington: Indiana University Press.

Held, Virginia. 1995. The meshing of care and justice. *Hypatia* 10(2): 128-132.

Ladd, John. 1991. The idea of collective violence. In *Jusitce, law and violence*, ed. James A. Brady and Newton Garver. Philadelphia: Temple University Press.

Mill, John Stuart. 1965. *Principles of political economy*, Vol. 3. Ed. J.M. Robson. Toronto: University of Toronto Press.

Said, Edward. 1993. *Culture and imperialism*. New York: Alfred A. Knopf.

Sen, Amartya. 1990. More than 100 million women are missing. *New York Review of Books*, December 1990.

Tronto, Joan. 1995. Care as a basis for radical political judgements. *Hypatia* 10(2): 141-149.

Zlotnick, Susan. 1994. Domesticating imperialism: Curry and cookbooks in Victorian England. Paper presented at the American Political Science Association meeting, New York City.

# [13]



# INDIVIDUALISM, CLASS, AND THE SITUATION OF CARE: AN ESSAY ON CAROL GILLIGAN

Kathleen League

Alison Jaggar maintains that feminist approaches to ethics, while varied, share a commitment to the view that "the moral experience of women should be treated as respectfully as the moral experience of men" (Jaggar, pp. 97-98). Perhaps this should be true, but it is not quite true. Some of the most visible efforts proclaimed and accepted as feminist are still, whether knowingly or not, accepting and using the terms associated with and predominantly defined by men, where I understand those terms, through Carol Gilligan's work, to be one-sidedly those of the "rights" and choices of the independent individual. Many feminists are allowing those terms to determine their causes such that they focus primarily or only on gaining for women the rights, opportunities, and choices traditionally accorded to men. This, rather than calling for fundamental changes in society that would be based, at least in part, on the alternative insights accorded by women's collective experiences. This is not a thesis that I wish to argue, but merely to evoke. One need only consider the rhetoric surrounding the abortion debate, or the careerist slant of much feminist rhetoric and organizing, to sense the slant in much feminism toward (if I may call it this) a rather "masculinist" conception of individual rights.

I agree with Carol Gilligan that the appeal to rights by feminists is not entirely inappropriate or misguided. It has its role to play in ending the subordination of women. But I also agree with Gilligan that the "rights" language, taken only by itself, has serious limitations as well, both in terms of its conception of social life and in its disregard of the insights of women into the nature of social life.

A strength of Gilligan's work is that she challenges not only the rights conception of ethics, but also the disregard that has been shown to women's ethical insights. She does so by thematizing an ethics of interdependence, contextuality, responsibility, and care of the particular other. Gilligan calls this ethic "the care ethic." She contrasts it with an ethics based on universal, hierarchical principles, formal abstractions, and notions of substitutability,

JOURNAL of SOCIAL PHILOSOPHY, Vol. 24 No. 3, Winter 1993 69-79 separateness, rights, and noninterference. She associates the care ethic with women because she finds it voiced more often by women. She also identifies ways in which the care ethic has been devalued by means of its omission in normative theories of moral development. Conveying the crucial value of the care ethic to human existence, Gilligan conveys the injustice done both to this ethic and to women by the disregard that has been shown them.

To be sure, there are problems with Gilligan's position in that it sounds, at least in places, as though Gilligan assumes an essential split of psycho-biological origin between the sexes in moral development. As a number of responses to Gilligan's work have pointed out, Gilligan's writing, in spite of her claims to the contrary, does generalize sex differences. Likewise, despite her stated wish and belief to the contrary, the weave of Gilligan's written claims and observations does not fundamentally leave room for considering the influence of social class and culture on gender and moral development (see, e.g., Lucia, pp. 318-19; Moody-Adams, p. 197; Stack, pp. 322-23).

Nevertheless, what many of Gilligan's critics seem to overlook, and what Gilligan herself points out in rejoinder, is that her fundamental point still stands. There is an ethical approach to life that is associated with and experienced by women that has not been officially or institutionally recognized or valued in any substantial way. Thus, to devalue or deny this ethic is to help perpetuate the devaluation of women's experience. It is also to forestall consideration of what advantages this ethic might offer if it were more thoroughly and substantially practiced and integrated into the grain of society. As Gilligan also points out, some of her critics go so far in denying sex differences that they strongly imply that there are no different voices at all. In so doing, they actually confirm Gilligan's point about the devaluation of the different voice represented by women, and thus confirm the need for her continued efforts on behalf of this different voice (Gilligan, 1986: 325). What Gilligan does not quite say, but I would add, is that when feminists go overboard in their reaction to Gilligan by asserting no differences between men and women, they not only imply that there are no important biologically-based differences, but no cultural or experiential ones as well. They thus undermine the reason for feminism, and also conjure a closed, monolithic, static world that allows no hope for change.

All of this is by way of background on Gilligan's position and the debate surrounding it. It is also by way of indicating my respect for Gilligan's work and why I think what she says is of continued importance and usefulness to feminists. That having been said, however, I do have three main problems with Gilligan's position. First, Gilligan's position overlooks the dialectical nature of women's strength in the care ethic. Second, class biases are apparent in the way she frames the sequence leading to the ethic of care.

Third, despite her emphasis on interdependence, Gilligan's appraisal of decision-making patterns betrays a strong individualistic bias. These three problems are closely intertwined and aid and abet each other. Nor are they trifling problems of merely philosophical interest. They are serious problems of practical importance.

In the remainder of this paper, I will spell out more thoroughly the nature of these problems and how they are manifest in Gilligan's writing. My focus will be chapters three and four of *In a Different Voice,* because that is where I find the problems to come out most clearly and strongly. These are the chapters where, in the context of a study of abortion decisions, Gilligan sets forth her view of the sequence that leads to the care ethic. What follows will therefore be critical of the way Gilligan develops her position; but this is not meant to undercut the respect I have for Gilligan's larger project.

There are at least two important ways in which Gilligan fails to take into account the dialectical nature of the care ethic. First, Gilligan implicitly operates from the view that one can cleanly separate choice from what is not choice, and accordingly separate the moral from the nonmoral. As she says, "The essence of moral decision is the exercise of choice and the willingness to accept responsibility for that choice" (Gilligan, 1982: 67). This view serves as the underpinning for the moral sequence that she identifies and the interpretations that she gives to various examples of decision making and self description. She thus identifies levels of and progression in morality on the basis of a proposed dichotomy between choice and not-choice, and the claiming of choice and the disclaiming of it. She implies that one can separate the disempowered voice from the empowered one, the passive from the active, the weak from the strong, and the nonmoral from the moral. In other words, Gilligan wants to cleanly separate the strength of women and the care ethic on one side from the passivity and lack of power traditionally associated with women on the other, rather than look into how they are related and affect and limit one another. One could also say with some justification that in associating women with the care ethic, Gilligan in effect excludes those women who do not have the care ethic from the category of real women, and thus compounds the errors that stem from her undialectical analysis.

At any rate, the root problem, as I see it, is Gilligan's lack of recognition, in the crucial instance, of the impossibility of separating the moral strength of women from their historical position of weakness, and the related impossibility of "choice" pure and simple. This impossibility arises in part because of the connection between women's strength in empathy and contextual thinking on one hand, and their traditionally lesser economic and bargaining power on the other. As Marxists such as Lukacs have pointed out, those who are at the mercy of others do not have the leisure to overlook power relations. Because they are subjected to them and dependent upon the mercy of the powerful, they must attend to those relations. Thus, to be in a position of subordination leads to a heightened use of contextual thinking (Jameson, pp. 185-187). This analysis applies to the situation of women as it concerns Gilligan. But Gilligan fails to follow the limits on women's choices to their logical conclusion. She fails to appreciate that any kind of dependence will complicate the issue of choice and place limits upon it. Instead, as will be seen more fully further on, Gilligan prefers and uses a simple model of choice that goes hand in hand with a psychologistic preference for isolating the field of inquiry to, and placing all responsibility with, the individual. This has serious consequences for her interpretations of women's varying degrees of frustration over the terminology of choice.

The second way in which Gilligan's account overlooks the dialectical nature of the care ethic is closely related to the first. In wanting to portray the care ethic in only a positive light, she presents it as a complete good that balances care for others with respect for oneself and responsibility with rights. Consequently, she neglects to deal with or mention the "undertow" for any ethic born in the context of exploitation. Just as one would question a male-centered or male-defined morality on the grounds that such a morality, no matter how noble it may be in some respects, is marked by its service to the beneficiaries of an exploitative system, so too one should question any woman-centered or woman-defined morality on the grounds that it will bear the marks of the exploited and oppressed. As Linda Kerber observes,

> But the reification of different spheres, now freshly buttressed by Gilligan's study of psychological development, poses major dangers of oversimplification. As Ellen DuBois warned..., single-minded focus on women's own culture brings with it the risk of ignoring "the larger social and historical developments of which it was a part" and does not "address the limitations of the values of women's culture," the ways that they restrained and confined. (Kerber, p. 308)

Jaggar likewise observes, "the feminine...has been construed inevitably in circumstances of male domination, and its value for feminism is likely, therefore, to be very questionable" (Jaggar, p. 90). Granted, as Gilligan points out in reply to her critics, she is not promoting all aspects of women's culture or the feminine. She is critical of the self-sacrificing mode that renders women into virtual doormats, so solicitous of others' feelings that they disregard their own, so empathic with their oppressors that they further their own oppression. I have no disagreement with Gilligan on that score. My problem with Gilligan is that she proceeds to treat one segment of women's culture as though it can be separated cleanly and unproblematically from the rest of women's culture and as though it is unmarked by any signs of coercion or exploitation. In fact, I think this gesture on Gilligan's part, like the gesture of the ethic that she singles out for favor, harbors the signs of an exploitative system, and does so in the very way it avoids confronting those signs within it, preferring instead to pull back into the "safe" contours of the status quo. I will develop this idea more in what follows.

Concerning the class-bias and individualism that inform Gilligan's moralizing, these emerge, as stated previously, in Gilligan's abortion study. Here she interprets how women deal, as she says, with "adult questions of responsibility and choice" (Gilligan, 1982: 71). In the process, she deduces a "sequence of women's moral judgment" that involves three moral perspectives linked by two transitions:

> In this sequence, an initial focus on caring for the self in order to ensure survival is followed by a transitional phase in which this judgment is criticized as selfish. ... The elaboration of this concept of responsibility...characterizes the second perspective. At this point, the good is equated with caring for others. However, ...the exclusion of herself gives rise to problems in relationships, creating a disequilibrium that initiates the second transition. ... The third perspective focuses on the dynamics of relationships and dissipates the tension between selfishness and responsibility through a new understanding of the interconnection between other and self. Care becomes the self-chosen principle of a judgment that remains psychological in its concern with relationships and response but becomes universal in its condemnation of exploitation and hurt. (Gilligan, 1982: 74)

In order to bring out the biases that inhere in this construction, I will follow the way Gilligan illustrates the different levels of morality that she has isolated as leading to the mature care ethic. Discussion of the first level will be my focus because it allows me to raise what I consider to be the main problems with Gilligan's position. After this discussion I will present brief responses to the other levels outlined by Gilligan.

Gilligan characterizes the lowest stage of moral development as "center[ing] on the self. The concern is pragmatic and the issue is survival" (Gilligan, 1982: 74). She repeatedly attributes this focus to a "feeling" of being disconnected, alone, helpless, and powerless, and a "perception" of the world as an "exploitative and threatening" place (Gilligan, 1982: 75, 109, 110, 114). Nowhere does she consider the possibility that these "feelings" may be anything more than that. The terms are deflating and dismissive as though the sense of aloneness, and so forth, is but an illusion: one is not really alone or powerless but just feels that she is. This implication is especially strong when Gilligan goes on to give a case with a happy ending: Betty, 16, is described by Gilligan as "feeling" alone and blaming others for her situation. But a year later she has made the "transition from selfishness to responsibility in her thought" (Gilligan, 1982: 112). She rises a full level in moral maturity in Gilligan's view because she "no longer feel[s] so powerless, exploited, alone, and endangered," but rather "feels more in control" and has adopted the outlook of responsibility, with the result that she is a happier person and describes herself as a "responsible person in her relationships with her family, her boyfriend, and in her school community" (Gilligan, 1982: 115). The clear implication is that if one would just change one's individual self, particularly one's feelings about the world and oneself, to thinking of oneself as being in control and able to do "the right thing," then there would no longer be a problem; the problem would go away because it only resided or consisted in one's bad and/or immature attitude.

There are many problems with this scenario as Gilligan has framed it. First, despite her indictment of the inadequacy and inflexibility of hierarchical systems or formulations, she has set the cornerstone of one of her own. She proceeds to posit degrees of maturity and morality where the locus of determination is said to be the person rather than the situation. Further, in adding, as previously seen, that morality consists in choice and the accepting of responsibility for choice, she is actually suggesting that a person at this first stage of the moral sequence is not yet a moral person, because that person denies that what befell her was the result of her choices. The implication is far too encompassing to be valid; it overlooks that just because a person has not been able to make a real choice in a given situation, and says so, it does not necessarily follow that the person is immature, is wrong about her situation, or is without access to moral decision and the acknowledged "exercise of choice" in other situations.

What I am saying is that Gilligan's focus, despite her emphasis on interdependence and her apparent criticism of individualism, is precisely individualistic in her outlook and prescription. She hastens to attribute shortcomings to the individual while blatantly downplaying the role that social conditions play in necessitating or eliciting certain responses. The reality of the need to respond in different ways to different situations is Gilligan's theme, yet she overlooks it in her individualistically-biased hierarchical ranking of responses to situations. She seems to automatically categorize some types as less valid, when indeed they may well be valid as related to or dictated by the situation. A situation-specific response may be less a reflection of the moral "goodness or maturity" of a person and more a reflection of what kind of social reality they are in; but Gilligan does not touch this issue or even bring it up. She instead operates as though the opposite is always true, in contradiction to her own basic theme of the web of relations that form us.

The problems with Gilligan's way of framing the issue of moral maturity and the care ethic go deeper still. They may, ironically, both reflect and serve to justify the prevailing social order and the sorts of institutional practices that blame the victim and deflect attention away from deeper social problems. This point is borne home well by Nanette Schorr in an article in *Tikkun* on the child-protective movement. Her discussion is not about Gilligan's work, but her observations are pertinent to Gilligan's work in that she addresses the problem posed by the focus in psychology on individual weaknesses. As she says, the focus of psychiatric labeling and casework "has remained the treatment of individual weakness" (Schorr, p. 21). She adds that "the focus of scrutiny" has particularly "turned to single parents, many of them women" (Schorr, p. 22). The problem is that "when these parents criticize a social order that gives their parenting efforts little material or emotional support, social welfare experts term this an 'externalization of blame'" (Schorr, p. 22). This move to label any complaint or expression of being overwhelmed as an externalization of blame is one which I see consistently and repeatedly carried out by Gilligan. In spite of challenging some aspects of her training in psychology, her psychologistic prejudices have not been fully rooted out and still run deep. Again, the problem with that is as Schorr points out:

> Instead of treating the crisis in meaning—the despair and emptiness born of lifelong experiences of physical or emotional violence, unemployment or meaningless work, broken families, inadequate education, loneliness, lack of stable long-term relationships, dangerous, dirty, and violence-ridden neighborhoods, decrepit housing, and lack of community—the symptoms of crisis are treated in isolation from their causes. (Schorr, p. 22)

In other words, therapeutic focus is on "learning acceptable outlets for anger—not [talking] about what you're really angry about" (Schorr, p. 22). This pulling back from, and resistance to, questioning the social order—this I see operating in full force in Gilligan's approach. This essentially conservative gesture, and the fact that it remains unthematized, unrecognized, and unproblematized in Gilligan, betrays in Gilligan a cozy and unwitting complicity with, and acceptance of, the status quo.

Operating both implicitly and explicitly throughout this acceptance of the status quo is a class bias. It is both a cause and effect of not challenging the social order, because such complacence involves and results in a failure to take seriously the prevailing divergences in material conditions. There is a meaning in this for the way Gilligan situates and formulates her care ethic. In her formulation, the practice of the care ethic does not involve questioning the social order or having an interest in doing so, but rather involves exercising rights and responsibilities in the playing field limited to individuals. Consequently, class differences and material conditions are papered over, and their importance is denied. After all, to point to them would be to invite accusations of "externalization of blame." What happens, then, is the exaltation of the point of view of those who have little or no conflict with the system but are relatively advantaged. Gilligan herself as much as says this: "the focus on care in moral reasoning, although not characteristic of all women, is characteristically a female phenomenon in the advantaged populations that have been studied" (Gilligan, 1986: p. 330). In other words, Gilligan gives preference to a relatively advantaged point of view without considering what might go into the advantages that could throw the advantaged values into question. What should then throw these values into question is precisely Gilligan's concerted avoidance of, and efforts to dissuade from, this line of inquiry. Also disconcerting is that, flying in the face of her principles, Gilligan follows the "male" pattern of initiating a universalizing move, in this case to install a white, middle-class view as representing the essence and interest of all women. Privileging the view that is most like her own, Gilligan embodies an example of how the class system replicates itself by claiming legitimacy for some viewpoints and denying that of others.

I have focused on the terms set by Gilligan in her characterization of the first level of a moral sequence. I have extrapolated from those terms the problems that I see inhering in Gilligan's project. What Gilligan says about the other two levels in the moral sequence and the transitions to them reinforces my points. I will now consider these other levels briefly.

Gilligan describes the first transition as involving an increase in self-esteem accompanying a sense of responsibility, control over one's life, and "a move toward social participation" (Gilligan, 1982: 77). As Gilligan says, "Whereas from the first perspective, morality is a matter of sanctions imposed by a society of which one is more subject than citizen, from the second perspective, moral judgment relies on shared norms and expectations" (Gilligan, 1982: 79). At the same time, this transition marks a move to a conventional understanding of goodness that identifies goodness with self-sacrifice. Gilligan at once characterizes this transition and the second level to which it leads as conventional, yet more developed than the first level.

In keeping with my line of criticism, I would question whether the point of view represented by the second perspective, with its conventional understanding of goodness, is necessarily more advanced or insightful than the perspective of the first level. Its simplistic and conventional notions of responsibility and choice may involve more self-deception than the outright rejection of the concept of choice. This possibility is bolstered by the fact that when women at this second level face a situation where no decision can be made such that no one is hurt, and any decision can be construed as selfish, many women, noticing the constraints upon them, back away from thinking of themselves as having meaningful choice and once again frame their "choice," as Gilligan calls it, as not a choice. Wanting to be responsible, and not wanting to be selfish, but seeing the pressures of the situation where there can be no good outcome to everyone involved, they prefer to "absolve" themselves of responsibility, as Gilligan says, rather than accept blame for selfishness or the situation (Gilligan, 1982: 81).

An interesting case in this regard is that of Josie, 17. By Gilligan's terms, she exhibits a slight backsliding in owning up to decisions. In her first interview in the abortion study, Josie claimed the abortion as her choice and labeled it a "responsible" decision as opposed to a "selfish" one. But looking back on that position in her second interview, she reconsiders and instead "says that she was 'pressured into it' and that she 'didn't have a choice'" (Gilligan, 1982: 116). Gilligan's interpretation of this is that Josie is simply exhibiting the conflict of the transition from selfishness to responsibility, and is so worried about being seen as selfish that she lets that conventional fear cloud her better judgment and steer her into disclaiming responsibility for hard decisions.

My interpretation of Josie's predicament is quite different from Gilligan's. I maintain that Josie's claim of being pressured is not without truth. It is true in the bigger social picture in which women's needs are not accommodated and they must to some extent take the rap for an inadequate society, such that they are constrained by concern for their own survival and sanity to do something that may be wrong, even if right for themselves. As Sandra, who is in a similar situation, remarks:

> I am saying that abortion is wrong, but the situation is right and I am going to do it. ... I don't think you can take something that you feel is morally wrong because the situation makes it right and put the two together. They are not together, they are opposite. They don't go together. Something is wrong, but all of a sudden, because you are doing it, it is right. (quoted in Gilligan, 1982: 86)

## 78 KATHLEEN LEAGUE

In my opinion, Josie's and Sandra's misgivings about abortion and their feeling that it is wrong should not simply be brushed aside and explained away as the product of an immature, transitional phase of conventional moralizing. Rather, what they are saying should be seen as an attempt on their part to preserve guilt, to lay the blame somewhere for an unnecessarily cruel and ugly world, while rightly deflecting the bulk of the blame from themselves. Gilligan provides all the pieces in support of this interpretation, while never allowing it to dawn upon her. Defending the crucial function of interdependence, Gilligan provides example after example of women who insist that a support network is necessary for the support of life and the raising of a child. But none of these women have such a support system, and none of them believe it is their fault that they do not. The prevalence of this problem in Gilligan's sample suggests a deep social problem, an absence of community, that goes beyond the foibles of individual women and that cannot be solved by blaming the victims. Gilligan blames the victims—the women of her study—by in effect telling them to accept and internalize responsibility for their conditions. At the same time, she attempts to make this blame palatable by trying to totally remove guilt from the picture. This is as though to say that the mature adult realizes that there is nothing so wrong going on that there needs to be guilt attributed to anyone or anything. But some of Gilligan's respondents stubbornly insist upon retaining the concept of guilt. Though Gilligan may chalk this up to inadequacy of moral development, I think the women who see the need to lay blame somewhere are onto something for which Gilligan's construction is inadequate.

According to Gilligan, the second transition introduces a return to concern with the self and culminates in the care ethic which combines responsibility to others with responsibility to oneself. This third and final level thus resolves the discrepancy between responsibility and selfishness, and thus removes the difficulty in "accepting responsibility for choice" (Gilligan, 1982: 85, 90). Again, this is an all-important consideration for Gilligan: acceptance of responsibility for choice is her main criterion for assessing moral maturity.

I have no problem with a call to responsibility, or even with the idea that responsibility and choice are the hallmarks of any moral decision. My problem is once again with the limits that Gilligan imposes on responsibility as well as with her failure to recognize the limits that do inhere in responsibility. As a result, I am not sure how responsible her responsibility is. For instance, when criticism of the social order becomes off limits, the possibilities for responsibility become severely gutted of substance. And criticism of the status quo is off bounds in Gilligan's scheme of things, because she in effect chastens those who lay blame anywhere than on themselves. She seems to want, by her moralizing, to beckon people back within the respectable borders of a stripped-down responsibility made safe for the comfort of the white middle class. Supporting prevailing conditions by deflecting attention away from them to individual attitudes, Gilligan has found a subtle way of telling people to adjust to reality. This is a cruel irony in a book purporting to offer a care-ethic.

**Works Cited**

Gilligan, Carol. *In a Different Voice: Psychological Theory and Women's Development*. Cambridge, Massachusetts: Harvard University Press, 1982.

—. "Reply," *Signs*. Winter 1986, pp. 324-333.

Jaggar, Alison M. "Feminist Ethics: Projects, Problems, Prospects," *Feminist Ethics*, ed. Claudia Card. Lawrence, Kansas: University Press of Kansas, 1991.

Jameson, Fredric. *Marxism and Form*. Princeton, New Jersey: Princeton University Press, 1971.

Kerber, Linda. "Some Cautionary Words for Historians," *Signs*. Winter 1986, pp. 304-310.

Luria, Zella. "A Methodological Critique," *Signs*. Winter 1986, pp. 316-321.

Moody-Adams, Michele M. "Gender and the Complexity of Moral Voices," *Feminist Ethics*, ed. Claudia Card. Lawrence, Kansas: University Press of Kansas, 1991.

Schorr, Nanette. "Foster Care and the Politics of Compassion," *Tikkun*. Vol. 7, No. 3, May/June 1992, pp. 19-22.

Stack, Carol B. "The Culture of Gender: Women and Men of Color," Signs. Winter 1986, pp. 321-324.

# [14]

# THE GENERALIZED AND THE CONCRETE OTHER: THE KOHLBERG-GILLIGAN CONTROVERSY AND FEMINIST THEORY*

**Seyla Benhabib**

Can there be a feminist contribution to moral philosophy? That is to say, can those men and women who view the gender-sex system of our societies as oppressive, and who regard women's emancipation as essential to human liberation, criticize, analyze, and when necessary, replace the traditional categories of moral philosophy such as to contribute to women's emancipation and human liberation? By focusing on the controversy generated by Carol Gilligan's work, this essay seeks to outline such a feminist contribution to moral philosophy.

## *I. The Kohlberg-Gilligan Controversy*

Carol Gilligan's research in cognitive, developmental moral psychology recapitulates a pattern made familiar to us by Thomas Kuhn.[1] Noting a discrepancy between the claims of the original research paradigm and the data, Gilligan and her co-workers first extend this paradigm such as to accommodate anomalous results. This extension then allows them to see some other problems in a new light; subsequently, the basic paradigm, namely, the study of the development of moral judgment, according to Lawrence Kohlberg's model, is fundamentally revised. Gilligan and her co-workers now maintain that Kohlbergian theory is valid only for measuring the development of one aspect of moral orientation, which focuses on the ethics of justice and rights.

In a 1980 article on "Moral Development in Late Adolescence and Adulthood: A Critique and Reconstruction of Kohlberg's Theory," Murphy and Gilligan note that moral-judgment data from a longitudinal study of 26 undergraduates scored by Kohlberg's revised manual replicate his original findings that a significant percentage of subjects appear to regress from adolescence to adulthood.[2] The persistence of this relativistic regression

* An earlier version of this paper was read at the Conference on "Women and Morality," SUNY at Stony Brook, March 22–24, 1985 and at the "Philosophy and Social Science" Course at the Inter-University Center in Dubrovnik, Yugoslavia, April 2–14, 1985. I would like to thank participants at both conferences for their criticisms and suggestions. Larry Blum and Eva Feder Kittay have made valuable suggestions for corrections. Nancy Fraser's commentary on this essay, "Toward a Discourse Ethic of Solidarity," read at the Women and Moral Theory Conference, as well as her paper, "Feminism and the Social State" (*Salmagundi*, April 1986), have been crucial in helping me articulate the political implications of the position developed here.

suggests a need to revise the theory. In this paper they propose a distinction between "post-conventional formalism" and "post-conventional contextualism." While the post-conventional type of reasoning solves the problem of relativism by constructing a system that derives a solution to all moral problems from concepts like social contract or natural rights, the second approach finds the solution in that "while no answer may be objectively right in the sense of being context-free, some answers and some ways of thinking are better than others" (Murphy and Gilligan, 1980: 83). The extension of the original paradigm from post-conventional formalist to post-conventional contextual then leads Gilligan to see some other discrepancies in the theory in a new light, and most notably among these, women's persistently low score when compared to their male peers. Distinguishing between the ethics of justice and rights, and the ethics of care and responsibility allows her to account for women's moral development and the cognitive skills they show in a new way. Women's moral judgment is more contextual, more immersed in the details of relationships and narratives. It shows a greater propensity to take the standpoint of the "particular other," and women appear more adept at revealing feelings of empathy and sympathy required by this. Once these cognitive characteristics are seen not as deficiencies, but as essential components of adult moral reasoning at the post-conventional stage, then women's apparent moral confusion of judgment becomes a sign of their strength. Agreeing with Piaget that a developmental theory hangs from its vertex of maturity, "the point towards which progress is traced," a change in "the definition of maturity," writes Gilligan, "does not simply alter the description of the highest stage but recasts the understanding of development, changing the entire account."[3] The contextuality, narrativity, and specificity of women's moral judgment is not a sign of weakness of deficiency, but a manifestation of a vision of moral maturity that views the self as a being immersed in a network of relationships with others. According to this vision, the respect for each other's needs and the mutuality of effort to satisfy them sustain moral growth and development.

When confronted with such a challenge, it is common that adherents of an old research paradigm respond by arguing (a) that the data base does not support the conclusions drawn by revisionists, (b) that some of the new conclusions can be accommodated by the old theory, and (c) that the new and old paradigms have different object domains and are not concerned with explaining the same phenomena at all. In his response to Gilligan, Kohlberg has followed all three alternatives.

a. *The Data Base*

In his 1984 "Synopses and Detailed Replies to Critics," Kohlberg argues that available data on cognitive moral development does not report differences among children and adolescents of both sexes with respect to justice reasoning.[4] "The only studies," he writes, "showing fairly frequent sex differences are those of adults, usually of spouse housewives. Many of the studies comparing adult males and females without controlling for education and job differences ... do report sex differences in favor of males" (Kohlberg,

1984: 347). Kohlberg maintains that these latter findings are not incompatible with his theory.[5] For, according to this theory, the attainment of stages 4 and 5 depends upon experiences of participation, responsibility, and role taking in the secondary institutions of society such as the workplace and government, from which women have been and still are to a large extend excluded. The data, he concludes, does not damage the validity of his theory but shows the necessity for controlling for such factors as education and employment when assessing sex differences in adult moral reasoning.

b. *Accommodation Within the Old Theory*

Kohlberg now agrees with Gilligan that "the acknowledgement of an orientation of care and response usefully enlarges the moral domain" (Kohlberg, 1984: 340). In his view, though, justice and rights, care and responsibility, are not two *tracks* of moral development, but two moral *orientations*. The rights orientation and the care orientation are not bipolar or dichotomous. Rather, the care-and-response orientation is directed primarily to relations of special obligation to family, friends, and group members, "relations which often include or presuppose general obligations of respect, fairness, and contract" (Kohlberg, 1984: 349). Kohlberg resists the conclusion that these differences are strongly "sex related"; instead, he views the choice of orientation "to be primarily a function of setting and dilemma, not sex" (Kohlberg, 1984: 350).

c. *Object Domain of the Two Theories*

In an earlier response to Gilligan, Kohlberg had argued as follows:

> Carol Gilligan's ideas, while interesting, were not really welcome to us, for two reasons. . . . The latter, we thought, was grist for Jane Loewinger's mill in studying stages of ego development, but not for studying the specifically moral dimension in reasoning. . . . Following Piaget, my colleagues and I have had the greatest confidence that reasoning about justice would lend itself to a formal structuralist or rationalist analysis . . . whereas questions about the nature of the "good life" have not been as amenable to this type of statement.[6]

In his 1984 reply to his critics, this distinction between moral and ego development is further refined. Kohlberg divides the ego domain into the cognitive, interpersonal, and moral functions (Kohlberg, 1984: 398). Since, however, ego development is a necessary but not sufficient condition for moral development, in his view the latter can be studied independently of the former. In light of this clarification, Kohlberg regards Murphy's and Gilligan's stage of "post-conventional contextualism" as one more concerned with questions of ego as opposed to moral development. While not wanting to maintain that the acquisition of moral competencies ends with reaching adulthood, Kohlberg nevertheless insists that adult moral and ego development studies only reveal the presence of "soft" as opposed to "hard" stages. The latter are irreversible in sequence and integrally related to one another in the sense that a subsequent stage grows out of, and presents a better solution to problems confronted at, an earlier stage.[7]

It will be up to latter-day historians of science to decide whether with these admissions and qualifications, Kohlbergian theory has entered the phase of "ad-hocism," in Imre Lakatos's words,[8] or whether Gilligan's challenge, as well as that of other critics, has moved this research paradigm to a new phase, in which new problems and conceptualizations will lead to more fruitful results.

What concerns me in this paper is the question: What can feminist theory contribute to this debate? Since Kohlberg himself regards an interaction between normative philosophy and the empirical study of moral development as essential to his theory, the insights of contemporary feminist theory and philosophy can be brought to bear upon some aspects of his theory. I want to define two premises as constituents of feminist theorizing. First, for feminist theory the gender-sex system is not a contingent but an essential way in which social reality is organized, symbolically divided, and lived through experientially. By the "gender-sex" system I understand the social-historical, symbolic constitution, and interpretation of the anatomical differences of the sexes. The gender-sex system is the grid through which the self develops an *embodied* identity, a certain mode of being in one's body and of living the body. The self becomes an I in that it appropriates from the human community a mode of psychically, socially, and symbolically experiencing its bodily identity. The gender-sex system is the grid through which societies and cultures reproduce embodied individuals.[9]

Second, the historically known gender-sex systems have contributed to the oppression and exploitation of women. The task of feminist critical theory is to uncover this fact, and to develop a theory that is emancipatory and reflective, and that can aid women in their struggles to overcome oppression and exploitation. Feminist theory can contribute to this task in two ways: by developing an *explanatory-diagnostic analysis* of women's oppression across history, cultures, and societies, and by articulating an *anticipatory-utopian critique* of the norms and values of our current society and culture, such as to project new modes of togetherness, of relating to ourselves and to nature in the future. Whereas the first aspect of feminist theory requires critical, social-scientific research, the second is primarily normative and philosophical: it involves the clarification of moral and political principles, both at the meta-ethical level with respect to their *logic of justification* and at the substantive, normative level with reference to their concrete content.[10]

In this paper I shall be concerned to articulate such an anticipatory-utopian critique of universalistic moral theories from a feminist perspective. I want to argue that the *definition* of the moral domain, as well as the ideal of *moral autonomy*, not only in Kohlberg's theory but in universalistic, contractarian theories from Hobbes to Rawls, lead to a *privatization* of women's experience and to the exclusion of its consideration from a moral point of view (section II). In this tradition, the moral self is viewed as a *disembedded* and *disembodied* being. This conception of the self reflects aspects of male experience; the "relevant other" in this theory is never the sister but always the brother. This vision of the self, I want to claim, is incompatible with the very criteria of reversibility and universalizability advocated by defenders of universalism. A universalistic moral theory restricted to the standpoint of the "generalized other" falls into epistemic incoherencies which jeopardize its claim to adequately fulfill reversibility and universalizability (section III).

Universalistic moral theories in the western tradition from Hobbes to Rawls are *substitutionalist*, in the sense that the universalism they defend is defined surreptitiously by identifying the experiences of a specific group of subjects as the paradigmatic case of the human as such. These subjects are invariably white, male adults that are propertied or at least professional. I want to distinguish *substitutionalist* from *interactive* universalism. Interactive universalism acknowledges the plurality of modes of being human, and differences among humans, without endorsing all these pluralities and differences as morally and politically valid. While agreeing that normative disputes can be rationally settled, and that fairness, reciprocity, and some procedure of universalizability are constituents, that is, necessary conditions of the moral standpoint, interactive universalism regards difference as a starting point for reflection and action. In this sense "universality" is a regulative ideal that does not deny our embodied and embedded identity, but aims at developing moral attitudes and encouraging political transformations that can yield a point of view acceptable to all. Universality is not the ideal consensus of fictitiously defined selves, but the concrete process in politics and morals of the struggle of concrete, embodied selves, striving for autonomy.

## *II. Justice and the Autonomous Self in Social Contract Theories*

Kohlberg defines the privileged object domain of moral philosophy and psychology as follows:

> We say that *moral* judgments or principles have the central function of resolving interpersonal or social conflicts, that is, conflicts of claims or rights.... Thus moral judgments and principles imply a notion of equilibrium, or reversibility of claims. In this sense they ultimately involve some reference to justice, at least insofar as they define "hard" structural stages (Kohlberg, 1984: 216).

Kohlberg's conception of the moral domain is based upon a strong differentiation between justice and the good life.[11] This is also one of the cornerstones of his critique of Gilligan. Although acknowledging that Gilligan's elucidation of a care-and-responsibility orientation "usefully enlarges the moral domain" (Kohlberg, 1984: 340), Kohlberg defines the domain of *special relationships of obligation* to which care and responsibility are oriented as follows: "the spheres of kinship, love, friendship, and sex that elicit considerations of care are usually understood to be spheres of personal decision-making, as are, for instance, the problems of marriage and divorce" (Kohlberg, 1984: 229–30). The care orientation is said thus to concern domains that are more "personal" than "moral in the sense of the formal point of view" (Kohlberg, 1984: 360). Questions of the good life, pertaining to the nature of our relationships of kinship, love, friendship, and sex, on the one hand, are included in the moral domain but, on the other hand, are named "personal" as opposed to "moral" issues.

Kohlberg proceeds from a definition of morality that begins with Hobbes, in the wake of the dissolution of the Aristotelian-Christian world-view. Ancient and medieval moral systems, by contrast, show the following structure: a definition of man-as-he-ought-to-be, a definition of man-as-he-is, and the articulation of a set or rules of precepts such as can lead man as he is into what he ought to be.[12] In such moral systems, the rules which govern just relations among the human community are embedded in a more encompassing conception of the good life. This good life, the *telos* of man, is defined ontologically with reference to man's place in the cosmos at large.

The destruction of the ancient and medieval teleological conception of nature through the attack of medieval nominalism and modern science, the emergence of capitalist exchange relations, and the subsequent division of the social structure into the economy, the polity, civil associations, and the domestic-intimate sphere, radically alter moral theory. Modern theorists claim that the ultimate purposes of nature are unknown. Morality is thus emancipated from cosmology and from an all-encompassing world-view that normatively limits man's relation to nature. The distinction between justice and the good life, as it is formulated by early contract theorists, aims at defending this privacy and autonomy of the self, first in the religious sphere and then in the scientific and philosophical spheres of "free thought" as well.

Justice alone becomes the center of moral theory when bourgeois individuals in a disenchanted universe face the task of creating the legitimate basis of the social order for themselves. What "ought" to be is now defined as what all would have rationally to agree to in order to ensure civil peace and prosperity (Hobbes, Locke), or the "ought" is derived from the rational form of the moral law alone (Rousseau, Kant). As long as the social bases of cooperation and the rights claims of individuals are respected, the autonomous bourgeois subject can define the good life as his mind and conscience dictate.

The transition to modernity does not only privatize the self's relation to the cosmos and to ultimate questions of religion and being. First with western modernity the conception of privacy is so enlarged that an intimate domestic-familial sphere is subsumed under it. Relations of "kinship, friendship, love, and sex," indeed, as Kohlberg takes them to be, come to be viewed as spheres of "personal decision-making." At the beginning of modern moral and political theory, however, the "personal" nature of these spheres does not mean the recognition of equal, female autonomy, but rather the removal of gender relations form the sphere of justice. While the bourgeois male celebrates his transition form conventional to post-conventional morality, from socially accepted rules of justice to their generation in light of the principles of a social contract, the domestic sphere remains at the conventional level. The sphere of justice from Hobbes through Locke and Kant is regarded as the domain where independent, male heads of household transact with one another, while the domestic-intimate sphere is put beyond the pale of justice and restricted to the reproductive and affective needs of the bourgeois *pater familias*. Agnes Heller has named this domain the "household of the emotions."[13] An entire domain of human activity, namely, nurture, reproduction, love, and care, which becomes the woman's lot in the course of the development of modern, bourgeois society, is excluded from moral and political considerations, and relegated to the realm of "nature."

Through a brief historical genealogy of social contract theories, I want to examine the distinction between justice and the good life as it is translated into the split between the public and the domestic. This analysis will also allow us to see the implicit ideal of autonomy cherished by this tradition.

At the beginning of modern moral and political philosophy stands a powerful metaphor: the "state of nature." This metaphor is at times said to be fact. Thus, in his *Second Treatise of Civil Government*, John Locke reminds us of "the two men in the desert island, mentioned by Garcilasso de la Vega.... or a Swiss and an Indian, in the woods of America."[14] At other times it is acknowledged as fiction. Thus, Kant dismisses the colorful reveries of his predecessors and transforms the "state of nature" from an empirical fact into a transcendental concept. The state of nature comes to represent the idea of *Privatrecht*, under which are subsumed the right of property and "thinglike rights of a personal nature" (*auf dingliche Natur persönliche Rechte*), which the male head of household exercises over his wife, children, and servants.[15] Only Thomas Hobbes compounds fact and fiction, and against those who consider it strange "that Nature should thus dissociate, and render men apt to invade, and destroy one another,"[16] he asks each man who does not trust "this Inference, made from the passions," to reflect why "when taking a journey, he arms himself, and seeks to go well accompanied; when going to sleep, he lockes his dores; when even in his house he lockes his chests. . . . Does he not there as much accuse mankind by his actions, as I do by my words?" (Hobbes, *Leviathan*, 187). The state of nature is the looking glass of these early bourgeois thinkers in which they and their societies are magnified, purified, and reflected in their original, naked verity. The state of nature is both nightmare (Hobbes) and utopia (Rousseau). In it the bourgeois male recognizes his flaws, fears, and anxieties, as well as dreams.

The varying content of this metaphor is less significant than its simple and profound message: in the beginning man was alone. Again it is Hobbes who gives this thought its clearest formulation. "Let us consider men.... as if but even now sprung out of the earth, and suddenly, like mushrooms, come to full maturity, without all kind of engagement to each other."[17] This vision of men as mushrooms is an ultimate picture of autonomy. The female, the mother of whom every individual is born, is now replaced by the earth. The denial of being born of woman frees the male ego from the most natural and basic bond of dependence. Nor is the picture very different for Rousseau's noble savage who, wandering wantonly through the woods, occasionally mates with a female and then seeks rest.[18]

The state-of-nature metaphor provides a vision of the autonomous self: this is a narcissist who sees the world in his own image; who has no awareness of the limits of his own desires and passions; and who cannot see himself through the eyes of another. The narcissism of this sovereign self is destroyed by the presence of the other. As Hegel expresses it:

> Self-consciousness is faced by another self-consciousness; it has come *out of*

> *itself*. This has a twofold significance: first, it has *lost* itself, for it finds itself as an *other* being; secondly, in doing so it has superseded the other, for it does not see the other as an essential being, but in the other sees its own self.[19]

The story of the autonomous male ego is the saga of this initial sense of *loss* in confrontation with the other, and the gradual recovery from this original narcissistic wound through the sobering experience of war, fear, domination, anxiety, and death. The last installment in this drama is the social contract: the establishment of the law to govern all. Having been thrust out of their narcissistic universe into a world of insecurity by their sibling brothers, these individuals have to reestablish the authority of the father in the image of the law. The early bourgeois individual not only has no mother but no father as well; rather, he strives to reconstitute the father in his own self-image. What is usually celebrated in the annals of modern moral and political theory as the dawn of liberty is precisely this destruction of political patriarchy in bourgeois society.

The constitution of political authority civilizes sibling rivalry by turning their attention from war to property, from vanity to science, from conquest to luxury. The original narcissism is not transformed; only now ego boundaries are clearly defined. The law reduces insecurity, the fear of being engulfed by the other, by defining mine and thine. Jealousy is not eliminated but tamed; as long as each can keep what is his and attain more by fair rules of the game, he is entitled to it. Competition is domesticized and channeled towards acquisition. The law contains anxiety by defining rigidly the boundaries between self and other, but the law does not cure anxiety. The anxiety that the other is always on the look to interfere in your space and appropriate what is yours; the anxiety that you will be subordinated to his will; the anxiety that a group of brothers will usurp the law in the name of the "will of all" and destroy "the general will," the will of the absent father, remains. The law teaches how to repress anxiety and to sober narcissism, but the constitution of the self is not altered. The establishment of private rights and duties does not overcome the inner wounds of the self; it only forces them to become less destructive.

This imaginary of early moral and political theory has had an amazing hold upon the modern consciousness. From Freud to Piaget, the relationship to the brother is viewed as the humanizing experience that teaches us to become social, responsible adults.[20] As a result of the hold of this metaphor upon our imagination, we have also come to inherit a number of philosophical prejudices. For Rawls and Kohlberg, as well, the autonomous self is disembedded and disembodied; moral impartiality is learning to recognize the claims of the other who is just like oneself; fairness is public justice; a public system of rights and duties is the best way to arbitrate conflict, to distribute rewards and to establish claims.

Yet this is a strange world: it is one in which individuals are grown up before they have been born; in which boys are men before they have been children; a world where neither mother, nor sister, nor wife exist. The question is less what Hobbes says about men and women, or what Rousseau sees the role of Sophie to be in Emile's education. The point is that in this universe, the experience of the early modern female has no place. Woman is simply what men are not; namely, they are not autonomous, independent, but by the same token, non-aggressive but nurturant, not competitive but giving, not public but private. The world of the female is constituted by a series of negations. She is simply what he happens not to be. Her identity becomes defined by a lack — the lack of autonomy, the lack of independence, the lack of the phallus. The narcissistic male takes her to be just like himself, only his opposite.

It is not the misogynist prejudices of early modern moral and political theory alone that lead to women's exclusion. It is the very constitution of a sphere of discourse which bans the female from history to the realm of nature, from the light of the public to the interior of the household, from the civilizing effect of culture to the repetitious burden of nurture and reproduction. The public sphere, the sphere of justice, moves in historicity, whereas the private sphere, the sphere of care and intimacy, is unchanging and timeless. It pulls us toward the earth even when we, as Hobbesian mushrooms, strive to pull away from it. The dehistoricization of the private realm signifies that, as the male ego celebrates his passage from nature to culture, from conflict to consensus, women remain in a timeless universe, condemned to repeat the cycles of life.

This split between the public sphere of justice, in which history is made, and the atemporal realm of the household, in which life is reproduced, is internalized by the male ego. The dichotomies are not only without but within. He himself is divided into the public person and the private individual. Within his chest clash the law of reason and the inclination of nature, the brilliance of cognition and the obscurity of emotion. Caught between the moral law and the starry heaven above and the earthly body below,[21] the autonomous self strives for unity. But the antagonism — between autonomy and nurturance, independence and bonding, sovereignty of the self and relations to others — remains. In the discourse of modern moral and political theory, these dichotomies are reified as being essential to the constitution of the self. While men humanize outer nature through labor, inner nature remains ahistorical, dark, and obscure. I want to suggest that contemporary universalist moral theory has inherited this dichotomy between autonomy and nurturance, independence and bonding, the sphere of justice and the domestic, personal realm. This becomes most visible in its attempt to restrict the moral point of view to the perspective of the "generalized other."

### *III. The Generalized versus the Concrete Other*

Let me describe two conceptions of self-other relations that delineate both moral perspectives and interactional structures. I shall name the first the standpoint of the "generalized"[22] and the second that of the "concrete" other. In contemporary moral theory these conceptions are viewed as incompatible, even as antagonistic. These two perspectives reflect the dichotomies and splits of early modern moral and political theory between autonomy and nurturance, independence and bonding, the public and the domestic, and more broadly, between justice and the good life. The content of the generalized as well as the concrete other is shaped by this dichotomous characterization, which we have inherited from the modern tradition.

The standpoint of the generalized other requires us to view each and every individual as a rational being entitled to the same rights and duties we would want to ascribe to ourselves. In assuming this standpoint, we abstract from the individuality and concrete identity of the other. We assume that the other, like ourselves, is a being who has concrete needs, desires, and affects, but that what constitutes his or her moral dignity is not what differentiates us from each other, but rather what we, as speaking and acting rational agents, have in common. Our relation to the other is governed by the norms of *formal equality* and *reciprocity*: each is entitled to expect and to assume from us what we can expect and assume from him or her. The norms of our interactions are primarily public and institutional ones. If I have a right to X, then you have the duty not to hinder me from enjoying X and conversely. In treating you in accordance with these norms, I confirm in your person the rights of humanity and I have a legitimate claim to expect that you will do the same in relation to me. The moral categories that accompany such interactions are those of right, obligation, and entitlement, and the corresponding moral feelings are those of respect, duty, worthiness, and dignity.

The standpoint of the concrete other, by contrast, requires us to view each and every rational being as an individual with a concrete history, identity, and affective-emotional constitution. In assuming this standpoint, we abstract from what constitutes our commonality. We seek to comprehend the needs of the other, his or her motivations, what s/he searches for, and what s/he desires. Our relation to the other is governed by the norms of *equity* and *complementary reciprocity*: each is entitled to expect and to assume from the other forms of behavior through which the other feels recognized and confirmed as a concrete, individual being with specific needs, talents, and capacities. Our differences in this case complement rather than exclude one another. The norms of our interaction are usually private, non-institutional ones. They are norms of friendship, love, and care. These norms require in various ways that I exhibit more than the simple assertion of my rights and duties in the face of your needs. In treating you in accordance with the norms of friendship, love, and care, I confirm not only your *humanity* but your human *individuality*. The moral categories that accompany such interactions are those of responsibility, bonding, and sharing. The corresponding moral feelings are those of love, care, sympathy, and solidarity.

In contemporary universalist moral psychology and moral theory, it is the viewpoint of the "generalized other" that predominates. In his article on "Justice as Reversibility: The Claim to Moral Adequacy of a Highest Stage of Moral Development," for example, Kohlberg argues that

> [M]oral judgments involve role-taking, taking the viewpoint of the others conceived as *subjects* and coordinating these viewpoints.... Second, equilibriated moral judgments involve principles of justice or fairness. A moral situation in disequilibrium is one in which there are unresolved, conflicting claims. A resolution of the situation is one in which each is "given his due" according to

> some principle of justice that can be recognized as fair by all the conflicting parties involved.[23]

Kohlberg regards Rawls's concept of "reflective equilibrium" as a parallel formulation of the basic idea of reciprocity, equality, and fairness intrinsic to all moral judgments. The Rawlsian "veil of ignorance," in Kohlberg's judgment, not only exemplifies the formalist idea of universalizability but that of perfect *reversibility* as well.[24] The idea behind the veil of ignorance is described as follows:

> The decider is to initially decide from a point of view *that ignores his identity* (veil of ignorance) under the assumption that decisions are governed by maximizing values from a viewpoint of rational egoism in considering each party's interest (Kohlberg, 1981: 200; my emphasis).

What I would like to question is the assumption that "taking the viewpoint of others" is truly compatible with this notion of fairness as reasoning behind a "veil of ignorance."[25] The problem is that the defensible kernel of the ideas of reciprocity and fairness are thereby identified with the perspective of the disembedded and disembodied generalized other. Now since Kohlberg presents his research subjects with hypothetically constructed moral dilemmas, it may be thought that his conception of "taking the standpoint of the other" is not subject to the epistemic restrictions that apply to the Rawlsian original position. Subjects in Kohlbergian interviews do not stand behind a veil of ignorance. However, the very *language* in which Kohlbergian dilemmas are presented incorporate these epistemic restrictions. For example, in the famous Heinz dilemma, as in others, the motivations of the druggist as a concrete individual, as well as the history of the individuals involved, are excluded as irrelevant to the definition of the moral problem at hand. In these dilemmas, individuals and their moral positions are represented by abstracting from the narrative history of the self and its motivations. Gilligan also notes that the implicit moral epistemology of Kohlbergian dilemmas frustrates women, who want to phrase these hypothetical dilemmas in a more contextual voice, attuned to the standpoint of the concrete other. The result is that

> though several of the women in the abortion study clearly articulate a post-conventional meta-ethical position, none of them are considered principled in their normative moral judgments of Kohlberg's hypothetical dilemmas. Instead, the women's judgments point toward an identification of the violence inherent in the dilemma itself, which is seen to compromise the justice of any of its possible resolutions (Gilligan, 1982: 101).

Through an immanent critique of the theories of Kohlberg and Rawls, I want to show that ignoring the standpoint of the concrete other leads to epistemic incoherence in universalistic moral theories. The problem can be stated as follows: according to Kohlberg and Rawls, moral reciprocity involves the capacity to take the standpoint of the other, to put oneself imaginatively in the place of the other, but under conditions of the "veil of ignorance," the *other as different from the self*, disappears. Unlike in previous contract theories, in this case the other is not constituted through projection, but as a consequence of total abstraction from his or her identity. Differences are not denied; they become irrelevant. The Rawlsian self does not know:

> his place in society, his class position or status; nor does he know his fortune in the distribution of natural assets and abilities, his intelligence and strength, and the like. Nor, again, does anyone know his conception of the good, the particulars of his rational plan of life, or even the special features of his psychology such as his aversion to risk or liability to optimism or pessimism.[26]

Let us ignore for a moment whether such selves who also do not know "the particular circumstances of their own society" can know anything at all that is relevant to the human condition, and ask instead, are these individuals *human selves* at all? In his attempt to do justice to Kant's conception of noumenal agency, Rawls recapitulates a basic problem with the Kantian conception of the self, namely, that noumenal selves cannot be *individuated*. If all that belongs to them as embodied, affective, suffering creatures, their memory and history, their ties and relations to others, are to be subsumed under the phenomenal realm, then what we are left with is an empty mask that is everyone and no one. Michael Sandel points out that the difficulty in Rawls's conception derives from his attempt to be consistent with the Kantian concept of the autonomous self, as a being freely choosing his or her own ends in life.[27] However, this moral and political concept of autonomy slips into a metaphysics according to which it is meaningful to define a self independently of *all* the ends it may choose and all and any conceptions of the good it may hold (Sandel, 1984: 47ff.). At this point we must ask whether the *identity* of any human self can be defined with reference to its capacity for agency alone. Identity does not refer to my potential for choice alone, but to the actuality of my choices, namely, to how I as a finite, concrete, embodied individual shape and fashion the circumstances of my birth and family, linguistic, cultural, and gender identity into a coherent narrative that stands as my life's story. Indeed, if we recall that every autonomous being is one born of others and not, as Rawls, following Hobbes, assumes, a being "not bound by prior moral ties to another,"[28] the question becomes: how does this finite, embodied creature constitute into a coherent narrative those episodes of choice and limit, agency and suffering, initiative and dependence? The self is not a thing, a substrate, but the protagonist of a life's tale. The conception of selves who can be individuated prior to their moral ends is incoherent. We could not know if such a being was a human self, an angel, or the Holy Spirit.

If this concept of the self as mushroom, behind a veil of ignorance, is incoherent, then it follows that there is no real *plurality* of perspectives in the Rawlsian original position, but only a *definitional identity*. For Rawls, as Sandel observes, "our individuating characteristics are given empirically, by the distinctive concatenation of wants and desires, aims and attributes, purposes and ends that come to characterize human beings in their particularity" (Sandel, 1984: 51). But how are we supposed to know what these wants and desires are independently of knowing something about the person who holds these wants, desires, aims and attributes? Is there perhaps an "essence" of anger that is the same for each angry individual; an essence of ambition that is distinct from ambitious selves? I fail to see how individuating characteristics can be ascribed to a transcendental self who can have any and none of these, who can be all or none of them.

If selves who are epistemologically and metaphysically prior to their individuating characteristics, as Rawls takes them to be, cannot be human selves at all; if, therefore, there is no human *plurality* behind the veil of ignorance but only *definitional identity*, then this has consequences for criteria of reversibility and universalizability said to be constituents of the moral point of view. Definitional identity leads to *incomplete reversibility*, for the primary requisite of reversibility, namely, a coherent distinction between me and you, the self and the other, cannot be sustained under these circumstances. Under conditions of the veil of ignorance, the other disappears.

It is no longer plausible to maintain that such a standpoint can universalize adequately. Kohlberg views the veil of ignorance not only as exemplifying reversibility but universalizability as well. This is the idea that "we must be willing to live with our judgment or decision when we trade places with others in the situation being judged" (Kohlberg, 1981: 197). But the question is, *which* situation? Can moral situations be individuated independently of our knowledge of the agents involved in these situations, of their histories, attitudes, characters, and desires? Can I describe a situation as one of arrogance or hurt pride without knowing something about you as a concrete other? Can I know how to distinguish between a breach of confidence and a harmless slip of the tongue, without knowing your history and your character? Moral situations, like moral emotions and attitudes, can only be individuated if they are evaluated in light of our knowledge of the history of the agents involved in them.

While every procedure of universalizability presupposes that "like cases ought to be treated alike" or that I should act in such a way that I should also be willing that all others in a like situation act like me, the most difficult aspect of any such procedure is to know what constitutes a "like" situation or what it would mean for another to be exactly in a situation like mine. Such a process of reasoning, to be at all viable, must involve the viewpoint of the concrete other, for situations, to paraphrase Stanley Cavell, do not come like "envelopes and golden finches," ready for definition and description, "nor like apples ripe for grading."[29] When we morally disagree, for example, we do not only disagree about the principles involved; very often we disagree because what I see as a lack of generosity on your part you construe as your legitimate right not to do something; we disagree because what you see as jealousy on my part I view as my desire to have more of your attention. Universalistic moral theory neglects such everyday, interactional morality and assumes that the public standpoint of justice, and our quasi-public personalities as right-bearing individuals, are the center of moral theory.[30]

Kohlberg emphasizes the dimension of ideal role-taking or taking the viewpoint of the other in moral judgment. Because he defines the other as the generalized other, however, he perpetrates one of the fundamental errors of Kantian moral theory. Kant's error was to assume that I, as a pure rational agent reasoning for myself, could reach a conclusion that would be acceptable for all at all times and places.[31] In Kantian moral theory, moral agents are like geometricians in different rooms who, reasoning alone for themselves, all arrive at the same solution to a problem. Following Habermas, I want to name this the "monological" model of moral reasoning. Insofar as he interprets ideal role-taking in the light of Rawls's concept of a "veil of ignorance," Kohlberg as well sees the silent thought process of a single self who imaginatively puts himself in the position of the other as the most adequate form of moral judgment.

I conclude that a definition of the self that is restricted to the standpoint of the generalized other becomes incoherent and cannot individuate among selves. Without assuming the standpoint of the concrete other, no coherent universalizability test can be carried out, for we lack the necessary epistemic information to judge my moral situation to be "like" or "unlike" yours.

### *IV. A Communicative Ethic of Need Interpretations and the Relational Self*

In the preceding sections of this paper I have argued that the distinction between justice and the good life, the restriction of the moral domain to questions of justice, as well as the ideal of moral autonomy in these theories, result in the privatization of women's experience and lead to epistemological blindness toward the concrete other. The consequence of such epistemological blindness is an internal inconsistency in universalistic moral theories, insofar as these define "taking the standpoint of the other" as essential to the moral point of view. My aim has been to take universalistic moral theories at their word and to show through an immanent critique, first of the "state of nature" metaphor and then of the "original position," that the conception of the autonomous self implied by these thought experiments is restricted to the "generalized other."

This distinction between the generalized and the concrete other raises questions in moral and political theory. It may be asked whether, without the standpoint of the generalized other, it would be possible to define a moral point of view at all. Since our identities as concrete others are what distinguish us from each other according to gender, race, class, cultural differentials, as well as psychic and natural abilities, would a moral theory restricted to the standpoint of the concrete other not be a racist, sexist, cultural relativist, discriminatory one? Furthermore, without the standpoint of the generalized other, it may be argued, a political theory of justice suited for modern, complex societies is unthinkable. Certainly rights must be an essential component in any such theory. Finally, the perspective of the "concrete other" defines our relations as private, non-institutional ones, concerned with love, care, friendship, and intimacy. Are these activities so gender-specific? Are we not all "concrete others"?

The distinction between the "generalized" and the "concrete other," as drawn in this essay so far, is not a *prescriptive* but a *critical* one. My goal is not to prescribe a moral and political theory consonant with the concept of the "concrete other." For, indeed, the recognition of the dignity and worthiness of the generalized other is a *necessary*, albeit not *sufficient*, condition to define the moral standpoint in modern societies. In this sense, the concrete other is a critical concept that designates the *ideological* limits of universalistic discourse. It signifies the *unthought*, the *unseen*, and the *unheard* in such theories. This is evidenced by Kohlberg's effort, on the one hand, to enlarge the domain of moral theory such as to include in it relations to the concrete other and, on the other hand, to characterize such special relations of obligation as "private, personal" matters of evaluative life-choices alone. Urging an examination of this unthought is necessary to prevent the preemption of the discourse of universality by an unexamined particularity. Substitutionalist universalism dismisses the concrete other, while interactive universalism acknowledges that every generalized other is also a concrete other.

From a meta-ethical and normative standpoint, I would argue, therefore, for the validity of a moral theory which allows us to recognize the dignity of the generalized other through an acknowledgment of the moral identity of the concrete other. The point is not to juxtapose the generalized to the concrete other or to seek normative validity in one or another standpoint. The point is to think through the ideological limitations and biases that arise in the discourse of universalist morality through this unexamined opposition. I doubt that an easy integration of both points of view, of justice and of care, is possible, without first clarifying the moral framework which would allow us to question both standpoints and their implicit gender presuppositions.

For this task a model of communicative need interpretations suggests itself. Not only is such an ethic, as I interpret it, compatible with the dialogic, interactive generation of universality, but most significant, such an ethic provides the suitable framework within which moral and political agents can define their own concrete identities on the basis of recognizing each other's dignity as generalized others. Questions of the most desirable and just political organization, as well as the distinction between justice and the good life, the public and the domestic, can be analyzed, renegotiated, and redefined in such a process. Since, however, all those affected are participants in this process, the presumption is that these distinctions cannot be drawn in such a way as to privatize, hide, and repress the experiences of those who have suffered under them, for only what all could consensually agree to be in the best interest of each could be accepted as the outcome of this dialogic process.

One consequence of this communicative ethic of need interpretations is that the object domain of moral theory is so enlarged that not only rights but needs, not only justice but possible modes of the good life, are moved into an anticipatory-utopian perspective. What such discourses can generate are not only universalistically prescribable norms, but also intimations of otherness in the present that can lead to the future.

In his current formulation of his theory, Kohlberg accepts this extension of his stage 6 perspective into an ethic of need interpretations, as suggested first by Habermas.[33] However, he does not see the incompatibility between the communicative ethics model and the Rawlsian "original position."[34] In defining reversibility of perspectives, he still considers the Rawlsian position to be paradigmatic (Kohlberg, 1984: 272, 310). Despite certain shared assumptions, the communicative model of need interpretations and the justice model of the original position need to be distinguished from each other.

First, the condition of ideal role-taking is not to be construed as a *hypothetical* thought process, carried out singly by the moral agent or the moral philosopher, but as an *actual* dialogue situation in which moral agents communicate with one another. Second, it is not necessary to place any epistemic constraints upon such an actual process of moral reasoning and disputation, for the more knowledge is available to moral agents about each other, their history, the particulars of their society, its structure and future, the more rational will be the outcome of their deliberations. Practical rationality entails epistemic rationality as well, and more knowledge rather than less contributes to a more rational and informed judgment. To judge rationally is not to judge as if one did not know what one could know, but to judge in light of all available and relevant information. Third, if there are no knowledge restrictions upon such a discursive situation, then it also follows that there is no privileged subject matter of moral disputation. Moral agents are not only limited to reasoning about primary goods which they are assumed to want whatever else they want. Instead, both the *goods* they desire and their *desires* themselves become legitimate topics of moral disputation. Finally, in such moral discourses agents can also change levels of reflexivity, that is, they can introduce meta-considerations about the very conditions and constraints under which such dialogue takes place and evaluate their fairness. There is no closure of reflexivity in this model as there is, for example, in the Rawlsian one, which enjoins agents to accept certain rules of the bargaining game prior to the very choice of principles of justice.[35] With regard to the Kohlbergian paradigm, this would mean that moral agents can challenge the relevant *definition* of a moral situation, and urge that this very definition itself become the subject matter of moral reasoning and dispute.

A consequence of this model of communicative ethics would be that the language of rights and duties can now be challenged in light of our need interpretations. Following the tradition of modern social contract theories, Rawls and Kohlberg assume that our affective-emotional constitution, the needs and desires in light of which we formulate our rights and claims, are private matters alone. Their theory of the self, and in particular the Rawlsian metaphysics of the moral agent, do not allow them to view the constitution of our inner nature in *relational* terms.

A relational-interactive theory of identity assumes that inner nature, while being unique, is not an immutable given.[36] Individual need-interpretations and motives carry within them the traces of those early childhood experiences, phantasies, wishes, and desires as well as the self-conscious goals of the person. The grammatical logic of the word "I" reveals the unique structure of ego identity: every subject who uses this concept in relation to herself knows that all other subjects are likewise "I"s. In this respect the self only becomes an I in a community of other selves who are also I's. Every act of self-reference expresses simultaneously the uniqueness and difference of the self as well as the commonality among selves. Discourses about needs and motives unfold in this space created by commonality and uniqueness, generally shared socialization, and the contingency of individual life-histories.

The non-relational theory of the self, which is privileged in contemporary universalist moral theory, by contrast, removes such need interpretations from the domain of moral discourse. They become "private," non-formalizable, non-analyzable, and amorphous aspects of our conceptions of the good life. I am not suggesting that such conceptions of the good life either *can* or *should* be universalized, but only that our affective-emotional constitution, as well as our concrete history as moral agents, ought to be considered accessible to moral communication, reflection, and transformation. Inner nature, no less than the public sphere of justice, has a historical dimension. In it are intertwined the history of the self and the history of the collective. To condemn it to silence is, as Gilligan has suggested, not to hear that other voice in moral theory. I would say more strongly that such discourse continues woman's oppression by privatizing their lot and by excluding from moral theory a central sphere of their activities.

As the Second Wave of the Women's Movement both in Europe and the United States has argued, to understand and to combat woman's oppression it is no longer sufficient to demand woman's political and economic emancipation alone; it is also necessary to question those psychosexual relations in the domestic and private spheres within which women's lives unfold, and through which gender identity is reproduced. To explicate woman's oppression it is necessary to uncover the power of those symbols, myths, and fantasies that entrap both sexes in the unquestioned world of gender roles. Perhaps one of the most fundamental of these myths and symbols has been the ideal of autonomy conceived in the image of a disembedded and disembodied male ego. This vision of autonomy was and continues to be based upon an implicit politics which defines the domestic, intimate sphere as ahistorical, unchanging, and immutable, thereby removing it from reflection and discussion.[37] Needs, as well as emotions and affects, become merely given properties of individuals, which moral philosophy recoils from examining, on the grounds that it may interfere with the autonomy of the sovereign self. Women, because they have been made the "housekeeper of the emotions" in the modern, bourgeois world, and because they have suffered from the uncomprehended needs and phantasies of the male imagination, which has made them at once into Mother Earth and nagging bitch, the Virgin Mary and the whore, cannot condemn this sphere to silence. What Carol Gilligan has heard are those mutterings, protestations, and objections which women, confronted with ways of posing moral dilemmas that seemed alien to them, have voiced. Only if we can understand why their voice has been silenced, and how the dominant ideals of moral autonomy in our culture, as well as the privileged definition of the moral sphere, continue to silence women's voices, do we have a hope of moving to a more integrated vision of ourselves and of our fellow humans as generalized as well as "concrete" others.

## NOTES

1 Thomas Kuhn, *The Structure of Scientific Revolutions* (Chicago: University of Chicago Press, 1970, second edition), pp. 52ff.

2 John Michael Murphy and Carol Gilligan, "Moral Development in Late Adolescence and Adulthood: A Critique and Reconstruction of Kohlberg's Theory," *Human Development* 23 (1980), pp. 77–104; cited in the text as Murphy and Gilligan, 1980.

3 Carol Gilligan, *In a Different Voice: Psychological Theory and Women's Development* (Cambridge, Mass.: Harvard University Press, 1982), pp. 18–19; cited in the text as Gilligan, 1982.

4 Lawrence Kohlberg, "Synopses and Detailed Replies to Critics," with Charles Levine and Alexandra Hewer, in L. Kohlberg, *Essays on Moral Development*, Vol. II, *The Psychology of Moral Development* (San Francisco: Harper & Row, 1984), p. 341. This volume is cited in the text as Kohlberg, 1984.

5 There still seems to be some question as to how the data on women's moral development is to be interpreted. Studies which focus on late adolescents and adult males and which show sex differences, include Fishkin, J., Keniston, K., and MacKinnon, C., "Moral Reasoning and Political Ideology," *Journal of Personality and Social Psychology* 27 (1973), pp. 109–19; Haan, N., Block, J., and Smith, M.B., "Moral Reasoning of Young Adults: Political-Social Behavior, Family Background, and Personality Correlates," *Journal of Personality and Social Psychology* 10 (1968), pp. 184–201; Holstein, C., "Irreversible, Stepwise Sequence in the Development of Moral Judgment: A Longitudinal Study of Males and Females," *Child Development* 47 (1976), pp. 51–61. While it is clear that the available evidence does not throw the model of stage-sequence development as such into question, the prevalent presence of sex differences in moral reasoning does raise questions about *what* exactly this model might be measuring. Norma Haan sums up this objection to the Kohlbergian paradigm as follows: "Thus the moral reasoning of males who live in technical, rationalized societies, who reason at the level of formal operations and who *defensively intellectualize and deny interpersonal and situational detail*, is especially favored in the Kohlbergian scoring system," in "Two Moralities in Action Contexts: Relationships to Thought, Ego Regulation, and Development" (*Journal of Personality and Social Psychology* 36 (1978), p. 287; emphasis mine). I think Gilligan's studies also support the finding that inappropriate "intellectualization and denial of interpersonal, situational detail" constitutes one of the major differences in male and female approaches to moral problems. This is why, as I argue in the text, the neat separation between ego and moral development, as drawn by Kohlberg and others, seems inadequate to deal with this problem, since certain ego attitudes — defensiveness, rigidity, inability to empathize, lack of flexibility — do seem to be favored over others — non-repressive attitude towards emotions, flexibility, presence of empathy.

6 L. Kohlberg, "A Reply to Owen Flanagan and Some Comments on the Puka-Goodpaster Exchange," in *Ethics* 92 (April 1982), p. 316. Cf. also Gertrud Nunner-Winkler, "Two Moralities? A Critical Discussion of an Ethic of Care and Responsibility Versus an Ethics of Rights and Justice," in *Morality, Moral Behavior and Moral Development*, ed. by W.M. Kurtines and J.L. Gewirtz (New York: John Wiley and Sons, 1984), p. 355. It is unclear whether the issue is, as Kohlberg and Nunner-Winkler suggest, one of distinguishing between "moral" and "ego" development or whether cognitive-developmental moral theory does not presuppose a model of ego development which clashes with more psychoanalytically oriented variants. In fact, to combat the charge of "maturationism" or "nativism" in his theory, which would imply that moral stages are a priori givens of the mind unfolding according to their own logic, regardless of the influence of society or environment upon them, Kohlberg argues as follows: "Stages," he writes, "are equilibriations arising from interaction between the organism (with its structuring tendencies) and the structure of the environment (physical or social). Universal moral stages are as much a function of universal features of social structure (such as institutions of law, family, property) and social interactions in various cultures, as they are products of

the general structuring tendencies of the knowing organism" (Kohlberg, "A Reply to Owen Flanagan," p. 521). If this is so, then cognitive-developmental moral theory must also presuppose that there is a *dynamic* between self and social structure whereby the individual learns, acquires or internalizes the perspectives and sanctions of the social world. But the mechanism of this dynamic may involve learning as well as resistance, internalization as well as projection and fantasy. The issue is less whether moral development and ego development are distinct — they may be conceptually distinguished and yet in the history of the self they are related — but whether the model of ego development presupposed by Kohlberg's theory is not distortingly *cognitivistic* in that it ignores the role of affects, resistance, projection, phantasy, and defense mechanisms in socialization processes.

7 For this formulation, see J. Habermas, "Interpretive Social Science vs. Hermeneuticism," in *Social Science as Moral Inquiry*, ed. by N. Haan, R. Bellah, P. Rabinow, and W. Sullivan (New York: Columbia University Press, 1983), p. 262.

8 Imre Lakatos, "Falsification and the Methodology of Scientific Research Programs," in *Criticism and the Growth of Knowledge*, ed. by I. Lakatos and A. Musgrave (Cambridge, England: Cambridge University Press, 1970), pp. 117ff.

9 Let me explain the status of this premise. I would characterize it as a "second-order research hypothesis" that both guides concrete research in the social sciences and that can, in turn, be falsified by them. It is not a statement of faith about the way the world is: the cross-cultural and trans-historical universality of the sex-gender system is an empirical fact. It is also most definitely not a normative proposition about the way the world *ought* to be. To the contrary, feminism radically challenges the validity of the sex-gender system in organizing societies and cultures, and advocates the emancipation of men and women from the unexamined and oppressive grids of this framework. The historian Kelly-Gadol succinctly captures the meaning of this premise for empirical research:

"Once we look to history for an understanding of woman's situation, we are, of course, already assuming that woman's situation is a social matter. But history, as we first come to it, did not seem to confirm this awareness.... The moment this is done — the moment that one assumes that women are part of humanity in the fullest sense — the period or set of events with which we deal takes on a wholly different character or meaning from the normally accepted one. Indeed what emerges is a fairly regular pattern of relative loss of status for women precisely in those periods of so-called progressive change.... Our notions of so-called progressive developments, such as classical Athenian civilization, the Renaissance and the French Revolution, undergo a startling re-evaluation.... Suddenly we see these ages *with a new, double vision — and each eye sees a different picture*" ("The Social Relations of the Sexes: Methodological Implications of Women's History," *Signs*, vol. 1, no. 4 (1976), pp. 810–11; emphasis mine).

10 For further clarification of these two aspects of critical theory, see my *Critique, Norm, and Utopia: A Study of the Foundations of Critical Theory* (New York: Columbia University Press, 1986), Part Two, "The Transformation of Critique."

11 Although frequently invoked by Kohlberg, Nunner-Winkler, and also Habermas, it is still unclear *how* this distinction is drawn and how it is justified. For example, does the justice/good life distinction correspond to sociological definitions of the public vs. the private? If so, what is meant by the "private"? Is women-battering a "private" or a "public" matter? The relevant sociological definitions of the private and the public are shifting in our societies, as they have shifted historically. I therefore find little justification for an examined reliance upon changing juridical and social definitions in moral theory. Another way of drawing this distinction is to separate what is universalizable from what is culturally contingent, dependent upon the specifics of concrete life-forms, individual

histories, and the like. Habermas, in particular, relegates questions of the good life to the aesthetic-expressive sphere (cf. "A Reply to My Critics," in *Habermas: Critical Debates*, ed. by John B. Thompson and David Held (Cambridge, Mass.: MIT Press, 1982), p. 262; "Moralbewusstsein und kommunikatives Handeln," in *Moralbewusstsein und kommunikatives Handeln* (Frankfurt: Suhrkamp, 1983), pp. 190ff.) Again, if privacy in the sense of intimacy is included in the "aesthetic-expressive" sphere, we are forced to silence and privatize most of the issues raised by the women's movement, which concern precisely the quality and nature of our "intimate" relations, fantasies, and hopes. A traditional response to this is to argue that in wanting to draw this aspect of our lives into the light of the public, the women's movement runs the risk of authoritarianism because it questions the limits of individual "liberty." In response to this legitimate political concern, I would argue that there is a distinction between questioning life-forms and values that have been oppressive for women, and making them "public" in the sense of making them accessible to reflection, action, and transformation, and in the sense of revealing their *socially constituted* character, on the one hand, and making them "public" in the sense that these areas be subject to legislative and administrative state-action. The second may, but need not, follow from the first. Because feminists focus on pornography as an "aesthetic-expressive" mode of denigrating women, it does not thereby follow that their critique should result in public legislation against pornography. Whether there ought to be this kind of legislation needs to be examined in the light of relevant legal, political, constitutional, etc., arguments. Questions of political authoritarianism arise at this level, but not at the level of a critical-philosophical examination of traditional distinctions that have privatized and silenced women's concerns.

12 Alasdair MacIntyre, *After Virtue* (Notre Dame: University of Notre Dame Press, 1981), pp. 50–51.

13 Agnes Heller, *A Theory of Feelings* (Holland: Van Gorcum, 1979), pp. 184ff.

14 John Locke, *The Second Treatise of Civil Government* in *Two Treatises of Government*, ed. and with an Introduction by Thomas I. Cook (New York: Haffner Press, 1947), p. 128.

15 Immanuel Kant, *The Metaphysical Elements of Justice*, trans. by John Ladd (New York: Liberal Arts Press, 1965), p. 55.

16 Thomas Hobbes, *Leviathan* (1651), ed. and with an Introduction by C.B. Macpherson (Middlesex, England: Penguin Books, 1980), p. 186. All future citations in the text are to this edition.

17 Thomas Hobbes, "Philosophical Rudiments Concerning Government and Society," in *The English Works of Thomas Hobbes*, ed. by Sir W. Molesworth, vol. II (Darmstadt, 1966), p. 109.

18 J.J. Rousseau, "On The Origin and Foundations of Inequality Among Men," in J.J. Rousseau, *The First and Second Discourses*, ed. by R.D. Masters, trans. by Roger D. and Judith R. Masters (New York: St. Martin's Press, 1964), p. 116.

19 G.W.F. Hegel, *Phänomenologie des Geistes*, ed. by Johannes Hoffmeister (Hamburg: Felix Meiner, 1952), 6th ed., p. 141 (Philosophische Bibliothek, Bd. 114), translation used here by A.V. Miller, *Phenomenology of Spirit* (Oxford: Clarendon Press, 1977), p. 111.

20 Sigmund Freud, *Moses and Monotheism*, trans. by Katharine Jones (New York: Vintage, Random House, 1967), pp. 103ff.; Jean Piaget, *The Moral Judgment of the Child*, trans. by Marjorie Gabain (New York: Free Press, 1965), pp. 65ff. Cf. the following comment on boys' and girls' games: "The most superficial observation is sufficient to show that in the main the legal sense is far less developed in little girls than in boys. We did not succeed in finding a single collective game played by girls in which there were as many rules and, above all, as fine and consistent an organization and codification of these rules as in the game of marbles examined above" (p. 77).

21 Kant, "Critique of Practical Reason" in *Critique of Practical Reason and Other Writings in*

*Moral Philosophy*, trans. and edited and with an Introduction by Louis White Beck (Chicago: University of Chicago Press, 1949), p. 258.

22 Although the term "generalized other" is borrowed from George Herbert Mead, my definition of it differs from his. Mead defines the "generalized other" as follows: "The organized community or social group which gives the individual his unity of self may be called the 'generalized other.' The attitude of the generalized other is the attitude of the whole community." George Herbert Mead, *Mind, Self and Society. From the Standpoint of a Social Behaviorist*, ed. and with Introd. by Charles W. Morris (Chicago: University of Chicago Press, 1955), tenth printing, p. 154. Among such communities Mead includes a ball team as well as political clubs, corporations, and other more abstract social classes or subgroups such as the class of debtors and the class of creditors (*Ibid.*, p. 157). Mead himself does not limit the concept of the "generalized other" to what is described in the text. In identifying the "generalized other" with the abstractly defined, legal and juridical subject, contract theorists and Kohlberg depart from Mead. Mead criticizes the social contract tradition precisely for distorting the psycho-social genesis of the individual subject, cf. *Ibid.*, p. 233.

23 Kohlberg, "Justice as Reversibility: The Claim to Moral Adequacy of a Highest Stage of Moral Judgment," in *Essays on Moral Development*, vol. I, *The Philosophy of Moral Development* (San Francisco: Harper & Row, 1981), p. 194, cited in the text as Kohlberg, 1981.

24 Whereas all forms of reciprocity involve some conceptions of reversibility these vary degree: reciprocity can be restricted to the reversibility of actions but not of moral perspectives, to behavioral role models but not to the principles which underlie the generation of such behavioral expectations. For Kohlberg, the "veil of ignorance" is a model of perfect reversibility, for it elaborates the procedure of "ideal role-taking" or "moral musical chairs" where the decider "is to successively put himself imaginatively in the place of each other actor and consider the claims each would make from his point of view" (Kohlberg, 1981, p. 199). My question is: are there any real "others" behind the "veil of ignorance" or are they indistinguishable from the self?

25 I find Kohlberg's general claim that the moral point of view entails reciprocity, equality, and fairness unproblematic. Reciprocity is not only a fundamental *moral* principle, but defines, as Alvin Gouldner has argued, a fundamental *social norm*, perhaps in fact the very concept of a social norm ("The Norm of Reciprocity: A Preliminary Statement," *American Sociological Review*, vol. 25 (April 1960), pp. 161–78). The existence of ongoing social relations in a human community entails some definition of reciprocity in the actions, expectations, and claims of the group. The fulfillment of such reciprocity, according to whatever interpretation is given to it, would then be considered fairness by members of the group. Likewise, members of a group bound by relations of reciprocity and fairness are considered equal. What changes through history and culture are not these formal structures implicit in the very logic of social relations (we can even call them social universals), but the criteria of inclusion and exclusion. Who constitutes the *relevant* human groups: masters vs. slaves, men vs. women, Gentiles vs. Jews? Similarly, *which* aspects of human behavior and objects of the world are to be regulated by norms of reciprocity: in the societies studied by Levi-Strauss, some tribes exchange sea shells for women. Finally, *in terms* of what is the equality among members of a group established: would this be gender, race, merit, virtue, or entitlement? Clearly Kohlberg presupposes a *universalist-egalitarian* interpretation of reciprocity, fairness, and equality, according to which all humans, in virtue of their mere humanity, are to be considered beings entitled to reciprocal rights and duties.

26 John Rawls, *A Theory of Justice* (Cambridge, Mass.: Harvard University Press, 1971; second printing, 1972), p. 137.

27 Michael J. Sandel, *Liberalism and the limits of Justice* (Cambridge, Mass.: Harvard University Press, 1982; reprented 1984), p. 9; cited in the text as Sandel, 1984.

28 Rawls, *A Theory of Justice*, p. 128.

29 Stanley Cavell, *The Claims of Reason* (Oxford: Oxford University Press, 1982), p. 265.

30 A most suggestive critique of Kohlberg's neglect of interpersonal morality has been developed by Norma Haan in "Two Moralities in Action Contexts: Relationships to Thought, Ego Regulation, and Development," pp. 286–305. Haan reports that "the formulation of formal morality appears to apply best to special kinds of hypothetical, rule-governed dilemmas, the paradigmatic situation in the minds of philosphers over the centuries" (p. 302). Interpersonal reasoning, by contrast, "arises within the context of moral dialogues between agents who strive to achieve balanced agreement, based on compromises they reach or on their joint discovery of interests they hold in common" (p. 303). For a more extensive statement see also Norma Haan, "An Interactional Morality of Everyday Life," in *Social Science as Moral Inquiry*, pp. 218–51. The conception of "communicative need interpretations," which I argue for below, is also such a model of interactional morality which, nonetheless, has implications for *institutionalized* relations of justice or for public morality as well, cf. note 50.

31 Cf. E. Tugendhat, "Zur Entwicklung von moralischen Begründungsstrukturen im modernen Recht," *Archiv für Recht und Sozialphilosophie*, vol. LXVIII (1980), pp. 1–20.

32 Although I follow the general outline of Habermas's conception of communicative ethics, I differ from him insofar as he distinguishes sharply between questions of justice and the good life (see note 11 above), and insofar as in his description of the "seventh stage," he equivocates between concepts of the "generalized" and the "concrete other"; cf. J. Habermas, "Moral Development and Ego Identity," in *Communication and the Evolution of Society*, trans. by T. McCarthy (Boston: Beacon Press, 1979), pp. 69–95. The "concrete other" is introduced in his theory through the back door, as an aspect of ego autonomy, and as an aspect of our relation to inner nature. I find this implausible for reasons discussed above.

33 See Habermas, *ibid.*, p. 90, and Kohlberg's discussion in Kohlberg, 1984: 35–86.

34 In an earlier piece, I have dealt with the strong parallelisms between the two conceptions of the "veil of ignorance" and the "ideal speech situation"; see my "The Methodological Illusions of Modern Political Theory: The Case of Rawls and Habermas," *Neue Hefte für Philosophie* (Spring 1982), no. 21, pp. 47–74. With the publication of the *Theory of Communicative Action*, Habermas himself has substantially modified the various assumptions in his original formulation of communicative ethics, and the rendition given here follows these modifications; for further discussion see my "Toward a Communicative Ethics," in *Critique, Norm, and Utopia*, ch. 8.

35 Cf. Rawls, *A Theory of Justice*, pp. 118ff.

36 For recent feminist perspectives on the development of the self, cf. Dorothy Dinnerstein, *The Mermaid and the Minotaur: Sexual Arrangements and Human Malaise* (New York: Harper, 1976); Jean Baker Miller, "The Development of Women's Sense of Self," work-in-progress paper published by the Stone Center for Developmental Services and Studies at Wellesley College, 1984; Nancy Chodorow, *The Reproduction of Mothering* (Berkeley: University of California Press, 1978); Jessica Benjamin, "Authority and the Family Revisited: Or, a World Without Fathers?" in *New German Critique* 13 (1978), pp. 35–58; Jane Flax, "The Conflict Between Nurturance and Autonomy in Mother-Daughter Relationships and Within Feminism," in *Feminist Studies*, vol. 4, no. 2 (June 1981), pp. 171–92; and I. Balbus, *Marxism and Domination* (Princeton: Princeton University Press, 1982).

37 The distinction between the public and the private spheres is undergoing a tremendous realignment in late-capitalist societies as a result of a complicated series of factors, the chief

of which may be the changing role of the state in such societies in assuming more and more tasks that were previously more or less restricted to the family and reproductive spheres, e.g. education, early child care, health care, care for the elderly, and the like. Also, recent legislation concerning abortion, wife battering, and child abuse, to name a few areas, suggests that the accepted legal definitions of these spheres have begun to shift as well. These new sociological and legislative developments point to the need to fundamentally rethink our concepts of moral, psychological, and legal autonomy, a task hitherto neglected by formal-universalist moral theory. I do not want by any means to imply that the philosophical critique voiced in this paper leads to a blue-eyed adumbration of these developments or to the neglect of their contradictory and ambivalent character for women. My analysis would need to be complemented by a critical social theory of the changing definition and function of the private sphere in late-capitalist societies. As I have argued elsewhere, these social and legal developments not only lead to an extension of the perspective of the "generalized other," by subjecting more and more spheres of life to legal norm, but create the potential for the growth of the perspective of the "concrete other," that is, an association of friendship and solidarity in which need interpretations are discussed and new needs created. I see these associations as being created by new social movements like ecology and feminism, in the interstices of our societies, partly in response to and partly as a consequence of, the activism of the welfare state in late-capitalist societies; cf. *Critique, Norm, and Utopia*, pp. 343–53. I am much indebted to Nancy Fraser for her elaboration of the political consequences of my distinction between the "generalized" and the "concrete" other in the context of the paradoxes of the modern welfare state in her "Feminism and the Social State" (Salmagundi, April 1986). An extensive historical and philosophical analysis of the changing relation between the private and the public is provided by Linda Nicholson in her forthcoming book, *Gender and History: The Limits of Social Theory in The Age of the Family* (Columbia University Press).

# [15]

# TOWARD A DISCOURSE ETHIC OF SOLIDARITY

**Nancy Fraser**

I approach Seyla Benhabib's paper as someone with a longstanding interest in Habermas and in the possible implications of a "discourse ethic" for the collective, political struggles of social movements, including but not limited to the feminist movement. Let me introduce my comments by explaining very generally how I understand these implications.

Suppose it were the case that dominant groups within society — here I include class and race dominance as well as gender dominance — had a privileged relation to what I shall call "the socio-cultural means of interpretation and communication." By socio-cultural means of interpretation and communication I mean things like: the officially recognized vocabularies in which one can press claims; the idioms available for interpreting and communicating one's needs; the established narrative conventions available for constructing the individual and collective histories which are constitutive of social identity; the paradigms of argumentation accepted as authoritative in adjudicating conflicting claims; the ways in which various discourses constitute their respective subject matters as specific sorts of objects; the repertory of available rhetorical devices; the bodily and gestural dimensions of speech which are associated in a given society with authority and conviction. Suppose it were the case that by and large such socio-cultural means of interpretation and communication expressed the point of view of dominant groups in society. Suppose that they were especially well-suited for giving voice to the experience, claims, interests and self-interpretations of members of such groups. Thus, for example, Nancy Hartsock, Virginia Held, Dorothy Smith, Sandra Harding and Seyla Benhabib have argued that the dominant moral and political vocabularies we have inherited articulate what Hartsock calls "the standpoint of exchange." That is, these vocabularies generally constitute people as rational, self-interested monads who transact with one another in transient, utility-maximizing encounters. It seems plausible that this standpoint reflects the experience and point of view of white European or European-descended male bourgeois property owners. A moral or political vocabulary which articulates this standpoint would hardly be able to give easy voice to experiences and relationships involving ongoing dependency, such as mother-child relations in the modern restricted nuclear family. Nor would it work well for experiences and forms of connectedness in more extended networks of community and solidarity, such as in subcultures of subordinated racial and ethnic groups. Thus, in sexist, racist and class societies, women, persons of color, the poor and other dominated persons would have a disadvantaged position with respect to the socio-cultural means of interpretation and communication. They would be structurally hindered from participating on a par with members of dominant groups in processes of communicative interaction. Unless they were to contest this situation and organize to win a greater measure of collective control over the means of interpretation and communication, it would appear that members of subordinated groups would have only two options: they could either adopt the dominant point of view and see their own experiences repressed and distorted; or they could develop idiolects capable of voicing their experience and see these marginalized, disqualified and excluded from the central discursive institutions and arenas of society. Or they could do both at once.

As I see it, then, the potential advantage of a discourse or dialogical ethic over what Benhabib has called a "universalist-formal" or monological ethic consists in the fact that the former, but not the latter, can allow for the situation I have been describing. That is, a discourse ethic could take into account that dominant and subordinated groups stand in different and unequal relations to the means of interpretation and communication. It could do this by maintaining a kind of suspicion or distance from any given vocabulary for interpreting needs, defining situations and pressing claims. It could keep open the possibility that it could come to pass that biases might become apparent in even what have been thought to be relatively neutral forms of discourse; that such forms could themselves become stakes in political deliberation; that subordinated groups could contest such forms and propose alternatives, and thereby gain a greater measure of collective control over the means of interpretation and communication. This, I take it, is the *political* point of Benhabib's arguments for the superiority of a discourse ethic over Rawls and Kohlberg. The former allows for the possibility that social divisions may run so deep as to permeate even the means of discourse themselves. Thus, a discourse ethic permits the thematization and critique of interpretations of needs, of definitions of situations and of the social conditions of dialogue, instead of establishing a privileged model of moral deliberation which effectively shields such matters from scrutiny.

Given this general perspective of sympathy with the project of a discourse or dialogical ethic, I find Benhabib's attempt to connect it to Carol Gilligan's work extremely important and interesting. I am especially intrigued by Benhabib's attempt to appropriate arguments for it for a justification of Gilligan's model of postconventional contextual moral reasoning and a new nonrepressive concept of moral and ego autonomy. On the other hand, I either have not understood or am not fully persuaded by the precise way in which Benhabib makes these connections.

As I understand her, Benhabib argues that in order to meet its own criteria of universalizability and reversibility, "universalist-formal moral theory" must abandon the monological model of moral deliberation in favor of a dialogical model. Moreover, it must also abandon the standpoint of the generalized other in favor of the standpoint of the concrete other. Thus, the discourse ethic is seen as the "truth" (in Hegel's sense) of universalist-formal moral theory. That is, it fulfills the latter's aims and resolves the latter's paradoxes and aporias. I presume that this entails that a discourse ethic can and should replace the latter; that it can and should handle the questions concerning political, collective institutions which Rawls handles, *as well as* the questions which Benhabib claims he does not. On the other hand, Benhabib's account of the *content* of the standpoint of the concrete other — as opposed to her account of its dialogical form — is presented in terms drawn largely from intimate relationships, and thus does not on the surface seem adequate for political contexts in which relationships are not intimate. So I am not clear how she gets from her arguments for the discourse-dialogical model of moral deliberation to a defense of the standpoint of the concrete other in the precise form in which she elaborates it, namely, as an ethic of care.

As I read her, the connecting link is the concept of the "relational-interactive model of identity." I want to look briefly at that concept and to sketch an alternative account of the content of the standpoint of the concrete other and an alternative concept of autonomy. I shall claim that these alternatives may be more useful in thinking about a feminist *political* ethic than the ones Benhabib has proposed.

Benhabib presents what she calls a relational-interactive model of identity. I do not mean to refer here to an empirical experience of oneself as connected in a web of relationships or as having permeable ego boundaries. I mean rather a general theoretical account of the concept of identity which applies to both sexes. Benhabib endorses a concept of identity in which one's emotional constitution, needs, motivations and desires are not simply private, inner and individual; but are rather intertwined with the history and culture of the collectivity in relation to which one individuates. For example, one's needs are interpreted in light of the available vocabularies elaborated within the collectivity. Similarly, the self is not a thing or substrate, but rather the protagonist of a life-story which must be constructed from the culturally specific narrative resources available within the collectivity. What strikes me as very important and right about this view is the careful tension and balance it maintains between individual and collective identity.

Now I want to suggest that in elaborating the ethical and interactive *content* (as opposed to the dialogical form) of the standpoint of the concrete other, there are two possibilities. One of these focalizes the dimension of individuality in the relational theory of identity, while the other focalizes the dimension of collectivity. As I read it, Benhabib's account of the ethical and interactive content of the standpoint of the concrete other focalizes the dimension of individuality. Thus, she emphasizes that in adopting this standpoint one attends to the specificity of a unique individual, with a unique affective-emotional constitution and life history. Similarly, she stresses that the moral demand which arises when one adopts this standpoint is the demand for confirmation of one's individuality. Likewise, she stresses that the norms and feelings which govern interactions undertaken from this standpoint are those of love, care and friendship, and she designates these as (usually) private, noninstitutional norms and feelings. From now on, I am going to call this elaboration of the content of the standpoint of the concrete other "the standpoint of the *individualized concrete other*."

I want to contrast the standpoint of the individualized concrete other with another possibility which focalizes the collective dimension of the relational concept of identity. I shall call this version "the standpoint of the *collective concrete other*." Here the stress is on the specificity of a collectivity: on the specificity of the vocabularies available to individuals and groups for the interpretation of their needs and for the definitions of situations in which they encounter one another. The stress is on the cultural specificity of the narrative resources available to individuals and groups for the construction of individual life-stories or group identities and solidarities. I hope it is clear that the stress on shared cultural vocabularies and narrative forms (as opposed to individual uniqueness) is not a return to the standpoint of the generalized other. There is no question here of orientation to some putative universal, atemporal, aspatial, acultural humanity. There is no bracketing of specificity, nor any exclusion of needs, motivations and desires. There is no projection of one's own perspective onto the place where another should be. There is dialogic interaction with actual others, although these are encountered less as unique individuals than as members of groups or collectivities with culturally specific identities, solidarities and forms of life. In short, the standpoint of the collective concrete other is contextual and hermeneutical, not "formal-universalist." It is flexible and nonrepressive with respect to emotions. And it acknowledges connectedness to specific human groups, though these are not restricted to intimate ones comprising family, lovers and friends.

If the elaboration of the standpoint of the individual concrete other eventuates in an ethic of care and responsibility, then perhaps the elaboration of the standpoint of the collective concrete other leads to an *ethic of solidarity*. As I envision it, this standpoint would require one to relate to people as members of collectivities or social groups with specific cultures, histories, social practices, values, habits, forms of life, vocabularies of self-interpretation and narrative traditions. Here one would abstract *both* from unique individuality *and* from universal humanity to focalize the intermediate zone of group identity. The most general ethical force of this orientation would be something like this: we owe each other behavior such that each is confirmed as a being with specific collective identifications and solidarities. The norms governing these interactions would be neither norms of intimacy such as love and care, nor those of formal institutions such as rights and entitlements. Rather they would be norms of collective solidarities as expressed in shared but non-universal social practices. The privileged moral feeling would be neither dignity nor love, but social solidarity. Finally, and most important, to be autonomous here would mean to be a member of a group or groups which have achieved a degree of collective control over the means of interpretation and communication sufficient to enable one to participate on a par with members of other groups in moral and political deliberation; that is, to speak and be heard, to tell one's own life-story, to press one's claims and point of view in one's own voice.

I claim that such an ethic of solidarity is superior to an ethic of care as a *political* ethic. It is the sort of ethic which is attuned to the contestatory activities of social movements struggling to forge narrative resources and vocabularies adequate to the expression of their self-interpreted needs. It is attuned also to collective struggles to deconstruct narrative forms and vocabularies of dominant groups and collectivities so as to show these are partial rather than genuinely shared and are incapable of giving voice to the needs and hopes of subordinated groups. In short, an ethic of solidarity elaborated from the standpoint of the collective concrete other is more appropriate than an ethic of care for a feminist ethic, if we think of a feminist ethic as the ethic of a social and political movement.

But here I do not see how I can avoid the conclusion that it is just as appropriate as a political ethic for movements of lesbians, gays, blacks, hispanics, other peoples of color and subordinated classes. In fact, it seems to me that when one develops the standpoint of the concrete other in this more collective dimension, as I believe one should, then the sense that it is tied specifically to women becomes attenuated. Or rather, women's specificity enters at a different level. It enters at the level of the concrete forms of solidarity among women which *may* develop *if* we are successful in building a movement inclusive of women of many different cultural, ethnic and class identities, a movement which, through dialogue and collective struggle, forges new vocabularies and narrative forms capable of giving voice to many different kinds of women. I think we need frankly to admit that such a specifically women's solidarity exists only in the most incipient, let us say prefigurative, form today. And its further and full flowering is by no means assured. It is a specific solidarity which must be achieved politically, not one that is simply given. In a society as complex as ours, it does not seem to me wise or even possible to extrapolate the specific content of such a solidarity from the current, prepoliticized experiences and idiolects of women, especially since it is likely, in my view, that these will turn out to be the current prepoliticized experiences and idiolects only of *some* women.*

*This work was supported by a much appreciated fellowship from The Stanford Humanities Center.

# Part IV
# Political Implications: Care/Dependency and Autonomy

# [16]

# Politics, Feminism, and the Ethics of Caring

MARY FAINSOD KATZENSTEIN & DAVID D. LAITIN

## Summary

There has been a recent trend among women, both from the right and the left, to appeal to an ethics of caring as a focal point for feminist politics. Opponents of this strategy argue that it is reactionary, enforcing existing systems of gender stratification. Rather than simply accept this critique, authors Katzenstein and Laitin outline three criteria that they deem necessary if an ethics of care is to be conjoined with a progressive feminist politics. Using these three standards, Katzenstein and Laitin analyze two political movements that appeal to an ethics of care: the women's suffrage campaign at the turn of the century, and the recent antipornography movement. The authors find that on the whole, the women's suffrage movement was a progressive one, and that the battle against pornography includes both reactionary and progressive possibilities. The point of these analyses however, is not simply to condemn or endorse either movement, but rather to demonstrate the complexity of all such movements, and to show the effectiveness of the suggested criteria for assessing the political promise of each. The progressive tendencies in both movements are evidence of the politically productive possibilities implicit in Gilligan's research. S.M.

Carol Gilligan's *In a Different Voice* (Gilligan 1982) offers the argument that two moral systems coexist: one based on the preservation of personal ties, contextualized judgments, and values of caring; the other based on a more abstract axial systemization of general rules. Theorists of moral development such as Lawrence Kohlberg, Gilligan maintains, wrongfully identify these different moral systems not as coequal but as lesser or more fully matured developmental stages. Kohlberg might well take comfort from the existence of hundreds of years of political theory on his side. The heroes, rulers, princes, and virtuous citizens of Western political theory are not those who

The authors thank Joan Brumberg, Zillah Eisenstein, Davydd Greenwood, Peter Katzenstein, and the volume's editors, Eva Feder Kittay and Diana Meyers for their useful comments.

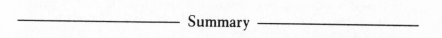

gave up lives, throne, and kingdom for the love of woman, friend, neighbor, or child. If the heroes of Western political theory sacrificed their personhood, it was in the pursuit of a "larger" glory—the conquest of nations or the well-being of the state. The hero was to be above family or personal ties. "Ties" after all, bind, limit, and constrict. The hero devoted himself to serving a cause greater than the well-being of self, or by extension, lover or family. Hanna Pitkin writes:

> From the political ideals of ancient Athens to their recent revival by Hannah Arendt, republican activism seems to be linked to 'manly' heroism and military glory and to disdain for the household, the private, the personal and the sensual. [1984, p. 5]

Were a morality of caring to be a core principle of a fully developed political theory, it would challenge the republican "disdain for the household, the private . . ." Feminist political theory, as it now stands, is hardly homogeneous. It is built on different theories of human nature, different conceptions of material and ideological forces, different views of the proper role of the state. (Jagger 1983). But a common thread in these theories is a shared refusal to ignore the household or to trivialize the personal. Those theories based on gender difference rather than gender sameness have, not surprisingly, given much attention to family and personal life (of both the psyche and the body).

In an important way, then, Gilligan's portrayal of the female mode of moral reasoning is in part confirmed by the very history and rhetoric of feminist politics. Summarizing the ideological history of the contemporary women's movement in the United States from a perspective of its moral "voice," we note two trends: (1) As has been accurately and vividly described elsewhere (H. Eisenstein 1980), feminism has moved from an attachment to ideals of androgyny to a debate over norms of difference; (2) the movement has also shifted from a commitment to ideals of individual rights to an insistence on moralities of caring.

In the earliest period of feminism's second wave (the mid- to late 1960s), feminists spoke the language of androgyny and sounded the rhetoric of abstract rights. The National Organization of Women (NOW) and feminist lobbies in Washington focused, during their first decade, on equal opportunities in employment and education. Matters traditionally defined as family issues were given little attention. Indeed, both the larger national groups (NOW, Women's Equity action League, and others) and the smaller consciousness-raising groups seemed to harbor a "disdain for family" that Pitkin speaks of as characterizing centuries of Western theory. But there was reason why this had to be the case. Before the family could be discussed in ways that could recreate intimacy free of women's subordination, the family had to be "deconstructed." As this project of "deconstruction" proceeded (with its attention to women's personal feeling and sexual experiences, with its analysis of heterosexuality and homosexuality) discussions of family and motherhood could once again become legitimate. By the mid-1970s, Adrienne Rich could thus criticize the experience of motherhood as found in patriarchy, but see in women's maternity the potential for unique joy and richness of life. (Rich 1976).

In search of new moralities of caring, feminism turned increasingly from arguments of sameness to ideas of difference. (Costain, forthcoming; Eisenstein 1980). By the mid- to late 1970s, the amount of writing that developed the thesis of women's difference expanded substantially within varied political concerns: spiritual feminism explored the possibility of women's alternative consciousness—what Mary Daly called the "spring into free space" (Echols 1984, p. 53).[1] Ecofeminism and pacifist feminists traced women's abhorrence of violence and aggression to their connection to nature and maternal experience. Conservative feminists sought to reclaim women's domestic role in the name of feminism. And a new body of radical feminist writing saw men and women defined by their sexuality into political opposites (with men driven by aggressive, irresponsible genital sexuality). This view was, in turn, vehemently criticized by other feminists (sometimes termed "pro-sex") who denounced these radical feminists as antisex and as absolutist, preaching a prescriptive morality that obscured individual differences in sexual tastes and preferences.[2]

Thus, there has been nothing simple about the evolution of contemporary feminist theory. Early ideas of androgyny that underlay the mobilization around equality at the work place appeared inattentive to issues of family and personhood. And yet arguments of difference embraced moralities of caring that had ambiguous implications for feminism. On the one hand, antifeminist Phyllis Schlafly's exhortation that women's special service to society lay with mothering and wifehood promised to return women to past inequalities.[3] On the other hand, spiritual, ecological, radical and conservative feminists insisted that they were speaking for difference in the name of feminism. Prosex feminists, to complicate the picture further, spoke against feminist advocates of sexual difference also in the name of difference. The issue of who spoke for women, who could claim to be on the side of feminist progress, and who spoke the language of political reaction became completely contested territory.

Despite these polemics, the political debate itself lent confirmation to a central Gilligan theme: all sides seemed to have agreed that caring and responsibility formed a focal point for feminist politics. Fundamental to this shared moral perspective was the conviction that the care and responsibility owed was not preeminently to principles of right or justice abstracted from their social context but was to ideas conjoined with named (and hence contextualized) persons—family, lovers, schoolchildren, victims of sexual violence, etc. Central to this conviction was the belief that the private and public spheres could not be set apart. To foster mutual caring and responsibility in the private domain required the exercise of political power on the public stage. To achieve responsibility and caring in public life demanded that values learned and exercised in personal relationships and family life had to be transported into public arenas of authority.

It is the feminist commitment to moralities of caring ***based on gender and sexual difference***[4] that engages us most directly in this chapter. On the one hand, arguments of difference (rather than sameness) seem to promise to evoke a female world of caring relationships and, yet, on the other hand, difference implies too readily a continuation of female subordination. We turn therefore to two particular cases that will allow us to question how moralities of caring based on gender difference have in fact been incorporated into political programs and events.

We propose, then, to focus our attention on the political manifestations of moralities of caring in two very different political contexts. The first is the movement among suffragists at the turn of the century that argued for enfranchisement on grounds that giving women voting rights would, among other things, strengthen the family, and permit greater attention to the needs of education, home, and children. These suffragists did not overtly challenge the long standing authority of separate spheres. Rather, they saw in women's separate and special place in society the possibility for creating a new morality and a reformed world. In our second case, we look at the present day antipornography movement that expresses a morality of caring by its insistence that the personal is political. Their appeal has been based on the moral premise that care and responsibility can only take place when sexual relationships are nonviolent, making possible equal dignity for both sexes. Antipornography proponents, too, have built their arguments around assumptions of gender and sexual difference, viewing pornography as the outcome of and instrument to preserve a sexually dichotomous and gender-stratified world. Women's sexual gentleness and capacity for intimacy, it is argued, can be practiced only when male sexual violence has been countered.

Our concern is with the question of where these gender-defined moralities of caring leave women. We come to this concern because as students of politics, we know the deep antagonisms that result from an aggrieved group claiming its moral perspectives to be equally valid to those held by the dominant group of society. These claims have been made in the past by representatives of ethnic groups (blacks in the United States; Basques in Spain; French in Canada; Tamils in Sri Lanka), and they have usually been associated with intergroup suspicions and violence. An oft-cited study in political science (Rabushka and Shepsle 1972) argues that democratic societies cannot survive when groups make claims based on their distinctive cultural or moral outlook; and a prominent anthropologist has claimed that such appeals to difference are exemplifications of a sick society, one which hasn't reached "civil" status. (Geertz 1973)

But the claims of moral difference hold other threats as well. For women (as for Basques, blacks, etc.) an emphasis on a moral perspective that is gender- or culture-related may obscure the differences between the haves and the have-nots within each group. So too, as Marxists have pointed out, such claims to moral difference may make alliances between have-nots of different groups more difficult to construct. But claims to moral or cultural difference (or superiority) have for women a particularly reactionary potential. Particular to women is the problem that claims of moral difference, based on the importance of family and personal ties, carries the ever present possibility of reinforcing rather than challenging existing systems of gender stratification. The question is then presented: under what formulations are arguments of moral difference likely to serve progressive ends and when are they likely to fulfill counter-progressive or reactionary purposes?

Thus, we are alerted to a major question in feminist political theory. Can an ethic of caring (for family, close friends) and can an effort to recreate the capacity for intimacy be combined with a commitment to a political program that delinks the "natural" and binding association of women to domestic roles? To answer this question, we must reconceptualize it. Rather than inquire whether moralities of caring based on gender difference are (simply) progressive or reactionary, we need to ask what conditions must be met in order for such moralities to be considered more (or less) of the former than of the latter?

The cases we have picked to discuss are, in a sense (and this is what makes them especially interesting), biased towards a more reactionary "outcome." Both cases advance arguments of gender difference rather than sameness and both are thus more likely to invite a return to old patterns, modes, and values that associate women with domestic, private concerns. We will thus need to ask to what extent the moral arguments to support suffrage in the early twentieth century or the movement of the 1980s to repress pornography can be seen, from an historical point of view, as progressive forces. To answer this question, we work to specify some preliminary criteria as to what would constitute a progressive or rectionary claim and examine these two particular claims of moral difference with an eye to whether their political programs meet such criteria.

Consider the following criteria:

(1) *Claims to moral distinctiveness by a group are progressive when they portray the group's social and political role in a dynamic, not static manner.* The idealization of a group's past may help to mobilize it into a reassertion of rights and privileges. But for a movement to be progressive, it must focus on the expansion of opportunities, the enrichment of autonomy, and not merely on the recalibrating of opportunity and autonomy at past levels. Moralities of caring tied to gender difference must attempt to foster intimacy and caring in personal relations among and between adults and children but, in so doing, cannot continue to restrict women to the primary caretaking role in these relationships.

(2) *Claims to moral distinctiveness by a group are progressive when its leaders seek to nurture and promote diversity across its ranks and to remedy differences in mobility prospects vertically among its members.* To promote diversity of tastes, interests and culture among a group's membership cannot be confused with or obscure the need to address inequality of well-being among a group's membership. The organizing of feminist events by both black and white women, for instance, may help to promote horizontal diversity. But vertical equality will be served only if both speak for the least privileged and only if they are ready to act on those claims.

(3) *Claims to moral distinctiveness by a group are progressive when its political project involves entry into an alliance or historical bloc that is committed to the expansion of opportunities and political power for other disadvantaged classes or groups.* While coalitions with some nonprogressive groups that have re-

sources and power are often necessary for tactical reasons, a movement that compromises its autonomy (or alternatively simply sustains its independence) by an alliance with a group committed to political suppression of other low-strata groups cannot be considered progressive.

These criteria constitute, in our judgment, the defining characteristics of a culturally or gender-based political movement that seeks to play a progressive role in the politics of its society. However tentative or arbitrary, we shall move on to examine our two cases in the American women's movement with an eye to sorting out their progressive and reactionary strands. In general, the suffrage arguments will be found to have a progressive slant, more so than is generally presumed; similarly, the antipornography movement will be found to have progressive possibilities as well as an ominous reactionary dimension. Our overall conclusion is that a morality of caring based on ideas of difference—despite a nervousness by many political scientists and anthropologists—should not be too easily dismissed as reactionary ideology.

## Suffrage, Social Housekeeping, and Moralities of Caring

Support for suffrage came out of several different theoretical positions. Some argued for enfranchisment on the basis of individual rights; others on the basis of the special contribution women might make in the public sphere. But no argument made by suffragists ignored the family. Elizabeth Cady Stanton (often seen as the leading proponent of an individual rights approach) devoted considerable thought to how the family might be changed to accommodate values of equality. Those who argued the case of women's special morality took a seemingly more conservative perspective on the family that appeared to invite the perpetuation of women's and men's separate spheres. This more conservative version of a caring morality is what we concern ourselves with here: what was it, and was it in its time, in fact, reactionary?

> DO YOU KNOW that extending the suffrage to women increases the moral vote; that in all states and countries that have adopted equal suffrage the vote of disreputable women is practically negligible, the slum wards of cities invariably having the lightest women vote and the respectable residence wards the heaviest; that only one out of every twenty criminals are women; that women constitute a minority of drunkards and petty misdemeanants; that for every prostitute there are at least two men responsible for her immorality; that in all the factors that tend to handicap the progress of society, women form a minority, whereas in churches, schools and all organizations working for the uplift of humanity, women are a majority? [Catt 1913, p. 9]

The elitist voice in Catt's appeal runs alongside the parallel appeal to women's special moral vision. Later, we take up the issue of racism and class exclusiveness. But first, we turn to the claims of women's moral voice. The "social housekeeping" dimension of the suffrage argument maintained that women's particular concerns with child labor, the exploitation of working mothers, decent standards of housing, and corruption in government constituted the preeminent reason for bringing women into the public domain. But was this social housekeeping argument, tied as it appeared to be to the distinction between the sexes, bound to maintain women's subordinate place in society? We turn to the three criteria offered earlier by which we argue that progressive and reactionary claims can be distinguished.

Did the argument of social housekeeping constitute a dynamic rather than static argument about women's place in American society? This "stasis" view would contend that as long as the argument for suffrage came out of a world view that posited women's and men's nature as different, the basic separation of spheres would go unchallenged. This first response relates to what suffragists may have *hoped* to achieve. The second argument is largely about what women did or did not achieve. Here, it has been argued that women did not "win" the vote but were "given" it for reasons unrelated to the recognition of gender claims. (Ginsberg 1982). This argument suggests further that, once "given" suffrage, women did little with it to venture outside the confines of the private sphere (as evidenced in part by the low percentages of women voting upon enfranchisement). (O'Neill 1969) We argue against these interpretations of suffrage.

On the first point, it seems clear that when exponents of social housekeeping referred to the difference in women's and men's natures, they did not feel tht these differences need confine women to the home. The social housekeeping argument grew naturally out of, but was very different from, the cult of domesticity which Charlotte Perkins Gilman had so scathingly criticized. (O'Neill 1969, p. 43) What the social housekeeping argument demanded was a place for women in the public domain. This was its radical contribution. From the vantage point of the 1980s, it is too easy to dismiss the nineteenth century demand for the vote as asking for something that could scarcely be termed radical. But at the turn of the century, the recognition of the right to a public voice—to participate in the affairs of men—constituted a radical break from the social order of the past. (Katzenstein 1984)

Had suffrage meant less, it would likely not have involved seven decades of active organization and the mass mobilization of women. (Catt 1923, p. 107). It is that long-waged extraordinary campaign that makes us reject the second "conservative argument"—that suffrage was bestowed, not won. This argument about the bestowal of suffrage by elites has been advanced in a provocative study of electoral institutions by political scientist Ben Ginsberg. (Ginsberg, 1982). He contends that enfranchisement often occurs because political elites seek to assert political control over new constituencies. Thus, he argues (convincingly) that there is reason to be skeptical when the Democratic party urged on the nation a lowering of the voting age in the 1960s since no such demand was forthcoming from the student movement. But the suffrage movement wanted *suffrage*—and it took over half a century and

> fifty-six campaigns of referenda to male voters, 480 campaigns to urge legislatures to submit suffrage amendments to voters; 47 campaigns to

induce state constitutional conventions to write women suffrage into state constitutions; 277 campaigns to persuade state party conventions to include women suffrage planks; 30 campaigns to urge presidential party conventions to adopt women suffrage planks in party platforms and 19 campaigns with 19 successive Congresses. [Catt 1923, p. 107]

No doubt there were political elites who thought they could benefit from women's enfranchisement. Some elites probably took seriously the suffragist "promise" that women's enfranchisement would help to counter the black and immigrant vote. Others, whether or not they were influenced by the feminist "extremists" who chained themselves to the White House fence, fasted, and publicly burned Wilson's speeches on democracy, no doubt felt that women's support and labor were needed for the war effort and that enfranchisement would be a reasonable *quid pro quo*. But the point is that all nations at war needed the support of their female populations; and yet, it was England and the United States (where the feminist movement had been extremely active), rather than France or Italy (where feminists were less conspiciously organized), that "gave" women the vote. What this suggests is that the mobilization of women, at the least, worked to shape elite perceptions of how they might "control" women's support.[6]

Suffragists, we thus argue, won the right to vote. And although they did not immediately fall headlong into active participation in electoral politics, women certainly used their right to fuller participation in the public sphere. The final point that must be made here is that it is likely that only particular suffrage arguments would have mobilized the multitude of women whose numbers made the issue of wartime support in exchange for suffrage a bargaining point: it was the incorporation of the "morality of caring" into the suffrage claim that helped to turn the movement from its limited size at the turn of the century into a mass effort. (O'Neill 1969, pp. 50-51) Like temperance campaigns that had always drawn numbers far in excess of the suffrage movement in the latter half of the century, the social housekeeping phase of the suffragist movement was able to attract women into the campaign who otherwise might have found suffrage threatening their attachment to the family. (Degler 1980, p. 359)

Although women did not vote in the numbers expected they were hardly passive actors in the political arena. Women were the major force behind preventive health legislation, the long fought (and still unsuccessful) campaign for equal rights, and the move to establish protective legislation. The movement of women into the public domain, begun in the nineteenth century, was thus given constitutional authority with the 19th amendment.[7]

Our second criterion—that women's claims advance diversity without aggravating class inequality—is more controversial. The suffrage movement made room for ideological diversity across the movement's leadership. In the nineteenth century, suffragists included those who supported temperance and those who did not; those who were ready to support advocates of free love and those who were not; those who were critical of the churches and those who were not. There were debates, then, and sometimes tempestuous ones. But there was still room for considerable diversity. Social housekeeping suffragists were generally critical of, but did not set out to undo, the activities of the extremists. While Carrie Chapman Catt sought to work with President Wilson to win over his support of the vote, members of the Woman's Party demonstrated feverishly outside the White House, fasted, and went to jail. But the diversity of views and/or tactics was tolerated and militant homogeneity eschewed.

But on issues of race and social class, suffragist spokeswomen were less ready to be open-minded. Carrie Chapman Catt joined social housekeeping arguments with strong expressions of elitism. Insisting that women had learned invaluable capacities for love and service as rearers and caretakers of children, she then maintained that government faced a great danger from

> votes possessed by the males in the slums of the cities and the ignorant foreign vote. . . . There is but one way to avert the danger—cut off the vote of the slums and give to women . . . the power of protecting herself that man has secured for himself—the ballot. [Kraditor 1965, pp. 110, 125]

In the twenty years before passage of the 19th amendment, suffrage was all too often advanced on grounds that the illiterate, Negro, and foreign male vote could be countered through the enfranchisement of educated women. Even working-class advocates like Florence Kelley, who railed against treating poor and foreign women as an undifferentiated mass, argued for the imposition of an educational requirement at the ballot place. (Kraditor 1965, p. 139)

In other respects, however, suffrage proved an avenue that connected the lives of middle-class and working women. The need to mobilize large numbers of supporters made it possible for individuals like Gertrude Barnum to argue against the xenophobia of her suffragist, middle-class sisters. At the 1906 convention of the National American Women Suffrage Association (NAWSA). Barnum insisted, "We have been preaching to wage earning women, teaching them, rescuing them, doing almost everything for them except knowing them and working with them for the good of the country." (Rothman 1978, p. 129). Eventually, some working-class advocates like Harriet Stanton Blatch left NAWSA to found independent local suffrage societies that would address working-class women directly. Historian Ellen Dubois (1984) makes an interesting case that the "militant" strategies of the suffrage movement (parades, street corner rallies) were actions middle-class suffragists learned from their working-class associates.

Although working-class issues were not seriously addressed by most suffragists, and although the participation of working-class women in suffrage organizations was erratic, it would be wrong to see suffrage simply as the political vehicle of white middle-class women.

Suffrage did, for example, lead indirectly to the participation of lower middle-class women in programs designed to assist the poor. In 1921, erstwhile suffragist supporters of the Sheppard-Towner Act won a stunning victory. The legislation not only brought the state into the business of preventive medicine with its funding of community health centers, but in the process, the act gave numbers of women a primary position as midwives and public health nurses in community health care.[8]

Suffragists, then, were not made from a single mold. Support for enfranchisement came from those who were advocates of different causes and different strategies. And suffrage found its spokeswomen among some who were quick to use arguments of racism and elitism and some whose values were far less easily seen as self-serving.

Although the racist and xenophobic strain of suffragist rhetoric remains a counter to the claim that social housekeeping was clearly progressive, this reactionary dimension of the suffragist argumentation can be better understood—although not explained away—by an understanding of the suffragists' political position. Had the suffragists been able to locate powerful allies in its claim to women's voting rights, it might have been less readily drawn to reactionary appeals. Suffragists had formed successful alliances with the Progressives. But (despite the very late concession of the Republican and Democratic parties to include suffrage in their platforms), no major political party had thrown itself behind women's enfranchisement. As Elizabeth Cady Stanton's daughter, Harriet Stanton Blatch commented, Negro enfranchisement had been championed by a major political party; so had the farm labor enfranchisement in England where Blatch saw the Liberal party under Gladstone extend the vote despite the fact that "only a few of the disfranchised class were active." She writes: "What a contrast the women suffrage movement! Perhaps some day men will raise a tablet reading in letters of gold: "All honor to women, the first disfranchised class in history who unaided by any political party won enfranchisement by its own effort alone." (Blatch/Lutz 1940, p. 293)

As Catt too described it, the effective alliances were the ones against the suffragist cause—the alliances of the brewers interest, workingmen, immigrants, etc. Had the suffragists found responsive allies in either of the major political parties, perhaps they would have felt it less necessary or expedient to use the appeals of race and class snobism in their effort to woo public opinion to their cause. The lack of support from party quarters helped edge suffragists into other opportunistic positions. NAWSA, Mary Ryan observes, withdrew from women's peace organizations at the outbreak of World War I, in order not to alienate President Wilson and potential supporters in Congress. (Ryan 1975, p. 245) These kinds of political pressure did not force suffragists into positions they found totally alien. But it would be naive on our part to think that suffrage organizers, at their cause for so long and with so little evidence of success, might not have tried, lawyer-like, a range of arguments, including reactionary ones, in the hope that something might move the deeply resistant political powers in American society.

The three criteria set out above help us to offer an historical account of social housekeeping and the use of a gender-linked caring morality that avoids a characterization of the movement as *either* progressive *or* reactionary. Rather, it allows us to specify more carefully the different dimensions of each element within the historical period being described. By the first criterion, suffragists clearly put moralities of caring to progressive usage: social housekeeping gave women the justification to enter the world of men—an argument that sought, despite its "separate spheres," rhetoric to change the status quo. By the second criterion, suffrage arguments come out as both forward looking and reactionary: a diversity of causes were espoused in connection with social housekeeping, and yet many of the main spokeswomen for suffrage fell into a pattern of political claims that used race and class appeals unabashedly. By our third criterion, exponents of a caring morality could not be considered reactionary. They did not go out searching for antiprogressive allies. In fact, early social housekeeping advocates had looked to Progressive party advocates for support. Unable to find sponsorship of women's emancipation in the major parties, however, suffragists lapsed into an opportunistic political rhetoric that seriously detracted from their otherwise progressive historical role.

## The Morality of Caring and the Antipornography Movement

The criteria we have specified above can be of particular use in a discussion of an issue like the antipornography campaigns of the last few years because they help us to avoid the kind of blanket characterizations that come too easily when polemics are intense. And such is surely the case of the present debate around pornography.

The antipornography "cause," which has long had supporters, picked up momentum with the proposal of Catharine MacKinnon and Andrea Dworkin that offered a civic ordinance making pornography a justiciable act of sex discrimination.[9] This movement represents one embodiment of a morality of caring. The symbolic power of this political crusade has appalled many of those who think in terms of abstract rights. The model antipornography ordinances, which are written in the language of rights, sound strained and unconvincing in their constitutional appeals. Without the counterpart moral message, these ordinances would ring hollow. For the moral message is that the unit of responsibility and care—that group with whom one has sexual or sensual relations—must be based on tenderness, not violence; equality, not hierarchy. The social construction of a kin-based network worthy of care and responsibility is the symbolic appeal—it seems to us—to the antipornography movement.

Not only is antipornography a powerful movement among women because it is built on a morality of caring, but it also mobilizes women with its emphasis on the notion of gender difference. As the writing of both Dworkin and MacKinnon suggest, antipornography is a public response warranted by the sexual differences that position women as victims of aggressive male sexuality. "Sexuality," MacKinnon writes, "is that social process which creates, organizes, expresses, and directs desire, creating the social beings we know as women and men as their relations create society" (MacKinnon 1983, 228). Just as work defines the difference for Marxist analysis between those who exploit and those exploited, so for MacKinnon, sex divides classes into "relations in which . . . some fuck and others get fucked." Although this analysis is not part and parcel, by any means, of the much more subdued rhetoric of the civic ordinances Dworkin and MacKinnon have authored, gender difference is indeed embodied in the proposed legislation. According to the ordinance, pornography is not sex-neutral. It means [only] "the graphic, sexually explicit subordination of women." (MacKinnon 1984, p. 501) It is discimination against *women* which MacKinnon and Dworkin seek to bar.[10] Because this movement has been so threatening to many members and allies of the women's movement who see it as nothing more than a bald attack on the First Amendment, it is important to evaluate it on the broader criteria we have developed. It is to this task we now turn.

The suffrage movement served a dynamic function by authorizing women's right to a place in domains from which they had been excluded. But does the antipornography movement help in some analagous fashion to push the boundaries outwards, permitting women greater opportunities in previously inaccessible or restricted realms? The negative response to this question (which we do not share) is that antipornography, at best, concerns the private, nonmaterial dimensions of women's lives and offers to protect women as though they were children. (Friedan 1985) At worst, the movement against pornography is seen as regulating, restricting that which women may choose to view, read, or think and distorting sexual pleasure into an ever present fear of sexual danger. (Vance 1984)

But we find neither of these arguments persuasive, and contend instead that at least on this first dimension—the generation of dynamic social change—antipornography politics must be seen as progressive. Friedan's relegation of pornography to the status of the immaterial rests on her assumption that sex is a private, personal matter and that it is less basic to women's subordination than material (economic) factors. It must be recognized, however, that just as women's opportunities in the nineteenth century depended on their success in establishing a claim to autonomy within the public domain, so women's claims now depend on their ability to evoke public (although not necessarily state) authority in the service of ending women's subordination in the private sphere. Women's sexual subordination in personal relations may be outside the realm of agreed upon issues demanding public action (pay, employment, welfare support of indigent mothers); but it is this very definition of what is properly political that feminist ethics of caring is attempting to address.

That sexuality is immaterial, in the sense of being peripheral to the way people make their living, is also unpersuasive. Leaving aside the fact that producers of pornography make a decent living from their four billion dollar industry (Almquist 1985, p. 42), it is simply undeniable that pornography is part and parcel of a sexual system of power that subordinates women. We need not go as far as MacKinnon and argue that sexuality is at the root of women's oppression.[11] The point is, however, that pornography is one of the significant causes (as well as mirrors) of a system that eroticizes sexual violence and sustains the continued physical and psychological derogation of women.[12]

In two senses, violent, women-degrading pornography is part of the causal chain in the system of women's subordination. First, purely at the level of ideas, violent pornography helps to maintain a normative order based on the making of sexual violence into erotica. Here a distinction between power and violence must be made. There is much that many women and men find erotic in the display of sexual and other manifestations of power. But when that display of sexual power causes harm, as is so much more likely to be the case when violent sexuality is depicted, pornography must be deemed unacceptable. Eva Feder Kittay argues:

> Regardless of how we draw the line between a legitimate and illegitimate sexuality, it appears that there are nonsexual grounds, purely moral considerations which apply to human actions and intentions, that render some sexual acts illegitimate—illegitimate by virtue of the moral impermissibility of harming another person and particularly for the pleasure of obtaining pleasure or other benefit from the harm another incurs. [1983. p. 150]

Second, at the level of behavior, it may be difficult to trace the link between word and deed—to predict as MacKinnon says which man will go out and rape after reading pornography (Blakely 1985, p. 40); but there *is* (laboratory) evidence from the studies of N. Malamuth and C. Donnerstein that pornographic viewing increases male acceptance of violence against women, that attitudes change as a result of exposure to pornography.[13] (MacKinnon 1984, p. 504)

If the antipornography movement helps to curtail these two forms of harm, it has moved women and men to a more elevated plateau of moral behavior. If it has helped to break down one link in the chain of sexual subordination (of which, rape, battering, harassment, incest are all a part), it has also created a dynamic for change in multiple domains of women's lives.

Although some might argue that the link in the chain that must be broken should be the sexual "act" (of prostitution, harassment, rape, battery) rather than the "depiction" of sexual violence, there are indeed good arguments for identifying pornography as a crucial link that can help to unravel the chain. What antipornography proponents have understood is that a campaign around pornography can have far greater mobilizational impact than similar campaigns against other forms of sexual abuse. Prostitution is too easily "ghettoized"—seen as limited to seamy neighborhoods and targeting only "bad girls" as its victims. Even rape (acknowledged to victimize more than just "bad girls" and recognized as widespread in its occurrence) is still often seen as a crime perpetrated by deviant, lawless men, someone else's husband or brother. But even though antipornography critics maintain that antipornography campaigns revitalize the notion of sex perverts committing sex crimes, such a notion is not easy to sustain. Pornography is commonplace—found in your son's bedroom, at the neighborhood drugstore, in the locker, the dormitory room, and now on television. If Jerry Falwell is right, one quarter of all pornography sold is marketed through 7-Eleven stores. (MacNeil-Lehrer Report 1985) If pornography is violence against women, then such violence is more likely to be seen as part of the fabric of society than rape or other forms of sexual abuse.

But if pornography is progressive on the first dimension (broadening the realms within which women can be equal), what about the second dimension we have identified: does the antipornography movement counter diversity? It is interesting that among feminists, the most vehement criticism of antipornography comes from those who share with antipornography proponents a belief that sexuality (albeit socially constructed) is absolutely crucial to the subordination of women. Their argument, however, is that antipornography further subordinates, rather than liberates, women (a) by identifying sex as danger to be feared and avoided, and (b) by its apparent assertion that only egalitarian, nonviolent sex is legitimate. (Vance 1984; Levine 1985)

This argument is real. There are clearly adherents of sado-masochism who mutually desire violent sex and for whom such sex is not harmful.[14] But to the extent that pornography both maintains a normative order that legitimizes the eroticization of violence, and to the extent that it constitutes even a remote cause of violent, nonconsensual, nondesired sex, the "rights" of such adherents to acquire pornographic products deemed important for their sexual gratification must take second place. It is surprising that while pro-sex advocates are ready to state that what is seen as violent by some may be pleasure for others, they are less ready to acknowledge that what is pleasure for some may be violence for others.[15] Racist cartoons abusive of minorities may and do give pleasure to some. But such rights to pleasure must surely be subordinated to the more fundamental right to be free from serious harm. From this point of view, there is a blindness in the pro-sex argument. Pro-sex theorists argue that sexual mores are not natural, but are socially constructed. They are reluctant to acknowledge, however, that sexual violence as a source of sexual pleasure too is socially constructed, and that therefore it can be politically deconstructed. What is the moral difference, they may ask themselves, between the social legitimation of nonheterosexual relations (one of their projects) and the delegitimation of violent sexual relations (the antipornography project)? If pro-sex advocates insisted that pornographic depiction did not cause violent behavior, their position would be more comprehensible.

Our final point here is that while the antipornography movement has made little attempt to mobilize support across socio-economic groups, the issue of pornography is certainly relevant across all strata of society.[16] Given the right linkages, it could well generate working-class as well as middle-class support. In any case, unlike the suffragist case discussed above, there is no outright racism or xenophobia embodied in the antipornography effort.

But the progressive character of the antipornography campaign falters on our third criterion. It is clear that an antipornography movement is found to invite reactionary alliances. Even if antipornography feminists endeavored to disassociate themselves from conservative "anti-smut" moralists as they did in Suffolk County (but did not do in Indianapolis where feminists worked with Beulah Coughenour, a Stop-ERA activist), the right can inevitably be expected to form a common cause even if not an outright alliance with feminist antipornography activists.[17] It is hardly a surprise that no lesser light than Jerry Falwell has spoken in praise of the feminist effort to bar pornography, and that the right has launched a campaign of its own against pornography kings and distributors. (MacNeil-Lehrer Report 1985). This interest from the right was bound to be sparked, whatever form a feminist antipornography campaign was to take.

But the fact that the feminist antipornography movement has pursued civic ordinances that would bar pornography makes the issue of alliances a deeply troubling one and inviting of more reactionary outcomes than if state authority were not to be invoked. By seeking to legitimize the use of state censorship, feminist antipornographers place in the hands of the right a new set of political instruments whose purpose can be put to quite different purposes from those feminists themselves intended.[18]

With the moral majority's interest in resurrecting a moral America, it is worrisome that censorship of pornographic materials could lead easily into censorship of erotica, health education, lesbian and gay literature, and, indeed, to the closing down of many a feminist bookstore. It could be a small step to the censorship of literature depicting homosexual intimacy on grounds that it promotes violence by encouraging sexual practices that cause the proliferation of AIDS.

The reply to these fears by antipornography advocates is that the ordinances are specific enough to bar only women-degrading (or violent and women-degrading) materials. But the distinction between sexually explicit materials that dehumanize women as sexual objects and those that are merely sexually explicit or erotic is not easily specified. Similarly the difference between violently degrading materials and those that are "merely" degrading can be highly contentious. To make these distinctions in clear, legally applicable language requires tools and indeed the motivation to "limit" the ban on pornography strictly to certain categories of sexually explicit material. In a political context in which the state is constituted by few feminists so motivated, it is naive to think that feminist antipornography proponents can keep control of how a ban on sexually explicit literature will be interpreted and used.

By the three criteria we have identified, then, the antipornography mobilization must be seen as incorporating both progressive and reactionary elements. It does offer a radical challenge to a system that helps to subordinate women by making sexual violence erotic; and it subdues diversity only to safeguard women against serious harm. But these progressive or at least acceptably nonreactionary features of the antipornography movement must be seen alongside the problems identified by our third criterion: the existence of unavoidable linkages to repressive alliances that can utilize new sources of state authority.

To label suffrage progressive due to its mobilizational successes, or the antipornography movement reactionary due to its approval by the Reverend Falwell, is to ignore the complex strands woven by any social movement. Clearly there are progressive and reactionary fibers connected with any social movement. In our discussion of suffrage and pornography, we have tried to demonstrate this complexity through a contextualized discussion of the three strands within each movement.

## Conclusion

Our perusal of the moral foundation of feminist political discourse confirms Carol Gilligan's central claim—that women reach moral maturity when they "see the actors in (a moral) dilemma arrayed not as opponents in a contest of rights (as do men) but as members of a network of relationships on whose continuation they all depend." (Gilligan 1982, p. 30) We saw in the suffrage movement an exemplification of this point; women felt comfortable making self-interest claims for the vote based on their moral perspective of social housekeeping. We also saw that in the early periods of the feminist revival of the 1960s, there was an attempt to reject a special women's morality. These feminists spoke the (male) language of rules and abstract rights. But the absence of a morality of caring left the women's movement without its own voice. From the left and right, as we saw, feminists quickly brought back the women's moral voice in political discourse. In this sense, women today have reached a new equilibrium—with their own voice—and Gilligan's work has enabled us to see this continuing moral fiber of feminist politics.

But Gilligan wants more than a distinctive women's voice in politics. She is quite explicit in her hopes that the recognition of this "different voice" will "lead to a changed understanding of human development and a more *generative* view of human life." (Gilligan p. 174, emphasis ours) This suggests to us that Gilligan intends that her findings *not* be used to defend the status quo or to bring back some mythical past. Rather, she sees her finding as opening up opportunities for women to use their voice to reform and broaden both public and private domains. Obviously, however, Gilligan's findings can serve as ammunition for reactionary as well as generative purposes. The question we have asked is whether we could state the criteria by which political claims by women based on a moral claim of difference can be judged as helping to create a world of greater vision and opportunity.

Gilligan does not address herself to this question. Her discussion leaves us with just a hope, but not a vision of how her findings could lead to a politics in which an "ethic of care rest[ing] on the premise of non-violence—that no one should be hurt," (Gilligan p. 174) might come about. To be sure, all politics is contextual and the same politics emerging in different settings can often serve very different interests. Nonetheless, it is important to specify criteria by which we can judge feminist political claims so that a work as significant as Gilligan's not be used merely to arrest the advances of women in modern America. We have therefore attempted to state criteria by which to evaluate the political meaning of feminist claims. We have contended that an ethic of responsibility and care is compatible with a more progressive politics when its claims (a) permit a dynamic role for women who employ their voice in an expanding number of public and private domains; (b) permit diversity among all women without ignoring the demands of the poor; and (c) are part of an historic bloc that is sensitive to the constraints faced by other social and cultural groups seeking justice for their causes. With these guidelines, we feel, an ethic of care can be conjoined with a politics of progress.

## Notes

1. For a discussion of spiritual feminism, see Spretnak 1982; Ochs 1983.
2. Jean Elshtain's work best exemplifies what we call conservative feminism: a desire to maintain a division between private and public based on a strong family

system built around distinctive male and female roles. (Elshtain 1981a, 1981b) What makes her writing feminist and not simply conservative is the critique she develops of women's historical oppression (including her use of such words as "oppression") and her desire to see the private sphere not limit women as it has done in the past. It is unclear, however, how the division of private and public that she envisions, based as it is on a view of women's and men's biologically-founded separate identities, will, in fact, prove more emancipatory than earlier paradigms. (Cohen and Katzenstein, forthcoming) For a discussion of eco-feminism, see Ynestra King, "Feminism and the Revolt of Nature," *Heresies* 13; for a discussion of the relationship of mothering to pacifism, see Sara Ruddick, 1982; for a discussion of radical or cultural feminism, see Echols, 1984 and her essay in Snitow, 1983.

3. See Zillah Eisenstein (1984) for a distinction between conservative, revisionary feminists.

4. The phrase, "moralities of caring based on gender/sex difference" requires further explication. By this phrase, we refer to the way in which some 20th century suffragists and 1980s antipornography feminists linked the capacity (or incapacity) to practice a morality of caring and responsibility to inequalities of power between men and women. Some suffragists believed that women were endowed with a special moral voice and unless this voice could be heard in public affairs, public life would continue to be degraded by corruption and grievous social ills. Whether this "voice" was part of women's biological makeup or was acquired experientially is left unclear in much of suffragist writing. Antipornography feminists too argue that the realization of a morality of responsibility based on true intimacy and caring is possible only when society is freed of sexual violence. This in turn is possible when men cease to eroticize violence as part of a quest for power. Antipornography feminists walk both sides of the very fine line between arguments of biologically determined and socially learned behavior. Andrea Dworkin for instance discusses the "immutable self of the male" (1979, p. 13) at the same time that she argues that male identity is "chosen" (1979, p. 49).

Hence we wish to make three points about the phrase "moralities of caring based on gender/sex difference." (1) It is the suffragist/antipornography feminist understanding that unless women acquire greater power, a morality of caring and responsibility cannot be realized; (2) The term, gender/sex difference, which we will shorten to "gender difference" in the text, incorporates both the biological and socially learned understanding of that term; (3) Whether suffragists or antipornography feminists ultimately visualize a society based on androgyny rather than difference is not addressed in this chapter, nor is the question of how men might acquire a capacity for caring and responsibility. The focus of the paper, rather, is on the consequences for women of political programs that grow out of a belief in gender-based moralities of caring. The question we ask is how such programs enhance or diminish women's strength as a collectivity and how such programs shape the kind of power women can exercise.

5. The term social housekeeping is used by Mary P. Ryan, 1975, pp. 193–251.

6. We are not suggesting that there is a unicausal (women's activism or any other single factor) explanation for suffrage. What we are suggesting is that women's mobilization has been an important contributant to the passage of suffrage in particular cases of which the United States was one. For a discussion of the circumstances around the passage of suffrage in different countries, see Lovenduski and Hills (1981).

7. That suffrage challenged the separation of spheres by giving constitutional authorization to women's place in the public domain is clear; whether the ballot *then* became instrumental in the challenge to the separation of spheres—whether that is why women used the vote to endorse or defeat candidates supportive of women's concerns is an interesting and researchable issue but not one addressed here.

8. Florence Kelley was called "the ablest legislative general communism had produced" (Rothman 1978, p. 152). Eight years later, the act was overturned, perhaps because by then congressmen knew they did not need to face the repercussions of a women's bloc vote (Lemons, 1973, pp. 153–81). Soon women's positions in public health were overtaken by private male physicians.

9. For sources, see note 13.

10. One clause in the proposed Minneapolis ordinance (sect. 1, 8, 2) states that "The use of men, children or transexuals in the place of women . . ." is pornography but the ordinance is about sex discrimination and is not set out in sex-neutral terminology.

11. See MacKinnon 1983, and MacKinnon June 1984 in which she says "Male domination permeates everything. There are other major issues such as the ones you mentioned. But as segregation was and is central to the second class status of Black people, pornography is central to the second class status of women. It is its embodiment, its way of being practiced, being made socially real." Critics of the antipornography feminists, however, often go to the other extreme. Vanda Burstyn writes, for instance, "sexist pornography is a product of the economic and social conditions of our society—not vice versa" (1985, p. 24). This position that views words and images as mere reflections of society seems uninformed by the rich insights of poststructuralist feminist criticism.

12. Eva Feder Kittay writes: "As symptom, pornography is reflective of certain social and political relations between men and women; although as a mirror, it reflects through hyperbolic distortions. As a cause, pornography is a contributing factor perpetuating a social order in which men dominate. In its casual aspect, pornography is hate literature . . . and is morally wrong for it contributes to a political and moral injustice" (1983 p. 145).

13. See MacKinnon, "Not a Moral Issue," 1984; MacKinnon 1983; MacKinnon, June 1984; Dworkin 1979; Duggan 1984; Blakely 1985; Copp, ed., 1983 and essays therein; *Harvard Law Review* (unsigned), 1984; Hentoff 1984.

14. See Kittay's analysis of the meaning of harm in this context (1983, pp. 153–54).

15. The prosex refusal to entertain seriously the possibility that pornography promotes attitudes conducive to violence is striking. In an attempted refutation of the charge that pornography may promote sexual violence, one prosex essayist writes, "The idea that every time women get a thrill from watching women TV cops Cagney and Lacey shoot a crime suspect, we want to kill . . . runs counter to most women's experience." (Diamond 1985, p. 47). The point is, rather, how would female viewers react if Cagneys and Laceys were regular fare, their victims sexually violated, their exploits the standard entertainment of groups of teenage girls and adult women? Would we really think such viewing matter completely nonformative of the ideas, values, behavior of Cagney/Lacey fans?

16. See Alice Walker's discussion of pornography (MS, February 1980) and Dworkin (1979).

17. In Indiana where the ordinance passed (but has now been declared unconstitutional) Beulah Coughenour, a Stop-ERA activist, introduced the law locally (Duggan, 1984). In Suffolk County, New York, a much broader antiobscenity measure was recently introduced and defeated. Antipornography feminists opposed the law. (Blakely 1985)

18. An antipornography campaign may usefully attempt to change public understanding of violent sexuality and its eroticization as morally repugnant and harmful to women. As Bryden argues (1985, p. 15), feminists have changed the image of the rapist as a victim of an unjust society to one of the woman as a victim of rape, and

have redefined faculty/student sex from a problem of sexual permissiveness to a problem of sexual exploitation. This change in understanding of pornography may have been advanced by the public stir created over the ordinances. But public mobilization that does not involve the state and thus does not invite the "right" to use the tools of censorship would, we argue, be far preferable.

## References

Almquist, Heidi. "The Civil Rights Approach to Control of Pornography." B.A. Honors Thesis, Department of Government, Cornell University, April 1985.

Blakely, Mary Kay. "Is One Woman's Sex Another Woman's Pornography: The Question Behind a Major Legal Battle." *MS*, XII, 16 (April 1985).

Blatch, Harriet Stanton and Alma Lutz. *Challenging Years: The Memoirs of Harriet Stanton Blatch*. New York: G.P. Putnam, 1940.

Bridenthal, Renate. "Professional Housewives: Stepsisters of the Women's Movement," in Renate Bridenthal, Atina Grossman, and Marion Kaplan, eds., *When Biology Became Destiny: Women in Weimar and Nazi Germany*. New York: Monthly Review Press, 1984, pp. 153–74.

Bryden, David. "Between Two Constitutions: Feminism and Pornography." *Constitutional Commentary*, vol. 2, no. 1 (Winter 1985).

Burstyn, Varda, ed. *Women Against Censorship*. Vancouver and Toronto: Douglas and McIntyre, 1985.

Catt, Carrie Chapman. "Do You Know," National American Woman Suffrage Association, 507 Fifth Avenue, New York (1913 [brochure, personal library]).

——— and Nettie Rogers Shuler. *Woman Suffrage and Politics: The Inner Story of the Suffrage Movement*. Seattle: University of Washington Press, 1923.

Cohen, Susan and Mary F. Katzenstein. "The War Over the Family Is Not Over the Family," in Sanford Dornbusch and Myra Strober, eds. *Feminism, Children and the New Families*. New York: Guilford Press, forthcoming.

Copp, D. *Censorship and Pornography*.

Costain, Anne N. "Will the Gender Gap Make Women an Electoral Interest in American Politics?" in Carol Mueller, ed. *The Gender Gap*. Beverly Hills, Calif. Sage Publishing Inc., forthcoming.

Cott, Nancy F. *The Bonds of Womanhood: "Women's Sphere" in New England, 1780–1835*. New Haven: Yale University Press, 1977.

———. "The Crisis in Feminism 1910–1930." Paper presented at the Berkshire Conference, Northampton, Mass., June 2, 1984.

Diamond, Sara, "Pornography, Image, and Reality" in Varda Burstyn et. al., *Women Against Censorship*. Toronto: Douglas & McIntyre, 1985.

De Lesseps, Emmanuele, "Female Reality: Biology or Society?" *Feminist Issues*, 1981, pp. 77–100.

Degler, Carl. *At Odds: Women and the Family in America from the Revolution to the Present*. Oxford: Oxford University Press, 1980.

Dubois, Ellen. "Harriot Stanton Blatch and the Progressive Era Women Suffrage Movement." Paper presented at the Berkshire Conference, Northampton, Mass., June 2, 1984.

Duggan, Lisa. "Censorship in the Name of Feminism." *Village Voice*, October 16, 1984.

Dworkin, Andrea. *Pornography: Men Possessing Women*. New York: G.P. Putnam, 1979.

Echols, Alice. "The Taming of the Id: Feminist Sexual Politics, 1968–83," in Carol Vance, ed., *Pleasure and Danger*. Boston: Routledge and Kegan Paul, 1984.
Eisenstein, Hester and Alice Jardine, eds. *The Future of Difference*. New Brunswick, N.J.: Rutgers University Press, 1980.
Eisenstein, Zillah R. *Feminism and Sexual Equality*. New York: Monthly Review Press, 1984.
Elshtain, Jean Bethke. *Public Man, Private Woman: Women in Social and Political Thought*. Princeton: Princeton University Press, 1981a.
———. "Against Androgyny," *Telos* 47 (Spring, 1981b).
Ferguson, Ann; Ilene Philipson, Irene Diamond, Lee Quimby, Carole S. Vance and Ann Barr Snitow. "Forum: The Feminist Sexuality Debates," *SIGNS*, no. 10 (Autumn, 1984), pp. 106-36.
Freedman, Estelle. "Separatism as Strategy: Female Institution Building and American Feminism, 1870-1930," *Feminist Studies* 5, no. 3 (Fall, 1979), pp. 512-29.
Freidan, Betty. "How to Get the Women's Movement Moving Again," *New York Times Magazine*, November 3, 1985.
Geertz, Clifford. *The Interpretation of Cultures*. New York: Basic Books, 1973.
Gilligan, Carol. *In a Different Voice: Psychological Theory and Women's Development*. Cambridge: Harvard University Press, 1982.
Ginsberg, Benjamin. *The Consequences of Consent: Elections, Citizen Control and Popular Acquiescence*. Menlo Park, Calif. Addison-Wesley Publishing Co., 1982.
*Harvard Law Review* (note) "Anti-Pornography Laws and First Amendment Values," vol. 98 (1984), pp. 460-81.
Hentoff, Nat. "Is the First Amendment Dangerous to Women?", *Village Voice*, October 16, 1984.
Jagger, Alison M. *Feminist Politics and Human Nature*. Totowa, N.J.: Rowman and Allanheld, 1983.
Jones, Ann Rosalind. "Writing the Body" in Elaine Showalter, ed. *Feminist Criticism*. New York: Pantheon, 1985.
Katzenstein, Mary Fainsod. "Feminism and the Meaning of the Vote." *SIGNS*, vol. 10, no. 1 (Autumn, 1984), pp. 106-36.
Kittay, Eva Feder. "Pornography and the Erotics of Domination," in Carol Gould, ed. *Beyond Domination: Perspectives on Women and Philosophy*. Totowa, N.J.: Rowman and Allanheld, 1983.
Kraditor, Aileen. *The Ideas of the Woman Suffrage Movement, 1890-1920*. New York: W.W. Norton, 1965.
Laitin, David D. "Linguistic Dissociation: A Strategy for Africa," in John Gerard Ruggie, ed. *The Antinomies of Interdependence: National Welfare and the International Division of Labor*. New York: Columbia University Press, 1983, pp. 317-69.
Lemons, J. Stanley. *The Woman Citizen: Social Feminism in the 1920s*. Urbana: University of Illinois Press, 1973.
Levine, Judith. "Sex: Threat or Menace? Perils of Desire." *Village Voice*, Supplement (March 1985).
Lovenduski, Joni and Jill Hills, eds. *The Politics of the Second Electorate: Women and Public Participation*. London and Boston: Routledge and Kegan Paul, 1981.
MacKinnon, Catharine (interview). On Defining Pornography, *Off Our Backs*, June 1984, pp. 14-15.
———. "Not a Moral Issue," *Yale Law and Policy Review*, vol. 2 (1984), pp. 501-25.
———. "Feminism Marxism Method and the State: An Agenda for Theory" in Elizabeth Abel and Emily Abel, eds. *The SIGNS Reader: Women, Gender and Scholarship*. Chicago: University of Chicago Press, 1983.
MacNeil-Lehrer Report, August 12, 1985, special program on pornography.

Malamuth, Neil M. and Edward Donnerstein, eds. *Pornography and Sexual Aggression*. Orlando: Academic Press, 1984.

Ochs, Carol. *Women and Spirituality*. New Jersey: Rowman and Allanheld, 1983.

O'Neill, William L. *Everyone Was Brave: The Rise and Fall of Feminism in America*. New York: Quadrangle Books, 1969.

Pitkin, Hanna Fenichel. *Fortune Is A Woman: Gender and Politics in the Thought of Niccolo Machiavelli*. Berkeley: University of California Press, 1984.

Rabushka, Alvin and Kenneth Shepsle. *Politics in Plural Societies: A Theory of Democratic Instability*. Columbus: Merrill, 1972.

Rich, Adrienne. *Of Woman Born: Motherhood as Experience and Institution*. New York: W.W. Norton, 1976.

Ruddick, Sara. "Preservative Love and Military Destruction: Some Reflections on Mothering and Peace," in Joyce Trebilcot, ed. *Mothering: Essays in Feminist Theory*. New York: Rowman and Allanheld, 1983.

Ryan, Mary P. *Womanhood in America from Colonial Times to the Present*. New York: Franklin Watts, 1975.

Schlafly, Phyllis. *The Power of the Positive Woman*. New York: Harcourt, Brace, Jovanovich, 1977.

Snitow, Ann, Christine Stansell, and Sharon Thompson, eds. *Powers of Desire: The Politics of Sexuality*. New York: Monthly Review Press, 1983.

Spretnak, Charlene. *The Politics of Women's Spirituality: Essays on the Rise of Spiritual Power Within the Feminist Movement*. Garden City: Anchor Books, 1982.

Vance, Carol, ed. *Pleasure and Danger*. Boston: Routledge and Kegan Paul, 1984.

Walkowitz, Judith R. "Male Vice and Female Virtue: Feminism and the Politics of Prostitution in 19th Century Britain," in Snitow, *Powers of Desire*, pp. 419-38.

Willis, Ellen, "Feminism, Moralism and Pornography," in Snitow, *Powers of Desire*, pp. 460-67.

Walker, Alice, "Porn at Home," *MS*. (February, 1980)

[17]

*Mary G. Dietz*

# Context Is All: Feminism and Theories of Citizenship

IN MARGARET ATWOOD'S POWERFUL NOVEL *The Handmaid's Tale*,[1] the heroine Offred, a member of a new class of "two-legged wombs" in a dystopian society, often thinks to herself, "Context is all." Offred reminds us of an important truth: at each moment of our lives our every thought, value, and act—from the most mundane to the most lofty—takes its meaning and purpose from the wider political and social reality that constitutes and conditions us. In her newly reduced circumstances, Offred comes to see that matters beyond one's immediate purview make a great deal of difference with respect to living a more or less free and fully human life. But her realization comes too late.

Unlike Offred, feminists have long recognized as imperative the task of seeking out, defining, and criticizing the complex reality that governs the ways we think, the values we hold, and the relationships we share, especially with regard to gender. If context is all, then feminism in its various guises is committed to uncovering what is all around us and to revealing the power relations that constitute the creatures we become. "The personal is the political" is the credo of this critical practice.

*Mary G. Dietz is assistant professor of political science at the University of Minnesota. Her publications include "Citizenship with a Feminist Face: The Problem with Maternal Thinking" (1985), "Trapping the Prince: Machiavelli and the Politics of Deception" (1986), and* Between the Human and the Divine: The Political Thought of Simone Weil *(forthcoming in 1988). Her primary areas of study are the history of ideas, democratic theory, and feminist theory. Professor Dietz is currently writing a book on patriotism and conceptual change.*

## 2 *Mary G. Dietz*

The political and ideological context that most deeply conditions the American experience is liberalism and its attendant set of values, beliefs, and practices. Without question, the liberal tradition can count many among its adherents, but it has its critics as well. Over the past decade in the United States, few critics of liberalism have been as persistent or as wide-ranging as the feminists. Certainly no others have been as committed to articulating alternatives to the liberal vision of gender, the family, the sexual division of labor, and the relationship between the public and the private realm.[2]

In this essay I shall focus on the aspect of the feminists' critique that concerns citizenship. First I will outline the dominant features of liberalism's conception of citizenship, and then I will introduce two current feminist challenges to that conception. What I ultimately want to argue, however, is that although both of these challenges offer important insights, neither of them leads to a suitable alternative to the liberal view or a sufficiently compelling feminist political vision. In the third section of the essay I will make a preliminary sketch of what such a feminist vision of citizenship might be. In part, I would have it reconfirm the idea that "equal access is not enough."

### I

The terrain of liberalism is vast, and its historical basis has over the past century been extensively surveyed in social, political, and moral theory.[3] All I shall present here is the bare bones of the liberal conception of citizenship, but this skeletal construction may sufficiently set off the feminist critiques that follow. With this in mind and the caveat that all conceptions change through time, we can begin by considering the features that have more or less consistently distinguished the views of liberal political thinkers.

First, there is the notion that human beings are atomistic, rational agents whose existence and interests are ontologically prior to society.[4] In the liberal society one might say that context is not "all." It is nothing, for liberalism conceives of the needs and capacities of individuals as being independent of any immediate social or political condition.[5] What counts is that we understand human beings as rational individuals who have intrinsic worth.

A second tenet of liberal political thought is that society should ensure the freedom of all its members to realize their capabilities. This is the central ethical principle of the Western liberal tradition. Perhaps the classic formulation is John Stuart Mill's observation that "the only freedom which deserves the name, is that of pursuing our own good in our own way, so long as we do not attempt to deprive others of theirs, or impede their efforts to obtain it."[6]

Closely associated with the principle of individual liberty is a third feature—an emphasis on human equality. Liberal theorists may differ in their formulations of this principle but not on its centrality. Locke, for example, held that "reason is the common rule and measure that God has given to mankind" and therefore that all men must be considered created equal and thereby worthy of the same dignity and respect. Bentham argued (not always consistently) that the case for equality rests on the fact that all individuals have the same capacity for pleasure and hence that the happiness of society is maximized when everyone has the same amount of wealth or income. In his "Liberal Legislation and Freedom of Contract," T.H. Green proclaimed that "every one has an interest in securing to every one else the free use and enjoyment and disposal of his possessions, so long as that freedom on the part of one does not interfere with a like freedom on the part of others, because such freedom contributes to that equal development of the faculties of all which is the highest good of all."[7] Since liberal theories usually begin with some version of the presumption of perfect equality among individual men, it is a relatively small step from this to the related argument that societal justice entails equal suffrage, in which every single person should count, in Herbert Spencer's words, "for as much as any other single individual in the community."[8] As Allison Jagger writes, "Liberalism's belief in the ultimate worth of the individual is expressed in political egalitarianism."[9]

This egalitarianism takes the form of what theorists call "negative liberty," which Sir Isaiah Berlin in his classic essay on freedom characterizes as "the area within which a man can act unobstructed by others."[10] It is the absence of obstacles to possible choices and activities. What is at stake in this liberal conception is neither the "right" choice nor the "good" action but simply the freedom of the individual to choose his own values or ends without interference from others and consistent with a similar liberty for others. At the core of negative liberty, then, is a fourth feature of liberalism that speaks to the individual in his political guise as citizen: the conception of the individual as the "bearer of formal rights" designed to protect him from the infringement or interference of others and to guarantee him the same opportunities or "equal access" as others.

The concept of rights is of fundamental importance to the liberal political vision. In *A Theory of Justice,* John Rawls offers this classic formulation of the liberal view: "Each person possesses an inviolability founded on justice that even the welfare of society as a whole cannot override. . . . The rights secured by justice are not subject to political bargaining or the calculus of social interests."[11]

Not only does the concept of rights reinforce the underlying liberal principles of individual freedom and formal equality; it also sets up the distinction between "private" and "public" that informs so much of the liberal perspective on family and social institutions. Individual rights correspond to the notion of a private realm of freedom, separate and distinct from that of the public. Although liberal theorists disagree about the nature and degree of state intervention in the public realm—and even about what counts as "public"—they nevertheless accept the idea that certain rights are inviolable and exist in a private realm where the state cannot legitimately interfere. For much of liberalism's past this private realm has subsumed, in Agnes Heller's phrase, "the household of the emotions"—marriage, family, housework, and child care. In short, the liberal notion of "the private" has included what has been called "woman's sphere" as "male property" and sought not only to preserve it from the interference of the public realm but also to keep those who "belong" in that realm—women—from the life of the public.[12]

Another feature of liberalism tied to all of the above is the idea of the free individual as competitor. To understand it, we might recall liberalism's own context, its distinctive history and origin.[13] Liberalism emerged amid the final disintegration of, in Karl Marx's words, those "motley feudal ties"—in the decline of aristocracy and the rise of a new order of merchants and entrepreneurs with a "natural propensity," as Adam Smith wrote, "to trade, truck, and barter." The life of liberalism, in other words, began in capitalist market societies, and as Marx argued, it can only be fully comprehended in terms of the social and economic institutions that shaped it. For Max Weber, liberal political thought inherited the great transformation wrought by Protestantism and a new ethic of self and work soon to replace privilege, prescription, and primacy of rank. As both Marx and Weber recognized, liberalism was the practical consciousness, or the theoretical legitimation, of the values and practices emanating from the newly emergent market society. Accordingly, liberalism lent support to the active pursuit of things beneficial to an economic system based on production for the sake of profit.

Among these "things beneficial" is the notion of the rational man as a competitive individual who tends naturally to pursue his own interest and maximize his own gain. Although it would be mistaken to suggest that all liberal theorists conceive of human nature as being egoistic, most do argue that people tend naturally in this direction and must work to develop moral capacities to counter their basic selfish, acquisitive inclinations.[14] Thus, we can at least generally conclude that, for liberals, the motive force of human action is not to be found in any noble desires to achieve "the good life" or "the morally virtuous society" but rather in the inclination toward individual advancement or (in capitalist terms) the pursuit of profit according to the rules of the market.[15] Taken in this light, then, the liberal individual might be understood as the competitive entrepreneur, his civil society as an economic marketplace, and his ideal as the equal opportunity to engage, as Adam Smith wrote, in "the race for wealth, and honors, and preferments."

Vital in this race is the very issue that concerns us in this issue of *Dædalus*—the equality of access to the race itself, to the market society. What liberty comes to mean in this context is a set of formal guarantees to the individual that he (and later she) may enjoy a fair start in Smith's "race." What citizenship comes to mean in this liberal guise is something like equal membership in an economic and social sphere, more or less regulated by government and more or less dedicated to the assumption that the "market maketh man."[16] To put this another way, under liberalism, citizenship becomes less a collective, political activity than an individual, economic activity—the right to pursue one's interests, without hindrance, in the marketplace. Likewise, democracy is tied more to representative government and the right to vote than to the idea of the collective, participatory activity of citizens in the public realm.

This vision of the citizen as the bearer of rights, democracy as the capitalist market society, and politics as representative government is

# 6 *Mary G. Dietz*

precisely what makes liberalism, despite its admirable and vital insistence on the values of individual freedom and equality, seem so politically barren to so many of its critics, past and present, conservative and radical. As far as feminism is concerned, perhaps Mary Shanley best sums up the problem liberalism poses when she writes:

> While liberal ideals have been efficacious in overturning restrictions on women as individuals, liberal theory does not provide the language or concepts to help us understand the various kinds of human interdependence which are part of the life of both families and polities, nor to articulate a feminist vision of 'the good life.' Feminists are thus in the awkward position of having to use rhetoric in dealing with the state that does not adequately describe their goals and that may undercut their efforts at establishing new modes of life.[17]

## II

For good and obvious reasons, one might expect that a feminist critique of liberalism would best begin by uncovering the reality behind the idea of equal access. Not only is equal access a central tenet of liberal thought; it is also a driving part of our contemporary political discourse that is used both to attack and to defend special pleas for women's rights. Just such a critique is what this volume undertakes.

But a complementary approach may be in order as well. There is merit, I think, to the argument that to begin with the question of equal access is already to grant too much, to deal too many high cards to the liberal hand. Quite literally, "access is not enough," for once in the domain of "equal access talk," we are tied into a whole network of liberal concepts—rights, interests, contracts, individualism, representative government, negative liberty. These open up some avenues of discourse but at the same time block off others. As Shanley implies, for feminists to sign on to these concepts may be to obscure rather than to illuminate a vision of politics, citizenship, and "the good life" that is appropriate to feminist values and concerns.

By this I do not mean to suggest that feminists who proceed from the question of access are doing something unhelpful or unimportant. On the contrary, by using gender as a unit of analysis, feminist scholars have revealed the inegalitarianism behind the myth of equal opportunity and made us aware of how such presumptions deny the social reality of unequal treatment, sexual discrimination, cultural stereotypes, and women's subordination both at home and in the marketplace. To the extent that this sort of gender analysis leads to positive political programs—the extension of pregnancy leaves, affirmative action plans, child-care facilities, comparable-worth wages, sexual harassment laws, health care benefits—feminists give indispensable assistance to liberal practice.

However, we should not overlook the fact that this sort of analysis has boundaries that are determined by the concepts of liberalism and the questions they entail. So, for example, when power is perceived in terms of access to social, economic, or political institutions, other possibilities (including the radical one that power has nothing to do with access to institutions at all) are left out. Or to take another example, if one establishes the enjoyment of rights or the pursuit of free trade as the criterion of citizenship, alternative conceptions like civic activity and participatory self-government are overlooked. Liberalism tends toward both an understanding of power as access and a conception of citizenship as civil liberty. What I want to emphasize is that neither of these formulations is adequate in and of itself or appropriate for a feminist political theory.

Of course, few feminist theorists would find these remarks startling or new. Indeed, much of recent feminist thought (liberal feminism notwithstanding) has been directed toward revealing the problems a liberal political theory poses for a vision of women's liberation and human emancipation. A variety of arguments and approaches has been articulated. Some have focused on the epistemological and ontological roots of liberalism, others on its implications for an ethical understanding of personhood, still others on the assumptions that underlie its methodology.[18]

On the political side and with regard to the liberal theory of freedom, the role of the state, the public and the private, and capitalism and democracy, feminist critics seem to fall into two camps—the Marxists and what I will call the maternalists.[19] These two camps are of primary concern in this essay because they address issues of "the good life" and, more precisely, the nature of political community. A brief look at each should suffice to bring us up to date on the feminist alternatives to the liberal conception of the citizen—alternatives that are, as I shall go on to argue, not fully satisfactory counters to the liberal view, although they provide suggestive and thought-provoking contributions to the political debate.

First, the Marxists. Feminists working within the Marxist tradition seek to reveal the capitalist and patriarchal foundations of the liberal state as well as the oppression inherent in the sexual division of labor—or, as one thinker puts it, "the consequences of women's dual contribution to subsistence in capitalism."[20] At stake in this economic critique, as another theorist argues, is the notion of the "state's involvement in protecting patriarchy as a system of power, much in the same way it protects capitalism and racism. . . . "[21] Insofar as they believe that the state participates in the oppression of women, Marxist feminists hold that the idea of the rights of citizenship granted by the state is a sham, a convenient ideological fiction that serves to obscure the underlying reality of a dominant male ruling class. Accordingly, so these theorists contend, the liberation of women will be possible only when the liberal state is overthrown and its capitalist and patriarchal structure dismantled. What will emerge is an end to the sexual division of labor and "a feminist politics that moves beyond liberalism."[22] What most Marxist feminists seem to mean by these politics is the egalitarian reordering of productive and reproductive labor and the achievement of truly liberating human relations, a society of "propertyless producers of use values."[23]

The strengths of this critique should be obvious. Marxist feminists would have us recognize that a system of economics and gender rooted in capitalist, male-dominant structures underlies much of liberal ideology, from the notion of independent, rational man to the conception of separate private and public realms, from the value of individualism to the equation of freedom with free trade. As such, the Marxist-feminist analysis reveals numerous inadequacies in the liberal feminist position, particularly in its mainstream view of women's work and its reliance on the law, the state, interest groups, and state-instituted reforms as the source of social justice, individual equality, and "access." The advantage of the Marxist-feminist approach is not only its critique of capitalism, which reveals the exploitative and socially constructed nature of women's work, but also its political critique, which challenges the liberal assumption that representative government is the sole sanctuary for politics and the legitimate arbiter of social change.

Nevertheless, even though the Marxist-feminist critique has much to offer from the standpoint of historical materialism, it has little to say on the subject of citizenship. As Sheldon Wolin has noted, "Most Marxists are interested in the 'masses' or the workers, but they dismiss citizenship as a bourgeois conceit, formal and empty. . . ."[24] Unfortunately, Marxist feminists are no exception to this generalization. *Citizenship* hardly appears in their vocabulary, much less any of the rest of its family of concepts: participation, action, democracy, community, and political freedom.

To the extent that Marxist feminists discuss citizenship at all, they usually conflate it with labor, class struggle, and socialist revolution, and with the advent of social change and certain economic conditions. In their view, true citizenship is realized with the collective ownership of the means of production and the end of oppression in the relations of reproduction. They associate both of these ideas with revolutionary action and the disappearance of the patriarchal state. In their approach to citizenship, Marxist feminists tend to reduce politics to revolutionary struggle, women to the category of "reproducers," and freedom to the realization of economic and social equality and the overthrowing of natural necessity. Once freedom is achieved, they seem to say, politics ends or becomes little more than what Marx himself once termed "the administration of things."

Now no one would deny that economic equality and social justice empower people. A society that values and strives for them with both men and women in mind deserves admiration and respect. What I am suggesting is that because Marxist feminism stops here, its liberatory vision of how things will be "after the revolution" is incomplete, for what emerges is a picture of economic, not political, freedom and a society of autonomous and fulfilled social beings, not a polity of citizens. As a result, a whole complex of vital political questions is sidestepped or ignored: What is political freedom? What does it mean to be a citizen? What does an expressly feminist political consciousness require? Or, to put the matter more bluntly, is there more to feminist politics than revolutionary struggle against the state?

The second camp of feminist theorists, the maternalists, would answer this last question with a resounding yes. They would have us reconsider both the liberal and the Marxist views of citizenship[25] and become committed to a conception of female political consciousness that is grounded in the virtues of woman's private sphere, primarily in mothering. Unlike the Marxist feminists, the maternal feminists hold that, as important as social justice is, it is not a sufficient condition for a truly liberatory feminist politics. Women must be addressed as mothers, not as "reproducers," and as participants in the public realm, not just as members of the social and economic orders.

Like the Marxist feminists, however, the maternal feminists eschew the liberal notion of the citizen as an individual holder of rights protected by the state. For the maternalist, such a notion is at best morally empty and at worst morally subversive since it rests on a distinctly masculine conception of the person as an independent, self-interested, economic being. When one translates this notion into a broader conception of politics, the maternal feminist argues, one is left with a vision of citizens as competitive marketeers and jobholders for whom civic activity is, at most, membership in interest groups. Thus, the maternal feminist would deny precisely what the liberal would defend—an individualist, rights-based, contractual conception of citizenship and a view of the public realm as one of competition. As one maternalist puts it:

> The problem—or one of the problems—with a politics that begins and ends with mobilizing resources, achieving maximum impacts, calculating prudentially, articulating interest group claims . . . and so on, is not only its utter lack of imagination but its inability to engage in the reflective allegiance and committed loyalty of citizens. Oversimply, no substantive sense of civic virtue, no vision of political community that might serve as the groundwork of a life in common, is possible within a political life dominated by a self-interested, predatory, individualism.[26]

Maternal feminism is expressly designed to counter what it thinks are the arid and unimaginative qualities of the prevailing liberal view and, more emphatically, to present an alternative sense of civic virtue and citizenship. As a first step, it wants to establish the moral primacy of the family. Although this may seem to some a strange start for a feminist politics, the maternalists would have us rethink the rigid, liberal distinction of public and private realms and consider instead the "private" as the locus for a possible public morality and as a model for the activity of citizenship itself. Or, to put this another way, maternal feminism criticizes "statist" politics and individualist persons, and offers in their place the only other alternative it sees—a politics informed by the virtues of the private realm, and a personhood committed to relational capacities, love, and caring for others.

What makes this view expressly feminist (rather than, say, traditionally conservative) is its claim that women's experience as mothers in the private realm endows them with a special capacity and a "moral imperative" for countering both the male liberal individualist world view and its masculinist notion of citizenship. Jean Bethke Elshtain describes mothering as a "complicated, rich, ambivalent, vexing, joyous activity" that upholds the principle that "the reality of a single human child [must] be kept before the mind's eye."[27] For her, the implications mothering holds for citizenship are clear: "Were maternal thinking to be taken as the base for feminist consciousness, a wedge for examining an increasingly overcontrolled public world would open immediately."[28]

Not only would maternal thinking chasten the "arrogant" (i.e., male) public; it would also provide the basis for a whole new conception of power, citizenship, and the public realm. The citizen that emerges is a loving being who, in Elshtain's words, is "devoted to the protection of vulnerable human life" and seeks to make the virtues of mothering the "template" for a new, more humane public world.

Much of the maternalist argument takes its inspiration from, or finds support in, the psychoanalytic object-relations theory of Nancy Chodorow and the moral development theory of Carol Gilligan.[29] These scholars argue that striking contrasts exist between men and women and can be understood in terms of certain experiential differences in the early stages of their development. At the crux of Chodorow and Gilligan's findings is the implication that women's morality is tied to a more mature and humane set of moral values than men's.[30] Gilligan identifies a female "ethic of care" that differs from the male "ethic of justice." The ethic of care revolves more around responsibility and relationships than rights, and more around the needs of particular situations than the application of general rules of conduct. Maternal feminists seize upon this psychological "binary opposition" and, in effect, politicize it. In their work, "the male voice" is that of the liberal individualist who stands in opposition to the female, whose voice is that of the compassionate citizen as loving mother. For maternal feminists, as for feminist psychologists, there is no doubt about which side of the opposition is normatively superior and deserving of elevation, both as a basis for political consciousness and as an ethical way of being. The maternalists might say that the female morality of responsibility "must extend its imperative to men," but they nevertheless grant a pride of place to women and to "women's sphere"—the family—as the wellspring of this new "mode of public discourse."[31] They also maintain that public discourse and citizenship should be informed by the virtues of mothering—love, attentiveness, compassion, care, and "engrossment"—in short, by all the virtues the liberal, statist, public realm disdains.

What are we to make of this vision of feminist citizenship? There is, I think, much to be gained from the maternalist approach, especially if we consider it within the context of the liberal and Marxist-feminist views. First, the maternalists are almost alone among other "feminisms" in their concern with the meaning of citizenship and political consciousness. Although we may disagree with their formulations, they deserve appreciation for making citizenship a matter of concern in a movement that (at least on its academic side) is too often caught up in the psychological, the literary, and the social rather than in problems of political theory that feminists must face. Second, the maternalists remind us of the inadequacy and limitations of a rights-based conception of the individual and a view of social justice as equal access. They would have us understand the dimensions of political morality in other ways and politics itself as potentially virtuous. Third, in an era when politics has on all sides become something like a swear word, the maternal feminists would have us rehumanize the way we think about political participation and recognize how, as interrelated "selves," we can strive for a more humane, relational, and shared community than our current political circumstances allow.

Despite these contributions, however, much is troubling about the maternalists' conception of citizenship. It has the same problems as do all theories that hold one side of an opposition to be superior to the other. For the maternalists, women are more moral than men because they are, or can be, or are raised by, mothers and because mothering itself is necessarily and universally an affective, caring, loving activity. Leaving aside what should be the obvious and problematic logical and sociological character of these claims, suffice it to say that the maternalists stand in danger of committing precisely the same mistake they find in the liberal view. They threaten to turn historically distinctive women into ahistorical, universalized entities.[32]

Even more serious is the conviction of the maternalists that feminists must choose between two worlds—the masculinist, competitive, statist public and the maternal, loving, virtuous private. To choose the public world, they argue, is to fall prey to both a politics and an ethic that recapitulates the dehumanizing features of the liberal-capitalist state. To choose the private world, however, is not only to reassert the value of a "women's realm" but also to adopt a maternal ethic potentially appropriate for citizenship, a deeply moral alternative to the liberal, statist one.[33]

When we look to mothering for a vision of feminist citizenship, however, we look in the wrong place—or, in the language of the maternalists, to the wrong "world." At the center of the mothering activity is not the distinctive political bond among equal citizens but the intimate bond between mother and child. But the maternalist would offer us no choice in the matter: we must turn to the "intimate private" because the "statist public" is corrupt. This choice is a specious one, however. Indeed, by equating the public with statist politics and the private with the virtue of intimacy, maternalist feminism reveals itself to be closer to the liberal view than we might at first suppose. Thus it is open to much the same charge as liberalism: its conception of citizenship is informed by a flawed conception of politics as impersonal, representative government. That liberalism is content to maintain such a conception and that maternalist feminism wants to replace it with a set of prescriptions drawn from the private is not the real issue. The problem for a feminist conception is that neither of the above will do, because both leave us with a one-sided view of politics and therefore of citizenship. What we need is an entirely different conception. For the remainder of this essay, I will sketch out an alternative basis for a feminist political vision, with a view to developing a more detailed feminist vision in the future. I offer the following recommendations more as a programmatic outline than as a comprehensive theory.

## III

My basic point is a straightforward one: for a vision of citizenship, feminists should turn to the virtues, relations, and practices that are expressly political and, more exactly, participatory and democratic. What this requires, among other things, is a willingness to perceive politics in a way neither liberals nor maternalists do: as a human activity that is not necessarily or historically reducible to representative government or "the arrogant, male, public realm." By accepting such judgments, the feminist stands in danger of missing a valuable alternative conception of politics that is historically concrete and very much a part of women's lives. That conception is perhaps best called the democratic one, and it takes politics to be the collective and participatory engagement of citizens in the determination of the affairs of their community. The community may be the neighborhood, the city, the state, the region, or the nation itself. What counts is that all matters relating to the community are undertaken as "the people's affair."[34]

From a slightly different angle, we might understand democracy as the form of politics that brings people together as citizens. Indeed, the power of democracy rests in its capacity to transform the individual as teacher, trader, corporate executive, child, sibling, worker, artist, friend, or mother into a special sort of political being, a citizen among other citizens. Thus, democracy offers us an identity that neither liberalism, with its propensity to view the citizen as an individual bearer of rights, nor maternalism, with its attentiveness to mothering, provides. Democracy gives us a conception of ourselves as "speakers of words and doers of deeds" mutually participating in the public realm. To put this another way, the democratic vision does not legitimize the pursuit of every separate, individual interest or the transformation of private into public virtues. Insofar as it derives its meaning from the collective and public engagement of peers, it sees citizens neither as wary strangers (as the liberal marketplace would have it) nor as "loving intimates" (as the maternalist family imagines).

To return to my earlier point, democratic citizenship is a practice unlike any other; it has a distinctive set of relations, virtues, and principles all its own. Its relation is that of civic peers; its guiding virtue is mutual respect; its primary principle is the "positive liberty" of democracy and self-government, not simply the "negative liberty" of noninterference. To assume, then, that the relations that accompany the capitalist marketplace or the virtues that emerge from the intimate experience of mothering are the models for the practice of citizenship is to misperceive the distinctive characteristics of democratic political life and to misconstrue its special relations, virtues, and principles.

The maternalists would have us believe that this democratic political condition would, in fact, flow from the "insertion" of women's virtues as mothers into the public world. There is no reason to think that mothering necessarily induces commitment to democratic practices. Nor are there good grounds for arguing that a principle like "care for vulnerable human life" (as noble as that principle is) by definition encompasses a defense of participatory citizenship. An enlightened despotism, a welfare-state, a single-party bureaucracy, and a democratic republic may all respect mothers, protect children's lives, and show compassion for the vulnerable.

The political issue for feminists must not be just whether children are protected (or any other desirable end achieved) but how and by whom those ends are determined. My point is this: as long as feminists focus only on questions of social and economic concern—questions about children, family, schools, work, wages, pornography, abortion, abuse—they will not articulate a truly political vision, nor will they address the problem of citizenship. Only when they stress that the pursuit of those social and economic concerns must be undertaken through active engagement as citizens in the public world and when they declare the activity of citizenship itself a value will feminists be able to claim a truly liberatory politics as their own.

I hope it is clear that what I am arguing for is the democratization of the polity, not interest-group or single-issue politics-as-usual. A feminist commitment to democratic citizenship should not be confused with either the liberal politics of pressure groups and representative government or the idea that after victory or defeat on an issue, the game is over and we can "go home." As one democratic theorist writes:

> The radical democrat does not agree . . . that after solving [a] problem it will be safe to abandon the democratic struggle and disband the organizations. . . . The radical democrat does not believe that any institutional or social arrangement can give an automatic and permanent solution to the main question of political virtue, or can repeal what may be the only scientific law political science has ever produced: power corrupts.[35]

16 *Mary G. Dietz*

The key idea here is that citizenship must be conceived of as a continuous activity and a good in itself, not as a momentary engagement (or a socialist revolution) with an eye to a final goal or a societal arrangement. This does not mean, of course, that democratic citizens do not pursue specific social and economic ends. Politics is about such things, after all, and the debates and discussions of civic peers will necessarily center on issues of social, political, and economic concern to the community. But at the same time the democratic vision is, and feminist citizenship must be, more than this. Perhaps it is best to say that this is a vision fixed not on an end but rather inspired by a principle—freedom—and by a political activity—positive liberty. That activity is a demanding process that never ends, for it means engaging in public debate and sharing responsibility for self-government. What I am pressing for, in both theory and practice, is a feminist revitalization of this activity.

The reader who has followed me this far is perhaps now wondering whether I have not simply reduced feminist political consciousness to democratic consciousness, leaving nothing in this vision of feminist citizenship for feminism itself. In concluding these reflections, let me suggest why I think the revitalization of democratic citizenship is an especially appropriate task for feminists to undertake. Although the argument can be made more generally, I will direct my remarks to feminism in the United States.

Like Offred in *The Handmaid's Tale*, we Americans live in reduced circumstances, politically speaking. How we understand ourselves as citizens has little to do with the democratic norms and values I have just defended, and it is probably fair to say that most Americans do not think of citizenship in this way at all. We seem hypnotized by a liberal conception of citizenship as rights, an unremitting consumerism that we confuse with freedom, and a capitalist ethic that we take as our collective identity.[36] Sheldon Wolin has noted that in the American political tradition there exist two "bodies" within the historic "body of the people"—a collectivity informed by democratic practices on the one hand and a collectivity informed by an antidemocratic political economy on the other.[37] The latter is a "liberal-capitalist citizenship" that has emerged triumphant today. Truly democratic practices have nearly ceased to be a part of politics in the United States. They exist only on the margins. More disturbing still, I think, even the memory of these practices seems to elude our collective imagination. As Hannah Arendt puts it, citizenship is the "lost treasure" of American political life.

What I want to argue is that we may yet recover the treasure. We may be able to breathe new life into the peoples' other "body"—into our democratic "selves." This prospect brings us back to feminism, which I think is a potential source for our political resuscitation. Feminism has been more than a social cause; it has been a political movement with distinctive attributes. Throughout its second wave in America, the movement has been informed by democratic organization and practice—by spontaneous gatherings and marches, diverse and multitudinous action groups, face-to-face assemblies, consensus decision making, nonhierarchical power structures, open speech and debate.[38] That is, embodied within the immediate political past of feminism in this country are forms of freedom that are far more compatible with the "democratic body" of the American experience than with the liberal-capitalist one.[39] These particular feminist forms are, potentially at least, compatible with the idea of collective, democratic citizenship on a wider scale.

I say "potentially" because feminists must first transform their own democratic practices into a more comprehensive theory of citizenship before they can arrive at an alternative to the nondemocratic liberal theory. Feminist political practice will not in some automatic way become an inspiration for a new citizenship. Instead, feminists must become self-conscious political thinkers—defenders of democracy—in a land of liberalism. To be sure, this task is neither easy nor short-term, but it is possible for feminists to undertake it in earnest because the foundation is already set in the movement's own experiences, in its persistent attention to issues of power, structure, and democracy, and in the historical precedent of women acting as citizens in the United States.[40]

A warning is in order, however. What a feminist defense of democracy must at all costs avoid is the temptation of "womanism." To turn to "women of the republic" and to feminist organization for inspiration in articulating democratic values is one thing; it is quite another to conclude that therein lies evidence of women's "superior democratic nature" or of their "more mature" political voice. A truly democratic defense of citizenship cannot afford to launch its appeal from a position of gender opposition and women's superiority. Such a premise would posit as a starting point precisely what a democratic attitude must deny—that one group of citizens' voices is generally better, more deserving of attention, more worthy of emulation, more moral, than another's. A feminist democrat cannot give way to this sort of temptation, lest democracy itself lose its meaning, and citizenship its special nature. With this in mind, feminists would be well advised to secure the political defense of their theory of democratic citizenship not only in their own territory but also in the diversity of other democratic territories historical and contemporary, male and female. We might include the townships and councils of revolutionary America, the populist National Farmers Alliance, the sit-down strikes of the 1930s, the civil rights movement, the soviets of the Russian Revolution, the French political clubs of 1789, the Spanish anarchist affinity groups, the KOR (Workers' Defense Committee) in Poland, the "mothers of the disappeared ones" in Argentina, and so on. In short, the aim of this political feminism is to remember and bring to light the many examples of democratic practices already in existence and to use these examples as inspiration for a form of political life that would challenge the dominant liberal one.[41] What this aim requires is not only a feminist determination to avoid "womanism" while remaining attentive to women but also a commitment to the activity of citizenship, which includes and requires the participation of men.

I began these reflections by agreeing with Offred that "context is all." I end on what I hope is a complementary and not an overly optimistic note. We are indeed conditioned by the contexts in which we live, but we are also the creators of our political and social constructions and we can change them if we are so determined. The recent history of democratic politics in this country has not been an altogether happy one, despite spontaneous movements and periodic successes. Rather than occasion despair, however, perhaps this realization can work to strengthen and renew our sense of urgency concerning our present condition and what is to be done.

First, however, the urgency must be felt, and the spirit necessary for revitalizing citizenship must be enlivened in the public realm. Democracy, in other words, awaits its "prime movers." My aim here has been to argue that one such mover might be feminism and to suggest why I think feminism is well suited to this demanding and difficult task that would benefit us all.

ENDNOTES

[1]Margaret Atwood, *The Handmaid's Tale* (New York: Simon & Schuster, 1986).

[2]For some idea of the wide-ranging nature of the feminist critique of liberalism, see the following: Irene Diamond, ed., *Families, Politics, and Public Policy: A Feminist Dialogue on Women and the State* (New York: Longman, 1983); Zillah Einstein, *The Radical Future of Liberal Feminism* (New York: Longman, 1981); Jean Bethke Elshtain, *Public Man, Private Woman* (Princeton, NJ: Princeton University Press, 1981); Sandra Harding and Merrill Hintikka, *Discovering Reality: Feminist Perspectives on Epistemology, Metaphysics, Methodology, and the Philosophy of Science* (Dordrecht: Reidel, 1983); Allison Jagger, *Feminist Politics and Human Nature* (New York: Rowman and Allenheld, 1983); Juliet Mitchell and Ann Oakley, *The Rights and Wrongs of Women* (Harmondsworth: Penguin, 1976); Linda Nicholson, *Gender and History* (New York: Columbia University Press, 1986); and Susan Moller Okin, *Women in Western Political Thought* (Princeton, NJ: Princeton University Press, 1979). For a feminist critique of social contract theory, see Seyla Benhabib, "The Generalized and Concrete Other: The Kohlberg-Gilligan Controversy and Feminist Theory," *Praxis International* 5 (4) (1986), pp. 402–24; Christine Di Stephano, "Masculinity as Ideology in Political Theory: Hobbesian Man Considered," *Women's Studies International Forum* 6 (6) (1983); Carole Pateman, "Women and Consent," *Political Theory* 8 (2) (1980), pp. 149–68; Carole Pateman and Teresa Brennan, "Mere Auxiliaries to the Commonwealth: Women and the Origins of Liberalism," *Political Studies* 27 (2) (1979), pp. 183–200; and Mary Lyndon Shanley, "Marriage Contract and Social Contract in Seventeenth-Century English Political Thought," *Western Political Quarterly* 32 (1) (1979), pp. 79–91. For a critique of the "rational man," see Nancy Hartsock, *Money, Sex, and Power* (New York: Longman, 1983); Genevieve Lloyd, *Man of Reason* (Minneapolis: University of Minnesota Press, 1984); and Iris Marion Young, "Impartiality and the Civic Public: Some Implications of Feminist Critiques of Moral and Political Theory," *Praxis International* 5 (4) (1986), pp. 381–401. On Locke, see Melissa Butler, "Early Liberal Roots of Feminism: John Locke and the Attack on Patriarchy," *American Political Science Review* 72 (1) (1978), pp. 135–50; Lorenne M.G. Clark, "Women and Locke: Who Owns the Apples in the Garden of Eden?" in Clark and Lynda Lange, eds., *The Sexism of Social and Political Theory* (Toronto: University of Toronto Press, 1979); and Carole Pateman, "Sublimation and Reification: Locke, Wolin, and the Liberal Democratic Conception of the Political," *Politics and Society* 5 (1975), pp. 441–67. On Mill, see Julia Annas, "Mill and the Subjection of Women," *Philosophy* 52 (1977), p. 179–94; Richard W. Krouse, "Patriarchal Liberalism and Beyond: From John Stuart Mill to Harriet Taylor," in Jean Bethke Elshtain, ed., *The Family in Political Thought* (Amherst: University of Massachusetts Press, 1982); and Jennifer Ring, "Mill's *Subjection of Women:* The Methodological Limits of Liberal Feminism," *Review of Politics* 47 (1) (1985). On liberal moral theory, see Lawrence Blum, "Kant and Hegel's Moral Paternalism: A Feminist Response," *Canadian Journal of Philosophy* 12 (1982), pp. 287–302.

[3]For a sense of the historical and intellectual development of liberalism over the past three centuries, see the following (in chronological order): L.T. Hobhouse, *Liberalism* (London, 1911); Guido De Ruggiero, *The History of European Liberalism* (Oxford: Oxford University Press, 1927); Harold Laski, *The Rise of*

## 20 *Mary G. Dietz*

*European Liberalism* (London: Allen & Unwin, 1936); George H. Sabine, *A History of Political Theory* (New York: Holt, 1937); Charles Howard McIlwain, *Constitutionalism and the Changing World* (New York: Macmillan, 1939); John H. Hallowell, *The Decline of Liberalism as an Ideology* (Berkeley: University of California Press, 1943); Thomas Maitland Marshall, *Citizenship and Social Class* (Cambridge: Cambridge University Press, 1950); Michael Polanyi, *The Logic of Liberty* (Chicago: University of Chicago Press, 1951); Louis Hartz, *The Liberal Tradition in America* (New York: Harcourt Brace, 1955); R.D. Cumming, *Human Nature and History, A Study of the Development of Liberal Democracy*, 2 vols. (Chicago: University of Chicago Press, 1969); C.B. MacPherson, *The Life and Times of Liberal Democracy* (Oxford: Oxford University Press, 1977); Alan Macfarlane, *Origins of English Individualism* (Oxford: Oxford University Press, 1978); Steven Seidman, *Liberalism and the Origins of European Social Theory* (Berkeley: University of California Press, 1983); and John Gray, *Liberalism* (Minneapolis: University of Minnesota Press, 1986).

[4]Although Thomas Hobbes was not within the main (and broadly defined) tradition of liberal theory that includes but is not limited to Locke, Kant, Smith, Madison, Montesquieu, Bentham, Mill, T.H. Green, L.T. Hobhouse, Dewey, and, recently, Rawls, Dworkin, and Nozick, he set the stage for the view of man that came to distinguish much of liberal thought. In *De Cive*, Hobbes wrote, "let us . . . consider men as if but even now sprung out of the earth, and suddenly, like mushrooms come to full maturity, without all kinds of engagement to each other." "Philosophical Rudiments Concerning Government and Society," in Sir W. Molesworth, ed., *The English Works of Thomas Hobbes* (London: Longman, 1966), p. 102. This invocation to view man as an autonomous "self" outside society is discernible, in varied forms, from Locke's state of nature to Rawls's "veil of ignorance." Contemporary critics of liberalism refer to this formulation as the "unencumbered self"; see Michael Sandel, "The Procedural Republic and the Unencumbered Self," *Political Theory*, 12 (1) (1984), pp. 81–96.

I will use the male referent in this discussion of liberalism for two reasons: first, it serves as a reminder of the exclusively male discourse used in traditional political theory, including that of the few theorists who are willing to concede that *he/him* means "all." Second, many feminist theorists have persuasively argued that the term *man* as used in liberal thought is not simply a linguistic device or a generic label but a symbol for a concept reflecting both masculine values and virtues and patriarchalist practices. See Brennan and Pateman, "Mere Auxiliaries to the Commonwealth."

[5]As Brennan and Pateman point out in "Mere Auxiliaries," the idea that the individual is by nature free—that is, outside the bonds of society, history, and tradition—was bequeathed to liberalism by social contract theorists. The emergence of this idea in the seventeenth century not only marked "a decisive break with the traditional view that people were 'naturally' bound together in a hierarchy of inequality and subordination" but also established a conception of "natural" individual freedom as the condition of individual isolation from others prior to the (artificial) creation of "civil society."

[6]John Stuart Mill, "On Liberty," in Max Lerner, ed., *The Essential Works of John Stuart Mill* (New York: Bantam, 1961), p. 266.

[7]T.H. Green, "Liberal Legislation and Freedom of Contract," in John R. Rodman, ed., *The Political Theory of T.H. Green* (New York: Crofts, 1964).

[8]Quoted in Sheldon Wolin, *Politics and Vision* (Boston: Little, Brown, 1963).

[9]Jagger, *Feminist Politics*, p. 33.

[10]Sir Isaiah Berlin, "Two Concepts of Liberty," in *Four Essays on Liberty* (Oxford: Oxford University Press, 1969), p. 122. Berlin goes on to note something that will be important to the argument I make in section III—that "freedom [as negative liberty] is not, at any rate logically, connected with democracy or self-government. . . . The answer to the question 'Who governs me?' is logically distinct from the question 'How far does government interfere with me?' " (pp. 129–30). The latter question, as we shall see, is the one that is of primary concern for the liberal citizen; the former must be of concern to the democratic citizen, and accordingly, to feminist political thought.

[11]John Rawls, *A Theory of Justice* (Cambridge, MA: Harvard University Press, 1971).

[12]The denial of citizenship to women is, of course, a historical but not a contemporary feature of liberalism. Nevertheless, it is worth noting that at least in early liberal thought, the ethical principles that distinguish liberalism—individual freedom and social equality—were not in practice (and often not in theory) extended to women, but solely to "rational men," whose "rationality" was linked to the ownership of property.

[13]Liberalism's context is actually a highly complex set of shifting social, political, and historical situations. We must not forget that in its earliest (seventeenth- and eighteenth-century) manifestations with the Levellers, the True Whigs, the Commonwealthmen, and revolutionary "patriots," the proclamation of individual rights and social equality were acts of rebellion against king and court. The domain of capitalist "possessive individualism" developed in a separate but related set of practices. Thus liberalism's legacy is a radical as well as a capitalist one.

[14]See Jagger, *Feminist Politics*, p. 31.

[15]As C.B. MacPherson rightly points out in *The Life and Times of Liberal Democracy*, p. 2, one of the prevailing difficulties of liberalism is that it has tried to combine the idea of individual freedom as "self-development" with the entrepreneurial notion of liberalism as the "right of the stronger to do down the weaker by following market rules." Despite attempts by J.S. Mill, Robert Nozick, and others to reconcile market freedom with self-development freedom, a successful resolution has not yet been achieved. MacPherson argues that the two freedoms are profoundly inconsistent, but he also asserts that the liberal position "need not be taken to depend forever on an acceptance of capitalist assumptions, although historically it has been so taken" (p. 2). That historical reality is the one I focus on here, and is what I think predominates in the liberal American view of citizenship. However, like MacPherson, I do not think liberalism is necessarily bound (conceptually or practically) to what he calls the "capitalist market envelope."

[16]Ibid., p. 1.

[17]Mary Lyndon Shanley, "Afterword: Feminism and Families in a Liberal Polity," in Diamond, *Families, Politics, and Public Policy*, p. 360.

[18]For example, see Jagger, *Feminist Politics;* Naomi Scheman, "Individualism and the Objects of Psychology," in Harding and Hintikka, *Discovering Reality*; Jean Grimshaw, *Philosophy and Feminist Thinking* (Minneapolis: University of Minnesota Press, 1986); Nicholson, *Gender and History;* and Young, "Impartiality and the Civic Public."

## 22 *Mary G. Dietz*

[19]I intentionally leave radical feminism out of this discussion, not because it is insignificant or unimportant, but because it has, to date, not arrived at a consistent political position on the questions that concern us here. For a helpful critique of radical feminism's theoretical failings, see Jagger, *Feminist Politics*, pp. 286–90, and Joan Cocks, "Wordless Emotions: Some Critical Reflections on Radical Feminism," *Politics and Society* 13 (1) (1984), pp. 27–57.

[20]By delineating this category I do not mean to blur or erase the very real distinctions between various kinds of Marxist feminists or to obscure the importance of the "patriarchy versus capitalism" debate. For a sense of the diversity of Marxist (or socialist) feminism, see: Mariarose DallaCosta and Selma James, *Women and the Subversion of Community: A Woman's Place* (Bristol: Falling Wall Press, 1981); Hartsock, *Money, Sex, and Power;* Zillah Eisenstein, *Capitalist Patriarchy and the Case for Socialist Feminism* (New York: Monthly Review Press, 1978); Catherine A. Mackinnon, "Feminism, Marxism, Method, and the State: An Agenda for Theory," in Nannerl O. Keohane, Michelle Rosaldo, and Barbara Gelpi, eds., *Feminist Theory: A Critique of Ideology* (Chicago: University of Chicago Press, 1981); Sheila Rowbotham, *Women, Resistance, and Revolution* (New York: Vintage, 1974); and Lydia Sargent, ed., *Women and Revolution* (Boston: South End Press, 1981). The quotations are from Hartsock, *Money Sex, and Power*, p. 235.

[21]Eisenstein, *The Radical Future of Liberal Politics*, p. 223.

[22]Ibid., p. 222.

[23]Hartsock, *Money, Sex, and Power*, p. 247.

[24]Sheldon Wolin, "Revolutionary Action Today," *Democracy* 2 (4) (1982), pp. 17–28.

[25]For various maternalist views see, among others, Jean Bethke Elshtain, "Antigone's Daughters," *Democracy* 2 (2) (1982), pp. 46–59; Elshtain, "Feminism, Family and Community," *Dissent* 29 (4) (1982), pp. 442–49; and Elshtain, "Feminist Discourse and Its Discontents: Language, Power, and Meaning," *Signs* 3 (7) (1982), pp. 603–21; also Sara Ruddick, "Maternal Thinking," *Feminist Studies* 6 (2) (1980), pp. 342–67; Ruddick, "Preservative Love and Military Destruction: Reflections on Mothering and Peace," in Joyce Treblicot, ed., *Mothering: Essays on Feminist Theory* (Totowa, NJ: Littlefield Adams, 1983); and Hartsock, *Money, Sex, and Power* (Hartsock incorporates both Marxist and maternalist perspectives in her "feminist standpoint" theory).

[26]Elshtain, "Feminist Discourse," p. 617.

[27]Elshtain, *Public Man, Private Woman*, p. 243, and Elshtain, "Antigone's Daughters," p. 59.

[28]Elshtain, "Antigone's Daughters," p. 58.

[29]See Nancy Chodorow, The Reproduction of Mothering: Psychoanalysis and the Sociology of Gender (Berkeley: University of California Press, 1978), and Carol Gilligan, *In a Different Voice: Psychological Theory and Women's Development* (Cambridge: Harvard University Press, 1982).

[30]I qualify this with "implication" because Gilligan is by no means consistent about whether the "different voice" is exclusive to women or open to men. For an interesting critique, see Joan Tronto, "Women's Morality: Beyond Gender Difference to a Theory of Care," in *Signs* 12 (4) (1987), pp. 644–63.

[31]Elshtain, "Feminist Discourse," p. 621.

[32]For a complementary and elegant critique of binary opposition arguments, see Joan Scott, "Gender: A Useful Category of Historical Analysis," *American Historical Review* 91 (2) (1986), pp. 1053–75.

[33]For a more detailed critique, see Dietz, "Citizenship with a Feminist Face: The Problem with Maternal Thinking," *Political Theory* 13 (1) (1985), pp. 19–35.

[34]The alternative conception introduced here—of politics as participatory and citizenship as the active engagement of peers in the public realm—has been of considerable interest to political theorists and historians over the past twenty years and has developed in detail as an alternative to the liberal view. Feminists now need to consider the significance of this perspective in regard to their own political theories. Perhaps the leading contemporary exponent of politics as the active life of citizens is Hannah Arendt, *The Human Condition* (Chicago: University of Chicago Press, 1958) and *On Revolution* (New York: Penguin, 1963). But alternatives to liberalism are also explored as "civic republicanism" in the work of J.G.A. Pocock, *The Machiavellian Moment: Florentine Political Thought and the Atlantic Republican Tradition* (Princeton, NJ: Princeton University Press, 1975), and in the recent "communitarian turn" articulated by Michael Sandel in his critique of the tradition of thinkers from Kant to Rawls, *Liberalism and the Limits of Justice* (Cambridge, England: Cambridge University Press, 1982). For other "democratic" critiques of liberalism, see Benjamin Barber, *Strong Democracy: Participatory Politics for a New Age* (Berkeley: University of California Press, 1984); Joshua Cohen and Joel Rogers, *On Democracy: Toward a Transformation of American Society* (New York: Penguin, 1983); Russell Hanson, *The Democratic Imagination in America* (Princeton, NJ: Princeton University Press, 1985); Lawrence Goodwyn, *Democratic Promise: The Populist Movement in America* (New York: Oxford University Press, 1976); Carole Pateman, *Participation and Democratic Theory* (Cambridge, England: Cambridge University Press, 1970); Michael Walzer, *Radical Principles* (New York: Basic Books, 1980); and Sheldon Wolin, *Politics and Vision* (Boston: Little, Brown, 1963). Also see the short-lived but useful journal *Democracy* (1981–1983).

[35]C. Douglas Lummis, "The Radicalization of Democracy," *Democracy* 2 (4) (1982), pp. 9–16.

[36]I would reiterate, however, that despite its historical propensity to collapse democracy into a capitalist economic ethic, liberalism is not without its own vital ethical principles (namely, individual freedom and equality) that democrats ignore to their peril. The task for "ethical liberals," as MacPherson puts it in *The Life and Times of Liberal Democracy*, is to detach these principles from the "market assumptions" of capitalism and integrate them into a truly democratic vision of participatory citizenship. By the same token, the task for participatory democrats is to preserve the principles of freedom and equality that are the special legacy of liberalism.

[37]Sheldon Wolin, "The Peoples' Two Bodies," *Democracy* 1 (1) (1981), pp. 9–24.

[38]I do not intend to imply that feminism is the only democratic movement that has emerged in the recent American past or that it is the only one from which we can draw examples. There are others—the civil rights movement, the populist resurgence, the collective political gatherings occasioned by the farm crises of the 1980s, gay liberation, and so on. But in its organization and decentralized practices, the feminist movement has been the most consistently democratic, its liberal, interest-group side (NOW) notwithstanding.

## 24 *Mary G. Dietz*

[39]The phrase "forms of freedom" comes from Jane Mansbridge, "Feminism and the Forms of Freedom," in Frank Fischer and Carmen Siriani, eds., *Critical Studies in Organization and Bureaucracy* (Philadelphia: Temple University Press, 1984), pp. 472–86.

[40]Some of the historical precedents I have in mind are developed in Linda Kerber's book, *Women of the Republic* (New York: Norton, 1980), especially in chapter 3, "The Meaning of Female Patriotism," in which she reconsiders the political activism of women in revolutionary America. Other activist precedents that contemporary feminists might recall and preserve are discussed in Sara M. Evans and Harry C. Boyte, *Free Spaces: The Sources of Democratic Change in America* (New York: Harper & Row, 1986); these include the abolitionist movement, the suffrage movement, the Women's Christian Temperance Union, the settlement house movement, and the National Women's Trade Union League, as well as contemporary forms of feminist organization and action.

[41]My point here is not that the soviets of 1917 or the Polish KOR of 1978 can serve as models for participatory citizenship in late twentieth-century America, but rather that an alternative to liberal citizenship can take root only if it is distilled into a framework of conceptual notions. The historical moments I mention (and others) provide the experiential and practical reality for such a conceptual framework and thus merit incorporation into feminist democratic politics. Or, as Arendt writes in *On Revolution*, "What saves the affairs of moral men from their inherent futility is nothing but the incessant talk about them, which in turn remains futile unless certain concepts, certain guideposts for future remembrance and even for sheer reference, arise out of it" (p. 20). The diverse practices mentioned above should be perceived as guideposts and references that might inspire a democratic spirit rather than as literal examples to be emulated in keeping with such a spirit.

# [18]

## SYMPOSIUM ON CARE AND JUSTICE

# Care as a Basis for Radical Political Judgments

JOAN C. TRONTO

*The best framework for moral and political thought is the one that creates the best climate for good political judgments. I argue that universalistic theories of justice fall short in this regard because they cannot distinguish idealization from abstraction. After describing how an ethic of care guides judgments, I suggest the practical effects that make this approach preferable. The ethic of care includes more aspects of human life in making political judgments.*

The ethic of care has much to recommend it as a systematic framework for moral and political thought. I assert, in fact, that care provides the basis for the most important form of contemporary radical political thinking. My remarks come under three headings. First, I discuss the ethic of care as a framework for moral and political judgment, with a quick comparison with justice theories. Second, I mention some of the elements that a care perspective suggests are important in making practical political judgments. Third, I conclude by pointing to what I think are some general practical effects of using the care framework for political judgments.

### CARE AS A FRAMEWORK

For me, the question of which framework for moral and political thought is best is not so much an epistemological or logical question as it is a question about the prospects for creating a climate for good political judgments. In this regard, my approach is inspired by an Aristotelian conception of the task of political science: what we need to do as political theorists is to make clear what the parameters and conditions are for individuals to make good judgments.

*Hypatia* vol. 10, no. 2 (Spring 1995) 

Care provides a radically different way to look at moral and political life. Although the analysis of care began with women's work and lives, I have argued that we make a mistake if we fail to generalize our analysis of care beyond gender. All humans must be engaged in care activities, both as receivers of care and, in most cases, also as care-givers.

Berenice Fisher and I defined care as "*a species activity that includes everything that we do to maintain, continue, and repair our 'world' so that we can live in it as well as possible*. That world includes our bodies, our selves, and our environment, all of which we seek to interweave in a complex, life-sustaining web" (Fisher and Tronto 1991, 40).

From this definition, it is obvious that care is a process, that judgments made about care arise out of the real, lived experiences of people in all of their variety. From this standpoint, we must reformulate our account of human nature (people qua people are interdependent rather than independent), of what activities count as centrally human (complicating the separation of realms of "freedom" and "necessity"), and our values, rethinking what we expect from our collective institutions.

As a process, care is amenable to closer analysis, and Fisher and I suggested four phases of care, each of which, I argued, has a concomitant virtue: caring about, attentiveness; taking care of, responsibility; care-giving, competence; and care-receiving, responsiveness. Ideally, care takes place in a holistic way. It is not necessarily privatized, individualized, or de-institutionalized, but any thorough analysis of care requires that we be attentive to the complete context of care.[1]

What kind of framework does care entail? Care may be ubiquitous in human life, but it has remained hidden from the conceptual lenses of social and political thought. As a result, to place care at the center of human life requires that we rethink many of the assumptions that we make about social and political theory. At the outset, care begins from a different understanding of human nature and human interaction. Rather than seeing people as rational actors pursuing their own goals and maximizing their interests, we must instead see people as constantly enmeshed in relationships of care. When individuals achieve autonomy, that is a valued point in human activity, but it does not happen automatically and therefore cannot serve as an accurate portrayal of human life. Individuals act politically, then, not only on the basis of their self-interests, but as a result of the particular constellation of caring relationships and institutions within which they find themselves. Families, welfare states, and the market are all institutions that provide care. Who people are, what interests they will take to heart, and so on, depend, to some extent, on the shape and culture of these institutions. The ethic of care therefore constantly forces us to place into the context of people's daily lived lives any political or moral concerns that we might wish to raise.

Furthermore, the ethic of care entails a basic value: that proper care for others is a good, and that humans in society should strive to enhance the quality of care in their world "so that we may live in it as well as possible." Perhaps the account closest to this view of the world offered by other contemporary philosophers is Martha Nussbaum's (1992) notion of human capacity and flourishing.

Let us quickly compare this standard of care with the Kantian-derived, deontological theories of justice that predominate in discussions of how moral theory should inform political theory. The standard attack on these positions is that they are too abstract. In these theories, moral standards are largely governed by universalized rules, such as the principle of fairness. The danger with such theories, as many commentators have noticed, is that these formal criteria may ignore and not provide any account of the concrete details of the moral and political life of individuals.

Onora O'Neill (1993) has provided a thoughtful response to such critics by distinguishing between *abstraction* and *idealization*. O'Neill argues that all philosophical discussion must engage in the process of abstraction; all thinking is a form of abstraction. The danger, O'Neill suggests, arises when our abstractions are inadequately general because, instead of including only the essential elements that should be abstracted for our philosophical concerns, they also include idealized elements. Hence, an assumption that philosophers are men, with its attendant sexism, is not an error of philosophical abstraction, but an error of philosophical idealization.

This is a useful distinction, but not completely sufficient. Nothing in the theory of justice, or in the distinction between abstraction and idealization, allows us to know when a philosophical position grows out of idealization rather than abstraction. As Nussbaum (1993) has noted, there is no guarantee that we will catch errors through use of this distinction. After others have pointed to the limits of our thought, then we can recognize that our abstractions are really idealizations.

To fix similar kinds of problems but to hold on to general theories of justice, justice theorists have added two different kinds of epicycles to their theories: one procedural and the other substantive. The procedural epicycle is the turn to discourse ethics: if all are engaged in the discussion, then the idealizations will be separable from the abstractions.[2] In answer to criticisms that these models do not take account of power differentials (e.g., Sanders 1992), theorists have proposed procedures to strengthen the positions of those less well off through such methods as providing a veto power to affected groups (Young 1990).

The substantive fix to these general theories of justice is the idea proposed by Robert Goodin (1985), advocated by Susan Moller Okin (e.g., 1989) and others, that we make certain in our philosophical frameworks to think to "protect the vulnerable." In this way our idealizations will cease to be at the expense of those who are least well off.

Nevertheless, neither of these remedies solves the basic problem of the limits of these theories of justice. All philosophical theories grow out of the perspectives of the individual philosophers who are engaged in thinking. All thinkers are likely to see their own perspectives as true rather than as idealizations. Thus the prescription to avoid idealization may carry no practical force.

Indeed, if we look at the ways in which theories of justice are applied to practical political problems, we see that there is a serious dropping off in adherents of philosophies when they arrive at practical political issues. We can put a more sinister cast to the distinction between abstraction and idealization, and note that the usual form of idealization might instead be called rationalization. Hence, Kant was aware of women and wrote about them in some essays, but excluded them from all rational beings (Schott 1988). Egalitarian republicanism and slavery were thought to be consistent earlier in American history by reducing the human status of African-captured slaves. Rationalization, as Brown (1933, 306) put it, serves as "inoculation against insight."

## SPECIFIC ELEMENTS OF ANALYSIS SUGGESTED BY A THEORY OF CARE

In the light of this ever-present philosophical danger, the care ethic requires that we constantly return to the real world of daily-lived lives in order to generate our philosophical and political positions. The ethic of care requires at least these focal points for moral and political discussion:

1. A full account of human needs
2. Careful analysis of the four phases of care
3. An analysis of power relationships within processes of care
4. Whether care processes fit together into a whole or remain incomplete.

Beyond providing us with a guide for practical judgments, the care ethic is also useful because it confounds many of the dividing lines that have led to the incompleteness of other ways of analyzing and thinking about human lives.

For example, the ethic of care requires that processes of care be understood in culturally specific ways. Thus, while the condition of needing care is universal, standards of care will vary by culture.[3]

Or, consider as another example: Both the broad political economic concerns that shape the material conditions of people's lives, the very local scope of interpersonal psychological mechanisms, and social interactions are incorporated into an ethic of care. Care requires the physical materials of enough food, shelter, and clothing and a rich complex of material resources needed to provide these essentials. Depending on the type and quality of the interaction, care may also involve a number of psychological aspects: rage at the powerful care-giver, fear of the care-giver, anger at the care-receiver, idealization (of either a positive or negative type) of others in the care relationships. Care requires that humans pay attention to one another, take responsibility for one another, engage in physical processes of care giving, and respond to those who have received care. As a result, the process of care, the dynamics of interaction, are also inevitably involved in understanding care. Further, because people can be in different positions vis-à-vis those who care for them, power dimensions are also deeply implicated in these interactions.[4]

And, another dimension: care is not solely private or parochial; it can concern institutions, societies, even global levels of thinking.

As this brief exegesis of some of the dimensions of care suggests, though,[5] starting from a care perspective is likely to prevent a simplistic avoidance of the elements of care. Although it is always possible for any set of ideas to be misapplied, I hope that an engagement in thinking about care, because it necessarily turns our attention to the concrete, avoids this danger.

The opposite danger is perhaps more likely: a care perspective might become too parochial and too narrow. Let me take that objection up in the final section, in which I consider some of the practical effects of a switch to a theory of care.

## Some General Practical Effects of Thinking in Terms of Care

Although our notions of care make philosophical and political thought considerably more complex, they also increase the likelihood that our thinking will better capture the reality of human experience. Let me suggest some practical effects of this position.

The first "virtue" of care, the first step in an analysis of care, is the requirement of attentiveness: until we care about something, the care process cannot begin. Thus, a constant impulse to return to the details of care processes and structures in life is the starting point of care as a theoretical perspective. This stance, it seems to me, is a better defense against idealization than the epicycles of a theory of justice.

To be attentive, furthermore, requires actual attention be paid to those who are engaged in care processes. To use a simple example, the public housing debate looks quite different to someone living in substandard housing who has to cope with that situation (which affects all other aspects of life: how to keep and prepare food, how to protect property, how to arrive safely home from school, etc.) than to an economist who focuses solely on "market forces." Thus, a shift occurs in what counts as "knowledge" in making philosophical and political judgments. This shift, then, is not only in terms of abstract ideas, but in whose voice should count. It is an attempt, in some ways, not to change the participants in a dialogue by inviting the previously excluded to join into pre-existing discourses on issues of justice, fairness, and so on. It is instead, an attempt to say that what discourses are important needs to change, and those who have the most to say may not be those who speak the eloquent language of the academy or of the realm of public policymakers. Hence, although care may continue to be parochial through its misapplication, I argue that a theory of care requires care to be the opposite of parochial, that is, attentive to others.

In very concrete ways, this shift requires a shift in what constitutes our notions of desert, and, hence, at the deepest level, our substantive notions of justice. To put the point in shortest form: even notions of justice as fairness rely on senses of desert, for example, that all people deserve rights. Virtually every political debate in the United States comes down, sooner or later, to a desert claim that grows out of the "work ethic": that people are entitled to what they have because they "earned" it. The care ethic posits a very different set of standards for desert: people are entitled to what they need because they need it; people are entitled to care because they are part of ongoing relations of care.[6]

Finally, let me make a somewhat counter-intuitive argument about the relationship of care and justice. We seem to invoke arguments from justice when arguments from self-interest fail. I propose, though, that in a society that took care seriously, people would perceive greater and wider forms of care as within their self-interest.[7]

Following Albert Hirschmann's (1977) suggestions about the "*doux*, sweet" effects of commerce on human behavior in the eighteenth century, we might want to think about the *doux* effects of care as a way to understand human interaction in an era in which the economic exploitation of others can appear as brutal as some earlier forms of physical violence against others. It is clear that being well-cared-for, being properly attended to as an infant, given space to develop autonomy in the context of caring relations where other needs are met, makes people happier.[8] To be well-cared-for requires further care, and an attentiveness to the caring needs of others. The absence of care, incomplete or disrupted care, creates anger, rage, violence. It creates the conditions for yet more incomplete care. Given a choice between cycles of care or cycles of incomplete care, it seems to me that people would, out of self-interest, prefer to participate in societies, communities, and institutions where care was complete.[9]

I began by asserting that care provides a radical basis for rethinking political judgments. I hope, however, that as utopian as these ideas sound, we recall that what most recommends care is the practical, daily, concrete way it forces us to think about moral and political life.

NOTES

1. In asserting the political nature of care I disagree most with theorists of care such as Noddings (1984) and Manning (1992).

2. In the context of the care debate, the foremost proponent of this turn is probably Benhabib (1992). Benhabib partly makes her position appealing, however, by exaggerating the flaws of her opponents' views. Hence, she asserts, "A morality of care can revert simply to the position that what is morally good is what is best for those who are like me. Such a claim is no different than arguing that what is best morally is what pleases me most" (187). This argument is not convincing. In the first place, the second claim does not follow from the first. Her claim requires that we equate "what is best for those who are like me" with "what pleases me most." In the second place, if we take the worst simplifications of Kantian categorical imperatives, they too can be distorted into claims for self-interest. Benhabib's caricature does not carry special weight against an ethic of care.

3. But what happens in the face of culturally specific standards for care that are patently unfair? For example, in some cultures the presumption is that women require less education than men. It is simply a fact of life, and given the division of caring work in society, that belief determines the outcome of the dispute.

This kind of argument is quite troubling for my position, obviously. Nevertheless, I suggest that grounding such disputes in the practices of everyday life rather than in abstract principles such as justice or fairness is likely to result in more change. A patriarch in a village might be more willing to recognize the changing needs for the education of women than to adopt a different worldview in which gender equity is brought to the fore. The accommodation of religions and other systems of beliefs to local circumstances have always required these kinds of philosophical negotiations: focusing on care is a way to hasten the process.

4. Clare Ungerson, drawing on the work of Kari Wærness, distinguishes here different care statuses: (1) personal service: an unequal relation between two people where the superior in status is cared for and could provide the care for himself or herself; (2) care-giving work: where the cared-for is incapable of self care and is dependent upon the care-giver; (3) spontaneous care: care that occurs in communities but is not consistent or reliable (Ungerson 1990, 14-15).

5. See Tronto 1993a for a more sustained discussion of these dimensions of care.

6. Many discussions of welfare policy have conceived this position as a type of reciprocity. Everyone may need welfare, or workers' compensation insurance, or social security, and so forth, at some point in their lives. Thus it is justifiable to require that all in the society take care of those who are now in such positions of need. The problems with this view are many; I will name two of them. In the first place, it requires people to make an assumption about themselves that, psychologically, they cannot feel pleased to make: they will someday give up what makes them socially valued and become "needy." In the second place, it does not change the assumption of responsibility inherent in the work ethic.

What the care ethic does is to change the assumptions about desert, about the regularity of the need to be cared for (*all* people need and provide care), and about responsibility. I cannot elaborate on these points here; see Tronto (1993b).

7. It can be argued that this principle is at work in the European welfare states.

8. And I surely do not mean to suggest that this development happens only, or best, in the upper middle class of modern industrial societies. See, inter alia, Giddings (1993).

9. I am not asserting that all violence, rage, or unhappiness arises from improper care, or that enough good care would solve all of these problems. Even if good care could solve all problems, there can never be enough care. Care itself often involves tragic choices: we cannot possibly meet all of the needs for care that exist in society. In this regard, this is not a perfectionist theory. Nevertheless, a society based on care would perhaps be less violent, rageful, and unhappy than many current societies are.

## REFERENCES


Benhabib, Seyla. 1992. *Situating the self: Gender, community and postmodernism in contemporary ethics*. New York: Routledge.

Brown, W. D. 1933. Rationalization of race prejudice. *International Journal of Ethics* 43(3): 294-306.

Fisher, Berenice, and Joan C. Tronto. 1990. Toward a feminist theory of caring. In *Circles of care: Work and identity in women's lives*, ed. Emily Abel and Margaret Nelson. Albany: State University of New York Press.

Giddings, Paula. 1993. Afterword. *Double stitch: Black women write about mothers and daughters*, ed. Patricia Bell-Scott et al. Boston: Beacon Press.

Gilligan, Carol. 1982. *In a different voice: Psychological theory and women's development*. Cambridge: Harvard University Press.

Goodin, Robert. 1985. *Protecting the vulnerable: A reanalysis of our social responsibilities*. Chicago: University of Chicago Press.

Hirschmann, Albert O. 1977. *The passions and the interests*. Princeton: Princeton University Press.

Manning, Rita C. 1992. *Speaking from the heart: A feminist perpsective on ethics*. Lanham, MD: Rowman and Littlefield.

Noddings, Nel. 1984. *Caring: A feminine approach to ethics and moral education*. Berkeley: University of California Press.

———. 1990. A Response. *Hypatia* 5(1): 120-26.

Nussbaum, Martha C. 1992. Human functioning and social justice: In defense of Aristotelian essentialism. *Political Theory* 20(2): 202-46.

———. 1993. Commentary. In *The quality of life*. See Nussbaum and Sen 1993.

Nussbaum, Martha C., and Amartya K. Sen, eds. 1993. *The quality of life*. Oxford: Clarendon Press.

Okin, Susan Moller. 1989. *Justice, gender, and the family*. New York: Basic Books.

O'Neill, Onora. 1993. Justice, Gender and International Boundaries. In *The quality of life*. See Nussbaum and Sen 1993.

Sanders, Lynn. 1992. Against deliberation. Paper presented at the annual meeting of the Midwestern Political Science Association.

Schott, Robin May. 1988. *Cognition and eros: A critique of the Kantian paradigm*. Boston: Beacon Press.

Tronto, Joan C. 1993a. *Moral boundaries: A political argument for an ethic of care*. New York: Routledge.

———. 1993b. Welfare policy and the ethics of care. Paper presented at the University of Pittsburgh, November.

Ungerson, Clare. 1990. The language of care: Crossing the boundaries. In *Gender and caring: Work and welfare in Britain and Scandinavia*, ed. Clare Ungerson. London: Harvester, Wheatsheaf.

Young, Iris M. 1990. *Justice and the politics of difference*. Princeton: Princeton University Press.

# [19]

# FEMINISM AND DEMOCRATIC COMMUNITY

JANE MANSBRIDGE

Advocates of individualism tend to assume a zero-sum game, in which any advance in community entails a retreat in protecting individuality. Advocates of greater community tend to assume no tradeoff between these goods, ignoring the ways community ties undermine individual freedom. This essay proposes advancing selectively on both fronts. Democracies need community to help develop their citizens' faculties, solve collective action problems, and legitimate democratic decisions. But community is in tension with individualism. The challenge for most polities is to find ways of strengthening community ties while developing institutions to protect individuals from community oppression. Women's experiences, traditionally neglected in political philos-

I would like to thank Pauline Bart, Nancy Fraser, Virginia Held, Christopher Jencks, Jennifer Nedelsky, Robert Merton, Susan Okin, Robert Post, my two NOMOS commentators, Carol Gould and David Richards, and Kenneth Winston, who read the manuscript carefully twice, for useful and insightful comments. In particular, I urge that Carol Gould's commentary be read in conjunction with this essay. Some of the ideas in the essay were developed earlier in my "Feminism and Democracy," *The American Prospect* vol. 1, no. 1 (1990). I would also like to thank the Center for Urban Affairs and Policy Research at Northwestern University and the Russell Sage Foundation for support.

ophy, help in both prongs of the challenge, by revealing undervalued components of community and underestimated threats to individual autonomy.

## I. First Prologue: Democratic Community

Social critics who write about community usually believe that American society in particular and Western societies in general need to redress the balance between individualism and community in favor of community. Redress, they contend, would be good both for the psychological health of the individuals in the society and for the society as a whole.[1] I argue that communal bonds can improve the competitive status of the group as a whole by providing an efficient way of solving problems of collective action.

In a "collective action problem," or social dilemma, each individual's self-interested action interacts with the self-interested actions of others to produce a lower overall product for the group, and, consequently, for the individuals involved. Faced with these dilemmas, communities often use the sanctions as well as the ties of love and duty at their disposal to induce their members to replace some aspects of their self-interested behavior with cooperation. These sanctions and ties can make the community more materially productive, enhancing its competitive status vis-à-vis other communities.[2]

I define a "community" as a group in which the individual members can trust other members more than they can trust strangers not to "free ride" or "defect" in social dilemmas, not to exploit the members of the group in other ways, and, on occasion, to further the perceived needs of other members of the group rather than their own needs. The trust that so defines community derives from ties of love and duty creating mutual obligation, from mutual vulnerability (including vulnerability to the others' sanctions), from mutual understanding and sympathy. The stronger the community, the stronger are the ties of mutual obligation, vulnerability, understanding, and sympathy.[3]

I define a "democratic" community as one that makes decisions in ways that respect the fundamental equality of each citizen, both as a participant in deliberation and as the bearer of potentially equal power in decisions. The appropriate forms of democracy differ depending on the degree of common interest in the polity. The stronger the community, the less useful are aggregative democratic forms like majority rule, developed to handle fundamentally conflicting interests, and the more useful are deliberative democratic forms developed to promote mutual accommodation and agreement. A democracy that is only minimally a "community," with few ties of mutual obligation, vulnerability, understanding, and sympathy, will experience as common interest little more than the coincidence of material interests. As ties of love and duty lead citizens to make the good of others and the whole their own, the incidence of common interest will increase.[4]

All societies depend for their success partly on the ties of community; democracies do so in their own way. Unlike polities based primarily on traditional or charismatic authority, for example, modern democracies claim part of their legitimacy from an egalitarian, individualistic rationality that assumes underlying conflict. The individualistic formula, "each counts for one and none for more than one," comes into play when the interests of some in the community conflict with the interests of others. Yet accepting this individualistic formula in practice requires motivations fostered by community. The socializing agents of a community must help develop citizen commitment to principles of justice such as the principle that each should count for one.

No democracy, however, can meet the absolute requirements of procedural fairness. No polity can guarantee that every individual will count equally in all decisions. Individual preferences are often ordered such that no one outcome is obviously just.[5] And procedures that are just in one context produce injustice in another. (Societies with many cross-cutting cleavages can support systems of majority rule, because each individual can expect, while losing on one, to win on other issues. But in segmented societies, in which one section of the population will be in a minority on most important issues, democratic justice requires proportional outcomes.) In response to these inevitable imperfections, members of a community develop habits and understandings, ideally subject to critical scrutiny, by which they come to accept certain institutions as sufficiently close approximations to the democratic ideal. Without such understandings, democracy cannot work.[6]

The stronger the community in a democracy, the more likely it is that losers will accept a decision by majority rule not only because it is fair (for it can never be perfectly fair), not only because it is a decision (and they benefit from any decision, compared to civil war), and not only because they believe (in polities with cross-cutting cleavages) that they will find themselves in the majority on other issues, but also because, as in traditional non-democratic communities, mutual ties give community members some interest in the fate of others. Even otherwise zero-sum losses may be perceived as not completely losses if the losers see the winners as part of their community.

Most importantly, many democratic decisions are made not by majority rule or even proportional outcomes but by a process of deliberation that generates mutual accommodation and agreement. This process usually requires a strong leaven of commitment to the common good. The classic writers in the liberal democratic tradition, such as John Locke, James Madison, and J. S. Mill, all assumed that democracy as they understood it could not function without such a commitment, at least on the part of the public's representatives. Communal ties of mutual obligation, vulnerability, understanding, and sympathy help create such commitments, making possible a vast range of democratic decisions based in part on common interest.

## II. Second Prologue: Gratuitous Gendering

### *a) "Women's Experiences"*

I use the phrase "women's experiences" to mean not just experiences that only women have had or that all women have had, but also experiences that women are more likely than men to have had and experiences that have been "gender-coded" in our society as primarily female rather than male.

Much gender coding is gratuitous, unrelated either to functional necessity or, in some cases, even to observable differences in men's and women's actual behavior. But what I call "gratuitous gendering" is a fact of intellectual life, past and present. Recognizing the subtle yet pervasive influence of gratuitous gendering helps explain why ways of thinking that Western society codes as female have had less influence on its intellectual evolution than ways the society codes as male. The pervasive past influence of gendering also helps explain why feminists want "female" experiences and ways of knowing to play a larger and more respected role in political and philosophical discourse.

To say that women's experiences can add to our understanding of democratic community does not imply that women's experiences are essentially different from those of men, only that the frequency of certain experiences differs by gender. A fairly small average difference in experience or behavior can create a large difference in self-image and an even larger difference in social image. When the social meaning of belonging to a group is strong, cultures magnify the group's distinctive features. Members of each group tend to cleave to the images that their common culture prescribes for them. If one group is dominant, it will tend to avoid the language and images the culture attributes to less powerful groups. Subordinate groups will be torn between pride in their own language and images and a desire to emulate the language and images of the dominant group.

### *b) The Magnification of Small Differences*

Gender is more salient in some societies than in others. Yet in every society gender is one of the three or four most salient traits that distinguish people from one another. When children are born, their gender is one of the few traits reported about them. Among adults, the possibility of sexual contact makes almost everyone notice the gender of others. Sex is sexy. Finally, gender is heavily implicated in reproduction, without which societies cannot continue. It is thus not surprising that some societies consider gender truly cosmic—an organizing principle that explains the fundamental relations in the universe.[7]

Human beings use the categories society gives them to make sense of the world. We learn new information through classification schemes that sort the information as we take it in. When information does not easily fit into familiar categories, we usually forget it. And when a category describes our identities as individuals, we pay even more attention than when it describes something unconnected with ourselves.

Children learn that they are boys or girls before they know much else about themselves, often even their last names. Once they know they are boys or girls, they try to learn what "boy" or "girl" means in order to be it better. Because healthy people want to be who they are, children usually value being a boy or a girl long before they understand the full social connotations of this identity. As a result, socialization to gender is not merely a passive response to punishment and reward, but an active, engaged building of positive self-image.[8]

Human beings also remember the vivid.[9] In two normal distributions, or bell-shaped curves, in which the means of the two groups differ only slightly, an observer would probably not notice differences between the groups for most of the people in that distribution. In a field like math, in which boys excel by a small amount, if the bell-shaped curve of boys is positioned only slightly farther along the skill dimension than the bell-shaped curve of girls and if the curves have generally the same shape, almost half the girls will do *better* than half the boys. For most of the students in a given school, gender differences will not be noticeable. But at the extremes, the differences will become more vivid. Boys will predominate noticeably in the upper "tail" of the distribution. This big difference at the tail provides an interpretative framework for differences elsewhere in the distribution. A girl who is doing better than half the boys at math but better than sixty percent in reading will think of herself as "not good at math."

When differences between groups are tied to relations of domination and subordination, the dominant group will also have an interest in magnifying the salience of these differences.

Because gender is so salient, and its salience has been for these reasons and others greatly reinforced, it has in many societies become an organizing feature for the whole universe. In such societies, every identifiable feature of the universe can be assimilated into either Yin or Yang, the female or the male principle. Every noun in the language can be given a gender, making a table feminine and a wall masculine.

The cultures of this world have produced a great deal of

gratuitous gendering ascribing gender definitions and taboos to many features of social and physical life. Anthropologists report that among the Aleut of North America, for example, only women are allowed to butcher animals. But among the Ingalik of North America, only men are allowed to butcher animals. Among the Suku of Africa, only the women can plant crops and only the men can make baskets. But among the Kaffa of the Circum-Mediterranean, only the men can plant crops and only the women can make baskets. Among the Hansa of the Circum-Mediterranean, only the men can prepare skins and only the women can milk. But among the Rwala of the Circum-Mediterranean, only the women can prepare skins and only the men milk.[10] In the culture of the United States, I would venture, we have created similar, though less mutually exclusive, patterns. We code empathy, for example, as women's work, so that the more both men and women are aware that empathy is the object of attention, the more they slide into their cultural roles.

If gender-coding followed a pattern of "separate but equal" and if all the actions of every individual perfectly fit the appropriate gender code, the pervasiveness of gender coding might be only a charming idiosyncrasy of the human race. But men's unequal power has made male practices and traits the norm for "mankind." In the United States, to give only a few examples from Catharine MacKinnon's impressive list, "men's physiology defines most sports, their needs define auto and health insurance coverage, their socially-designed biographies define workplace expectations and successful career patterns."[11] In practice, the labor, traits, and even philosophical terms that are coded as male are usually more highly valued.

### *c) Gendered Meanings in the Concept of Community*

In the United States today, the term "community" is not gender-free. Its two components, local geographical rootedness and emotional ties, have female connotations. Local communities are the province of women far more than are state or national affairs. Women organize, run, and staff many activities of local communities, which as a cause and consequence feel close to home, almost domestic. Even in the formal political realm, from which women have been excluded in almost every traditional society, local communities in the United States have allowed women the most access. Considerably before women won the vote nationally, several states and localities allowed women to vote in local school elections; today, the percentage of women in city and town councils and the percentage of women mayors far exceeds the percentage of women in state and national legislatures or executive positions. In the recent past, the gendered division of labor insured that when men earned the family wage, and particularly when they worked away from the community, women became the caretakers of local community life.

An even more salient component of "community" involves the quality of human relations.[12] In the United States today, women have particular responsibility for intimate human relations. Talcott Parsons and Robert Bales codified the reigning gender schema in 1955 when they wrote that in households men generally took the more "instrumental" roles and women the more "expressive" roles, maintaining "integrative" relations among the household members.[13] Mothers and wives still tend disproportionately to take on the family's "emotion work" and "kinwork," fostering the relations of connection.[14] One recent review of psychological research noted that the two orientations it studied "have been labeled *masculine* and *feminine, instrumental* and *expressive,* and *assertive* and *communal.*"[15] In this analysis, "communal" is almost synonymous with "feminine."

As the triad "liberty, equality, fraternity" has evolved into "liberty, equality, community," the third element has experienced a gender evolution from male to female.[16] In this evolution, the term has lost legitimacy in a way that affects the balance between individual and community. As a consequence, those who today urge renewed emphasis in liberal individualism on ties of connection in the social world and on the possibility of common interests in politics have to fight not only the well-founded fears of those who see in any move toward commonality the potential for domination, but also, more insidiously, the subtle association of connection and commonality with womanliness. Pamela Conover suggests, for example, that among political scientists eager to be seen as tough-minded, altruism has come to seem sissified.[17] It seems likely that several components of community—the legitimation of intimate connection, emotional ties, particularity, and common interests—suffer the same disability.

In making the case for ties of love and duty, for mutual vulnerability, and for the possibility of common interest in democratic politics, proponents of democratic community are hampered by the female connotations of love, certain kinds of duty, vulnerability, and even common interest. Some feminist theorists have therefore attempted a radical revaluation, recognizing the gender connotations of these elements of community and insisting on their worth. As the next section demonstrates, these theorists draw heavily from women's experiences of intimate human "connection." A later section explores the ways women's experiences of unequal power reveal the potential oppression, blatant and subtle, inherent in communal ties.

## III. Connection

Empathy, the quality of being able to put oneself emotionally in another's place, exemplifies the process through which gender differences take on magnified social significance. In the United States, both men and women see women as intuitive, good at understanding others, and sensitive to personal or emotional appeals. Empirical research on empathy shows, however, that gender differences in empathy vary dramatically according to the measure used. The more the person being measured knows that empathy is being measured, the more a gender difference appears. When psychologists try to take physiological measurements of empathy—such as galvanic skin responses on seeing others receive an electric shock; skin conductance, blood pressure, heart rate, or pulse on seeing or hearing newborn infants cry; or sweating while seeing another take a test—they usually find no significant difference between women and men or between girls and boys. When psychologists tell stories to children of other children experiencing happiness, sadness, fear, and anger, and ask after each story, "How do you *feel?*" "Tell me how you *feel?*" or "How did that story make you *feel?*"—a procedure that might lead the child to think that responsive feelings were being measured—either girls score higher than boys on empathy when the experimenter is female and boys score higher than girls when the experimenter is male, or else the differences are not significant. Yet when either children or adults are asked to fill out a questionnaire asking individuals to describe themselves with statements like "I tend to get emotionally involved with a friend's problems" and "Seeing people cry upsets me," the difference between males and females is consistently significant and in the expected direction. On these measures, females always appear more empathetic. The differences are larger among adults than children, and larger still among those who rate themselves high on other measures of stereotypical "femininity" and "masculinity."[18] The more the person knows what is being measured, the older the person is, and the more attached to gender stereotypes, the stronger the relations between gender and empathy.

Gender differences on other themes involving intimate connection may well follow the same pattern as gender differences in empathy. If research on nurturance, care, and other correlates of intimate connection parallels that on empathy, the largest differences will be obtained from female experimenters, fully socialized adults, stimuli likely to elicit empathetic-nurturance responses from women, and clear cues in the stimuli that empathy, nurturance, and care are the subject of investigation. This pattern would not make the differences less "real." When women define themselves and are defined as more attuned to empathy or intimate connection, specific practices draw from and reinforce that connection. Women allow themselves, for example, to demonstrate their empathy openly. Girls and women look more for emotion and expression in their friendships, centering their conversations with friends more on discussions of relations, whereas men develop more instrumental or goal-oriented friendships, based more on shared activities.[19] These gender-coded practices then have effects on the way both genders view the political and social world.

The gender-coding of intimate connection has had a long history in American feminist political argument. The first wave of feminism evolved the idea that women were likely to act more nurturantly not only in the home but also in political life. Six years before women won the vote, Charlotte Perkins Gilman's classic novel *Herland* envisioned a utopia composed only of women, whose communal form of maternal nurturance produced a politics of loving cooperation.[20] Particularly toward the end of the struggle for women's suffrage, arguments for the vote stressed the virtues women would bring to the polity from their experiences as wives and mothers.[21]

The second wave of the feminist movement almost from the beginning incorporated interest in the ways that "women's culture" could be more caring and less rapacious than men's. A 1970 movement article on women's culture quoted Marlene Dixon's derivation of the special skills of "intuition" and "empathy" from women's relative powerlessness, and three years later Jane Alpert attributed to the experience of motherhood the empathy, intuitiveness, and protective feelings toward others of the developing feminist culture.[22]

Related ideas entered the academy a decade or so later. In 1976, the psychologist Dorothy Dinnerstein argued that it is harder for women than men to separate themselves from their mothers.[23] Her work, and in 1978 Nancy Chodorow's greatly more influential *The Reproduction of Mothering,* set the stage through psychoanalytic speculation for academic feminists to recognize and celebrate women's "connection." Chodorow ascribed what she called "women's relatedness and men's denial of relation" to the male child's need to differentiate himself from his mother and create a separate, oppositional, entity. Although for both boys and girls mothers represent lack of autonomy, for boys dependence on the mother and identification with her also represent the not-masculine; a boy must "reject dependence and deny attachment and identification."[24] "The basic feminine sense of self," Chodorow concluded, "is connected to the world, the basic masculine sense of self is separate."[25]

The theme moved into philosophy when in 1980 Sara Ruddick drew attention to the strengths of "maternal thinking,"[26] and in 1981 Sheila Ruth concluded that male philosophers tended to shun or show contempt for female connection: "Flight from woman is flight from feeling, from experiencing, from the affective; it is flight into distance."[27]

In 1982, Carol Gilligan's *In a Different Voice* adopted much of Chodorow's analysis, arguing that "since masculinity is defined through separation while femininity is defined through attachment, male gender identity is threatened by intimacy while female gender identity is threatened by separation. Thus males tend to have difficulty with relationships, while females tend to have problems with individuation."[28] Gilligan's investigations of women's reactions to moral dilemmas led her to conclude that women define themselves "in a context of human relationship" and judge themselves according to their ability to care.[29] Chodorow and Gilligan inspired an outpouring of theoretical writing, including Nel Noddings's 1984 argument that the approach to ethics through law and principle "is the approach of the detached one, the father," whereas the caring approach, the "approach of the mother," is "rooted in receptivity, relatedness, and responsiveness."[30]

I suggest that feminist analyses of maternal and other forms of intimate connection can generate new insights into democratic community. Yet the relation of these insights to actual differences in experience between American men and women is not clear. Chodorow's psychoanalytic theory, although intellectually suggestive, remains to be tested empirically. Gilligan's finding—that in the United States today women are more likely than men to adopt a morality based on preserving relations rather than one based on individual rights—appears primarily among the highly educated, because it is primarily in this class that men distinctively adopt a "rights" or "justice" orientation to which Gilligan's "care" or "relationships" orientation can be compared.[31] Even within this group, we do not yet know how large are the differences between men and women, and whether they might not, like differences in empathy, appear only or most dramatically when the persons being interviewed have some idea of what is being measured. In the population as a whole, the differences are unlikely to be large, since several studies cannot find any difference.[32]

Research since Gilligan's *In a Different Voice* has made it clear that even when no differences appear between men and women on the dimensions of relationships and rights, when researchers describe two orientations to moral conflict, one based on relationships and one on rights,[33] those men and women distinguish between the two orientations in a way that fits traditional gender stereotypes. Both men and women tend to rate Gilligan's care orientation as more feminine and the rights orientation as more masculine.[34] If the American public in the late twentieth century codes connection as female and separation as male, it would not be surprising if the women and feminist theorists of that society tended to make the value of connection their "own."

I find it most useful to treat this literature not as demonstrating any large difference between the actual behavior or even the normative orientations of most men and women in American society, but as drawing attention to the deeply gender-coded nature in this society of the dichotomy of separation versus connection. It is not simply that some groups of modern American women seem in fact to be somewhat more deeply embedded in intimate relationships than some groups of men. It is also, more importantly, that the cultural reification and exaggeration of these gender differences in behavior has influenced popular and philosophical thinking about the various possibilities in human relations.

Anglo-American democratic theory, for example, often portrays the polity as constructed by free and unencumbered individuals who associate to promote self-interest. Such a theory cannot easily draw inspiration from or use metaphors derived from the typically "female" experiences of empathetic interdependence, compassion, and personal vulnerability.

Drawing from experiences of intimate connection, on the other hand, makes it easier to envision preserving individuality and furthering community at the same time. These experiences help generate a vision of democratic community in which autonomy derives from social nurturance, some obligations are given, communal ties derive from emotional connection as well as from principle, the local and particular has legitimately a special moral weight, and a leaven of common interest makes possible a politics based on persuasion as well as power. I consider each of these ideas briefly, pointing out how they draw on metaphors and experiences relatively untapped in Western political discourse, and suggesting either problems or directions for further exploration.

*a) Autonomy*

In classic liberal theory, Jennifer Nedelsky argues, autonomy is "achieved by erecting a wall (of rights) between the individual and those around him." An understanding of autonomy based on more typically female experiences would make connection a prerequisite for autonomy:

> If we ask ourselves what actually enables people to be autonomous, the answer is not isolation, but relationships—with parents, teachers, friends, loved ones—that provide the support and guidance necessary for the development and experience of autonomy. The most promising model, symbol or metaphor for autonomy is not therefore property, but childrearing.[35]

In a parallel vein, Virginia Held writes that if we begin our theorizing about society with the social tie between mothering person and child instead of with isolated, rational contractors "the starting condition is an enveloping tie, and the problem is individuating oneself." For both parent and child, "the progression is from society to greater individuality rather than from self-sufficient individuality to contractual ties."[36]

The easily accessible idea that autonomy requires nurturance in a web of relationships undermines the "either/or" character of parts of the individualism/communitarian debate. It does not require claiming that a source in nurturance exhausts the meanings of autonomy,[37] that the idea is in all respects new,[38] or that all childrearing produces autonomy.[39] Nor does it require claiming that the ideal of motherhood is impervious to abuse.

Drawing from an idealized version of motherhood to enrich our vision of the potential relation between individual and community is no less subject to abuse as a cover for unequal power relations than is drawing from idealized models of property or freely contracting individuals. As with all idealized models, we need to ask whether the everyday experience on which the model is based holds in it material from which to draw a critique of the model itself, and whether the norms inherent in the ideal lend themselves to misuse less than other ideals.

At least in the United States today, the experience of mothering evokes an active and conscious critique of the potential in that practice for suppressing individuality. Contracting, experienced primarily through participation in the labor force, does not as often put the parties in the kind of sustained and intimate relation that makes the information on which a critique may be based as easily accessible. While the history of any patriarchal society indicates that familial models can powerfully obfuscate individual interests, access to a language of critique stemming from the image of a "bad father" or "bad mother" is easily available to all.

Moreover, in a model of community based on idealized maternity, the members of the group take as one of their primary responsibilities the growth into individuality of each member. The potential vices in motherhood—attempts at total control or total unity—are obvious. But the model itself reflects the simple impossibility of these goals. It is not possible for mother and child to be one. The child always grows up; the child is always different; the child is dynamic, not static, and cannot in adulthood remain easily under the power of the mother. No model of motherhood can escape this fact, and good models embrace it. This feature of the maternal model, with its in-built assurance that each is in the end separate as well as connected, should make this model preferable to others for those who see potential totalitarian dominance or mob rule in the communitarian reaction to liberal individualism.[40] A nuanced understanding of the nurturing ties usually coded as maternal makes it easier to see how the members of a polity require nurturance and mutual support, varying greatly by the context and the individual's current needs and always subject to criticism, from communities constituted by mutual obligation, vulnerability, understanding, and sympathy.

*b) Nonvoluntary Obligation*

The communities in which citizens must make democratic decisions are in some respects given. Although in our mobile and cosmopolitan era most of us can "shop" for geographical and workplace communities we like, the demands of geography, work, and birth also land us in communities with characteristics not totally of our choosing. Ideally, the democratic process should help citizens work through the obligations embedded in the communities in which they live and work, testing those obligations against the selves that develop in the course of living and participating in the relevant democracies. An understanding of the obligations of community based in an evolving process of public and private decision makes these obligations manifold and complex, partly formally "political" and partly not, and as dynamic as a parent's relation with a child. Such obligations are always a mixture of the given and the voluntary, moving back and forth between these poles over the lifetime of the individual and the community, depending on obligation and context.

Theories of obligation based in liberty, such as that of Thomas Hobbes, see all genuine obligations as in some way voluntarily contracted. Theories based in justice stress the natural duty to act justly. Theories based in the experience of nonvoluntary connections add to these forms of obligation—obligations that are neither voluntary nor just or unjust. A mother may think "I *must* help this baby," at moments when "I want to," "I contracted to," and "It is just to" do not accurately describe the sense of obligation she feels.[41]

Some feminist theorists explicitly link a greater consciousness of involuntary obligation to women's greater embeddedness in intimate relationships. Nancy Hirschmann argues, for example, that voluntarist liberal consent theory, based on independence as separation, rests on the principle that "one has control over one's bonds and connections because one creates those bonds."[42] Her own "feminist model," by contrast, "beginning with connection, tries to determine how to carve out a space for the self without violating care." The freedom that is created by "stepping away from, or out of, obligations" must be achieved, and justified with good reasons; it is not a given.[43]

The traditional philosophical literature on nonvoluntary obligation, which produced the "Good Samaritan" dilemmas[44] and the distinction between duty and obligation,[45] has been revived by recent communitarians.[46] Feminists can add women's experiences in negotiating the meaning and demands of given obligations. Understanding how to incorporate given obligations into a fundamentally voluntarist theory of democracy requires drawing both from typically male experiences, like the wartime demand that one risk one's life, and from typically female experiences, like the occasionally life-consuming obligations to children, parents, and kin.[47]

Nancy Hirschmann argues that "if an obligation is given, it does not really make sense to ask how it can arise."[48] But because of the role of power in creating obligation, both women and men are best served by theories of obligation, to the community or to individuals, that are open to critical scrutiny. Women, and all groups with less than equal power, cannot simply accept all the obligations they are "given" without asking how they arose.

When the communitarians Michael Sandel and Alasdair MacIntyre advance the idea of nonvoluntary obligations, they do not explore in depth the possible sources of obligation beyond justice and promising. Intuitionists get us no further than that what we "know" to be true must be confirmed by critical scrutiny. MacIntyre and Rawls, in addition, suggest that obligations of greater and less importance might be attached to socially defined roles and practices, so that for example, a bricklayer might have some obligation to be a good bricklayer, a mother some larger obligation to be, or try to be, a good mother, and a citizen of a given community some obligation to support that community. The "ought" in these cases would derive from the purpose or function that the incumbent of the role is traditionally expected to perform.[49]

The more one explores the potential sources of obligations, however, the harder it becomes to escape all voluntarism. Most real obligations have many sources, including some form of voluntary act. An obligation attached to a role is certainly more binding if one has freely chosen to become, say, a bricklayer or a mother. For a non-voluntary mother, the obligation to the child may be no more than the obligation from natural duty on anyone who has it in his or her power to harm or help an extremely vulnerable human being. For children, born without their consent into particular families and communities, the obligation to care for parents and other members of the community may consist of no more than a combination of the obligation to reciprocate benefits received and the obligation of those strategically placed to protect the vulnerable.[50]

In the domestic realm, the content of given obligations is at least to some degree negotiable. Obligation in families emerges from a process of mutual soundings, trials that end in partial success or failure, and advance or retreat through nuance as well as overt conflict on several often unspecified and simultaneous fronts. This continuous process of negotiation magnifies and diminishes both feelings of obligation and the obligations themselves, solidifying or moderating the norms of what ought to be expected, even creating or eliminating mutual "given" obligations. This familial process matches the ways most obligations are formed in political communities better than do derivations from contract or abstract justice.[51] Through negotiation, the given becomes to some extent voluntary, even if the quality of voluntarism is at times more akin to handing over one's wallet to a mugger than to choosing between a concert or a movie on Saturday evening.

Moreover, obligations attached to roles, the community's conceptions of one's natural duties, and even consciously chosen obligations are structured by social power relations, which one may later conclude are unjust. To be considered binding against one's own contrary desires or interests, any duty or obligation should be able to withstand critical scrutiny, employing emotions and principles drawn from religion, natural law, hypothetical agreement, utilitarianism, empirical understanding (including an understanding of the relevant power relations), gut conviction, and other sources.[52] To the degree that one's obligations withstand scrutiny, and to the degree that in the process of building an identity one reaches out and makes those obligations one's own, the obligations become less "given" and more voluntary.

When the losers in majority rule feel some obligation to support the winners and when citizens feel some obligation to make the good of the community their own, these obligations have a "given" component, for one often did not choose to be obligated to the specific others in one's political community. If we allow our experience of "domestic" given obligations to inform our understanding of "political" ones, we can begin to understand the processes by which those obligations can be rejected in whole or in part, and how they can become more willed, or more one's own without conscious willing, in the course of each individual's life in several interlocking and separate, perhaps conflicting, communities.

*c) The Moral Emotions*

The mother's "I must" grows not only out of cognitive conviction but out of moral emotions, psychological feelings, and impulses. So too in democratic community, the bonds of mutual obligation, vulnerability, understanding, and sympathy that lead its members to cooperate with one another grow as much from emotional identification as from rational, principled commitment.

"Emotion" and "reason" are today strongly gender-coded, at least among the college-educated. And although the association of "emotional" qualities with women and "rational" qualities with men is almost world-wide, this association has particular strength in the English-speaking world, especially the United States.[53] The strength of this gender-coding gives feminist theorists a special interest in understanding the role of the emotions in creating democratic community.

In moral theory, feminist theorists have recently urged a revitalization of the sympathy-based theories of David Hume and others of the Scottish Enlightenment, as against the reason-based theories of Immanuel Kant.[54] Kant had maintained, in his 1785 *Foundations of the Metaphysics of Morals,* that only actions done from duty, not sympathy, had "true moral worth." It is true, he conceded, that

> there are many minds so sympathetically constituted that, without any other motive of vanity or self-interest, they find pleasure in spreading joy around them, and can take delight in the satisfaction of others as far as it is their own work. But I maintain that in such a case an action of this kind however proper, however amiable it may be, has nevertheless no true moral worth, but is on a level with other inclinations.

If an inclination, such as a sympathetic inclination, is "happily directed to that which is in fact of public utility and accordant with duty," then it "deserves praise and encouragement, but not esteem."[55] More than twenty years earlier, Kant had revealed the "gender subtext" of this distinction:

> Women will avoid the wicked not because it is unright, but only because it is ugly.... Nothing of duty, nothing of compulsion, nothing of obligation!... They do something only because it pleases them.... I hardly believe that the fair sex is capable of principles.[56]

Today, feminist theorists argue that the person who acts spontaneously and emotionally, on impulse, from a personal identity as someone who wants to make another happy, is as moral and deserves as much moral credit ("esteem" as well as "praise and encouragement") as the person who acts cognitively and thoughtfully, though possibly grudgingly, from duty.[57] Their debate with the Kantians draws attention to the restrictive elision of the dichotomies "reason/emotion" and "male/female." If developing democratic community requires developing the capacity for sympathy, men as well as women and the parents of boys as well as girls must consider developing the sympathetic capacities an important part of civic education. The goal is not to substitute sympathy for justice, but to integrate the two in ways that give more weight to the cultivation of sympathetic understanding.

Susan Moller Okin points out that John Rawls argues toward the end of *A Theory of Justice* that a just society requires the development of empathetic sensitivity in the family. The traditional gendered division of labor, she suggests, may have led him to separate reason from feeling (and focus on reason) in the outline and central exposition of his theory while relying on their integration in the theory's development.[58] Liberal democratic theories that begin with fully grown, independent, rational citizens similarly assume the emotional, characterological prerequisites for community that must develop in part in the family.[59] Theories of democracy based entirely on rational self-interest will not work in practice without a non-self-interested leaven of public spirit that derives not only from rational commitment but also from sympathy.[60] Theories that see democracy as rational deliberation will not work in practice without citizens' emotional capacities to understand their own and others' needs.[61]

Sympathy is by no means always good; nor are the emotions, benevolent or malevolent, sure guides to correct action. But the traditional neglect of emotion as compared to reason or rational calculation in the study of philosophy and political science makes it harder to understand the costs and benefits of community to democracy.

*d) Particularity*

Although it is possible to think of a community of all humankind, the word "community," with its connotations of greater than usual mutual obligation, suggests a unit smaller than the planet, more narrow than humankind. "Community," in most cases, entails particularity.

To argue, as most democratic theorists do, for decisions by one person/one vote on a scale smaller than all humanity requires justifying the decisional boundaries.[62] Such justifications are impossible without invoking some notion of community, and consequently of particularistic obligations.

If democratic community rests in part on particularistic obligations, these might be justified in at least three ways. First, psychologically we feel more responsibility to those closest to us. Although on an extreme Kantian reading that feeling may be irrelevant to our moral duty, the feminist project of giving moral status to the emotions begins to justify favored treatment of some through the mutual emotions engendered by continuing relationship.[63] If we recognize more than one legitimate source of obligation—justified both through principled commitment and emotional ties—we can then begin to envision a world of interlocking spheres of greater and lesser mutual obligation, in which boundaries, though at times set by law to settle certain questions by administrative fiat, are usually in practice negotiable. If communities are groups in which people can trust one another more than they can trust a stranger, then families, friendships, workplaces, towns, ethnic groups, states, nations, international alliances, and humanity all become communities of mutual trust, obligation, vulnerability, understanding, and sympathy in varying degrees.[64] As members of more than one community, individuals must negotiate their identities and obligations with themselves and the other members of those communities, taking into account emotional ties as well as rational commitments.

Second, our obligations to the members of more proximate communities might be constituted, as Michael Walzer once suggested, by the implicit promises created through interaction.[65]

Third, these proximate obligations might be justified by utilitarian functionality, on the grounds that a system based on heightened obligation to those closest works more efficiently than a system of universal obligation, precisely because it is congruent with desire.[66] These two last arguments provide universalistic justifications for particularity.[67]

As we shall see, aspects of the normative mandate to see and credit particularity inspire not only feminists who promote connection but also those who warn against communal domination. Iris Marion Young, Seyla Benhabib, and Martha Minow contend that the universalistic ideal of impartiality entails treating everyone according to the same rules, thus ignoring difference and seeking to "eliminate otherness."[68] Particularity in their analysis entails fostering, noticing, and respecting difference.

### *e) Persuasion Based on Common Interests*

Finally, some feminists who write from the experience of connection emphasize the possibilities of common interest in politics, making possible decisions based in persuasion rather than power. This approach breaks radically from the dominant contemporary definition of politics as power.

As early as 1818, Hannah Mather Crocker stated in print that persuasion was a particularly female art, which may have been a common perception.[69] By the time of women's suffrage, feminists such as Charlotte Perkins Gilman espoused a vision of women's approach to politics that eschewed power.[70] In the mid-twentieth century, a woman, Mary Parker Follett, invented the concepts of "integration" (what some today call "win/win solutions"), and "power with" rather than "power over."[71] In the second wave of the women's movement, Nancy Hartsock suggested that feminism could lead to the "redefinition of political power itself" as not domination but "energy, strength, and effective interaction."[72] Kathy Ferguson similarly urged women to use the "values that are structured into women's experience—caretaking, nurturance, empathy, connectedness" to create new organizational models not dependent on domination.[73] Although these formulations do not deny that power, defined as getting people to do something by threat of sanction or force,[74] plays a legitimate role in human relations, they stress the generalizability to democratic politics of relations based on persuasion. Legitimate persuasion in turn requires common interests, that derive from the ties of community—mutual obligation, vulnerability, understanding, and sympathy—as well as from the simple coincidence of material interests.

Women's frequent stress on persuasion is probably related to the "consultative" style of leadership that, in the United States today, women are more likely to adopt than men. The researchers who find this difference in study after study speculate that gender socialization, organizational positions of lesser power, bias against female leaders, and the greater social skills of women may all contribute to women's more persuasive, consultative style.[75]

If it is not to be manipulative, however, persuasion requires a common interest between the leaders and the led. Leaders committed to the use of persuasion rather than power may exaggerate the degree of common interest on a given issue, and avoid the necessity of exercising power, that is, threats of sanction or force, on issues involving irreconcilable conflict. Yet democratic politics also requires handling irreconcilable conflicts through fair procedures that often involve forcing some, on any given issue, to conform to a policy not in their interests. As the next section shows, feminist theorists who warn against communal domination are particularly aware of the potential, in a politics that works primarily through persuasion, of more powerful groups assuming a common interest or convincing the less powerful of a common interest that does not in fact exist.

## IV. Unequal Power and Democracy

Among women, the experience of unequal power is as universal as the experience of connection. Accordingly, for every positive aspect of community into which the experience of intimate connection can give further insight, the experience of pervasive inequality provides a caution. A social role that prescribes empathy, for example, can at the same time proscribe a legitimate concern for self-interest. A social role that prescribes caring can make the carer asymmetrically vulnerable. A social role that prescribes particularity, deriving from bonds that go beyond justice, can eliminate the protection and the moral direction of justice. A social role that prescribes persuasion can make the bearer unfamiliar with, repulsed by, or blind to power.

Women have experienced a long historical legacy of unequal power, particularly in the public realm. Believed incapable of fully human reasoning, barred from owning property, vigorously excluded from the political arena in almost every human society, and until recently deprived of the vote even in Western democracies, women have long been denied equal power, often on the grounds that their interests were the same as the men who exercised power, specifically their husbands and fathers.

Yet women have had, and still have, a unique relation to the class that has benefitted from this unequal power. Many women, no matter how active as feminists, love or have loved individual men—their fathers, their sons, their male lovers or husbands. Moreover, many men love or have loved women, sometimes, at least in the modern era, with a genuine belief in the underlying equality of the relations and sometimes with a strong conscious commitment to recreating in the existing social and political world the equality they see "underneath." As a consequence, women, more than most groups that struggle to redress inequalities of power, have come to learn the subtle as well as the obvious forms that unequal power can take, and its private as well as public faces. Of the many forms of subtle and private power that feminist scholarship and theory have begun to expose, I give just two examples.

*a) Subtle Power*

One subtle political inequality that particularly affects democratic community emerges in speech. In the United States today, girls and women speak noticeably less than boys and men in mixed settings, both in private and in public.[76] In New England town meetings, women speak half as often as men. Female state legislators speak less than their male counterparts.[77] When women speak, moreover, they adopt more linguistic usages that connote uncertainty.[78] In public meetings, they tend to give information or ask questions rather than stating opinions or initiating controversy. In private, they submit to male interruptions.[79] Since at least the fifth century B.C., when Sophocles warned that "a modest silence is a woman's crown," women have been disciplined by proverbs that criticize their talking.[80]

Training for listening and supportive speech is disempowering. But because this training is also vital for a politics based on persuasion rather than power,[81] women and feminist theorists face the difficult but urgent task of disentangling the evil from the good. The double edge and the subtlety of many forms of unequal power explains the attraction of some feminist thinkers to certain of the writings of Michel Foucault, particularly his concept of "capillary" power, power that carries the lifeblood of the system into the smallest part of the body.[82]

The problem is that the very obligations, vulnerabilities, understandings, and sympathies that make members of a community engage in acts of social cooperation against their narrow self-interest will in many cases subtly or unsubtly privilege the most powerful. If, for example, a democracy relies on face-to-face or consensual procedures to maintain its ties of community, those procedures will usually discriminate subtly against women and other less powerful groups.

On the level of the small group, democracies can fight these subtle biases against women's speech with institutional innovations like breaking into smaller like-minded groups for discussion, rationing speaking time in some way, or making space for the patterns of non-dominant cultures.[83] On the national level, activists and writers in democratic politics have long realized not only that power over decisions in any existing democratic polity is highly unequal but also that the broader process of democratic deliberation is permeated with large, though often subtle and interstitial, inequalities.[84] The women's movement worldwide fights the subtle inequalities of speech by bringing women together in their own groups to speak, decide, make allies, and strategize, usually without the presence of men. The movement also relies heavily on women coming together in domestic contexts. Outside formal politics women find out from one another how their common and divergent experiences let them shape new preferences, new underlying goals and interests, and ultimately new political identities. Precisely because the formal political arena will not usually advance agendas that appropriately address the concerns of non-dominant groups, members of those groups often deliberate in a way that best serves their political needs in associations formed to address traditionally "private" or "domestic" concerns. Just as Marx predicted factories would bring workers together in ways that fomented revolution, so today health, credit, and cooperative shopping associations bring women together across the world in ways that undermine the political dominance of men.

### b) Private Power

Sexual intercourse is an archetypically private act. Yet patterns of sexual interaction encode and maintain patterns of unequal power that reverberate far beyond the private realm. Being raped or battered, typically a woman's experience, is a private act that reflects and reinforces public power.

Catharine MacKinnon and Andrea Dworkin point out that dominance is intertwined with heterosexual activity.[85] Marital rape is still legal in some states, partly because sexual possession, by force if necessary, is still often considered a husband's right. Looking at the power implicitly or explicitly involved in sexuality opens up to political analysis an arena previously off limits. As Catherine MacKinnon puts it, the quintessentially private sphere of sexuality "is to feminism what work is to marxism: that which is most one's own, yet most taken away."[86]

Physical violence expresses this private power. Women and children are the primary victims of private battering.[87] Women's traditional primary responsibility for childrearing produces unequal power in the economic marketplace, which in turn produces unequal power in the family. That unequal power results not only in battering but also, in countries subject to food shortages, in inadequate nutrition and higher mortality for female children.[88]

On a less dramatic level, feminists have also begun to investigate the power imbalances inherent in many small, repeated, private acts—the clothing the two genders use, their hairstyles, makeup, laughter, and their attitudes toward food or their own bodies. For women, a significant part of the struggle of self-construction is trying to parse out which of the gendered elements of private, everyday life they want to make their own, as authentic expressions of their individuality, love of life, and sexual desire, and which ones they must discard as whispering to them, every time they take a step or look in a mirror, a message, often the "community's" message, of fundamental inadequacy and inequality.

In developing this analysis, feminist theorists can ally, however uneasily, with Foucault and with the anthropologists and political scientists who have developed in their study of exploited populations the concept of "resistance."[89] Resistance describes any act, no matter how small or private, by a member of a subordinate class that is intended either to mitigate or deny claims made by superordinate classes or to advance its own claims against those classes.[90] To the degree that any community is constructed from ties of mutual obligation, vulnerability, understanding, and sympathy, the struggle against domination will often be a struggle against the obligations imposed by, vulnerabilities exploited by, understandings created by, and sympathies directed toward the dominant classes. The struggle against those classes in the private and public realms will therefore become a struggle against that community, often by creating communities of resistance among the subordinates. If a dominant community is not to overwhelm its members, its social organization must facilitate the creation of communities of resistance.

*c) The Critique of Community*

Their experiences of the pervasive effects of subtle and private inequalities alert many feminist theorists to the dangers of "community."

On the broadest front, Iris Young writes that the very ideal of community "devalues and denies difference."[91] Although actual communities differ on this dimension, some explicitly valuing diversity, all communities nevertheless generate norms that some of their members cannot meet. Indeed, in a world dominated by men, when communities are precisely the given, involuntary communities in which relations are most like the maternal relation, they are most likely to generate norms that women cannot meet—norms, for example, that it is better to be a man.[92]

Looking at some of the constituent features of community, Susan Okin documents the deep gender inequalities in the traditions on which Alasdair MacIntyre relies in his defense of a tradition-based morality of the virtues. Contemplating the shared understandings on which Michael Walzer relies to conclude that different spheres have different criteria for justice, she points out that oppressors and oppressed often disagree fundamentally, generating out of the linguistic meanings they share two irreconcilable accounts of what is just.[93]

Recent understandings of community focus on language in a way that feminists find telling. Michael Sandel writes that a community "in the constitutive sense" is marked by "a common vocabulary of discourse and a background of implicit practices and understandings."[94] Charles Taylor adds that the least alienated human life is lived in communities "where the norms and ends expressed in the public life of a society are the most important ones by which its members define their identity as human beings,"[95] suggesting that these norms, and the institutions and practices that embody them, function "as a kind of language" that is necessary for human interaction, but "can only grow in and be sustained by a community."[96]

For feminists, the analogy to language conjures up the way Western languages reiterate the message of male as norm and female as other. The "common vocabulary" is not neutral among those who use it. Beyond male and female, feminists point out that any word implies, as words must, the dominant or majority subcategory in the category covered by that word, thereby excluding by implication the less powerful or the minority. The use of "men" to mean "human beings" theoretically includes women, except that the word "men" has connotations and establishes expectations that exclude women. Similarly, the word "women" theoretically includes African-American women, except that because white women comprise in the United States the great majority of women, the word in that context has connotations that exclude experiences characterizing the majority of African-American women. In the same way, the phrase "African-American women" implies "heterosexual African American women," and the phrase "heterosexual African-American women" implies "able-bodied heterosexual African-American women."[97] Each category, conjuring up its dominant or majority referent, implicitly excludes those whose experiences differ from that majority.

Community dominance through language thus cannot be avoided. It requires conscious effort to include in one's thinking those who do not fit the dominant or majority image, particularly when the interests of members of that group conflict with the dominant group's interests. Because we must use words, and cannot maintain in consciousness the potentially infinite regress of the implicitly unincluded, we need to recognize that all communication encodes power, and be sensitive both to the worst abuses and to those who bring that power to the surface for conscious criticism.

The feminist sensitivity to the subtle and private forms of communal exclusion may seem to the more powerful somewhat strained. I have argued here that this sensitivity is based on a serious evaluation of the potentially far-reaching cumulative effects of a constellation of large and small violations of self, acts of domination, and inequalities, often hidden from overt public discourse in the realms of private behavior. Women's experience heightens feminists' sensitivity to the problems of the excluded, a sensitivity further heightened by Black, Asian, Latin American, Near Eastern, and African feminists, who point out in racial and international contexts how easily the language and practices of the dominant group exclude and subordinate the less culturally, socially, and politically powerful.[98]

## V. Women's Perspectives on Community

### *a) Drawing from the Personal for the Political*

The spheres of formal government and personal life, crossed with the politics of power and the politics of persuasion, produce four cells. The cell that combines formal government and power needs no further explanation. It is the cell of traditional pluralist democracy. The cell that combines personal life and persuasion also needs no further explanation. It is the cell of the traditional idealized family. Feminist theory, however, directs us to the two least examined cells. Combining formal government with persuasion produces a theory of democracy that assumes the possibility of creating on some issues a common good. Combining the personal sphere with power produces a theory of interstitial power that manifests itself, for women, in pervasive sexual subordination.

I have drawn from women's experiences in the familiar sphere of intimate and domestic connection to argue that the formal politics of democratic community must use persuasion as well as power. I have drawn from women's experiences in the less familiar sphere of private power to argue that the formal politics of democratic community will be permeated by subtle and "private" forms of domination. For formal politics, this analysis gets its edge from infusing the formally political with the personal. Crossing the line that divides the personal from the political also frequently means resisting a sharp distinction between moral and political obligation, and between moral and political theory more broadly.

Simply to dissolve the governmental into the domestic, or define as "public" every human group, would deprive language and thought of important meanings and connections. This is not usually the goal of those who develop the feminist insight that "the personal is political."[99] Rather, the aim of feminists who focus on "connection" is to release from the realm of taboo, for incorporation into political discourse, a host of experiences and referents related to intimate personal connection. The aim of feminists who focus on subordination is to point out how closely and subtly linked are private and public forms of power.

No borrowing from one experience to another can be perfect. Childrearing and some forms of sexuality, for example, involve an intimacy that renders moot or mutes many outstanding political questions, that have to do quintessentially with relations among relative strangers.[100] But it would be a mistake to make impermeable and mutually exclusive the categories of household and polis.[101] If we assume that neither conceptual end of a spectrum running from the total assimilation of every individual in every other to the total alienation of each from all can support what we think of as "politics," intimate personal life, by standing relatively close to the end of assimilation, suggests various models of human relations, with their attendant problems, from which any theory of political community should be able to borrow. As medieval and non-Western patriarchies have drawn heavily from family relations in conceiving their nondemocratic polities, contemporary theories should be able to draw from other forms of private relations in conceiving democracy. When nineteenth-century feminists suggested "organized mother love" or "social housekeeping" as ideals of democratic political organization, their borrowing from the experience of family relations was no different in kind from the ancient Greek borrowing of "civic friendship" from the personal relation of friends.

### *b) Maximalism versus Minimalism*

In drawing political insight from various realms of private life, this essay embodies a tension, but not a logical contradiction, between "minimalist" and "maximalist" approaches to gender differences. Pointing out the extent of gratuitous gendering in every society suggests a "minimalist" approach to gender differences. This approach, to which I subscribe, holds that although men and women undoubtedly differ in biological characteristics like the ability to give birth and upper body strength, technological advances in contraception, childrearing, and material production have significantly reduced the social importance of these differences in the last several centuries.

Much of the remaining social stress on gender differences is "gratuitous," resting on differences or magnitudes of difference that are neither innate nor socially efficient.[102]

In this essay, however, I also emphasize gender differences throughout, in a way that may seem to align implicitly with the "maximalist" school of feminist analysis, which emphasizes the differences between men and women.[103] Members of this school sometimes suggest that these differences are large and perhaps impossible to change, although few, if any, conclude that they are innate.[104] Nor is innateness the issue. The great variation in women's experience by class and across individuals even in one culture suggests that whether or not the roots of some differences are innate, the differences are susceptible to social change. Moreover, the psychological differences implicated in intimate connection do not seem large compared to many cultural differences.[105]

To make the points about cultural dominance that I have been making, it is not necessary to argue that women are "essentially connected" to other human beings through their biology in a way that differs from men, or even that they have a more connected relation than men to their mothers. There may be some truth to both points. But if there were no truth to either, simply typing women as connected and men as separate would do the trick. If many women grew up thinking of themselves as relatively connected with others and men grew up thinking of themselves as relatively separate, and if men produced the dominant literature, that literature would tend to emphasize the virtues of separation. Connection, or at least "going on" about connection, would have about it just a touch of the effeminate.

In this situation one obvious intellectual strategy would be simply to point out and try to eliminate the gratuitous gendered implications that accrue to various philosophical positions, make the case on its own grounds for the "feminine" position, and move on from the subject of gender. This is a good strategy, with much to recommend it, including prefiguring its goal in its form of argument. It has, however, several weak points.

Most importantly, it is a better strategy for what I perceive as a distant goal than for the present. In the different cultures of the world, the association of gender with various social ideals will presumably begin to wither away as women and men have more of one another's "typical" experiences and recognize the diversity within their own and the other group. However, because it is unlikely that the salience of gender will ever be eliminated, and because the full androgynization of childrearing and workplace roles is in any existing society almost unimaginably distant, it will be hard in the imaginable future to reach a stage at which, when arguments for one or another ideal imply constellations of linked behaviors, those implications could be teased apart and examined without inferences derived from gender. Moreover, if in the future some gendered division of labor should prove socially efficient and normatively acceptable, some ideals would probably remain gendered. A more proximate goal than the abolition of all gender implications, a goal aimed at a world in which some association of gender with particular social ideals persists, prescribes first, that gendering should be reduced to a realistic minimum, and second, that ideals for which there are equally good independent normative arguments should enjoy an equal normative status.

These two prongs of the proximate goal are in tension. Reducing gendering to a minimum, that is, eliminating "gratuitous" gendering, requires downplaying gender implications when they arise in social and philosophical discourse. But arguing for the equal normative status of "female" ideals requires bringing those ideals to center stage and trumpeting their virtues. Moreover, because "male" virtues will be better in some ways and contexts and worse in others, and "female" virtues will be better in some ways and contexts and worse in others, trying to achieve equality in an already hierarchical world will require stressing the ways in which "female" virtues are better.

This essay tries to accomplish both goals. It is logically possible, and I believe an accurate description of much of today's social reality, to say, first, that much of the human race's carrying on about gender could be eliminated without much loss and with a good deal of gain, and second, that so long as gender is still extremely salient and society is still hierarchically organized in regard to gender, some of the ideals more frequently associated with women should be valued more highly than they are now—indeed, that in some ways and contexts those ideals serve human needs better than some ideals more frequently associated with men. Simply pointing out the gendered component of ideals and passing on is not enough.

Another problem with the idea that an argument should stand "on its own," regardless of the gender-coding of its content or the gender of those who espouse it, is that this proposition, while generally an excellent guide to productive thought, tends to obscure the many ways that arguments themselves are gendered. Normative arguments do not consist solely, or even primarily, of deduction from agreed or self-evident principles. These arguments involve telling stories, making analogies, and asking readers to imagine themselves in situations they have never experienced. They can be persuasive only to the degree that they build on something in a reader's experience that the reader values either positively or negatively. To the degree that experience is heavily gendered, and readers do not share in an experience from which an author draws, it becomes possible for readers of a gender different from that of an author simply not to understand the point the author is making. If gendered differences in experience are unequally valued socially, it becomes even harder for readers with the more valued experience to understand points drawn from the less valued experience. (To succeed in the dominant world, however, those with less valued experiences must be able to understand at least in part the dominant experiences.) An argument "standing on its own" may be surreptitiously an argument that draws heavily on male experience. To make this possibility conscious, women must draw consciously on specifically women's experiences. Before we set out to "translate" our insights to men, as to some extent I try to do here, women must also sometimes write as women to women, working out those insights in a context of greater common experience, particularly in those areas neglected by traditional male discourse.

Finally, the strategy of simply pointing out the gender connotations of existing values and moving on fails to take full account of the role in intellectual life of emotional identification with ideas. People often come to think differently about their ideas and values because others exert effort to persuade them to change. Those who exert effort often do so because they identify themselves emotionally with the ideals they are promoting. "Schools of thought" often advance intellectually through emotional as well as cognitive reinforcement, each member reassuring the others that the ideas on which they are working deserve their efforts. Academics who think of the methodological structuralism they espouse as "French" or the methodological individualism they espouse as "Anglo-American" draw some of their intellectual energy from identification with their nation. Women theorists as a group will put more effort into unfolding certain arguments when they identify as women with those ideas.

Even insight itself sometimes requires commitment. Women are more likely than men to have insights on connection and unequal power not only because women are more likely to have had experiences that generate these insights, but also because they are more likely to feel strongly about their insights. Anger, pride, and other of the more disreputable emotions also fuel the intellectual machine. As a woman, I feel angry, and deserve to feel angry, that "our" values have been denigrated. I also feel proud, and deserve to feel proud, of those values, adopting some version of them after scrutiny even more consciously as my own. When the anger women feel on these issues touches off an opposing anger in men, and our pride an opposing pride, these are often acceptable costs of a process that brings the ideas to the surface for critical examination.

Because anger and pride by and large tend to obscure rather than illuminate, this stage in the intellectual process works best if it is only one stage in an ongoing dialectic. It may well be a recurring stage until greater social equality is achieved, because ultimately, in spite of the best efforts of feminist theorists, "female" values are unlikely to be accorded equal worth until women are perceived as the social, political, and intellectual equals of men. But harnessing now for the process of revaluation the anger and resentment generated by the existing system of gendered ideals is likely to make a useful difference in how future generations, at least of philosophers, think of autonomy, obligation, emotion, particularity, persuasion, power, privacy, and other components of a dual stance of welcome and vigilance toward democratic community.

## VI. Deepening Community: Enhancing Individuality

"Ties" tie you down. Increasing the number and strength of communal ties usually decreases personal freedom. But recognizing the frequent tradeoff between ties and choices does not entail accepting the present mix between the two. Just as a child who has mastered the bicycle must learn street safety before venturing forth, so progress from a previous equilibrium often requires a move and a countermove to regain a satisfactory equilibrium farther along. Although American society has established an equilibrium of sorts between the competing claims of individualism and community, thought and experimentation should allow us to create a better equilibrium strengthening the community ties that most advance the ends we desire while at the same time creating and strengthening institutions that guard against community domination.[106]

Individualists and communitarians would both gain from recognizing that any step that strengthens people's ties to a democratic community usually requires heightened, institutionalized vigilance against the illusion that all members of the community have common interests. If we look to long-standing groups for cues to which equilibria work in practice, we see that in the realm of democratic procedure, groups that pursue the quest for democratic community to an extreme, by refusing to make any decisions not perceived by all as in the common good, also institutionalize safeguards against the creation of false consensus. Quaker communities make decisions only by consensus, but also fight the social pressure not to disrupt a consensus by making it a religious duty to hold out against a decision one genuinely thinks is immoral or wrong. The Bruderhof, an even more communal association, institutes similar mechanisms.[107] Other smoothly functioning groups that make many decisions by consensus find ways of investigating verbal or nonverbal signs of dissatisfaction to give the possibly silenced members a hearing, to meet their needs in ways not included in the formal decision, or to reopen the question. In all these cases, a move toward community works in tandem with moves to recognize and protect individual difference.

Individualists and communitarians need to recognize the possibility that a polity can strengthen community ties and respect for the individual at the same time. Contemporary feminist theory helps us think about how to perform these seemingly contradictory tasks simultaneously. If, as I argue, liberal individualism and an adversary system of democracy overemphasize atomistic conflict, the greater self-consciousness of women regarding intimate connection makes available metaphors and experiences in which individuals are not so starkly pitted against one another. If, as I argue, all moves toward assuming commonality need monitoring, feminist insights into pervasive and unequal power provide for all individuals conceptual defenses against the pronouncements of the community on who we are or what our good should be.

The main task of feminist theory must be to clarify and help redress gender inequality. In doing so, however, it contributes to a more general understanding of democratic community in ways not available to a liberalism restricted to individuals sprung into adulthood fully grown and a politics that excludes the private.

## NOTES

1. E.g., Robert H. Bellah, Richard Madsen, William M. Sullivan, Ann Swidler, and Steven M. Tipton, *Habits of the Heart: Individualism and Commitment in American Life* (Berkeley: University of California Press, 1985); Alan Wolfe, *Whose Keeper: Social Science and Moral Obligation* (Berkeley: University of California Press, 1989); Elizabeth Fox-Genovese, *Feminism without Illusions: A Critique of Individualism* (Chapel Hill: University of North Carolina Press, 1991).

2. On communal bonds as a way of solving collective action problems, see Jane J. Mansbridge, "On the Relation between Altruism and Self-Interest," in Mansbridge, ed., *Beyond Self-Interest* (Chicago: University of Chicago Press, 1990). Communal bonds can also deter material success, as when the community expectation that members will share accumulated wealth produces disincentives for individuals to exert effort in earning.

3. Roberto Mangabeira Unger characterizes communities as "those areas of social existence where people stand in a relationship of heightened mutual vulnerability and responsibility toward each other" (*The*

*Critical Legal Studies Movement* [1982] [Cambridge: Harvard University Press, 1986], p. 36), and considers sympathy "the sentiment that animates community" (*Knowledge and Politics* [New York: Free Press, 1975], p. 220). Thomas Bender (*Community and Social Change in America* [New Brunswick: Rutgers University Press, 1978], p. 7) describes communities as "held together by shared understandings and a sense of obligation." Although conflict also creates and maintains mutual ties, it undermines "community" when it lowers the trust between members below that which they would feel with strangers.

4. In *Beyond Adversary Democracy* [1980] (Chicago: University of Chicago Press, 1983) I elaborate on these distinctions, including the forms of equality democracy requires in contexts of common and conflicting interests, and the use of friendship, based on equality of respect, as a model for democratic community. I assume there and elsewhere that both forms of democracy require the protection of minority rights.

5. Kenneth Arrow, *Social Choice and Individual Values* [1951] (New York: Wiley, 1963). William H. Riker, *Liberalism against Populism: A Confrontation between the Theory of Democracy and the Theory of Social Choice* [1982] (Prospect Heights, Ill.: Waveland Press, 1988).

6. Community understandings of what constitutes "good enough" (sufficing rather than maximizing) democracy parallel similar understandings of "good enough" (or "mediated") morality (see Mansbridge, "On the Relation between Altruism and Self-Interest," 1990). Such broad understandings facilitate democracy, while not constituting an "agreement on fundamentals," which Carl Friedrich (*The New Belief in the Common Man* [Boston: Little, Brown, 1942], p. 153ff) argued democracies do not require.

7. Whereas "gender" has social connotations and "sex" connotations of biology and sexual intercourse, I do not make a sharp distinction between the two. On interchangeable usage, see, from different perspectives, Francine Watman Frank and Paula A. Treichler, *Language, Gender, and Professional Writing* (New York: Modern Language Association, 1989), pp. 10–14; and Catharine A. MacKinnon, *Toward a Feminist Theory of the State* (Cambridge: Harvard University Press, 1989), pp. xiii, 113.

8. Lawrence Kohlberg, "A Cognitive-Developmental Analysis of Children's Sex-Role Concepts and Attitudes," in Eleanor E. Maccoby, ed., *The Developmental Sex Differences* (Stanford: Stanford University Press, 1966).

9. See Amos Tversky, Daniel Kahneman, and Paul Slovic, eds., *Judgment under Uncertainty: Heuristics and Biases* (Cambridge: Cambridge University Press, 1982), on the availability heuristic.

10. Analysis derived from data in George P. Murdoch and Caterina Provost, "Factors in the Division of Labor by Sex: A Cross-Cultural Analysis," *Ethnology* 12 (1973): 203–225, Table 8. "Circum-Mediterranean" is Murdoch's own neologism. Data of this kind derive from the reports of anthropologists who often did not check their conclusions with the people they described. Had they done so, they might have found that these practices were contested, changing, or more ambiguous than reported (personal communication from David Cohen, Professor of History and Director of African Studies, Northwestern University).

11. Catharine MacKinnon, "Difference and Dominance," in *Feminism Unmodified* (Cambridge: Harvard University Press, 1967), pp. 32–45, p. 36. See also Mary Austin, *Earth Horizon* (Boston: Houghton Mifflin, 1932), cited by Nancy Cott, "Feminist Theory and Feminist Movements," in Juliet Mitchell and Ann Oakley, eds., *What Is Feminism?* (New York: Pantheon, 1986); and Martha Minow, "Justice Engendered," a feminist "Foreword to the Supreme Court 1986 Term," *Harvard Law Review* 101 (1987): 10–95, pp. 32ff.

12. Although in 1955 George A. Hillary, Jr. concluded after inspecting ninety-four different definitions of community that "social interaction within a geographic area" was part of a "minimum" definition ("Definitions of Community: Areas of Agreement," *Rural Sociology* 20 [1955]: 111–123), subsequent thinkers have downplayed the importance of locality. Raymond Plant reported in 1987 that compared to the dispute over whether locality is a necessary component of the meaning of community, "all are agreed that it is something about the quality of the relationships that makes a social grouping into a community" ("Community," in *The Blackwell Encyclopedia of Political Thought* [Oxford: Basil Blackwell, 1987], p. 90). Reviewing "the meanings of community" in 1978, Thomas Bender concluded that it "is best defined as a network of social relations marked by mutuality and emotional bonds," or, in a formal definition, "a community involves a limited number of people in a somewhat restricted social space or network held together by shared understandings and a sense of obligation" (*Community and Social Change in America* [New Brunswick: Rutgers University Press, 1978], p. 7).

13. Talcott Parsons and Robert F. Bales, *Family, Socialization, and Interaction Process* (New York: Free Press, 1955), p. 47.

14. For "emotion work," see Arlie Russell Hochschild, "The Sociology of Feeling and Emotion: Selected Possibilities," in Marcia Millman and Rosabeth Moss Kanter, eds., *Another Voice: Feminist Perspectives on Social Life and Social Science* (New York: Doubleday/Anchor, 1975), pp. 280–307; for "kinwork," see Micaela di Leonardo, "The Female

World of Cards and Holidays: Women, Families and the Work of Kinship," *Signs* 12 (1987): 440–453.

15. Alice H. Eagly and Blair T. Johnson, "Gender and Leadership Style: A Meta-Analysis," *Psychological Bulletin* 108 (1990): 233–256, p. 236, emphasis in original.

16. For the strong male content of "fraternity," see Wilson Carey McWilliams, *The Idea of Fraternity in America* (Berkeley: University of California Press, 1973), chap. 1; and Carole Pateman, "The Fraternal Social Contract," in *The Disorder of Women* (Stanford: Stanford University Press, 1989), and *The Sexual Contract* (Stanford: Stanford University Press, 1988).

17. Pamela Johnston Conover, "Who Cares? Sympathy and Politics: A Feminist Perspective," paper presented at the annual meeting of the Midwest Political Science Association, 1988.

18. Nancy Eisenberg and Randy Lennon, "Sex Differences in Empathy and Related Capacities," *Psychological Bulletin* 94 (1983): 100–131.

19. Ruth Sharabany, Ruth Gershoni, and John E. Hofman, "Girl Friend, Boy Friend: Age and Sex Differences in Development of Intimate Friendships," *Developmental Psychology* 17 (1981): 800–808; Margery Fox, Margaret Gibbs, and Doris Auerbach, "Age and Gender Dimensions of Friendship," *Psychology of Women Quarterly* 9 (1985): 489–502; E. Douvan and J. Adelson, *The Adolescent Experience* (New York: Wiley, 1966); Matya A. Caldwell and Letitia A. Peplau, "Sex Differences in Same-sex Friendships," *Sex Roles* 8 (1982): 721–732; Lynne R. Davidson and Lucile Duberman, "Friendship: Communication and Interactional Patterns in Same-Sex Dyads," *Sex Roles* 8 (1982): 809–822. For a recent review of the literature, see Hazel Markus and Daphna Oyserman, "Gender and Thought: The Role of Self-Concept," in Mary Crawford and Margaret Gentry, eds., *Gender and Thought: Psychological Perspectives* (New York: Springer-Verlag, 1989). There is no meta-analysis of psychological studies involving connection. Much of the work cited in support of greater connection among women is, in the original research, more ambiguous than the citations suggest.

20. Charlotte Perkins Gilman, *Herland* [1915] (New York: Pantheon, 1979).

21. Aileen Kraditor, *The Ideas of the Woman Suffrage Movement* (Garden City: Doubleday, 1971). Although Kraditor stresses the predominance of arguments from women's special virtues toward the end of the suffrage movement, more recent historians (cited in Cott [1986], pp. 50–51) demonstrate that both kinds of arguments flourished throughout the period from 1792 (Mary Wollstonecraft's *Vindication of*

*the Rights of Women*) to 1921. Cott (1986) provides an excellent short account of "sameness" versus "difference" strands in the first wave of feminism in the United States.

22. Marlene Dixon in *It Ain't Me Babe*, April 7, 1970, p. 8; Jane Alpert, "Mother Right: A New Feminist Theory," *off our backs* 3 (8 May 1973): 6; *Ms.* 2 (1973): 52–55, 88–94. Alice Echols, *Daring to be Bad: Radical Feminism in America, 1967–1975* (Minneapolis: University of Minnesota Press, 1989), p. 7, dates the term "cultural feminism" to 1972, but indicates correctly that the ideas predated the term. Echols, who wants to associate the "rise of cultural feminism" with a turn "away from opposing male supremacy" (p. 5), attributes to "conceptual confusion" (pp. 6, 7, 10) the interlacing of concern with women's culture through much of the early radical women's movement.

"Women's culture" undoubtedly has its roots in women's powerlessness as well as other sources. But as Dixon suggests, roots in a harmful situation do not automatically invalidate a cognitive or emotional insight. A brush with death can make one more appreciative of life in a way one may want to maintain after reducing the threat of death. Per contra, see MacKinnon (1989), pp. 51–58, 153.

23. Dorothy Dinnerstein, *The Mermaid and the Minotaur: Sexual Arrangements and Human Malaise* [1976] (New York: Harper Colophon, 1977), p. 193. Dinnerstein also concludes that the need to invest major energy in perpetuating the species tended to make women specialists in the exercise of capacities "crucial for empathic care of the very young and for maintenance of the social-emotional arrangements that sustain everyday primary-group life" (p. 20). See also p. 68 on the more permeable boundaries of self among women. Dinnerstein drew from Norman O. Brown's conclusion that male domination is the product of the boy's "revolt against biological dependence on the mother" (p. 182, citing Norman O. Brown, *Life against Death* [Middletown: Wesleyan University Press, 1959], n.p.).

24. Nancy Chodorow, *The Reproduction of Mothering: Psychoanalysis and the Sociology of Gender* (Berkeley: University of California Press, 1978), p. 181. Chodorow linked connection with empathy: "Girls emerge from this [oedipal] period with a basis for 'empathy' built into their primary definition of self in a way that boys do not. Girls emerge with a stronger basis for experiencing another's needs or feelings as one's own (or of thinking that one is so experiencing another's needs or feelings)" (p. 167).

25. Chodorow (1978), p. 169.

26. Sara Ruddick, "Maternal Thinking," *Feminist Studies* 6 (Summer 1980): 353; see also Jean Bethke Elshtain, *Public Man, Private Woman:*

*Women in Social and Political Thought* (Princeton: Princeton University Press, 1981), p. 336, and "Feminist Discourse and Its Discontents: Language, Power and Meaning," *Signs* 7 (1983): 603–621, p. 621.

27. "Methodocracy, Misogyny and Bad Faith: The Response of Philosophy," in D. Spender, ed., *Men's Studies Modified: The Impact of Feminism on the Academic Disciplines* (New York: Oxford University Press, 1981), p. 47 cited in Jean Grimshaw, *Philosophy and Feminist Thinking* (Minneapolis: University of Minnesota Press, 1986), p. 54. See also Jane Flax, "Political Philosophy and the Patriarchal Unconscious: A Psychoanalytic Perspective on Epistemology and Metaphysics," in S. Harding and M. Hintikka, eds., *Discovering Reality: Feminist Perspectives on Epistemology, Metaphysics, Methodology, and the Philosophy of Science* (London: D. Reidel, 1983), for a critique, based on Chodorow, of the denial of primary relatedness in philosophy.

28. Carol Gilligan, *In a Different Voice* (Cambridge: Harvard University Press 1982), p. 8. Several years later, however, in "Moral Orientation and Moral Development," in Kittay and Meyers, eds. *Women and Moral Theory* (Totowa, N.J.: Rowman and Littlefield, 1987), Gilligan criticized Chodorow for tying self-development to the experience of separation, thus sustaining "a series of oppositions that have been central in Western thought and moral theory, including the opposition between thought and feelings, self and relationship, reason and compassion, justice and love" (p. 29). Although I concentrate here on the empirical question of gender differences in "connection," Gilligan was reacting to a line of research that, for reasons probably linked in part to implicit gender coding, considered a rights, or Kantian, orientation higher than other moral orientations. See below on the moral emotions for the feminist critique of this form of Kantian orientation. See also Joan C. Tronto, "Women and Caring: What Can Feminists Learn about Morality from Caring?" in Alison M. Jaggar and Susan R. Bordo, eds., *Gender/Body/Knowledge* (New Brunswick: Rutgers University Press, 1989); and Owen Flanagan and Kathryn Jackson, "Justice, Care and Gender: The Kohlberg-Gilligan Debate Revisited," *Ethics* 97 (1987): 622–637 for a review and critique of the literature.

29. Gilligan (1982), p. 17. Like Chodorow, Gilligan explicitly linked care with empathy, concluding that women's moral judgments "are tied to feelings of empathy and compassion" (p. 69), and that girls' smaller and more intimate playgroups foster the development of "empathy and sensitivity" (p. 11).

30. Nel Noddings, *Caring: A Feminine Approach to Ethics and Moral Education* (Berkeley: University of California Press, 1984), p. 2.

31. Diana Baumrind, "Sex Differences in Moral Reasoning: Re-

sponse to Walker's (1984) Conclusion that There Are None," *Child Development* 57 (1986): 511–521.

32. Nona Plessner Lyons reports the largest differences of any of Carol Gilligan's students. In her sample of 30 upper-middle-class people, identified through personal contact and recommendation, 63 percent of the 16 women were coded as "predominantly connected" compared to none of the 14 men, and 79 percent of the men as "predominantly separate" compared to 13 percent of the women (Nona Plessner Lyons, "Two Perspectives: On Self, Relationships, and Morality," in Carol Gilligan, J. Victoria Ward, and Jill McLean Taylor, eds., *Mapping the Moral Domain: A Contribution of Women's Thinking to Psychological Theory and Education* [Cambridge: Harvard University Press, 1988]).

Other studies do not find significant gender differences, even in college-educated populations. See Maureen R. Ford and Carol R. Lowery, "Gender Differences in Moral Reasoning: A Comparison of the Use of Justice and Care Orientations," *Journal of Personality and Social Psychology* 50(1986): 777–783 (college students); William J. Friedman, Amy B. Robinson, and Britt L. Friedman, "Sex Differences in Moral Judgments? A Test of Gilligan's Theory," *Psychology of Women Quarterly* 11(1987): 37–46 (college students); Robbin Derry, "Moral Reasoning in Work-related Conflicts," *Research in Corporate Performance and Policy* 9 (1987): 25–49 ("first-level managers"). On Kohlberg's measures, see Laurence J. Walker, "Sex Differences in the Development of Moral Reasoning: A Critical Review," *Child Development* 55 (1984): 677–691.

Such differences may be highly context specific. When no other cues are given, the classic Bem Sex-Role Inventory finds American college students linking the words "understanding," "sensitive to the needs of others," and "compassionate" to the "feminine" role (Sandra L. Bem, "The Measurement of Psychological Androgyny," *Journal of Consulting and Clinical Psychology* 42 [1974]: 155–162; and Hazel Markus, Marie Crane, Stan Bernstein, and Michael Siladi, "Self-Schemas and Gender," *Journal of Personality and Social Psychology* 42 [1982]: 38–50). When no cues are given, students also associate the "communal goals" of "selflessness, concern with others and a desire to be at one with others" with women more than men (women 3.81, men 3.03 on a 5-point scale). Yet the same students also see male *homemakers* as more likely to have communal traits than female *employees* (4.11 vs. 3.31), suggesting that the stereotypes derive at least in part from the work in which the two sexes are thought typically to engage. Alice H. Eagly and Valerie J. Steffen, "Gender Stereotypes Stem from the Distribution of Women and Men into Social Roles," *Journal of Personality and Social Psychology* 46 (1984): 735–754.

The anthropologist Ronald Cohen concludes that "empathy" is "not a proper way to behave" in some African tribal societies, and suggests that the Anglo-European focus on empathy may be the historical result of many generations of small, inwardly focussed nuclear families with a relatively low instance of infant death. "Altruism: Human, Cultural, or What?", *Journal of Social Issues* 28 (1972): 39–57. On the other hand, Sandra Harding, "The Curious Coincidence of Feminine and African Moralities," in Kittay and Meyers, eds. (1987), and Patricia Hill Collins, *Black Feminist Thought* (London: Allen and Unwin, 1990), pp. 206ff., suggest that an ethics of "connection" and "caring" may typify the behavior and norms not only of women in the United States, but also of both men and women in Africa. Empirical research on these issues is in its infancy.

33. That a researcher can construct two distinct operationalizations of these two orientations does not mean that analytically the two are entirely separate. On the overlap, see Susan Moller Okin, "Thinking Like a Woman," in Deborah L. Rhode, ed., *Theoretical Perspectives on Sexual Difference* (New Haven: Yale University Press, 1990); George Sher, "Other Voices, Other Rooms? Women's Psychology and Moral Theory," in Kittay and Meyers, eds. (1987); and Flanagan and Jackson (1987). Nondiscretionary rights can be based on relations, as when the primary caretaker has the right to custody after divorce (Mary Becker, University of Chicago Law School, personal communication). Moreover, although about two-thirds of D. Kay Johnston's ("Adolescents' Solutions to Dilemmas in Fables" in Gilligan et al. [1988]) eighty middle-class students focussed on one orientation rather than another in interpreting a moral fable, all were eventually able to adopt the other orientation (about half spontaneously, after being asked, "Is there another way to think about this problem?" and the rest after prompting).

34. Ford and Lowery (1986).

35. Jennifer Nedelsky, "Reconceiving Autonomy," *Yale Journal of Law and Feminism* 1 (1989): 7–36, p. 12. See also Nancy J. Chodorow, "Gender, Relation, and Difference in Psychoanalytic Perspective" [1979], in *Feminism and Psychoanalytic Theory* (New Haven: Yale University Press, 1989), p. 106.

36. Virginia Held on the "mothering parent" in "Mothering versus Contract," in Mansbridge, ed. (1990), p. 300. For summaries of feminist thought and quandaries regarding autonomy, see Christine Di Stefano, "Rethinking Autonomy," paper delivered at the 1990 Annual Meeting of the American Political Science Association, San Francisco.

37. An autonomous self develops not only through the help and care of others, but also through having the material, legal, and psychological wherewithal to create and maintain some form of independence from others and from the state.

38. Like many philosophical points in recent feminist theory, the realization that community precedes autonomy is as old as Aristotle, without the feminist emphasis on nurturance. However, after Aristotle and most subsequent Western philosophers excluded the domestic sphere from the political (indeed defined the political in contradistinction to the domestic), language, analogies, and stories derived from women's experiences in the domestic sphere could have little place in descriptions of what politics is or ought to be.

39. No feminist theorist using experiences from motherhood to illuminate the potential in democratic community wants to suggest that actual mothers have with actual children only the relations conjured up by the ideal. While arguing that the ideal mothering relation empowers the child, Held (1990), for example, would not ignore mothers' frequent exercise of naked power over children in their own rather than the children's interests. Both negative and positive aspects of the practice of childrearing illuminate the values, human processes, and problems inherent in helping develop democratic citizens (Jennifer Nedelsky, University of Toronto Law School, personal communication).

40. For critiques of the maternal model, see Mary G. Dietz, "Citizenship with a Feminist Face: The Problem with Maternal Thinking," *Political Theory* 13 (1985): 19–37; and "Context Is All: Feminism and Theories of Citizenship," in J. K. Conway, S. C. Bourque, and J. W. Scott, eds., *Learning about Women: Gender, Politics, and Power* (Ann Arbor: University of Michigan Press, 1987).

41. Held, (1990), pp. 297–299.

42. Nancy J. Hirschmann, "Freedom, Recognition, and Obligation: A Feminist Approach to Political Theory," *American Political Science Review* 83 (1989): 1227–1244, p. 1238.

43. Hirschmann (1989), p. 1242.

44. See, e.g., references in Robert E. Goodin, *Protecting the Vulnerable* (Chicago: University of Chicago Press, 1985).

45. In *A Theory of Justice* (Cambridge: Harvard University Press, 1971), pp. 113–116, John Rawls follows H. L. A. Hart, C. H. Whiteley, and R. B. Brandt in distinguishing between "obligations," which must arise through promising or tacit understandings, and natural "duties." See also Lawrence A. Blum, *Friendship, Altruism and Morality* (London: Routledge and Kegan Paul, 1980), p. 142, and Noddings (1984), pp. 81–84. Hirschmann ([1989], p. 1243 n. 1) argues that "duty" has not been

as central to liberal theory as "obligation" precisely because "obligation" has been defined as voluntary. I use the word "obligation" broadly, assuming that both moral and political obligations can have multiple sources, some reinforcing and some undermining the others.

46. Michael Sandel (*Liberalism and the Limits of Justice* [Cambridge: Cambridge University Press, 1982], p. 179) writes that certain allegiances "go beyond the obligations I voluntarily incur and the 'natural duties' I owe to human beings as such. They allow that to some I owe more than justice requires or even permits, not by reason of agreements I have made but instead in virtue of those more or less enduring attachments and commitments which taken together partly define the person I am." These attachments, he specifies, are not chosen but discovered. Alasdair MacIntyre writes that "I inherit from the past of my family, my city, my tribe, my nation, a variety of... obligations. These constitute the given of my life" (*After Virtue* [1981] [Notre Dame: Notre Dame University Press, 1984], p. 220). Roberto Unger, making room for chosen as well as given communities, nevertheless points out that communities "arise from relationships of interdependence that have been only partly articulated by the will," and concludes that "received ideas about... the sources of obligation cannot readily inform even the existing varieties of communal experience" (*The Critical Legal Studies Movement* [1983] [Cambridge: Harvard University Press, 1986], p. 37).

47. In the United States and most other countries, when children are born, when they get sick, or when parents grow old and get sick, women are expected to care for them and usually accept that responsibility. Women also accept more responsibility for helping in the crises of kin and friends (Carol Heimer, "On Taking Responsibility," presented at the Seminar on Contemporary Social and Political Theory, University of Chicago, April 6, 1989; Janet Finch and Dulcie Groves, eds., *A Labour of Love: Women, Work, and Caring* [London: Routledge and Kegan Paul, 1983]).

48. Hirschmann (1989), p. 1241.

49. MacIntyre (1981/1984), pp. 58–59, 220. Rawls (1971), on learning "the virtues of a good student" and other roles whose content "is given by the various conceptions of a good wife and husband, a good friend and citizen, and so on... the morality of association includes a large number of ideals each defined in ways suitable for the respective status or role" (p. 468).

50. Goodin (1985) makes a powerful case for the obligation to protect the vulnerable as the root of many specific obligations that liberal philosophers have derived from some form of voluntarism. His discussion of the family, however, provides a less satisfactory account of

why any particular person has such an obligation to any particular other. He argues first, that certain people are the "obvious" candidates to bear such responsibilities, with obviousness coming to have moral significance "by virtue of the reactions of other people" (p. 82). But this criterion seems to provide no recourse against unjust cultural expectations. He also argues that when emotional rather than material interests are at stake, individuals enmeshed in affective ties have obligations to the specific others whose emotional welfare depends on them. But as he points out, if affection is lacking, this criterion absolves family members of any special obligation beyond the "general duty to help those in need" (pp. 88–89). A slightly more utilitarian approach would argue that those strategically placed to be most useful to others in their vulnerability have an obligation deriving from that placement. The nearest person is obliged to rescue a drowning swimmer at least in part because he is objectively the best placed to do so, not simply because others expect him to, as in Goodin's explanation (p. 82). Obligations created this way are then subject to scrutiny over the justice of the underlying placement.

51. Some "political" obligations, for example, are also obligations to specific people with whom one has developed stronger or weaker relations of mutual trust or expectation. The obligation to obey the law may derive from considerations of the justness of a law or of the institutions that produced it, but the obligation to take community office—a complexly negotiated obligation, partaking both of the voluntary and the given—is often in part an obligation to specific members of the community, who would bear the costs of one's reneging on that obligation. Parallels with the domestic realm multiply as one conceives the obligations of political community to extend beyond the traditional political obligation of obeying the law to the obligation to vote against one's self-interest for the community good, or the obligation to give time to political projects.

52. The critical scrutiny I have in mind has affinities with Rawls's (1971) "reflective equilibrium."

53. When university students from 28 countries were asked to rate a set of 300 adjectives as being "more frequently associated with men rather than women, or more frequently associated with women than men," students in all but 1 country associated the adjective "emotional" with women, and in all but 5 countries associated the adjective "rational" with men. A score of 0 indicates complete agreement that the adjective is associated with women, 100 complete agreement on association with men. For the adjective "emotional," the average score in Pakistan was 51, neutral between 0 and 100; the average score across all countries

was 12 and across English-speaking countries 4. Students in the United States were unique in giving "emotional" a score of zero, indicating complete association with women. With 100 indicating complete association with men, the average score for the adjective "rational" across all countries was 75, across English-speaking countries 76, and in the United States, 90. (Students in Bolivia, Norway, Pakistan, Scotland, and Venezuela gave "rational" the relatively neutral average scores of 60, 57, 49, 61, and 62 respectively.) In only one country, the Netherlands (with an average score of 94), did students type "rational" as more masculine than in the United States. Analysis from data in John E. Williams and Deborah L. Best, *Measuring Sex Stereotypes* (Beverly Hills: Sage, 1982), Appendix A.

54. Annette C. Baier, "Hume, the Woman's Moral Theorist?" in Kittay and Meyers, eds. (1987); Joan C. Tronto, "Political Science and Caring," *Women and Politics* 7 (1987): 85–97.

55. Immanuel Kant, *Fundamental Principles of the Metaphysic of Morals*, trans. Thomas K. Abbott [1785] (Indianapolis: Bobbs-Merrill, 1949), pp. 15–16.

56. *Observations on the Feeling of the Beautiful and the Sublime*, trans. John Goldthwait, [1763] (Berkeley: University of California Press, 1960), p. 81. See Carol C. Gould, "Philosophy of Liberation and Liberation of Philosophy," in Carol C. Gould and Marx W. Wartofsky, eds., *Women and Philosophy* (New York: Capricorn/G. P. Putnam, 1976), p. 18; Laurence A. Blum, "Kant and Hegel's Moral Rationalism: A Feminist Perspective," *Canadian Journal of Philosophy* 12 (1982): 287–302; and Grimshaw (1986), pp. 42–44. See also G. W. F. Hegel in *The Philosophy of Right:* "Women regulate their actions not by the demands of universality but by arbitrary inclinations" (Oxford: Oxford University Press, 1952), p. 263, cited in Genevieve Lloyd, "Reason, Gender and Morality in the History of Philosophy," *Social Research* 50 (1983): 491–513, p. 511.

57. Blum (1980); Blum (1982); and Lawrence A. Blum, "Gilligan and Kohlberg: Implications for Moral Theory," *Ethics* 98 (1988): 472–491, in which he suggests a typology of the ways moral theories based on the will can coexist with moral theories based on emotion. See David A. J. Richards, chap. 15 in this volume; Virginia Held, "Feminism and Moral Theory," in Kittay and Meyers (1987) eds., pp. 119ff; and Sher (1987) especially the comment on Bernard Williams on p. 185, for the point that morality requires generalizable principles, although those principles may derive from, and encode distinctions drawn from, particularistic commitment. See also Grimshaw (1986), pp. 205–211.

Blum ([1988], p. 475) makes the moral goal "achieving knowledge of the good for another," not just making an effort to know. Bernard

Williams objects that there is some problem, even an "ultimate and outrageous absurdity" in the idea that "the achievement of the highest kind of moral worth should depend on natural capacities [including "a capacity for sympathetic understanding"] unequally and fortuitously distributed as they are" (Bernard Williams, "The Idea of Equality," in Peter Laslett and W. G. Runciman, eds., *Philosophy, Politics, and Society* [2nd. ser.] [Oxford: Basil Blackwell, 1969], p. 115). Williams thus praises effort rather than success in the act of sympathy. Each human being, he concludes, is owed an "effort" at identification and understanding (p. 117). In Simone Weil and Iris Murdoch's understanding of "attention," the moral mandate also requires noticing and asking rather than succeeding in putting oneself in another's place (see Ruddick [1980], p. 359). Finally, Martha Minow ([1987], pp. 77, 79) and Alasdair MacIntyre ([1981/1984], p. 149), following David Hume (see Baier [1987], p. 41), both seem to make morality at least partly a matter of effort in cultivating the capacity for sympathy.

58. "Reason and Feeling in Thinking about Justice," *Ethics* 99 (1989): 229–249.

59. Seyla Benhabib, "The Generalized and Concrete Other," pp. 32ff, in Seyla Benhabib and Ducilla Cornell, eds., *Feminism as Critique* [1987] (Minneapolis: University of Minnesota Press, 1988).

60. See Mansbridge, "The Rise and Fall of Self-Interest" and "On the Relation between Altruism and Self-Interest" in Mansbridge, ed. (1990).

61. For the role of emotion in deliberation, see Jane Mansbridge, "A Deliberative Theory of Interest Representation," in Mark Petracca, ed., *The Politics of Interests: Interest Groups Transformed* (Boulder: Westview Press, 1992), p. 35; Charles E. Lindblom, *Inquiry and Change* (New Haven: Yale University Press, 1990), p. 32; and Benjamin Barber, *Strong Democracy: Participatory Politics for a New Age* (Berkeley: University of California Press, 1984), p. 174.

62. Michael Walzer, *Spheres of Justice* (New York: Basic Books, 1983); Robert A. Dahl, *After the Revolution* (New Haven: Yale University Press, 1970). Arguments for justice within one nation require similar justifications. See Rawls (1971) and Charles R. Beitz, *Political Theory and International Relations* (Princeton: Princeton University Press, 1979).

63. Robert E. Goodin, *Protecting the Vulnerable* (Chicago: University of Chicago Press, 1985) makes the best modern case for identifying " 'particularity' as the principal enemy of justice" (p. 1). In doing so, he provides a masterly summary of the conclusions of those philosophers, from Maimonides to Bernard Williams, who have argued the claims of particular relations to particular persons. Goodin does not

argue "that we have *no* responsibilities toward those with who we enjoy 'special relationships.' That would be absurd. Nor for that matter shall I deny our firm intuitions that our responsibilities toward them tend to be particularly strong ones" (pp. 10–11). It is not his task, however, to justify those special relations.

64. Although the limiting case of "humanity" undermines the opposition between a community member and a stranger, even here one could treat as relative strangers animals, extraterrestrial beings, and "enemies of humanity." One might also include some animals in the membership of certain primarily human communities, depending on the existence and strength of mutual relations of obligation, vulnerability, understanding, and sympathy between the animals and human members of those communities.

65. Michael Walzer, *Obligations* (Cambridge: Harvard University Press, 1970).

66. C. D. Broad, "Self and Others" [1953], in David R. Cheney, ed., *Broad's Critical Essays in Moral Philosophy* (London: George Allen and Unwin, 1971). I thank Marx Wartofsky for first drawing this point to my attention.

67. Carol A. Heimer, "Doing Your Job *and* Helping Your Friends: Universalistic Norms about Obligations to Particular Others in Networks," in Nitin Nohria and Robert Eccles, eds., *Networks and Organizations: Theory and Practice* (Cambridge: Harvard Business School, 1992).

68. Iris Marion Young, "Impartiality and the Civic Public," in Seyla Benhabib and Drucilla Cornell, eds., *Feminism as Critique: On the Politics of Gender* (Minneapolis: University of Minnesota Press, 1987), pp. 61–62. Benhabib and Minow retain a greater respect than Young for the norms of universalism or impartiality. Benhabib ([1987], p. 81) would replace "substitutionalist" universalism, which surreptitiously "identifies the experiences of a particular group of human beings as the paradigmatic case of the human as such," with "interactive" universalism, which "acknowledges the plurality of modes of being human, and differences among humans, without endorsing all these pluralities and differences as morally and politically valid." Interactive universalism agrees that "normative disputes can be settled rationally, and that fairness, reciprocity and some procedure of universalizability are . . . necessary conditions of the moral standpoint." Minow ([1987], pp. 75–76) accepts a form of impartiality as a goal when she argues that "only by admitting our partiality can we strive for impartiality." "If I embrace partiality, I risk ignoring . . . your alternate reality. . . . I must acknowledge and struggle against my partiality by making an effort to understand your reality and what it means for my own." See also "Symposium on Im-

partiality and Ethical Theory" in *Ethics* 101 (1991), especially Marilyn Friedman, "The Practice of Partiality," pp. 818–835.

69. "Observations on the Real Rights of Women" [1818], in Aileen Kraditor, ed., *Up from the Pedestal* (Chicago: Quandrangle Books, 1968), p. 40.

70. Gilman (1915/1979).

71. Mary Parker Follett, "Coordination" in *Freedom and Coordination: Lectures in Business Organization* (London: Management Publications Trust, 1949), p. 66; see also "Constructive Conflict," in Henry C. Metcalf, ed., *Dynamic Administration: The Collected Papers of Mary Parker Follett* (New York: Harper, 1942), p. 32. Follett is sometimes misinterpreted on this point. She made it clear "definitely that I do not think integration is possible in all cases" (p. 36), and argued that in trying to "find the real demand as against the demand put forward," the first rule for obtaining integration is to "face the real issue, uncover the conflict, bring the whole thing into the open" (p. 38). For a modern use of both Follett's ideas and her concrete examples, see Roger Fisher and William Ury, *Getting to Yes* [1981] (New York: Penguin Books, 1983), esp. p. 41. Dorothy Emmett revived Follett's distinction between "power over" and "power with" (Mary Parker Follett, "Power," in Metcalf, ed. (1942) pp. 101, 109) in "The Concept of Power," *Proceedings of the Aristotelian Society* 54 (1953–1954), pp. 1–26, her presidential address to that society and argued that the Laswellian definition of politics as a struggle for power to obtain deference did not "represent a view of politics in the round," which would include using power for coping with "problems set by events or social situations" (p. 9). Follett and Emmett were the most distinguished women in their professions; although neither considered herself a feminist, their experiences and socialization as women may well have contributed to their unorthodox alternatives to "power over."

72. Nancy Hartsock, "Political Change: Two Perspectives on Power," *Quest* 1 (1974): 10–25, reprinted in Charlotte Bunch, ed., *Building Feminist Theory: Essays from Quest* (New York: Longman, 1981), pp. 9, 10. See also Berenice Carroll, "Peace Research: The Cult of Power," *Journal of Conflict Resolution* 4 (1972): 585–616. For similar points without a feminist perspective, see William E. Connolly, "Power and Responsibility," in *The Terms of Political Discourse* (Lexington: D. C. Heath, 1974) and less directly C. B. Macpherson, "The Maximization of Democracy," in *Democratic Theory: Essays in Retrieval* (Oxford: Oxford University Press, 1973).

73. Kathy E. Ferguson, *The Feminist Case against Bureaucracy* (Philadelphia: Temple University Press, 1984) pp. 25, 119–203. See also

Carol Gould, "The Woman Question: Philosophy of Liberation and the Liberation of Philosophy," in C. Gould and M. W. Wartofsky, eds., *Women and Philosophy: Toward a Theory of Liberation* (New York: G. P. Putnam's Sons, 1976), pp. 5–44; and Held (1990), p. 300. Bertrand de Jouvenel confirms the gendering of this concept by making politics as power through imposition not only the source of "incomparable pleasure" but also manly: "A man feels more of a man when imposing himself and making others the instrument of his will" (Bertrand de Jouvenel, *Power* [1945], cited in Hannah Arendt, "Reflections on Violence," *Journal of International Affairs* 23 [1969]: 1–35, p. 12). See Carroll (1972), p. 588.

74. Peter Bachrach and Morton Baratz, "Decisions and Non-Decisions," *American Political Science Review* 57 (1963): 632–644.

75. Alice H. Eagly and Blair T. Johnson, "Gender and Leadership Style: A Meta-Analysis," *Psychological Bulletin* 108 (1990): 233–256. Socialization, lesser power, and anticipation of bias may also explain why, in the research of Lynn R. Offerman and Pamela E. Schrier, "Social Influence Strategies: The Impact of Sex, Role, and Attitudes toward Power," *Personality and Social Psychology Bulletin* 11 (1985): 286–300, p. 295, fear of having power was significantly correlated with gender.

76. Literature reviews in Nancy Henley, *Body Politics* (Englewood Cliffs: Prentice-Hall, 1977), p. 74; Adelaide Haas, "Male and Female Spoken Language Differences: Stereotypes and Evidence," *Psychological Bulletin* 86 (1979): 616–626); Virginia P. Brooks, (1982), "Sex Differences in Student Dominance Behavior in Female and Male Professors' Classrooms," *Sex Roles* 8 (1982): 683–690; and Cynthia Fuchs Epstein, *Deceptive Distinctions: Sex, Gender, and the Social Order* (New Haven: Yale University Press and Russell Sage Foundation, 1988), pp. 217ff. Epstein's excellent review points out that speaking patterns vary depending on the situation and the definition of that situation. In one study, "when women were told they would be assessed on their leadership ability in a discussion group, they spoke up as much as the men did" (p. 219). I know of no meta-analysis of this literature.

77. On town meetings, see Frank M. Bryan, "Comparative Town Meetings: A Search for Causative Models of Feminine Involvement in Politics," paper delivered at the annual meeting of the Rural Sociological Society, 1975; and Mansbridge (1980/1983), p. 106 and ns. 19–23. On state legislatures, see Lyn Kathlene, "The Impact of Gender on the Legislative Process," a study of the Colorado state legislature, in Joyce McCarl Nielsen, ed., *Feminist Research Methods* (Boulder: Westview, 1990), pp. 246–247.

78. For women's use of constructions such as "can" or "could," tag

questions such as "didn't I?" and imperative constructions in question form, such as "Will you please close the door?" See Julie R. McMillan, A. Kay Clifton, Diane McGrath, and Wanda S. Gale, "Women's Language: Uncertainty or Interpersonal Sensitivity and Emotionality?" *Sex Roles* 3 (1977): 546–559. For women's use of questions and supportive interjections like "mm," and "yeah," see Pamela M. Fishman, "Interaction: The Work Women Do," *Social Problems* 25 (1978): 397–406. In three hearings before the Colorado state legislature in 1989 (Kathlene [1990], p. 247) women were more likely to use qualifiers in their testimony. See also Robin Lakoff, *Language and Woman's Place* (New York: Harper and Row, 1975). A few studies, however, show no gender differences in some of these areas (see Haas [1979] for literature review).

79. On meetings, see Mansbridge (1980/1983), p. 106; on interruptions, see Donald H. Zimmerman and Candace West, "Sex Roles, Interruptions, and Silence in Conversation," in Barry Thorne and Nancy Henley, eds., *Language and Sex* (Rowley: Newbury House, 1975).

80. On modest silence, see Aristotle, *Politics*, 1260a. On men's negative reactions to women's assertiveness, see review in Brooks (1982). See Haas (1979), citing Otto Jesperson's *Language* (New York: Henry Holt, 1922), for proverbs from France ("Où femme il y a, silence il n'y a" ["Where there's a woman, there's no silence"]), China ("The tongue is the sword of a woman, and she never lets it become rusty"), Jutland ("The North Sea will sooner be found wanting in water than a woman at a loss for a word"), and elsewhere. In Williams and Best's study of twenty-eight countries in the late 1970s, the adjective "talkative" was associated primarily with females in all but the Latin countries (analysis from data in Williams and Best [1982], Appendix A).

81. Barber (1984), p. 175.

82. Michel Foucault, "Prison Talk" [1975], in Colin Gordon, ed., *Power/Knowledge* (New York: Pantheon, 1980), p. 39.

83. See Mansbridge (1980/1983) on devices for spreading the opportunity to speak, and on gender and class differences in hesitations and not speaking until angry. See Thomas Kochman, *Black and White Styles in Conflict* (Chicago: University of Chicago Press, 1981) on cultural differences between American Blacks and whites in the public expression of anger.

84. On reducing deliberative inequalities on the national scale, see my "A Deliberative Inquiry of Interest Representation," in Mark P. Petracca, ed., *The Politics of Interests: Interest Groups Transformed* (Boulder, Colo.: Westview Press, 1992) and theorists cited therein.

85. Catharine A. MacKinnon, *Feminism Unmodified* (Cambridge:

Harvard University Press, 1987), pp. 7, 217–218; and Andrea Dworkin, *Intercourse* (New York: Free Press, 1987), passim.

86. MacKinnon (1989), p. 3.

87. Although women report hitting or slapping their spouse in marital disputes as often as men (Murray A. Straus, Richard J. Gelles, and Suzanne K. Steinmetz, *Behind Closed Doors: Violence in the American Family* [Garden City: Doubleday, 1980]), they are more likely to be injured in those disputes (Lisa D. Brush, "Violent Acts and Injurious Outcomes in Married Couples: Methodological Issues in the National Survey of Families and Households," *Gender & Society* 4 [1990]: 56–67). It is also possible that men initiate the physical part of the dispute more often than women and that men act violently more often outside the context of a delimited dispute. The greatest differences appear at the extremes: records for one year in Scotland show 98.5 percent of all reported domestic assaults to be assaults of a husband on a wife, and only 1.5 percent of wife on husband (R. Emerson Dobash and Russell P. Dobash, "Wives: The 'Appropriate' victims of Marital Violence," *Victimology* 2 [1978]: 426–442). Although some of this difference may be due to proclivity to report, great differences also show up in hospital admissions. In one year, 70 percent of the assault victims in Boston Hospital were women attacked in the home (Center for Women Policy Studies, Fact Sheet, 1977, cited in Elaine Hilberman, "Response," in U.S. Commission on Civil Rights, *Battered Women: Issues of Public Policy* [n.p., n. pub: Jan 30–31, 1978]).

88. Susan Moller Okin, *Justice, Gender, and the Family* (New York: Basic Books, 1989), p. 152; Amartya Sen, "More than 100 Million Women Are Missing," *New York Review of Books*, December 20, 1990, pp. 61–66.

89. Foucault (1975/1980), pp. 142, 163; Louise Lamphere on "informal resistance in an apparel plant," in *From Working Daughters to Working Mothers: Immigrant Women in a New England Industrial Community* (Ithaca: Cornell University Press, 1987), pp. 289–325; Jean Comaroff, *Body of Power, Spirit of Resistance* (Chicago: University of Chicago Press, 1985).

90. This definition is adapted from James C. Scott's in *Weapons of the Weak: Everyday Forms of Peasant Resistance* (New Haven: Yale University Press, 1985), p. 290. Scott makes it clear that such resistance has "political" features even when it is individual, unorganized, has only tiny consequences, and combines self-interest with collective motivation.

91. Iris Marion Young, "The Ideal of Community and the Politics of Difference," *Social Theory and Practice* 12 (1986): 1–26, p. 2. See also

"Polity and Group Difference: A Critique of the Ideal of Universal Citizenship," *Ethics* 99 (1989): 250–274.

92. See the prayer from the Jewish morning service: "Blessed art thou, Oh Lord our God, King of the universe, who hast not made me a woman."

93. Okin (1989), chap. 3, whose title, "Whose Traditions? Which Understandings?" responds to MacIntyre's *Whose Justice? Which Rationality?* (Notre Dame: Notre Dame University Press, 1988). For another trenchant critique, see Marilyn Freidman, "Feminism and Modern Friendship: Dislocating the Community," *Ethics* 99 (1989): 275–290.

94. Sandel (1982), pp. 172–173.

95. Charles Taylor, *Hegel and Modern Society* (Cambridge: Cambridge University Press, 1979), p. 90.

96. Taylor (1979), pp. 87, 89.

97. I take these examples from Katharine T. Bartlett, "Feminist Legal Methods," *Harvard Law Review* 103 (1990): 829–888, p. 848, commenting on Elizabeth Spelman's *Inessential Woman: Problems of Exclusion in Feminist Thought* (Boston: Beacon Press, 1988).

98. E.g., Angela Harris, "Race and Essentialism in Legal Theory," *Stanford Law Review* 42 (1990): 581–616.

99. On protecting the particular virtues of the public and private realms, see Elshtain (1981), pp. 217–218, 331–353. On the mutual interpenetration of the spheres, see Okin (1989), pp. 124–133; Young (1987), p. 74; Benhabib (1987), p. 177, n. 12; and MacKinnon (1989), p. 120.

100. See Dietz (1985) and (1987).

101. Aristotle, much of whose work rested on categorization, distinguished relatively sharply between a family, a village, and a polis. The political begins at the polis, which Aristotle described as having reached full self-sufficiency (*Politics* 1252b), existing for the sake of a good life (1252b), exemplifying justice (1253a), demanding a common place of residence, (1260b), and being composed of different kinds of men (1261a). The interdependence of different elements distinguishes a polis from a military alliance or a tribe (1261a), and by implication, from a village and household.

Yet Aristotle may not have drawn as sharp a line regarding the nature of the "political" as some subsequent commentators assume. Careful in his classifications, and sensitive not only to sharp demarcations but to the variety of "mixed" states and continua that occur in nature, Aristotle might have believed that elements of the political existed even in the household, and certainly in the village, although those elements were not fully developed until the polis itself. He pointed out, for example, that every polis has "itself the same quality as the earlier associations from which it grew" (1252b), and argued that association in language and the ability to declare what is just and unjust "makes a family and a polis" (1253a). By explicitly including a family with the polis in the process of perceiving and speaking about justice, Aristotle may have suggested that the two are parts of a continuum rather than radically separate.

102. In some philosophic readings, neither innateness nor efficiency is automatically good. Nor does innateness or efficiency automatically trump other goods. Societies work hard and often successfully to reduce or eliminate the effects of many innate impulses, such as the impulse to defecate spontaneously. Societies may also decide against implementing certain efficient ways of functioning, such as plantation slavery, on the grounds that these forms of efficiency are incompatible with other social ideals.

103. The terms "minimalist" and "maximalist" derive from the work of Catharine R. Stimpson, e.g., "Knowing Women," the Marjorie Smart Memorial Lecture, St. Hilda's College, University of Melbourne, August 1990. For divisions in the women's movement on this issue, see Ann Snitow, "Gender Diary," in Marianne Hirsch and Evelyn Fox Keller, eds., *Conflicts in Feminism* (New York: Routledge, 1990).

104. Robin West, "Jurisprudence and Gender," *University of Chicago Law Review* 55 (1988): 1–72, comes close to making a claim for innateness when she says that "women, uniquely, are physically and materially 'connected' to those human beings when the human beings are fetuses and then infants. Women are more empathic to the lives of others because women are physically tied to the lives of others in a way that men are not" (p. 21). West states the "connection thesis" as follows: "Women are actually or potentially materially connected to other human life. Men aren't. This material fact has existential consequences" (p. 14). West also somewhat exaggerates the evidence of gender difference by writing, "According to the vast literature on difference now being developed by cultural feminists, women's cognitive development, literary sensibility, aesthetic taste and psychological development, no less than our anatomy, are all fundamentally different from men's, and are different in the same way: unlike men, we view ourselves as connected to, not separate from, the other" (p. 17). Or, "Intimacy is not something which women fight to become capable of. We just do it. It is ridiculously easy. It is also, I suspect, qualitatively beyond the pale of male effort" (p. 40). In her conclusion West modifies her emphasis on biology by saying that "material biology does not *mandate* existential value: men *can* connect to other human life. . . . *Biology is destiny only to the extent of*

*our ignorance*" (p. 71, emphases in original), but her stress throughout on "material" and "physical" connection, and her use of phrases like "fundamentally" and "qualitatively beyond the pale of... effort" make the differences sound insurmountable.

105. My own experience suggests that the differences between college-educated men and women in the United States today are no greater than the differences between college-educated residents of France and the United States. I have found no systematic comparison, across different norms or behaviors, of the size of gender differences to the size of class or other cultural differences. Janet Shibley Hyde's recent study, demonstrating that gender differences in cognitive abilities are generally not large and differences in social behavior depend greatly on context, implies that comparisons of the size of gender differences with the size of class or other cultural differences are rare or non-existent. Janet Shibley Hyde, "Meta-Analysis and the Psychology of Gender Differences," *Signs* 16 (1990): 5–73, esp. 63–64, 72.

106. Community may be valued both as an end in itself and as a means to other ends. When community is at least in part a means, clarity about ends allows us to look for ways of achieving those ends with lower costs. Communities cohering through interdependence, for example, allow more individuality than communities cohering through sameness (Emile Durkheim, *The Division of Labor in Society* [1893], trans. George Simpson [New York: Free Press, 1964]); chosen communities with easy exit allow individuality than "given" communities with non-voluntary obligations (Friedman [1989]). Evaluating these alternatives requires asking what aspects of community different kinds of people most value, and why.

107. Benjamin Zablocki, *The Joyful Community* (Baltimore: Penguin, 1971).

# [20]

# Reconceiving Autonomy: Sources, Thoughts and Possibilities

Jennifer Nedelsky†

## I. Feminism and the Tensions of Autonomy

### A. *Feminist Guidance*

Feminism requires a new conception of autonomy. The prevailing conception stands at the core of liberal theory and carries with it the individualism characteristic of liberalism. Such a conception cannot meet the aspirations of feminist theory and is inconsistent with its methodology.[1] The basic value of autonomy is, however, central to feminism. Feminist theory must retain the value, while rejecting its liberal incarnation.

Feminism is not, of course, alone in its rejection of liberal individualism. The individualistic premises of liberal theory (and their inadequacies) have become an important subject of debate in contemporary political and legal theory.[2] Feminism offers us a particularly promising avenue for advancing this debate, not because it provides a fully articulated alterna-

---

† Assistant Professor, Faculty of Law and Department of Political Science, University of Toronto. This project began when I was a postdoctoral fellow at the Russell Sage Foundation. The Foundation provided a wonderful community of scholars, who gave me many helpful comments and suggestions. I am particularly grateful to Robert Merton for his encouragement, probing questions, and general assistance with this and related projects. Circulating the draft I wrote at Russell Sage first introduced me to the exciting range of overlapping projects other feminist scholars are engaged in. I received encouraging and helpful responses from Drucilla Cornell, Kathy Ferguson, and Susan Sherwin. I would also like to thank the participants in the Yale Legal Theory Workshop for their questions and comments. Finally, I owe a special thanks to my colleague Hudson Janisch, who first planted the seed of my interest in administrative law and who has helped me in the area since. Naturally, any errors are mine alone.

1. Among the many discussions of feminist theory and methodology are: Alison Jagger, Feminist Politics and Human Nature (Totowa, N.J.: Rowman & Allanheld, 1983); Lorraine Code, Sheila Mullett, and Christine Overall, eds., Feminist Perspectives: Philosophical Essays on Method and Morals (Toronto: University of Toronto Press, 1988); Sandra Harding, ed., Feminism and Methodology: Social Science Issues (Bloomington: Indiana University Press, 1987); Carol Gilligan, In a Different Voice: Psychological Theory and Women's Development (Cambridge: Harvard University Press, 1982); Tronto, *Beyond Gender Difference to a Theory of Care*, 12 Signs 644 (1987) (applying Gilligan's work to political theory); MacKinnon, *Feminism, Marxism, Method, and the State: Toward Feminist Jurisprudence*, 8 Signs 635 (1983); Scales, *The Emergence of Feminist Jurisprudence: An Essay*, 95 Yale L.J. 1373 (1986).

2. Among the best known critics of liberal individualism are Alasdair MacIntyre, After Virtue: A Study in Moral Theory (Notre Dame, Ind.: University of Notre Dame Press, 1981); Michael J. Sandel, Liberalism and the Limits of Justice (Cambridge: Cambridge University Press, 1982); Charles Taylor, Philosophy and the Human Sciences (Cambridge: Cambridge University Press, 1985), particularly Ch. 7, "Atomism." Michael Sandel has edited an excellent collection of essays on this debate entitled Liberalism and Its Critics (New York: New York University Press, 1984).

tive to liberal theory, but because feminist concerns so effectively capture the problems such an alternative must address.

Feminism appears equivocal in its stance toward liberalism because it simultaneously demands a respect for women's individual selfhood and rejects the language and assumptions of individual rights that have been our culture's primary means of expressing and enforcing respect for selfhood. This apparent equivocation is not the result of superficiality or indecision. On the contrary, it reflects the difficulties inherent in building a theory (and practice) that adequately reflects both the social and the individual nature of human beings. Feminist perspectives and demands can guide the inquiry: they point to dangers, define aspirations, and indicate the contours of an approach that transcends the limitations of liberal theory while fostering its underlying values. This article is part of that process: an inquiry into the meaning of autonomy, guided by feminist objectives.

### B. *Self-Determination and Social Construction*

The notion of autonomy goes to the heart of liberalism and of the powerful, yet ambivalent, feminist rejection of liberalism. The now familiar critique by feminists and communitarians is that liberalism takes atomistic individuals as the basic units of political and legal theory and thus fails to recognize the inherently social nature of human beings. Part of the critique is directed at the liberal vision of human beings as self-made and self-making men (my choice of noun is, of course, deliberate). The critics rightly insist that, of course, people are not self-made. We come into being in a social context that is literally constitutive of us. Some of our most essential characteristics, such as our capacity for language and the conceptual framework through which we see the world, are not made by us, but given to us (or developed in us) through our interactions with others.

The image of humans as self-determining creatures nevertheless remains one of the most powerful dimensions of liberal thought.[3] For all of us raised in liberal societies, our deep attachment to freedom takes its meaning and value from the presupposition of our self-determining, self-making nature: that is what freedom is for, the exercise of that capacity. No one among the feminists or communitarians is prepared to abandon freedom as a value, nor, therefore, can any of us completely abandon the notion of a human capacity for making one's own life and self.

Indeed, feminists are centrally concerned with freeing women to shape our own lives, to define who we (each) are, rather than accepting the definition given to us by others (men and male-dominated society, in par-

3. Charles Taylor provides a particularly compelling statement of the importance of this vision in the origins and enduring power of liberal thought. Taylor, "Justice After Virtue," paper presented at Legal Theory Workshop Series, University of Toronto Faculty of Law, 23 October 1987. *See also* "Atomism," *supra* note 2.

ticular). Feminists therefore need a language of freedom with which to express the value underlying this concern. But that language must also be true to the equally important feminist precept that any good theorizing will start with people in their social contexts. And the notion of social context must take seriously its constitutive quality; social context cannot simply mean that individuals will, of course, encounter one another.[4] It means, rather, that there are no human beings in the absence of relations with others. We take our being in part from those relations.

The problem, of course, is how to combine the claim of the constitutiveness of social relations with the value of self-determination.[5] The problem is common to all communitarians but is particularly acute for feminists because of women's relations to the traditions of theory and of society. It is worth restating the problem in terms of these complex and ambivalent relations. Feminists angrily reject the tradition of liberal theory that has felt so alien, so lacking in language and ability to comprehend our reality, and that has been so successful in defining what the relevant questions and appropriate answers are.[6] Anyone who has listened closely to academic feminists will have heard this undercurrent of rage at all things liberal.[7] Yet liberalism has been the source of our language of freedom and self-determination. The values we cherish have come to us embedded in a theory that denies the reality we know: the centrality of relationships in constituting the self.

That knowledge has its own ironies: women know this centrality through experience, but the experience has been an oppressive one. One of the oldest feminist arguments is that women are not seen and defined as themselves, but in their relations to others. The argument is posed at the philosophical level of de Beauvoir's claim that men always experience women as "Other" (a perverse, impersonal form of "relationship") and in the mundane, but no less important, form of objections to being defined as someone's wife or mother. We need a language of self-determination that

4. I once heard a(n otherwise) thoughtful liberal theorist dismiss with exasperation the critique that liberal theory fails to take seriously the social nature of human beings. "Of course it does," he said. "Liberal theory is all about the proper rules governing the interaction among people, so, of course it recognizes their social nature." This observation completely misses the point. Drawing boundaries around the sphere of individual rights to protect those individuals from the intrusions of others (individuals or the state) naturally takes for granted the existence and interaction of others. Such an assumption, however, has nothing in common with the claim that a person's identity is in large part constituted by her interactions with others. On this view there is, in an important sense, no "person" to protect within a sphere protected from all others, for there is no pre-existing, unitary self in isolation from relationships.

5. The parallel with old theological debates about the freedom of man and the omnipotence of God is really quite striking. Taylor comments on the relevance of these debates to the emergence of liberalism. "Justice After Virtue," *supra* note 3.

6. It is, of course, not some disembodied Theory, but those who practice it who arouse these feelings. The convention is, however, to indulge in the more polite (and safer) sounding reification.

7. Excepting, of course, liberals who think of themselves as feminists. They take their theoretical framework from liberalism and thus are not part of the enterprise of developing a distinctive feminist theory.

avoids the blind literalness of the liberal concept.[8] We need concepts that incorporate our experience of embeddedness in relations, both the inherent, underlying reality of such embeddedness and the oppressiveness of its current social forms.[9] I think the best path to this end is to work towards a reconception of the term "autonomy."

C. *Finding One's Own Law*

The word "autonomy" is so closely tied to the liberal tradition that it is often treated as symbolizing the very individualism from which I am trying to reclaim it. Among critics of liberalism one can hear the phrase "autonomous individuals" uttered with the contempt meant to express the absurdity of conceiving of individuals in isolation from one another. But one also hears the word used with approbation, usually in the context of the problem of achieving true autonomy (as opposed to the false liberal autonomy). I think the word itself carries with it the complexity of the issue. The literal meaning of the word is to be "governed by one's own law." To become autonomous is to come to be able to find and live in accordance with one's own law.

I speak of "becoming" autonomous because I think it is not a quality one can simply posit about human beings. We must develop and sustain the capacity for finding our own law, and the task is to understand what social forms, relationships, and personal practices foster that capacity. I use the word "find" to suggest that we do not make or even exactly choose our own law. The idea of "finding" one's law is true to the belief that even what is truly one's own law is shaped by the society in which one lives and the relationships that are a part of one's life. "Finding" also permits an openness to the idea that one's own law is revealed by spiritual sources, that our capacity to find a law within us comes from our spiritual nature.[10] From both perspectives, the law is one's own in the deepest sense, but not made by the individual; the individual develops it, but in connection with others; it is not chosen, but recognized. "One's own law" connotes values, limits, order, even commands just as the more conventional use of the term does. But these values and demands come from within each person rather than being imposed from without. The idea

8. The fact that contemporary liberals know all about "social conditioning" doesn't seem to change the structure of their concepts. It may mean that they, too, face similar dilemmas but do not hoose to make them central to their theoretical inquiries.

9. In developing such concepts, feminists have an advantage in avoiding one of the pitfalls of challenges to liberal individualism: women's experience of relationships as oppressive as well as essential has the virtue of making us less likely to be romantic about the virtues of community as such.

10. Indeed, it may be that the idea of one's own law, as opposed to one's own wishes, presupposes some transcendent, spiritual order of which we are a part. Such a notion need not, of course, be anything like Kant's categorical imperative with its exclusive reliance on man's rationality. *See* Immanuel Kant, GROUNDWORK OF THE METAPHYSIC OF MORALS, trans. H.J. Paton (New York: Harper & Row, 1964).

that there are commands that one recognizes as one's own, requirements that constrain one's life, but come from the meaning or purpose of that life, captures the basic connection between law and freedom[11]—which is perhaps the essence of the concept of autonomy. The necessary social dimension of the vision I am sketching comes from the insistence, first, that the capacity to find one's own law can develop only in the context of relations with others (both intimate and more broadly social) that nurture this capacity, and second, that the "content" of one's own law is comprehensible only with reference to shared social norms, values, and concepts.

This concept has inherent tensions between the idea of autonomy as both originating with oneself *and* being conditioned and shaped by one's social context. Those tensions are the tensions of feminism, and they come from feminism's recognition of the nature of human beings. The word "autonomy" is thus a suitable vehicle for achieving feminist objectives. It is capable of carrying the full dimensions of feminist values and perspectives. And sticking with the word, working toward reconceiving it, has the further virtue of rescuing not only a term, but a basic value, from the confines of liberalism. That is the project of this article.

### D. *The Objective: Understanding and Overcoming Pathology*

So far we have only a general sense of what some of the ingredients of autonomy must be. I have already mentioned the (problematic) notion of self-determination. I think comprehension, confidence, dignity, efficacy, respect, and some degree of peace and security from oppressive power are probably also components. (Note that these ingredients are both characteristics of individuals and states of being which presuppose certain conditions in intimate and social-structural relationships.) But we have as yet no full or integrated articulation of the values and perspectives I have mentioned. There are many different ways of trying to come to the articulation of a new value or, as in the case of autonomy, to help that value

11. There is a passage in Ursula K. Le Guin's novel, THE BEGINNING PLACE (New York: Harper & Row, 1980), which expresses this connection: "There was no boundary. It was all his country. But this time, this was far enough: he would go no further now. Part of the pleasure of being here was that he could listen for and obey such impulses and commands coming from within him, undistorted by external pressures and compulsions. In that obedience, for the first time since early childhood, he sensed the headiness of freedom, the calmness of power" (p. 27).

Of course this connection is played out in the political realm as well, and entails the same paradox: in a democracy, limited government means self-limiting government. The people must limit themselves. The fictions of constitutionalism try to obscure the paradox: a constitution spells out the limits the people have placed on themselves; those limits once set need not be reconsidered (except in the exceptional circumstances of amendments). The fiction works particularly nicely in the United States, where the Constitution was written so long ago. The reality is, of course, that the limits must be constantly reinterpreted. The "people," in the form of their representatives in the judiciary, must constantly set and reset the limits that they will treat as clear, fixed, and unquestioned. Within these self-defined limits, the collective finds its own law, which is an essential element of collective freedom. I discuss the paradox of self-limiting government more fully in "American Constitutionalism and the Paradox of Private Property," in CONSTITUTIONALISM AND DEMOCRACY, J. Elster and R. Slagstad, eds. (Cambridge: Cambridge University Press, 1988), 241-273.

emerge from the process of transforming an old one. Here I want to focus on a particular dimension of our current conception of autonomy that stands in the way of the necessary transformation: the dichotomy between autonomy and the collectivity.

This dichotomy is grounded in the deeply ingrained sense that individual autonomy is to be achieved by erecting a wall (of rights) between the individual and those around him. Property (as I will discuss more fully later) is, not surprisingly, the central symbol for this vision of autonomy, for it can both literally and figuratively provide the necessary walls. The most perfectly autonomous man is thus the most perfectly isolated.[12] The perverse quality of this implicit ideal is, I trust, obvious. This vision of the autonomous individual as one securely isolated from his threatening fellows seems to me to be a pathology that has profoundly affected western societies for several centuries.[13]

If we ask ourselves what actually enables people to be autonomous, the answer is not isolation, but relationships—with parents, teachers, friends, loved ones—that provide the support and guidance necessary for the development and experience of autonomy. I think, therefore, that the most promising model, symbol, or metaphor for autonomy is not property, but childrearing. There we have encapsulated the emergence of autonomy through relationship with others. We see that relatedness is not, as our tradition teaches, the antithesis of autonomy, but a literal precondition of autonomy, and interdependence a constant component of autonomy. This model of what actually sustains autonomy is, appropriately, the opposite of the isolated, distancing symbol of property. We may, in fact, have more to learn about the nature of autonomy by thinking about childrearing than by the sort of inquiry into law and bureaucracy that I undertake here. But there are advantages to avoiding the problems of extrapolating from intimate relationships to large-scale ones. And some of the relationships which either foster or undermine autonomy are not of an intimate variety, but rather are part of the more formal structures of authority (which include employment relations as well as the officially "public" sphere I deal

---

12. There is an interesting corroboration of my view of property-based independence as isolation in J.G.A. Pocock's analyses of the relationship between property and autonomy in 17th century liberal thought: "The point about freehold in this context is that it involves its proprietor as little as possible in dependence upon or ***even in relations with other people*** and so leaves him free for the full austerity of citizenship in the classical sense" (emphasis added). J.G.A. Pocock, POLITICS, LANGUAGE, AND TIME: ESSAYS ON POLITICAL THOUGHT AND HISTORY (New York: Atheneum, 1971), 91.

13. For a brilliant discussion of the western conception of the separate self, see Catherine Keller, FROM A BROKEN WEB: SEPARATION, SEXISM, AND SELF (Boston: Beacon Press, 1986). She also points to another connection between feminism and the reconception of autonomy: men's fear of women is tied to their fear of the collective. She begins her book (p. 1) with a telling quotation from C.S. Lewis's SURPRISED BY JOY: "You may add that in the hive and the anthill we see fully realized the two things that some of us most dread for our own species—the dominance of the female and the dominance of the collective."

with here). Ultimately, I think the different approaches (and I plan eventually to pursue both) will complement each other.

Here I will focus on how the pathological conception of autonomy as boundaries against others has played itself out in some of the central public institutions of the United States. This approach has the virtue of addressing immediate problems while at the same time moving toward a fuller conception of autonomy. The approach is also suggested by my belief that abstract theorizing alone is not likely to get us where we want to go. If we want to understand the social forms that foster autonomy, we need first to look at actual practices of collective organization that can reveal for us the possibilities of a new understanding of autonomy and help us understand the nature and sources of the limitations of the prevailing conception. Let me turn therefore to the particular problems of autonomy in the American bureaucratic state.

## II. Bureaucracy, Collectivity, and Autonomy

The American bureaucratic state threatens individual autonomy because it threatens to transform the objects of its action from citizens to subjects—dependent, passive, helpless before the power of the collective. This threat is not peculiar to American forms of bureaucracy. Whenever a democratic society assumes collective responsibility for individual welfare, it faces the task of implementing this responsibility in ways that foster rather than undermine citizens' sense of their own competence, control, and integrity. The traditional American conception of autonomy impedes this task and thus limits our understanding of the problem and the potential for its solution. The tradition of American political thought sets individual autonomy in opposition to collective power.[14] This opposition now distorts our perceptions. The characteristic problem of autonomy in the modern state is not, as our tradition has taught us, to shield individuals from the collective, to set up legal barriers around the individual which the state cannot cross, but to ensure the autonomy of individuals when they are *within* the legitimate sphere of collective power. The task is to render autonomy compatible with the interdependence which collective power (properly used) expresses.

The problem of interdependence, individual autonomy, and collective power takes its characteristic modern form in the relations between citizens and administrative bodies.[15] The dependence of citizens on those who

14. This focus on American political thought provides specificity in looking at how the problem of autonomy fits within a larger framework of political theory. The American treatment of autonomy is particularly focused on boundaries (as we shall see later), but it is not unique. On the contrary, I think it helps us understand a problem characteristic of all liberal thought.

15. In the course of my discussion I will use both the terms "state power" and "collective power." I am addressing the broad problem of the tension between individual autonomy and the power of the collective. In our political system that power is ordinarily exercised by the state, and thus in most contexts it is appropriate to refer to state or governmental power; but part of my argument is that the

apply policy to their particular cases poses a problem distinct from the traditional issues of democracy. The extent to which the policies administered are formulated by bodies (e.g., elected legislatures) which citizens have democratic access to and control over continues to be an important issue. But it is no longer the only one.

Even if legislative policy-making were democratically optimal, citizens in the modern state would still be subject to the decisions of administrators. People's knowledge that the policies behind these decisions were made in some distant way with their consent may do little to ease their sense of dependence and helplessness. (The distant quality of consent seems likely to prevail in any large-scale society, even when the forms of democracy make citizen participation active, widespread, and effective.) The nature of people's interactions with bureaucratic decision-making may be as important as the nature of legislative policy-making[16] in determining whether citizens are autonomous members of a democratic society or dependent subjects of collective control.

The objective of making the direct exercise of collective power conducive to the autonomy of those subject to it requires more than a shift in focus from legislation to administration. We also need to see that our traditional focus on protecting the individual from the collective has given us a distorted image of the problem of autonomy and of alternative visions of society. The prevailing conception of autonomy sets alternatives in the context of a false choice: when autonomy is identified with individual independence and security from collective power, the choice is posed between admitting collective control and preserving autonomy in any given realm of life. It is as though the degree of collective responsibility for, say, the material needs of citizens must result in a corresponding decrease in the autonomy of those receiving the benefits. Such a dichotomy between autonomy and collective power forecloses a whole range of social arrangements—at least to anyone who values autonomy. A classic example of a choice premised on this dichotomy is the claim that a free press is possible only if newspapers are privately owned. This claim rests on a notion of what the law can and cannot do which is unfounded. It assumes, first, that the law can protect property against the power of the collective and that this protection will provide the necessary insulation and foundation for freedom of expression. At the same time, the claim assumes that the

---

tension will endure however collective power is organized. The analysis therefore should be relevant both to alternative political systems and to the non-governmental power exercised by such "private" entities as corporations.

16. The legislative and bureaucratic "models" of democratic citizenship are in some ways in tension with one another. If the legislature managed to make all policy decisions, if it were possible to formulate rules which neutral, efficient bureaucrats could apply mechanically (i.e., without evil degrees of discretion), citizens would be spared the sense of being subject to arbitrary control. But they would also have little scope for participation in the decisions on their own cases. While this may be advantageous from one point of view, it may seriously undermine the autonomy of citizens directly subject to governmental action over which they feel they have no control.

law cannot provide comparable *direct* protection of this freedom by legal limits on the power of the state to control expression. The implicit conclusion is that if there were public rather than private ownership of the press, those wishing to express their views would require the (virtually uncontrollable) "permission" of the state.

This conclusion denies the possibility of structuring the relations between citizen and public press, their corresponding rights and powers, in a way compatible with freedom of expression. But we need no more assume that the relationship would take the form of "asking permission" to use the press than we assume the necessity of asking permission to use public schools, parks, or water. There is nothing in the nature of the legal protections themselves (as I shall return to later) nor in our experience of public resources to justify the stark dichotomy between freedom founded on private property and tyranny produced by collective control.[17]

State control of resources always poses problems, but the American legal system has found ways of distinguishing control from caprice, of rendering dependence upon state services (imperfectly) compatible with freedom and autonomy. Were the dichotomy between state power and autonomy exhaustive and inevitable, we would be forced either to give up on autonomy in large spheres of our lives or to advocate a vast limitation on state power, which would be incompatible both with modern economic and political realities and with aspirations for a more communal and equitable society. This choice is not necessary. Despair about individual freedom in the face of collective power reflects a poverty of imagination about the possibilities for protection and control.

Belief in the false choice between autonomy and collective power is the product of a powerful tradition of political thought. Paradoxically, the tradition (mis)shapes the perception of the problem while pointing in the direction of solutions. Our legal tradition itself suggests the possibilities of protection and control. To see both the problem and the possibilities more clearly, we need first to examine the tradition.

## III. Autonomy and Property in the American Tradition[18]

### A. *Boundaries and Dichotomies*

Our political tradition has virtually identified freedom and autonomy with the private sphere, and posed them in opposition to the public sphere of state power. The idea of a boundary between these spheres, a line di-

17. The example of airwaves, of course, points to the complexity of governmental control. The government has assumed a much larger role in regulating the electronic than the written media, on the grounds of regulating a finite public resource. One need not be sanguine about the history of this regulation to see that public control can take a wide range of forms.

18. The arguments in this section are spelled out more fully in Jennifer Nedelsky, Private Property and the Limits of American Constitutionalism: A View From the Formation, forthcoming from University of Chicago Press.

viding individual autonomy from the legitimate scope of state power, has been central to the American conceptions of freedom and limited government. The notion of a boundary took shape in the early development of our Constitution, and it was property which was the focal point for this idea. While parts of this story are well known, they bear a retelling (and reformulation) here as the framework for the prevailing conception of autonomy.

The revolutionary slogan "no taxation without representation" posed consent as the basis for legitimacy. It asserted not that private property could never be taken by the state, but that such taking was legitimate only if consented to by the governed. This idea also took the form of claims that a government which could take property without consent was tyrannous and reduced men to slaves. These claims reflected the sense that the major threat to freedom and autonomy was the inability to have some say in the decisions which affected important aspects of one's life. But this emphasis on consent shifted with the grim realization that consent alone was no guarantee against injustice or tyranny.[19]

In the 1780s duly elected state legislatures passed a variety of debtor relief laws which were widely viewed as violations of property rights and as evidence of the intrinsic vulnerability of property (and, more generally, minority) rights under popular government. The concern turned to making popular government compatible with the security of individual rights and to asserting as a matter of political principle that consent was not a sufficient basis for legitimacy. "Rules of justice"[20] and the concept of basic rights formed independent standards against which to measure the legitimacy of democratic outcomes. The need to inculcate these independent standards, and the particular preoccupation with protecting property against tyranny by the majority, led to a differentiation between civil and political rights and a clear hierarchical relation between them. Political rights were merely means to the true end of government: the security of private or civil rights. This security itself, as well as the principle of consent, required some form of representative government. But for the Federalists—whose views triumphed in the writing of the Constitution and in the dominant tradition of American political thought—the focus of concern was not on designing means for men to have an active share in their own governance, but rather designing means to contain, control, and minimize the threat of popular political power. There is virtually nothing in Federalist thought which treats political participation as an important component of individual autonomy, as a dimension of self-determination with intrinsic value.[21]

19. *See* Gordon Wood, CREATION OF THE AMERICAN REPUBLIC, 1776-1787 (Chapel Hill: University of North Carolina Press, 1969).
20. THE FEDERALIST No. 10 (J. Madison).
21. The Anti-Federalists did treat political participation in this way. *See* Nedelsky, *Confining*

The Federalists drew on a tradition (Locke, for example) which emphasized rights as the object of legitimate government and hence the limit to it. But in the context of the American fear of *popular* tyranny, the conception of rights as limiting values hardened into opposed categories of state vs. individual and public vs. private. Individual autonomy was conceived of as protected by a bounded sphere—defined primarily by property—into which the state could not enter. The sphere of rights, freedom, autonomy was private. And the means of assuring those rights, that autonomy, was to keep the public realm distant, separate, at bay. The people (in a highly mediated, carefully structured system of government) would control the public realm: collective decisions would be taken on democratic principles. But every effort was made to minimize the chances of those decisions encroaching on the private realm. The idea of a boundary to the legitimate scope of the public realm then crystallized in judicial review. And, as in the earlier conception of divided spheres, property was the central issue around which the idea of judicially enforceable boundaries developed.

There was, finally, another dimension to the parallel divisions between state and individual, public and private: the opposition between politics and market. This dichotomy was part of the conceptual framework which placed freedom and autonomy on the side of the "individual," "private," and "market" and coercion on the side of the "state," "public," and "politics." The coercive power of the collective was given free expression in legislation. The rights of individuals (private rights), by contrast, were given order, protection and scope through the common law, which permitted market transactions—ostensibly without the coercive intervention of the state, without the purposive, collective decision-making of the legislature.[22] Free, private, individual (trans)actions stood in defensive opposition to coercive control by collective (public, legislative) power.

We now have a picture of a legal and political ideology which identified autonomy with a private sphere defined and bounded by property. This was the conceptual framework which prevailed (despite major deviations from it in practice) until 1937,[23] and which continues to haunt and shape both theory and practice.

Three things need to be said about this picture of law, state, and autonomy. The first (which in its full dimensions is beyond the scope of this paper) is that the dichotomous categories of liberal theory have always been illusory. Second (and only apparently in contrast), these categories

---

*Democratic Politics: Anti-Federalists, Federalists, and the Constitution* (Book Review), 96 HARV. L. REV. 340 (1982).

22. Friedrich A. Hayek offers a particularly clear statement of (and argument for) these contrasts in our tradition in his LAW, LEGISLATION, AND LIBERTY, Vol. 1, Chs. 5 and 6 (Chicago: The University of Chicago Press, 1973).

23. This was the date of West Coast Hotel v. Parrish, 300 U.S. 379 (1937), which is the conventionally recognized turning point in a long process.

and constellations of beliefs, and their related concepts of the rule of law and the sanctity of property, could not have had such power and endurance if they were based on illusion only. If I am right that their meaning was not what it purported to be, then our task is to discover the truths which lay behind them. Third, whatever the subtle truths behind the tradition, its basic components of property and boundary are no longer adequate to the contemporary problems of autonomy. I shall begin with the illusions, turn to the particular inadequacy of property, and then note the insights this misleading tradition nevertheless provides.

### B. *Illusions*

The dichotomies of state-individual, public-private, politics-market, legislation-common law were always illusory. The central part of the illusion was the association of freedom with the second term of each dichotomy and coercion with the first. It is not simply that things have changed so much that the categories no longer make sense. Rather, the dichotomies from the beginning served to mask the role of state power in the second set of terms.[24]

To take a central example, property rights are defined by the legal system. The security they provide rests on the power of the state to punish those who trespass on those rights. And the power and independence which individuals derive from property rests on the rules the legal system has set up to define what constitutes legitimate and enforceable transactions, what goods can be demanded on the basis of what sorts of claims. Property takes its power and importance in large part from "the market"—which is itself defined by the legal system. "The market" is not a freestanding, natural phenomenon, but consists of rules defined by law and backed by the power of the state.[25]

Only a radical difference between common law and legislation (such as Friedrich Hayek eloquently, but in the end unpersuasively, defends[26]) can maintain the claim to the essential privateness and freedom of property and the market. But the actual workings of the common law have not

---

24. Theodore Lowi, THE END OF LIBERALISM, 2d ed. (New York: W.W. Norton and Company, 1979), and Robert Dahl and Charles Lindblom, POLITICS, ECONOMICS, AND WELFARE (Chicago: University of Chicago Press, 1976), offer graphic illustrations of the inaptness of similar traditional categories.

25. There can, of course, be markets where there is no legal system like ours. Custom alone may define both rules and sanctions. Even in our society there are areas of commercial transaction governed largely not by law, but by agreement among parties with adequate enforcement power of their own. I leave aside for the moment whether these customary norms constitute a form of collective power radically different from that exercised through legislation. But, in any case, in our system "the market" consists essentially of legal rules and is in that sense a creature of the state.

26. Hayek, *supra* note 22, argues that the common law is neutral, non-purposive, and the articulation of spontaneously arising custom. It is "the law of freedom" because it merely provides the framework for the exercise of freedom. Legislation, by contrast, is aimed at the achievement of some collective purpose and must by its nature be coercive.

been Hayekian.[27] They have not had the essential lack of purposiveness he claims. The common law has been informed and shaped by particular conceptions of fairness, freedom, and progress. The "neutral" rules of the game correspond to a particular vision of the good society which gives advantages to some players over others in systematic, if not perfectly predictable ways.

I have embarked on this both overly long and too abbreviated argument about property, the market, and the common law to show that the long prevailing conception of autonomy was embedded in a set of categories and oppositions that were in basic ways illusory. And to the extent that the contrasts are illusory, the choices they point to are false.

Property is the creature of the state. To replace property as the symbol and source of autonomy may redefine the relations between citizens and the state. But the choice to do so (as in the free press example above) is not a choice between private and free on the one hand and collective and coercive on the other. Because reality has never corresponded to these neat oppositional categories, there is no need to choose between them. Freeing ourselves from misleading categories and false choices opens the possibility for individual autonomy in the context of collectivity.

### C. *Contemporary Inadequacies*

While the dichotomies of liberal theory have always been illusory, there is a particular inadequacy to the role played by property today. Private property was for 150 years the central and defining instance of the boundary between governmental authority and individual autonomy. Property can, however, no longer serve this function because it has lost its original political significance.

Property no longer provides people with the basis for independence and autonomy in the eighteenth-century sense. For the farmer who tilled his own land or the craftsman who owned his tools, property was a real source of independence. However much they depended on good weather or customers, their property gave them a control over their livelihood, and hence their independence, which was radically different from that of modern wage earners, salaried professionals, or stockholders. The dependence of wage earners on their employers is obvious. But even stockholders, who own their shares, have little control over the source of their income. Their income, like that of most professionals, embeds them in a network of relationships characterized by interdependence rather than independence. The percentage of Americans for whom property provides the traditional inde-

27. Morton J. Horwitz's THE TRANSFORMATION OF AMERICAN LAW, 1780-1860 (Cambridge: Harvard University Press, 1977) provides the clearest evidence of this. Even critics who challenge many of Horwitz's claims do not present a picture of the common law as having the natural and undirected quality which is a central part of Hayek's picture.

pendence of the yeoman farmer is now so small that the idea of property as the basis for autonomy has lost most of its original meaning.[28] In addition, property itself is now subject to regulation to such an extent that it cannot serve symbolically or substantively as the boundary between individual rights and governmental power.[29]

Moreover, the very idea of an inviolable sphere can no longer be the central issue of autonomy in the modern state.[30] As more and more issues are seen in terms of collective rather than individual responsibility, there will be fewer and fewer spheres of activity in which the state is not involved. As the reality of interdependence shapes the scope of collective action and control, citizens will increasingly be subject to governmental authority to license, regulate, and distribute benefits. The model for autonomy must be integration, not isolation. The task is to make the interdependence of citizen and state conducive to, rather than destructive of, autonomy.

We have some reason to be optimistic about finding the means of doing so. The old dichotomies prove to be misleading. And, as the final section of this article will suggest, contemporary administrative law gives glimpses of what such means might be like. But in reconceiving autonomy, in reconstituting its sources and protections, we should also try to uncover the truths which have sustained the traditional framework for so long.

## D. *Lessons for Reconceiving Autonomy*

There are, of course, explanations other than truth for the endurance of ideology. Those in power usually have considerable resources for fostering

---

28. The importance of property has never been simple. Even in 1787, many of the Framers derived an important part of their income from complicated transactions in bonds and speculative ventures in joint stock companies. Certainly not all of these men shared Jefferson's vision of an agrarian republic. But they did see a close connection between wide-spread, small-scale ownership of property and political independence, and they feared the day when wage labour would sever that connection. Important dimensions of the connection have now disappeared, leaving behind, perhaps, residual dreams of home ownership as the last widely available form of autonomy sustained and protected by property. The receding reality of the property-autonomy nexus is not the same as the advantages and insulation wealth continues to provide.

29. There is, of course, the related but distinct question of whether some form of property is essential for autonomy. If property is so broadly defined that it means the concrete expression of autonomous action, then, practically tautologically, autonomy requires property. Such a definition leaves entirely open the practices of use, possession, alienation, and advantage that we associate with property. Margaret Radin has tried to distinguish between those dimensions of conventional property essential for what she calls personhood and those unsuitable to and even destructive of that value (which, I think, includes, but is not synonymous with autonomy). *See* Radin, *Property and Personhood*, 34 STAN. L. REV. 957 (1982). The extent of my claim here is that the current meaning of property no longer stands in any clear or necessary relation to autonomy.

30. The problem of boundaries does not disappear. Part of the task of ensuring the good society is to redefine the relation between citizen and state, individual and collective. That task includes identifying those realms which should be considered private, beyond the scope of collective control. My point is that the definition of such boundaries cannot be the only basis for autonomy in a society which recognizes individual responsibility to the collective and collective responsibility for social and individual welfare.

beliefs which sustain the status quo. But it seems likely that when particular conceptions have endured for centuries in both the popular imagination and theoretical writings, they can provide insights into the problems they address. It is not possible here to unpack everything embedded in the tradition I have outlined. But we can examine some of the directions the tradition points to, some of the problems it alerts us to in the effort to reconceive autonomy.

The first is that while the stark opposition between autonomy and collectivity presumed in the American tradition is misleading, that opposition also reflects a basic truth. There is a real and enduring tension between the individual and the collective, and any good political system will recognize it. The problem with our tradition is that it not only recognizes, but highlights the tension, and has a limited view of the non-oppositional aspects of the relation and of the social dimension of human beings. There is thus a twofold objective in reconceiving autonomy: (1) to recognize that the irreducible tension between the individual and the collective makes choices or trade-offs necessary; and (2) at the same time, to move beyond a conception of human beings which sees them exclusively as separate individuals and focuses on the threat of the community. The collective is not simply a potential threat to individuals, but is constitutive of them, and thus is a source of their autonomy as well as a danger to it.[31] For some purposes it makes sense to talk about the separate constructs of "the individual" and "the community." But those constructs are misleading[32] if they obscure the fact that people do not exist in isolation, but in social and political relations. People develop their predispositions, their interests, their autonomy—in short, their identity—in large part out of these relations. The very way one experiences and perceives the world, for example, is shaped by the social constructions of language. The task, then, is to think of autonomy in terms of the forms of human interactions in which it will develop and flourish.[33] And the starting point of this inquiry must be

31. The childrearing model is helpful here: parents are both a source of a child's autonomy and a potential threat to it. It is easy to see that the powerful relationship of dependency children have with their parents is a necessary foundation for the child's autonomy. But the relationship can also be structured in ways that undermine autonomy, that maintain dependence. It is probably the case that all relationships necessary for autonomy can easily be perverted to undermine it.

32. In our current discourse it is hard to avoid such misleading language. The concept of "self-determination," which I described as central to autonomy, carries the tension implicit in the problem itself. Few people in our culture believe that people are truly self-determining. It is commonly accepted that people are shaped to a great extent by their culture and genetic make-up. Yet self-determination remains an important value and aspiration. The new conception of autonomy must give force to the aspiration while incorporating a recognition of interdependence.

33. Bruno Bettelheim offers a brief but fascinating discussion of the kinds of relations which foster autonomy. In his account they are direct and personal rather than large scale, anonymous, or abstract. If his views are correct, we can both understand something about why autonomy has been associated with the private sphere and see that the relevant characteristics are possible in spheres not conventionally considered private. Bettelheim offers as examples both the relation to parents and to teachers. Bruno Bettelheim, THE INFORMED HEART: AUTONOMY IN A MASS AGE (Glencoe, Ill.: Free Press, 1960), 95–97.

an attention both to the individuality of human beings and to their essentially social nature. The hope is that a society with such an outlook could escape some of the problems of our more limited perspective and could structure relations of community which also fostered autonomy.

The tradition warns us, however, that there is probably an inevitable trade-off between collective cohesion and responsibility on the one hand, and individual freedom and autonomy on the other—at least as we currently understand these concepts. The individualism of liberal capitalism has never actually provided all citizens with its proclaimed values of freedom and independence. But our system has made comparatively few demands on its citizens and has left a wide scope for individual choice. American democratic capitalism has neither demanded nor fostered excellence, virtue, commitment, social or civic responsibility (which is not, of course, to say that none of these ever emerged). A society which seeks to promote these characteristics will have a far greater interest in the values its members hold, the relationships they form, and the way they choose to spend their time and their talents. Such a society will almost certainly be more demanding and constraining in those areas, leaving fewer spheres of action to private choice.

Ultimately, the objective is to find the optimal relation between individual and collective and, more particularly, to understand the core of human autonomy and the forms and scope of collective activity that will foster it. We can take from the tradition a recognition that the new forms of autonomy within collectivity will involve choices, even trade-offs. But the limitations of our current conceptions should lend us confidence that to choose new forms of autonomy is to reconstitute it, not abandon it.

The tradition also offers us a way of grasping the essence of autonomy. An understanding of the powerful associations between property, security, and autonomy is likely to provide a better sense of the nature of autonomy and the requirements for it. (This despite the fact that autonomy in a collective state will be quite different from the individualistic, oppositional model associated with property.)

The rhetorical, even mythical power of the identification of property with freedom goes beyond the literal power and advantages of property under liberal capitalism. And the experience of the rights of property as qualitatively different from and more secure than other legal rights cannot be accounted for by the legal history of property rights. Property rights have in fact been subject to a great deal of state interference and to redefinition which amounted to destruction.[34] As I argued earlier, there is nothing intrinsic about legal rights of property which make them a more promising basis for freedom than other legal rights. Property rights, like

---

34. *See* M. Horwitz, *supra* note 27, and Scheiber, *Property Law, Expropriation, and Resource Allocation by Government in the United States, 1789–1910*, 33 J. ECON. HIST. 232 (1973).

all legal rights, take their formal meaning from definitions and guarantees provided by the state. The security which property provides rests, on an institutional level, on the state's power to protect what it defines as property. And the forms and means of defining and protecting property are, at root, indistinguishable from those of other legal rights.

What then accounts for the enduring associations between property and autonomy? Two striking and distinguishing characteristics of property are its concreteness and the relative unobtrusiveness of the state power which lies behind it.[35] The concreteness of property makes it an effective symbol. It is easy for people to see the relationship between owning property and autonomy, and it seems (deceptively) easy to know what property is and when it is violated. And most people do not think of their ownership of property as in any way involving the state; it is simply theirs. It is not granted to them by the state or administered by the state. Most property rights can be exercised most of the time without the obvious intervention of the state. The fact that property rights only have meaning when backed by the power of the state seems an abstraction that students have a hard time grasping, many sophisticated theorists ignore entirely, and the general population has no idea about. Due process, by comparison with property, is abstract rather than concrete and clearly requires official action. If these are the characteristics which make the association of property with freedom so compelling, we should be alerted to the probable limitations of due process as an alternative source, symbol, or protector of autonomy.

Finally, my comments about property reflect a more general approach to the problem of autonomy and to what tradition and current practices can teach us about it. Autonomy is an elusive problem in part because it is practically inseparable from an experience or feeling.[36] In an earlier version of this article I added the qualification that "It would, of course, seriously distort any political analysis of autonomy to treat it as a 'mere' feeling. One can evaluate the degree of autonomy an individual is actually capable of exercising, and there can be disparities between experience and reality." This qualification was an effort to meet the objection that people

35. This argument is elaborated in J. Nedelsky, *supra* note 11.

36. It is important to avoid a misunderstanding about the "mere subjectivity" of feelings. In my view, feelings have two dimensions not commonly associated with the word: (1) There is a truth about feelings. One can be right or wrong about them. Thus while they are subjective in the sense that only the person having the feeling is "authoritative" on whether she feels something, her true feelings are not simply whatever impression, or experience, or sensation she has at the moment. A person must inquire internally to determine her true feelings. They may be hard to discern, there may be confusion, but there is in the end a right answer to what she really feels. (2) The related point is that feelings are, at least in our culture, not always immediately ascertainable. There is a commonplace association between the word "feeling" and something like the experience of a pin prick. One feels pain. No inquiry is necessary. The experience is immediate and obvious. The perception is instantaneous and (under normal circumstances, excluding states of hypnosis or delusion) infallible. But this association is misleading. Even a feeling like anger is by no means always obvious. Only the "feeler's" statements are authoritative, but she can be mistaken. In our culture most people seem to need to learn to recognize the signs by which one can tell the truth of a feeling.

may be deluded about what provides them with autonomy.[37] In fact, I think people may be very wrong in their opinions about the relation between autonomy and institutions or practices. But I doubt that it makes sense to say they could actually feel autonomous and not be so.[38] However, just as we need to develop a new conception of autonomy, probably most of us need to learn what real autonomy feels like.

Our actual experiences of autonomy—those rare moments when we feel that we are following an inner direction rather than merely responding to the pushes and pulls of our environment—are so fleeting that it is often difficult to know or remember what it is like to live by one's own law. And our society misleads us about the very nature of autonomy as well as the conditions for it. We not only learn, as I noted above, that the essence of autonomy is the power to close out others; we are also taught that money is power and power is freedom—and the power is from and over others, not inner power.[39] We are taught that the capacity to manipulate our environment is the power of freedom. A participant at the Yale Legal Theory Workshop, where an earlier version of this article was presented, suggested that those who feel autonomous are those who believe that their actions generate predicted and desired results, as opposed to those who feel powerless to control their lives, who feel buffeted about by forces beyond their control. (This notion of autonomy, he pointed out, has the virtue of being measurable.) In fact, many people learn to "play the game" effectively, to do what is wanted of them, and to confidently reap the rewards handed out for compliance. This counts as success and generates the feeling he described. It is not autonomy. Playing someone else's game well is not defining the path of one's own life.

These perverse messages about autonomy contain a germ of truth: powerlessness is destructive of autonomy. And the question of power points to the ways autonomy entails, but does not consist in, a feeling. Autonomy is a capacity, but it is unimaginable in the absence of the feeling or experience of being autonomous. The capacity can be destroyed by being subjected to the arbitrary and damaging power of others.[40] Power relations are, in that sense, an external, "objective" reality. To be autono-

---

37. I think the qualification was also, less consciously, a response to the sense that taking subjectivity seriously was unacceptable in academic theorizing about law and politics. And, indeed, despite the disclaimer, a commentator on the paper wittily objected that, "If autonomy is a feeling, there are pharmacological solutions to the problem." I think that is clever, but wrong. Perhaps I have too little faith in modern technology and/or too little experience with drugs, but I can imagine a drug making one feel euphoric, maybe even happy, but not autonomous.

38. Of course, to ascertain someone's feeling of autonomy, it would be necessary to communicate effectively about the content of the value and the experience, not simply ask for a response to a term, "autonomy."

39. The distinction between power over others and empowerment, a power from within, is discussed in Starhawk, TRUTH OR DARE: ENCOUNTERS WITH POWER, AUTHORITY, AND MYSTERY (San Francisco: Harper & Row, 1987).

40. Bettelheim's THE INFORMED HEART, *supra* note 33, is a study of the extreme case of such destruction in concentration camps.

mous a person must feel a sense of her own power (which does not mean power over others), and that feeling is only possible within a structure of relationships conducive to autonomy. But it is also the case that if we lose our feeling of being autonomous, we lose our capacity to be so. Autonomy is a capacity that exists only in the context of social relations that support it and only in conjunction with the internal sense of being autonomous.

Although I define autonomy as a capacity and not a feeling, I insist upon the feeling of autonomy as an inseparable component of the capacity for several reasons. First, I think the capacity does not exist without the feeling. Second, I think the feeling is our best guide to understanding the structure of those relationships which make autonomy possible. Third, focusing on the feelings of autonomy defines as authoritative the voices of those whose autonomy is at issue. Their autonomy is then not a question that can be settled for them by others. The focus on feeling or internal experience defines whose perspective is taken seriously,[41] and by turning our attention in the right direction it enhances our ability to learn what fosters and constitutes autonomy. For the purpose of evaluating institutions, one can generate a list, or at least a sense, of the components or dimensions of autonomy and then try to identify the practices that seem to foster some or all of those components. To that extent one would be engaged in an "objective" inquiry. But the underlying concern would be the actual experience of autonomy. We cannot understand or protect, much less reconceive, autonomy unless we attend to what gives citizens a sense of autonomy, to what makes them feel competent, effective, able to exercise some control over their lives, as opposed to feeling passive, helpless, and dependent.[42]

But this ingredient of subjectivity introduces an added complication. The institutions, social practices, and relations that foster the feeling of autonomy may vary considerably across cultures and over time within a culture.[43] These variations raise the question of whether one form and experience of autonomy (and the institutions that sustain it) can be judged to be superior to another. (Such a judgment is, of course, implicit in this article.) Recognizing subjective experience as an essential component of

41. I owe this insight to Lucinda Finley.

42. A government's efforts to encourage its subjects to feel autonomous when they are not is obviously a perversion. The recent history of administrative hearings may provide evidence of the relation between the actual effectiveness of citizen-participation and the way hearings make participants feel about the process, the decision, and their role in it. *See* Handler, *Justice for the Welfare Recipient: Fair Hearings in AFDC—The Wisconsin Experience*, 43 Soc. Serv. Rev. 12 (1969); Hammer and Hartley, *Procedural Due Process and the Welfare Recipient: A Statistical Study of AFDC Fair Hearings in Wisconsin*, 1978 Wis. L. Rev. 145.

43. For example, the much vaunted freedom of mainstream North-American life seems to many Native Americans to entail patterns of work with such extreme regimentation as to be incompatible with freedom or autonomy. (Brian Slattery of Osgoode Hall Law School provided me with this example from his work with Native peoples.) Of course, this observation leaves open the question whether the participants in the mainstream patterns of life actually experience their lives as autonomous.

autonomy invites all the much debated problems of objectivity and universal truths—which are beyond the scope of this article. Here I want only to draw attention to feelings as a basic dimension of the abstract concept of autonomy, and to note that feminist theory is becoming increasingly practiced in dealing with these issues.

Recognizing the subjective element of autonomy is also important because the very fact that autonomy is in part a feeling may make people particularly resistant to changes in its form. Bruno Bettelheim, for example, suggests that the ancient nomads, as they watched society shifting to agriculture, may have responded with anxiety and contempt as they saw their fellows give up "for greater economic ease and security, a relative freedom to roam."[44] In this instance, Bettelheim is willing to make a tacit judgment that the new settled life was not, in fact, a diminished one. But he does suggest that real accommodations had to be made. Because, as I argued above, trade-offs are probably inevitable, hostility to new approaches to autonomy may be based on real perceptions of loss. Perhaps it is even likely that the new approach will draw the contempt Bettelheim mentions. Perhaps all alternatives to what has been perceived as the essence of freedom are likely to be cast by anxious critics in terms of the basic (and base) needs, as libertarians, for example, dismiss as mere envy or greed claims that economic equality is a precondition of autonomy.

Acknowledging the complexities of understanding, comparing, and evaluating feelings of autonomy, it is still useful to look to actual practices that seem to have fostered this feeling, or at least have been associated with the concept. Past practices, however deficient, may provide important clues to new sources of autonomy and to the problems they are likely to entail. And present practices offer concrete examples of the efforts to reconcile autonomy with collective control. Let us turn therefore to what the present has to offer us.

## IV. The Insights of Administrative Law

### A. *The Potential of Due Process*

My objective in this section is to point to those aspects of contemporary administrative law which suggest the kinds of values and practices needed to make autonomy more viable in a bureaucratic state.[45] I shall start with

44. Bettelheim, *supra* note 33, at 45.

45. I do not mean to suggest anywhere in this article that a bureaucratic state is inevitable. And it seems quite possible that, ultimately, bureaucracy is incompatible with autonomy. Kathy Ferguson certainly thinks so. She has argued very persuasively that whenever people are being "managed" by others, something is wrong. The main point of her book (The Feminist Case Against Bureaucracy [Philadelphia: Temple University Press, 1984]) is the claim that there are viable and vastly preferable alternatives to bureaucracy. But as I noted at the outset, the hope is to find in our present practices clues to better solutions to the general problem that arises when there is both collective control and the mediate application of collective decisions. Only a very small community could avoid the latter. I remain agnostic on the question of whether that is what we should aspire to. And without

the positive contributions of contemporary American law and then identify some of its problems—problems that reflect the errors our tradition invites and the difficulty of avoiding them.

Administrative law mediates between governmental agencies and the citizens subject to their decisions. It defines the rights and obligations of both parties, and it has in recent years shown impressive—if flawed—attention to the problem of making dependence upon governmental benefits compatible with autonomy. The chief contributions of the law are to be found in the "due process explosion" (followed by retrenchment) signalled by *Goldberg v. Kelly.*[46] In that now famous case, the Supreme Court adopted the idea that welfare payments were the kind of benefit—a form of "new property"[47]—which could not be taken away without due process. Specifically, the Court held that a welfare recipient was entitled to a hearing *before* benefits were terminated.

The Court stressed the fact that welfare recipients were dependent on government for their basic necessities and that this made the provision of a pre-termination hearing particularly important. This case seems to be an instance of an effort to provide some degree of control and effectiveness to those in the most dependent relation to the government. The opportunity to be heard by those deciding one's fate, to participate in the decision at least to the point of telling one's side of the story, presumably means not only that the administrators will have a better basis for determining what the law provides in a given case, but that the recipients will experience their relations to the agency in a different way. The right to a hearing declares their views to be significant, their contribution to be relevant. In principle, a hearing designates recipients as part of the process of collective decision-making rather than as passive, external objects of judgment. Inclusion in the process offers the potential for providing subjects of bureaucratic power with some effective control as well as a sense of dignity, competence, and power. A hearing could of course be a sham, or be perceived to be so even if it were not. But the possibility of failure or perversion of the process leaves its potential contribution to autonomy unchanged.

This case and the (shifting) trend it started is of interest because it suggests something important about the possibility of achieving autonomy within a context of dependence. Dependence is a reality, and will be a reality in any system based on collective responsibility for the material well-being of some or all of its citizens. The problem is to avoid making autonomy a casualty of such collective responsibility. *Goldberg v. Kelly* suggests that there are forms of participation in administrative decisions

waiting to figure that one out, I think we can make progress on the question of autonomy.

46. 397 U.S. 254 (1970).

47. The phrase and the idea come from Reich, *The New Property*, 73 YALE L.J. 733 (1964).

which may prevent citizens from becoming passive subjects. The relationship can be shaped by the nature of the decision-making and the citizen's role in it. The nature of the citizen's relation to the agency to which he or she is subject need not be dictated by the substance of the agency's power, e.g., to grant or withhold basic necessities. This enormous power and corresponding dependency will affect, but need not destroy, the citizen's autonomy.

Most of the contributions of contemporary administrative law are of this order: provisions for participation in one form or another. (The expansion of standing—the rules defining who may challenge agency decisions in court—is a related development.[48]) My purpose here is not to analyze the line of cases through which the rights to hearings have been elaborated and restricted, but rather is to suggest that the cases reveal something important about the possibility of autonomy in the modern state and the requirements for it. The components of autonomy to which these legal developments seem responsive are dignity, efficacy, competence, and comprehension, as well as defense against arbitrariness. However mixed the cases, they provide some hope that there are ways of structuring bureaucratic decision-making so that the relations between citizen and state foster rather than undermine these values.

### B. *The Limits of Due Process*

Of course, legal rules alone will not determine whether bureaucratic encounters actually promote autonomy. Joel Handler offers an account of the failures of a federal law (Education for All Handicapped Children Act, P.L. 94-142) which seems designed to ensure optimal conditions for interaction between parents of handicapped children and the officials who will determine the children's placement.[49] The law has all the ingredients one might want: its requires ongoing participation by the parents in the decision-making, flexibility, individual tailoring of programs, hearings, and full rights of appeal. But stipulating these requirements does not make them a reality. In particular, it does not mean that parents actually take an active part, that they are listened to, or that they feel as though they are actors in the decision-making rather than (indirect) subjects of it.[50] The schools have strong incentives of time and money not to have the

48. *See* Sierra Club v. Morton, 405 U.S. 727 (1972); *compare* United States v. Students Challenging Regulatory Agency Procedures (SCRAP), 412 U.S. 669 (1973).

49. In terms of substantive outcomes, the provision of education for handicapped children, Handler considers the law largely a success. It is specifically with regard to the relationship between the clients and the official decision-makers that there is a striking disparity between the admirable intentions and language of the law and its actual effects. Joel F. Handler, THE CONDITIONS OF DISCRETION: AUTONOMY, COMMUNITY, BUREAUCRACY, Ch. 5 (New York: Russell Sage Foundation, 1986).

50. There is, of course, an unusual quality to these decisions since their actual subject, the child, is often not a participant (although the Madison plan calls for them to be when appropriate). The more general problem of structuring autonomous dependence, when the subject of the decision must

parents actively involved, and they have been successful in complying with the formal requirements of the law while undermining its purposes.

Handler's message is not, however, that bureaucratic encounters cannot be structured so that clients are genuinely autonomous actors; it is merely that formal law alone cannot achieve this end. Indeed, he provides a detailed example[51] of the schools in Madison, Wisconsin, which seem to have achieved genuine participation, and to have done so with similar (only this time actually realized) means: participation, information, and flexibility, as well as formal rights of appeal. Among the many factors that account for the difference, the most important seems to be that the relevant personnel in the Madison schools actually wanted parental participation; they thought it was necessary for the special education programs to work effectively. Given this goal, they were able to design the process of decision-making to encourage participation and to make it meaningful. For example, parents participated in the earliest stages of assessing the child's needs and planning a program, rather than being called in merely to consent to a diagnosis and plan already formulated (as was generally the case in the other systems). The teachers saw the parents' information and judgment about the child as valuable and thus treated them as actual partners in the decision-making. By contrast, in other systems studied, parents who raised questions were treated as "trouble makers."[52] Handler thinks that it is particularly important that in Madison conflict between the parents and the schools was not deflected, suppressed or avoided, but treated as part of a constructive process through which a better decision could be reached. The Madison schools also recognized that even with their positive attitude toward the parents and their acceptance of conflict, there was a power imbalance of resources and information that had to be addressed if the parents were to be able to take part effectively. "Parent advocates" were made available to try to redress the imbalance. In Massachusetts, by contrast, in the meetings at which the parents were presented with plans (made in their absence), the parents "were outnumbered, they were strangers confronting a group of people who had struck a bargain between them, and the discussion was often in technical jargon with the subtle implication that the child or the parent or both were at fault."[53] In Madison, information in clear, ordinary language was provided. The decision-making process was ongoing and open-ended, with room for readjustment. In most other school districts what

---

also be able to participate in the decision, is thus not the problem Handler addresses. There is some question whether he adequately considers the *children's* autonomy in his analysis. *See* Minow, *Part of the Solution, Part of the Problem* (Book Review), 34 UCLA L. REV. 981 (1987).

51. Handler, *supra* note 49, Ch. 4. Handler notes that his is a case study based on interviews with the full range of system participants, conducted during the 1983 school year. The data, he says, are not systematic.

52. Ibid., 66.

53. Ibid., 67.

was supposed to be an ongoing process of consultation was usually collapsed into one or two meetings.

In short, "the conclusion of virtually all the research is that whereas P.L. 94-142 seems to have resulted in more parental *contact* with the school authorities, there has not been much change in parental *involvement* in the actual decision-making process."[54] Throughout the Madison approach, there is a recognition that the parents are in a continuing relationship with the school. The objective is not simply to arrive at a decision to which the parents will not object, but to sustain a relationship such that the necessary ongoing decisions can be collectively made in the best interests of the child (which in turn are recognized to involve relations with the parents and with the school and relations between the school and the parents).

The parents' own testimony is the most compelling evidence that the system in Madison was "working," that the parents were not subordinated objects of bureaucratic decision-making, but were partners in a relationship that fostered their dignity, efficacy, comprehension, and competence and that protected them from arbitrary power. The parents were dependent on the schools (although not as starkly as a welfare recipient is dependent on the welfare bureaucracy), but their relationship was nevertheless characterized by autonomy. The dependence was not removed, it was transformed. The autonomy was thus, of course, not based on independence, on the capacity to make decisions without being subject to anyone else's preferences, judgments, or choices (the sort of autonomy Reich associates with property[55]). It was autonomy within relationship. And for some parents, the autonomy fostered in the relationship with the school seems to have made them feel more generally competent and secure in their ability to understand and help make decisions about their child.[56]

There are also cautionary dimensions to the Madison story. First, Handler notes that Madison has a long history of active citizen participation which may have made possible both the inception and the success of this experiment. But while that means that one should not be overly sanguine about simply transporting the model elsewhere, it also suggests that patterns of social and political interaction can foster autonomous relationships. It further invites us to inquire into the details of the institutional and social practices that have fostered this participatory culture.

A little more troubling is the suggestion that participation actually dropped off once parents developed a high level of trust in the school. A successful relationship seemed to make parents feel that they need not work to sustain it. This is, of course, easily understandable. With all the

54. Ibid., 68.
55. Reich, *supra* note 47.
56. Handler, *supra* note 49, at 79.

competing pressures on one's time, why not delegate time-consuming decision-making to those one trusts? (And of course genuine participation is very time-consuming. Handler suggests that is one of the reasons most school districts comply with the legal requirements for parental participation in a perfunctory way.) In Madison, it was the school officials who complained about the parents' lack of participation.

Of course it is an old problem that genuine power-sharing and democracy are time-consuming. One would need to know more about the Madison story to tell whether the parents' stepping back from active involvement necessarily undermined the autonomy fostered by the original relationship. It may be that the Madison parents were exercising their autonomy to make a reasonable choice of delegation—a choice that has nothing in common with forced acquiescence in the presumed superior authority of school officials. Perhaps it is enough if the parents continue to feel able to understand and evaluate what is happening with their child, and able to become involved whenever it seems necessary to them. Their sense of a *capacity* to participate may be what is crucial, rather than participation itself. Unfortunately, it may also be that while the parents' autonomy remains intact, the child's education suffers when participation drops off.

There are other problems (e.g., the question of whether the "parent advocates" are actually used and what their role should be) and quibbles (Handler's language of negotiation and bargaining does not capture my image of an optimal relationship, and even the parental statements he likes best have hints that the primary decision-makers are the school professionals).[57] But overall, Handler's argument shows both that the participatory move in American law can foster autonomy and that legal requirements alone are insufficient.

### C. *Conceptual Failures of Liberal Rights*[58]

These developments in administrative law grew out of the best in the American liberal tradition: its emphasis on the protection of individuals from the power of the state. But the tradition has also been the source of problems with the judicial response to conflicts between individuals and the bureaucracies upon which they are dependent. It is hardly surprising that a tradition which has conceived of the relationship between the individual and the collective primarily in terms of the threat of the latter does not provide an adequate basis for defining individual rights in the context

57. The quote he uses to open the chapter on Madison reads: "Our family has never been criticized, they've never said, 'you're failing him.' They've encouraged us to allow him to do more and try more, and not to be afraid. They've convinced us he can do more than we think he can do." Ibid. One can see that the relationship has been helpful, supportive, and respectful, but to me it does not quite convey the sense of fully equal partnership.

58. Handler also treats the failures of due process as a conceptual failure.

of affirmative responsibilities of the state. The dichotomy between individual rights and state power has meant that the courts have particular trouble in cases which require them both to accept the state's intrusion into previously private spheres *and* to develop a useful framework of individual rights.

*Wyman v. James*[59] dramatically illustrates the justices' inability to analyze rights in the context of dependence. The Supreme Court held that a social worker did not need a warrant for a "home visit" to a woman receiving Aid for Families with Dependent Children. Justice Blackmun's underlying argument for the majority was essentially this: in accepting the state's offer of responsibility for the welfare of her child, Mrs. James had declared her home life to be the state's business. She could not then turn around and stand on the traditional rights of individuals against state intrusion. In dissent, Justice Douglas made an impassioned argument against the state's capacity to "buy up" rights when it distributes largesse and convincingly argued that if Mrs. James were a businessman objecting to administrative searches, she would win. But Douglas showed virtually no acknowledgement of the ways in which traditional rights may have to be reconceived as the state takes on responsibilities that transform its relations to the individual. Neither approach seems to recognize that the task is to think creatively about the protections of autonomy given the realities of overlapping spheres of public and private interest. Neither a denial of rights nor a denial of realities can solve the problem.

Even when courts do try to protect individual rights in the face of collective power, they tend to use a private-rights model to define and justify the rights in question. Thus *Goldberg v. Kelly* uses the concept of "new property" to explain why welfare recipients are entitled to pre-termination hearings. The choice of property is understandable, but particularly unfortunate. As subsequent developments[60] have shown, characterizing dependents' rights as property invites a focus on entitlement that misses the point and facilitates retrenchment. Property also carries with it a powerful tradition of inequality which should not be incorporated into new conceptions of autonomy.

But the problem with the concept of new property is more general. It is a mistake to tie protections for citizens' autonomy to particular substantive rights. The objective is to protect the autonomy of citizens in their interactions with government. The appropriate forms of those interactions may vary depending on the kind of interest involved. But the entitlement to autonomy, and to bureaucratic encounters conducive to autonomy, should

59. 400 U.S. 309 (1971).

60. These developments began with Board of Regents v. Roth, 408 U.S. 564 (1972), in which the Court held that a one-year position at a state university did not constitute a property interest and did not, therefore, bring with it an entitlement to due process.

not depend upon or be deduced from the particular interest at stake.[61] What is at issue here is autonomy and democratic citizenship, which are not relevant only to particular rights.

And for reasons suggested in my discussion of *Wyman v. James*, the use of a private-rights model may only lead to the abandonment of any judicial protection. Jerry Mashaw's similar argument about private law and public law models suggests that the evident inappropriateness of private law models for state undertakings such as welfare may lead courts to cede complete authority to legislatures to define the terms on which benefits are granted or withdrawn.[62]

## V. Democracy and Autonomy

The possibility of such abandonment points to another, quite different error or danger of contemporary administrative law: the tendency to treat autonomy exclusively as a matter of process rather than as a substantive value. The danger arises because so many of the protections for autonomy rest on forms of participation. These forms are indeed the strength of the legal response, but the focus on process may easily be confused with a powerful trend in contemporary legal theory: the effort to build a constitutional theory based on the values of democracy and consent alone.

This seems to me a fundamental error—a misunderstanding not only of our constitutional system, but of the kind of political system which can foster the good society, and autonomy in particular. Property was once the core of a tension between democratic values of popular rule and liberal values of individual rights as limits on state power. Property neither can nor should continue to serve this role. But we should not abandon the tension itself. It has been the strength of our system and captures the irreducible tension between the individual and the collective which any good society must recognize and find ways of dealing with. Autonomy should be contrasted with democratic values in the following related senses: democracy is not itself sufficient to ensure autonomy; autonomy is a substantive value which can be threatened by democratic outcomes, even though the democratic process is itself a necessary component of autonomy; and the outcomes of democratic processes should respect the autonomy of all citizens and should be held accountable for doing so.

The confusion and correspondence between democracy and autonomy do not, of course, rest with prevailing legal theories alone; the correspondence between the two is real. Participation seems central to both. Its importance to democracy is obvious. It has been my basic point here that

61. In constitutional terms, which I have so far avoided, one might argue that there is a "liberty interest" in autonomy itself, rather than that individuals are entitled to be treated in a manner compatible with autonomy only when they can demonstrate a property or liberty interest.

62. Mashaw, *"Rights" in the Federal Administrative State*, 92 Yale L.J. 1129 (1983).

citizens who participate directly[63] in the decisions affecting them are less likely to relinquish their autonomy as they accept the benefits or control of the state. But participation here is a means to autonomy, not its substantive content. The fact that the means of protecting autonomy may primarily be forms of participation should not lead to the confusion that autonomy can be subsumed under democracy. We should not collapse democracy and autonomy into a single value, despite their close connection.

The perfection of democracy thus cannot alone assure protection of autonomy. To believe that it can is to believe that a democratically organized collective would never do violence to the autonomy of any of its members. That seems to me implausible. What is required is an understanding of the substance of autonomy and of the practices that foster it so that citizens can ask whether the actions or institutions proposed in their collective decision-making are consistent with the autonomy of all. We must, for example, ask whether official action in any particular circumstance denies clients basic respect or treats them in ways that makes them less able to understand what is happening to them, less able to participate effectively in the decisions affecting their lives, less able to define and pursue their own goals—in short, in ways that undermine rather than foster their capacity to find and live by their own law.

It may be that if such failings are found, increased participation will be a partial remedy. Or the client may need information or support. Or the outlook of the official (e.g., seeing parents as time-consuming sources of trouble rather than as participants valued for their information and judgment) may be the source of the problem. Or it may be that the interaction, such as intrusive home visits, is inherently incompatible with the autonomy of the client and can only be justified under exceptional circumstances (e.g., the sort of probable cause needed for a warrant). And impasses such as that over home visits may be evidence that the whole relationship between client and authority must be restructured if it is to foster the client's autonomy.

Further, some mechanism would probably be needed to encourage and facilitate the posing of questions about institutional compatibility with autonomy. In other words, there must be means of measuring the content of collective decisions against the (separate and substantive) value of autonomy. Such means would include appropriate institutions, language, and habits of inquiry through which citizens and representatives of some kind (including judges) could check whether the laws, rules, or patterns of official behavior fostered or undermined autonomy. Such an inquiry is only

63. As noted earlier, I do not think that the more general form of participation in elections of democratic bodies can substitute for direct participation in administrative decision-making.

possible if we have a concept of autonomy that is distinct from the democratic processes which may threaten it.

It is important to distinguish the above (somewhat vague and awkwardly stated) ideas from the conventional liberal understanding of individual rights, and of autonomy in particular. First, the wordy awkwardness arises from a deliberate effort to avoid the neat and pithy claim that autonomy should be a substantive limit to democratic outcomes. That powerful vision of rights-as-limits no longer seems to me the best way of thinking about or trying to institutionalize the notion that in any society there will be competing values and that groups of people exercising democratic power may be inclined to override even basic values. What seems important is the clear articulation of the values a society considers basic (surely an ongoing process), together with the idea that democratic outcomes are not (at least in the first instance) dispositive of the meaning of those values or what counts as a violation of them. But that is a long way from saying that rights are trumps. A society should, as I argued above, acknowledge the inherent tension between the collective and the individual and find means of mediating as well as sustaining the tension. I say "sustaining" because the values of neither the individual nor the collective should be collapsed into the other. Treating rights as limits on democracy is one way of maintaining both distinct values; but it is a method that throws its weight too heavily to the side of the individual.[64]

There is a second distinction that is best put as an answer to the following challenge: You started by saying that you were going to break down the conventional dichotomies, but aren't we right back in the conventional choices and conflicts between collective goods and individual rights? Aren't you just restating the old liberal argument that, of course, rights (including autonomy) sometimes have to be balanced against the public good—only without the willingness to guarantee rights against collective oppression? How is this a new conception of autonomy?[65] The answer is that in measuring and weighing collective choices against the value of autonomy, the meaning of autonomy will be different. The autonomy I am talking about does remain an individual value, a value that takes its meaning from the recognition of (and respect for) the inherent individuality of each person. But it takes its meaning no less from the recognition that individuality cannot be conceived of in isolation from the social con-

64. The Canadian Charter of Rights and Freedoms designates rights as basic values, but it does not treat them as absolute limits. The very first section of the Charter says that it "guarantees the rights and freedoms set out in it subject only to such reasonable limits prescribed by law as can be demonstrably justified in a free and democratic society." CAN. CHARTER OF RIGHTS AND FREEDOMS § 1. There is also an "override" provision that permits legislatures to pass a law notwithstanding its violation of the Charter. *Id.* at § 33(1). The "notwithstanding" clause must be part of the bill and any law so passed ceases to have effect after five years (and thus would have to be passed again). *Id.* at § 33(3). Canada is likely, therefore, to generate a jurisprudence and a set of institutional practices that put into effect some version of the notion of rights that I have articulated.

65. My thanks to my colleague Alan Brudner for posing this challenge.

text in which that individuality comes into being. The value of autonomy will at some level be inseparable from the relations that make it possible; there will thus be a social component built into the meaning of autonomy. That is the difference. But the presence of a social component does not mean that the value cannot be threatened by collective choices; hence the continuing need to identify autonomy as a separate value, to take account of its vulnerability to democratic decision-making, and to find some way of making those decisions "accountable" to the value of autonomy.

## VI. Conclusion

This inquiry has been prompted more by an interest in future possibilities than by hopes for the perfection of autonomy under the current American legal system. Forms of bureaucratic decision-making—however participatory or otherwise optimal—cannot change basic power relations and structures of inequality. These more than anything determine the potential for autonomy for all citizens, for subordination and powerlessness are incompatible with autonomy. But even in a quite imperfect society, experiments with forms of collective (bureaucratic) power and with the relations between those implementing it and those dependent upon it can give us insight into what optimal forms and relations would look like. What I have tried to do is suggest a framework which we can use to help extract what is useful out of current experiments—since I believe that a new conception of autonomy is not likely to spring full-blown from theory.

I see the development of such a conception as essential for working out alternatives to our present system. The alternatives which seem compelling to me all involve a far greater role for collective power and responsibility than does our current system. Those who aspire to such alternatives must be able to persuade themselves as well as their critics that such changes need not diminish, though they will certainly change, autonomy. More importantly, we must have language that adequately captures our highest goals, in terms that reflect both the individual and the social dimensions of human beings. That language will take some time to emerge, but in the meantime we cannot cede to liberal convention a monopoly on the value of autonomy.

# [21]

# STRUCTURES OF POLITICAL ORDER: THE RELATIONAL FEMINIST ALTERNATIVE

ROBERT E. GOODIN

## I. Political Order and the Problem of Evil

Evil has many faces, many sources.[1] Not all of them are interpersonally hurtful. Sometimes the wicked harm only themselves. Neither are all forms of evil publicly actionable. Sometimes the only remotely plausible preventives or remedies are necessarily private ones. That said, it would be widely (if not, perhaps, universally) agreed that, first and foremost, political arrangements should strive to forestall evil where they can and to rectify its effects as they are able.

A variety of arguments converge on setting that as the first priority of political order. Some of the most compelling have to do with the "fear of fear." Living under constant threat of suffering gross evil engenders a sort of fear that we find utterly crippling in all our ordinary, everyday actions. If we are to live our ordinary lives at all, government must protect us from such crippling fear of extraordinary interventions. Protection from that sort of fear would rank as the primary primary good, in

I am grateful to Moira Gatens, Jenny Mansbridge, Jenny Nedelsky, and Carole Pateman for helping to clarify these issues for me.

much the same way and for much the same reason as "self-respect" is said to do in Rawls's *Theory of Justice.*[2]

Other arguments converging on the same conclusion about the political preeminence of preventing evil have to do with the problems of knowledge facing public officials. The causes of happiness are many and varied, the causes of misery few and common to all. Public officials are able to act with more confidence in rooting out evils, on which almost everyone agrees, than in promoting The Good, which almost everyone understands differently.[3]

Whichever path we take to that conclusion, it certainly is a common proposition that the problem of evil is *the* problem to which political order is a solution. That is widely agreed among liberal political theorists and many others besides. Indeed, it is almost the defining tenet of a liberal political theory that the state ought strive to prevent evils, or at least a certain well-defined subset of evils, rather than to promote The Good; and circumscribing the state's response to the problem of evil, creating a state strong enough to control evil without its being so strong as to submerge the moral personality of its citizens, is liberal political theory's preeminent task.

Within other, more optimistic traditions—anarchist, utopian, socialist, feminist—the problem of evil looms less large and politics performs various other important tasks. Outside the liberal canon order is taken as more natural and evil as more aberrant. Even there, however, the problem of evil remains a (if not the) central problem that political order is required to solve. That is in part because, on those other more optimistic accounts, there will be fewer problems to be solved, politically or otherwise. It is also in large part because those other gentler forms of social arrangement are more susceptible to being undermined by evil influences, however rare.

In short, wherever you start you come quickly to the same conclusion: the problem of evil occupies center-stage, politically. Politics is a matter of "imposing order." That is almost the whole story according to liberalism; it is at least a large part of the story according to most other traditions. And on all accounts, institutional order is designed first and foremost to control the knaves, many or few, among us.[4]

## II. Structures of Political Order

Political structures for pursuing that purpose are themselves many and varied. At root, however, there seem to be only three fundamentally different ways of structuring political order.

One classic style of political order is *authoritarian.* This is the Hobbesian approach, adopted and adapted by many others besides. Its core components are a strong central authority, which issues rules and edicts directly to subjects who in turn have minimal discretion in interpreting their content and virtually none in applying them. This is the world of crude legal positivism, Austin's sovereign handing down laws understood as orders backed by threats.[5]

A second style of political order is broadly *hierarchical.* What all these many subspecies of hierarchical rule have in common are notions of superiors and subordinates, with the former empowered by the rules of the system to issue orders (of certain kinds, within certain limits) to the latter—and to empower them (within limits) to issue orders in turn. In the final analysis, the force of the orders comes down, once again, to the threat of force. From within, however, it is the authority of the rules empowering hierarchs to issue the orders, rather than the force with which they can back them up, that is the felt force behind the order.[6]

That is how, subjectively, life in a hierarchy feels different from life in an autocracy. Structurally, the more crucial difference lies in the fact that hierarchical forms of political order devolve authority from the central authority (who still is the ultimate source of all authority) to other lower-level authorities in the political order. Structurally, hierarchy is essentially a matter of *subcontracting* political order.

The clearest case of hierarchical political order, understood in this way, is feudalism. The lord of the manor enjoys his authority by the grace of the monarch, to be sure; but within his realm he is (perhaps within certain limits, perhaps not) the absolute ruler of all those who are tied to him. Likewise, the master is empowered by the crown and its successors to rule (with more limits) over his servants and employers to rule (with still more limits) over their employees.

This model is not without its contemporary advocates. Corporatists, syndicalists, and guild socialists all appeal to essentially this same model.[7] Nor is the model without practical contemporary relevance. The family was traditionally organized on just such a basis, with the law of marriage historically empowering the husband to be (within increasing limits) absolute ruler of his wife and household; and much contemporary feminist writing is devoted to demonstrating the myriad ways in which that basic model still prevails even after formal legal shells have been notionally changed.[8]

Most interesting for present purposes is the limiting case of hierarchical models of political order. That, I submit, is what a regime of rights amounts to. Ascribing to individuals rights, understood as legally protected spheres within which the right-holder's choices will be respected, is tantamount to empowering the right-holder as absolute sovereign within that (admittedly, tightly circumscribed) sphere.[9] It is a model of Everyman his own King—and, ideally, every woman too.

The right-holder's authority is subcontracted authority, to be sure. It is derived from the higher authority of the legal system ascribing those rights in the first place. But being subcontracted in that way is precisely what makes it, structurally, an instance (albeit the limiting one) of hierarchical models of political order. Insofar as we are acting within our rights we are absolute rulers, and others must simply bow to our sovereign determinations.

The defining feature of the third mode of political order, the *decentralist* mode, is its opposition to hierarchy in any form. The ideal there is, somehow, to establish order by everyone controlling everyone. There are no central authorities, no superiors and subordinates, no spheres within which anyone can rule supreme.

Such models have long formed the backbone of radical programs of one sort and another. Anarchists have always insisted upon the possibilities of achieving order without any central authority structures.[10] More recently, decentralization conceived in roughly this way has formed the core of a great many practical (as well as a great many impractical) proposals eminating from New Social Movements in general and Green parties in particular.[11]

Within more narrowly academic discussions, a classic example of such a model would be the market, sufficiently idealized to ensure that no one has any power to dictate (or even to shape significantly) the outcome of market transactions.[12] Democratic pluralism, in its various forms, is another example of this sort of decentralized-control model. The aspiration for everyone to control everyone without the intervention of any (independent) central authority is one which is shared by democratic theorists ranging from populists to advocates of deliberative democracy and communicative ethics to advocates of checks and balances and countervailing power.[13]

There is another variation on essentially decentralist themes. Remembering that the problem to which political order is a solution is the problem of evil, another way of solving the problem would be to make people less evil in the first place. Instead of trying to construct mechanisms to control people's evil impulses, we might strive to remake people so they are less in need of being controlled at all. There are many ways of attempting to achieve that outcome, some more authoritarian, some less so. Once people's characters have been reformed in this way, however, they are in effect controlling themselves, checking their own evil impulses before they issue in action. For this reason, this strategy is properly classed as a decentralized one, although of course the mechanisms by which the character reform was achieved in the first place may have been of a very different sort.

This strategy represents an important, albeit often idealistic, alternative. It was the aspiration of certain sorts of state socialist systems to create the New Socialist Man (and, typically, woman in his image).[14] It is one of the central arguments in favor of participatory democracy, for its potential in furthering people's self-development and the growth of their moral capacities.[15] And it is into this broad mode that "relational feminism" fits.[16] All those represent attempts not so much to *solve* the problem of evil by manipulating the political order in such a way as to contain evil, but to make evil *disappear* altogether—by, in the case of relational feminism, ensuring the right relations among people.

The contrast between these three ideal types is perhaps too strong. Perhaps none can exist in pure form. Just as the second sort of strategy requires a certain element of the first, perhaps so too does the third.[17] Hierarchies, as I have already observed, require central authority to ground the authority of subcontractors. So too do most decentralized mechanisms likewise require or presuppose centralized authority structures of some sort or another. Markets presuppose the structure of property law, contracts and torts; democracy presupposes electoral law, fairly enforced; relational feminism, in so far as it is to be undergirded by and reinforced through socio-legal instruments, presupposes a formal legal code. Any given political order will, therefore, probably always be a blend of these several styles. Even so, it genuinely matters how much of each ingredient you blend in. The contrast among these styles of structuring political order is nonetheless useful for its being something less than absolute.

## III. Feminist Critiques of the Liberal Political Order

Contemporary feminist critiques of the received wisdom about the problem of political order focus largely upon the problem of too much (artificially imposed) order—and, of course, upon whose interests are served by that order.[18] While sympathizing with the liberal animus against the oversupply of central state power in authoritarian regimes, feminists are equally anxious to avoid a parallel oversupply of publicly licensed private power being exercised by the state's subcontractors. The problem is power and authority, domination and oppression, whether public or (notionally) private.[19]

The classic liberal solution to the problem of tyranny was to create a "sphere of rights, freedom and autonomy [that] was private . . . [and] to keep the public realm distant, separate, at bay."[20] This system of rights and the public/private split it serves to create, so cherished by liberals, has traditionally had the effect of lending the liberal state's authority to authoritarian rule within the household.[21] Carving out a protected private sphere traditionally protected the husband and father from the state, while within that sphere leaving the wife and children utterly at his mercy.[22]

Of course the details of that traditional settlement can be, and have been, adjusted at the margins. Any grant of authority to subcontractors is always circumscribed to some extent or another. If subcontractors are misbehaving, then their authority can always be circumscribed still further. In the limiting case, the same sort of rights that liberals traditionally granted husbands against the state could be granted to wives and children against brutal husbands and parents.[23]

Some feminist critics of the liberal order would insist that none of this addresses the real problem, however. "Our project," they say, "should not be to try to shore up women's boundaries . . . nor should it be, at least in the long run, to find ways to draw circles of protection around women that are the same as men's."[24] For such feminists, the problem with the liberal solution lies in its structure, not in its details. The problem lies in the use of liberal rights to carve out separate private spheres at all, not in how those private spheres are delimited.

Giving women or children a private sphere within which they, by right, are sovereign simply reinforces separateness rather than encouraging us to think about what sorts of relationships we have and what sorts we want.[25] Liberal rights claims are egoistic in tone and preemptory in form. Relational feminists would join communitarians more generally in saying that in both those respects rights are powerfully subversive of the sort of cooperative thinking required to undergird any proper form of community morality.[26]

Furthermore, any grant of power to some people to act as (more or less) free agents within a sphere defined by liberal rights brings with it the hierarchical subcontracting of authority. Within that hierarchy, in turn, necessarily comes the subordination of those who must yield to the will of others. By their very nature, subordinates are (to some extent or another) dominated by superiors in the authority structure created by liberal rights, as surely as by autocratic rules.

The feminist program, in all its varieties, essentially aims to end domination in all its forms. Its aspiration is to ensure equality, which can be undercut as powerfully by private exercises of power that are at most only implicitly sanctioned by state authority. (The example of Southern lynchings keeping blacks in their place is indeed a powerful case in point.)[27] Feminists typically shy away from seeking the solution in more intervention from central state authorities, however—and understandably so, given their animus against hierarchical authority, with its inevitable corollary of domination and subordination.[28]

## IV. Feminist Alternatives: Politics as Personal Relations

There are all those forces pushing feminists away from reliance upon the traditional instruments of the liberal state to protect women and children against many of life's greatest evils. That, however, is only part—and perhaps the lesser part—of the story. Feminists also feel a powerful attraction to alternative, non-state remedies to the forms of domination and subordination that they hope to eradicate.

For many of them, the preferred solution is to be found in what is said to be a peculiarly female "ethic of care," arising principally out of the experience of mothering.[29] That seems to be an essential part, anyway, of what is meant by "relational feminism." The emphasis there is upon getting personal relations right. Caring affection of the sort found within a good friendship is offered as a general model for political life.[30]

This is almost the flip side of the old slogan, "the personal is political." Within this style of relational feminism, the political is personal. Or, more precisely, the personal is the best model for and best ground on which to build the good polis. And since the personal is peculiar to individuals and groups, the emphasis within this strand of feminism (as within many others) is upon respect for "difference," upon particularity rather than universalistic abstractions.[31]

Working within this broad framework, relational feminism reconstructs all manner of received socio-legal instruments—notions of "rights" conspicuously among them—to its own peculiar ends. Of course, rights have always been regarded as being inherently relational: by their very nature, rights connect holders of the rights with those who bear the correlative duties.[32] While that would remain true for relational feminists' rights, as well, that is not the most important sense in which they see their preferred model of rights as being relational.[33]

The goal of rights, on the relational feminist model, would be to cultivate the right relationships at a personal level. A decent political order would follow from that. Rights, on this view, are not so much devices to protect people from one another as devices for binding people together. Rights do not carve out a private sphere within which anyone is sovereign. Rather, they carve out a shared sphere within which we who are bound together by them must act somehow in concert.[34]

On this relational feminist model, invoking rights amounts less to lodging a preemptory claim than to initiating a conversation.[35] Rights conceived in this way would call for negotiation rather than litigation, for mediation rather than adjudication.[36] On this view, disputes betoken the breakdown of ordinary social relations, and the proper goal (or, anyway, highest aspiration) for systems of dispute resolution should be to restore decent social relations among parties to that dispute.[37]

The aim would be not just to find some modus vivendi, not just some common ground upon which all parties can stand, nor even come to that to find some fair compromise to end the controversy. Ideally the aim would instead be genuinely to dissolve the dispute—to find, through this conversation, some way of recasting relationships so that a new consensus genuinely emerges to replace what were previously points of contention.

## V. An Assessment: Feminism versus Liberalism

Relational feminists are dead set against models of order achieved by fence building and boundary maintenance. They are appalled by the stark individualism, the neglect of community ties and social relations built into such models. Insofar as those models are given social meaning through regimes of liberal rights, relational feminists are further appalled by the hierarchical authority structures thereby created, and the possibilities (yea, inevitabilities) of domination built into such models. Their preferred alternative might be characterized as decentralized systems of order achieved by subsuming people into relationships—"we"ness, to borrow Buber's term employed by self-styled "new communitarians" to similar effect.[38]

The trouble with subsuming individuals into relationships of "we"ness, however, is precisely that we then risk losing track of the "separateness of people." Within a full Buberian relationship of "we"ness, we are a single entity, a single personality. Then any can speak for all. That, in turn, makes it easy for everyone to impose upon (to exploit, if not strictly dominate) any or indeed every other. Sacrifice of the few for the many, or of the many for some higher group-defining cause—precisely the sort of thing liberal rights were designed to protect against in the first place[39]—is then very much on the cards. Indeed, so too is the sacrifice of the many for the few, for in relationships of "we"ness each one can make in principle limitless claims against all others in the name of the collective "we."

Of course, relational feminists may have something less than the full Buberian program in mind here. They may, for example, mean no more than that we develop our own separate identities in the context of social (primarily family) relationships.[40] They may just be saying that to understand, and hence to alter, socially undesirable differences between men and women we need to understand and to alter socially undesirable differences in the way these family relationships impact upon boys and girls in early childhood socialization.

If that is all the relational feminist emphasis upon relationships amounts to, then it is unexceptionable but also unexceptional. Ameliorating social ills through improved childhood socialization is an old and familiar strategy. Furthermore, it is one with which liberalism has long ago made its peace. Much though it may prefer to focus upon fully-formed, autonomous agents, liberalism needs some account of the genesis of such agents. Insofar as relational feminism merely offers a better account of preference formation and character development than liberalism's own, the two models might be seen as complements to one another rather than as alternatives to one another.

Typically, however, the two are presented as stark alternatives. Relational feminism rejects the stark individualism of liberalism, and not just because of its inadequate account of the shaping of individuals' personalities. Rather, it seems, relational feminists are typically advocating an "ethic of care" that involves subsuming self into relationships in a stronger Buberian sense. Insofar as that is the aim, then relational feminists are as much at risk of losing track of the separateness of people as are Buberians.[41]

Relational feminists thus hope to ground moral and political responsibilities on concrete, existing relationships. But where do those relationships come from, and how far do they stretch?[42] Some relationships clearly exist independently of choice and were in no sense voluntarily assumed. Family relations, especially relations between children and their parents, are the paradigm case of that, as I have remarked elsewhere.[43] But wherever such relations came from, it is at least clear in that case that there is a relationship in existence once the children are on the doorstep.

Within relational feminism, it is unclear what criteria are to be employed for saying whether a relationship does or does not exist. Does an analogous relationship arise when a bag lady appears on your doorstep, for example? It is undeniably true that her well-being is affected (maybe weakly, maybe powerfully) by your actions and choices with respect to her. That is enough on my reckoning to impose some responsibility (weak or strong) upon us for helping her. But that, on my reckoning, is because our acts and omissions will help or harm her, not because we have any "relationship" in any other sense with her. My point would be precisely opposite to that of the relational feminists. I would say that we bear that responsibility regardless of whether or not we have any special relationship, whereas they would insist that we have such responsibility precisely because we have some sort of a relationship with her.

Maybe the relational feminist point could be rephrased to assert not that we *do* have a relationship to her but rather that, because of that power of ours to help or harm her, we *should*.[44] Once we have started rendering assistance, and she has started relying on it, then a relationship clearly will have come into existence; law and morals converge on the conclusion that we then have a strong duty to continue that assistance. Maybe what relational feminists are suggesting is merely that we should cultivate ongoing relationships of interdependence of that sort. But if that is the argument, then the reason for cultivating the relationship is not the existence of a preexisting relationship. Rather, the reason must have to do with the excellence of a life built around relationships, or some such.

There are occasional passages in the writings of relational feminists to suggest that we ought strive to form just such positive relationships with anyone and everyone. More often, though, the appeal is not to universality but rather to particularity. It is our relations with particular others that we ought cherish in these ways. Then, however, that particularized ethic of care threatens to make us literally careless of others outside our particular circle of relations.[45] "Care as a political ideal," Joan Tronto acknowledges, "could [then] quickly become a way to argue that everyone should cultivate one's own garden, and let others take care of themselves, too."[46]

Relational feminists such as Tronto clearly hope to avoid that conclusion. But if they succeed in stretching their notion of relationships far enough that it can in principle embrace large groups, further questions arise. How are those larger groups of "related others" supposed to come to some collective determinations? Given relational feminists' emphasis upon the particularity and situatedness of each party to the relation, and the particular needs and interests arising from that, it would be fatuous for them to postulate some facile consensus to get around the problem. Inevitably, some perspectives will prevail over others, certainly on any given occasion and perhaps systematically across all occasions. Thus we see reemerging *within* relationships risks akin to familiar problems of majority tyranny.

## VI. Rights and Right Relations

Why, exactly, should we suppose that relational feminism and liberal rights are necessarily at odds? What exactly is it about structures of order built around liberal notions of rights that is thought to make them inherently hostile to right relations, and what is it about structures of order built around notions of right relations that is thought to make them inherently hostile to liberal-style rights?

The central intuition underlying the analysis at that point seems to be just this: standing on your rights is inimical to close personal relationships. As arbitrators keen to avoid premature hardening of positions often say, standing on your rights gets in the way of sitting down at the table. Close personal relationships, at their best, are "characterized by intimacy, genuine care, love, and emotional involvement." All that is antithetical to the sort of arms-length "respect" that one shows for the other's rights, to say nothing of the sort of "demanding one's due" that is involved in asserting rights claims.[47] Liberal rights are essentially fence-building, boundary-enforcing exercises, and fencing others out is no way to foster a relationship with them.[48]

This is a familiar proposition, in law and in ethics alike. Traditionally courts refused to entertain litigation of any form between husband and wife.[49] At least one of the central rationales for that policy had to do with the way in which "domestic harmony" would be disturbed if husbands and wives were living their lives in the shadow of the courts. In the words of one nineteenth-century case, "The flames which litigation would kindle on the domestic hearth would consume in an instant the conjugal bond."[50] Even as late as the mid-1970s, dissenting members of the U.S. Supreme Court could still mount a spirited challenge to due-process rights for pupils suspended from school on analogous grounds that legalistic remedies would upset the delicate and complex ongoing relationships between teachers and pupils.[51]

Of course all that reflects an attitude toward the sanctity of private spheres that has now been superseded in the courts.[52] And rightly so, feminists would be the first to agree.[53] They are properly keen for ordinary legal remedies to be readily available to battered wives and abused children. They are rightly suspicious of "just so" stories about "domestic harmony" that serve only to shelter abusive behavior in distinctly nonharmonious settings.

Anxious though feminists might be for such legal remedies to be available to battered wives and abused children when ordinary affection has broken down, relational feminists in particular retain strong elements of this old animus against liberal rights as being destructive of ongoing relationships when they are going well. Much though we may need standard liberal rights when things are going badly, they would say, recourse to such remedies is also much to be avoided when things are going well. Liberal-style boundary-protecting rights might be an unfortunate necessity, to which we appeal when relationships have already been destroyed. But by the same token they are destructive of relationships and therefore ought not be invoked prematurely to settle matters that might still admit of other modes of resolution.

The sorts of rights that relational feminists would most like to use most of the time are the other sorts of rights, ones designed to create good relationships and to bind us into cooperative communities with one another. That more positive side of the relational feminists' program amounts, in effect, to equating rights of their preferred sort with right relationships.

That move seems to me to involve a simple fallacy, already familiar in only a slightly different form. It is something of a saw in recent moral philosophy that there is a difference between rights and right conduct.[54] If people have rights, then the right conduct toward them follows (in part) from that fact. But even then, there may be more to right conduct toward them than merely respecting their rights: it might be *wrong* to let them starve, even if they have no right against you to food. Just as there is more to right conduct than just respecting rights, even where there are rights, it is all the more true that there can be notions of right conduct where there are no rights.

The connection within relational feminism between rights and right relations is, I think, similarly deceptive. The best way to build the right sort of relationships might be to forget about our rights altogether; and, conversely, the best way to construct our lists of rights might be to forget about relationships. It is not at all clear that notions of rights, of whatever sort, will ever facilitate relationship-tending on a day to day basis. As Waldron rightly says, rights do not specify how you live your life. They are merely fallback positions, telling you how to govern the unraveling of relations when ordinary affection fails.[55]

It is important for relational feminists and liberals alike to realize that this is precisely how we use liberal rights in our everyday affairs, of both a personal and an impersonal sort. Just as no one within a thriving family would dream of "standing on their rights," so too does no one even within an ongoing business relationship.

Business, of course, typically proceeds through contracts, and those standardly specify what will happen push come to shove.[56] It is an important fact, however, that even in the business world push rarely comes to shove—not just in the sense that things rarely come to actual litigation, but also in the more important sense that accommodations to shifting circumstances are most typically made without reference to the terms of the existing contract at all. Macaulay's classic paper on "Noncontractual Relations in Business" quotes one businessman as explaining,

> If something comes up, you get the other man on the telephone and deal with the problem. You don't read legalistic contract clauses at each other if you ever want to do business again. One doesn't run to lawyers if he wants to stay in business because one must behave decently.

Another says, more succinctly, "You can settle any dispute if you keep the lawyers and accountants out of it. They just do not understand the give and take needed in business."[57]

Upon reflection, there is nothing surprising in that. It simply would not be a particularly effective business firm in which all partners, all customers, all employees were always governing every act every day according to contractual entitlements and how best to defend themselves should the matter end in court. Whatever the formal authority structure within an organization, subordinates almost always enjoy substantially more latitude than the formal organization chart suggests.[58] Whatever the formal rights flowing from their ownership of a firm, shareholders and Boards of Directors inevitably cede almost all effective control to managers technically employed merely to carry out their orders.[59]

That is not to deny that Boards of Directors have rights over managers, and managers over subordinates. Nor is it to deny they can and will stand on them, in extremis. The point is merely that those rights are very much in the background rather than in the foreground in the course of everyday affairs, even in the most impersonal business-like corners of liberal society.

### VII. Toward a Reconciliation of Liberalism and Relational Feminism

The upshot would seem to be just this: even relational feminists would (for certain purposes) want rights of the standard liberal sort, and even liberals would (for the most part) lead their ordinary lives in relationships of trust and reciprocity rather than always standing on their rights. In short, more sophisticated forms of liberalism and relational feminism may tend in the end to converge.

The crucial move toward convergence on the side of relational feminism comes with the recognition that relationships encode power as well as affection.[60] The program of these more sophisticated relational feminists consists, in part, in recognizing existing relationships for what they are. But often what they are are relationships of domination and subordination, exclusion, and inclusion.

That recognition leads to the other, more important part of the sophisticated relational feminist program—of recasting power relations in such a way as to empower those who are excluded or subordinated under existing social arrangements. In this reconstructivist "social-relations model for law," a crucial element in recasting power relations works through notions of rights. The aim is "remaking rights so that they do not recreate the differences etched . . . into the structures and crevices of inherited institutions."[61] In effect, that amounts to giving subordinated groups resources for negotiating their way in the world on an improved footing.[62]

The crucial move toward convergence on the liberal side comes with the recognition that formal structures of rights and duties merely set the parameters for bargaining.[63] The lived reality of a liberal world is the experience not merely of formal authority structures and entitlements but of the negotiated order that results from accommodation and exchanges arising from that initial distribution of power and resources. In an ongoing relationship, reliance and trust inevitably emerge as the most profitable strategy, even among arch-liberal agents.[64]

A sophisticated relational feminist, therefore, would be sensitive to power relations and reallocate rights in such a way as to get the power balance more nearly right.[65] She would do so not in the expectation that people would live their lives according to the strict letter of the law thus laid down, but rather in the expectation that relationships would grow and develop in the interstices of the formal structures thus created.

By the same token, a sophisticated liberal would expect formal allocations of rights and duties and authority to be opening gambits in a bargaining game. Assuming society is sufficiently small and stable for people to know one another and their reputations, repeat-players would cultivate relationships of trust and reciprocity among those with whom they will have continuing involvement.

The upshot, therefore, is that the two worlds of liberalism and relational feminism do not really look so very different after all. The differences are largely ones of emphasis, of whether we should focus primarily on formal allocations of power and authority or primarily on the ongoing relationships that grow up in their shadow. The latter may well be the more apt characterization of social life in general. But the former is the more appropriate model of political order, characterized at the outset as primarily a response to the problem of evil.

## NOTES

1. See, e.g.: Judith N. Shklar, *Ordinary Vices* (Cambridge: Harvard University Press, 1984); Ronald D. Milo, *Immorality* (Princeton: Princeton University Press, 1984); and S. I. Benn, "Wickedness," *Ethics* 95 (1985): 795–810.

2. Judith N. Shklar, "The Liberalism of Fear," in *Liberalism and the Moral Life*, ed. Nancy Rosenblum (Cambridge: Harvard University Press, 1989), 21–38; John Rawls, *A Theory of Justice* (Cambridge: Harvard University Press, 1971), sec. 67.

3. Barrington Moore, Jr., *Reflections on the Causes of Human Misery* (Boston: Beacon Press, 1970).

4. David Hume, "Of the Independency of Parliament," *Essays: Literary, Moral, and Political* (London: A. Millar, 1760), part 1, chap. 6.

5. John Austin, *Province of Jurisprudence,* as explicated by H. L. A. Hart, *The Concept of Law* (Oxford: Clarendon Press, 1961), chaps. 2–4.

6. If the first model is essentially Austin's, the second is essentially H. L. A. Hart's alternative of power-conferring rules: see his *Concept of Law,* esp. chaps. 5–6.

7. Bob Jessop, "Corporatism and Syndicalism," in *A Companion to Contemporary Political Philosophy,* ed. Robert E. Goodin and Philip Pettit (Oxford: Blackwell, 1993), 404–10.

8. Carole Pateman, *The Sexual Contract* (Oxford: Polity Press, 1988), esp. chaps. 5 and 6; Susan Moller Okin, *Justice, Gender, and the Family* (New York: Basic Books, 1989).

9. H. L. A. Hart, "Definition and Theory in Jurisprudence," *Essays in Jurisprudence and Philosophy* (Oxford: Clarendon Press, 1983), 21–49 at 35 and "Are There Any Natural Rights?" *Philosophical Review* 64 (1955): 175–91.

10. Richard Sylvan, "Anarchism," in *A Companion to Contemporary Political Philosophy,* ed. Robert E. Goodin and Philip Pettit (Oxford: Blackwell, 1993), 215–43.

11. Kirkpatrick Sale, "Bioregionalism—A New Way to Treat the Land," *Ecologist* 14, no. 4 (1984): 167–73; Claus Offe, "New Social Movements: Challenging the Boundaries of Institutional Politics," *Social Research* 52 (1985): 817–68; Robert E. Goodin, *Green Political Theory* (Oxford: Polity Press, 1993), chap. 4.

12. The contrast is nicely drawn by Oliver E. Williamson, "Markets and Hierarchies: Some Elementary Considerations," *American Economic Review (Papers and Proceedings)* 63 (1973): 316–25.

13. Robert A. Dahl, *A Preface to Democratic Theory* (Chicago: University of Chicago Press, 1956); Jürgen Habermas, *Legitimation Crisis,* trans. Thomas McCarthy (London: Heinemann, 1976). See, more generally, Robert A. Dahl and Charles E. Lindblom, *Politics, Economics, and Welfare* (New York: Harper and Row, 1953).

14. Peter Clecak, "Moral and Material Incentives," *Socialist Register* (1969): 101–35.

15. C. B. Macpherson, *Democratic Theory* (Oxford: Clarendon Press, 1973), chaps. 1–3 and *The Life and Times of Liberal Democracy* (Oxford: Clarendon Press, 1977), chap. 3.

16. See Section IV of this chapter for further elaboration and references.

17. So, I shall argue below, do both of the other modes in effect

enshrine something of the third model, in the form of bargaining among those in relations of notional authority.

18. See, e.g.: Catharine A. MacKinnon, *Toward a Feminist Theory of the State* (Cambridge: Harvard University Press, 1989); Martha Minow, *Making All the Difference: Inclusion, Exclusion, and American Law* (Ithaca: Cornell University Press, 1990); and, for an overview, Jane J. Mansbridge and Susan Moller Okin, "Feminism," in *A Companion to Contemporary Political Philosophy,* ed. Robert E. Goodin and Philip Pettit (Oxford: Blackwell, 1993), 269–90.

19. Some feminist writers (MacKinnon, especially) would of course say that an important part of the remedy involves the imposition of different sorts of power and order, regulating even more tightly what sorts of activities we can engage in, what sorts of images we may view, and so on.

20. Jennifer Nedelsky, "Reconceiving Autonomy: Sources, Thoughts, and Possibilities," *Yale Journal of Law and Feminism* 1 (1989): 7–36 at 17.

21. Just as, in the *Lochner* era, enforcement of liberal rights of contract had the effect of protecting employers from the power of the state while lending state authority to their authoritarian rule over their employees (Minow, *Making All the Difference,* 277–83).

22. Note, for example, the way in which courts process child abuse cases and the way in which public policy-makers, when finally forced to face the fact of child abuse, insistently recast it in ways least intrusive into the existing structures of family relations. On the former, see Robert Dingwall, John Eekelaar, and Topsy Murray, *The Protection of Children: State Intervention and Family Life* (Oxford: Blackwell, 1983). On the latter, see Barbara J. Nelson, *Making an Issue of Child Abuse* (Chicago: University of Chicago Press, 1984), esp. chap. 7.

For more general feminist critiques of the public/private dichotomy, see: Jean Elshtain, *Public Man, Private Woman* (Princeton: Princeton University Press, 1981); Mary G. Deitz, "Citizenship with a Feminist Face: The Problem with Maternal Thinking," *Political Theory* 13 (1985): 19–37; Okin, *Justice, Gender and the Family,* chap. 6; and Carole Pateman, "Feminist Critiques of the Public/Private Dichotomy," *The Disorder of Women* (Oxford: Polity Press, 1989), 118–40.

23. Dingwall, Eekelaar, and Murray, *The Protection of Children,* chap. 11; "United Nations Declaration of the Rights of the Child (1959)," reprinted in *Having Children,* ed. Onora O'Neill and William Ruddick (New York: Oxford University Press, 1979), 112–14.

24. Jennifer Nedelsky, "Law, Boundaries, and the Bounded Self," *Representations* 30 (1990): 162–89 at 170.

25. Nedelsky, "Law, Boundaries, and the Bounded Self" and "Reconceiving Autonomy." Cf. Minow, *Making All the Difference,* chaps. 8 and 9.

26. Mary Ann Glendon, *Rights Talk* (New York: Free Press, 1991). For the more general "new communitarian" case against rights, see "The Responsive Communitarian Platform: Rights *and* Responsibilities," *The Responsive Community* 2 (1991/2): 4–20, and Amitai Etzioni, *The Spirit of Community* (New York: Crown Books, 1993).

27. Gunnar Myrdal, *An American Dilemma* (New York: Harper and Row, 1944), chaps. 25–27. Cf. James M. Inverarity, "Populism and Lynching in Louisiana, 1889–1896," and Whitney Pope and Charles Ragin, "Mechanical Solidarity, Justice, and Lynching in Louisiana," *American Sociological Review* 41 (1976): 262–80 and 42 (1977): 363–69 respectively.

28. In some cases, though, the liberal state and the rights it confers can be a powerful force for liberation. That certainly was true in the case of civil rights in the American South, for example. What makes the case of gender so very different from that of race, here?

29. Carol Gilligan, *In a Different Voice* (Cambridge: Harvard University Press, 1982); Virginia Held, "Mothering versus Contract," in *Beyond Self-Interest,* ed. Jane J. Mansbridge (Chicago: University of Chicago Press, 1990), 287–304; Sara Ruddick, "Maternal Thinking," *Feminist Studies* 6 (1980): 342–67 and *Maternal Thinking* (New York: Ballantine Books, 1989); Kathleen B. Jones, *Compassionate Authority* (London: Routledge, 1993), esp. chap. 4; Cass R. Sunstein, ed., *Feminism and Political Theory* (Chicago: University of Chicago Press, 1990); Mansbridge and Okin, "Feminism." Other feminists would, of course, reject the sort of "essentialism" that ascribes to women any such natural caring or nurturing tendencies.

30. On friendship, see Lawrence A. Blum, *Friendship, Altruism, and Morality* (London: Routledge and Kegan Paul, 1980) and Neera Kapur Badhwar, "The Circumstances of Justice: Pluralism, Community, and Friendship," *Journal of Political Philosophy* 1 (1993): 250–76. On caring, see especially: Nel Noddings, *Caring* (Berkeley: University of California Press, 1984); Joan C. Tronto, "Beyond Gender Difference to a Theory of Care," *Signs* 12 (1987); 644–63 and *Moral Boundaries: A Political Argument for an Ethic of Care* (London: Routledge, 1993); and Jeffrey Blustein, *Care and Commitment: Taking the Personal Point of View* (New York: Oxford University Press, 1991).

31. Iris Young, *Justice and the Politics of Difference* (Princeton: Princeton University Press, 1990); Minow, *Making All the Difference.*

32. Wesley N. Hohfeld, *Fundamental Legal Conceptions as Applied in*

*Judicial Reasoning* (New Haven: Yale University Press, 1923). Hart, "Definition and Theory in Jurisprudence" and "Are There Any Natural Rights?"

33. Minow, *Making All the Difference*, 277–78; Nedelsky, "Law, Boundaries, and the Bounded Self," 171, concedes that "the function of boundaries *is* to structure relationships," but she goes on to argue that "the boundary metaphor consistently inhibits our capacity to focus on the relationships it is in fact structuring."

34. This formulation is meant to pick up the "anti-boundary, antiseparateness" strand in Nedelsky ("Law, Boundaries, and the Bounded Self" and "Reconceiving Autonomy") and Minow (*Making All the Difference*, chaps. 8 and 9).

35. "By invoking rights, an individual or group claims the attention of the larger community and its authorities. At the same time, this claim acknowledges the claimant's membership in the larger group, participation in its traditions, and observation of its forms. . . . Although the language of rights, on its surface, says little of community or convention, those who exercise rights signal and strengthen their relation to a community" (Minow, *Making All the Difference*, 293–94, see similarly 296–97).

36. "The powerful vision of rights-as-limits no longer seems to me the best way of thinking about or trying to institutionalize the notions that in any society there will be competing values. . . . A society should . . . acknowledge the inherent tension between the collective and the individual and find means of mediating as well as sustaining the tension. I say 'sustaining' because the values of neither the individual nor the collective should be collapsed into one another" (Nedelsky, "Reconceiving Autonomy," 35).

37. See especially Lon L. Fuller, "Mediation—Its Forms and Functions" and "The Forms and Limits of Adjudication," in *The Principles of Social Order*, ed. Kenneth I. Winston (Durham: Duke University Press, 1981), 125–57 and 86–124 respectively. This Alternative Dispute Resolution program, advocated by Derek Bok and others, is fairly summarized and roundly challenged by Owen M. Fiss, "Against Settlement," *Yale Law Journal* 93 (1984): 1073–91.

38. Amitai Etzioni, *The Moral Dimension* (New York: Free Press, 1988). See also Mansbridge, ed., *Beyond Self-Interest*.

39. H. L. A. Hart, "Between Utility and Rights," *Essays in Jurisprudence and Philosophy* (Oxford: Clarendon Press, 1983), 198–222.

40. Often "communitarians" seem to be saying no more than that; see, e.g., Michael Sandel, *Liberalism and the Limits of Justice* (Cambridge: Cambridge University Press, 1982).

41. While relational feminists might be enamored of the "ethic of care," there are of course other strands of feminism that would be keenly sensitive to the costs to women of being relied upon to provide disproportionate shares of such caregiving. See, e.g., Diane Gibson and Judith Allen, "Parasitism and Phallocentrism in Social Provision for the Elderly," *Policy Sciences* 26 (1993): 79–98.

42. Tronto raises these issues in her early paper ("Beyond Gender Difference to a Theory of Care," 659–61) but does not get very far toward resolving them in the book that grew out of that work (*Moral Boundaries*, 142–43, 170–73).

43. Robert E. Goodin, *Protecting the Vulnerable* (Chicago: University of Chicago Press, 1985).

44. On such themes, see the title essay in Harry Frankfurt, *The Importance of What We Care About* (Cambridge: Cambridge University Press, 1998).

45. This might be rationalized, in terms of "respect for difference," in terms of not being imperialistic about unknown others' values. But ignorance is always a weak excuse, carrying with it a duty to find out.

46. Tronto, *Moral Boundaries*, 171. She continues, lamely, "The only solution that I see . . . is to insist that care needs to be connected to a theory of justice and to be relentlessly democratic in its disposition," suggesting that "what would make care democratic is . . . its focus on needs, and on the balance between care-givers and care-receivers." That might make the theory democratic, and instill a concern for justice, but I cannot see how that would do anything (except via the sort of extrapolation and abstraction that relational feminists eschew) to instill a concern for justice or democracy that would go beyond those particular individuals thus linked by caring relations.

47. John Hardwig, "Should Women Think in Terms of Rights?" in *Feminism and Political Theory*, ed. Cass R. Sunstein (Chicago: University of Chicago Press, 1990), 53–67 at 54–55.

48. To borrow the terminology of Nedelsky, "Law, Boundaries, and the Bounded Self."

49. The principle was taken to absurd extremes: if a man negligently driving a car hits a woman pedestrian, causing her serious injuries, she ordinarily could sue for damages; but not, traditionally, if the driver in question were her husband. See "Note: Litigation between Husband and Wife," *Harvard Law Review* 79 (1966): 1650–65 at 1650–51.

50. *Ritter v. Ritter*, 31 Pa. 396, 398 (1858), quoted ibid., 1650–51.

51. Justice Lewis Powell, dissenting, in *Goss v. Lopez*, 419 US 565 (1975), at 593–94.

52. "Developments in the Law—Legal Responses to Domestic Violence," *Harvard Law Review* 106 (1993): 1499–620.

53. Minow, *Making All the Difference,* 289–95.

54. And not-so-recent moral philosophy, come to that: see George Cornewall Lewis, *Remarks on the Use and Abuse of Some Political Terms* (London: Fellowes, 1832), 7–32, distinguishing between the very different uses of "right" as an adjective and as a noun. See similarly Jeremy Waldron, "A Right to Do Wrong," *Ethics* 92 (1981): 21–39.

55. Jeremy Waldron, "When Justice Replaces Affection: The Need for Rights," *Harvard Journal of Law and Public Policy* 11 (1988): 625–47; Onora O'Neill, "The Prerogatives of the Premature," *Times Literary Supplement,* March 26, 1982, 332.

56. Surprisingly often, however, there are no contracts at all or no default clauses written into them; see Stewart Macaulay, "Noncontractual Relations in Business: A Preliminary Study," *American Sociological Review* 28 (1963): 55–67.

57. Macaulay, "Noncontractual Relations in Business," 61.

58. Herbert A. Simon, *Administrative Behavior,* 2d ed. (New York: Free Press, 1957), esp. chap. 7; Peter M. Balu, *The Dynamics of Bureaucracy,* rev. ed. (Chicago: University of Chicago Press, 1963), chaps. 7–9; Richard Cyert and James G. March, *A Behavioral Theory of the Firm* (Englewood Cliffs: Prentice-Hall, 1963); David M. Kreps, "Corporate Culture and Economic Theory," in *Perspectives on Positive Political Economy,* ed. James E. Alt and Kenneth A. Shepsle (Cambridge: Cambridge University Press, 1990), 90–143.

59. Adolf A. Berle, Jr., and Gardiner C. Means, *The Modern Corporation and Private Property* (New York: Macmillan, 1932); Oliver E. Williamson, "Corporate Governance," *Yale Law Journal* 93 (1984): 1197–230.

60. For a particularly clear statement of this proposition, see Catharine A. MacKinnon, "Difference and Dominance: On Sex Discrimination," in *The Moral Foundations of Civil Rights,* ed. Robert K. Fullinwider and Claudia Mills (Totowa: Rowman and Littlefield, 1986), 144–58.

61. Minow, *Making All the Difference,* 228.

62. In ways akin to the "protective state" of liberalism: see Macpherson, *Life and Times of Liberal Democracy,* chap. 2.

63. Thomas C. Schelling, "An Essay on Bargaining," *The Strategy of Conflict* (Cambridge: Harvard University Press, 1960), 21–52.

64. On the theory, see: Russell Hardin, "Exchange Theory on Strategic Bases," *Social Science Information* 21 (1982): 251–72 and *Collective Action* (Baltimore: Johns Hopkins University Press, 1982); Robert Axelrod, *The Evolution of Cooperation* (New York: Basic Books, 1984); Mi-

chael Taylor, *The Possibility of Cooperation* (Cambridge: Cambridge University Press, 1987); and Partha Dasgupta, "Trust as a Commodity," in *Trust,* ed. Diego Gambetta (Oxford: Blackwell, 1988), 49–72. For practical examples, see Elinor Ostrom, *Governing the Commons* (Cambridge: Cambridge University Press, 1990) and Robert C. Ellickson, *Order without Law: How Neighbors Settle Disputes* (Cambridge: Harvard University Press, 1991).

65. That arguably is what is going on in Nedelsky's prize example of Canadian rape law, resetting the standard of proof in rape cases in such a way as to advantage victims as against perpetrators.

# [22]

# Human Dependency and Rawlsian Equality

EVA FEDER KITTAY

> *"That all men are created free and equal." . . .*
> *That's a hard mystery of Jefferson's.*
> *What did he mean? Of course the easy way*
> *Is to decide it simply isn't true.*
> *It may not be. I heard a fellow say so.*
> *But never mind, the Welshman got it planted*
> *Where it will trouble us a thousand years.*
> *Each age will have to reconsider it.*
> —**Robert Frost, from "The Black Cottage"**

## 1. Introduction

### *1.1. Defining the Problem*

The liberal tradition in ethics and political theory is based upon the view that within a just society all persons should be treated as free and equal. 'All persons' would include the formerly disenfranchised—for example, women and black men. It would also include persons with special needs who are dependent upon others in basic ways—that is to say, children, the disabled, and the frail elderly. In order for persons with the special needs of dependents to be included in the community of equal citizens, however, these persons' needs require special consideration. There is, furthermore, a class of persons upon whom the dependent persons depend. These persons I call *dependency workers.* They are individuals who devote a major part of their lives (whether full or part time and through paid or unpaid labor) to attending to the dependency needs of others. As long as any of us are dependent, and as long as dependency care is a primary responsibility, our capacity to participate as equals in a community of free and equal persons is restricted by natural and social circumstance. Although the bounds of justice are drawn within reciprocal relations among free and equal persons, dependents will continue to remain disenfranchised, and dependency workers who are otherwise fully capable and cooperating members of society will continue to share varying degrees of the dependents' disfranchisement.

John Rawls, the most distinguished contemporary representative of the liberal view, defines the political in terms articulated by traditional Western political philosophies; he joins those who have omitted responsibility for dependents from, or relegated it to the periphery of, the political.[1] The presumption has been that these responsibilities belong to citizens' *private* rather than *public* concerns—a dichotomy that appears reasonable only by virtue of the neglect of dependency in delineating the political. The particular situation of those who care for dependents becomes invisible in the *political* associations of equals. Enlightenment's progeny, equality for all, fails to illuminate the nether world of dependency or shine its beneficent light on the inhabitants, the dependent and the dependency worker.

The dependency care I want to spotlight centers on the most acute moments of human dependency: helpless infancy and early childhood, frail old age, and incapacitating illness and disability. I focus on utter dependency because the inequities in the organization and distribution of dependency work, and the impact of these inequities on the possibility of equality for all, are most evident when dependency is a feature of our human condition rather than a consequence of socially prescribed roles, privileges, or distribution policies.[2] As such, dependency has a number of features that are separable in its lesser forms but inexorably linked in utter dependency, the form that concerns us here. First, the dependent requires care and caring persons to meet fundamental needs for survival and basic thriving. Second, while in the condition of dependency, the dependent is unable to reciprocate the benefits received.[3] And, third, the intervention of another is crucial to ensure that the needs of the dependent are met and that the interests of the dependent are recognized in a social context.[4] Dependency so understood underscores not only the limitations of an individual's capability but also the necessary labor of a dependency worker. The dependency worker, clearly, is not dependent in the sense outlined above. Nonetheless, the dependency worker, by virtue of her attention to her charge, becomes vulnerable to a *derived*[5] dependence: a dependence upon others to secure her own interests, which is derived from her responsibilities to turn her efforts to the individual who is dependent because she is too young, too feeble, too ill, or too disabled to fend for herself.[6]

Rawls may be said to address these concerns indirectly, in terms of either his presupposition that the needs of dependents are met in the nonpolitical domestic domain or his concern for "the least well-off"; but he does not deal with them directly. Most important, Rawls does not consider these concerns as central to the political aim of his theory. Especially as he refines the political focus of his work in *Political Liberalism* (1992), concerns of this sort are excluded. The exclusion is not trivial, nor is it Rawls's alone.

It is my view that liberal political theory and Rawls's theory, in particular, are flawed in that they do not take this issue of dependency to be central. All of us are dependent in childhood; most of us are dependent in old age; and many of us are dependent for long periods of time (sometimes throughout a life) because of ill health. Dependency is thus a matter for us all in our lives as social beings. Most women—by virtue of their traditional roles and the ineluctable demands of dependency—and some men, primarily those from marginalized classes, find themselves with the responsibility to care for dependents. In assuming these duties, they have too often found themselves stigmatized as dependents. As such, they have not been able to function as equals in a society of equals.

Because dependency strongly affects our status as equal citizens (i.e., as persons who, as equals, share the benefits and burdens of social cooperation), and because it affects all of us at one time or another, it is not an issue that can be set aside, much less avoided. Its consequences for social organization cannot be deferred until other traditional questions about the structure of society have been settled, without distorting the character of a just social order. Dependency must be faced from the beginning of any project in egalitarian theory that hopes to include *all* persons within its scope.

### *1.2. The Dependency Critique of Liberal Equality*

Collecting and refashioning the work of the years since his singularly influential *A Theory of Justice* (1971), Rawls, in his most recent book, *Political Liberalism* (1992), pares down the concept of "justice as fairness" to what he considers its political heart. The task is to refine the argument and answer his critics. Rawls, who has insisted throughout his work that gender, along with race, is irrelevant in considering persons as equal, briefly addresses feminist commentators (see Kittay 1994). He acknowledges the theory's dependence on a "few main and enduring classical problems" of political philosophy (Rawls 1992, xxix). These underlie much of the criticisms from feminist quarters, criticisms aimed at the masculine bias of the tradition's conception of the person. Defending the theory's conception of the person as merely a "device of representation," as opposed to a characterization of persons in a full sense, he opines optimistically that "alleged difficulties in discussing problems of gender and the family can be overcome" (1992, xxix).

With the publication of *Political Liberalism*, it is fitting to reexamine the Rawlsian construction with respect to the equality of women—a population too often excluded even in the most egalitarian liberal theories. Rawls intends to include women within the scope of his theory. But given the starting points of the work, can he succeed?

Rawls's theory begins, as do all contractarian theories, by construing society as an association of equals, conceived as individuals who are more or less equal in their ability to compete for the benefits of social cooperation. Equality forms one of the two pillars (the other being liberty) on which liberal political theory is erected; and, appropriately, equality is at the core of Rawls's theory. Indeed, equal divisions of the benefits and burdens of social cooperation serve as a benchmark for "justice as fairness" (Rawls 1992, 282). Equality plays its role both foundationally and normatively. The theory is based on the conception of all persons as moral equals; and it develops a concept of justice that issues in a relatively egalitarian society—a society in which basic political liberties are enjoyed equally by all and in which a fair economic distribution, in combination with equal opportunity, advantages the least well-off.[7]

Historical formulations of this fundamental level of equality betray an androcentric view of society. The historical development of this ideal since its emergence as a challenge to feudalism has been an ideal for male heads of households only.[8] The equality of heads of households banishes feudalistic dependencies that were the product of hierarchical political organization. The dependencies and resultant hierarchies that attend human development, disease, and decline remain within the household. Yet accompanying the egalitarian challenge to patriarchal, feudalistic hierarchies was a stress on individuals—that is, on the individualism championed in the theory of rights and political liberties. This overlay of individualism creates a conceptual illusion that dependencies do not exist—or at least are not a political matter. The illusion makes it appear that the extension of equality to all, not only to heads of households, is an easy matter.

From interdependencies that grow out of our dependencies emerge the central bonds of human life—bonds based on the vulnerabilities of the dependent person, on the one hand, and on the trust invested in the dependency worker, on the other. Those vulnerable in the sense that they require care are also vulnerable in that they often have no voice—at least no public voice—save that of their caretaker, the dependency worker, who is charged with articulating and meeting their needs.

But the voice of the dependency worker is not the independent voice of the equal autonomous agent of liberal political theory; it is a voice sometimes blending the interests of the caregiver and care-recipient, sometimes torn between conflicting interests. Either because the obligation devolves on the dependency worker, or because it is one of a very few options available, or because she freely chooses it from a wide variety of possibilities, she enters the "fair and equal" competitive arena with a handicapping condition: Along with the same responsibilities other citizens have to each other and to themselves, the dependency worker has the added responsibility of meeting the needs of another who is unable to care for himself. Given the cycle of human life, and given the pivotal place of *dependency work* in social life, its just organization is as central to the formation of a just society as is development of the principles of distribution under conditions of moderate scarcity.

Calling attention to the neglect of dependency, and to the consequences of that omission in theories of equality and social justice, constitutes what I call the *dependency critique*.[9] To the extent that the responsibility for providing the care required by dependents has traditionally fallen to women, this critique of liberal theories of equality is inspired by feminist concerns. As such, it provides a framework for rethinking the distribution of goods and responsibilities across gender lines, without staking the interests of some women against the interests of others.[10]

### *1.3. Dependency as a Criterion of Adequacy Applied to Rawls's Theory of Justice*

The principles of justice proposed by Rawls are intended to govern the basic structures of a well-ordered society; these principles, he argues, would be chosen by reasonable and rational persons under certain specified conditions—conditions simulated in the *original position*. In the context of Rawls's constructivism,[11] the *original position* (henceforth OP) is a hypothetical position from which representatives of citizens in a well-ordered society choose the principles of justice that they want their basic social structures (i.e., their laws and institutions) to embody. The participants in the OP are all modeled on equal and free moral persons, who are rational and mutually disinterested. They know general facts about human nature and society but are ignorant of their own station in life, their "conceptions of the good," and "their special psychological propensities" (Rawls 1971, 11). This *veil of ignorance* over participants in the OP should ensure that the choice of principles is unaffected by knowledge of one's own place in society, one's own vision of the good, or one's particular psychological proclivities; it should guarantee that parties choose principles impartially and, therefore, fairly. Parties in the OP are representatives of mutually disinterested *rational* agents concerned primarily with their own well-being. The constraints of the OP reflect fair terms of social cooperation to which rational persons could agree.

In "Kantian Constructivism in Moral Theory: The Dewey Lectures 1980" (1980, 520), Rawls exhibits the methodology and foundational concepts of *A Theory of Justice* (1971) in what he later calls "model-conceptions." (Rawls

1980, 520). The OP mediates between the "model-conceptions" of a *well-ordered society* and of a *moral person*, modeling the "way in which the citizens in a well-ordered society, viewed as moral persons, would ideally select first principles of justice for their society" (Rawls 1980, 520). Answering criticisms addressed to his model-conceptions, Rawls asserts, in one of his later works,[12] that thinking of ourselves as participants in the OP is analogous to "role-playing" (1992, 27).[13] Thus the OP and the model-conceptions are meant "to show how the idea of society as a fair system of social cooperation can be unfolded so as to find principles specifying the basic rights and liberties and the forms of equality most appropriate to those cooperating, once they are regarded as citizens, as free and equal persons" (Rawls 1992, 27).

My claim is that those within relations of dependency fall outside the conceptual perimeters of Rawls's egalitarianism. I shall trace the conceptual shape of this exclusion in Rawls through an analysis of the five presuppositions standing behind the concept of equality as we find it in Rawls's constructivism. In the concluding section, I return to the principles selected in the OP. I argue that they cannot accommodate the objections of the dependency critique if the foundational assumptions are not altered. In pointing to omissions in the theory, I contemplate ways in which the Rawlsian position could be amended. Whether the suggestions put forward suffice to make the theory amenable to dependency concerns without introducing new incoherencies for the theory is a question I leave for Rawlsians. My aim is neither to reform Rawls's political theory nor to say that it cannot be reformed. Rather, I offer the arguments of the dependency critique as a criterion of adequacy, one applicable to *any* political theory claiming to be egalitarian.

### *1.4. The Arguments in Outline*

"Equal justice," writes Rawls, "is owed to those who have the capacity to take part in and to act in accordance with the public understanding of the initial situation" (1971, 505). The moral equality of all members of a well-ordered society is represented in the model-conception of the person. In the "Dewey Lectures," he writes, "The representation for equality is an easy matter: we simply describe all the parties in the same way and situate them equally, that is, symmetrically with respect to one another. Everyone has the same rights and powers in the procedure for reaching agreement" (1980, 550). 'Equality' in this passage refers to the identity of members with respect to certain salient features: their rights and their powers in the procedure for reaching agreement. It also means that the parties are equally situated with respect to one another.[14] Representing equality here seems unproblematic. But, I wish to argue, what makes it an "easy matter" is that so much has been presumed already. Let us see if we can make the presumptions evident.

First, note that this representation of moral equality begins with an "idealization" of citizens in a well-ordered society, initially introduced when Rawls attempts to state the sense in which citizens in a well-ordered society are equal moral persons, that "all citizens are fully cooperating members of society *over the course of a complete life*" (1980, 546; emphasis added).

For Rawls this means that no one has particularly taxing or costly needs to fulfill, such as unusual medical requirements. In *Political Liberalism*, he writes, "The normal range [of functioning] is specified as follows: since the fundamental problem of justice concerns the relations among those who are full and active participants in society, and directly or indirectly associated together over the course of a whole life, it is reasonable to *assume that everyone has physical needs and psychological capacities within some normal range. Thus the problem of special health care and how to treat the mentally defective are set*. If we can work out a viable theory for the normal range, we can attempt to handle these other cases later" (1992, 272: note 10). That is, the case must initially be made for the "normal" situation and then be modified to include important but unusual considerations such as special medical requirements.[15]

Second, as everyone is equally capable of understanding and complying with the principles of justice (to a certain minimal degree), and is equally capable of honoring them, and insofar as each person is free (i.e., is a "self-originating" or "self-authenticating source of valid claims"),[16] each views her- or himself as worthy of being represented in a procedure by which the principles of justice are determined. An equality with respect, first, to a sense of justice and, second, to freedom as being a self-authenticating source of valid claims establishes the grounds for the claim to equal worth.

Third, the realization of equality assumes a common measure. But insofar as each person forms his or her own conception of the good, Rawls proposes an index composed of those goods all persons require given the two moral powers of a person: an ability to form and revise one's conception of one's own good and a sense of justice. The possession of these two moral powers is itself a feature of the modeling of the parties as equals.[17]

Fourth, the representation of the parties as equals turns on a conception of social cooperation. The equality of those representing citizens requires that persons possess the two moral powers and have normal capacities because these are the only requirements for establishing fair terms of social cooperation.[18]

And, finally, the entire edifice rests on what are identified as the "circumstances of justice." These are the circumstances under which a society of free and equal persons who share the benefits and the burdens of social organization is constituted.

Rawls's account, by his own insistence, is an idealization. Still, he acknowledges that it must take into account "an appropriate conception of the person that general facts about human nature and society allow" (1980, 534). Unfortunately, however, Rawls's idealization neglects certain scarcely acknowledged facts bearing on "an appropriate conception of the person" that are of the utmost importance in social organization—namely, facts of human dependency. The question then arises as to whether, given the Rawlsian idealization, the equality of citizens applies to those individuals who are dependent either in the primary sense or in the derived sense, even in a fully compliant well-ordered society.

The succession of the above considerations follows the reliance of each idea upon its successor. To bring us closer to the logic of theory construction, I invert the order. I argue that the fact of human dependency is excluded from each of the following considerations, and that we must not exclude such concerns if we are to develop a just social organization capable of meeting dependency needs:

1. The *circumstances of justice* that determine a well-ordered society's conceptual perimeters.
2. The *conception of social cooperation* that supposes equality between those in cooperative arrangements.
3. The *moral powers of a person* relevant to justice as (a) a sense of justice and (b) a conception of one's own good; and list of *primary goods* based on these moral powers that serves as index for interpersonal comparisons of well-being.
4. The *conception of free persons* as those who think of themselves as "self-originating sources of valid claims."
5. The *norm* appealed to and projected into the *idealization* that *"all citizens are fully cooperating members of society over the course of a complete life."*

These points are addressed in the five major sections that follow.

## 2. The Circumstances of Justice for a Well-Ordered Society

### *2.1. Dependency as Both an Objective and a Subjective Circumstance of Justice*

The general facts about human nature and society that constrain the conception of the person and of the well-ordered society constitute the most fundamental presuppositions for the conception of equality and justice evoked in Rawls's scheme. The most general of these facts are encapsulated in what Rawls, invoking Hume, calls the *circumstances of justice*. These are either objective or subjective (see Rawls 1971, 126–127; 1980, 536). Because each is so fundamental, the effect of overlooking an important circumstance has serious consequences for the whole theory.

According to current estimates, as many as one-third of the people in the United States are dependent. In complex societies nearly two decades are required to train people to be "fully cooperating members of society," and in all societies approximately ten childhood years are spent in nearly total dependence on an adult. As we live longer and longer, a greater portion of our lives is led in a state of frail old age when, once again, we cannot be fully cooperating members of society.[19] Indeed, despite advanced medical care, serious disabling conditions strike as much as 10 percent of the U.S. population. Surely, one would think, such a fundamental feature of our lives would be included among the circumstances of justice.

At the same time, we have to recognize dependency in its subjective forms—that is, as it affects our needs and desires. We have the need and desire both to be cared for and to care (or have someone care for) those who are important to us. Having these desires satisfied and these needs met are part of any conception of the good (see Section 4 below). By contrast, not everyone's conception of the good will include doing what is necessary to take care of these needs and desires. A just distribution of the burdens and responsibilities attached to meeting these needs is required in the same way that adjudicating between differing conceptions of the good is required of a just form of social cooperation. Furthermore, the subjective conditions resulting from inevitable human dependencies, such as the fact of differing conceptions of the good, are at the heart of considerations that propel us into social and political associations.

## 2.2. *The Absence of Dependency Considerations*

From the "Dewey Lectures" onward, Rawls speaks only of the objective circumstance of moderate scarcity—that is, of the condition in which natural resources are neither so abundant that distributive problems do not arise nor so scarce that cooperative arrangements cannot be realized. With respect to the subjective circumstances of justice, Rawls speaks primarily of the condition that "persons and associations have contrary conceptions of the good as well as of how to realize them" (1980, 536).

But even under conditions of affluence, there are important questions to raise with respect to both the distribution of resources devoted to meeting dependency needs and the distribution of the burdens and responsibilities of dependency work. Distributive questions with respect to dependency needs are not traceable to circumstances of justice concerning moderate scarcity. Yet nowhere in Rawls's work is human dependency explicitly cited among the circumstances of justice.

In the earlier works, we can find allusions to dependency concerns in two passages. First, Rawls (1971, 127) includes the equal vulnerability of all to attack and to being hindered by the united force of the others in the more complete enumeration of objective circumstances. This vulnerability, however, should not be confused with the vulnerability of dependency. Rawls speaks of an *equal* vulnerability (consider, for example, our equal vulnerability to being attacked). Vulnerability originating in dependency is not a condition in which all are *equally* vulnerable but, rather, one in which some are *especially* vulnerable.[20] The unequal vulnerability of the dependent and, secondarily, of the dependent's caretaker is an inequality in starting positions that, if left unaddressed, will be injected into the political situation.

Second, and more promising, is a passage in which Rawls says it is "essential . . . that each person in the original position should care about the well-being of some of those in the next generation . . . [and that] for anyone in the next generation, there is someone who cares about him in the present generation" (1971, 129). These remarks are provoked by Rawls's worry that if the generations are mutually disinterested, then there is no impetus to prevent the depletion of resources for future generations. Thus Rawls is led to propose a "motivational assumption" that will generate a "just savings principle"(1971, 285). Specifically, he proposes that the parties to the OP represent generational lines and that they be heads of households, thereby securing the interests of subsequent generations.

Although Rawls speaks of each person in the OP caring about the welfare of some in the next generation, the concern is with a scarcity of resources across generations, not the care of dependents. Even as he talks about a member of each generation "caring about" one in the next, he urges us not to presuppose extensive ties of natural sentiment.[21]

### *2.3. Can Dependency Concerns Be Introduced Through the Device of Representation?*

Rawls does not introduce representation by heads of households to solve problems arising from dependency; in *Political Liberalism*, in fact, he abandons the idea altogether. Might this device, nonetheless, be helpful in considering the circumstance of dependency, by having household heads represent the interests of dependents and familial caretakers?

In real politics, having one's own interests represented by someone who is differently situated is always a risky matter. Abigail Adams thought herself *represented* by her husband, but in the constitutional assembly, composed only of male heads of households, no one seemed to have heeded her call to "remember the Ladies."[22] But the OP posits a hypothetical representation: Why not just stipulate that those represented are represented faithfully?

The difficulty with such hypothetical representation in the Rawlsian framework was pointed to first by Jane English (1977) and later by Susan Okin. Using heads of households as representatives means that, although the family is one of the basic structures of society, justice cannot be said to pertain *within* it—a difficulty for gender equality among those who share a household.[23] If parties to the OP already have a determined social position relative to the family, they will not choose the principles of justice in ignorance of their social position. And in the framework of Rawlsian constructivism, only principles that we choose in ignorance of our social position will issue in fair principles with respect to the basic institutions. Since Rawls does want to say that the family is a basic institution, and since justice should then pertain to the family, the parties cannot be heads of households.

Okin's suggestion is that individuals, not heads of households, should be representatives. My question, then, is whether the parties representing individuals will represent the interests of both dependents and caretakers. If human dependency counts among the general facts to which representatives in the OP have epistemic access, they know that when the veil is lifted they may find themselves dependent or having to care for dependents. And if the representatives are individuals instead of household heads, they should be considering such contingencies in choosing their principles.

Although the theory allows an individual in the OP to imagine her- or himself to be a dependent or a dependency worker, the construction of the OP does not guarantee that the principles of justice chosen will reflect the concerns of either. Whereas the Rawlsian construct allows for the possibility that a representative *may* imagine her- or himself as a dependent or as having responsibility for a dependent's care, it does not necessitate that a representative *will* do so when choosing the principles for a well-ordered society. Indeed, dependents do not form an obvious constituency within the Rawlsian construct.[24] Surely, some persons, envisioning themselves as having dependency responsibilities, may choose to adopt other-directed interests as their own. But in this case, the representation of these dependents is a contingent matter and not one integral to the procedure of determining the principles of justice. (For a related discussion, see Subsection 6.2 below.)

If we insist, instead, that the parties represent generational lines,[25] we face still another predicament. If the rational choices of individual parties modeled in the OP (along with the other conditions stipulated of the OP) sufficed, there would be no need for any additional motivational assumptions, such as the one securing resources for future generations. The motivational assumption is necessary just because we may find too few in any one generation willing take responsibility for those in the next, if we must rely on individual voluntary decisions to ensure that everyone in a future generation will have someone who cares about his or her interest.[26] The choice not to take on such responsibility is neither irrational nor unreasonable, and it accords with our reflective judgments, as the social acceptance of remaining childless shows.[27] The mandating of such a responsibility could be seen as a serious constraint on individual conceptions of the good. The "just savings principle" stands in lieu of a mandate that each person in a society care about another in the next generation. But if the mandate itself is an undue constraint on each person's conception of the good, why is the substitute more acceptable, since it requires that we refrain from the enjoyment of at least some of our resources for the sake of a future generation whose well-being may play no role in our own conception of the good? Either Rawls's motivational assumption fails or it allows into his scheme principles that constitute an unpalatable constraint on each person's choice of the good.

Now, if the presumption that each party in the OP is a head of household—which still precludes supposing extensive ties of natural sentiment—and if this presumption is too strong to accommodate certain rational and reasonable conceptions of the good, then it surely cannot be helpful in addressing the needs of dependents whose care requires a commitment stronger still than the preservation of resources for the future. Therefore, we are confronted with the problem that however we conceive of the parties in the OP, as representatives of individuals or as representatives of households (or generational lines), the representation of dependents and those caring for dependents is not ensured by the construction of the OP. And this is so even if we include facts concerning dependency among those that parties in the OP would know while under the veil of ignorance.

### *2.4. Chronological Unfairness and Intergenerational Justice*

Rawls (1992) revised his strategy to ensure the just savings principle. Acknowledging a proposal previously suggested by English (1977), he now maintains that "the parties can be required to agree to a savings principle subject to the further condition that they must want all *previous* generations to have followed it" (Rawls 1992, 274). Thus the motivational assumption that "constrains the parties from refusing to make any savings at all" remains (Rawls 1992, 274: note 12) and is captured by a form of reciprocity peculiar to the savings principle. Rawls had earlier noted:

> Normally this [reciprocity] principle applies when there is an exchange of advantages and each party gives something as a fair return to the other. But in the course of history no generation gives to the preceding generations, the benefits of whose saving it has received. In following the savings principle, each generation makes a contribution to later generations and receives from its predecessors. (1971, 290)

It is a natural fact that "[w]e can do something for posterity but it can do nothing for us" (Rawls 1971, 291). This fact involves "a kind of chronological unfairness since those who live later profit from the labor of their predecessors without paying the same price" (Alexander Herzen, cited in Rawls 1971, 291); being unalterable, however, this condition is itself not a question of justice but a consideration that we have to acknowledge in fashioning the just society.

Similarly, there are unalterable conditions proceeding from the facts of human development, disease, and decline. First, the dependent needs care and is not equal in situation or power to those who are relatively independent. Second, the dependency worker has a particular interest in the welfare of others, and her independence as a self-originator of desires and claims is constrained in a way not characteristic of the unemcumbered independent agent (see Subsection 5.1 below). What is not unalterable is the level of support extended to the dependent and the dependency worker. If we need a just savings principle (however formulated) to ensure that the well-being of future generations is not jeopardized, we need a similar principle to ensure that the well-being of dependents and their caretakers is not jeopardized, since the natural developmental process to which the first is addressed is mirrored within the life history of each individual as well—and if the first needs to be addressed by a theory of justice, so does the second.

The essential point is this: To capture these circumstances of justice in the OP, we need to provide additional motivational assumptions that constrain the parties from choosing principles that fail to address dependency concerns. If dependency concerns are among the circumstances of justice, then our conceptions of social goods and social cooperation need to be reexamined in light of the consequences of human dependency—that is, with attention to the ties between persons, and to the costs in human and material terms effected by human dependency.

## 3. The Public Conception of Social Cooperation

### *3.1. Dependency Concerns in Rawls's Conception of Social Cooperation*

For Rawls, social cooperation is more than "simply . . . coordinated social activity efficiently organized and guided by publicly recognized rules to achieve some overall end" (1992, 300). Indeed, it also demands "fair terms of cooperation" among citizens—namely, terms that citizens can accept not only because they are *rational* (in that they satisfy each person's view of their rational advantage) but also because they are *reasonable* (in that they recognize and accept that not all people have the same ends when engaging in social interaction).

In another work (Kittay 1995a), I claim that the Rawlsian position should, but does not, include dependency concerns as part of an adequate conception of social cooperation.[28] Dependency concerns fall within the purview of a notion of social cooperation pertinent to political justice for at least three reasons: first, because they are rational and reasonable considerations in choosing a conception of justice; second, because a society that does not care for its dependents or that cares for them only by unfairly exploiting the labor of those who do the caring cannot be said to be well-ordered (see Subsection 3.3); and, third, because when we reorient our political insights to see the centrality of human relationships to our happiness and well-being, we recognize dependency needs as basic motivations for creating a social order. In short, the reorientation of our political insights focuses our attention on the justice of providing *both* for dependents—who, even in their neediness, contribute to the ongoing nature of human relationships—*and* for those who care for dependents—whose social contribution is obscured when we are looking only at the social cooperation between independent and fully functioning persons.

### *3.2. Fair Terms of Agreement and Reciprocity*

One way to construe the arguments summarized here is to say that dependency concerns fall within political justice but outside of justice as fairness. Rawls, who notes that justice as fairness may not be entirely coincident with political justice, remarks, "How deep a fault this is must wait until the case itself can be examined" (1992, 21). He reminds us that political justice needs to be complemented by additional virtues (1992, 21). I suggest another possibility. We can reconceive fairness. By enlarging the concept of reciprocity, we return to some of the ideas expressed in Subsection 2.4, but now applied to relations in which not all are independent and fully functioning.

The reciprocity and mutuality articulated in fair terms of cooperation apply to "all who cooperate." Each, then, must "benefit, or share in common burdens, in some appropriate fashion judged by a suitable benchmark of comparison" (Rawls 1992, 300). Because the relations of dependents and dependency workers to one another and to the larger society do not fit standard models of reciprocity, it is difficult to include dependency concerns within a conception of justice as fairness. This conception implicitly excludes severely disabled, permanently dependent people, especially those who are mentally incapacitated, from social cooperation and therefore citizenship.[29] They can neither reciprocate the care they receive nor, in relevant senses, "restrict their liberty in ways necessary to yield advantages to all."[30] Temporarily dependent persons may be able to collect on benefits they had bestowed on others when they were fully functioning, or they may be able to defer reciprocation. But the opportunity to reciprocate may never come:

A child may not reach maturity; an ill person may die or become permanently incapacitated; a now needy and elderly parent may never have been an adequate provider or nurturer. How then is the caretaker's contribution to be reciprocated? Unless the needs of the caretaker are to be met through or by means of some other form of reciprocity, the only available moral characterization of the caretaker's function is that it constitutes exploitation or supererogation.

### *3.3. Doulia*

The need, then, is to expand the notion of reciprocity and, in so doing, to open a conceptual space for dependency concerns within social cooperation in a just society. To fix our ideas, we consider the situation of the postpartum mother caring for her infant. The extreme neediness of the infant and the physiological trauma of having given birth create a special vulnerability for the mother. Some traditional cultures and religions mark this period of maternity: The mother is enjoined to care for her child while others attend to her needs and household and familial duties. Some assign a "doula," a postpartum caregiver who assists the mother and, at times, relieves her. Today, in the United States, where families are geographically dispersed and lack community support as well as adequate workers' leave policies, a fledgling effort is being made to adopt the idea of the doula. By contrast to the time-worn paid help known as the "baby nurse," who displaces the mother by taking over care of the infant, the doula assists by caring for the mother as the mother attends to the child.[31]

The word 'Doula' originally meant slave or servant in Greek. So it is rather intriguing to redirect the concept and signify instead a caretaker who cares for those who care for others. In place of the notion of a servant fulfilling the function of a doula, then, we need a concept of interdependence that recognizes a relation not so much of reciprocity as of nested dependencies, linking those who help and those who require help in order to give aid to those who cannot help themselves. Extending the notion of the service performed by the doula, let us use the term 'doulia' to refer to an arrangement by which service is passed on so that those who become needy by virtue of tending to those in need can be cared for as well.[32] Doulia is part of an ethic that is captured in the colloquial phrase "What goes around comes around."[33] If someone helps another in her need, someone in turn will help the helper when she is needy—regardless of whether the neediness derives from her position as caretaker or from circumstances that pertain to her health or age. We can state a principle of doulia: *Just as we have required care to survive and thrive, so we need to provide conditions that allow others—including those who do the work of caring—to receive the care they need to survive and thrive.*

Since society is an association that persists through generations, an extended notion of "reciprocity," a transitive (if you will) responsiveness to our dependence on others, is needed for justice between generations. As Rawls recognizes, the care we take to hand over a world that is not depleted is never reciprocated to us by those whom we benefit. Rather, the benefit we bestow on the next generation ought to be the benefit we would have wanted the previous generation to bestow on us. The resemblance between this extended notion of reciprocity and doulia is not accidental.[34] In both contexts, we deal with human development and with its "chronological unfairness." Moreover, just as the gains and savings from a previous generation pass from us to the next generation, the care a mother bestows on her child calls for reciprocation from the adult child not only back to the parents but also forward to a future generation.[35]

The doula, who serves as our paradigm, is engaged in private interactions. Rawls's concerns are limited to the public—to the basic structure of society. Although the paradigm concerns domestic interactions, I am arguing for an analogical extension of the idea of doulia to the public domain. The caretaker has a responsibility to care for the dependent, and the larger society seeks ways to attend to the well-being of the caretaker, thereby allowing the caretaker to fulfill responsibilities to the dependent without exploiting the labor and concern of the caretaker. This is a *public* conception of doulia. As human dependency is inevitably a circumstance of justice that marks our most profound attachments, and as care of a dependent morally obliges the dependency worker to give a certain priority to the welfare of her charge (see Subsection 5.2), a public conception of doulia is needed to accomplish the tripartite goal of treating the dependency worker equitably, providing care for dependents, and respecting the dependency relations in which fundamental human attachments grow and thrive.

"Although a well-ordered society is divided and pluralistic . . . the public agreement on questions of political and social justice supports ties of civic friendship and secures the bonds of association," writes Rawls (1980, 540). But as potent as the bonds of association created by public agreement may be, they are not as powerful as those created by caring relationships. The latter are bonds that tie individuals together into families, kin, and other intimate relations, bonds that allow individuals at different stages of life to withstand the forces that act upon them. Indeed, these intimate bonds make civic order and civic friendship possible (see Held 1987a). A political theory must therefore attend not only to the well-being of dependents *and* of their caretakers but also to the *relation* of caretaker and dependent upon which all other civic unions depend.[36] Without practices based on an implicit principle of care, human beings would either not survive or survive very poorly—and surely would not thrive.[37] Principles of right and traditional notions of justice depend upon a prior and more fundamental principle and practice of care. Roughly stated, such a principle holds that, in order to grow, flourish, and survive or endure illness, disability, and frailty, each individual requires caring relationship with significant others who hold that individual's well-being as a primary responsibility and a primary good.

In constructing a just social order, then, we need a theory that acknowledges the fact that humans are dependent for periods of their lives—rather than ignoring that fact through idealizations in which men (to use Hobbes's term) spring from the earth "like mushrooms," or ones in which citizens are fully functioning throughout a life span, or ones that merely presuppose that caring is done, somehow, by someone. Such theories and the societies they envision occlude any principle of care and the fundamental associations it would create. But for a society to attend to the need for care and do so justly, it is not sufficient for the dependency worker alone to be caring. Indeed, this objective requires the establishment of a social principle that provides the basis for social institutions that aid and support dependency workers in their caring responsibilities. But then such a principle, in turn, requires the broadened conception of reciprocity (and a suitably modified sense of fairness *within* each generation) expressed in the concept of doulia. Such a principle would be instantiated when the value of receiving care and giving care is publicly acknowledged; when the burdens and cost incurred by doing the work of caring for dependent do not fall to the dependency worker alone (even when that dependency work is freely assumed); and when the commitment to preserving caring *relations* is assumed by the society. Such a principle would mandate, first, a *social responsibility* (derived from political justice realized in social cooperation) for enabling dependency relations satisfactory to dependency worker and dependent alike; and, second, social institutions that foster an attitude of caring and a respect for care by enabling caretakers to do the job of caretaking without becoming disadvantaged in the competition for the benefits of social cooperation—a competition that now favors those situated as equal and independent persons unencumbered by dependency demands.

The Rawlsian (and the liberal) account of a well-ordered society as characterized by the narrower notions of justice and of right, then, is either incomplete or inadequate. And this is so not for the reason communitarians have stressed—namely, that, on the one hand, it purports more of a conception of the good life than it admits to, and that, on the other hand, it fails to provide enough of a guide to the good life to be fully satisfying. Rather, a society cannot be well-ordered—that is, it cannot sustain its members and provide them with a basis for self-respect (see Subsection 4.4)—if it fails to be a society in which care is publicly acknowledged as a good for which the society as a whole bears a responsibility to provide in a manner that is just to all.

Rawls, speaking of the need to give priority to the basic liberties, points out that even when the political will does not yet exist to do what is required (as it might not in a society that is less than well ordered), "part of the political task is to help fashion it" (1992, 297). Likewise, if the political will to imbue citizens with sensitivity and a sense of priority for care does not yet exist, it is "part of the political task . . . to help fashion it" (1992, 297).

## 4. The Two Powers of a Moral Person and the Index of Primary Goods

### *4.1. The Omission of Care as a Primary Good*

Social cooperation, as Rawls understands it, is achievable among persons conceived as having certain moral capacities, a sense of justice, and a conception of their own good. Presupposing "various general facts about human wants and abilities, their characteristic phases and requirements of nurture, relations of social interdependence, and much else" (1992, 307), Rawls generates an index of *primary goods*, goods that presume the possession of the two moral powers and that serve as a basis for making comparative assessments of interpersonal well-being.

The list of primary goods has remained unaltered since *A Theory of Justice:*

1. The basic liberties (freedom of thought and liberty of conscience) . . . .
2. Freedom of movement and free choice of occupation against a background of diverse opportunities . . . as well as [the ability] to give effect to a decision to revise and change them. . . .
3. Powers and prerogatives of offices and positions of responsibility . . . .
4. Income and wealth. . . .
5. The social bases of self-respect. . . . (Rawls 1980, 526)[38]

Without questioning the merit of such a gauge as a measure for interpersonal well-being,[39] I want to ask: Does this list adequately address needs of dependents[40] and those who care for them?

The question presumes that the two moral powers Rawls attributes to citizens are the only ones relevant to persons as citizens. Indeed, the list of goods is supposed to have been motivated by a conception of moral persons as those possessing a sense of justice and the capacity to form and revise a rational life-plan. Assuming, then, that individuals in dependency relations count as citizens, assessing the adequacy of the list requires asking whether these moral powers suffice as the moral powers of citizens in a society that takes dependency needs seriously.

An ethic reflecting concern for dependents and those who care for them demands, first, a sense of attachment to others; second, an empathetic attention to their needs;[41] and, third, a responsiveness to the needs of another. Such an ethic goes well beyond duties traditionally assigned to justice, but in the context of caring relations they are not supererogatory. Fulfillment of these duties requires the cultivation of capacities that, although they are not required by justice as traditionally conceived, *are* required by a state which recognizes that taking dependency seriously is a requirement of justice.

Neither of Rawls's two moral powers requires such concern nor yields such an ethic. First, for some the good will include attachments of sentiment, leading them to cultivate capacities to care for others; still, this remains a private matter requiring no responsibility on the part of the society at large and no assurance that dependents can be cared for without extracting undue sacrifices from those upon whom the responsibilities fall. (See Subsections 2.3 and 6.2.) Second, unlike the ability to form and revise a conception of one's own good, a sense of justice is necessarily an other-directed moral power. Though one that involves reciprocity, it does not necessarily entail an empathetic attention to the needs of another who may be incapable of reciprocating. Thus, the moral capacities for care are never invoked in the moral capacity of justice as construed in Rawlsian constructivism.[42]

A construction adequate to meeting dependency needs justly would expand the list of moral powers and amend the list of primary goods.[43] The moral powers of the person should include not only (a) a sense of justice (construed in the more narrow sense that Rawls suggests) and (b) a capacity to pursue a conception of the good but also (c) a capacity to respond to vulnerability with care.[44] Neither (a) nor (b) addresses citizens who are vulnerable to the dependencies of age, illness, or disability, or who have to care for others in that state of dependency. Although justice and caring have often been seen as distinct, even opposing, virtues, the arguments put forward in this chapter press for a different view. In short, a justice that does not incorporate the need to respond to vulnerability with care is incomplete, and a social order that ignores care will itself fail to be just.

### *4.2. Care as a Primary Good Issuing from the Moral Power to Care*

Rawls's list of primary goods neglects the goods that issue from a commitment to care: (a) the understanding that we will be cared for if we become dependent, (b) the support we require if we have to take on the work of caring for a dependent, and (c) the assurance that if we become dependent, someone will take on the job of caring for those who are dependent upon us. We can possess basic liberties, freedom of movement and choice of occupation, the powers and prerogatives of public office, even income and wealth, without the assurance that we will be cared for if we become dependent; that when we are called upon to do the work of caring for a dependent, we will be adequately supported in our undertaking; and that, as we focus our energies and attention on another, we do not thereby lose the ability to care for ourselves.

Must these concerns be reflected in a list of *primary goods?* That is, are they goods basic for any individual who is capable of fashioning a conception of the good for herself and needed whatever her life-plan happens to be? And, if this is so, are they also among those needs "relevant in questions of justice?"(Rawls 1982, 172).[45]

The answer to both queries is "yes." Regardless of how we fashion our conception of the good, we would want to be cared for when we are dependent and would want to be adequately supported if we find ourselves having to be responsible for the care of a dependent. Moreover, if, as I shall demonstrate in the next section, the failure to secure these conditions impairs the capability of those most vulnerable to dependency and dependency work to participate as equals in an otherwise well-ordered society,[46] then these conditions are indeed relevant to questions of justice. Therefore, the good *to be cared for in a responsive dependency relation if and when one is unable to care for oneself, as well as to meet dependency needs of others without incurring undue sacrifices oneself,* is a primary good in the Rawlsian sense because it is a good of citizens as they pursue their own conception of the good and exercise their moral faculties of justice and care.

Furthermore, like all the other primary goods, such a good has a bearing on the social bases of self-respect for the members of the well-ordered society. In this connection, consider Patricia Williams's (1991, 55) citation of the following passage from Marguerite Duras's *The Lover* (1985): "We're united in a fundamental shame at having to live. It's here we are at the heart of our common fate, the fate that [we] are our mother's children, the children of a candid creature murdered by society. We're on the side of society which has reduced her to despair. Because of what's been done to our mother, so amiable, so trusting, we hate life, we hate ourselves."

To the extent that we grow into a relatively safe and secure adulthood in consequence of care secured through the sacrifice of another, a sacrifice that can never be adequately restored, we carry with us a shame that diminishes self-respect. We are diminished in this way as long as we live in a society where care can be had only through such a sacrifice.

If women, through their maternal roles, have been sacrificial lambs, they have also been the ones who have recognized care as a primary good and have engaged in political struggle when their ability to care has been undermined. Indeed, as historian Temma Kaplan (1982, 1992) has documented, the political participation of women in diverse nations, cultures, and historical periods is tied to circumstances rendering women unable to give care to their families. Through their willingness to engage in political struggles to ensure their ability to care for their families, women, at least, have contended that being able to care for others is a primary social good. The political nature of these struggles is consistent with Rawls's conception of self-respect, which is contingent not only on the way the individual conducts herself privately but also on "the public features of basic social institutions" and "publicly expected (and normally honored) ways of conduct" (Kaplan 1992, 319).

## 5. Free Persons Are "Self-Originating Sources of Valid Claims"

Equal persons in a well-ordered society must also be regarded as free. In fact, our contemporary sensibility refuses to tolerate slavery, serfdom, or any similar bondage within a well-ordered society. Rawls contrasts the free citizen to the slave or bondsman. In the "Dewey Lectures" he depicts citizens in the well-ordered society as "self-*originating* sources of valid claims" (1980, 543; emphasis added), and in *Political Liberalism* he depicts them as "self-*authenticating* sources of valid claims" (1992, 33; emphasis added).[47] Rawls also contrasts claims originating from ourselves with those derived from our social role, wherein we act for others upon whose rights and powers our own depend. In the next two subsections, I will argue that being a "self-*authenticating* source of valid claims" is an inapt characterization of freedom for the dependency worker. But because it is an important feature of the freedom that Rawls attributes to the "free and equal citizen," parties to the OP who are modeled on free persons (in this sense) do not represent the dependency worker.

### *5.1. Is the Dependency Worker a Self-Originator of Claims?*

What should we say of the mother and her claim to, say, the right to education—not for herself, but for her child? Is hers a self-originating claim, or is it a claim derived from prior duties or obligations owed to society or to other persons—that is, one derived from or assigned to her particular social role? The parent who presses the claim on behalf of the child also sees it—appropriately, I believe—as her own interest.[48] A caring and responsible parent is one whose self-respect is bound up with the care she attempts to provide and the opportunities she attempts to make available to her children. Therefore, the claims she makes on their behalf are reasonably experienced as self-originating claims, although they are claims made on behalf of another within the context of a social role.

The dependency worker whose relation to the charge is more distant, and so whose own well-being is less intimately tied to her charge, may nonetheless make claims on the other's behalf—claims that exceed the dependency worker's prescribed duties. When her claims (in contrast to the mother's) go beyond prescribed duties, the *specific* claims cannot be said to originate in her social role, even if, in general, her claims on behalf of her charge derive from her social role. Thus, *both* for the mother (who, in making claims for her child, remains within her socially defined role but experiences those claims as her own) *and* for the other dependency worker who does not so closely identify her good with that of her charge (yet whose claims on behalf of her charge will exceed her specified responsibility), freedom is as bound up with claims that originate from others (i.e., the cared-for) as with those that originate independently.[49]

It is important to stress here that a thick involvement of the dependency worker in the welfare of her charge is generally not, as so often portrayed, a neurotic, compensatory action on the part of an individual who has no hope of being a person in her own right. Because dependency work is frequently accomplished under oppressive conditions, it is easy to miss the fact that deep involvement is a normal and necessary part of good dependency work—whereas overinvolvement and self-abnegation may not constitute good caretaking. A feverish child who wakes in the middle of the night has a claim on her caretaker's attention, even if the caretaker is very tired or even ill.[50] Whether a dependency worker presses for a child's educational opportunities or ignores her own fatigue to care for the ill child, her actions are good caring—not, generally speaking, neurotic overidentification or self-abnegating self-sacrifice. Caring about the welfare of persons for whom we are responsible and care for is entailed in normal and *effective* caring. In fact, the failure of much institutionalized caretaking is traceable to the difficulty of evoking this thick involvement on the part of the caretakers—who, so often, *don't care*.

The dependency worker cannot be said to be a self-originating source of claims, at least not in the terms suggested in the "Dewey Lectures." Any retort that it is only the dependency worker, *qua* dependency worker, who fails to be a self-originating source of claims (since these claims issue from her as she fills a particular social role) fails to recognize an important difference between dependency work and most other forms of labor. Because of the moral demands of the work (see Subsection 4.2), dependency worker's moral self cannot easily be peeled from her social role.[51] Therefore, freedom that demands a view of oneself as a self-originator of valid claims is not a freedom applicable to the situation of the dependency worker.

Of course, Rawls's theory is normative, not descriptive. Slaves, for example, would not count among the free individuals who have an equal claim to the fruits of social cooperation, since they, too, are not self-originating sources of valid claims. But in a well-ordered society all should be treated as free and equal, and so slavery would be impermissible. We cannot similarly interdict dependency work, nor would we want to.[52] If, as Rawls writes, the members of a well-ordered society are to "view their common polity as extending backward and forward in time over generations" (1980, 536), and given that the course of human development inevitably requires that some care for dependents, we cannot tell the dependency worker to abandon her concern for the well-being of her charge, even though this concern renders her freedom—construed as the self-origination of valid claims—an empty abstraction.

The etymology of doulia as slavery is instructive here. Whereas slavery is a morally impermissible form of service, dependency work is an inescapable one. Whereas slavery, under even the most favorable conditions, is demeaning and dehumanizing, dependency work, under the right conditions, reaches into the core of our humanity. And whereas slavery is the most debased of human relations, dependency work forms the most fundamental of social relations. Nonetheless, the restraint on freedom that dependency work shares with slavery has tainted this form of labor—especially now, at a time when freedom as the self-origination of valid claims is so highly prized. Only by naturalizing dependency work (consider, for example, the assumption that women are *naturally* better with children, the sick, the elderly) have ideologues made its constraints on freedom palatable to a modern sensibility.[53] Indeed, as a result of the naturalization of this labor, the coercion required for the *modern* woman to engage in dependency work has been overlaid with sentimentality (see Badinger 1980). This is not to say that dependency work cannot be intensely rewarding. Not only *can* it be, but, under favorable conditions, it *is*. When we highlight this sense of freedom, however, we are less likely to see dependency work as the vital, fulfilling, humanizing work it is.

### *5.2. Is the Dependency Worker a Self-Authenticator of Claims?*

The criticism launched here is against an individualistic view of citizens and their representatives in the OP. And the formulation in the "Dewey Lectures" may be most susceptible to such a reading.[54] Earlier, Rawls had explicitly warned against construing the self-interestedness of the participants of the OP as reflecting interest only in their selfish pursuits: "There is no inconsistency, then, in supposing that once the veil of ignorance is removed, the parties find that they have ties of sentiment and affection, and want to advance the interests of others and to see their ends attained" (1971, 129). Thus the parties in the OP may represent the wants and interests of others (and when the parties are heads of families they presumably do), and self-originating claims need not be self-interested. For example, if I want whatever *J* wants, then although the content of my wants is determined not by me but by *J*, the claim is self-originating if *my* want is to want what *J* wants. This is a noncoerced, other-linked, second-order wanting. One who voices such a want is less like the slave, and more like the churches, voluntary agencies, and so on, that press claims on behalf of others.[55]

This wanting can be assumed in a variety of ways, not all of which have the same moral standing or the same moral consequences. We need to distinguish between two kinds of relations based on noncoerced, other-linked wanting. In the first instance, if we exit we do so without jeopardizing the vital interests of those in the relationship. In the second, we do not have such an exit option. Labor regulations prohibiting certain workers from striking because others are vitally dependent upon them recognize this distinction.

The dependency worker—especially one who is unpaid and whose responsibilities are familial—rarely has a morally acceptable option of exiting from her relation to the dependent. Even when she no longer wants to want what her charge wants, she feels morally obliged to continue assuming the other's interests. At best, the daily hour-to-hour responsibilities can be given over to a paid dependency worker. But this substitute's obligation is as morally (even legally) compelling as that of the original dependency worker until the substitute is herself relieved. For example, in group homes for the retarded, as in many other facilities that provide twenty-four-hour care, workers are mandated to work overtime if their replacements fail to show up, and they must remain on duty until they are relieved. Clearly, the interests of a paid dependency worker in such a situation *must* be subservient to those of her charges, whether or not she wants them to be.

Well, one can respond, to some extent all workers must subordinate their own wants in a work situation. Yet they would ordinarily be held to that obligation only for a contracted period of time or amount of work. For the dependency worker, however, mandated overtime, unlike the hours for which she contracted, is work-time controlled—both legally and morally—by the needs of a dependent. The dependency worker does not have the option to leave because she has a better-paying job awaiting her after-hours, or because she doesn't need the extra pay, or because she just doesn't want to work anymore. Although the dependency worker either need not or does not distinguish between self-interested preferences and non-self-interested preferences, when there is a conflict she may be so situated that the moral, and sometimes legal, obligation falls upon her to favor the latter.[56]

Perhaps the disparity between the demands of dependency work and the status of the individual as a self-originator of valid claims is not irreconcilable. In Rawls's (1971) portrayal of the party in the OP as the head of a generational line, that party—like the dependency worker—would, in a less-than-voluntary-yet-not-coerced manner, assume the responsibility of representing the claims of third parties and be morally compelled to protect the interests of the members of the household under the same constraints-of-exit options as the dependency worker. And the representatives of generational lines or heads of households would similarly be morally obliged to balance their self-interest against the interests of those they represent, and may even have to prefer the interests of third parties over and above their own. The Rawlsian would thus remind us that only the mutual disinterestedness of the parties—not the mutual disinterestedness between the individuals of the society—is important for the OP.

Although Rawls has dropped the notion of generational lines, he has replaced the idea of parties being self-originators of valid claims, as used in the "Dewey Lectures," with the idea that parties are "self-authenticating" sources of valid claims. The revision seems to address some communitarian and feminist objections to a metaphysical conception of a person that is highly individualist—a problem aggravated when we relinquish the idea of parties as representing generational lines or heads of households. By shifting to the "self-authenticating" formulation, Rawls allows himself to state: "Claims that citizens regard as founded on duties and obligations based on their conception of the good and the moral doctrine they affirm in their own life are also, for our purposes here, to be counted as self-authenticating" (1992, 32).

This new formulation opens a space for an expanded notion of "self"-interest, compatible with the interest of the dependency worker. The mother who insists on a child's right to an education may not be acting on a self-originating claim, but she surely is acting on a self-authenticating one. The particular claims she makes as a dependency worker may be self-authenticating in this sense. But the solution is only partial, for it returns us to the vagaries of the relatively arbitrary choices that individuals make about their work and their conception of the good, and to the uncertainty of whether or not their representatives in the OP will choose principles that will take care of dependency needs in a just and equitable fashion, as judged by our considered reflections (see Subsection 2.3 above). Indeed, without the assurance that dependency concerns will be handled equitably, we still have to question the self-authenticating nature of the choice to be a dependency worker.

If dependency work were well paid, had a high status, or received some other social recognition, we could conclude that the constraint of freedom and its other demands explain the sufficient supply of dependency workers. The disparity, however, between the rewards offered in the labor market and the vital interest to have good dependency care makes it clear that market forces have not been relied upon to supply adequate dependency work. Indeed, a clear-eyed look at the nearly universal twin features of female caregiving and female subordination reveals (a) that a certain class of persons has been subjected to and socialized to develop the character traits and the volitional structure needed for dependency work;[57] (b) that certain sexual behaviors commensurate with forming attachments, being submissive to another's will, and so forth, have been made compulsory for women (see Rich 1978); and (c) that poor women and women of color have been forced into paid employment as dependency workers by the scanty financial resources and limited employment opportunities available to them, and middle-class women have been forced out of paid employment not commensurate with their (largely unpaid) duties as dependency workers. It has not merely "happened" that women have consistently "chosen" to make dependency relations and dependency work central to their vision of the good life, whereas men have chosen a wider variety of options.[58] Because care of dependents is nonoptional in any society, some societal measures are inescapably taken to meet the inevitable need for care. If the means by which a society distributes responsibility for dependency work is not guided by principles of justice, then coercive measures—often in the guise of tradition and custom, sometimes in the guise of merely apparent voluntary life choices—are the predictable response.

The contention that dependency work is freely chosen and results in self-authenticating, if not self-originating, claims pushes the problem of distributing dependency work back into the realm of the private—into private choice and so outside the purview of public demands of justice. The consequence is that many claims are presumed to be "self-authenticated" when they are really heteronomous. The dependency worker who fits this description will be no more a self-authenticated source of valid claims than a self-originating source of such claims.[59]

The self-origination of claims may be an inapt characterization of the dependency worker's freedom in any society; but a "well-ordered society" that is not yet a society in which the principles of care and doulia are operative is also not one in which dependency workers can be said to be self-authenticating sources of valid claims. The dependency worker would not yet be among the free citizens of such a putatively well-ordered state. If only those who are equals and free in the Rawlsian sense are eligible to participate in social cooperation, then dependency workers cannot be included among the "free" individuals who have an equal claim to the fruits of social cooperation.

## 6. The Idealization That "All Citizens Are Fully Cooperating Members of Society"

### *6.1. Fully Cooperating Throughout a Life—The Strong Interpretation*

Representing the equality of citizens in a well-ordered society, claims Rawls, requires the idealization that "all are capable of honoring the principles of justice and of being full participants in social cooperation *throughout* their lives" (1980, 546; emphasis added). Rawls presumes this to be an innocent idealization, thereby greasing the wheels of the theoretical apparatus that allows us to pass over the few difficult cases—for example, persons with "unusual and costly medical requirements." He justifies his exclusion of "hard" cases" such as disabilities and special health needs by claiming that they are "morally irrelevant" and can "distract our moral perception by leading us to think of people distant from us whose fate arouses pity and anxiety" (Rawls 1975a, 96).

But this idealization is seriously misleading. Amartya Sen remarks that leaving out disabilities, special health needs, or physical or mental defects, "for fear of making a mistake, may guarantee that the *opposite* mistake will be made" (1987, 157).[60] The opposite mistake, I contend, is to put too much distance between the "normal functioning individual" and the person with special needs and disabilities. Not a single citizen approaches the ideal of full functioning *throughout* a lifetime. The idealization, in contrast, suggests that those who are not fully functioning are relatively few, and that the consequences of special needs are brokered only in monetary terms.

Perhaps by pressing the phrase "*throughout* their lives" I have interpreted Rawls too strongly, inasmuch as this phrase suggests that full functioning at *every point* in a complete life is the requirement for equal citizenship. Rawls also uses the phrase "over the course of a complete life" (which survives the revision of the "Dewey Lectures" in *Political Liberalism*). A weaker requirement is to be a fully cooperating member of society at just those points when it would be reasonable to expect an individual to be fully functioning. The fact, for example, that one-third of the population is dependent at any given time doesn't necessarily imply that those within that one-third are not "equal," since they may well be equal *over* the course of a complete life.[61] Even though individuals who are underage, or disabled, are equal citizens only *in potentia*, their representatives in the OP are modeled as rational, symmetrically situated, fully functioning parties, with equal powers.

### *6.2. Fully Cooperating over a Lifetime— The Weak Interpretation*

If we accept the weaker reading of the idealization of full functioning, then parties all come to the "bargaining table" of the OP with a knowledge that they are dependent at some time in their lives (and may have to take on dependency responsibilities), even though as rational autonomous representatives (Rawls 1992, 316), they come to the bargaining table of the OP in full possession of their power. Since those whom the parties represent are dependent *in potentia* (and possibly dependency workers *in potentia*), it seems as if the situation of the dependent (at least) should be robustly represented in the party to the OP. Behind the veil of ignorance we do not know if we are dependent or independent, dependency workers or unencumbered persons. It should be the case that either the nature of the representative or the construction of the situation in which the representative deliberates will allow the interests of the dependent and the dependency worker to be taken into account in choosing the principles of justice. Indeed, as I argued in Subsection 2.3, although nothing in the construction of the OP prevents a representative in the hypothetical situation of the OP from thinking about her- or himself as a dependent or a dependency worker, nothing ensures it either, so these concerns will not necessarily be represented. Since only the least well-off is guaranteed representation, I will argue in Subsection 7.1 that assimilating either dependent or dependency worker to the position of the least well-off is warranted neither by Rawls's theory nor by our considered reflections.

However, *if* dependency is recognized as one of the circumstances of justice, then the dependent, at least, *is* represented—as a fully functioning citizen in a period of dependency, such as early childhood. If I imagine myself as a party to the original position, I consider that I will have such periods of dependency and will want to choose my principles of justice in such a way that, while I am in this state, my interests are protected. Since I will also think that, in all likelihood, I will not always be dependent, I will want to choose principles capable of generating policies that balance my concerns during periods of dependency with those during periods of full functioning. In this way, the weak interpretation does allow for the concerns of the dependent to be included.

However, as long as nothing in the construction of the OP ensures that any parties to the OP will imagine that their own conception of the good, or their own rational self-interest, necessitates that they be the ones who will meet the needs of the dependent, the problem of representing the dependency worker has not yet been solved. If we think of citizens as fully functioning and ignore periods of dependency, there is no internal incoherence in a theory that does not ensure that parties to the OP represent dependency workers, since the theory simply is not concerned with such needs nor with the justice or injustice of how these needs come to be met. But because such a theory has completely neglected dependency concerns, it is not true to the realities of human life that move us to seek social alliances. Once we stop ignoring dependency, we are obliged to think of how dependency needs are met in a manner that is equitable to all.

Yet as a representative in the OP who knows that we all have periods of dependency, I *do* consider that I may choose (or may be called upon to take on) dependency work. What kind of bargaining position would I need, then, with respect to the other parties? I would be situated symmetrically to the other parties only if they too envision the possibility of becoming dependency workers themselves. They may do so; but because nothing in the moral psychology that Rawls sketches for us ensures that they will,[62] they may not.

Why is being situated symmetrically to the other parties a problem for the representative of the dependency worker? The reason is that, if I am a dependency worker, I cannot think only about my own interests but must also consider those of the dependent (see Section 5). The egalitarian benchmark that constrains the OP is that each participant counts for one when choosing the principles of justice. The idealization of citizens as fully functioning over the course of their lives is needed for this modeling of the parties because only then are we *able* to think of each citizen as counting for one in the distribution of both the benefits and the burdens of social cooperation. All representatives of such citizens in the OP go to the bargaining table knowing that, whatever position they hold in society, whether successful at a lucrative profession or employed as street sweepers, they have an equal voice in the choice of the fundamental principles governing the basic structure because they are each fully capable of participating according to the terms of fair social cooperation.

Reflect on what happens during those periods when we are not fully functioning and are dependent. The question of whether we are (temporarily) too disabled or too young to cooperate fully in benefits and burdens is morally irrelevant. Those so incapacitated still must have rights. But these rights would thus be in need of protection by others whose powers are intact. The dependent, however, cannot assume the burdens and responsibilities of social cooperation while in a state of dependency, even though as a citizen she or he should be able to enjoy the benefits of social cooperation. A dependent can define the terms of political participation *only* to the extent that she can speak on her own behalf, can be heard as an independent voice (neither is generally true of "underage" individuals), and can act on her own behalf (an option that is circumscribed by virtue of the dependency). For the rest, she must depend on those responsible for her well-being. Another must hold the rights of the dependent in trust,[63] just as another must take on the care for the physical well-being of the dependent. In this connection, recall Section 5, where I argue that the dependent's neediness not only poses burdens of maintaining the dependent but also compromises the dependency worker's status as a "self-originating source of claims."

If we all took turns being dependent and dependency workers, we would repay the debt, incurred during periods of dependency, of benefits-received-without-burdens-assumed. But there is no reason to suppose such a state of affairs exists—that is not what is implied in the norm of all citizens being fully functioning over the course of a life. Therefore, the burdens and responsibilities of the dependent, which are assumed by the dependency worker, make the interests of the dependency worker importantly different from those of the unencumbered and fully functioning citizen. In the economy of social cooperation, the dependency worker assumes the burdens and responsibilities of more than one, and the dependent those of less than one, whereas the independent, full-functioning citizen counts for one. In terms of benefits, however, the dependent, like the full-functioning citizen, counts as one. In contrast, if the dependency worker must also secure rights and benefits for her charge, even at the expense of her own rights and benefits, her own welfare comes to count for *less* than one.

If parties representing citizens who take on dependency work can be said to do so simply as one among many possible conceptions of the good, then they should accept the disadvantage along with the advantage of that individual's autonomous choice, as must all citizens who form a conception of the good. But taking on dependency work is not one choice of the good life among others. For (a) if none made such a choice, society could not continue beyond a single generation (see Subsection 2.1), so this conception of the good would be one that occupies a special place with respect to the welfare of society. And (b) when one takes on dependency responsibilities, one becomes poorly situated in a system of social cooperation in which each counts as one (see Subsection 3.1).

Unless some device acknowledges the fact that some citizens will be disadvantaged even as they provide the labor needed to care for and reproduce other citizens, and provides a mechanism for equalizing the prospects of all, situating their representatives symmetrically to those of unencumbered citizens cannot do the job of fairly representing all. The veil of ignorance won't suffice as such a device, because it gets us only the reasonableness needed for social cooperation when all the rational agents represent free and equal citizens—but we must remember, first, that dependency workers are not free in the requisite sense and, second, that the social cooperation in which dependents and dependency workers engage is not social cooperation among equals. That is why, at the very least, we need a motivational assumption akin to the just savings principle (see Subsection 2.4), but one that recognizes the role of dependency and care in the lives of each of us.

The symmetries that allow the rational party to simulate the commitments of a rational and reasonable person do not hold for conditions pertinent to the dependency relation; moreover, they arise even on the weaker interpretation of the norm of full functioning. So whether we say that we are fully cooperating members of society throughout our lives, or over the course of our lives, the idealization is questionable at best, pernicious at worst. Its virtue springs from the Kantian position that autonomy is that feature of human existence which gives us our dignity. But it fosters a fiction that the incapacity to function as a fully cooperating societal member is an exception in human life, not a normal variation; and that the dependency is a phase normally too brief and episodic to concern political life, rather than a periodic, and often prolonged, phase of our lives whose costs and burdens ought to be justly shared.

Autonomy in the sense of self-governance is surely of special importance. But this Kantian consideration must find its way into a more adequate representation of persons, one capable of acknowledging dependency as an obligatory limitation to self-governance. Neither the condition of the self-governing adult (the liberal Kantian model) nor the condition of a minor (the secular and religious authoritarian model) ought to serve as the "normal" condition of persons when choosing the design of a social order. I am proposing instead that the full range of human functioning[64] is the "normal" condition. Otherwise, representing dependents and their caretakers within the OP and within the well-ordered society becomes *a problem;* and the demands on those who care for them, a personal issue standing outside considerations of equality and justice.

The adoption of the norm that all are fully cooperating members over the course of a lifetime makes plausible the modeling of citizens in the well-ordered society as parties in the OP who are symmetrically situated. But between the idealization (of equal situation and equal powers) and the reality (of asymmetries of situation and inequalities of capability) lies the danger that dependents and dependency caretakers will fall into a worst-off position. The procedure of construction modeled by the OP "shows how the principles of justice follow from the principles of practical reason in union with conceptions of society and person" (Rawls 1992, 90). Although Rawls believes that the conception of the person he employs is itself an idea of practical reason (1992, 90), it is an idea inadequate to the fact of humans vulnerable to dependency. To model the representative party on a norm of a fully functioning person, then, is to skew the choice of principles in favor of those who can function independently and who are not responsible for assuming the care of those who cannot.

## 7. Conclusion: The Principles of Justice and Dependency Concerns

Sections 2 through 6 have shown that Rawls's model-conceptions omit dependency concerns and, hence, are inadequate for a truly egalitarian theory of justice. Can we now conclude that the presumably egalitarian suppositions do not yield sufficiently egalitarian outcomes? Ultimately, a definite answer rests on the capacity of the chosen principles to accommodate dependency concerns. The principles of justice chosen by the parties to the OP are selected from a "short list" of principles drawn from traditional Western political thought—none of which consider the justice of dependency arrangements for dependency worker and dependent alike. Therefore, no principle on the short list is more likely than any other to accommodate such concerns. For example, some of the argument in Subsection 6.2 not only runs counter to contractarian assumptions but also points to a difficulty with at least one form of utilitarianism: preference-satisfaction utilitarianism. Do the preferences of a mother for the goods pertaining to the well-being of a child count as the preferences of one individual, the concerned mother, or of two, mother and child? If they count for one only, then how are we to tally the preferences of the child? If they count for two, we violate the egalitarian principle that each counts for just one. Few, if any, political theories have focused on the consequences of dependency and dependency work, because few, if any, have seriously concerned themselves with the lives led by those persons (e.g., women) who have had to deal with inevitable dependencies.

Now that these concerns have been raised, however, we can use the notion of reflective equilibrium to "test" the adequacy of the principles that emerge. If those principles yield an egalitarian outcome for dependents and dependency workers, the arguments in Subsections 2 through 6 could be rendered superfluous. The first principle, the principle of equal liberties, is irrelevant to our concerns, although dependency concerns introduce a worry that those who do dependency work will not be guaranteed the fair value of the political liberties. But I shall not take up this matter here. I proceed to demonstrate that the second principle, the difference principle, fails in the relevant respects.

### *7.1. Dependents and Dependency Workers as the Least Well-Off*

The latest formulation of the difference principle states, "Social and economic inequalities are to satisfy two conditions: first, they are to be attached to positions and offices open to all under conditions of fair equality of opportunity; and second, they are to be to the greatest benefit of the least advantaged members of the society" (Rawls 1992, 6).

Dependency work, when done for pay, is poorly paid. Furthermore, it is largely gender-determined. If the second principle is to ensure a fair distribution of goods to those in dependency relations, it must be interpreted in such a way that (a) the group that is least advantaged includes paid dependency workers and that (b) fair equality of opportunity precludes all forms of sex discrimination that restrict women to poorly paid or unpaid work. If fair equality of opportunity is realized, then the question is: Will distributive policies favoring the least well-off ensure adequate fulfillment of the needs of dependents and caretakers?

I do not believe they will. Fair equality of opportunity would mean that a woman who chooses dependency work as paid labor, even when the work is poorly paid, makes her choice unconstrained by gender discrimination. And if that choice puts her among the ranks of the least advantaged, she would know that justice required distributive policies that would not favor any other group unless they ameliorated her condition—an outcome that would doubtless be an improvement over today's situation.

But would such an outcome be good enough? Paying workers so poorly that this indispensable contribution to the well-being and sociality of any society places the paid dependency worker in the least-favored situation seems not to cohere with our reflective judgments of what is fair. The least-favored situation, we would think, is the condition inhabited by those so poorly endowed that they simply cannot take advantage of fair equality of opportunity to better their condition. Moreover, is it reasonable to expect the dependency worker to continue to be sufficiently motivated to give the *caring* care critical to good dependency work, all the while assuming the status of the least well-off, when truly fair equality of opportunity is in the offing? Normally, some degree of coercion is present when dependency labor is had "on the cheap."

Perhaps, then, market forces will push up the monetary value of dependency work: If we want good day care for our children, then we will have to pay good money for it—and both children and their caretakers will be well situated. So it may seem if we look only at paid dependency work. But much dependency work has been done as unpaid labor, and because such work involves affective bonds and is infused with social meaning, it is likely to remain so. Due to the importance of these bonds to the quality of care—*who* does the caring is frequently as important as the care itself—the dependency worker is nonfungible. (Though especially true of dependency workers who are familial and unpaid, this conclusion also applies to paid dependency workers.) I would venture to say that, as long as dependency work continues to be unpaid and filled with social and affective significance, even fair equality of opportunity for all is unlikely to alter wages significantly because the value of such work will not be assessed in market terms. Under the best scenario, assimilating the dependency worker to the level of the least well-paid worker will make the dependency worker better off than she is now. But this solution does not reach into the situation of the unpaid dependency worker, nor does it touch the individual whose dependency caregiving is a major responsibility along with waged work. The nonfungible nature of much dependency work not only vitiates much of the *freedom* assumed to be available to the caretaker under equality of opportunity; indeed, it also constrains her, by ties of affection and sentiments of duty to her charge.[65]

### *7.2. The Dependency Relation as a Social Position*

A less Rawlsian option would be to count the position of the dependency worker, along with that of the citizen and the least advantaged, as a distinct social position (see Rawls 1971, 95ff.) Although Rawls does not encourage us to multiply social positions, this strategy would ensure that no advantage in the distribution of goods could accrue to those better off than the dependency worker unless the inequality benefited the dependency worker. However, given Rawls's two moral powers and his list of primary goods, there is no basis within his theory upon which to construct such a new social position. To create a special social position for the dependency worker would seem arbitrarily to favor one form of socially useful labor over others—a form of labor, moreover, that a person would choose because it somehow fits with his own conception of the good life.

If, however, we add to the other moral powers the capacity to give care, and if we include goods related to our interdependence in states of vulnerability in the index of primary goods, we can make a case for adding the dependency worker and the dependent to the short list of social positions from which to consider issues of fairness and just distributions. For example, we can make a case for a paid employee who is in a dependency relation, and so has dependency responsibilities, to receive additional pay, benefits, time off, or services, which would enable her to support the dependency relation in a manner suitable to the situation. She could then opt to pay another *adequately* to do all or some of the dependency work or do the dependency work herself by virtue of the freed-up time and added support. This outcome would be seen not as a privilege but, rather, as what is properly due citizens of a just and caring society—enabling us each to be cared for without extracting an undue burden from those charged with our care. But if being cared for by one upon whom you depend and being able to give care to one who depends on you are not seen as primary goods, then there would be no reason for principles of justice to be chosen that would facilitate such policy-making. Inasmuch as the difference principle is based on a list of primary goods blind to dependency, it fails to accomplish this task.[66]

### *7.3. A Third Principle of Justice?*

The social position of the citizen gives rise to the first principle of justice. The social position of the least advantaged gives rise to the difference principle with fair equality of opportunity. If we were to amend the theory of justice as fairness to include the social position of the participants in a dependency relation, it would most likely give rise to a third principle of justice, one based not on our equal vulnerability or on our having some minimal powers of rationality, a sense of justice, and a vision of our own good, but, rather, on our unequal vulnerability in dependency, on the moral power to respond to others in need, and on the primacy of human relations to happiness and well-being. The principle of the social responsibility for care would read something like this: *To each according to his or her need for care, from each according to his or her capacity for care, and such support from social institutions as to make available resources and opportunities to those providing care, so that all will be adequately attended in relations that are sustaining.*

I see no natural way of converting such a principle to either of Rawls's two principles of justice. Therefore, it remains the claim of this chapter that the theory of justice as fairness, relying as it does on the suppositions outlined and contested above, falls short of meeting dependency concerns and so fails to sustain the egalitarian vision that purports to inform it.

Once we understand that we cannot neglect the circumstance of human dependency within the sphere of the political, that it is a fact that pervades social structures, that it extends throughout our lives, and that it connects us with one another and spans the generations, the significance of care and the centrality of those who give care recast and refocus the political considerations of equality and of freedom as well as the moral understanding of the person and the nature of moral and political obligation and responsibility.[67]

## Notes

1. See, for example, Rawls (1992, xxviii–xxix) for the characterization of his project. Rawls acknowledges that a conception of justice "so arrived at may prove defective" (1992, xxix). My claim is that it is defective because it is so arrived at.

2. I am not assuming that any features of human life are untouched by social factors, nor that these social factors can be neatly bracketed. Nonetheless, development, decline, and disease are inescapable conditions for natural beings, and these set the parameters for the dependency that is equally inescapable.

3. In one sense, the inability to reciprocate is a function of dependency only in the context of certain socially based distribution policies. Such policies also make those who are or become dependent especially vulnerable to impoverishment and, hence, unable to reciprocate benefits they have received. In an other sense, however, during the time people are very ill or very young, they are at the mercy of others to dispense whatever resources those people have. In *this* sense, the infant heir and the beggar's child both require a third-party intervention to repay their caretakers. I focus on the second sense inasmuch as I am looking at dependency through dual lenses, that of the dependent and that of the dependency worker. In this connection, it may be helpful to see the difficulties raised by dependency in terms of capability rather than resources (see Sen 1992). Thus, although the child of the poor and the child of the wealthy have differing resources, by virtue of their dependency their inability to convert those resources into functionings and capabilities is more similar than their resources are different.

4. The person who intervenes may or may not be the same person who provides hands-on care. But the person who provides hands-on care is virtually always in a position of having to interpret the needs and desires of her charge. This person is not always, however, the one empowered to translate those needs into socially understood interests.

5. The terms 'inevitable dependency' and 'derived dependency' were independently arrived at by Martha Albertson Fineman (1995) and myself (Kittay 1991)

6. Henceforth, all references to a "dependent" will be to the primary dependent.

7. Rawls says that equality operates on three levels: (a) the administrative and procedural (i.e., the impartial and consistent application of rules, constituted by the precept to treat likes alike); (b) "the substantive structure of institutions" (Rawls 1971, 505), requiring that all persons be assigned equal basic rights; and (c) the situation of the original position addressing the basis of equality, those "features of human beings in virtue of which they are to be treated in accordance with the principles of justice"

(Rawls 1971, 504). At the first of these levels there are inequalities for dependency workers and dependents that could be defended. One can argue, for example, that persons unable to fill a job because of a disability, or because they have dependency responsibilities, cannot be eligible for equal opportunity considerations. We can justify some inequalities at the second level as well. Minors do not have the right to vote. And severely retarded individuals cannot be assigned rights and freedoms requiring higher mental abilities. Rights, after all, can be granted only to those capable of understanding and acting on them. Responsibilities of dependency work, in contrast, should not affect the equal assignment of basic rights. (Note that, formerly, women's responsibilities as dependency workers were deemed sufficient to exclude them from many economic and political rights. If we count pregnancy as "dependency work"—insofar as it involves the care and nurture of a completely dependent being—then, as shown by the abortion debate, along with controversies concerning surrogate mothering, suitable work environments of pregnant women, and the prosecution of pregnant women abusing drugs, the assignment of equal basic rights to these dependency workers is still not a resolved issue.) Accordingly, the objective of this chapter is to show that even though we can grant that some inequalities are justified, there is a more fundamental problem for the achievement of full moral equality at the third, and most fundamental, level.

8. See Okin (1979) for a deft interpretation of canonical texts. See also Pateman (1989) and Benhabib (1987) for further discussion of this issue.

9. A number of feminist theorists have regarded the work of Rawls and other liberal philosophers with an eye toward issues of dependency, but without articulating the dependency critique. Overall, there are too many feminist criticisms of liberal political philosophy to list in a single chapter such as this one; suffice to say that some of them are more closely tied to dependency than others. These writers have spoken of "the need for more than justice," as Annette Baier entitles one work (1987) expounding this theme. Baier expands on this theme in a number of other works as well (1985, 1986, 1987, 1994). Other writers—for example, Minow (1990), Pateman (1989), and Held (1978, 1987a, 1987b)—have shed light on the unacknowledged gender considerations that undergird legal theory and a social contract engaged in by men. In this connection, also see the essays in Phillips (1987). Fineman (1991, 1995) comes very close to articulating the dependency critique as I conceive it. And Susan Okin (1979, 1989a, 1989b) brings both the historical and the contemporary neglect of women's involvement in dependency to the forefront of her political considerations. I owe much to her systematic analysis and feminist, but sympathetic, critique of Rawls. My examination of Rawls is deeply indebted to these writers and others too numerous to mention, and intends to carry these discussions further.

10. I take this framework to be a central thrust of the dependency critique, an issue that I discuss further in Kittay (1995b). The objective underlying my adoption of the dependency critique is precisely to understand how a more equitable arrangement of dependency can be established not only between men and women but among women themselves. As bell hooks (1987) asks: "Since men are not equals in white supremacist, capitalist, patriarchal class structure, which men do women want to be equal to?" The point captured by bell hooks and stressed by a number of feminists is that the striving for equality on the part of the largely white and middle-class women's movement presumes an egalitarianism into which women can integrate themselves.

The force of this critique emerges with special poignancy when one looks at the complexion of dependency workers in countries blighted by racial and social inequities. The figures concerning, for example, the employment of immigrant women tell much of the story. Consider the findings reported by the National Council for Research on Women: "The International Labor Office estimates that more than 350,000 illegal immigrant women work as domestics in the current U.S. market (Stalker 1994, 149). Although these women are ultimately statistically invisible, the effects of their labor are more than apparent in the lives of professional families throughout the U.S." (Capek and Kenny, 1995).

11. This method is characterized by Rawls, first, as a procedural interpretation of Kantian moral conceptions (particularly those principles regulative of the kingdom of ends (1971, 256)); then, as *Kantian constructivism* (1980); and, later, as *political constructivism* (1992). These alterations do not affect the argument presented here, however. The method is supposed to be constructivist in that "it does not accept any intuitions as indubitable and does not begin with the assumption that there are first principles in moral theory" (Baynes 1992, 55).

12. These later writings are intended to answer criticisms that the conception of the person is a metaphysical one specific to certain liberal theories and that the principles of justice chosen are not as purely constructivist as Rawls claims. See especially Nagel (1973), Hart (1975), and Sandel (1982). Rawls's (1992) response is to distinguish "political liberalism" from liberalism as a "comprehensive moral doctrine" (also see Rawls 1985). In addition, he clarifies the basis on which parties in the OP adopt the basic liberties and their priority, avoiding both metaphysical conceptions of the person and particular psychological propensities (see Rawls 1982, 1992). The argument in this chapter is, nonetheless, that the individualism at the core of the theory—which Nagel (1973, 228) notes is augmented by the motivational assumption of mutual disinterestedness—does predispose the parties in the OP to ignore the concerns of both dependents and dependency workers.

13. Also see Rawls (1975b, 542ff.).

14. In *Political Liberalism*, Rawls writes, "To model this equality in the OP we say that the parties, as representatives of those who meet the condition, are symmetrically situated. This requirement is fair because in establishing fair terms of social cooperation (in the case of the basic structure) the only relevant feature of persons is their possessing the moral powers . . . and their having the normal capacities to be . . . cooperating member[s] of society over the course of a lifetime" (1992, 79). The OP is regarded as fair because it presumably models this equality. Rawls further writes that "citizens are equal in virtue of possessing, to the requisite minimum degree, the two moral powers and other capacities that enable us to be normal and fully cooperating members of society. All those who meet this condition have the same basic rights, liberties and opportunities and the same protections of the principles of justice" (1992, 79). He then continues, "To model this equality in the OP we say that the parties, as representatives of those who meet this condition, are symmetrically situated" (1992, 79).

15. In the "Dewey Lectures," Rawls writes simply: "[T]he idealization means that everyone has sufficient intellectual powers to play a *normal* part in society, and no one suffers from *unusual* needs that are *especially difficult* to fulfill, for example, *unusual and costly medical requirements*" (1980, 546; emphasis added). Thus the idealization requires the condition not only of adulthood but also of health. Since both children

and the temporarily disabled merely temporarily and contingently fail to meet the requirements for equal moral worth, they are included in the category of equal citizen (see Rawls 1971, 509). The appropriate treatment of those who are permanently disabled seems to be another matter, one that is further explicated in Note 29.

16. In *Political Liberalism* Rawls drops 'self-originating source of claims' (1980, 544) and substitutes 'self-authenticating source of valid claims' (1992, 32). See Section 5.2 for a discussion of the difference between these two phrases.

17. Rawls acknowledges that some will have a more developed sense of justice than others. Equality with respect to a sense of justice demands only that persons have a sense of justice "equally sufficient relative to what is asked of them" (1980, 546), insofar as they are "fully cooperating members of society over a complete life" (1980, 546).

18. See Note 17. Rawls also writes of "the equally sufficient capacity (which I assume to be realized) to understand and to act from *the public conception of social cooperation*" (1980, 546; emphasis added).

19. According to the *New York Times* (November 14, 1989, pp. A1, B12), a 1985 survey found that "about one in five employees over the age of 30 was providing some care to an elderly parent." The same article reported that almost one-third of part-time workers in the United States spent more than twenty hours a week helping older relatives and, of those not employed who had previously held jobs, 27 percent had taken early retirement or resigned to meet their responsibilities.

20. See Goodin (1985) for a very useful discussion of the obligation to protect those who are vulnerable.

21. Rawls is not concerned here with the dependencies at issue in this chapter, at least not insofar as these are the ones to which *women* usually attend. This is evident in his language: "Nevertheless, since it is assumed that a generation cares for its immediate descendants, as *fathers, say, care for their sons*, a just savings principle . . . would be acknowledged" (1971, 288; emphasis added). And on the following page he writes, "Thus imaging themselves to be *fathers*, say, they are to ascertain how much they should set aside for their *sons* by noting what they would believe *themselves* entitled to claim of their *fathers*" (1971, 289; emphasis added). No mothers or daughters appear on these pages. During a discussion in April 1993, Professor Rawls indicated to me that he meant to include both parents—the mother as well as the father—among the representative heads of households. How different would the theory look if fathers *and mothers* had been included among the parties in the OP? That would depend, I think, on whether the dependency concerns for which mothers have traditionally been responsible are included as well.

22. So she admonished her husband. Still, the representation granted the paterfamilias is different from the one necessitated by dependency work, when the heads of households represent those who are capable of speaking for themselves. The dependency worker must represent the needs of those too young, frail, weak, or ill to come before a public forum and speak for themselves.

23. Okin (1989b) makes the additional point that the phrase 'head of household' is gendered masculine. If we want to speak of a woman who heads a household, we say 'female head of household'. The latter phrase invariably denotes a household in which there is no healthy adult male.

24. Contrast the case of dependents to what Rawls calls the "relevant positions" of "equal citizenship and that defined by [an individual's] place in the distribution of income and wealth" (1971, 96).

25. The representatives in the OP are envisioned by Rawls to be of the same generation. One who adopts the standpoint of the OP thus assumes a "present time of entry" into the OP and that the representatives can communicate with other parties in the OP (see Rawls 1971, 136–142) If parties represent generational lines, there is little point in asking what temporal position they occupy relative to one another with respect to the issue of mutual disinterestedness. But if the representatives represent individuals, the question is pertinent. Now, however, the requirement of mutual disinterestedness is questionable. If one representative is representing an individual living today and another is representing the other's ancestor, we cannot say with assurance that the parties are mutually disinterested.

26. It may seem possible to construe an ambiguity in Rawls's notion that each individual in a future generation should have someone who cares about her or him—that is, an ambiguity between (a) each assuming a special responsibility for someone in the next generation, as in the case of a parent to a child, and (b) each acting responsibly to the next generation. Yet Rawls himself seems to see not an ambiguity but a relation between these seeming alternatives. He writes: "Those in the OP know, then, that they are contemporaries, so unless they care for at least their immediate successors, there is no reason for them to agree to undertake any savings whatever" (1971, 292).

27. This acceptance, however, is culturally relative. Even within liberal societies where no moral stigma attaches to remaining childless, the choice is better tolerated in the case of men than of women. (see Meyers 1993). For a different cultural view, see the powerful drama of Frederico Garcia Lorca entitled *Yerma*.

28. One plausible exception is health care, which, arguably, *is* a dependency concern. And Rawls wants an extension of his theory to cover "*normal* health care" (1992, 21; emphasis added). But excluded from this category are the daily care of infants and children—which is not *health* care as such—and the care of persons with long-term medical or disabling conditions—which is generally not included within *normal* health care. (In this connection, see also Note 43.)

29. Rawls writes that "we take the two moral powers as the necessary and sufficient condition for being counted a full and equal member of society in questions of political justice. Those who can take part in social cooperation over a complete life, and who are willing to honor the appropriate fair terms of agreement, are regarded as equal citizens" (1992, 302). This is a very strong claim, and a puzzling one. For why should the contingent fact that some people are born, let us say, "sufficiently" mentally disabled necessitate their exclusion from citizenship? There are some political activities they may not be able to engage in—for example, they may lack the political understanding required to vote—but surely they need to receive the protections of political justice all the same. (I thank Susan Okin for her discussions with me on this point.) The only rationale consistent with the aforementioned theory is that although their condition is no less due to contingent factors, they will never be able to participate in the social cooperative situation as understood by Rawls.

30. The full passage reads as follows: "The main idea is that when a number of persons engage in a mutually advantageous cooperative venture according to rules, and

thus restrict their liberty in ways necessary to yield advantages for all, those who have submitted to the restrictions have a right to a similar acquiescence on the part of those who have benefitted from their submission" (Rawls 1971, 112).

31. See Aronow (1993). One of the doulas "recalls arriving at homes late morning to find mothers who haven't eaten or dressed. 'They are so concerned that the baby is O.K., they forget to take care of themselves'" (Aronow, 8).

32. I wish to thank Elfie Raymond for helping me search for a term with the resonance necessary to capture the concept articulated here.

33. The importance of this ethic within the African American community is documented in Stacks (1974).

34. It may be unclear whether Rawls's new principle of intergenerational justice and my principle of doulia are truly instances of reciprocity, inasmuch as we are enjoined to give back to a party other than the one from whom we have received, but also inasmuch as both principles enjoin us to give what we would have *wanted* to receive, not necessarily what we have *in fact* received. Nonetheless, the survival of a generation depends on its having received a world not entirely depleted of resources, and the survival of an individual depends on care sufficient to bring her or him to adulthood. So there is a minimal sense in which both are principles of reciprocity, for we are enjoined not only to give but also to give *back*. That is, we would not be in a position to consider what we would want others to provide us if we were not already recipients, even to a minimal degree, of those goods. But it is not reciprocity in the sense of returning *either* to the *same party* or in the *same measure* that which we have received.

35. This is not to say that we have a duty to *have* children because we have been cared for, but I do suggest that, to any children we have, we owe the care we would have wanted to receive (and, at the very least, the care that was necessary to allow us to survive and thrive). I further suggest that the care bestowed on us—and some care must have been bestowed on us if we survived—should in fact be *reciprocated* through care to the next generation.

36. For a concrete public-policy example of the difference effected by this understanding of social cooperation, see Kittay (1995a).

37. Even a Hobbesian state of nature is barely conceivable without some principle of care (however attenuated). *Contra* Hobbes, we mischaracterize social organizations if we conceive of men springing from the earth "like mushrooms," already fully grown. (See Hobbes 1966, 109; also see Benhabib 1987 for a discussion of this passage.)

38. Rawls later (1992, 308–309) gives essentially the same list but accompanies it with explanations of why each element is included. Conspicuously absent from the considerations adduced in these explanations, however, are the elements of "nurture," "interdependence," and "phases of life," all of which are mentioned as general facts about human life on the preceding page (1992, 307). Effectively, these elements are still omitted in the hard-core center of Rawls's theory.

39. See Nagel (1973, 228) for the criticism that the ignorance concerning one's own conception of the good does not necessarily result in an index of primary goods that is equally fair to all parties, "because the primary goods are not equally valuable in pursuit of all conceptions of the good." One may claim that my argument is already

implicit in Nagel's if one supposes that dependency concerns are important to some conceptions of the good—more important, perhaps, than many of the other goods currently in Rawls's index. But the criticism that I put forward differs from Nagel's. I am arguing that, regardless of one's conception of one's own good, the dependency concerns would belong on a list of primary goods. For an excellent discussion of the controversy surrounding the claim that such an index is the best way to make interpersonal comparative assessments of well-being, see Daniels (1990).

40. See Arrow (1973) and especially Sen (1987, 1989, 1990) for arguments that the variations in capabilities between persons may be so significant that one index cannot be adequate to meet the needs of all citizens. Also see Rawls (1992, 182 ff.) for his answer to this objection.

41. Meyers (1993, 1994) speaks of the necessity of empathetic thought as a feature of a moral person. What I am considering is precisely such a moral capacity.

42. As I remarked above, a number of writers have urged the need for "more than justice." See especially Baier (1987), Held (1993), Tronto (1993), and Ruddick (1995).

43. Norman Daniels argues that the Rawlsian primary good of opportunity can be extended to cover health-care needs. First the health-care needs of "normally active and fully functioning" persons are calculated at the legislative stage; then "special needs" can be considered. Health care demands "those things we need in order to maintain, restore, or provide functional equivalents (where possible) to normal species function" (1990, 280). Daniels not only emphasizes the relevance of normal functioning to equality of opportunity but also proposes the concept of "normal opportunity range." Appropriate health care, as determined partially by culture and partially by individual talents and skills, can allow a person to "enjoy that portion of the range to which his full array of talents and skills would give him access, assuming that these too are not impaired by special social disadvantages (e.g., racism and sexism)" (1990, 281). The handicap with respect to normal functioning refers to one of Rawls's two moral powers, the power to form and revise our own vision of the good. Rawls takes up this suggestion: "The aim is to restore people by health care so that once again they are fully cooperating members of society" (1992, 184ff.). However, though health care is an integral part of dependency care, Daniels's solution will not be adequate for three reasons. First, "normal opportunity range" is ill-defined for many sorts of disabilities and illnesses—for example, Down's syndrome and, especially, severe mental retardation. Second, providing the "functional equivalents" to "normal species functioning," even when doing so falls far short of a complete restoration, can require resources extensive enough that an explicit commitment in the founding principles themselves may be needed for its realization. And, third, we need to consider whether a social commitment to restore, when possible, the dependent to full functioning will also compensate dependency workers without exploiting them. This final point is not Daniels's concern, but it is integral to any adequate reckoning of justice that includes dependency. Since no dependent can be restored to any degree of functioning without a significant infusion of caring labor, we have to ask about the cost to the dependency worker and the level of compensation. In this connection, see Kittay (forthcoming).

44. I emphasize that (c) calls for the *capacity* to respond, not for the response itself. We must understand such a capacity (along with a sense of fairness) as fundamental to moral persons, if we want basic institutions to incorporate principles ensuring

support for relations in which dependents are cared for without sacrificing the interests of caretakers. *Response* to the needs of another is itself a normal moral behavior, but one that may not always be required for justice.

45. As Rawls (1982) stresses, we assess needs in many different contexts and for many different reasons, but the index of primary goods includes only those needs relevant to justice.

46. In criticizing Rawls's use of primary goods, Sen (1990) argues that guarantees of primary goods do not serve justice for those so handicapped that they cannot make use of the goods. Sen's important argument is orthogonal to my own. The demands of care are primary goods that reflect a relation between persons and the resources for their well-being. (See also Note 59.)

47. In the "Dewey Lectures" Rawls also writes: "[S]laves are human beings who are not counted as self-originating sources of claims at all; any such claims originate with their owners or in the rights of a certain class in society" (1980, 544). And in an analogous passage in *Political Liberalism* he writes: "[S]laves are human beings who are not counted as sources of claims, not even claims based on social duties or obligations. . . . Laws that prohibit the maltreatment of slaves are not based on claims made by slaves, but on claims originating from slaveholders, or from the general interests of society (which do not include the interests of slaves). Slaves are, so to speak, socially dead: they are not recognized as persons at all." (1992, 33).

48. One might reply, as did a reviewer, that the valid claim is the *child's*. The mother may have a valid claim to her own education, but the claim to her child's education should not be expressed as *her* claim. To this I say that the child's is *one* relevant valid claim, and usually, at least when the child is very young, not a self-originating one. The child's claim originates with an adult responsible for the child's well-being. In fact, that claim lacks efficacy as long as the child's status as a minor excludes her from political participation. The claim not only originates with, but must also be pressed by, an adult whose voice can be heard in the relevant arena.

49. The communitarian critique expounded by Sandel (1982) raises some similar points about a self-definition that includes centrally the well-being of others. But whereas Sandel's account locates the difficulty in Rawls's prioritization of the self over its ends (1982, 19), I locate it in a conception of self so individuated that dependency concerns are not normally comprehended as intrinsic to it.

50. Perhaps we should interdict dependency work if it demands a psychology in which the dependency worker's self-worth is more a function of another's accomplishments and welfare than of her own. Some jobs do seem inherently oppressive—say, coal-mining. One may argue that no wage can compensate for the diminution in well-being that a coal-miner must suffer, and that justice demands abolishing coal-mining. But dependency work has another character, and justice could never demand that we abolish it. A tension between maintaining that dependency work be more highly valued and that dependency work is too oppressive and ought not to be foisted on anyone is not inevitable. If dependency work appears oppressive it is because the norm of freedom is shaped without attention to the role of dependency in our lives. If it is oppressive, it is so within a social setting that fails to foster the well-being of dependency workers and their charges.

51. Chodorow (1978) and Gilligan (1982) are only two of the most prominent thinkers who argue that for many women the self is experienced as a relational self

and that such a relational self is importantly tied to women's functions as caretakers. In this chapter, I have relied on the persuasiveness of these and other feminist discussions of the self-conception of many women as relational.

52. See Note 50.

53. Rousseau's writings not only embody this image, linking it to an Enlightenment ideal of freedom for male citizens, but have also exerted much influence on women's actual behavior. See Rousseau (1762), Wollstonecraft (1792), Badinger (1980), and Held (1993, esp. ch. 6).

54. Yet even in the "Dewey Lectures," Rawls writes, "These remarks . . . [are] to indicate the conception of the person connected with . . . the principles of justice that apply to its basic institutions. By contrast, citizens in their personal affairs, or within the internal life of associations, may . . . have attachments and loves that they believe they would not, or could not, stand apart from" (1980, 545).

55. This way of putting the criticism is taken nearly verbatim from some very interesting and useful comments provided by John Baker.

56. Consider the horror that yielded the *New York Times* story about the physically and mentally handicapped children who were abandoned in a besieged Bosnian hospital. The reporter, John Burns, wrote about Edin, one of the children who died: "Unlike 200,000 others whom the Bosnian Government estimates to have died in the war, Edin was not blown apart by heavy artillery, cut down by snipers, tortured or burned alive. He was simply left to fend for himself, an infant in a cot who was so severely handicapped that he had spent most of his life at the hospital" (July 20, 1993, p. 1). The sentiment expressed is one of moral horror at the abandonment such helpless individuals. "It's monstrous," said Brigadier General Vere Hayes, chief of staff for the United Nations protection force in Bosnia. There is, at least *prima facie*, a special obligation not to abandon such helpless persons—regardless of the cost to the staff.

57. See, for example, Beauvoir (1952), Chodorow (1978), Dinnerstein (1977), Gilligan (1982), and Bartky (1990).

58. In this connection, see the essays in Trebilcot (1987).

59. The relation between dependency worker and dependent seems to hover between servitude and paternalism. On the one hand, the dependency worker's self-respect is partially a function of how well she meets the needs of another; on the other, she has the awesome power to respond to and interpret the needs of a helpless other. In short, she has too little power with respect to those who stand outside the dependency relation and potentially too much power with respect to her charge. In arguing against the powerlessness of the dependency worker vis-à-vis the world outside the dependency relation, we must be sensitive as well to the dependent's vulnerability to her caretaker's power within this relation. But though paternalism in dependency relations is always a danger, it is not one augmented by any of the proposals made here. On the contrary, the dependency worker who has her interests taken care of in an appropriate and just manner will be less, not more, likely to live her life through her charge, and less, not more, likely to find other ways to discharge ambition and power than through paternalistic behavior. But a system that pays adequate attention to the dependency relation will be one seeking not only to empower the dependency worker with respect to her own interests but also, whenever possible, to decrease the dependency of the dependent as well. When dependency is relegated to the status of an afterthought, neither caretaker nor charge is well served.

60. Sen argues that because people have very different needs, an index of primary goods is not a sufficiently sensitive measure of interpersonal comparison of well-being. Primary goods are the "embodiment of advantage," whereas advantage itself ought to be understood as "a *relationship between persons and goods*" (Sen 1987, 158; original emphasis). Rawls replies that he assumes that citizens do have, "at least to the essential minimum degree, the moral, intellectual, and physical capacities that enable them to be fully cooperating members of society over a complete life" (1992, 183). "The aim," he continues, "is to restore people by health care so that once again they are fully cooperating members of society" (1992, 184). Variations in physical capacities due to disability or disease can be dealt with at the legislative stage.

61. I thank Annette Baier for calling this alternative interpretation to my attention. The reading consistent with the weaker claim gains support, first, in Rawls (1971, part 3, especially section 77), where he is careful to insist that the mere potentiality to have the features of a moral person is sufficient to bring into play the claims of justice; second, in Rawls (1982, 15); and, third, in Rawls (1992, 301), where he identifies the points of entry and exit into society as birth and death.

62. See, for example, the moral psychology that Rawls outlines in section 7 of *Political Liberalism* (1992), especially the enumerations on page 86. If these included dependency concerns and relational capacities, then perhaps there would be motivation sufficient for all parties to consider that they may be taking on responsibilities for dependents.

63. See Schwarzenbach (1986) regarding the notion that parents are "stewards" to their children.

64. I use the term in a manner similar to that in Sen (1992) and Nussbaum (1988a, 1988b).

65. Recently, the U.S. Congress seriously entertained the notion of orphanages in which to place children whose parents were deprived of the public assistance they depended upon to care for their children. This policy recommendation epitomizes a disregard for the value and integrity of the relation of dependency worker and dependent. The recommendation was dropped because it was reckoned to be too costly, not because its severing of the bonds of the dependency relation was considered immoral or unjust.

66. The difference principle is the distributive principle applicable to certain goods on the list of primary goods (especially income and wealth) and not others (e.g., the basic liberties). To determine if it would be applicable to the added primary good(s) concerning care, we would have to consider whether and how the Rawlsian project could coherently be reworked to include dependency concerns. This is too large a project for the present chapter, which aims to be a critique rather than a reconstruction. Suffice to say that I do not mean to suggest that a difference principle that applies to distributive problems concerning dependency care and dependency work is, in principle, not possible.

67. This chapter is the result of an effort in which many have participated. I would like to thank Annette Baier, Susan Brison, Ellen Feder, Susan Okin, William Kymlicka, and Michael Simon for their helpful comments on the initial shorter version of the paper. And I would especially like to thank the many friends and colleagues who have read and supplied extensive comments on later drafts of the present long version: Jonathan Adler, John Baker, Kenneth Baynes, Robert Goodin, Alistair

MacLeod, Diana Tietjens Meyers, Elfie Raymond, George Sher, and Anthony Weston, as well as a number of anonymous reviewers. I have benefited from these comments, even if the current version does not reflect all the sage advice I received. A special thanks is reserved for Leigh Cauman, Neil Tennant, and Jeffrey Kittay for the painstaking care they took in both philosophical content and stylistic matters. I also wish to thank Barbara Andrew, Barbara LeClere, and Eric Steinhart, my research assistants. This chapter emerges in part out of research made possible by a Founders Fellow grant from the American Association of University Women (AAUW).

## References

Aronow, Ina. 1993. Doulas step in when mothers need a hand. *New York Times (Westchester Weekly*, Sunday), August 1, 1993, pp. 1, 8.

Arrow, Kenneth J. 1973. Some ordinalist utilitarian notes on Rawls's *Theory of justice*. *Journal of Philosophy* 70: 245–263.

Badinger, Elisabeth. 1980. *Mother love: Myth and reality*. New York: MacMillan.

Baier, Annette. 1985. Caring about caring: A reply to Frankfurt. In *Postures of the mind: Essays on mind and morals* (pp. 93–108), ed. Annette Baier. Minneapolis: University of Minnesota Press.

______. 1986. Trust and antitrust. *Ethics* 96: 231–260.

______. 1987. The need for more than justice. In *Science, morality and feminist theory* (pp. 41–56), ed. Marsha Hanen and Kai Nielsen. Minneapolis: University of Minnesota Press.

______. 1994. *Moral prejudices: Essays on ethics.* Cambridge, Mass.: Harvard University Press.

Bartky, Sandra. 1990. *Femininity and oppression*. New York: Routledge.

Baynes, Kenneth. 1992. *The normative grounds of social criticism: Kant, Rawls, and Habermas*. Albany: State University of New York Press.

Beauvoir, Simone de. 1952. *The second sex,* trans. H. M. Parsley. New York: Alfred Knopf.

Benhabib, Seyla. 1987. The generalized and the concrete other. In *Women and moral theory* (pp. 154–177), ed. Eva F. Kittay and Diana T. Meyers. Totowa, N.J.: Rowman and Littlefield.

Capek, Mary Ellen, and Lorraine Delia Kenny. 1995. *Issues Quarterly*, Vol. 1, No. 3 (a publication of the National Council for Research on Women, New York).

Chodorow, Nancy. 1978. *The reproduction of mothering: Psychoanalysis and the sociology of gender*. Berkeley: University of California Press.

Daniels, Norman. 1988. *Am I my parents' keeper? An essay on justice between the younger and the older*. New York: Oxford University Press.

______. 1990. Equality of what: Welfare, resources, or capabilities? *Philosophy and Phenomenological Research* 50 (suppl. vol.): 273–296.

Dinnerstein, Dorothy. 1977. *The mermaid and the minotaur: Sexual arrangements and human malaise.* New York: Harper and Row.

English, Jane. 1977. Justice between generations. *Philosophical Studies* 31(2): 91–104.

Fineman, Martha Albertson. 1991. *The illusion of equality*. Chicago: University of Chicago Press.

_____. 1995. *The neutered mother, the sexual family and other twentieth century tragedies*. New York: Routledge.

Gilligan, Carol. 1982. *In a different voice*. Cambridge, Mass: Harvard University Press.

Goodin, Robert. 1985. *Protecting the vulnerable*. Chicago: University of Chicago Press.

Hart, H.L.A. 1975. Rawls on liberty and its priority. In *Reading Rawls: Critical studies of* A Theory of Justice (pp. 230–252), ed. Norman Daniels. New York: Basic Books.

Held, Virginia. 1978. Men, women, and equal liberty. In *Equality and Social Policy* (pp. 66–81), ed. Walter Feinberg. Urbana: University of Illinois Press.

_____. 1987a. Feminism and moral theory. In *Women and moral theory* (pp. 111–128), ed. Eva F. Kittay and Diana T. Meyers. Totowa, N.J.: Rowman and Littlefield.

_____. 1987b. Non-contractual society: A feminist view. *Canadian Journal of Philosophy* 13: 111–137.

_____. 1993. *Feminist morality: Transforming culture, society, and politics*. Chicago: University of Chicago Press.

Hobbes, Thomas. 1966. Philosophical rudiments concerning government and society. In *The English works of Thomas Hobbes*, Vol. 2, ed. Sir W. Molesworth. Darmstadt.

hooks, bell. 1987. Feminism: A movement to end sexist oppression. In *Equality and Feminism* (pp. 62–76), ed. Anne Phillips. New York: New York University Press.

Kaplan, Temma. 1982. Female consciousness and collective action. *Signs* 7(3): 545–566.

_____. 1992. *Red city blue period: Social movements in Picasso's Barcelona*. Berkeley: University of California Press.

Kittay, Eva Feder. 1991. Dependency, vulnerability and equality. Paper delivered at the Department of Philosophy Colloquium, SUNY/Purchase, November.

_____. 1994. A Review of John Rawls's *Political Liberalism. APA Newsletter of Feminism and Philosophy* (Fall).

_____. 1995a. Taking dependency seriously: The Family and Medical Leave Act considered in light of the social organization of dependency work and gender equality. *Hypatia* 10(1, Winter): 8–29.

_____. 1995b. Dependency work, political discourse and a new basis for a coalition amongst women. Paper delivered at the Women, Children, and Poverty: Feminism and Legal Theory Workshop, Columbia Law School and Barnard College Institute for Research on Women, June.

_____. forthcoming. *Some mother's child: Equality, dependency and women*. New York: Routledge.

Kittay, Eva F., and Diana T. Meyers, eds. 1987. *Women and moral theory*, ed. Eva F. Kittay and Diana T. Meyers. Totowa, N.J.: Rowman and Littlefield.

Meyers, Diana T. 1993. Moral reflection: Beyond impartial reason. *Hypatia* 8: 21–47.

_____. 1994. *Subjection and subjectivity*. New York: Routledge.

Minow, Martha. 1990. *Making all the difference*. Cambridge, Mass: Harvard University Press.

Nagel, Thomas. 1973. Rawls on justice. *Philosophical Review* 82: 220–234.

Nussbaum, Martha. 1988a. Nature, function, capability: Aristotle on political distribution. *Oxford Studies in Ancient Philosophy* 1 (suppl. vol.): 145–184.

______. 1988b. Non-relative virtues: An Aristotelian approach. *Midwest Studies in Philosophy* 13: 32–53.

Okin, Susan. 1979. *Women in western political philosophy*. Princeton: Princeton University Press.

______. 1989a. Humanist liberalism. In *Liberalism and the moral life*, ed. Nancy Rosenbaum. Cambridge: Harvard University Press.

______. 1989b. *Justice, gender and the family*. New York: Basic Books.

Pateman, Carole. 1989. *The sexual contract*. Stanford: Stanford University Press.

Phillips, Anne, ed. 1987. *Feminism and equality*. New York: New York University Press.

Rawls, John. 1971. *A theory of justice.* Cambridge, Mass.: Harvard University Press.

______. 1975a. A Kantian concept of equality. *Cambridge Review* (February).

______. 1975b. Fairness to goodness. *Philosophical Review* 84.

______. 1982. Social unity and primary choice. In *Utilitarianism and beyond*, ed. Amartya Sen and Bernard Williams. New York: Cambridge University Press.

______. 1980. Kantian constructivism in moral theory: The Dewey lectures 1980. *Journal of Philosophy* 77(9): 515–572.

______. 1985. Justice as fairness. *Philosophy and Public Affairs* 14: 227–251.

______. 1992. *Political liberalism*. New York: Columbia University Press.

Rich, Adrienne. 1978. Compulsory heterosexuality and lesbian existence. *Signs* 5(4): 632–660.

Rousseau, Jean-Jacques. 1762. *Emile, or On education*, trans. Allan Bloom. New York: Basic Books. (Reprinted in 1979.)

Ruddick, Sara. 1995. Injustice in families: Assault and domination. In *Justice and care: Essential readings in feminist ethics*, ed. Virginia Held. Boulder, Colo.: Westview Press.

Sandel, Michael J. 1982. *Liberalism and the limits of justice*. Cambridge: Cambridge University Press.

Schwarzenbach, Sybil. 1986. Rawls and ownership: The forgotten category of reproductive labor. In *Science, morality and feminist theory*, ed. Marsha Hanen and Kai Nielsen. Minneapolis: University of Minnesota Press.

Sen, Amartya. 1987. Equality of what? The Tanner lecture on human values. (Delivered in 1979.) In *Liberty, equality and law: Selected Tanner lectures* (pp. 137–162), ed. Sterling M. McMurrin, Cambridge: Cambridge University Press.

______. 1989. Gender and cooperative conflict. In *Persistent inequalities* (pp. 123–149), ed. Irene Trinker. New York: New York: Oxford University Press.

______. 1990. Justice: Means v. freedom. *Philosophy and Public Affairs* 19(2): 111–121.

______. 1992. *Inequality reexamined.* Cambridge, Mass: Harvard University Press.

Stacks, Carol B. 1974. *All our kin: Strategies for survival in a black community*. New York: Harper and Row.

Stalker, Peter. 1994. *The work of strangers: A survey of international labor migration*. Geneva, Switzerland: International Labor Office.

Trebilcot, Joyce, ed. 1987. *Mothering: New essays in feminist theory*. Totowa, N.J.: Rowman and Littlefield.

Tronto, Joan. 1993. *Moral boundaries: A political argument for an ethic of care*. New York: Routledge.

Williams, Patricia. 1991. On being the object of property. In *At the boundaries of the law*, ed. Martha Albertson Fineman and Nancy Thomadson. New York: Routledge.

Wollstonecraft, Mary. 1792, 1988. *A vindication of the rights of woman* (2nd ed.), trans. and ed. Carol Poston. New York: W. W. Norton.

# Part V
# Care Versus Justice: Must We Choose?

# [23]

# Moral Understandings: Alternative "Epistemology" for a Feminist Ethics

MARGARET URBAN WALKER

*Work on representing women's voices in ethics has produced a vision of moral understanding profoundly subversive of the traditional philosophical conception of moral knowledge. I explicate this alternative moral "epistemology," identify how it challenges the prevailing view, and indicate some of its resources for a liberatory feminist critique of philosophical ethics.*

---

When Annette Baier asked a few years ago what women wanted in a moral theory, the answer she arrived at was that moral *theory* was just what women *didn't* want, if a moral theory is a "fairly systematic account of a fairly large area of morality, with a keystone supporting all the rest" (Baier 1985, 55). Yet the latter is what a still dominant tradition of moral philosophy—stretching from Socrates through Sidgwick to Rawls—*does* want: a fairly compact system of very general but directly action-guiding principles or procedures. Current philosophical practice still largely views ethics as the search for moral knowledge, and moral knowledge as comprising universal moral formulae and the theoretical justification of these.

If one asks the somewhat different question of what a *feminist ethics* is, or should look like, one might have in mind some different things. One is that feminist ethics is one which clarifies the moral legitimacy and necessity of the kinds of social, political, and personal changes that feminism demands in order to end male domination, or perhaps to end domination generally.[1] Another conception of feminist ethics is that of one in which the moral perceptions, self-images, and senses of moral value and responsibility of women have been represented or restored. Philosophical ethics, as a cultural product, has been until recently almost entirely a product of some men's thinking. There are the usual reasons to suspect that those men will not have represented, or will not have represented truly, modes of life and forms of responsibility which aren't theirs, or which they could recognize fully only at the cost of acknowledging their interlocking gender, race and class privileges. While

*Hypatia* vol. 4, no. 2 (Summer 1989) © by Margaret Urban Walker

female voices alone may not be sufficient correctives to this, they promise to be important ones. Here the tasks of restoration, reconstruction, and new construction are not sharply divided; all involve suspension and re-examination of unquestioned assumptions and standard forms.

The reconstructive project has been pioneered in work by Baier (1985; 1986; 1987), Carol Gilligan (1982), Nel Noddings (1984), Adrienne Rich (1976; 1979), Sara Ruddick (1984), Caroline Whitbeck (1983), and others. While the result in each case is distinctive, a lattice of similar themes—personal relations, nurturance and caring, maternal experience, emotional responsiveness, attunement to particular persons and contexts, sensitivity to open-ended responsibilities—has become the object of sharp criticism from *other* feminist quarters. While the criticisms too are varied, they include a variety of cognate concerns about whether the values and paradigms valorized in the reconstructive work are not mistaken and politically retrograde. Jean Grimshaw (1986), Claudia Card (1985), Jeffner Allen (1986), Lorraine Code (1987), Barbara Houston (1987), and others have asked whether maternal paradigms, nurturant responsiveness, and a bent toward responsibility for others' needs aren't our oppressive history, not our liberating future, and whether "women's morality" isn't a familiar ghetto rather than a liberated space.[2] It is fair, if oversimple, to say that some feminists question whether the reconstructive project can meet and nourish the politically normative one.[3]

The many crossing strands of this conversation beg for close consideration, but I will pull one thread loose from the reconstructive project and commend it to our further deliberation as a part, but only part, of an adequate and flexible feminist ethic. The thread I refer to in the reconstructive work is a profound and original rebellion against the regnant paradigm of moral knowledge mentioned in my opening paragraph. Hence, it might be called an *alternative moral epistemology*, a very different way of identifying and appreciating the forms of intelligence which define responsible moral consideration. This view does not imagine our moral understandings congealed into a compact theoretical instrument of impersonal decision for each person, but as deployed in shared processes of discovery, expression, interpretation, and adjustment between persons. Facets of this alternative view which appear repeatedly in reconstructive discussions are: attention to the particular; a way of constructing morally relevant understandings which is "contextual and narrative" (Gilligan 1982, 19); a picture of deliberation as a site of expression and communication.

Here are my limited aims. First, I model this alternative epistemology of moral understandings by describing its three elements and their affinities. Second, I identify how its features challenge the still hardy mainstream universalist tradition on moral knowledge. Finally, too briefly, I indicate some ways this particular result of the reconstructive approach to feminist ethics answers to some concerns of the first, politically normative approach. Refusing the canonical "theory" option does not mean going without guidance in judgments and practices of countering domination. Neither does the alternative moral epistemology by itself require commitments to the specific moral values and paradigms lately in dispute among feminists.

## I. Elements of an Alternative Moral Epistemology

A substantial number of contemporary women writers on morality have sounded the theme of attention to "particular others in actual contexts" (Held 1987, 118). Iris Murdoch (1970) sets an oft-cited precedent for this theme in her defense of *attention* ("loving regard" (40); "patient and just discernment" (38)) as the "characteristic and proper mark of the active moral agent" (34). In pointed opposition to the emphasis in most moral philosophy on conscientious adherence to principle, Murdoch insists instead on the "endless task" (28) of "good vision: unsentimental, detached, unselfish, objective attention" (65-66), which she calls *love*.[4] More recent women writers who see acute and unimpeded perception of particular human beings as the condition of adequate moral response concur in Murdoch's epistemological point—her emphasis on a certain kind of understanding as central to morality.[5]

Ruddick (1984), for example, finds in the normative structure of maternal practices a rich display of that openness which allows for revelation of the particular individual. Maternal responsibility to foster growth, on Ruddick's account, requires certain recognitions: of the separate consciousness of another making its own sense of the world; of the common humanity of the other's familiar longings and impulses; of the need to give up expectations of repeatability in order to follow the distinct trajectory of a particular life (218-220). Such maternal virtues are ones Ruddick thinks it urgent to cultivate more widely. Whitbeck (1983) sees a similar sensibility enabling practices (such as teaching the young, nursing the sick, tending the body) for "the (mutual) realization of people" (65) which are typically considered "women's work." Related themes are sounded by others: Gilligan's reconstruction of the "care ethic" involves "the ability to perceive people in their own terms and to respond to their needs" (1984, 77); Benhabib (1987, 164) explores the "epistemic incoherence" of strategies of reversability and universalization once the concreteness of other individuals has been covered over by the "generalized" conception of others in terms of an abstract *status*.[6]

Attention to particular persons as *a*, if not *the*, morally crucial epistemic mode requires distinctive sorts of understanding. Gilligan has usefully described the pattern of this thinking as "contextual and narrative" rather than "formal and abstract," where the latter "abstracts the moral problem from the interpersonal situation" (1982, 32), while the former invokes a "narrative of relationships that extends over time" (1982, 28). Two elements are at work here: context and concreteness of individuals with specific "history, identity, and affective-emotional constitution" (Benhabib 1987, 163), and the special context that is a relationship, with *its* history, identity, and affective definition.

The two are linked by the notion of a narrative, of the location of human beings' feelings, psychological states, needs, and understandings as nodes of a story (or of the intersection of stories) that has already begun, and will continue beyond a given juncture of moral urgency. Conceptually, this means that we don't and can't identify people's emotions, intentions and other mental states with momentary (and especially not momentary inner, private) phenomena. Instead, we identify these features of people by attending to how their beliefs, feelings, modes of expression, circumstances and more, arranged in characteristic ways and often spread out in time, configure into a recognizable kind of story. Practically, this means that individual embroideries and idiosyncracies, as well as the learned codes of expression and response built up in particular relationships, and built up culturally around kinds of relationships, require of us very acute attention to the minute and specific, to history and incident, in grasping cases in a morally adequate way. If the others I need to understand really are actual others in a particular case at hand, and not repeatable instances or replaceable occupants of a general status, they will require of me an understanding of their/our story and its concrete detail. Without this I really cannot know *how it is* with others towards whom I will act, or what the meaning and consequence of any acts will be.

Whitbeck argues for a relational view of persons, of their historical being as "fundamentally a history of relationships to other people," and their actions as responses to the "whole configuration of relations" (1983, 76). She connects this view with the essentially responsive, discretionary character of moral responsibilities that relationships generate, responsibilities that cannot then be reduced to obligations and specified in uniform terms. Sharon Bishop (1987) has also examined the different light cast on moral responsibilities, problems, deliberation, resolution and guilt when one sees moral response as the attempt to mediate multiple, sometimes conflicting, moral claims that arise out of our many actual connections with other people and our needs to maintain them with integrity and sensitivity. This intertwining of selves and stories in narrative constructions which locate what is at stake, what is needed, and what is possible is at the heart of moral thinking for many women and feminist writers. The understanding of such stories requires many forms of intelligence; all are at work in the competent moral agent, according to these views.[7]

One form of intelligence that very often, if not typically, offers crucial resources for the resolution of moral problems is the *ability to communicate* among persons involved or affected. While this avenue to understanding is not always open, it often enough is, and its efficacy is so obvious that it is astonishing how little attention is paid it in most nonfeminist moral philosophy. Even in that strain of theory that postulates or simulates an original agreement or compact, the role of communication in, as it were, the moral event is routinely ignored, and the moral agent on the spot is depicted in lonely cogitations (or sometimes in admirable but solo display of fixed habits of virtue). Given the particularistic paradigm of understanding and the situated conception of responsibility already discussed, it is not surprising that the resource of communication is often stressed in women's writing on morality. Gilligan stresses the commitment in the "care" ethic she describes to "activating the network [of relationships] by communication" (1982, 30); and Bishop's reconstrual of moral response as "offering compensation and mediating settlements" (1987, 12) pictures us as engaging those affected by our moral choices in tight places in a common search for constructive ways of answering unsatisfiable or competing claims. Benhabib even more directly challenges the "monological model of moral reasoning" with a proposal for a "communicative ethic of need interpretation," in which actual dialogue replaces hypothetical methods and fixed, prior constraints on "admissible" concerns (1987, 167; 169). Murdoch speaks of a mutual "obscurity" which makes the work of love endless (1970, 33), and urges on us the study of literature as an education in how to "picture and understand human situations" (34). We need not make our obscurity to each other worse by unnecessarily unilateral decision. We might just try turning to each other: talking and listening and imagining possibilities together.

## II. From Moral Knowledge to Moral Understandings

The three elements of attention, contextual and narrative appreciation, and communication in the event of moral deliberation might be seen, in their natural interdependence, as an alternative epistemology of moral understanding, or the basis of one. This view, gleaned from the works of a variety of female and feminist writers, provides an alternative to a now standard and canonical (which is to say: professionally institutionalized) view of the form and point of ethics (or its philosophical elaboration).[8] This view is both old and continuous enough to be called a tradition in the strongest sense, and we might call it the *universalist/impersonalist tradition*. In the words of one of its most explicit proponents, nineteenth-century utilitarian philosopher Henry Sidgwick,[9] its goal is systematization of moral understanding, and its ideal of system is that of "precise general knowledge of what ought to be" (1907, 1), encoded in "directive rules of conduct" (2) which are "clear and decisive" (199) and "in universal form" (228). The rationale for pursuing a "scientifically complete and systematically reflective form" (425) in morals is that it "corrects" and "supplements" our scattered intuitions, and resolves "uncertainties and discrepancies" in moral judgment. By useful abstraction it steers us away from, in Sidgwick's words, "obvious sources of error" which "disturb the clearness" of moral discernment (214). For Sidgwick, such distractions include complexity of circumstances, personal interests, and habitual sympathies. Thus, according to Sidgwick, only precise and truly universal principles can provide for "perfection of practice no less than for theoretical completeness" (262).

This capsule description of standard intent and methodology aims to bring into relief its very general picture of morality as individuals standing before the bar of impersonal truth. Moral responsibility is envisioned as responsiveness to the impersonal truths in which morality resides; each individual stands justified if he or she can invoke the authority of this impersonal truth, and the moral community of individuals is secured by the conformity (and uniformity) guaranteed by obedience to this higher authority.[10] From an epistemological angle, one might gloss this view as: adequacy of moral understanding increases as this understanding approaches systematic generality.

The alternative moral epistemology already outlined, holds, to the contrary, that: adequacy of moral understanding decreases as its form approaches generality through abstraction. A view consistent with this will not be one of individuals standing singly before the impersonal dicta of Morality, but one of human beings connected in various ways and at various depths responding *to each other* by engaging together in a search for shareable interpretations of their responsibilities, and/or bearable resolutions to their moral binds. These interpretations and resolutions will be constrained not only by how well they protect goods we can share, but also by how well they preserve the very human connections that make the shared process necessary and possible. The long oscillation in Western moral thought between the impersonal and the personal viewpoints is answered by proposing that we consider, fully and in earnest, the *interpersonal* view.

The result of this alternative epistemology is not, then, an "opposite number" or shadow image of impersonalist approaches; it is instead a point of departure for a *variety* of different problematics, investigations, focal concerns, and genres of writing and teaching about ethics, many of which we have not, I suppose, yet clearly imagined. Some philosophical endeavors are obviously relevant. We might pay greater attention to the pragmatics of communication (of what people mean and do when they address each other, and not just what their words mean). We could explore more fully how moral paradigms and exemplary particular cases are made points of reference for shareable judgments, how they are explicated and how analogies are drawn with them. A lively interest in understanding how various factors (semantic, institutional, political) shape our ability to arrive at shared interpretations is needed, as is a questioning of barriers between philosophical, literary, critical, and empirical investigations of moral life. These endeavors can, however, be carried out in a cheerfully piecemeal fashion; we need not expect or require the results to eventuate in a comprehensive systematization.

The analogue of this on the practical level is the expectation of constant "moral remainders," to adopt a phrase in recent philosophical use. 'Moral remainders' refers to some genuine moral demands which, because their fulfillment conflicted with other genuine moral demands, are "left over" in episodes of moral choice, and yet are not just nullified.[11] Whether this sort of thing is even possible is an issue in contemporary moral philosophy.[12] But if moral life is seen as a tissue of moral understandings which configure, respond to, and reconfigure relations as they go, we should anticipate residues and carry-overs as the rule rather than the exceptions: one's choice will often be a selection of one among various imperfect responses, a response to some among various claims which can't all be fulfilled. So there will just as often be unfinished and ongoing business, compensations and reparations, postponements and returns. Moral problems on this view are nodal points in progressive histories of mutual adjustment and understanding, not "cases" to be closed by a final verdict of a highest court.

## III. From Epistemology to Practice

Although I've cast the discussion here in terms of moral "epistemology," my point has been that there is a way of looking at the understanding critical to and distinctive of full moral capacity on which this understanding is *not* really an *episteme*, not a nomologically ordered theory. From the alternative view, moral understanding comprises a collection of perceptive, imaginative, appreciative, and expressive skills and capacities which put and keep us in unimpeded contact with the realities of ourselves and specific others.[13]

It's also true that a picture of moral understanding is not a whole moral view. Indeed, the alternative moral "epistemology" sketched here leaves open to consideration many questions about which sorts of values enable moral agents to express themselves and hear others, to interpret wisely, and to nourish each other's capacities for supple attentiveness. It also leaves open what other values not directly related to these expressive and receptive capacities are those a feminist ethics ought to endorse. It does not promote one kind of relationship as paradigmatic of moral encounter, and invites us to explore the resources and impediments to expression, reception and communication in relationships of many kinds. Yet the priority it gives to voicing and hearing, to being answerable in and for specific encounters and relationships promises, I believe, potent critical resources. The most obvious ones I see are its structural capacity to challenge "principled" moral stances in the concrete, where these are surrogates for, or defenses against, responsiveness in actual relationships; to export an insistence on the primacy of personal acknowledgement and communication to institutional and "stranger" contexts;

and on a philosophical plane to pierce through the rhetoric of ethics to the *politics of ethics* as a routine matter.[14]

In the first instance, an ethic based on this alternative picture of moral understanding is set to challenge fundamentally and consistently the way the universalist tradition has institutionalized *indirect* ways of relating as moral *paradigms*. By 'indirect' here I mean ways of appreciating persons and situations mediated through what are typically some few, entrenched parameters of status, right, principle, or duty. The alternative picture discussed here confronts this "policed sociability" (Skillen 1978, 170) of universalism with an alternative ideal of *moral objectivity*: that of unimpeded, undistorted, and flexible appreciation of unrepeatable individuals in what are often distinctive situations and relationships. Morally relevant categories on this view include the full, nuanced range of expressive resources for articulating and constructing interpersonal life. By contrast, the ways of describing and expressing to which universalist morality permits moral relevance are typically limited to those which are "repeatable," "universalizable," "impartial," or "impersonal," i.e., those that embody the forms of detachment that are taken by universalism as constitutive of "the moral point of view."

Universalism presses me to view you, for instance, as a holder of a certain right, or a promisee, or a satisfaction-function, or a focus of some specifiable set of obligatory responses. I am pressed to structure my response or appeal to you in terms which I can think of as applying repeatably to any number of other cases. If we step into the alternative framework, however, we see universalist morality as thus "curbing our imaginations" (Lovibond 1983, 199) by enforcing communicative and reflective strategies which are interpersonally *evasive*. Universalism, for example, tends to regiment moral thinking so that negligent or willful inattention to need and expectation in the course of daily life is readily seen as "mere insensitivity," a non-moral failing, when it is not in dereliction of explicit "duties." Worse, it legitimates *uniformly* assuming the quasi-administrative or juridical posture of "the" (i.e., universal) moral point of view. Yet in many cases assuming that viewpoint may foreclose the more revealing, if sometimes painful, path of expression, acknowledgement, and collaboration that could otherwise lead to genuinely responsive solutions.

A principled appeal to "fairness" or "what one promised" or what "right" one has to something or why "anyone" should expect a certain response may be a summarily effective arguing point. But if it is brought forth in an intricate situation of an ongoing relationship, it may also be the most effective way to stymie or silence your interlocutor—spouse, lover, friend, student, partner, patient—without addressing many questions. The avoided questions may include just the morally relevant ones about the particular needs and harms, the expectations and forms of trust, and the character and future of *that* relationship. Feminists have special and acute needs to fend off this systematic de-personalizing of the moral and de-moralizing of the personal. For on a practical level what feminists aspire to depends as much on restructuring our senses of moral responsibility in intimate partnerships, sexual relations, communities of personal loyalty, and day-to-day work relations as it clearly does on replacing institutional, legal, and political arrangements.

The alternative picture also invites us not to be too tempted by the "separate spheres" move of endorsing particularism for personal or intimate relations, universalism for the large-scale or genuinely administrative context, or for dealings with unknown or little-known persons. While principled, generalized treatments may really be the best we can resort to in many cases of the latter sort, it is well to preserve a lively sense of the *moral incompleteness* or inadequacy of these resorts. This is partly to defend ourselves against dispositions to keep strangers strange and outsiders outside, but it is also to prevent our becoming comfortable with essentially distancing, depersonalizing, or paternalistic attitudes which may not really *be* the only resorts if roles and institutions can be shaped to embody expressive and communicative possibilities. It is often claimed that more humanly responsive institutions are not practical (read: instrumentally efficient). But if moral-practical intelligence is understood consistently in the alternative way discussed (the way appropriate to relations among persons), it may instead be correct to say that certain incorrigibly impersonal or depersonalizing institutions are too morally impractical to be tolerated. It is crucial to examine how structural features of institutionalized relations—medical personnel, patients and families; teachers, students and parents; case workers and clients, for example—combine with typical situations to enable or deform the abilities of all concerned to hear and to be heard. Some characteristically modern forms of universalist thinking may project a sort of "moral colonialism" (the "subjects" of my moral decisions disappear behind uniform "policies" I must impartially "apply") precisely because they were forged historically with an eye to actual colonization—industrial or imperial.[15]

Finally, this kind of moral epistemology reminds us that styles of moral thinking are not primarily philosophical brain-teasers, data begging for the maximally elegant theoretical construction, but are ways of answering to *other people* in terms of some responsibilities that are commonly recognized or recognizable in some community. Philosophical representations of these styles will both reflect and reinforce the relations of authority, power, and responsibility they encode. Hence, for moral philosophy to be sincerely reflective, it must attend focally to questions heretofore considered "philosophically" inappropriate: questions about the rhetoric and politics of ethics. These are questions about the discursive and expressive formats which have been declared appropriate to the task of representing moral life, and about who has the standing (and the access to institutionalized forums) to make, and to challenge, the "rules" (including substantive assumptions) of the genre. When we construct and consider representations of our moral situations, we need to ask: what actual community of moral responsibility does this representation of moral thinking purport to represent? Who does it actually represent? What communicative strategies does it support? Who will be in a position (concretely, socially) to deploy these strategies? Who is in a position to transmit and enforce the rules which constrain them? In what forms of activity or endeavor will they have (or fail to have) an application, and who is served by these activities?

These questions are hard for philosophers to ask; it flies in the face of the professional self-image of supposedly disinterested searchers after timeless moral truth to recognize that a moral philosophy is a particular rhetoric too, situated in certain places, sustained and deployed by certain groups of people. Its apparent form may belie its real application and meaning. For example, philosophers have long insisted on "the universal" in ethics, and continue, I find, to insist on formal universality of norms, concepts, or procedures as the key moral bulwark against bias and injustice. Yet the rhetoric of universality has been entirely compatible, as feminist philosophers have repeatedly shown, with the most complete (and often intentional) exclusion of women as moral agents from such loftily universal constructs as the social contract, pure practical rationality, or the good life for man, and with bypassing altogether in application whole areas of life that are the province of women (voluntarily or not), such as the rearing of children.[16]

Further, not only the substance and presuppositions but also the standard discursive forms of moral philosophy—its canonical styles of presentation, methods of argument, characteristic problems —require pragmatic evaluation. These forms include stark absence of the second person and the plural in projections of philosophical deliberation; virtual exclusion of collaborative and communicative modes of formulating and negotiating moral problems; regimentation of moral "reasoning" into formats of deductive argument; reliance on schematic examples in which the few "morally relevant" factors have already been selected and in which social-political context is effaced; and omission of continuing narratives that explore the interpersonal sequels to moral "solutions." These are rhetorical conventions which curb the moral imaginations of academic philosophers drastically. Alarmingly, we visit them on our students as we "refine" their moral thinking, obscuring morally significant features of everyday life, personal relations, and the social conditions which structure them.

There are alternatives to the abstract, authoritarian, impersonal, universalist view of moral consciousness. The picture of direct mutual response and responsibility is not a whole ethics, but it is one way of rotating the axis of our investigation around the fixed point of our real need.[17]

## Notes

1. This view of feminist ethics does not rule out in principle that some currently prominent view in philosophical ethics, properly applied, can be a feminist ethics. Although this possibility seems less promising currently, early feminist discussions of issues like abortion, rape, and pornography often invoked standard notions of rights, respect, or the promotion of happiness. And it is still a fact that in our given political culture appeals to moral standards which cohere with liberal political ideas are potent and indispensable tools in pursuing feminist social and legal objectives.

2. Grimshaw is specially critical of claims that women's moral *thinking* is characteristically different; Code criticizes "maternalism;" Houston discusses objections by Card, Allen and others. For critical reactions to Gilligan's work, see Nails et al. (1983), Kerber et al. (1986) and Michaels (1986).

3. I don't mean to make this dialogue sound too bipolar. Virginia Held (1987) is cautious on the issue of jettisoning principles to particularism. Marilyn Friedman (1987) combines a plea for the integration of justice and caring values with the view that the character of particularized moral commitments does not combine with rule-based respect. Both Held and Friedman tentatively suggest the application of different moral approaches to different "spheres" of life or different kinds of relationships. But see my section III, below, on the "separate spheres" idea.

4. Murdoch herself credits her conception of a "just and loving gaze directed upon an individual reality" (34) to Simone Weil, whose views are complicated enough, (and ambivalent enough, from the viewpoint I'm discussing here) to require quite separate consideration.

5. Many may not share the Platonism, Freudian psychology, theory of art, or other views to which Murdoch joins her views on love. One subtle critique of the deep social conservatism of Murdoch's views is provided by Sabina Lovibond (1983, 189-200).

6. See Held (1987); Noddings (1984, chapters 1 and 4). See also Nussbaum (1983) on reviving the Aristotelian notion of perception as "appropriate acknowledgement" of the particular person in the face of the blinding urge to preserve preconceived, harmonious orderings of abstracted value.

7. See also Diamond (1983) on the importance of grasping the moral "texture" of individuals (an idea she attributes to Iris Murdoch).

8. The difference between representing morality and "rationally reconstructing" it philosophically is not always clear, and this is itself a source of deep problems, substantively and methodologically. Addelson (1987), for example, deeply challenges the appropriateness and moral legitimacy of an academic practice of philosophical ethics (if I understand her correctly). I take this challenge quite seriously, even as I right now continue to do a version of academic philosophical ethics.

9. Sidgwick's work richly repays study if one wants to see in explicit and self-conscious form the "rules" of the genre of today's philosophical ethics. But one could find the same rules formulated (or implicitly honored) in any number of mainstream twentieth century authors.

10. Since writing this I have discovered a parallel characterization in Anthony Skillen's description of modern bourgeois moral consciousness as a blend of "abstract authoritarianism" and "generalized disciplinarianism" (Skillen 1978, 153).

11. A standard example would be that in which two promises, each sincerely and responsibly made, turn out to be contingently incapable of both being kept. In such cases, whichever commitment I fulfill, another will have been neglected. Bishop (1987, 13ff.) discusses the importance of taking the longer view of such cases.

12. A number of widely known essays which debate the issues about dilemmas and moral remainders are collected in Gowans (1987).

13. A moral epistemology of the sort described finds common or overlapping cause with a number of other contemporary deviations from dominant views. For critics of impartiality on behalf of the personal life, see Williams (1981), Blum (1980), and Stocker (1976). On interrogating moral views for their concrete social and historical conditions, see MacIntyre (1981). For insistence on the primacy of judgments in particular cases, see the new Aristotelians, Nussbaum (1986) and Wiggins (1978). For other versions of "responsibility ethics" which situate moral claims in relational structures of power and dependency, see Goodin (1985) and Jonas (1984).

On morality as a tissue of acknowledgements and refusals, see Cavell (1979, Parts 3 and 4). And on morality as constituted by social practices and as expressive of relations of authority in, respectively, a Marxist and a Wittgensteinian-Hegelian vein see Skillen (1978) and Lovibond (1983). All these may be, used selectively, resources for a different kind of ethics. Yet feminists might remain wary of unwanted residues and omissions in some of these views.

14. On the political aspects of construction and deployment of modes of rationality and styles of thought with respect to gender, see essays by Ruddick, Addelson, and Harding in Kittay and Meyers (1987). See also Calhoun (1988) for a discussion of the way philosophers' neglect of certain topics reinforces moral ideologies.

15. In this connection see Skillen (1978, Chapter 4) on both Kantian and utilitarian disciplinarianism and Williams (1985, Chapter 6) on Sidgwickian "government house utilitarianism."

16. Baier (1986; 1987) is particularly humane and lucid on this topic.

17. Special thanks to Sandra Bartky for very good suggestions on an earlier and briefer draft of this paper, and to the editors and readers for helpful suggestions.

## References


Addelson, Kathryn. 1987. Moral passages. In *Women and moral theory*. Eva Feder Kittay and Diana T. Meyers, eds. Totowa, New Jersey: Rowman and Littlefield.

Allen, Jeffner. 1986. *Lesbian philosophy: Explorations*. Palo Alto, California: Institute of Lesbian Studies.

Baier, Annette. 1985. What do women want in a moral theory? *Nous* 19: 53-63.

Baier, Annette. 1986. Trust and anti-trust. *Ethics* 96: 231-260.

Baier, Annette. 1987. The need for more than justice. In *Science, morality & feminist theory*. Marsha Hanen and Kai Nielsen, eds. Calgary, Canada: University of Calgary Press.

Benhabib, Seyla. 1987. The generalized and the concrete other. In *Women and moral theory*. Eva Feder Kittay and Diana T. Meyers, eds. Totowa, New Jersey: Rowman and Littlefield.

Bishop, Sharon. 1987. Connections and guilt. *Hypatia* 2(1):7-23.

Blum, Lawrence. 1980. *Friendship, altruism and morality*. London: Routledge & Kegan Paul.

Calhoun, Cheshire. 1988. Justice, care, gender bias. *The Journal of Philosophy* 85: 451-463.

Card, Claudia. 1985. Virtues and moral luck. Working Series I, No. 4, Institute for Legal Studies, University of Wisconsin, Madison, Law School.

Cavell, Stanley. 1979. *The claim of reason*. Oxford: Oxford University Press.

Code, Lorraine. 1987. Second persons. In *Science, morality & feminist theory*. Marsha Hanen and Kai Nielsen, eds. Calgary, Canada: University of Calgary Press.

Diamond, Cora. 1983. Having a rough story about what moral philosophy is. *New Literary History* 15: 155-169.

Friedman, Marilyn. 1987. Beyond caring: The de-moralization of gender. In *Science, morality & feminist theory*. Marsha Hanen and Kai Nielsen, eds. Calgary, Canada: University of Calgary Press.

Gilligan, Carol. 1982. *In a different voice*. Cambridge: Harvard University Press.

Gilligan, Carol. 1984. The conquistador and the dark continent: Reflections on the psychology of love. *Daedalus* 113: 75-95.

Goodin, Robert. 1985. *Protecting the vulnerable*. Chicago: University of Chicago Press.

Gowans, Christopher. 1987. *Moral dilemmas*. New York: Oxford University Press.

Grimshaw, Jean. 1986. *Philosophy and feminist thinking*. Minneapolis: University of Minnesota Press.

Hanen, Marsha and Kai Nielsen, eds. 1987. *Science, morality & feminist theory*. Calgary, Canada: University of Calgary Press.

Held, Virginia. 1987. Feminism and moral theory. In *Women and moral theory*. Eva Feder Kittay and Diana T. Meyers, eds. Totowa, New Jersey: Rowman and Littlefield.

Houston, Barbara. 1987. Rescuing womanly virtues: Some dangers of moral reclamation. In *Science, morality & feminist theory*. Marsha Hanen and Kai Nielsen, eds. Totowa, New Jersey: Rowman and Littlefield.

Jonas, Hans. 1984. *The imperative of responsibility*. Chicago: University of Chicago Press.

Kerber, Linda, et al. 1986. On *In a different voice*: An interdisciplinary forum. *Signs* 11: 304-333.

Kittay, Eva Feder and Diana T. Meyers, eds. 1987. *Women and moral theory*. Totowa, New Jersey: Rowman and Littlefield.

Lovibond, Sabina. 1983. *Realism and imagination in ethics*. Minneapolis: University of Minnesota Press.

MacIntyre, Alasdair. 1981. *After virtue*. Notre Dame, Indiana: University of Notre Dame Press.

Michaels, Meredith. 1986. Morality without distinction. *The Philosophical Forum* 17: 175-187.

Murdoch, Iris. [1970] 1985. *The sovereignty of good*. London: Routledge & Kegan Paul.

Nails, Debra, Mary Ann O'Loughlin and James C. Walker, eds. 1983. *Social research* 50.

Noddings, Nel. 1984. *Caring: A feminine approach to ethics and moral education*. Berkeley and Los Angeles: University of California Press.

Nussbaum, Martha. 1983. Flawed crystals: James's *The golden bowl* and literature as moral philosophy. *New Literary History* 15: 25-50.

Nussbaum, Martha. 1986. *The fragility of goodness*. Cambridge: Cambridge University Press.

Rich, Adrienne. 1976. *Of woman born*. New York: W. W. Norton & Company.

Rich, Adrienne. 1979. *On lies, secrets, and silence*. New York: W. W. Norton & Company.

Ruddick, Sara. 1984. Maternal thinking. In *Mothering*. Joyce Trebilcot, ed. Totowa, New Jersey: Rowman and Allanheld.

Sidgwick, Henry. [1907] 1981. *The methods of ethics*. Indianapolis: Hackett Publishing.

Skillen, Anthony. 1978. *Ruling illusions*. Atlantic Highlands, New Jersey: Humanities Press.

Stocker, Michael. 1976. The schizophrenia of modern ethical theories. *The Journal of Philosophy* 73: 453-466.

Whitbeck, Caroline. 1983. A different reality: Feminist ontology. In *Beyond domination*. Carol C. Gould, ed. Totowa, New Jersey: Rowman and Allanheld.

Wiggins, David. 1978. Deliberation and practical reason. In *Practical reasoning*. Joseph Raz, ed. Oxford: Oxford University Press.

Williams, Bernard. 1981. *Moral luck*. Cambridge: Cambridge University Press.

Williams, Bernard. 1985. *Ethics and the limits of philosophy*. Cambridge: Harvard University Press.

# [24]

*Human Studies* **16:** 143–162, 1993.


# Moral voices, moral selves: About getting it right in moral theory

SUSAN HEKMAN
*Department of Political Science, University of Texas at Arlington, Arlington, TX 76019*

## 1. Introduction

In 1982 Carol Gilligan published an empirical analysis of the decision-making processes of a sample of girls and young women confronted with real-life moral dilemmas. Gilligan claimed that these girls and women articulated their moral situations in a "different" moral voice, a voice distinct from the moral voice defined in previous studies that involved primarily male subjects. Nearly a decade later the moral and epistemological ramifications of Gilligan's study are still being explored. A wide array of claims have been made on the basis of Gilligan's analysis. Moral philosophers, feminist theorists and moral psychologists have asserted, variously, that Gilligan's "different voice" represents a significant departure in moral theory, that it is empirically unjustified, that it establishes the superiority of a distinctively feminine moral voice, and that it provides a complement to the unitary voice of moral theories that have dominated moral philosophy in the west.

Some of these claims are made explicitly in *In a Different Voice* or in Gilligan's subsequent work, while others are implicit in it. Some contradict Gilligan's analysis or try to supercede it. The different claims that allegedly arise from her work, furthermore, are not consistent. In the following I will sort through several of these claims and examine them from an epistemological perspective. My larger goal, however, it to do more than make some sense of this extensive literature, as difficult as that task is. My thesis is that most of the claims made by Gilligan and her commentators are not sufficiently radical. The claims fall under two headings: first, the contention that the unitary moral theory of the Western tradition should be replaced by a dualistic theory, or, second, that the justice perspective in moral theory should be replaced with the more superior care perspective. The problem with these claims is that neither challenges the epistemology that characterizes Western moral theory, an epistemology that attempts to define one true moral theory. What I would like to suggest, in contrast to these claims, is that if we take seriously Gilligan's understanding of the creation of moral voices, voices that arise from relational, discursively constituted subjects, then much more radical implications flow from her work. In her analysis of how moral voices are constituted Gilligan wants to reduce the moral voices to two, masculine and feminine, and, furthermore, to fit her theory into the epistemological space of Western moral theories. In the following I will argue that neither of these moves is epistemologically viable. If it is the case that subjects are constituted through discursive relationships and, further, that central to the constitution of the subject is the creation of a moral voice, then the moral epistemology that flows from this entails a radical alteration of existing moral theories. It follows that moral voices will be as diverse as the subjects that produce them, that many moral voices must be defined, not only two. It also follows that it is impossible to define one true moral theory based on the definition of one or even two true moral voices. In short, I will argue that the relational self that Gilligan describes effectively deconstructs the metanarrative of moral theory that has dominated Western thought since its inception. Gilligan's theory cannot, as she and many of her commentators suggest, be accomodated by a reworking of the epistemology of existing moral theory, but, rather, demands a new epistemological space for the moral.

## 2. Care and justice

In *In a Different Voice* Gilligan presents a thesis that is, on the surface, quite simple. She argues that the women and girls that she studied articulate their moral dilemmas in a voice that differs from that of the men and boys studied by her colleague Lawrence Kohlberg and, before him, Piaget. She argues that the girls and women articulate what she defines as a "care" perspective, while the boys and men that Kohlberg studied articulate a "justice" perspective.[1] The relationship that she posits between the masculine justice orientation and the feminine care orientation, however, is far from simple. In the course of her book she suggests at least three possible relationships between the two perspectives. Some of these are overlapping, some contradictory. All have implications both for moral theory and for the social scientific methodology that Gilligan employs.

The first relationship between justice and care that Gilligan posits is that the two orientations are separate but equal. Kohlberg's stage sequence of moral development relegated the care perspective that Gilligan identifies in women's moral voices to a lower level of moral development. Gilligan's principle thesis is that the care perspective represents a separate but equal pattern of moral development. Her researches constitute an attempt to rescue the care perspective from Kohlberg's inferior categorization by positing a different, yet equally valid developmental pattern for women. In *In a Different Voice* Gilligan (1982:26) states this aim very succinctly:

> Adding a new line of interpretation, based on the imagery of the girls' thought, makes it possible not only to see development where previously development was not discerned, but also to consider differences in the understanding of relationships without scaling these differences from better to worse.

Although Gilligan (1982:14) concedes that it is difficult to say "different" without saying better or worse, she does not deviate from the claim that the voice of care is both distinct from and equal to that of justice.

In her subsequent empirical work Gilligan has expanded the separate but equal perspective in terms of what she calls the "focus phenomenon" (1987a:28). In these studies Gilligan and her colleagues (1989:xviii) have found that the majority of those studied describe moral conflict from either a justice or a care perspective. Gilligan concludes that justice and care are not opposites, but, rather, different ways of organizing moral problems. At one point she utilizes the duck/rabbit figure to make her point. Just as it is impossible for an observer to see the figure as both a duck and a rabbit simultaneously, she (1987a:22) argues that moral problems can be seen as problems either of care or of justice, but not as both at once. What we must do, she claims, is educate both moral voices and abandon the notion of a single right answer to moral questions. She (1987b:88) hopes that this will lead to ways of speaking about differences that do not lead to "invidious comparisons" between justice and care.

It is tempting to move from Gilligan's argument to the claim that different kinds of moral problems are appropriate to care reasoning, others to justice reasoning. It is significant that Gilligan herself does not make this move. Several of her commentators, however, have done so. John Hardwig (1984), for example, argues that the justice orientation is appropriate to the public sphere, the care orientation to the private. Virginia Held (1987) argues that Gilligan's position entails "domain relativism," and thus a pluralistic, tolerant moral theory that is richly diverse rather than unitary and hierarchical.[2] The separate but equal thesis, however, either in the version posited by Gilligan or that advanced by Hardwig and Held, creates dangerous pitfalls for feminist theory. The particular separation of moral domains suggested by these approaches reifies the public/private distinction that has defined the inferior role of women in Western thought. The hope that, at this point in history, woman's "private morality" will be elevated to equal status with man's public domain seems at best naive. Even though Gilligan avoids the association of care with the private realm and justice with the public, her argument that the separate but equal position she advocates will eschew "invidious comparisons" is unrealistic. The difference that she describes reifies the inferior status of women central to western history and epistemology. The "invidious comparisons" she wants to eschew are inseparable from that epistemology.

A second possible relationship between justice and care that runs through Gilligan's work is that of complementarity. At the end of *In a Different Voice* Gilligan (1982:174) states that in a mature person the perspectives of justice and care converge, resulting in a "dialogue between fairness and care." In a more recent work she describes this dialogue in terms of a "double fugue" in which the themes of justice and care are woven into a harmonious whole (Gilligan, Rogers and Brown 1990:321). Several of the essays in her edited book, *Making Connections*, emphasize that the girls that were studied integrate considerations of justice and care in their definitions of moral problems (Bernstein and Gilligan, 1990; Stern, 1990). What this entails is that justice and care are not separate, but intertwined. In making this argument Gilligan specifically relates the two moral perspectives to conceptions of self: the care perspective entails a relational self, the justice perspective a separate one. Gilligan argues that these two conceptions of self are likewise intertwined. Unlike many of her commentators Gilligan does not separate the relational and autonomous selves, defining them as different modes of being. Rather, she argues that they are two aspects of human existence: one can only experience self in the context of relationship with others and, conversely, one can only experience relationship by differentiating other from self (Gilligan, Rogers and Brown, 1990:328).

Gilligan's complementarity theme raises more problems than it solves. First of all it contradicts the separate but equal thesis she simultaneously advances: complementarity entails convergence, not separation. More importantly, it once more associates women with the caring, relational aspects of moral life, men with the autonomous and separate, yet denies the hierarchy that this move necessarily entails within the confines of Western epistemology. Gilligan's claim that the two moral perspectives are complementary is, of course, far from unique. The understanding of woman as complement to man goes all the way back to Eve's creation as Adam's helpmate. Throughout Western history woman's moral perspective has been understood as an inherently inferior supplement to man's moral principles. Gilligan is here taking a familiar understanding of woman's voice and trying to raise it from inferiority to equality. Once more her effort is noble but futile; complements are always inferior to that which they complement.[3]

An important aspect of Gilligan's complementarity thesis is a claim that raises even more difficult epistemological questions. Gilligan asserts that the justice perspective is incomplete without the addition of the care perspective and, thus, that the addition of this perspective brings us closer to an understanding of the "truth" of human moral development. This effort to find the "truth" of moral development by "completing" the justice perspective with that of care is a theme that runs strongly through Gilligan's discussion in *In a Different Voice*. At the outset she claims that her aim is to "yield a more encompassing view of the lives of both sexes" (1982:4) by looking for the "truth of woman's experience" (1982:62). But it is important to note that Gilligan's search for "truth" is not limited to women's experience alone. She (1982:98) wants to claim that the care perspective describes a truth characteristic of the *human* life cycle:

> To admit the truth of the women's perspective to the conception of moral development is to recognize for both sexes the importance throughout life of the connection between self and other, the universality of the need for compassion and care. The concept of the separate self and of moral principles uncompromised by the constraints of reality is an adolescent ideal, the elaborately wrought philosophy of a Stephen Daedalus whose flight we know to be in jeopardy.

Furthermore, she (1982:173) wants to claim that her work provides "a new perspective on relationships that changes the basic constructs of interpretation." Thus the "marriage" she (1982:174) proposes between men's and women's developmental patterns "could lead to a changed understanding of human development and a more generative view of human life."

The themes of universality and truth that are introduced in *In a Different Voice* have become stronger in Gilligan's subsequent work. She now claims that there are two universal dimensions of early childhood relationships, inequality and attachment, and that these experiences produce the dual perspectives of justice and care. Because girls are more attuned to attachment the care perspective is more developed in women; the opposite is true of men. Her point, however, is that both perspectives are rooted in universal truths of human existence (Gilligan and Wiggins, 1988:114–16). Gilligan is not shy about the revolutionary implications of her theory. She claims that it refutes Piaget's claim that egocentrism is inherent, identifying it instead as the result of boys' childhood experience (Gilligan and Wiggins, 1988:136). Her theory challenges the definition of "human" as separate, autonomous and egocentric that has dominated not only moral psychology, but moral philosophy as well (1987a:31). Finally, she (1987b:93, 77) claims that her work replaces the unitary theory of moral development with a dualistic theory resulting in a new, and better, "map of development."

In the next section I will argue that Gilligan's pursuit of the universal truth of human moral development in these passages contradicts other aspects of her theory. At this point, however, I would like to make the narrower point that the position that Gilligan is adopting in these passages is what Sandra Harding has labelled "feminist empiricism." Feminist empiricists do not challenge the basic structure of the masculine tradition of science, but, rather, attempt to correct or complete it (Harding 1987). They argue that masculine scientific approaches have been incomplete because they have ignored the "truth" of feminine experience. Their solution is to add the dimension of feminine experience to the masculine account and, thus, with a more complete analysis, achieve the male scientist's goal: truth and objectivity. This accurately describes Gilligan's goal as she states it in these passages. She does not challenge Kohlberg's methodology outright, but merely argues that it is incomplete. More importantly, she does not challenge the *goal* of Kohlberg's work, uncovering the "truth" of human experience. On the contrary, she adopts truth and objectivity as her goals as well and faults Kohlberg for failing to attain them.

In all of her work, Gilligan only hints at a third possible relationship between justice and care: the superiority of care to justice. In 1985 at a conference on "Women and Moral Theory" Gilligan (1987a:32) stated: "The promise of joining women and moral theory lies in the fact that human survival, in the late twentieth century, may depend less on formal agreement than on human connection."

As far as I know this is the only time that Gilligan has privileged the care perspective over that of justice. In all of her other work she has argued that the implication of her analyses is to institute a dual conception of moral theory in which justice and care are equally valid. Furthermore, she has argued that although the care perspective is dominant in women, it is not exclusively defined by gender. But although Gilligan is, with this one exception, scrupulous in her assertion of the equality of justice and care, the argument that care is superior to justice is worth noting because it has been one of the major consequences of Gilligan's work. Given Gilligan's hesitancy on this issue, it is ironic that one of the most striking results of her researches has been the development of the argument, first, that the care perspective is essentially feminine and, second, that it is superior to the masculine-defined justice perspective. Sarah Ruddick (1989) and Nel Noddings (1984) in particular have argued that the caring, connected moral perspective of women is superior to the abstract, formalistic morality of men. Frequently citing Gilligan's work in support of their arguments, Ruddick, Noddings and other feminist theorists have asserted that the justice perspective of men has been instrumental in creating the domination, racial discrimination and rape of nature that characterizes the modern world.

The advantages and disadvantages of this approach to moral theory have been extensively discussed in contemporary feminist theory. I will only make two brief points here that are relevant to my argument. First, the discourse of care advanced by these theorists does nothing to displace the monistic, hierarchical and universalistic epistemology of the masculinist theories they attack. Rather, these theorists simply reverse the hierarchy implicit in the masculinist theories by arguing that the morality that they privilege is, in actuality, inferior. Second, the care perspective as it is presented by these theorists is inconsistent with the over-all tenor of Gilligan's approach. Unlike Ruddick and Noddings, Gilligan seeks to advance a dualistic rather than a monistic theory. Her goal is to develop a theory that attempts to probe the truth of the human condition, a truth that encompasses both justice and care.

## 3. Truth and objectivity

The different perspectives on the relationship between care and justice that Gilligan offers raise a number of epistemological problems. In this section I will focus on one of those problems, a problem that has been the focus of much of the criticism of *In a Different Voice*. A major component of Gilligan's argument is her assertion that her approach captures the "truth" of human development more adequately than her rivals. She claims that her studies are more "objective" because they encompass the truth of both women's and men's moral experiences. Many of Gilligan's critics, both moral psychologists and moral theorists, understand Gilligan's claim to be essentially an empirical one. Hence, subsequent to the publication of *In a Different Voice*, a heated debate has raged over the empirical accuracy of Gilligan's claim, that is, whether the existence of a different voice can be scientifically documented.[4] Kohlberg, the principal target of her attack, treats Gilligan's challenge as essentially an empirical claim, arguing that, as an empirical psychologist, he (1982:528) is open to "new data and new findings" despite his misgivings about Gilligan's approach. Several of Gilligan's critics fault her work on the grounds of its failure to conform to standard social scientific methodology. Some of these criticize the "bias" in her account, resulting in, as one critic puts it, "social science at sea without an anchor" (Nails 1983:664). Others cite the paucity of evidence that Gilligan offers to establish her position (Eisenberg and Lennon, 1983; Walker 1984). In some of her rejoinders to these critics, furthermore, Gilligan meets these criticisms by defending the empirical support for her theory. For example, in a recent work she defends her central claim, the existence of sex differences in empathy, citing the larger male prison population as evidence (Gilligan and Wiggins, 1988:113).

In 1986 *Signs* published a review symposium on *In a Different Voice*. This review is instructive for a number of reasons. First, it reveals that even within the bastion of feminist theory and in a journal that has been on the forefront of the feminist critique of science, feminist empiricism was, at least in this instance, the dominant discourse. In her introduction to the review the editor asks whether the dialogue on *In a Different Voice* constitutes a break from "the male-dominated tradition of confrontational debate" (Kerber *et al.*, 1986:304). The answer to this question must be a resounding "no." Had the editor asked whether the review represents a departure from the androcentric standards of science, the answer would also be "no." Most of the authors of the review articles argue that the evidence does not support Gilligan's claim of a different voice and that "claims about these differences should be subjected to the empirical tests that are the basis of social science" (Greeno and Macoby, 1986:316).

The second notable aspect of this review is Gilligan's reply. In a forceful argument that effectively destroys her critics' positions, Gilligan asserts that her claim in *In a Different Voice* was not statistical or empirical but interpretive. She asserts that her point against Kohlberg was not that men and women differ on his scale but, rather, that his scale only fits men's experiences. Even more significantly she (1986:328) argues that "There is no data independent of theory, no observations not made from a perspective. Data alone do not tell us anything; they do not speak, but are interpreted by people."

Although none of her critics noted it, this same position is clearly stated at the beginning of *In a Different Voice*: (1982:6) "Then the presumed neutrality of science, like that of language itself, gives way to the recognition that the categories of knowledge are human constructions."

Anyone familiar with recent discussions in the phiiosophy of the natural and social sciences will recognize the origin of Gilligan's argument here. She is utilizing current critiques of social scientific methodology to argue against the presumption of a theory-free observation language for social inquiry. On the basis of these critiques she argues that Kohlberg's theory is "biased" in that he begins with the assumption of what constitutes moral behavior and then proceeds to find data that fit his theory. She is further arguing that women's moral "underdevelopment" is the result of the bias inherent in Kohlberg's theory, that is, that there is a discrepancy between his theory and the data of women's moral experience (1987b:78). All of these assertions are consistent with the critique of social scientific "objectivity" that has flourished in recent decades, a critique that, significantly, has been central to feminist critiques of science. What does *not* follow from this critique, however, is Gilligan's claim, both in *In a Different Voice* and her subsequent work, that her researches lead to the "truth" of human moral development. This claim is inconsistent with the critique-of-objectivity position that she uses to attack Kohlberg and reveals a significant contradiction in her work.

Despite the existence of this contradiction, however, Gilligan's critique of Kohlberg's moral theory has significant implications. It follows from Gilligan's critique of Kohlberg that it is impossible to "objectively assess" moral development patterns because anyone who attempts to do so will bring to that investigation assumptions of what constitutes "morality." It is particularly easy to criticize Kohlberg along these lines because, although he (1982:525) claims that his goal is "the rational reconstruction of the deep structure of a morally educated adult's moral judgments and intuitions," it is quite clear that what he designates as "moral" is a pattern of thought that has been identified as moral in a very long tradition of Western moral theory. Thus Kohlberg's theory of moral development obviously determines his assessment of the "data" he "discovers." But other conclusions follow from Gilligan's critique that she does not discuss. If it is the case that all theories of moral development are human constructions informed by preconceptions, then this is true of her theory as well. Gilligan's theory of the moral development of women is as much "biased" by her preconceptions as is that of Kohlberg. It further follows that, despite her claims to the contrary, Gilligan is not "discovering" the "truth" of women's experiences, but, rather, interpreting the data in light of her own preconceptions as to what constitutes the "moral."

Instead of condemning Gilligan for this contradiction in her work, however, it is more fruitful to examine exactly what is at issue here. Kohlberg's definition of the moral realm is a quite literal translation of a tradition of moral theory rooted in a discourse that was first articulated by the Greeks. In this discourse moral reasoning based on abstract, formal principles is defined as the "true" and "highest" form of moral thought. In this discourse considerations that involve particularistic, relative and perspectival elements are declared to be inferior or, more precisely, outside the moral realm altogether. What Gilligan has done is to examine these particulartistic, relative elements and, in opposition to the Western moral tradition in general and Kohlberg in particular, to declare them to be within the sphere of the "moral." She extends her heresy by declaring this realm to be on an equal footing with abstract, formalistic moral reasoning. In making this declaration she is, undoubtedly, making a significant conceptual breakthrough. But it is not simply the case that she is imposing her own personal definiton of the "moral" on the data she collects. Rather, she is documenting a self-understanding that many women possess. In our culture women are expected to exhibit caring and nurturing qualities, while men are expected to exhibit qualities associated with abstract considerations of justice. By defining the nurturing qualities of women as a legitimate moral sphere Gilligan is simultaneously opposing the tradition of Western moral theory and tapping into understandings of the gendered division of moral labor that is a product of that tradition. She is not discovering the "truth" of moral development any more than Kohlberg is. What she is doing is labelling as "moral" the concerns that women are supposed to and, indeed, do have in this culture. It is for this reason that the "different voice" has resonated so strongly for so many women that have read Gilligan's work. Gilligan is correct in her assertion that statistical "proof" of the different voice is irrelevant.[5] What is relevant is that she is documenting a self-understanding that is common to most women in our society.

## 4. Discourses of morality

What I am arguing, then, is that the epistemological import of Gilligan's work is not, as she claims, that she is adding to or correcting the masculine moral theories of theorists such as Kohlberg, or that she is discovering the "truth" of human moral development, but, rather, that she is offering a new discourse of morality that redefines what is to count as "moral." In opposition to the unitary moral tradition that Kohlberg is articulating, a tradition in which *only* abstract, formalistic thought counts as moral, Gilligan claims that she is advancing a dual conception of moral discourse in which both considerations of care and those of justice are defined as equally valid moral domains. In advancing this claim, Gilligan is accutely aware of the strength of the moral tradition against which she is arguing. In her work and that of her associates she cites several instances in which adolescent girls are reluctant to describe the ethical dilemmas that they confront as "moral problems" because they have been told that "morality" is the sphere of abstract rules and obligations, not a realm concerned with the particularity of relationships. One of Gilligan's associates notes that because what is morally imperative for these girls is not considered "moral" by society, the result is a loss of trust in their judgment and moral integrity (Brown 1990:107). Gilligan (1990:26) puts it this way: "The wind of tradition blowing through women is a chill wind because it brings a message of exclusion."

What I would like to suggest, however, is that Gilligan's assertion of a dualistic moral theory is not consistent with the nature of her challenge to masculine moral theory. Although she is clear in her claim that the Western tradition of morality excludes the moral concerns traditionally associated with women, she goes on to argue that we can add this "different voice" to that moral tradition as a separate (or compatible) but equal component. There are two compelling sets of arguments that reveal this position to be both epistemologically confused and theoretically undesirable. First, the epistemological space defined by the Western moral tradition does not allow for the addition of an element that is equal to the standard of universal, absolute, formal principles that defines that tradition. This is particularly the case with Gilligan's theory because she proposes the addition of "feminine" elements of particularity and connection that contradict the very basis of the masculinist tradition. What I am arguing here is similar to Foucault's argument with regard to the human sciences in *The Order of Things* (1971). Foucault asserts that the epistemological space of modernity leaves no room for the human sciences. My assertion is that the same is true of Gilligan's theory relative to the western moral tradition: the *episteme* of moral theory explicitly prohibits the introduction of a rival element and, most particularly, a rival element with radically different epistemological assumptions. It follows that Gilligan's advocacy of a dualistic, non-hierarchical moral theory is simply not viable. My second argument is that if we assume that Gilligan's theory effectively deconstructs the unitary, abstract principles of masculine moral theory, then we are left with a much more radical conclusion than Gilligan herself advances. Gilligan claims that the "different" moral voice that women articulate is constituted by the relational experience of girls in childhood. Less explicitly she claims that men's more abstract and autonomous moral voice is also a result of childhood relationships. But if moral voices are a result of particular relational experiences, an expression of the subject that is constituted from these experiences, then it must follow that there are many different moral voices, not only two. The forces that constitute subjectivity are not encompassed by gender alone. Race, class, culture, and historical locatedness are also constitutive factors. The moral theory that is implicit in Gilligan's work demands that we must confront the problem of identifying and legitimizing the variety of moral voices that are linked to diversely constituted subjects. What I am suggesting, in other words, is that Gilligan's theory leads us into a radically new epsitemological space, but that space is not, as she envisions, one in which two identifiable and familiar voices interact, but, rather, one in which a plurality of voices are heard.

Gilligan and her commentators have much to say about the tradition of moral theory that they oppose and the alternatives that they propose. I will attempt to establish both of the above points through an analysis of these discussions. Gilligan casts her argument in opposition to the work of Kohlberg, but it is evident, not least of all to Gilligan herself, that Kohlberg is far from original, that he is a loyal son of the western moral tradition.

That the moral discourse of modernity has been dominated by formal, abstract principles, particularly as they were expressed by Kant, needs no argument here. Kohlberg relies heavily on one of the most prominent twentieth century representatives of the formalistic tradition, John Rawls. In *A Theory of Justice* Rawls presents a theory of moral development that is divided into three stages, the morality of authority, association and principles. The morality of authority which, Rawls stresses, is temporary, is based on love. The morality of principles, in contrast, is based on abstract "first principles" that rise above "contingencies" (1971:456). Kohlberg's stage sequence is a direct reflection of Rawls' theory. Kohlberg posits three levels of moral development, pre-conventional, conventional and post-conventional, with two stages within each level. The culmination of his sequence is Stage 6 which he characterizes as a morality of individual principles or conscience (1984:xxix).

Kohlberg makes many claims for these stages. First, he (1981:178) claims that they are scientific and empirical. Second, he claims that they are universal. Although he concedes that moral philosophy is not itself universal, he is adamant in his assertion that the basic moral principles are. Anyone who attains Stages 5 and 6 in any culture, he (1981:98) asserts, will attempt to formulate universal principles. Third, he claims that the stages are evolutionary both culturally and individually: the two highest stages are absent in preliterate cultures, and within particular cultures individuals progress to higher stages of moral development as they mature. His fourth claim is a negative one: he asserts that he does not mean to imply that the individuals who attain the higher stages are more moral. His claim, rather, is that the universal principles of the higher stages are more *adequate*, that they are more likely to resolve moral problems (1984:331). Unfortunately for the consistency of his theory, this claim seems to fly in the face of his additional assertion that Stage 6 is "what it means to judge morally. If you want to play the moral game, if you want to make decisions which anyone could agree upon in resolving social conflicts, Stage 6 is it" (1981:172).

This perspective on Kohlberg's work reveals the liability of his methodological presuppositions. Kohlberg begins with a precise conception of what morality *essentially* is – Stage 6 – and sets out to gather evidence to support his theory. He finds this evidence for a reason that Gilligan's researches clarified: educated people in this culture have been taught that "morality" consists of a set of abstract, universal principles. In defending the empirical evidence for his thesis Kohlberg is undaunted by his findings that only 5% of adult Americans test out at Stage 6, that these are people with extensive philosophical training, and that the majority of adult Americans (and nearly all women) are at the conventional level of morality (1981:100, 146, 192). Many critics of Kohlberg have attacked him for his elitism, sexism and ethnocentrism. These charges are accurate, but few of these critics have gone on to examine the methodological and epistemological presuppositions that lead him to his conclusions. "Moral judgments," Kohlberg (1981:170) declares, "unlike judgments of prudence or aesthetics, tend to be universal, inclusive, consistent and grounded on objective, impersonal or ideal grounds." It follows that other kinds of judgments will be declared *not to be moral* from Kohlberg's perspective. The girls that Gilligan interviews are hesitant to call their relational problems "moral" because they, too, have been taught that "morality" is the sphere of formalistic principles. The problem here is not that Kohlberg is "biased" and that this leads to his sexism and elitism. Gilligan is just as "biased" when she wants to extend the concept "moral" to the non-principled, relational, particularistic realm that has been associated with women. What Kohlberg has done is simply to define the "moral game" as it has been articulated in the western tradition and then confirmed his theory by interviewing men and boys who were educated in the rules of that game.

Given Kohlberg's perspective, it is not surprising that he is unimpressed by Gilligan's researches. He dismisses her work in a manner consistent with the moral tradition he espouses. Gilligan, he claims, is dealing with "special" relationships, those of the family. He (1984:338) concedes that his studies did not include the full domain of moral development and "welcomes" Gilligan's attempt to add to that domain. He (1984:232) proposes a conception of the dimensions of morality with the personal at one end, impartial justice at the other. He (1984:348) further asserts that as women enter men's occupations, they, too, will adopt the morality of justice over care. Kohlberg's "refutation" of Gilligan here fits her theory quite neatly into his traditional perspective: women's care relationships deal with private, "special," and hence inferior concerns; as women move out of this realm they, like men, will recognize the superiority of the justice perspective.

Some commentators on the Gilligan-Kohlberg controversy have argued that the dilemma that it poses can be resolved by looking at an alternative tradition in moral theory, one that opposes the universalism of the masculinist tradition. The theorists most often cited in the attempt to establish an alternative tradition are Simone Weil and Iris Murdoch.[6] Both Weil and Murdoch reject the unitary, abstract formalism of Kantian ethics and instead propose a contextual morality that is very similar to Gilligan's ethic of care. Weil argues against the tradition of individualism and rights that has defined moral thought in the western tradition. As an alternative she proposes a redefinition of justice as love and a separation of rights and justice. She (1977:325, 334) claims that "Justice consists in seeing that no harm is done to men" and that rights have no connection with love. Weil argues that central to the moral experience is the practice of a form of "attention." Iris Murdoch employs this concept of attention in her theory, making it the centerpiece of her account. Morality, Murdoch asserts, is constituted by "attention" to individuals. Against the dominant moral tradition Murdoch argues that morality is not usually a matter of choice that a rational, autonomous individual freely exercises through the application of abstract principles. Rather, moral choice is historically conditioned by the lives we lead and the loving connections we establish with other people (1970:37–8).

Many of the themes that Gilligan takes up in her description of the ethic of care are also expressed by Murdoch. Just as Gilligan attacked the presumption of the autonomous self, Murdoch attacks the Cartesian concept of self and argues that it offers an inadequate description of morality. Morality, she (1970:56–66) claims, is not an act of will, but the practice of attention tied to love. She (1970:28, 76, 87) criticizes the attempt to make morality a branch of science and logic, arguing that a better model would be that of art, which, unlike science, presents us with truthful images of the human condition. She (1970:71) concludes *The Sovereignty of Good* by arguing that moral philosophy needs a new "more realistic, less romantic terminology if it is to rescue thought about human destiny from a scientifically minded empiricism which is not equipped to deal with real problems."

Strictly speaking, Murdoch and Gilligan diverge on this point. Murdoch advocates replacing the justice tradition with the care perspective while Gilligan argues for a non-hierarchical dualism. A moral theorist more congruent with Gilligan's position is Lawrence Blum. Blum argues that the Kantian ethical tradition must be supplemented by the moral value of altruism. He (1980:5–6) argues that "The good we do our friends cannot be expressed within Kantian categories" because altruistic emotions are not grounded in universal moral principles. In a long and complex argument Blum seeks to establish what would seem to be an obvious point: that friendship is a legitimate moral phenomenon and that the caring love that we bestow on our friends is a moral good. Blum is careful not to deny Kantian ethics; his aim is rather to assert that there are other types of moral goodness. Although praising Murdoch for her emphasis on the particularity of morals, Blum argues that her view is incomplete; it must be supplemented by the Kantian, impartial view. Morality, he claims, has different spheres; from Blum's point of view Kant and Murdoch are simply expressing those different spheres (1986:360).

Weil, Murdoch and Blum all lend philosophical sophistication to Gilligan's advocacy of a different voice. Advocates of the philosophies of Weil and Murdoch argue that they supply precisely what Gilligan's theory lacks, the articulation of an alternative moral tradition. The argument for the existence of an alternative moral tradition, however, is difficult to sustain. Both Weil and Murdoch argue against what they themselves recognise is the dominant tradition in moral theory. Their voices do not constitute a recognised alternative, however, but, rather, amount to only faint voices of protest. Both are marginal figures in moral philosophy and both, not coincidentally, are women. Their position is more accurately described by Foucault's term "subjugated knowledges." The very existence of this knowledge establishes the power of the hegemonic discourse against which they argue.

Another objection to the existence of an alternative moral tradition is indicated by Blum. He (1988:482) notes that Kohlberg dismisses the care perspective as a junior partner in the justice/care union he proposes. What both Gilligan and Blum are claiming is that the private sphere of personal, particularistic relationships is not, as the justice tradition dictates, an amoral sphere but, rather, a legitimate moral realm equal to the abstract, formalistic sphere of justice and rights. The problem with this claim, however, is precisely the problem that Blum identified in Kohlberg's redefined theory. The logic of the justice tradition excludes the addition of particularistic, relativistic elements. If these elements are added they must, following the logic of that tradition, be relegated to an inferior status. Care cannot be added as an equal partner with justice because, as Kohlberg puts it so clearly, Stage 6 is simply what morality *is*. The justice tradition is epistemologically exclusive. It cannot incorporate the addition of a perspective that deconstructs its epistemological foundations.[7]

In addition to the advocacy of an alternative moral tradition, contemporary moral theorists have suggested another solution to the problems posed by Gilligan's discussion of the ethic of care: redefining justice in terms of care. This tactic was suggested by Weil whose separation of justice and rights was predicated on the definition of justice as love. This approach has been more extensively developed in two recent contributions to feminist political theory. In *Justice, Gender and the Family* Susan Moller Okin (1989:15) argues that the distinction between justice and care is overdrawn and that the best theorizing about justice includes care. What Okin tries to do in her book is nothing short of the transformation of the public/private distinction that restricts justice to the public sphere. Arguing that if families are unjust, we cannot create a just polity, Okin asserts that we must evaluate the justice of families in our society. Although she concedes that we do not now associate justice with intimacy, she argues that we would gain much from doing so (1989:135). Iris Young adopts a similar approach, but emphasizes a different aspect of the problem. Attacking Gilligan's separation of justice and care, Young asserts that feminists who retain the public/private distinction in moral theory fail to challenge impartiality in the public sphere (1990:97). Against this, Young argues that impartiality is an impossible ideal that masks the domination of the hegemonic group. A better ideal, she (1990:112) argues, is public fairness in a context of heterogeneity and partial discourse.[8]

The approaches of Okin and Young, however, like that of the other theorists discussed above, fail to assess the radical implications suggested by Gilligan's work. Okin and Young attempt to redefine the relationship between justice and care, but like the other theorists, they attempt to do so within the epistemological space that defines traditional moral theory. None of these approaches offers a radical challenge to that epistemology, an epistemology that defines the space of the "moral" within our tradition. They are attempts at redefinition, not transformation. More importantly, none challenges the notion that there is one "correct" approach to moral questions and that moral theory is unitary, or, in the case of Gilligan and Blum, a dualistic unity. All of these approaches are tyring to "get it right" without challenging the epistemological assumptions that compel them to look for the one right answer.[9] The search for the right answer, a new and "better" moral theory, however, will always be a futile one. First, it will run up against the solid wall of tradition that has already decreed the right answer to the question of morals (abstract principles) and allows for no other correct answers to this question. Second, attempts to find the right answer, however it is defined, will perpetuate the epistemology that grounds the tradition of moral theory these solutions purport to attack, an epistemology of absolute truths. What is required, on the contrary, is an approach that displaces that epistemology and, specifically, abandons the search for a single right answer.

Such an approach is entailed by Gilligan's understanding of the relational origins of moral voices, but she fails to draw out the implications of it in her work. Gilligan argues that two kinds of subjects evolve out of childhood experiences, masculine subjects whose moral voices speak in terms of separation and abstract principles and feminine subjects whose moral voices resonate with considerations of care and connection. There are several radical moves in this formulation of the self and morality. By deconstructing the absolutism of the justice tradition, Gilligan has moved us into a new epistemological space. What her work suggests is that discourses of morality have internal criteria of rightness and development, and that the unitary moral universe that has been presupposed in the Western tradition must be displaced. This entails a profound change in our understanding of the rules of the moral language game; it means that we cannot fit morality back into the epistemological space from which it has escaped. What Gilligan does not explore, however, is the question of whether there are more than two moral voices.[10] If Gilligan is correct in her assertion that moral voices are the product of the experiences through which the subject is constituted, then it would surely follow that there are more than the two subjects she posits. Although Gilligan's discussion of the constitution of masculine and feminine subjects is profound and insightful, she misses the opportunity to assess the different kinds of masculine and feminine subjects that will arise from different childhood experiences, differences caused by the influence of class, race and culture. These forces, along with gender, will exert a profound effect on the constitution of the subject and, hence, on the moral voices that these subjects speak.

Gilligan began by examining the "different" moral voice of women in our society. Her researches have spawned an examination of the masculine bias of moral theory and the valuation of an ethic of care defined in gender terms. What I am arguing here is that a very different line of investigation is suggested by Gilligan's researches: an exploration of the constitution of multiple moral voices. Gilligan's work effectively deconstructs the metanarrative of traditional moral theory. What is entailed by the rejection of the metanarrative of truth has been extensively explored in recent discussions of epistemology. What is entailed by the rejection of the metanarrative of morality and the positing of a heterogeneity of moral voices and moral selves, however, has been less extensively explored. Bernard Williams (1985:173) argues that we would be better off without the "peculiar institution" of morality. Iris Murdoch (1970:44) asserts that the abstract reasoning that characterizes traditional moral theory is a special case of moral reasoning, not the paradigm for all moral thinking. But we have to go much beyond this to explore the parameters of this approach to moral questions. Moral notions, like the subjects who hold them, are contextual and relational. They are constituted by the discourses or language games of the societies in which those subjects live. Gilligan claims that there are two moral voices constituted by the different childhood experiences of girls and boys. But this approach is too simple. It ignores the fact that masculinity and femininty are constituted differently in different cultures; racial and class differences also result in a variety of constructions of masculine and feminine subjects. It follows that there are many different moral voices even within a given society; moral standards will vary respective to these moral voices. Critics of this approach to morality will argue that this obviates the possibility of moral judgments. But although this position does eliminate reference to a moral metanarrative, it does not entail arbitrariness. It entails, rather, that our definition of the moral and the patterns of our moral thinking are, like all other aspects of our lives, constituted by discursive formations. The result is not moral anarchy, but, rather, an attention to the particularity of moral notions and the internal dynamics that constitute them. That this is a very different approach to morality is undeniable. That it is necessary to account for the different moral voices in particular human societies seems unavoidable.

## Notes

1. Gilligan is careful to avoid the gendered connection of these two perspectives, denying that the care perspective is exclusively feminine and the justice perspective exclusively masculine. But in her studies the gendered association of the perspectives is rarely challenged.
2. Flanagan and Jackson (1987) make a similar point.
3. See Walker (1984) for a discussion of complementarity and opposition. It is interesting that John Stuart Mill also posits the complementarity of male and female moral voices. His formulation, however, also fails to relieve the inferiority of the female voice.
4. Among others, see Eisenbery and Lennon (1983), Walker (1984), Broughton (1983), Nails (1983), Kohlberg (1982), Kerber *et al.* (1986), and Baumrind (1986).
5. See Friedman (1987) for a discussion of the irrelevance of statistical proof of the different voice. Deborah Tannen (1990) documents how the empathetic voice of women structures their self-understanding.
6. Annette Baier (1987) also cites Hume's moral theory as an example of this alternative tradition.
7. Two other theorists are frequently mentioned in this context: MacIntyre and Frankena. MacIntyre's theory of virtue is cited as compatible with Gilligan's ethics of care. But MacIntyre's communitarian ethics (1984) is profoundly hostile to women. Frankena (1963) is cited as advocating two moral axes, benevolence and justice. But for Frankena both benevolence and justice are defined as *abstract* moral principles.
8. See Benson (1990) for a redefinition of free agency along these lines.
9. See Tronto (1987) for another attempt to find the right answer, in this case by more securely grounding the ethic of care.
10. See Blum (1988) for a discussion of more than two moral voices.

## References

Baier, A. (1987). Hume: The women's moral theorist? In E. Kittay and D. Meyers (Eds.), *Women and moral theory*, 37–55. Totowa, NJ: Rowman and Littlefield.

Baumrind, D. (1986). Sex differences in moral reasoning: Response to Walker's [1984] conclusion that there are none. *Child Development* 57:511–521.

Benson, P. (1990). Feminist second thoughts about free agency. *Hypatia* 5(3):47–64.

Bernstein, E. and Gilligan, C. (1990). Unfairness and not listening: Converging themes in Emma Willard girls' development. In C. Gilligan, N. Lyons and T. Hanmer (Eds.), *Making connections*, 147–161. Cambridge, MA: Harvard University Press.

Blum, L. (1980). *Friendship, altruism and morality*. Boston: Routledge and Kegan Paul.

Blum, L. (1986). Iris Murdoch and the domain of the moral. *Philosophical Studies* 50:343–367.

Blum, L. (1988). Gilligan and Kohlberg: Implications for moral theory. *Ethics* 98(3):472–491.

Broughton, J. (1983). Women's rationality and men's virtues: A critique of gender dualism in Gilligan's theory of moral development. *Social Research* 50(3):597–642.

Brown, L. (1990). When is a moral problem not a moral problem? In C. Gilligan, N. Lyons and T. Hanmer (Eds.), *Making connections*, 88–109. Cambridge, MA: Harvard University Press.

Eisenberg, N. and Lennon, R. (1983). Sex differences in empathy and related capacities. *Psychological Bulletin* 94(1):100–131.

Flanagan, O. and Jackson, K. (1987). Justice, care and gender: The Kohlberg-Gilligan debate revisited. *Ethics* 97:622–637.

Foucault, M. (1971). *The order of things*. New York: Random House.

Frankena, W. K. (1963). *Ethics*. Englewood Cliffs, NJ: Prentice-Hall.

Friedman, M. (1987). Care and context in moral reasoning. In E. Kittay and D. Meyers (Eds.), *Women and moral theory*, 190–204. Totowa, NJ: Rowman and Littlefield.

Gilligan, C. (1982). *In a different voice*. Cambridge, MA: Harvard University Press.

Gilligan, C. (1986). Reply by Carol Gilligan. *Signs* 11(2):324–333.

Gilligan, C. (1987a). Moral orientation and moral development. In E. Kittay and D. Meyers (Eds.), *Women and moral theory*, 19–33. Totowa, NJ: Rowman and Littlefield.

Gilligan, C. (1987b). Remapping development: The power of divergent data. In C. Farnham (Ed.), *The impact of feminist research in the academy*, 77–94. Bloomington, IN: Indiana University Press.

Gilligan, C. (1989). Adolescent development reconsidered. In C. Gilligan et al. (Eds.), *Mapping the moral domain*, vii-xxxix. Cambridge, MA: Harvard University Press.

Gilligan, C. (1990). Preface. In C. Gilligan, N. Lyons and T. Hanmer (Eds.), *Making connections*, 6–29. Cambridge, MA: Harvard University Press.

Gilligan, C. and Wiggins, G. (1988). The origins of morality in early childhood relationships. In C. Gilligan et al. (Eds.), *Mapping the moral domain*. Cambridge, MA: Harvard University Press.

Gilligan, C., Rogers, A. and Brown, L. (1990). Epilogue. In C. Gilligan and T. Hanmer (Eds.), *Making connections*, 314–334. Cambridge, MA: Harvard University Press.

Greeno, C. and Maccoby, E. (1986). How different is the "different voice"? *Signs* 11(2):310–316.

Harding, S. (1986). *The science question in feminism*. Ithaca, NY: Cornell University Press.

Hardwig, J. (1984). Should women think in terms of rights? *Ethics* 94(3):441–455.

Held, V. (1987). Feminism and moral theory. In E. Kittay and D. Meyers (Eds.), *Women and moral theory*, 111–128. Totowa, NJ: Rowman and Littlefield.

Kerber, L. et al. (1986). On *In a different voice*: An interdisciplinary forum. *Signs* 11(2):304–333.

Kohlberg, L. (1981). *The philosophy of moral development*. San Francisco: Harper and Row.

162

Kohlberg, L. (1982). A reply to Owen Flanagan and some comments on the Puka-Goodpaster exchange. *Ethics* 92(3):513–528.
Kohlberg, L. (1984). *The psychology of moral development: Essays on moral development*, vol. 2. San Francisco: Harper and Row.
McIntyre, A. (1984). *After virtue*. 2nd ed. Notre Dame, IN: University of Notre Dame Press.
Murdoch, I. (1970). *The sovereignty of good*. London: Routledge and Kegan Paul.
Nails, D. (1983). Social-scientific sexism: Gilligan's mismeasure of man. *Social Research* 50(3):643–664.
Noddings, N. (1984). *Caring*. Berkeley, CA: University of California Press.
Okin, S. M. (1989). *Justice, gender and the family*. New York: Basic.
Rawls, J. (1971). *A theory of justice*. Cambridge, MA: Harvard University Press.
Ruddick, S. (1989). *Maternal thinking*. Boston: Beacon Press.
Stern, L. (1990). Conceptions of separation and connection in female adolescents. In C. Gilligan, N. Lyons and T. Hanmer (Eds.), *Making connections*, 73–87. Cambridge, MA: Harvard University Press.
Tannen, D. (1990). *You just don't understand: Women and men in conversatio*. New York: William Morrow.
Tronto, J. (1987). Women's morality: Beyond gender differences to a theory of care. *Signs* 12(4):644–663.
Walker, L. (1984). Sex differences in the development of moral reasoning: A critical review. *Child Development* 55:677–691.
Weil, S. (1977). *The Simone Weil reader*. Ed. G. Fanichas. New York: David McKay.
Williams, B. (1985). *Ethics and the limits of philosophy*. Cambridge, MA: Harvard University Press.
Young, I. M. (1990). *Justice and the politics of difference*. Princeton, NJ: Princeton University Press.

SYMPOSIUM ON CARE AND JUSTICE

# Hearing the Difference: Theorizing Connection

CAROL GILLIGAN

*Hearing the difference between a patriarchal voice and a relational voice defines a paradigm shift: a change in the conception of the human world. Theorizing connection as primary and fundamental in human life leads to a new psychology, which shifts the grounds for philosophy and political theory. A crucial distinction is made between a feminine ethic of care and a feminist ethic of care. Voice, relationship, resistance, and women become central rather than peripheral in this reframing of the human world.*

---

When I began the work that led to *In a Different Voice* (1982), the framework was invisible. To study psychology at that time was like seeing a picture without seeing the frame, and the picture of the human world had become so large and all-encompassing that it looked like reality or a mirror of reality, rather than a representation. It was startling then to discover that women for the most part were not included in research on psychological development, or when included were marginalized or interpreted within a theoretical bias where the child and the adult were assumed to be male and the male was taken as the norm.

Bringing women's voices into psychology posed an interpretive challenge: how to listen to women in women's terms, rather than assimilating women's voices to the existing theoretical framework. And this led to a paradigm shift. Men's disconnection from women, formerly construed as the separation of the self from relationships, and women's dissociation from parts of themselves, formerly interpreted as women's selflessness in relationships, now appeared problematic. Framed within an ethic of care, disconnections and dissociations which had been taken as foundational to conceptions of self and morality

*Hypatia* vol. 10, no. 2 (Spring 1995) © by Carol Gilligan

appeared instead to be careless and harmful. This is what I meant by a different voice, on a theoretical level.

It is said that a tuning fork, tuned to a particular pitch, will stop the vibrations in eight or nine others that are tuned to a different frequency (Noel 1995). Listening to human voices, Noel finds that one voice, speaking in a particular emotional register can stop the emotional vibrations in a group of people so that the environment in the room becomes deadened or flat. When this happens, she observes, it looks like silence but in fact the feelings and thoughts—the psychological energy—often move into the only place they can still live, and vibrate in silence, in the inner sense, until it becomes possible to bring them back into the world (Noel 1995).

I began writing about a different voice when I heard what George Eliot called the "still, small voice" speaking in a different psychological register. The voice that set the dominant key in psychology, in political theory, in law and in ethics, was keyed to separation: the separate self, the individual acting alone, the possessor of natural rights, the autonomous moral agent. Because the paradigmatic human voice conveyed this sense of separation as foundational, it was difficult to hear connection without listening under the conversation.

I was listening at the time to women who were pregnant and thinking about abortion in the immediate aftermath of the Roe v. Wade decision. Women's concerns were often driven by experiences of disconnection which rendered relationships difficult to maintain, but their voices carried a sense of connection, of living and acting in a web of relationships which went against the grain of the prevailing discourse of individual rights and freedom. Speaking of connection, of responsiveness and responsibility in relationships, women heard themselves sounding either selfish or selfless, because the opposition of self and other was so pervasive and so powerfully voiced in the public discourse. It was as if women's experience of connection was unnatural, unhealthy or unreal. But it was also ironic, because the Supreme Court had given women a legal voice in a matter of relationship and at the same time had framed that voice within a discourse of rights which made it impossible to speak about relationship, except in terms of justice—equality, fairness, reciprocity—or in terms of contractual obligation, neither of which had much bearing on many women's situation. In developing a different voice as a key to a new psychology and politics, I found that human voices and also relationship became more resonant and more vibrant.

On a theoretical and political level, on a personal and psychological level, this change in voice seemed essential. The existing paradigm was patriarchal; it was built on a disconnection from women which became part of the psychology of women and men. Theories of psychological and political development took this separation as foundational to the development of a sense of self, and as a result, the separate self and the selfless woman—the artifacts of a patriarchal psychology and politics—appeared natural and inevitable, necessary and good.

I come then to a crucial distinction: the difference between a feminine ethic of care and a feminist ethic of care. Care as a feminine ethic is an ethic of special obligations and interpersonal relationships. Selflessness or self-sacrifice is built into the very definition of care when caring is premised on an opposition between relationships and self-development. A feminine ethic of care is an ethic of the relational world as that world appears within a patriarchal social order: that is, as a world apart, separated politically and psychologically from a realm of individual autonomy and freedom which is the realm of justice and contractual obligation.

A feminist ethic of care begins with connection, theorized as primary and seen as fundamental in human life. People live in connection with one another; human lives are interwoven in a myriad of subtle and not so subtle ways. A feminist ethic of care reveals the disconnections in a feminine ethic of care as problems of relationship. From this standpoint, the conception of a separate self appears intrinsically problematic, conjuring up the image of rational man, acting out of relationship with the inner and outer world. Such autonomy, rather than being the bedrock for solving psychological and moral problems itself becomes the problem, signifying a disconnection from emotions and a blindness to relationships which set the stage for psychological and political trouble. This reframing of psychology in terms of connection changes the conception of the human world; in doing so, it establishes the ground for a different philosophy, a different political theory, a change in ethics and legal theory.

From this perspective, it becomes easier to see how the disconnection of the self from relationships and the separation of the public world from the private world define a realm of human activity which can only be maintained as long as someone cares about relationships, takes care of the private world and feels bound to other people. Historically this labor of caring has been the special obligation and unpaid labor of women, or the poorly paid labor of women who by virtue of class or caste difference are doubly excluded from the general domain of human freedom. Women living in patriarchal families, societies, and culture are bound internally and externally by obligations to care without complaint, on pain of becoming a bad woman: unfeminine, ungenerous, uncaring. Following women's psychological development, I found that for a woman to free herself from these moral strictures generally involves undoing a process of psychological dissociation and retrieving a voice that has been driven into silence (Gilligan 1982; Gilligan, Rogers and Noel 1992; Jack 1991; Linklater 1976). When this inner voice surfaces and comes into relationships, it sets off different vibrations and resonances. Then a discourse of relationship can replace the patriarchal construction of relationships. The tension between a relational psychology and a patriarchal social order is caught by a paradox:

living within the structures of patriarchy, women find themselves giving up relationship in order to have relationships (Gilligan 1990b; Gilligan n.d.b; Miller 1988). A feminist ethic of care became the voice of the resistance.

This brings me to my central point. Theorizing connection as primary and fundamental in human life directs attention to a growing body of supporting evidence which cannot be incorporated within the old paradigm. Studies of the infant as a member of a couple refute the depiction of the infant as locked up in egocentrism and provide compelling data showing that the desire for relationship, pleasure in connection, and the ability to make and maintain relationship are present at onset of development. Research on women and girls provides evidence of psychological capacities and relational knowledge that raises the most fundamental questions about the nature of cognitive and emotional and social development; otherwise, it would seem impossible that women and girls know what they know. These psychological studies of infants and women recast the understanding of the developmental process in relational terms; they have relied on new research methods and they demonstrate the power of a relational approach in research as well as in psychotherapy (Murray and Trevarthen 1985; Stern 1985; Tronick 1989; Brown and Gilligan 1992; Gilligan 1982; Gilligan, Kreider, and O'Neill n.d.; Jordan et al. 1991; Miller and Stiver 1994; Relke 1993).

In *History After Lacan*, Brennan describes the ending of the ego's era. It began with the joining of the Cartesian self and capitalism in the seventeenth century. Brennan characterizes the separate self or the autonomous ego as a foundational fantasy which does not appear as a fantasy as long as the ego's omnipotence and control are socially constructed as reality, wrapping the imperial "I" in a cultural cocoon.

> To allow that my feelings physically enter you, or yours me, to think that we both had the same thought at the same time because it was literally in the air, is to think in a way that really puts the subject in question. In some ways, the truly interesting thing is that this questioning has begun. (Brennan 1993, 41)

I am interested in women's relationship to this societal and cultural transformation because the history of this relationship is in danger of being buried. Listening to women's voices clarified the ethic of care, not because care is essentially associated with women or part of women's nature, but because women for a combination of psychological and political reasons voiced relational realities that were otherwise unspoken or dismissed as inconsequential. A patriarchal social order depends for its regeneration on a disconnection from women, which in women takes the form of a psychological dissociation: a process of inner division that makes it possible for a woman not to know what she knows, not to think what she thinks, not to feel what she feels. Dissociation cuts through experience and memory, and when these cuts become part of cultural history, women lose the grounds of their experience and with it, their sense of reality.

In studies of girls' psychological development, my colleagues and I have witnessed the onset of dissociative processes at adolescence (Brown and Gilligan 1992; Gilligan, Brown, and Rogers 1990; Rogers 1993). Girls at this time face a relational crisis or developmental impasse which has its parallel in the relational crisis of boys' early childhood. Freud called this crisis the Oedipus complex and theorized it as a turning point in psychological development, marking a definitive intersection between psychological development and the requisites of civilization. The resolution of the Oedipus Complex structures the connection between inner and outer worlds.

I have come to theorize a similar crisis in girls' lives at adolescence as a crisis of voice and relationship, also marking a definitive joining between psychological development and civilization. This is the time when girls are pressed from within and without to take in and take on the interpretive framework of patriarchy and to regulate their sexuality, their relationships, their desires and their judgments in its terms. As for boys in early childhood, this internalization of a patriarchal voice leads to a loss of relationship or a compromise between voice and relationships, leaving a psychological wound or scar. The asymmetry I have posited between boys' and girls' development finds confirmation in the considerable evidence showing that boys are more psychologically at risk than girls throughout the childhood years and that girls' psychological strengths and resilience are suddenly at risk in adolescence (see Gilligan n.d.a; Debold 1994).

Girls' initiation into womanhood has often meant an initiation into a kind of selflessness, which is associated with care and connection but also with a loss of psychological vitality and courage. To become selfless means to lose relationship or to lose one's voice in relationships. This loss of relationship leads to a muting of voice, leaving inner feelings of sadness and isolation. In effect, the young woman becomes shut up within herself.

When the release of women's voices in the 1970s put an end to this house arrest and brought the disconnection from women out into the open, women revealed the startling omission of women from psychology and from history and also discovered the extent of women's dissociation: women's ignorance of their bodies, themselves and other women. The association of women with care became problematic for many women because when care is framed as a ethic of selflessness and self-sacrifice in relationships it enjoins these inner divisions in women and catches women in a psychological and political trap. Claiming human status, women brought themselves and their concerns about relationship into the public arena, placing high on the political agenda relationships with children, family relationships, relationships with the environment, relationships with the future as developed through education and health care, and above all, the problem of violence in domestic as well as national and international relationships. In this way, women reframed women's problems as human concerns.

Any discussion of a care ethic, then, has to begin with the issue of framing. What is the framework within which we will compare and contrast justice and care? When I hear care discussed as a matter of special obligations or as an ethic of interpersonal relationships, I hear the vestiges of patriarchy. When I listen to care versus justice debated as if there was no framework, I hear the implicit patriarchal framework silently slipping back into place.

In analyzing psychological theory and women's psychological development, I have attempted to show how a feminist ethic of care repudiates a feminine ethic of care on the grounds that a feminine ethic of care rests on a faulty notion of relationship. This fault erupts in women's lives in the form of a psychological crisis. A paradox then becomes evident: women are "doing good and feeling bad" (Miller 1976); women are silencing themselves in order to be with other people; women are giving up relationship for the sake of having relationships, and then missing themselves and missing relationship or feeling stranded in a confusing isolation which is often filled with self-condemnation (Gilligan 1977; Gilligan 1982; Gilligan 1990b; Jack 1991; Miller 1988; Miller 1991; Stern 1990).

Hearing the difference between a patriarchal voice and a relational voice means hearing separations which have sounded natural or beneficial as disconnections which are psychologically and politically harmful. Within a relational framework, the separate self sounds like an artifact of an outmoded order: a disembodied voice speaking as if from nowhere. In the absence of relational resonances, the exposure of an inner voice is psychologically dangerous because its openness to vibrations heightens vulnerability. Hearing a relational voice as a new key for psychology and politics, I have theorized both justice and care in relational terms. Justice speaks to the disconnections which are at the root of violence, violation and oppression, or the unjust use of unequal power. Care speaks to the dissociations which lead people to abandon themselves and others: by not speaking, not listening, not knowing, not seeing, not caring and ultimately not feeling by numbing themselves or steeling themselves against the vibrations and the resonances which characterize and connect the living world.

The talking cure or cure through relationship which Freud and Breuer discovered to be so psychologically powerful and effective finds its analogue in the public arena which Arendt saw as essential to the health of a democratic society: a place where people can come and speak freely. The antidote to psychological repression is the antidote to totalitarianism. When a relational voice sets the key for psychology, political theory, law, ethics and philosophy, it frees the voices of women and men and also the voices of the disciplines from patriarchal strictures.

Hope is a dangerous emotion because it creates such vulnerability to disappointment, and the process of change is never straightforward. The desire for relationship may jeopardize relationships; the desire to speak will heighten vulnerability and may lead to psychological harm. The psychological knowledge that has been gained in the past quarter century provides a map for the resistance and a guide to relationship, marking the pitfalls of disconnection and dissociation. However arduous the terrain and however conflicted the journey, however strong the pulls toward repetition and return, a different voice has been heard and a new direction charted.

## REFERENCES


Belenky, Mary F., Blythe Clinchy, Nancy Goldberger, and Jill M. Tarule. 1986. *Women's ways of knowing*. New York: Basic Books.

Bordo, Susan. 1994. *Unbearable weight: Feminism, the body and western culture*. New York: Routledge.

Brennan, Teresa. 1993. *History after Lacan*. New York: Routledge.

Brown, Lyn Mikel and Gilligan, Carol. 1991. Listening for voices in narratives of relationship. In *Narrative and storytelling: Implications for understanding moral development*, ed. M. Tappan and M. Packer. New Directions for Child Development. San Francisco: Jossey-Bass.

———. 1992. *Meeting at the crossroads: Women's psychology and girls' development*. New York: Ballantine Books.

Debold, Elizabeth. 1994. Toward an understanding of gender differences in psychological distress: A Foucauldian integration of Freud, Gilligan and cognitive development theory. Qualifying Paper, Harvard Graduate School of Education. Cambridge, MA.

Freud, Sigmund and Josef Breuer. [1895] 1974. *Studies on hysteria*. London: Penguin Books.

Freud, Sigmund. [1899/1900]. *The interpretation of dreams*. London: Penguin Books.

Gilligan, Carol. 1977. In a different voice: Women's conceptions of self and morality. *Harvard Educational Review* 47: 481-517.

———. 1982. *In a different voice: Psychological theory and women's development*. Cambridge: Harvard University Press.

———. 1990a. Teaching Shakespeare's sister: Notes from the underground of female adolescence. In *Making connections*, ed. Gilligan, Lyons, and Hamner. Cambridge: Harvard University Press.

———. 1990b. Joining the resistance: Psychology, politics, girls and women. *Michigan Quarterly Review* 29(4): 501-36.

———. n.d.a. The centrality of relationship in human development: A puzzle, some evidence, and a theory. In *Development and vulnerability in close relationships*, ed. G. Noam and K. Fischer. New Jersey: Erlbaum.

———. n.d.b. Remembering Iphigenia: Voice, resonance, and a talking cure. In *The inner world in the outer world*, ed. E. Shapiro. New Haven: Yale University Press.

Gilligan, Carol, Lyn Mikel Brown, and Annie G. Rogers. 1990. Psyche embedded: A place for body, relationships, and culture in personality theory. In *Studying persons and lives*, ed. Albert Rabin et al. New York: Springer.

Gilligan, Carol, Annie G. Rogers, and Deborah Tolman, eds. 1991. *Women, girls and psychotherapy: Reframing resistance*. Birmingham, NY: Haworth Press.

Gilligan, Carol, Annie G. Rogers, and Normi Noel. 1992 Cartography of a lost time: Women, girls and relationships. Paper presented at the Lilly Conference on Youth and Caring, Daytona Beach, Florida, and at the Harvard Conference, Learning From Women, April, 1993.

Gilligan, Carol, Holly Kreider, and Kate O'Neill. n.d. Transforming psychological inquiry: Clarifying and strengthening connections. *Psychoanalytic Review*. In press.

Jack, Dana Crowley. 1991. *Silencing the self: Depression and women*. New York: Harper Collins.

Jordan, Judith V., Jean Baker Miller, Irene P. Stiver, and Janet Surrey. 1992. *Women's growth in connections*. New York: Guilford Press.

Linklater, Kristin. 1976. *Freeing the natural voice*. New York: Drama Book Publishers.

Miller, Jean Baker. 1976. *Toward a new psychology of women*. Boston: Beacon Press.

———. 1991. The development of women's sense of self. In *Women's growth in connections*, ed. Jordan et al. New York: Guilford Press.

———. 1988. Connections, disconnections and Violations. Wellesley, MA: Stone Center Works in Progress.

Miller, Jean Baker and Irene P. Stiver. 1994. A relational reframing of therapy. Wellesley, MA: Stone Center Works in Progress.

Murray, Lynne and Colwyn Trevarthen. 1985. Emotional regulation of interactions between two-month-olds and their mothers. In *Social perception in infants*, ed. T. Field and N. Fox. New Jersey: Ablex.

Noel, Normi. 1995. Personal communication.

Nussbaum, Martha C. 1986. *The fragility of goodness*. Cambridge, England: Cambridge University Press.

Relke, Diana M. 1993. Foremothers who cared: Paula Heimann, Margaret Little and the female tradition in psychoanalysis. *Feminism and Psychology* 3(1): 89-109.

Rogers, Annie. 1993. Voice, play and a practice of ordinary courage in girls' and women's lives. *Harvard Educational Review*. 63(3): 265-95.

Rogers, Annie G. 1995. Exiled voices: Dissociation and repression in women's narratives of trauma. Wellesley, MA. Stone Center Works in Progress.

Stern, Daniel. 1985. *The interpersonal world of the infant*. New York: Basic Books.

Stern, Lori. 1991. Disavowing the self in female adolescence. In *Women, girls and psychotherapy: Reframing resistance*, ed. Carol Gilligan et al. Birmingham, NY: Haworth Press.

Taylor, Jill McLean, Carol Gilligan, and Amy Sullivan, eds. n.d. *Holding difference, sustaining hope: Women and girls, race and relationship*. Cambridge: Harvard University Press. In press.

Tronick, Edward Z. 1989. Emotions and emotional communication in infants. *American Psychologist* 44(2): 112-19.

# [26]

SYMPOSIUM ON CARE AND JUSTICE

# The Meshing of Care and Justice

VIRGINIA HELD

*This essay attempts to work out how justice and care and their related concerns fit together. I suggest that as a basic moral value, care should be the wider moral framework into which justice should be fitted.*

Feminist understandings of justice and care have by now made clear, in my view, that these are different values, reflecting different ways of interpreting moral problems and of expressing moral concern. And feminist discussion has also made clear that neither can be dispensed with: both are highly important for morality. Not all feminists agree, by any means, but this is how I see the debates of the last decade on these issues (Baier 1994; Card 1991; Friedman 1993; Gilligan et al. 1988; Held 1993; Noddings 1984; Okin 1989; Tronto 1993).

What remains to be worked out, as I see it, is how justice and care and their related concerns fit together. How does the framework that structures justice, equality, rights, and liberty mesh with the network that delineates care, relatedness, and trust? Or are they incompatible views we must, at least at a given time and in a given context, choose between?

One clearly unsatisfactory possibility is to think that justice is a value appropriate to the public sphere of the political, while care belongs to the private domains of family and friends and charitable organizations. Feminist analyses have shown how faulty are traditional divisions between the personal and the political, but even if we use cleaned-up versions of these concepts, we can see how unsatisfactory it is to assign justice to public life and care to private, although I myself in earlier work may have failed to say enough along these lines (Held 1984). I have argued that we need different moral approaches for different domains, and have tried to map out which are suitable for which domains. And there is an initial plausibility, certainly, in thinking of justice as

*Hypatia* vol. 10, no. 2 (Spring 1995) © by Virginia Held

a primary value in the domain of law, and care as a primary value in the domain of the family. But more needs to be said.

Justice is badly needed in the family as well as in the state: in a more equitable division of labor between women and men in the household, in the protection of vulnerable family members from domestic violence and abuse, in recognizing the rights of family members to respect for their individuality. In the practice of caring for children or the elderly, justice requires us to avoid paternalistic and maternalistic domination.

At the same time, we can see that care is badly needed in the public domain. Welfare programs are an intrinsic part of what contemporary states provide, and no feminist should fail to acknowledge the social responsibilities they reflect, however poorly. The nightwatchman state is not a feminist goal. Almost all feminists recognize that there should be much more social and public concern for providing care than there now is in the United States, although it should be provided in appropriate and empowering ways very different from the current system of welfare. There should be greatly increased public concern for child care, education, and health care, infused with the values of care.

Caretaking is needed by everyone when they are children, ill, or very old, and it is needed by some most of their lives. Assuring that care is available to those who need it should be a central political concern, not one imagined to be a solely private responsibility of families and charities. Providing care has always fallen disproportionately to women and minorities, who do the bulk of unpaid or badly paid actual work of caring for those needing it. But in addition to a fairer division of responsibilities for care, the care made available through the institutions of the welfare state needs to be strengthened as well as reformed. Care and justice, then, cannot be allocated to the separate spheres of the private and the public. But they are different, and they are not always compatible.

Consider the category of "welfare" in its narrower sense rather than what is referred to by the term "welfare state." One way of thinking about the issues surrounding welfare and recommending action would be from a perspective of justice, equality, and rights. We could then recognize welfare as something to which each person is entitled by right under conditions of need. Welfare rights would be recognized as basic rights guaranteeing persons the resources needed to live. Against the traditional liberal view that freedom is negative only, we would recognize the positive rights of persons to what they need to act freely. And persons in need would be seen as entitled to the means to live, not as undeserving suppliants for private or public charity. An interpretation of such rights within the framework of justice would then be likely to yield monetary payments such as social security checks and unemployment insurance supplemented by other such payments for those in need. For many competent persons whose only major problem is a lack of money or a temporary lack of employment, such arrangements would seem recommended, and would be preferable to an array of social workers who are expected to practice care but who, whether because of paternalistic tendencies or bureaucratic constraints, often threaten the autonomy of persons in need.

Many persons, however, are not competent, autonomous, and only temporarily unemployed. Due to deficiencies of care at earlier stages or in various areas of their lives, their needs are complex and persistent. Inadequately cared for as children, at home, in school, and elsewhere, or inadequately provided with work and earning experience, they have grown up with more serious problems than a lack of money, or they suffer from illness or disability. In such cases care itself is needed. It should be addressed to specific persons and their needs. Dealing with these needs requires other specific persons to provide actual care and caring labor, not a machine turning out equal payments to all in a given category. The care should be sensitive and flexible, allowing for the interaction of care provider and care receiver in such a way that the care receiver is empowered to develop toward needing less care when such a decrease is part of a process of growth or training or recovery. When the care needed will be lasting, practices should evolve that preclude the provision of care from becoming dominating, and the receiving of care from becoming humiliating.

Whether we employ the perspectives of justice or care will affect how we interpret the moral problems involved and what we recommend as institutional policies or individual actions. We might try to combine care and justice into a recommendation concerning welfare that each person is entitled to the care needed for appropriate development, but such a recommendation will remain an abstract and empty formulation until we deal with just the kinds of very different policies and practices I've tried to outline.

If we try to see justice and care as alternative interpretations that we can apply to the same moral problem, as I think Carol Gilligan recommends, we can try to think of care and justice as different but equally valid. But we are still left with the question of which interpretation to apply when we act, or which to appeal to when we draw our recommendations. If we are merely describing the problem and possible interpretations of it, as in alternative literary accounts of it, we could maintain both of these alternative moral frameworks and not have to choose between them. But if policy decisions must be made about the problem, we will sometimes have to choose between these interpretations. If we use the analogy Gilligan suggests, should we see the figure as a duck or a rabbit? Moral theory should provide guidance for choice about actions and policies, and the problem of choosing between the interpretive frameworks of justice and care often persists after we have clarified both frameworks.

When the concerns of justice and care conflict, how should we try to reconcile these values? Does either have priority? Many philosophers have supposed that justice is the primary value of political institutions, but the example concerning welfare that I have been discussing is one from an important function of the modern state, and it did not yield the clear priority of justice over care. To suppose that the "justice system" of courts and law enforcement is the primary function of the contemporary state is surely unhelpful; to what extent it should or should not be would be among the very questions to be addressed by an adequately integrated ethic.

One possibility I have considered in the past is that justice deals with moral minimums, a floor of moral requirements beneath which we should not sink as we avoid the injustices of assault and disrespect. In contrast, care deals with what is above and beyond the floor of duty. Caring well for children, for instance, involves much more than honoring their rights to not be abused or deprived of adequate food; good care brings joy and laughter. But as a solution to our problem, I am coming to think that this is not clear. Perhaps one can have ever more justice in the sense of more and more understanding of rights, equality, and respect. And certainly there are minimums of care that *must* be provided for persons to live, though excellent care will far exceed them.

Another possible metaphor is that justice and rights set more or less absolute bounds or moral constraints within which we pursue our various visions of the good life, which would for almost everyone include the development of caring relationships. But this metaphor collapses for many of the same reasons as does that of justice as a floor of moral minimums. For instance, if there is anything that sets near absolute constraints on our pursuit of anything, including justice, it is responding to the needs of our children for basic care.

I now think—somewhat tentatively—that care is the wider moral framework into which justice should be fitted. Care seems to me the most basic moral value. As a practice, empirically described, we can say that without care we cannot have life at all. All human beings require a great deal of care in their early years, and most of us need and want caring relationships throughout our lives. As a value, care indicates what many practices ought to involve. When, for instance, necessities are provided without the relational human caring children need, children do not develop well, if at all. And when, in society, individuals treat each other with only the respect that justice requires, the social fabric of trust and concern can be missing or disappearing.

Though justice is surely a most important moral value, much life has gone on without it, and much of that life has been moderately good. There has, for instance, been little justice within the family, but much care; so we can have care without justice. Without care, however, there would be no persons to respect, either in the public system of rights—even if it could be just—or in the family. But care is not simply causally primary, it is more inclusive as a value. Within a network of caring, we can and should demand justice, but justice should not then push care to the margins, imagining justice's political embodiment as the model of morality, which is, I think, what has been done.

From a perspective of care, persons are relational and interdependent, not the individualistic autonomous agents of the perspective of justice and rights. This relational view is the better view of human beings, of persons engaged in developing human morality. We can decide to treat persons *as* individuals, to be the bearers of rights, for the sake of constructing just political and other institutions. But we should not forget the reality and the morality this view obscures. Persons *are* relational and interdependent. We can and should value autonomy, but it must be developed and sustained within a framework of relations of trust.

At the levels of global society and of our own communities, we should develop frameworks of caring about and for one another as human beings. These will of course be different from caring about and for the human beings who are members of our families or who are friends. We should care for one another as persons in need of a habitable environment with a sufficient absence of violence and with sufficient provision of care for human life to flourish. We need to acknowledge the moral values of the practices and family ties underlying the caring labor on which human life has always depended, and we need to consider how the best of these values can be better realized. Within a recognized framework of care we should see persons as having rights and as deserving justice, most assuredly. But we should embed this picture, I think, in the wider tapestry of human care.

Of course, in these short remarks, I cannot elaborate or fill in this tapestry. What I am trying to do is to suggest the directions in which I think we should be heading as we explore these issues of feminist morality.

## REFERENCES


Baier, Annette. 1994. *Moral prejudices: Essays on ethics*. Cambridge: Harvard University Press.

Card, Claudia, ed. 1991. *Feminist ethics*. Lawrence: University Press of Kansas.

Friedman, Marilyn. 1993. *What are friends for? Feminist perspectives on personal relationships and moral theory*. Ithaca: Cornell University Press.

Gilligan, Carol, Janie Victoria Ward, and Jill McLean Taylor, eds. 1988. *Mapping the moral domain: A contribution of women's thinking to psychological theory and education*. Cambridge: Harvard University Graduate School of Education.

Held, Virginia. 1984. *Rights and goods: Justifying social action*. New York: Free Press.

———. 1993. *Feminist morality: Transforming culture, society, and politics*. Chicago: University of Chicago Press.

Noddings, Nel. 1984. *Caring: A feminine approach to ethics and moral education*. Berkeley: University of California Press.

Okin, Susan Moller. 1989. *Justice, gender, and the family*. New York: Basic Books.

Tronto, Joan C. 1993. *Moral boundaries: A political argument for an ethic of care*. New York: Routledge.

[27]

# Liberating Care

Critical thinking about care and caring relationships is a burgeoning area of moral theory. The widespread attention shown by most of the theorists in this area to women's experiences and perspectives is utterly unique in the history of philosophical ethics and a momentous, if sadly belated, achievement. This is not to suggest, however, that all theorists of care ethics share similar approaches or concerns. In the growing and lively field of care ethics, there is a great deal of diversity and debate. The previous chapter touched on one major area of controversy: the relationship between considerations of care and considerations of justice. This chapter addresses the adequacy—or inadequacy—of an ethic of care to illuminate women's cultural subordination.

A brief review of Gilligan's approach to the interconnections between care and justice will soon bring issues of women's subordination into view. In the previous chapter, I argued that morally adequate care incorporates considerations of justice. Gilligan herself, at times, proposes this integration by suggesting that the highest level of moral reasoning, the postconventional level, combines considerations of care with those of justice.[1] In Gilligan's view, the important assumption that a justice and rights perspective adds to a care perspective is that "self and other are equal." The concept of rights also carries with it the notion that "the interests of the

1. Carol Gilligan, *In a Different Voice* (Cambridge: Harvard University Press, 1982), e.g., p. 174.

self can be considered legitimate." On the basis of this insight, women, as care givers, are enabled "to consider it moral to care not only for others but for themselves."[2] Beyond this point, psychologist Gilligan understandably does not develop in detail the philosophical possibilities of her own proposed integration.

Feminists diverge over the relevance of justice to care. Some agree with Gilligan that the integrative route is very promising and have further developed the philosophical details of this approach.[3] Others eschew the integrative approach altogether. Nel Noddings, for example, regards the ethic of universal justice as a masculine illusion.[4]

It is noteworthy that Gilligan's later writings do not claim that care and justice are the *only* two moral perspectives available. These are the only two perspectives she investigates, however, and she regards them as the two most widely preferred orientations.[5] On

2. Ibid., p. 149.

3. These works include Annette Baier, "The Need for More than Justice," in Marsha Hanen and Kai Nielsen, eds., *Science, Morality, and Feminist Theory, Canadian Journal of Philosophy* suppl. vol. 13 (1987): 41–56; Owen Flanagan and Kathryn Jackson, "Justice, Care, and Gender: The Kohlberg-Gilligan Debate Revisited," *Ethics* 97 (April 1987): 622–37; Susan Moller Okin, "Reason and Feeling in Thinking about Justice," *Ethics* 99 (January 1989): 229–49; Susan Moller Okin, *Justice, Gender, and the Family* (New York: Basic Books, 1989); and Claudia Card, "Gender and Moral Luck," in Owen Flanagan and Amélie Oksenberg Rorty, eds., *Identity, Character, and Morality* (Cambridge, Mass.: MIT Press, 1990), pp. 199–218. In the previous chapter, after suggesting that the equality of self and other is not all there is to the full-blown notion of justice, I went on to outline other considerations of justice that integrate in a relevant way with considerations of care in intimate relationships.

4. Nel Noddings, *Caring: A Feminine Approach to Ethics and Moral Education* (Berkeley: University of California Press, 1984), p. 90. More recently, in response to debate over this point, Noddings has postponed her final verdict on the relevance of justice to care; see her "A Response," *Hypatia* 5 (Spring 1990): 120.

5. Gilligan writes, "The tendency for people to organize experiences of conflict and choice largely in terms of justice or of care has been a consistent finding of research on moral orientation": "Prologue: Adolescent Development Reconsidered," in Carol Gilligan, Janie Victoria Ward, Jill McLean Taylor, with Betty Bardige, eds., *Mapping the Moral Domain* (Cambridge: Harvard Center for the Study of Gender, Education, and Human Development, 1988), p. xviii.

Gilligan's view, "people tend to focus their attention either on problems of unfairness or on problems of disconnection."[6]

Many feminists criticize care ethics for its relative silence about oppressive social practices and the cultural subordination of women. Gilligan seems to regard a concern for "problems of oppression" and "problems stemming from inequality" as reflecting the justice perspective.[7] Although many feminist concerns about oppression and subordination do reflect an orientation to matters of justice and injustice,[8] not all of them have this foundation. Not all problems of oppression are problems of unfairness or the violation of rights.

Some features of women's subordination pertain to the varied forms of care, the nature of traditional caretaking practices in our culture, and the complications of moral personality and moral identity that emerge with deep, long-term involvement in care giving. Care ethics has neglected the way caring practices themselves have been bound up with women's subordination. As a result of this neglect, care ethics as currently formulated seems incapable of sufficiently grounding the efforts to overcome the diverse forms of subordination affecting women. This is the issue to which we now turn.

I begin in section 1 by surveying some feminist criticisms of care ethics that point to its failure to illuminate women's cultural subordination or the means necessary to overcome it. This survey is followed, in section 2, by an exploration of the importance of care for female care givers themselves and some of the varied forms that care should take. Bernard Williams's quasi-hypothetical example of a painter seeking moral luck, who abandons his family to pursue his art, sets the stage for my query, in section 3, about the heavier caretaking responsibilities that befall women as compared to men. My discussion concludes in section 4 with a comparative exploration of the different sorts of care that women and

6. Ibid., p. xix.

7. Ibid., pp. xvii–xviii.

8. See Susan Moller Okin, *Justice, Gender, and the Family* (New York: Basic Books, 1989).

men provide each other in the context of heterosexual relationships and the way this difference contributes to women's subordination.

## 1. A Critical Feminist Overview of Care Ethics

Care ethics offers at least one very alluring feature: high moral esteem for the traditional caring work done by women. Yet, because of certain problems in care ethics, feminists wonder whether, on balance, this ethic hinders more than it helps women seeking to overcome their cultural subordination. Claudia Card and Joan Tronto, for example, observe that merely presenting care ethics as a distinctively female ethic is not enough to establish its moral adequacy or its moral superiority to other ethical perspectives.[9] Barbara Houston worries that to celebrate feminine virtues and perspectives is to risk glorifying the oppressive conditions under which they arose.[10]

Card and Tronto point out that relationships differ in their worth, that not every relationship is valuable, and that care ethics provides no basis for critical reflection on relationships.[11] Card suggests that, having developed under conditions of oppression, the

9. Card, "Gender and Moral Luck," p. 201; Joan Tronto, "Beyond Gender Difference to a Theory of Care," *Signs* 12, no. 4 (1987): 646.

10. Barbara Houston, "Rescuing Womanly Virtues: Some Dangers of Moral Reclamation," in Hanen and Nielsen, *Science, Morality, and Feminist Theory*, p. 247. On this point, Houston draws extensively upon Joan Ringelheim, "Women and the Holocaust: A Reconsideration of Research," *Signs* 10, no. 4 (1985): 759–60. In that essay, Ringelheim offers a newly cautious rereading of some of her own previous research findings which had adopted a "cultural feminist" approach. Cultural feminism, in general, honors the behavior, values, and perspectives of women more highly than those of men, even when the former have arisen under conventional conditions. Ringelheim's later skepticism about a cultural feminist approach directly responds to the temptation that a feminist might feel to regard care ethics as a sign of women's moral superiority.

11. Card, "Gender and Moral Luck," p. 215; Tronto, "Beyond Gender Difference to a Theory of Care," p. 660.

care perspective has been needed for adaptation to those oppressive conditions and may not embody genuine virtue.[12] In the views of both Card and Houston, care ethics ignores the possibility that a history of oppression has inflicted moral damage on women. Of special concern to feminists is the moral damage that further entrenches women's subordination,[13] for example, the morally hazardous forms of deference that are a frequent risk when women care for men.[14]

Card and Sarah Hoagland, in addition, both point out that care ethics lacks a political or institutional focus. It ignores the institutionally structured differentials of power and authority among different persons, especially those that constitute the gender hierarchy. It is thereby incapable of conceptualizing the oppressive, institutionally patriarchal context in which care takes place and that may compromise the otherwise high moral value of care.[15] In Jeffner Allen's view, the nonviolence of care is a liability to women under oppressive circumstances, for it disables women from resisting whatever abuse they experience in heterosexual relationships.[16]

Hoagland and Tronto, furthermore, recognized that care ethics ignores moral responsibilities to distant strangers and those for whom we do not feel particularly caring; care ethics thereby threat-

12. Card, "Gender and Moral Luck," pp. 204–5, 215–16.

13. Ibid., p. 216; Houston, "Rescuing Womanly Virtues," p. 253.

14. See Sandra Bartky, *Femininity and Domination* (New York: Routledge, 1990), especially chap. 7, "Feeding Egos and Tending Wounds: Deference and Disaffection in Women's Emotional Labor"; also see my "Moral Integrity and the Deferential Wife," *Philosophical Studies* 47 (January 1985): 141–50.

15. Card, "Gender and Moral Luck," p. 205; Sarah Hoagland, "Some Thoughts about 'Caring,' " in Claudia Card, ed., *Feminist Ethics* (Lawrence: University Press of Kansas, 1991), pp. 253, 260. For a good, early discussion of how care may be compromised by an institutionally oppressive context, see Larry Blum, Marcia Homiak, Judy Housman, and Naomi Scheman, "Altruism and Women's Oppression," in Sharon Bishop and Marjorie Weinzweig, eds., *Philosophy and Women* (Belmont, Calif.: Wadsworth, 1979), pp. 190–200; reprinted from *Philosophical Forum* 5 (1975).

16. Jeffner Allen, *Lesbian Philosophy* (Palo Alto, Calif.: Institute for Lesbian Studies, 1986), p. 35.

ens to devolve into a mere defense of conventional relationships.[17] Care ethics also fails to represent diversity among women. Either it suffers from positive biases of race, class, ethnicity, and national culture, as Michele Moody-Adams charges,[18] or, at the very least, it suffers by its simple failure to represent specific differences among women, such as the racial diversity discussed by Carol Stack.[19]

Despite such limitations, care ethics, in my view, makes a profound contribution to contemporary moral theory. This contribution is qualified but not fundamentally undermined even by the limitations mentioned above.[20] Care ethics raises caring, nurturing, and the maintenance of interpersonal relationships to the status of foundational moral importance. It directs our attention to the realms of human life in which these activities have been the primary focus, especially family life, friendship, and sexual and other close personal relationships. These realms of life have, until the last two decades or so, been neglected or relegated to a derivative and

17. Hoagland, "Some Thoughts about Caring," pp. 260–61; Tronto, "Beyond Gender Differences to a Theory of Care," ibid., pp. 659–60.

18. Michele Moody-Adams, "Gender and the Complexity of Moral Voices," in Card, *Feminist Ethics*, pp. 198–200.

19. Carol Stack, "The Culture of Gender: Women and Men of Color," *Signs* 11 (Winter 1986): 321–24. Gilligan does occasionally note, of her various findings, that they are based on "a small and highly educated sample.": *In a Different Voice*, p. 156. However, the language in which she reports those findings fails to repeat this limitation. Thus, she introduces certain of her findings in this way: "I want to restore in part the missing text of *women's development*, as *they* describe their conceptions of self and morality in the early adult years. In focusing primarily on the differences between the accounts of *women and men*, my aim is to enlarge developmental understanding by including *the perspectives* of both the sexes. While the judgments considered come from a small and highly educated sample, they elucidate a contrast and make it possible to recognize not only what is missing in *women's* development but also what is there" (p. 156).

20. Houston also applauds current work on care ethics even while worrying about the limitations of that work. The risk in abandoning care ethics altogether is that, to borrow Houston's terms, "a very large part of women's moral experience will again become invisible or will suffer a devaluation": "Rescuing Womanly Virtues," p. 260.

secondary theoretical status by most (although not all) of the major theorists of modern moral philosophy, both those who founded and those who further developed Kantian moral philosophy and utilitarianism.[21]

Care ethics, furthermore, makes an important contribution to contemporary moral theory by raising esteem for women in virtue of their primary identification with the caring and nurturing realms of social life. Cheshire Calhoun sees this development as a crucial step in overcoming ethical theory's own tendency to reinforce the pervasive societal bias toward the masculine.[22] This tendency is manifested both in an explicit devaluing of (traditionally female) moral experiences in the domestic and familial realm, and in selective attention only to (traditionally male) realms of moral experience in the public world. For advocates of care ethics to have turned women's traditional moral concerns into a fundamental focus of attention for moral theory was a ground-breaking endeavor. The importance of such an advance in moral philosophy and, in particular, its importance for feminism, should not be underestimated.

Care ethics is inspired and engaged by a respect for women's traditional domestic and familial care-giving labor. Any system of thought that shows such esteem combats the aspect of women's

21. Annette Baier finds much in the writings of David Hume that bears on contemporary feminist ethics; see "Hume, The Women's Moral Theorist?" in Eva Feder Kittay and Diana T. Meyers, eds., *Women and Moral Theory* (Totowa, N.J.: Rowman & Littlefield, 1987), pp. 37–55. John Stuart Mill, in collaboration with Harriet Taylor, is noteworthy for his extensive writings on the subordination of women; see their *Essays on Sex Equality*, ed. Alice S. Rossi (Chicago: University of Chicago Press, 1970). These investigations, however, do not appear in his major work of moral theory, *Utilitarianism*, and the subsequent tradition in moral philosophy has not canonized his writings on women. The major metaethical developments that dominated the early- to mid-twentieth century in moral philosophy, e.g., intuitionism, emotivism, and linguistic analysis, also ignored the realm of caring. This observation is scarcely noteworthy, however, since those trends tended to neglect important matters of moral substance in *most* realms of human activity.

22. Cheshire Calhoun, "Justice, Care, Gender Bias," *Journal of Philosophy* 85 (1988): 451–63.

oppression that has to do with the cultural devaluation of women's work. Feminist critics of care ethics, however, worry that, on balance, more harm than good may arise from promoting care ethics as a distinctively *female* ethical perspective. The subordination of women has included many more dimensions than simply the devaluation of women's traditional forms of labor, and it is not clear what contribution is made by care ethics toward alleviating these other problems. Women's subordination has included the denial to women of opportunities for full participation in public life and the concomitant confinement of women to traditionally female forms of labor, whether as unpaid or (under)paid workers. It has included whatever constriction of moral competency follows upon the loss of opportunity to cope with the circumstances, persons, and relationships of the public sphere. These concerns are ignored by care ethics.

Care ethics also neglects the historical male control of women's sexual and reproductive capacities and activities, whether by obstetric practitioners and other scientific experts,[23] by governments,[24] or by husbands and male lovers, as made possible by the practice of obligatory heterosexuality and prohibitions against lesbianism.[25] Care ethics tends to ignore the distinctive forms of violence and violation to which women, far more than men, have been subjected. The lamentably familiar examples include incest, rape, sexual harassment, and domestic battering.[26] Although a care ethic certainly condemns any form of violence and brutality, it is by no means clear what response it will advise for a woman or girl who has been the victim of, say, rape or battering by someone close to her.

23. Barbara Ehrenreich and Deirdre English, *For Her Own Good: 150 Years of the Experts' Advice to Women* (Garden City, N.Y.: Anchor Books, 1978).

24. For a discussion of the legal aspects of governmental control of reproductive and family policy, see Deborah L. Rhode, *Justice and Gender* (Cambridge: Harvard University Press, 1989), esp. chaps. 6, 7, and 9.

25. See Adrienne Rich, "Compulsory Heterosexuality and Lesbian Existence," *Signs* 5 (Summer 1980): 631–60.

26. For a recent discussion of the legal aspects of these social problems, see Rhode, *Justice and Gender*, chap. 10, "Sex and Violence."

## CARE AND JUSTICE

Traditional moral theories and traditional concepts of justice and rights may fare better than care ethics in handling problems of violence. Traditional moral theories offer grounds for judging that one has been harmed or wronged in certain important ways, and they also articulate rationales for the criminal punishment of wrongdoers.[27] Theorists of care ethics have been notably silent about these matters.[28]

Gilligan touches on the issue of violence in intimate relationships when she discusses some empirical data that summarize the reactions of female and male research subjects to certain suggestive visual images. In one study, women and men had to tell a story about two trapeze artists who were pictured performing a dangerous aerial act. Women, more often than men, added safety nets in their stories. Partly on the basis of such data, Gilligan concludes that, unlike men, women do not generally regard personal relationships as dangerous: "the women saw the scene on the trapeze as safe because, by providing nets, they had made it safe."[29] Perhaps, on the contrary, women added nets as external safety devices precisely because they perceived the relationships as being, in themselves, *un*safe.

It would be a mistake to think that a care perspective need not countenance the possibilities of harm in close personal relation-

27. Feminists debate the legal and moral adequacy of traditional conceptions of rights for dealing with such problems as that of violence against women; see Carol Smart, *Feminism and the Power of Law* (London: Routledge, 1989), esp. chap. 7, "The Problem of Rights." I do not assume that traditional conceptions have been rendered fully adequate to the problem. However, as stated in the text, they "may fare better" than care ethics. In addition, we should not underestimate the dynamic power of such systems of thought to grow and change in light of feminist concerns; see Carl Wellman, "Doing Justice to Rights," *Hypatia* 3 (Winter 1989): 153–58.

28. Moody-Adams argues persuasively that moral perspectives quite different from that of care might have emerged in Gilligan's studies had the underlying research been based on interviews with women who were coping with the experience of rape or domestic battering rather than (as was the case) on interviews with women who were struggling with abortion decisions: "Gender and the Complexity of Moral Voices," pp. 202–3.

29. *In a Different Voice*, p. 43; the entire discussion appears on pp. 39–45.

ships, and that such concerns are imported into morality only by way of a concern with justice. Sara Ruddick, for example, systematically confronts issues concerning violence as an inherent part of her care-based maternal ethic.[30] Ruddick examines "maternal practice through the lens of nonviolence" and asks "if there are principles in the practices of mothering that coincide" with ideals of nonviolence.[31] However, the mothering relationship, which is the focus of Ruddick's investigation, has limited usefulness as a source of insight about everyday adult interrelationships. Morally competent adults, in relationships with each other, do not usually have motherlike responsibilities for each other's preservation, growth, or social acceptability.[32] In addition, the domain to which Ruddick primarily applies, and in which she expands, the nonviolent insights of mothering is that of military politics, not the domain of domestic or sexual violence.

To sum up: resisting the varied forms of female subordination calls for more than simply elevating esteem for women's traditionally sanctioned forms of labor and attendant modes of consciousness. To elevate social esteem for care ethics is to combat women's subordination to the extent of resisting only one of its many manifestations. This approach, by itself, does not (yet) constitute a sufficiently rich or fully liberatory *feminist* ethic. Worse yet, care ethics appears to bolster some of the practices and conceptions that subordinate women.

To portray care ethics as a distinctively female ethic reinforces the stereotypic gender assumptions that women are especially suited for the domestic, nurturing realm, that men are unsuited for this realm, and that women are particularly unsuited for the traditionally masculine worlds of public work and activity. The apparent incapacity of care ethics to deal with the moral relationships of public life, relationships among strangers, or among persons who share no affective ties, contributes greatly to this

30. Sara Ruddick, *Maternal Thinking: Towards a Politics of Peace* (New York: Ballantine Books, 1989).

31. Ibid., p. 161.

32. These are the three demands that, in Ruddick's view, are imposed by maternal work and that "constitute" such work: ibid., p. 17.

impression. If care ethics is supposed to represent the preferred perspective of substantial numbers of women, and if its mutual integration with justice considerations is not widely convincing, then the promotion of care ethics as a female ethic cannot help but reinvigorate stereotypes of women's incapacity to handle the moral challenges of public life.

Furthermore, care ethics might also undermine women's resolve to resist, say, violence or reproductive control by others, by appearing to endorse the *overridingness* of the moral duties to care, nurture, and maintain relationship with anyone with whom one comes into intimate contact, regardless of the moral quality of the relationship. Gilligan's focus on what she sees as the inclusiveness of the caring attitude suggests this unqualified orientation simply to maintaining connections with others.[33] A care ethic, in this respect, is vulnerable to Hoagland's objection that it morally nullifies some of the most effective strategies available to women for resistance to abuse, exploitation, and coercion, strategies such as withdrawal altogether from relationship.[34]

It is noteworthy that Gilligan's writings are not univocal on this point. In one passage, for example, she writes approvingly of a decision by "Sarah," a research subject, to end a heterosexual relationship that seemed to Sarah to reduce her to a "nonentity." Sarah resolves to leave the relationship in a way that does not compromise her own needs. For Gilligan, this example illustrates mature, postconventional care reasoning. Gilligan emphasizes, however, that Sarah strives to end the relationship "in a responsible way," still attentive to the needs of her soon-to-be former partner and seeking to minimize his hurt.[35] Sarah exhibits supposed mature care reasoning by departing caringly from the very partner in af-

33. For example, *In a Different Voice,* p. 160.

34. Hoagland, "Some Thoughts about 'Caring,' " p. 256. Nel Noddings explicitly rejects the appropriateness of withdrawal from a relationship as a response to someone else's wrongdoing; see "A Response," *Hypatia* 5 (Spring 1990): 124.

35. Gilligan, *In a Different Voice,* p. 95. I am grateful to Diana Meyers for bringing this passage to my attention.

filiation with whom she felt effaced.[36] Thus, although Gilligan's care perspective does permit withdrawal as one resolution for relationships that oppress women, the moral option of withdrawal as such is deemphasized and attention is refocused elsewhere. This brief reference by Gilligan to withdrawal from relationship, furthermore, contrasts with her characteristic formulation of a mature care ethic in terms of a recognition of *everyone*'s need for care and a sense of personal responsibility for answering to that omnipresent need.[37]

Another way that care ethics fails to challenge the subordination of women is through its neglect of the wider sense of female community or collectivity that has been so crucial for feminist activism. The formulations of care ethics by Gilligan and Noddings tend to focus on dyadic relationships, relationships between two persons considered in isolation from any larger relational network. With the exception of Ruddick's work, care ethics usually fails to attend to the larger social context in which such relationships are embedded, the wider social networks or the communities at large.

Even those women who are comfortable with traditional heterosexual lives usually depend heavily, if not exclusively, on female relatives and friends for the practical advice and help, companionship, and emotional support that they need to cope with the minor and major relational challenges of daily life. Financial need and outright poverty, social marginalization, child rearing, domestic labor, the stresses and strains of marital and other sexually intimate relationships, illness, injury, bereavement, and the rest are borne more easily with support. Women have long been one anothers' primary supporters in such matters.[38] Female relational networks, so crucial for women, are radically underrepresented and underappreciated in our culture, a culture which, like most others, never-

36. "Reduced to a nonentity," are Sarah's own words, as quoted by Gilligan from her interviews with Sarah (ibid.).

37. Ibid., p. 100.

38. See Carroll Smith Rosenberg, "The Female World of Love and Ritual: Relations between Women in Nineteenth Century America," *Signs* 1, no. 1 (1975): 1–29.

theless depends profoundly on the labors of women who are sustained by such networks.[39] Care ethics unfortunately replicates this omission. Care ethics, in addition, ignores the sense of solidarity or commonality that most women share with at least some other women. It neglects those relationships among women that foster political consciousness and, thereby, enable some of them to resist the societal subordination of women and to work to improve the lot of women's lives on a broader scale.

One might say that the caring perspective as advanced by Gilligan and Noddings treats relationships *too individualistically*. Although human individuals are understood in terms of their relationships to other human individuals, those relationships themselves are abstracted from the wider social context of governmental, economic, and familial institutions and practices of which they are a part. "Atomistic" or abstractly isolated relationships are as much a theoretical misrepresentation as are atomistic (human) individuals. Removing relationships from their institutional settings obscures the way relationships are defined, structured, sustained, limited, and domesticated by those institutions and practices.

In light of the risks posed by promoting care ethics as a distinctively female ethic, we can retain the theory but work to modify its counterfeminist implications, or we can jettison the theory altogether and start anew. At the most general level, the key question is whether a female-associated care ethic in its current rudimentary state of development does more harm than good or more good than harm to the liberatory interests of diverse groups of women.

In light of how recently care ethics was articulated in moral theory—Gilligan's most famous statement of it was published in 1982, Nodding's in 1984, and Ruddick's book on maternal thinking in 1989—it seems premature to seek definitive answers to those questions now. A tentative compromise stance, however, is already available to us. In the previous chapter, I suggested that even if there is no gender gap between women and men in their moral perspectives, nevertheless, ethical theory should take account of

39. See the illuminating discussion of these networks in Adrienne Rich, "Compulsory Heterosexuality."

the different voice represented by care ethics. Recent moral theory has neglected the moral activities and experiences involved in caring and nurturing, both the caring by mature persons for those dependent on them[40] and the caring that can and should go on among morally competent adults. These themes are worth developing for contemporary moral theory even if care ethics is not a distinctively female moral orientation.

In addition, it may be premature to conclude that care ethics cannot expand to encompass such concerns as violence and oppression in personal relationships. As Card puts it, we need an understanding of "the capacity for love" that is "comparable in sophistication to Immanuel Kant's understanding of the capacity for acting on principle," an understanding that would illuminate the ways that "not every passionate attachment to persons is valuable" while still recognizing the ethical worth of those attachments that are valuable.[41] Thus, a conception of what we can call "enlightened care" should enable us to grasp that, in close personal relationships with morally competent adults, women deserve as much care and nurturing as we provide. Furthermore, enlightened care should enable women to discern appropriate ways to modify, refuse, or end those relationships that threaten to neglect our interests or to harm us. In the next section, I begin to explore the sorts of care that women, as care givers, should seek for ourselves.

## 2. Care for Women as Care Givers

A fully liberatory feminist ethic must legitimate a woman's care for herself and her pursuit of caring and nurturing from others. From the standpoint of care ethics, it is important to recognize that women, who are normally relied upon to provide the bulk of nur-

40. This way of emphasizing what is missing from modern moral theory is particularly prominent in the work of Sara Ruddick, *Maternal Thinking;* and Virginia Held, for example, in her "Non-Contractual Society," in Hanen and Nielsen, *Science, Morality, and Feminist Theory*, pp. 111–37.

41. "Gender and Moral Luck," p. 215. In Chapters 2 and 3, I explore some ways of distinguishing valuable from worthless close personal relationships.

turant care for others, are vulnerable in various ways. The forms of care that women need are not vouchsafed in the course of our caring for others. Even though women's caring for others sustains networks of interpersonal relationships, the existence of these relationships does not guarantee women's safety or equality of social status with men. Caring remains a risky business for women.

The care that can make a moral difference to a woman's life is roughly twofold. On the one hand, there is the kind of care involved in resisting our own devaluation, denigration, harassment, marginalization, exclusion, exploitation, subordination, domination, or openly violent abuse. Systematic attempts to overcome such harms may take the form of petitioning or pressuring societal institutions either to alter their own structures toward greater gender equity or to intercede more effectively on behalf of women in so-called private affairs, as in woman-battering cases. But rescue is not always available, and some of the problems in question arise out of social institutions and practices that are culturally sanctioned and widely tolerated. To protect ourselves, we as women must often rely on our own self-assertive efforts against oppressive practices. Thus, one major form of care for oneself concentrates on the variously necessary ways of protecting oneself against harm by others.

The second major category of care for self that a fully liberatory feminist ethic should offer involves positive flourishing, self-development that goes beyond merely resisting subordination or oppression. To be fully liberatory for women, such an ethic must develop ideals for a variety of personal achievements and excellences (other than those that center around self-protection). Care ethics does, of course, glorify the virtue of caring for and nurturing others. But this is not the only sort of human excellence that women can attain. Thus, a fully liberatory feminist ethic, with an eye toward the lives of women as typical care givers, should idealize forms of personal flourishing in addition to excellent care giving.[42]

42. I do not have in mind asocial concepts of human flourishing. In my view, no distinctively human excellence is possible apart from a human social context. The reference to excellences as "personal" indicates merely that the

The sort of care for oneself involved in flourishing is significantly different from the sort that concentrates on protecting oneself from harm. The familiar criticisms that the women's movement in the United States concentrates on the needs of middle-class, white women and ignores the needs of low-income women or women who are not white have much to do with this distinction. Many women in our culture lack access to the resources for forms of personal development that extend beyond self-protective and survival needs. To sue the Rotary Club for barring female applicants from membership is a different sort of feminist project from volunteering support services at a battered women's shelter.[43] Yet each is, in its own way, a quest by women to care for themselves and for some other women, a quest to surmount some facet of subordination or oppression facing some women and to live as well as conditions permit.[44] Both of these wide-ranging sorts of concerns, self-protection as well as personal flourishing, require moral anchorage in a notion of care for oneself.

On Nodding's formulation of care ethics, not much primary importance is attached to caring for oneself.[45] As Hoagland ob-

traits are ascribed to persons. In their origin, development, meaning, and manifestation, such traits are (I would argue) necessarily social.

43. I am not suggesting that domestic violence is a problem to which only low-income women or women of color are subject. The point is that low-income women, with few resources of their own and few alternative support systems available to them, are the ones who need special battered women's shelters to protect them from domestic violence. Women with more money can check into motels and, later, can afford to leave their abusive relationships.

44. As many feminist writers have emphasized, it is crucial that women with greater social privileges and advantages not presume that their experiences universally typify those of all women or exemplify woman's lot in life. It is also crucial that battles for the opportunities for (some) women's flourishing not be waged at the expense of other, less-advantaged women or articulated as if they were currently relevant for all women, or thought to be the only changes that women in general need in their lives. For an important philosophical discussion of how, in practice, to give due recognition to the cultural and ethnic differences among women, see Elizabeth V. Spelman, *Inessential Woman: Problems of Exclusion in Feminist Thought* (Boston: Beacon Press, 1988).

45. Noddings, *Caring*, p. 100.

serves,[46] the responsibility to care for oneself is derivative in Noddings's system; it derives from the responsibility to maintain one's capacity to care for others, a goal that requires staying in good, care-giving shape. Caring for oneself as such appears to have no intrinsic value.

Hoagland has noticed a unidirectional nature to Noddings's care ethics. Noddings explores what she herself calls "the logic of caring" as it flows from a care giver to one who is cared for. Someone in the role of care giver is not to seek or expect reciprocal care giving from the one for whom she cares. The only reciprocity that should be sought by the one who renders care is that of mere "recognition" by the recipient of the care.[47] In Noddings's view, the sole "major contribution" made by the care *recipient* to the relationship is a "willing and unselfconscious revealing of self."[48]

Such a conception of caring is inappropriate for intimate relationships among morally competent adults. On Hoagland's view, such unidirectional caring threatens to devolve into self-sacrificing care.[49] This problem arises whether or not the relationship between the adults is oppressive in any way. An oppressive relationship, however, worsens the problem. It is difficult to see how someone can strive to overcome oppressive conditions facing her unless, at the very least, she has begun to feel intrinsically entitled to care for herself and to demand reciprocal caring in return for the care she provides others.

Noddings has recently made it clear that her care ethic formulates a call for each person to foster caring relations in which the care giver is a recipient as well as a giver of care. No one is supposed to be "stuck" in a position of being one or the other.[50] Nevertheless, on Noddings's view, the relationship, and not the care giver, remains primary. Noddings has not yet explored, to the same depth or level of complexity as she has examined the attitude of caring for others, an adult care giver's own need for care. Con-

46. Hoagland, "Some Thoughts about 'Caring,' " p. 255.
47. Noddings, *Caring*, p. 71.
48. Ibid., p. 73.
49. Hoagland, "Some Thoughts about 'Caring,' " pp. 253–59.
50. Noddings, "A Response," p. 123.

trary to care giving, ensuring that one is well cared for by others does not appear to constitute a major moral problem for Noddings—not even under historical conditions of women's cultural subordination or other sorts of vulnerability. Noddings's recent clarification thus leaves caring and relationship as the central foci of care ethics while relegating the caring self to a status of only derivative importance. The risk of self-sacrifice remains present.

In Gilligan's formulation of care ethics, the threat that care might devolve into self-sacrifice is somewhat ameliorated. Gilligan regards self-sacrificing care as a manifestation of conventional femininity, a mode of behavior that is surmounted by the postconventional caring that at least some women manage to attain. Postconventional caring involves the recognition that self and other are equally deserving of care. In the school of developmental moral psychology out of which Gilligan's work initiated, postconventional moral reasoning of any sort is thought to be more morally adequate than conventional moral reasoning.[51] Gilligan's formulation of a mature caring perspective has the advantage, then, of making a woman's care for herself intrinsically valuable, and not valuable merely in so far as it derives from the responsibility to care for others or to foster caring relationships.

Gilligan's mature care ethic thus permits the care giver to grasp the legitimacy of including herself in the scope of her own caring. Gilligan's formulation, however, does not go far enough. Gilligan's mature, postconventional care ethic leads someone to "include herself among the people whom she considers it moral not to hurt" but does not afford the insight that she deserves to be cared for in return by those she loves.[52]

This is not, of course, to argue that there should be a quid pro quo accounting of services in personal relationships. Something is amiss, however, if a close personal relationship between morally competent adults lacks an overall approximate reciprocity in the

51. See Lawrence Kohlberg, *The Philosophy of Moral Development: Moral Stages and the Idea of Justice* (San Francisco: Harper & Row, 1981), e.g., pp. 147–73.

52. Gilligan, *In a Different Voice*, pp. 149, 165.

diverse ways of caring. This mutuality seems, on the face of it, to be a moral requirement for those morally competent persons who genuinely care for each other.[53] A care ethic such as Gilligan's, which does not illuminate caring as a mutual relationship, seems, in that respect, still to be incomplete. In close relationships among such morally competent adults, it is critical for a woman to avoid exploitation and to be nurtured herself by the relationship and by those for whom she cares.[54]

The gendered nature of our caretaking practices means that women are held accountable for continuing to provide care even under conditions in which women are mistreated by those for whom they care. The pressures on a woman to forgive and forget her injuries, to kiss and make up, for example, in those wife-battering cases that manage to reach family court, are infamous.[55] And it is in relationships with male peers, especially intimate relationships, that women have historically encountered substantial subordination and much of the abuse to which they are subject.

In Noddings's view, the perspective of caring calls upon us to

53. My generalization is intended to allow for exceptional cases; sometimes one partner is infirm or otherwise deeply needful of care and unable to reciprocate this care for a prolonged period of time. This notion introduces the concept of reciprocity into an understanding of care. Reciprocity is one of the formal features that define justice reasoning on a Kohlbergian model; see Kohlberg, *Philosophy of Moral Development*, pp. 147–67. Perhaps "mutuality" is a more appropriate term than "reciprocity" for the realm of personal interrelationships. "Reciprocity" suggests that specific actions are met with corresponding actions as repayments; "mutuality" suggests, in addition, the sharing of interests or concerns. "Mutuality" identifies a richer relationship than that of mere repayment for good turns rendered. Nevertheless, reciprocity is not irrelevant to personal relationships; it would seem to be a part, even though only a part, of what mutuality involves.

54. Ann Ferguson investigates the physical-social interaction that sustains human sexuality, parenting, family relationships, and other nurturant social relationships. She construes the sustaining interactions as a form of labor which, like the productive labor of the marketplace, may be exploited. The exploitation of women's sexual and caregiving labor is the system of male dominance; see her *Blood at the Root: Motherhood, Sexuality, and Male Dominance* (London: Pandora, 1989), pp. 7–8 and passim.

55. See Rhode, *Justice and Gender*, p. 239.

stop abuse and "nothing in the ethic of caring . . . disables" a woman from asserting that she will "not allow" it. Noddings also concedes that sometimes the need for self-protection might make "physical withdrawal" necessary. Physical withdrawal, however, is not the same thing as severance of the relationship, and Noddings opposes severance. Noddings's only other counsel to an abused woman is that she and her supporters "surround the abusive husband with loving models who would not tolerate abuse in their presence and would strongly disapprove of it whenever it occurred in their absence."[56] Aside from the difficulty a battered woman faces in orchestrating such a collective response, there is no reason why a care reasoner must settle for nothing more than "loving" moral persuasion when challenging men who beat up women. Care ethics, in my view, should begin by taking seriously the intrinsic worth of care-giving individuals (as well as that of individual care receivers) and the intrinsic value of whatever protects all of them from violence and violation.

Contemporary statements of care ethics figure prominently in the recent trend in moral theory to conceive of individuals as fundamentally social beings, relationally and communally defined. An ethics of care thus incorporates into its conception of personhood a much-needed recognition of the role of the social at the constitutive level of human identity and agency. Such an approach is a welcome challenge to those forms of individualism that treat only individual persons, abstracted from social connection, as the loci for moral agency and obligation. This virtue of care ethics is, however, also a source of one notable weakness. Care ethics neglects the well-being of individual persons to the extent that *it can* be conceptualized separately from that of other persons and the relationships with which the individual is nevertheless deeply intertwined.

My emphasis on the importance of caring for oneself and of being cared for in return by those for whom one cares introduces into care ethics an emphasis on self that is lacking in Noddings's formulation and that appears only in undeveloped form in Gilli-

56. Noddings, "A Response," p. 125.

gan's version. On the approach I am recommending, the self is still defined, at least in part, by her relationships. My approach, however, incorporates the recognition that the care-giving self is herself someone who needs care and that her needs as such make legitimate moral demands on those to whom she is close.

There is room in care ethics for a cautious strain of individualism, one that is consistent with a theoretical emphasis on interconnection and the social nature of persons. Responsibilities to care should not eclipse those features of the care giver that constitute her as an individual, nor should they obscure those dimensions of meaning in her life that are independent of her care-giving role. Subordination, exploitation, abuse, and oppression occur to individuals—individuals in relationships,[57] to be sure, but individuals nevertheless. Care ethics requires a notion of individuality (together with an adequate conception of human groups) in order to illuminate who is subordinated, who is oppressed, and why and how this occurs on a daily piecemeal basis.

A moral concept of individual personhood need not isolate the individual from social context and need not view individuals merely as mutually disinterested rational contractors. A person's needs and wants may well be social constructions arising out of relationships. Nevertheless, when a relatively mature person enters a new relationship, she brings with her needs and wants that were forged in the context of prior relationships. Such needs and wants give her an identity and a perspective that are, at the outset, independent of the new relationship. It is not inconsistent with an ontology of human relationships to recognize our relative independence of newcomers in our lives or to suppose that our preexistent needs and wants may remain stable and persistent through the vicissitudes of new relationships. This concept of relative mutual independence (on the parts of relatively mature adults) may be of special relevance to women entering relationships that threaten to subordinate or engulf them. Thus, the notion of caring for oneself is

57. For an in-depth development of the ontology and morality of individuals in relationships outside the context of care ethics, see Larry May, *The Morality of Groups* (Notre Dame, Ind.: University of Notre Dame Press, 1987).

a conceptual hybrid, exemplifying both relationality and individuality.

More so than Noddings and Gilligan, then, I construe the needs, wants, hopes, fears, and so forth of the care-giving self as legitimately helping to set the moral agenda for her relationships with other adults. The caring self, in such relationships, should care for herself and should expect her loved ones to reciprocate the care that she provides for them to the extent that they are able to do so. Self-assertion is not inimical to caring but, rather, helps to ensure that caring is mutual and undefiled by subordination of the care-giver.

In the next section, I turn to a different problem raised by actual caring practices. These practices impose greater responsibilities for care giving on women than on men and call for greater personal sacrifices by women in the provision of that care. A sufficiently liberatory care ethic should presume at the outset that these gender differences are morally unacceptable.

## 3. Women Who Don't . . . Care

Bernard Williams, in developing his conception of moral luck, offers a provocative discussion of how it might, in retrospect, be justified to have abandoned one's caretaking responsibilities to one's close family members.[58] His discussion provides a useful backdrop for exploring the full social significance of women's caretaking roles.

Williams's discussion of moral luck pertains to a theoretical matter not directly relevant to our present concern. Williams was seeking to challenge a background assumption of modern ethical theory, namely, that one's morally significant choices are either justified or not depending only on one's intentions and on other

58. Bernard Williams, "Moral Luck," in his *Moral Luck* (Cambridge: Cambridge University Press, 1981), pp. 20–39. This example was discussed in Chapter 3 to show the limitation it exposes in Williams's commitment to partiality toward beloved wives. On the general relevance of Williams's notion of moral luck to matters of gender and morality, see Card, "Gender and Moral Luck."

matters that are, in some sense, under one's control. Williams argues, contrary to this, that the actual outcomes of one's actions and projects—whether or not they are successful—also matter for the justification of one's choices. Such a view makes justification depend on factors beyond one's control and, from the agent's standpoint, makes justification a function of luck.

Although the notion of moral luck is paradoxical from the perspective of modern ethical theories, nevertheless, our daily moral (and legal) practices of holding people responsible for their actions do incorporate considerations of the (lucky or unlucky) outcomes of those actions. An actual murder, for example, is legally treated as a more serious offense than an unsuccessful attempt. Outcomes are partly determined by the nature of the situations that one faces, the circumstances that are not fully known, foreseen, or predictable (what Williams calls "incident" moral luck), and partly by the kind of person one is, one's abilities and temperament (what Williams calls "constitutive" moral luck).

Williams originally discussed incident moral luck in relation to moral dilemmas, situations in which one must unavoidably do harm in order to attain some good; his concern was with the justification for doing such harm. The famous quasi-hypothetical case study explored by Williams involved a man who turned away "from definite and pressing human claims on him" in order to be an artist and who later produced works of singular artistic merit.[59] The historical Gauguin is the model for Williams's study. Paul Gauguin deserted his wife and five children and embarked on a style of life which was to involve sojourns across France, close contact with other young artists of the day, and travels to the exotic islands of Martinique and Tahiti in search of artistic inspiration.[60] Gauguin, in other words, abandoned those persons for whose care he was most of all responsible, his five children among them, in order to paint pictures.

59. Williams, *Moral Luck,* p. 22. In the ensuing discussion, I consider artwork to be a metaphor for any project other than caring for one's intimates and for the sake of which one might abandon those care-giving responsibilities.

60. See Yann le Pichon, *Gauguin: Life, Art, Inspiration* (New York: Harry N. Abrams, 1987).

Williams encourages us to regard the (lucky) achievement of great art as an outcome that sufficiently justifies a man's forsaking the "definite and pressing human claims" of his wife and children.[61] Williams is subtle enough to sense the complexity that characterizes justification in such a case. Those who have been harmed by the artist do continue to have justified complaints against him, in Williams's estimation, and are not bound to regard the artist's choice as justified.[62] By contrast, Williams, who was *not* harmed by the artist, does consider that the success of Gauguin's project justifies the injury to Gauguin's family. After all, it is the sort of project, in Williams's estimation, that "can yield a good for the world."[63]

61. Williams's discussion evokes what Linda Nochlin has disparagingly called the "myth of the Great Artist—subject of a hundred monographs, unique, godlike—bearing within his person since birth a mysterious essence, rather like the golden nugget in Mrs. Grass's chicken soup, called Genius or Talent, which, like murder, must always out, no matter how unlikely or unpromising the circumstances." See her "Why Have There Been No Great Women Artists?" (originally published in 1971), in her *Women, Art, and Power* (New York: Harper & Row, 1988), p. 153. Nochlin recounts the way this conception of "the apparently miraculous, nondetermined, and asocial nature of artistic achievement" was "elevated to hagiography in the nineteenth century," as art historians and critics came to view the artist as someone who "struggles against the most determined parental and social opposition [those 'pressing human claims'], suffering the slings and arrows of social opprobrium like any Christian martyr, and ultimately succeeds against all odds . . . because deep within himself radiates that mysterious, holy effulgence: Genius" (p. 155). Williams's illustration of moral luck evokes this romantic notion of artistic talent.

62. Williams, *Moral Luck*, p. 37.

63. Ibid., p. 37. This justification sounds a surprisingly utilitarian note in Williams's writings. Tangentially, we might also note that the notion of justification becomes extraordinarily complex on the supposition that distinct standpoints might warrant mutually contradictory judgments and attitudes. To speak, then, of justification in a sense that is independent of standpoint requires either the sort of omniauthoritative impartial standpoint that Williams himself rejects (see ibid., "Persons, Character and Morality," pp. 1–19), or it requires identifying certain sorts of partial standpoints as morally more authoritative than others—a suspect theoretical maneuver. (From what standpoint would the ranking itself be justified?)

Williams does not clarify just how good the resultant art must be in order to justify the desertion of wife and children. If it is only works of the canonical stature of Gauguin's paintings that justify the abandonment of pressing human claims, then Williams's notion of justification in virtue of the luck of great subsequent accomplishment becomes a mere theoretical curiosity in ethics, having virtually no commonplace moral relevance. Only a few individuals in any generation would ever have such prodigious moral luck—although many more might be willing to sacrifice the welfare of their loved ones in the hope of attaining it. Williams's discussion, on that interpretation, has little practical relevance for people in general.

On the other hand, if one need not attain the rank of the Great Masters but need merely attain a more accessible level of excellence in one's subsequent accomplishments in order to justify abandoning one's loved ones, then Williams's notion has wide relevance for people of more ordinary talents. They need merely have some ambition and a willingness to shirk their own responsibility for the "pressing human claims" that weigh upon them.

If Williams's example is to constitute a moral examplar of the sort of justification he has in mind, then it is a troubling example for several reasons. First, the moral risk undertaken by the would-be artist imposes definite costs on those human beings whose pressing claims are thereby abandoned. In terms of a care ethic, the pressing human claims forsaken by Williams's artist were precisely those of close family relations for whose care the artist was responsible. For these persons, there is no risk of good or bad luck but rather a near certainty of suffering and, possibly, of tragedy. (Gauguin's wife was able to ameliorate her family's hardship by obtaining financial support from her own family of origin,[64] but the average mother who is abandoned with five dependent children is not so comfortably situated.)

Second, a would-be artist may never personally have to acknowledge the possible failure of his artistic endeavor or accept final responsibility for abandoning his loved ones. So long as the artist manages to eke out a living, he can sustain a life centered

64. Le Pichon, *Gauguin*, p. 25.

around the production of his art. Even if the artist does not find artistic acclaim in his lifetime, the continuing absence of great success or reward need not reveal the artistry to be mediocre, the project to have failed. After all, many historically revered artists achieved their acclaimed reputations only posthumously, following a lifetime's neglect, even ridicule, of their works. Conversely, success during the artist's lifetime can also be ephemeral and inconclusive; it does not always foreshadow enduring artistic repute.

The artist may, thus, endlessly defer a final accounting, a final assessment of the overall (moral as well as artistic) justifiability of his abandonment of wife and children. Only history will render the final accounting, and, by the time it does so, the artist, the wife, and the children will all be dead. No moral rectification will then be possible for the failure of artistic ambition. The artist can, thus, in a kind of perpetual moral adolescence, endlessly defer coming to terms with the ethical significance of his life.[65]

The two problems raised above are not specifically feminist in perspective. In turning to my more specifically feminist concern, I may seem to be reversing my attitude toward Williams's notion of incident moral luck. Having just pointed out some moral problems with it, I may seem now to be endorsing it by arguing that it should simply be extended to women. This is not my view. Let us proceed cautiously, then, for the terrain is uncertain.

The third problem with Williams's example is that the different genders have very unequal access to the sort of moral luck Williams describes. On the one hand, the success of artistry depends on more than mere talent; it also depends on how others respond to one's art. Such responses are "intrinsic," in Williams's term, to the success of the project.[66] Great art is, in important ways, a social construction; art critics and historians, art dealers and investors,

65. Williams fails to consider the fads and fancies of critical veneration or neglect that often delay the final accounting of artwork beyond an artist's own lifetime. This feature of art criticism and of other forms of cultural assessment complicates Williams's reflections on how a moral-risk-taking life might be assessed in retrospect from the (still-living) standpoint of the risk taker: ibid., pp. 34–37.

66. Ibid., p. 36.

the public at large, and other artists enable the production of great art and constitute its greatness in part through their reactions to it. (Can a painting be genuinely great if it does not profoundly stir other human beings?) In their readiness to view, purchase, display, emulate, find significance in, and derive creative inspiration from an artist's work, the people of a culture constitute the historical greatness of that work and of that person as a would-be great artist.

Careful assessment of Williams's quasi-hypothetical example and its full significance for matters of gender and moral theory calls for a brief digression, an excursion into some art history. Though limited to the field of pictorial art, this history is typical of a vast and pervasive problem, one that has yet to be entirely solved.

Until recently, no women achieved the enduring artistic acclaim afforded to some men. Linda Nochlin argues that the reason for this difference "lies not in the nature of [women's] individual genius or the lack of it, but in the nature of given social institutions and what they forbid or encourage in various classes or groups of individuals."[67] From the time of their inception in the late sixteenth century until the late nineteenth century, British and European art academies barred women from life-drawing classes (except as models) and, thus, from critically important formal training in drawing the nude. Until the twentieth century, this deprivation alone virtually precluded women from creating major works of art by consigning women "to the 'minor' fields of portraiture, genre, landscape, or still life."[68] In nineteenth-century France, where a surprising one-third of all artists were female, women were, nevertheless, not admitted to the Ecole des Beaux Arts until the end of the century, by which time the academic system had lost importance.[69] As late as the mid-nineteenth century, in addition, to attain any success as a painter, a woman required, without exception, the moral good luck of having been born to and raised by an artist father.[70]

67. Nochlin, *Women, Art, and Power*, p. 158.
68. Ibid., pp. 159–60.
69. Ibid., pp. 162–63.
70. Ibid., p. 169. The moral luck of personal origins—the kinds of caretakers one has, their degree of wealth or poverty, etc.—does not fit either of

Most cultures, furthermore, have not been sanguine about the possibility that a *woman's* subsequent art or other public achievement could justify her abandonment of the pressing claims of husband and children. In Europe, the nineteenth century witnessed the birth of the image of the "lady painter," someone who was permitted to be a proficient amateur but whose artistry would not interfere with the major caring work for husband and children that she was expected, on all sides, to undertake.[71] To attempt to be an artist, a woman had to defy all these restrictions and suffer grave personal costs. Barred from formal study of the human nude, for example, the nineteenth-century French painter Rosa Bonheur turned to livestock: "at a certain period," she once wrote, "I spent whole days in the slaughterhouses. Indeed, you have to love your art in order to live in pools of blood."[72]

Contemporary American culture is nearly unanimous in condemning a mother who turns away from familial responsibilities, no matter what she does afterward, while at the same time entertaining the possible justification of a father's similar desertion. Indeed, abandoning fathers often do not have to produce great art (or anything else great) at all in order, nevertheless, to win sympathy, even approval, for abandoning their families. The flight of men from familial responsibilities has long been a tolerated motif of American fiction.[73] In addition, as Barbara Ehrenreich contends, this theme began to attain great cultural prominence in the 1950s with the advent of several major trends.[74] One was the rise of the

Williams's categories; it is not incidental moral luck, nor is it, in itself, constitutive moral luck, although it has a great bearing on the development of character and talents.

71. Ibid., p. 164.

72. Quoted in ibid., p. 174.

73. See Judith Fetterley, *The Resisting Reader: A Feminist Approach to American Fiction*, Bloomington: Indiana University Press, 1978, esp. pp. 1–12.

74. Barbara Ehrenreich, *The Hearts of Men: American Dreams and the Flight from Commitment* (New York: Anchor Press/Doubleday, 1983), esp. chaps. 4 and 5. Ehrenreich suggests that the masculine-oriented trends of the 1950s did more to promote the current breakdown of "the" American family than anything the feminist movement is accused of perpetrating. She contrasts this period with earlier decades of the twentieth century in the United States, during

beat generation, which made a virtue out of cutting domestic ties and hitting the road. Another trend was the proliferation of what can be called "coffee table pornography," particularly *Playboy* magazine, which glamorized a model of male sexuality utterly devoid of marital or familial commitment.[75]

Thus, women and men have had radically different degrees of access to the artistic and other successes that can, on Williams's view, justify their having foresaken the pressing moral claims of those for whom they are supposed to care. It is a woman's moral luck to be expected by our culture to devote herself to the care of her family even at substantial personal cost to herself. In the case of a woman who deserts husband and children altogether, the justificatory stakes are raised appreciably.

Gauguin once wrote that "one man's faculties can't cope with two things at once, and I for one can do *one thing only:* paint. Everything else leaves me stupefied."[76] The woman who deserts her husband and children because caring for them left her "stupefied" can expect condemnation, no matter how great her subsequent achievements. Unlike Gauguin, she will not be canonized; she would be lucky to be remembered.

For all we know, of course, Williams himself might willingly accept a revision in his example, a female artist who takes the moral risk of abandoning husband and five children to pursue her art. The gender configuration of Williams's original example, however, remains an apt illustration of a widespread and gender-asymmetric cultural attitude. In those cases in which the meaning or success of our projects lies in awakening certain receptive attitudes in others, what Williams calls "moral luck" discloses a form of social control that we exercise over the outcomes of one another's project—a control that is deployed differently across lines of gender.

Claudia Card has investigated the way our genders determine the sorts of virtues open or closed to us in a hierarchical gender

---

which the adult male role of breadwinner supporting wife and children was much more widely honored; see chap. 2.

75. Ibid., chap. 4.

76. Le Pichon, *Gauguin*, p. 26.

system.[77] Furthermore, we might add, they determine how much weight our projects will have when weighed in the balance, and they determine how much gravity will be assigned to the familial obligations over against which these projects are set.

Why do we have such difficulty forgiving women for deserting their families for the sake of art or other projects of singular achievement while tolerating men who do so for lesser reasons? The feminist aim of equality for women has never sought the opportunity for women to be as villainous as men have been permitted to be. Still, it challenges moral thinking to say why, if women are to attain cultural and moral equality with men, they should be denied the moral excuses that men are permitted to use. Of course, one can always argue that men should not be so readily forgiven for their excuses, that feminist equality entails holding men to as high a moral standard as women. But what are the practical implications of such a view? Gauguin will hardly be dethroned; his artistic acclaim will not be rescinded. His cultural eminence remains an exemplar of what men—but not women, it seems—can attain who free themselves from the pressing human claims of their dependent families, those for whom they are supposed to care.

Our cultural practices hold mothers to a higher standard of accountability than fathers for the nurturant and attentive day-to-day labor of child care. Part of what this difference means in its full significance is exemplified by the justifiability that Williams finds in Gauguin's desertion of his family. What moral conception will sustain this gendered moral differentiation? What moral notions would undergird the view that the responsibilities for care, especially for dependents, fall more heavily on women than on men? Perhaps we fear that if women stop caring for children and the infirm, then *no one* will care for them. However realistic this observation may be, it yields a strategy of practical compromise but not a moral insight.

Care giving, especially when women's caretaking labors are in question, is not usually construed as a constraint but rather as a moral opportunity and a personally fulfilling venture. It is some-

77. Card, "Gender and Moral Luck," passim.

times thought sacrilegious, toward motherhood in particular, to contest this view. One sure way to derogate feminism is to portray it, contrary to its most representative formulations, as a theory that recommends that women abandon their familial responsibilities.[78] In these antifeminist maneuvers, the notion of profound responsibilities toward children, with which most of us would agree wholeheartedly, are used as an umbrella to shield other relationships of female care giving, especially those toward husbands, from careful scrutiny. Besides misrepresenting feminism, such positions seem to presume without argument that traditional conceptions of women's overriding caretaking responsibilities are virtually unassailable, no matter what the circumstances are.

How will a gender difference in caretaking responsibilities be handled by a care ethic? (Notice that this is not to ask how a gender difference in actual caretaking practices can be *explained*.)[79] Most recent moral philosophy aspires to gender neutrality. Contemporary ethics does not offer theoretical resources to sustain a differentiation of moral duties grounded in gender per se. In this respect, academic ethics diverges radically from popular morality, which features distinct gender differentiations. The gender-differentiated standards of care giving responsibility in close personal relationships are bùt one example of gender differences in the popular morality of care. Even in the workplace, typically female occupations are more likely than typically male occupations to call for friendly behaviors and pleasing attitudes toward those who are

78. Christina Hoff Sommers, "Philosophers against the Family," in George Graham and Hugh LaFollette, eds., *Person to Person* [Philadelphia: Temple University Press, 1989], pp. 82–105) portrays feminists, along with contractarians, as showing a "hostility to family morality" (p. 83) and contributing to the growing divorce rate. Sommers's main argument against divorce is that children are hurt by it (pp. 98–102), an argument that, in the context of Sommers's paper, preposterously suggests that feminists are unconcerned about the welfare of children.

79. The most familiar explanation is to be found in the work of Nancy Chodorow (*The Reproduction of Mothering* [Berkeley: University of California Press, 1978]), who offers an account of differences in female and male personalities which would explain why women, more than men, identify themselves in relational terms and seek nurturant affiliation with others.

served by the occupations in question.[80] What is it that so appalls or frightens us in women who do not care, who do not nurture us or greet us with a ready smile?

Can tradition per se constitute the rationale for gender-differentiated caretaking roles? If so, changes in tradition or legitimate moral criticisms of those traditional practices will undermine their moral authority and that of the corresponding gender differentiation.[81] Can utility be the rationale, that is, the sheer utilitarian value of the traditional practices and not their status as tradition? If so, changing circumstances, the economic transformations of our times, for example, may readily upset the relevant calculations and call for altogether new, possibly nongendered, arrangements. The notion of universalizability does not offer much help, nor do those of virtue or human flourishing, unless essentialist gendered natures are tacitly, question-beggingly assumed in specifying what is to be universalized or what is to count as a virtue.

It seems that not only care ethics but also moral theory as a whole still owe an accounting of the moral difference that gender makes in determining moral responsibilities—or, failing such an account, a critique of popular morality for its continued gender-based, moral differentiation.

## 4. Instrumental Care and Social Empowerment

Care ethics attracts the attention of feminist philosophers because it appears to introduce typically female moral concerns into moral theory. This view of the importance of care ethics reflects an assumption that women do the bulk of caring work in our culture, a view I took for granted in the foregoing discussion. Common experience appears to support this assumption. Women, it seems, are still the primary caretakers for infants and young

80. See Arlie Hochschild, *The Managed Heart: The Commercialization of Human Feeling* (Berkeley: University of California Press, 1983).

81. See Chapter 9 below for a critique of certain communitarian writings and their inadequate treatment of the cultural traditions surrounding women's caretaking roles in marriage and family.

children as well as for elderly and infirm persons, whether nonprofessionally for their own family members or professionally in the capacity of child-care workers, nurses, and so forth. Women still find themselves defined in terms of their intimate relationships; witness the continued use of "Miss" and "Mrs."

Women are still widely expected to need and desire relationships in which they will be primary carers for others, particularly for husbands and children. It continues to be assumed without question that women who do not have such caring responsibilities have failed to find fulfillment in their lives.[82] In addition, the prospect of living a life devoid of family relationships is used as a threat to scare women away from challenging the traditional patriarchal family.[83] The underlying presumption of such threats is that women are desperate for marriage and babies regardless of the costs. Such threats are seldom made to men who avoid or criticize the institutions of marriage and family. Caring, it seems, is *the* presumptive domain of women. Or is it?

We care about and for others in various ways. To care *about* someone is to take an interest in her, be concerned about her, have regard for her. To care *for* someone is to protect her and attend to her needs, to take responsibility for her well-being, perhaps by providing material sustenance or emotional support and nurturance. Care may involve feelings of affection and solicitude for someone, as well as respect and esteem. Protecting someone may include watching over her, defending her against dangers, and tending to her wounds and infirmities. Care may also include formal guardianship, involving custody and managerial control.

82. For a wide-ranging survey of various contemporary media and the endless ways they promote this assumption, see Susan Faludi, *Backlash: The Undeclared War against American Women* (New York: Crown, 1991), e.g., chap. 2, "Man Shortages and Barren Wombs: The Myths of the Backlash."

83. Christina Hoff Sommers, for example, warns that those who avoid or divorce themselves from the patriarchal family "often" suffer harm and "might" feel "betrayed by the ideology" that led them to this state: "Feminist Philosophers Are Oddly Unsympathetic to the Women They Claim to Represent," *Chronicle of Higher Education*, October 11, 1989, p. B3. These veiled threats are unexplained and unsupported.

The ways of caring are diverse. When we consider the wide variety of modes of caring, it becomes clear that much of the positive support that men provide to their intimates, the traditional breadwinning, for example, also falls under the rubric of care. In addition to earning income support for the family, the traditional husband and father may fix the car or the plumbing when it needs repair, do most of the tedious driving on long trips, undertake home carpentry projects, and, weapon in hand, venture forth to investigate suspicious nighttime noises in the home. From these examples, it begins to appear that women have no society-wide monopoly over caring practices.

On the one hand, this insight is good news; men indeed are capable of the practices and moral orientations of care. On the other hand, this insight obscures the distinctive nature of the care that men provide. Most important, I contend, the sort of care men typically provide for women manifests, consolidates, and perpetuates male power with respect to women. In heterosexual relationships, men do reciprocate the care that women provide, but in forms that preserve their dominant and privileged social positions.

Francesca Cancian's exploration of typical female and male patterns of loving in the context of heterosexual relationships helps to illuminate a wide-ranging and complex conception of care and the way its practice by both women and men promotes female subordination.[84] Speaking of love, Cancian differentiates expressive from instrumental forms. Expressive love has to do with intimate self-disclosure and the expression of feelings. Instrumental love pertains to protection and material forms of help. In the context of adult heterosexual relationships, argues Cancian, women tend to prefer and to be more skillful than men at expressive love while instrumental forms of love appear to be more distinctively the domain of men.[85]

84. Francesca M. Cancian, "The Feminization of Love," *Signs* (Summer 1986): 692–709.

85. Ibid., pp. 692–96, 699–705. Male philosophers who defend partiality tend to exhibit a preference, in their discussions, for illustrations of love or care of the instrumental variety, especially those that exhibit the resources or prowess of the care giver. Their most common examples of defensible partiality

CARE AND JUSTICE

The gentleness, tenderness, emotional revelation, and talkativeness of expressive love are sterotyped as feminine in our culture. In Cancian's view, "both contemporary scholarship and public opinion" are dominated by a definition of love that tends to treat these modes of interaction as paradigmatic of love per se.[86] By contrast, instrumental ways of loving are not widely recognized as love. Cancian refers to this interrelated complex of ideas as the "feminization of love." Women are, accordingly, regarded as better at loving than men, a view that is bolstered by psychological studies following the works of Gilligan and of Nancy Chodorow which treat love and attachment thus feminized as fundamental to women's personalities in ways not typical of men.[87]

Cancian challenges the feminization of love. In her view, it works to devalue and exploit women. Among other problems, it reinforces an ideology of separate spheres by continuing to stereotype female and male modes of intimate interrelationship along a conventional expressive-instrumental dichotomy. In Cancian's view, these stereotypes obscure the way (men's) helping behaviors are genuinely loving and they obscure the fact that women, too, provide instrumental forms of support to their loved ones.[88]

Most intriguing, Cancian observes that, in the context of heterosexual relationships, the differences between women's and men's typical ways of loving put women at a relative social disadvantage. In part, this is because men's instrumental ways of loving "reinforce men's power over women." Much of what men do as love "involves giving women important resources, such as money and protection that men control and women believe they need." Cancian states that women control resources on which men depend. This reliance, however, is not widely grasped as a form of dependency; being covert and unrecognized, it does not result

are those of saving a loved one, rather than a stranger, who is in danger and of providing financial and material resources to a loved one rather than to a stranger; see my discussion of this literature in Chapter 2.

86. Ibid., pp. 694–95.

87. Gilligan, *In a Different Voice;* Chodorow, *Reproduction of Mothering;* see Cancian's discussion of this literature: "Feminization of Love," p. 696.

88. Cancian, "Feminization of Love," pp. 705–8.

in empowering women.[89] In addition, the "intimate talk about personal troubles that appeals to women" requires or manifests "vulnerability, a willingness to see oneself as weak and in need of support." Thus, the expressive forms of women's love "involve admitting dependency and sharing or losing control."[90]

Women, too, provide instrumental love for others; cooking and doing laundry are common examples. Cancian argues, however, that because love is conceptualized in terms of its expressive manifestations, these activities are not viewed as love. The result is to ignore women's instrumentality. Since our culture "glorifies instrumental achievement," the net effect is that love is devalued for not being instrumental and women are accordingly devalued for their preoccupation with (supposedly noninstrumental) love.[91]

Cancian's suggestion that women's instrumental behavior toward loved ones is not viewed as love by our culture is puzzling. If instrumental achievement per se is highly valued in our society, then it would be valued wherever it were to be found, whether done by women or men, whether labeled as "love" or not. Upon more careful inspection, it appears that women's instrumental efforts for the sake of love are indeed often recognized as love. Women used to be routinely advised that the way to a man's heart is through his stomach; and, as the old Pillsbury commercial put it, "nothin' says lovin' like somethin' from the oven." The problem, it seems to me, is not that our culture fails to grasp women's instrumental support as love. Rather, the problem is that women's traditional caretaking instrumentalities are *ranked lower* than those of men, laundry and housecleaning, for example, as compared to, say, home carpentry and auto repair. More on this below.

Cancian's conclusion is to call for what she (qualifiedly) refers to as an androgynous conception of love.[92] Her analysis, outlined above, supports this call with two major overall observations. The important point about women is that, in loving relationships, they

89. Ibid., pp. 705–6; Cancian does not specify the resources controlled by women.

90. Ibid., p. 706.

91. Ibid.

92. Ibid., pp. 692, 708–9.

actually provide both expressive interaction and instrumental assistance. The important point about men, however, is not that they provide both expressive and instrumental love. Rather, the instrumental help that men provide, in Cancian's view, should be seen as genuinely loving, contrary to the feminized conception of love.

Overall, Cancian's observations suggest that the bulk of what men provide to women in loving relationships is instrumental help, whereas instrumental help is a part, but only a part and perhaps the lesser share, of what women provide to men. These combined revelations appear to suggest that men provide women with more instrumental love than they receive from women in return. If women's labors of love are already socially devalued relative to whatever it is that men are thought to do, then Cancian's recommendation will not help to correct that imbalance. Given our culture's esteem for instrumental achievement, the net result of recognizing that instrumental love is genuinely love would be to raise esteem somewhat for women's ways of loving, but to raise esteem for men's ways of loving even more. It seems that the mere alteration of our view of love to admit instrumentality will do little by itself to prevent the devaluation of women.

Despite this drawback, some features of Cancian's analysis seem right. There are varied ways of loving, and protection and material help should count among them as well as emotional expressiveness and intimate self-disclosure. A class bias, as Cancian suggests, may well lie behind the tendency to omit instrumental help from the contemporary conception of love as emotional intimacy; "poorer people [women as well as men] are more likely [than affluent people] to see practical help and financial assistance as a sign of love."[93] Applied to the larger domain of caring connections, of which heterosexual love relationships are but one example, this insight seems even more plausible. Instrumental ways of caretaking, such as feeding or sheltering someone and protecting her from harm, are obviously of critical importance in care overall. It may well be true that "man" does not live by bread alone; still less will an infant survive on her caretaker's emotional expressiveness

93. Ibid., p. 695; also see p. 704.

alone, however critical it may be for her later psychological maturation.

Cancian's concept of instrumental love bears further exploration. She has discerned that instrumental love is more socially powerful than expressive love in virtue of manifesting, consolidating, and perpetuating greater control of social resources, privileges, and status. Cancian does not appear to notice that there are power differences among the various forms of instrumental assistance. Although Cancian ranks preparing meals as instrumental, this form of assistance, especially on a routine daily basis, is, in important respects, far less powerful than, say, fixing someone's car.

One important difference among forms of instrumental care has to do with the extent to which the activity is governed by the desires and tastes, the subjective viewpoint, of the recipient of the care. The subjective viewpoint of the recipient may play a major, minor, or nonexistent role in determining the details, even the overall aim, of what the caretaker does. The difference is one of relative autonomy in the rendering of care. In a culture obsessed with autonomy and self-reliance, it seems that a great dependence on the desires, the mere whims, of the recipient of care reduces the status of the care rendered and the corresponding power of the care giver.

Consider the difference between fixing someone's car and feeding her. Fixing someone's car depends on relatively independent standards of car functioning, the principles of auto mechanics. The person whose car I fix may be entirely ignorant of those principles, even while the help I render her and on which she thereby depends is governed by (my apprehension of) them. Her desires and tastes will have relatively little to do with how I help her. As the person with greater car expertise, I will have substantial control over the assistance I render; my judgment, in the main, will ground what I decide to do and will determine whether or not I have done it well. I will not have to please her or cater to her tastes; my aim is to get her car running again.

Providing food for someone who is old enough to express her eating preferences is an altogether different matter. This sort of instrumental care is supposed to be especially attendant on the expressed desires of the one being cared for. It is true that independent standards of both culinary arts and good nutrition do apply to food preparation. A mother cooking for her family, for example, must master numerous cooking techniques and is not supposed to feed her children only junk food. A gourmet cook may become relatively autonomous in her gastronomic caretaking activity. Nevertheless, in the realm of everyday cooking, the mother who keeps serving the tuna casserole that her family detests, however nutritious or well prepared it is, does not earn wide esteem as a cook and will seem a bit cranky, to boot. Even a gourmet cook will not be a successful care giver if her exotic creations displease her family's palates.

At the extreme end, caretaking that is driven largely by the expressed desires and tastes, the very whims, of those who are cared for, devolves into servility. Servile behavior has never been much respected, either by philosophers or by people in general. Women's traditional forms of instrumental caring for husbands include numerous activities in which she is supposed to defer to his preferences, from what she cooks to how she looks. The more deferential the caretaking is supposed to be, deferential to the subjective viewpoint of the one cared for, the less autonomous is the caretaker and the less powerful she becomes with respect to the recipient of her care.

Another key to the social ranking of forms of instrumental care is the extent of the formal training that is publicly recognized as required to perform the care in question. Income-producing labors in the marketplace, traditionally assigned as the primary caretaking responsibility of men with families, usually require either formal education or special on-the-job training. Although much of women's traditional domestic work also requires training (e.g., cooking), nevertheless, many domestic chores (e.g., laundering clothes, cleaning house) are widely regarded as menial forms of labor needing little or no special instruction.

Sometimes, the facility and preparation required to perform women's traditional care-giving labor is quite high but, for various reasons, it goes unacknowledged. Most girls in our culture have engaged extensively in forms of socialization that prepare them to care for children, typically, playing with dolls, playing house, babysitting, and caring for younger siblings under maternal supervision. This training goes on in the private realm, however, and is not publicly recognized as training; it is simply child's "play." In addition, the educative role of this girlhood socialization has been effectively eclipsed by the concept of a "maternal instinct." Thus, the undeniably advanced level of proficiency engaged by child care and the training required to attain it are masked by a cultural stereotype that treats the adult competence in question as a spontaneous and innate propensity.

Protection against external dangers and enemies is another culturally revered form of instrumental caretaking. In our society, it seems that men do most of the physical dirty work of defending against "enemies" and contending with dangers, whether prowlers in the stairwell, rodents in the cellar, or storms on the horizon.[94] Contemporary films elevate the man furiously avenging his wife's rape to the status of cultural demigod. To be able to protect someone is a powerful stance with respect to her. It manifests one's greater capacity for discerning and guarding against danger, one's greater strength and cunning for fighting enemies. Protectiveness may carry with it the privilege of managing the affairs of the protected one, even to the point of dictating what she must do "for her own good." Displays of superior strength or practical intelli-

94. Protecting women against sexual violence by other men is also a traditional form of protective care men render to women in heterosexual relationships. Feminists, however, have discerned disturbing complications in this form of care. It is a form of protection that arises when sexual violence by some men drives women into the arms of other men. Many heterosexual men thus benefit from sexual violence by some among them. The unsettling result is to give most heterosexual men a kind of stake in the societal perpetuation of male sexual violence against women. (That stake obviously does not impute the conscious desires or motives of any particular man.) At any rate, my aim in this chapter is not to uncover either covert or unconscious hypocrisy at the heart of men's care-giving practices but, rather, to show how men's *genuine and sincere* forms of traditional care giving nevertheless subordinate women. Thus, I avoid delving into the complicated topic of men protecting women from sexual violence by other men.

gence consolidate greater relative social status. To save a damsel in distress is, after all, to be a hero, an achievement with clear masculine connotations.

Thus, both women and men provide care for others and, in heterosexual relationships, for each other. As Cancian has illuminated, both women and men provide instrumental forms of care, having to do with food, clothing, shelter, protection, and the other material bases of life. The forms of instrumental care that men typically provide, however, reflect and promote their more powerful social positions. The particular forms of instrumental care that a man traditionally renders, in the context of heterosexual relations and family life, manifest and promote his autonomy and expertise. In return, a woman provides her male partner with both expressive care and forms of instrumental care that tend to subordinate her activities to his desires. The overall effect of this exchange of care is to reinforce his, but not her, independent personhood. The consequence is a promotion of women's continued subordination to men, even in the domain of genuinely mutual care.

To subvert this caretaking hierarchy, we could challenge it along at least three different lines. We could call for a more equitable distribution of instrumental (and expressive) caretaking labor between women and men. Or we could try to show that women's expressive and instrumental forms of caring are really more powerful (more autonomous, expertise-based, or physically protective) than is commonly thought. Or we could challenge the higher status of the more powerful forms of care. We could also combine elements of all three strategies.

An awareness of class differences should govern our approach. A low-income woman might willingly accept some subordination to a husband-provider if he could ensure the material well-being of her children and herself. Given her precarious conditions, she may view this exchange as an attractive bargain. It is important not to underestimate the critical importance of protection and material well-being to those whose circumstances make such security elusive.[95]

95. See, however, bell hooks's discussion of the importance to low-income

The fact that a woman might accept subordination under such circumstances, however, does not indicate that there is nothing wrong with the social conditions that require a woman to make such a sacrifice in exchange for her security. Nor does it indicate that subordination made comfortable and alluring is thereby morally vindicated. To cover such cases, our best theoretical strategy might involve challenging the higher status of protective care and trying to raise esteem for the counterbalancing caretaking values which women, as traditional care givers, provide in return. The most important practical strategy, with respect to low-income women, must surely be to challenge the economic and social arrangements that make it necessary for many women to relinquish a substantial degree of personal autonomy in exchange for material support.

However we respond to this assessment of caretaking practices, it seems that we can no longer take a wholly benign view of the role of caring in women's lives, especially in the context of heterosexual relationships. If my analysis is correct, then it, together with the other feminist criticisms of care ethics outlined at the beginning of this chapter, yields a complex portrait of care. On the one hand, care is essential for the survival and development of both individuals and their communities, and care giving is a noble endeavor as well as being often morally requisite. On the other hand, care is simultaneously a perilous project for women, requiring the sacrifice of other important values, its very nobility part of its sometimes dangerously seductive allure. An ethic of care, to be fully liberatory for women, must not fail to explore and reflect this deep complexity.

---

women of equally shared parenting, where feasible: *Feminist Theory: From Margin to Center* (Boston: South End Press, 1984), pp. 140–41. If a man's participation in a heterosexual family relationship is explicitly defined at the outset in terms of his sharing child caretaking responsibilities equally, then, even in a low-income household, a woman would not have to bargain away her autonomy in order to secure a man's care for the children.

# Name Index